Contents

D0530049

The BPP Learning Media Study Text

Aims of this Study Text

To provide you with the knowledge and understanding, skills and application techniques that you need if you are to be successful in your exams

This Study Text has been written to cover the 2011 **Fundamentals of Ethics, Corporate Governance and Business Law** syllabus.

- It is **comprehensive**. It covers the syllabus content. No more, no less.

- It is written at the **right level**. Each chapter is written with CIMA's precise learning outcomes in mind.

- It is targeted to the **assessment**. We have taken account of guidance CIMA has given and the assessment methodology.

To allow you to study in the way that best suits your learning style and the time you have available, by following your personal Study Plan (see page (vii))

You may be studying at home on your own until the date of the exam, or you may be attending a full-time course. You may like to (and have time to) read every word, or you may prefer to (or only have time to) skim-read and devote the remainder of your time to question practice. Wherever you fall in the spectrum, you will find the BPP Learning Media Study Text meets your needs in designing and following your personal Study Plan.

To tie in with the other components of the BPP Learning Media Effective Study Package to ensure you have the best possible chance of passing the exam (see page (v))

Learning to Learn Accountancy

BPP Learning Media's ground-breaking **Learning to Learn Accountancy** book is designed to be used both at the outset of your CIMA studies and throughout the process of learning accountancy. It challenges you to consider how you study and gives you helpful hints about how to approach the various types of paper which you will encounter. It can help you **focus your studies on the subject and exam**, enabling you to **acquire knowledge, practise and revise efficiently and effectively**.

BPP
LEARNING MEDIA

The BPP Learning Media Effective Study Package

Recommended period of use	The BPP Learning Media Effective Study Package
From the outset and throughout	**Learning to Learn Accountancy** Read this invaluable book as you begin your studies and refer to it as you work through the various elements of the BPP Learning Media Effective Study Package. It will help you to acquire knowledge, practise and revise, efficiently and effectively.
Three to twelve months before the assessment	**Study Text and Interactive Passcards** Use the Study Text and Interactive Passcards to acquire knowledge, understanding, skills and the ability to apply techniques.
Throughout	**i-Pass** **i-Pass**, our computer-based testing package, provides objective test questions in a variety of formats and is ideal for self-assessment.
One to six months before the assessment	**Practice & Revision Kit** Try the numerous assessment-format questions, for which there are full worked solutions where relevant prepared by BPP Learning Media's own authors. Then attempt the two mock assessments.
From three months before the assessment until the last minute	**Passcards** Work through these short, memorable notes which are focused on what is most likely to come up in the assessment you will be sitting.

Help yourself study for your CIMA assessment

Assessments for professional bodies such as CIMA are very different from those you have taken at college or university. You will be under **greater time pressure before** the assessment – as you may be combining your study with work. There are many different ways of learning and so the BPP Study Text offers you a number of different tools to help you through. Here are some hints and tips: they are not plucked out of the air, but **based on research and experience**. (You don't need to know that long-term memory is in the same part of the brain as emotions and feelings - but it's a fact anyway.)

The right approach

1   **The right attitude**

Believe in yourself	Yes, there is a lot to learn. Yes, it is a challenge. But thousands have succeeded before and you can too.
Remember why you're doing it	Studying might seem a grind at times, but you are doing it for a reason: to advance your career.

2   **The right focus**

Read through the Syllabus and learning outcomes	These tell you what you are expected to know and are supplemented by Assessment focus points in the text.

3   **The right method**

The whole picture	You need to grasp the detail - but keeping in mind how everything fits into the whole picture will help you understand better. • The **Introduction** of each chapter puts the material in context. • The **Syllabus content, Learning outcomes** and **Assessment focus points** show you what you need to **grasp**.
In your own words	To absorb the information (and to practise your written communication skills), it helps to **put it into your own words**. • **Take notes.** • Answer the **questions** in each chapter. You will practise your written communication skills, which become increasingly important as you progress through your CIMA assessments. • Draw **mindmaps**. • Try **'teaching' a subject** to a colleague or friend.
Give yourself cues to jog your memory	The BPP Learning Media Study Text uses **bold** to **highlight key points**. • Try **colour coding** with a highlighter pen. • Write **key points** on cards.

BPP LEARNING MEDIA

Review, review, review	It is a **fact** that regularly reviewing a topic in summary form can **fix it in your memory**. Because **review** is so important, the BPP Learning Media Study Text helps you to do so in many ways.
	• **Chapter roundups** summarise the 'fast forward' key points in each chapter. Use them to recap each study session.
	• The **Quick quiz** is another review technique you can use to ensure that you have grasped the essentials.
	• Go through the **Examples** in each chapter a second or third time.

Developing your personal Study Plan

BPP Learning Media's **Learning to Learn Accountancy** book emphasises the need to prepare (and use) a study plan. Planning and sticking to the plan are key elements of learning success.

There are four steps you should work through.

Step 1   How do you learn?

First you need to be aware of your style of learning. The BPP Learning Media **Learning to Learn Accountancy** book commits a chapter to this **self-discovery**. What types of intelligence do you display when learning? You might be advised to brush up on certain study skills before launching into this Study Text.

BPP Learning Media's **Learning to Learn Accountancy** book helps you to identify what intelligences you show more strongly and then details how you can tailor your study process to your preferences. It also includes handy hints on how to develop intelligences you exhibit less strongly, but which might be needed as you study accountancy.

Are you a **theorist** or are you more **practical**? If you would rather get to grips with a theory before trying to apply it in practice, you should follow the study sequence on page (viii). If the reverse is true (you like to know why you are learning theory before you do so), you might be advised to flick through Study Text chapters and look at examples, case studies and questions (Steps 8, 9 and 10 in the **suggested study sequence**) before reading through the detailed theory.

Step 2   How much time do you have?

Work out the time you have available per week, given the following.

- The standard you have set yourself
- The time you need to set aside later for work on the Practice & Revision Kit and Passcards
- The other exam(s) you are sitting
- Very importantly, practical matters such as work, travel, exercise, sleep and social life

Hours

Note your time available in box A.   A [   ]

Step 3   Allocate your time

- Take the time you have available per week for this Study Text shown in box A, multiply it by the number of weeks available and insert the result in box B.

       B

- Divide the figure in box B by the number of chapters in this text and insert the result in box C.

       C

Remember that this is only a rough guide. Some of the chapters in this book are longer and more complicated than others, and you will find some subjects easier to understand than others.

Step 4   Implement

Set about studying each chapter in the time shown in box C, following the key study steps in the order suggested by your particular learning style.

This is your personal **Study Plan**. You should try and combine it with the study sequence outlined below. You may want to modify the sequence a little (as has been suggested above) to adapt it to your **personal style**.

BPP Learning Media's **Learning to Learn Accountancy** gives further guidance on developing a study plan, and deciding where and when to study.

Suggested study sequence

It is likely that the best way to approach this Study Text is to tackle the chapters in the order in which you find them. Taking into account your individual learning style, you could follow this sequence.

Key study steps	Activity
Step 1 **Topic list**	Each numbered topic is a numbered section in the chapter.
Step 2 **Introduction**	This gives you the big picture in terms of the context of the chapter, the learning outcomes the chapter covers, and the content you will read. In other words, it sets your objectives for study.
Step 3 **Fast forward**	Fast forward boxes give you a quick summary of the content of each of the main chapter sections. They are listed together in the roundup at the end of each chapter to provide you with an overview of the contents of the whole chapter.
Step 4 **Explanations**	Proceed methodically through the chapter, reading each section thoroughly and making sure you understand.
Step 5 **Key terms and Assessment focus points**	<ul><li>Key terms can often earn you *easy marks* (and they are highlighted in the index at the back of the text).</li><li>Assessment focus points state how we think the examiner intends to examine certain topics.</li></ul>
Step 6 **Note taking**	Take brief notes, if you wish. Avoid the temptation to copy out too much. Remember that being able to put something into your own words is a sign of being able to understand it. If you find you cannot explain something you have read, read it again before you make the notes.

BPP LEARNING MEDIA

Key study steps	Activity
Step 7 **Examples**	Follow each through to its solution very carefully.
Step 8 **Questions**	Make a very good attempt at each one.
Step 9 **Answers**	Check yours against ours, and make sure you understand any discrepancies.
Step 10 **Chapter roundup**	Work through it carefully, to make sure you have grasped the significance of all the fast forward points.
Step 11 **Quick quiz**	When you are happy that you have covered the chapter, use the Quick quiz to check how much you have remembered of the topics covered and to practise questions in a variety of formats.
Step 12 **Question(s) in the question bank**	Either at this point, or later when you are thinking about revising, make a full attempt at the Question(s) suggested at the very end of the chapter. You can find these at the end of the Study Text, along with the Answers so you can see how you did.

Short of time: Skim study technique?

You may find you simply do not have the time available to follow all the key study steps for each chapter, however you adapt them for your particular learning style. If this is the case, follow the **skim study** technique below.

- Study the chapters in the order you find them in the Study Text.
- For each chapter:
  - Follow the key study steps 1-2
  - Skim-read through step 4, looking out for the points highlighted in the fast forward boxes (step 4)
  - Jump to step 10
  - Go back to step 5
  - Follow through step 7
  - Prepare outline answers to questions (steps 8/9)
  - Try the Quick quiz (step 11), following up any items you can't answer
  - Do a plan for the Question (step 12), comparing it against our answers
  - You should probably still follow step 6 (note-taking), although you may decide simply to rely on the BPP Leaning Media Passcards for this.

Moving on...

However you study, when you are ready to embark on the practice and revision phase of the BPP Learning Media Effective Study Package, you should still refer back to this Study Text, both as a source of **reference** (you should find the index particularly helpful for this) and as a way to **review** (the Fast forwards, Assessment focus points, Chapter roundups and Quick quizzes help you here).

And remember to keep careful hold of this Study Text – you will find it invaluable in your work.

More advice on Study Skills can be found in BPP Learning Media's **Learning to Learn Accountancy** book.

Learning outcomes and Syllabus

Paper C05 Fundamentals of Ethics, Corporate Governance and Business Law

Syllabus overview

The learning outcomes in this paper reflect the legal framework for business and provide the underpinning for commercial activity. It includes the areas of contract law, employment law, financing, administration and management of companies. The globalisation of business is recognised by the inclusion of alternative legal systems, as well as the English legal system. Judicial precedent is included in relation to professional negligence.

Wherever business is conducted, the highest professional standards must be demonstrated for the benefit of all stakeholders. With this in mind, the place of ethics and ethical conflict is considered, as well as the role of corporate governance and its increasing impact in the management of organisations.

Syllabus structure

The syllabus comprises the following topics and study weightings:

A	Ethics and business	15%
B	Ethical conflict	10%
C	Corporate governance	10%
D	Comparison of English law with alternative legal systems	10%
E	The law of contract	20%
F	The law of employment	10%
G	Company administration and finance	25%

Assessment strategy

There will be a two hour computer based assessment, comprising 75 compulsory questions, each with one or more parts. In addition, a 15 minute tutorial is available before the start of the assessment to help familiarise yourself with the software and assessment environment.

A variety of objective test question styles and types will be used within the assessment.

BPP
LEARNING MEDIA

Learning outcomes and syllabus content

Learning Outcomes			
On completion of their studies students should be able to:			
Lead		**Component**	**Level**
CO5 - A. Ethics and busienss (15%)			
1.	demonstrate an understanding of the importance of ethics to business generally and to the professional accountant.	(a) apply the values and attitudes that provide professional accountants with a commitment to act in the public interest and with social responsibility;	3
		(b) explain the need for a framework of laws, regulations and standards in business and their application;	2
		(c) explain the nature of ethics and its application to business and the accountancy profession;	2
		(d) distinguish between detailed rules based and framework approaches to ethics.	2
2.	explain the need for CIMA members to adopt the highest standards of ethical behaviour.	(a) explain the need for continual personal improvement and lifelong learning;	2
		(b) explain the need to develop the virtues of reliability, responsibility, timeliness, courtesy and respect;	2
		(c) explain the ethical principles of integrity, objectivity, professional competence, due care and confidentiality;	2
		(d) identify concepts of independence, scepticism, accountability and social responsibility;	2
		(d) explain the reasons why CIMA and IFAC each have a 'Code of Ethics for Professional Accountants'.	2
CO5 – B. Ethical conflict (10%)			
1.	explain the various means of regulating ethical behaviour.	(a) explain the relationship between ethics, governance, the law and social responsibility;	2
		(b) describe the consequences of unethical behaviour to the individual, the profession and society.	2
2.	explain how ethical dilemmas and conflicts of interest arise and may be resolved.	(a) identify situations where ethical dilemmas and conflicts of interest occur;	2
		(b) explain how ethical dilemmas and conflicts of interest can be resolved.	2

Learning Outcomes

On completion of their studies students should be able to:

Lead		Component		Level
C05 – C. Corporate governance (10%)				
1.	explain the development of corporate governance to meet public concern in relation to the management of companies.	(a)	define corporate governance;	1
		(b)	explain the interaction of corporate governance with business ethics and company law;	2
		(c)	describe the history of corporate governance internationally;	2
		(d)	distinguish between detailed rules based and principles based approaches to governance.	2
2.	explain the impact of corporate governance on the directors and management structure of public limited companies and how this benefits stakeholders.	(a)	explain the effects of corporate governance on directors' powers and duties;	2
		(b)	describe different board structures, the role of the board and corporate social responsibility;	2
		(c)	describe the types of policies and procedures that constitute 'best practice';	2
		(d)	explain the regulatory governance framework for companies and benefits to stakeholders.	2
C05 – D. Comparison of English law with alternative legal systems (10%)				
1.	explain the essential elements of the English legal system and the tort of negligence.	(a)	explain the manner in which behaviour within society is regulated by the civil and the criminal law;	2
		(b)	explain the sources of English law;	2
		(c)	illustrate the operation of the doctrine of precedent by reference to the essential elements of the tort of negligence and its application to professional advisers.	2
2.	describe the essential elements of alternative legal systems.	(a)	describe the characteristics of the legal systems found in other countries;	2
		(b)	describe elements of Shari'ah law;	2
		(c)	describe the role of international regulations.	2

BPP
LEARNING MEDIA

Lead		Component		Level
C05 – E. The law of contract (20%)				
1.	explain how the law determines the point at which a contract is formed and the legal status of contractual terms.	(a)	identify the essential elements of a valid simple contract and situations where the law requires the contract to be in a particular form;	2
		(b)	explain how the law determines whether negotiating parties have reached agreement and the role of consideration in making that agreement enforceable;	2
		(c)	explain when the parties will be regarded as intending the agreement to be legally binding and how an agreement may be avoided because of misrepresentations;	2
		(d)	explain how the terms of a contract are established and their status determined;	2
		(e)	describe the effect of terms implied into contracts by sale of goods and supply of goods and services legislation;	2
		(f)	describe how the law controls the use of excluding, limiting and unfair terms.	2
2.	explain when the law regards a contract as discharged and the remedies available for breach and non-performance.	(a)	describe the factors which cause a contract to be discharged;	2
		(b)	explain how the law of frustration provides an excuse for non-performance of the contract;	2
		(c)	explain the remedies which are available for serious and minor breaches of contract.	2
C05 – F. The law of employment (10%)				
1.	explain the essential elements of an employment contract and the remedies available following termination of the contract.	(a)	explain the differences between employees and independent contractors;	2
		(b)	explain how the contents of a contract of employment are established;	2
		(c)	explain the distinction between unfair and wrongful dismissal.	2
2.	explain the impact of health and safety law on employers and employees.	(a)	explain how employers and employees are affected by health and safety legislation;	2
		(b)	describe the consequences of a failure to comply with health and safety legislation.	2

Learning Outcomes			
On completion of their studies students should be able to:			
Lead		**Component**	**Level**
CO5 – G. Company administration and finance (25%)			
1.	explain the nature, legal status and administration of business organisations.	(a) describe the essential characteristics of the different forms of business organisations and the implications of corporate personality;	2
		(b) explain the differences between public and private companies and establishing a company by registration or purchasing 'off the shelf';	2
		(c) explain the purpose and legal status of the articles of association;	2
		(d) explain the ability of a company to contract;	2
		(e) explain the main advantages and disadvantages of carrying on business through the medium of a company limited by shares;	2
		(f) explain the use and procedure of board meetings and general meetings of shareholders;	2
		(g) explain the voting rights of directors and shareholders;	2
		(h) identify the various types of shareholder resolutions.	2
2.	explain the law relating to the financing and management of companies limited by shares.	(a) explain the nature of different types of shares, the procedure for their issue and acceptable forms of payment;	2
		(b) explain the maintenance of capital principle and the reduction of share capital;	2
		(c) explain the ability of a company to take secured and unsecured loans, the different types of security and the registration procedure;	2
		(d) explain the procedure for the appointment, retirement, disqualification and removal of directors;	2
		(e) explain the powers and duties of directors when in office;	2
		(f) explain the rules dealing with the possible imposition of personal liability upon the directors of insolvent companies;	2
		(g) explain the rights of majority and minority shareholders;	2
		(h) explain the division of powers between the board of a company and the shareholders;	2
		(i) explain the qualifications, powers and duties of the company secretary.	2

BPP LEARNING MEDIA

The assessment

Format of computer-based assessment (CBA)

The CBA will not be divided into sections. There will be a total of seventy five objective test questions and you will need to answer **ALL** of them in the time allowed.

Candidates **may not** take a calculator into their assessment. Instead, an onscreen calculator will be available in the assessment environment.

Frequently asked questions about CBA

Q   What are the main advantages of CBA?

A   • Assessments can be offered on a continuing basis rather than at six-monthly intervals

     • Instant feedback is provided for candidates by displaying their results on the computer screen

Q   Where can I take CBA?

A   • CBA must be taken at a 'CIMA Accredited CBA Centre'. For further information on CBA, you can email CIMA at cba@cimaglobal.com.

Q   How does CBA work?

A   • Questions are displayed on a monitor

     • Candidates enter their answers directly onto a computer

     • The computer automatically marks the candidate's answers when the candidate has completed the examination

     • Candidates are provided with some indicative feedback on areas of weakness if the candidate is unsuccessful

Q   What sort of questions can I expect to find in CBA?

Your assessment will consist entirely of a number of different types of **objective test question**. Here are some possible examples.

• **MCQs.** Read through the information on page (xvi) about MCQs and how to tackle them.

• **Data entry.** This type of OT requires you to provide figures such as the correct figure for payables in a statement of financial position.

• **Multiple response.** These questions provide you with a number of options and you have to identify those which fulfil certain criteria.

This text provides you with **plenty of opportunities to practise** these various question types. You will find OTs **within each chapter** in the text and the **Quick quizzes** at the end of each chapter are full of them. The Question Bank contains exam standard objective test questions similar to the ones that you are likely to meet in your CBA.

Further information relating to OTs is given on page (xvii).

The **Practice and Revision Kit** for this paper was published in **December 2012** and is **full of OTs**, providing you with vital revision opportunities for the fundamental techniques and skills you will require in the assessment.

Tackling multiple choice questions

In a multiple choice question on your paper, you are given how many **incorrect** options?

A   Two
B   Three
C   Four
D   Five

The correct answer is B.

The MCQs in your assessment contain four possible answers. You have to **choose the option that best answers the question**. The three incorrect options are called distracters. There is a skill in answering MCQs quickly and correctly. By practising MCQs you can develop this skill, giving you a better chance of passing the exam.

You may wish to follow the approach outlined below, or you may prefer to adapt it.

Step 1   **Skim read** all the MCQs and **identify** what appear to be the easier questions.

Step 2   Attempt each question – **starting with the easier questions** identified in Step 1. Read the question thoroughly. You may prefer to work out the answer before looking at the options, or you may prefer to look at the options at the beginning. Adopt the method that works best for you.

Step 3   Read the four options and see if one matches your own answer. **Be careful with numerical questions**, as the distracters are designed to match answers that incorporate common errors. Check that your calculation is correct. Have you followed the requirement exactly? Have you included every stage of the calculation?

Step 4   You may **find that none of the options matches your answer**.

   •   Re-read the question to ensure that you understand it and are answering the requirement.

   •   Eliminate any obviously wrong answers.

   •   Consider which of the remaining answers is the most likely to be correct and select the option.

Step 5   If you are still **unsure** make a note **and continue to the next question**.

Step 6   **Revisit unanswered** questions. When you come back to a question after a break you often find you are able to answer it correctly straight away. If you are still unsure have a guess. You are not penalised for incorrect answers, so **never leave a question unanswered!**

Assessment focus. After extensive practice and revision of MCQs, you may find that you recognise a question when you sit the exam. Be aware that the detail and/or requirement may be different. If the question seems familiar read the requirement and options carefully – do not assume that it is identical.

BPP Learning Media's i-Pass for this paper provides you with plenty of opportunity for further practice of MCQs.

BPP LEARNING MEDIA

Tackling objective test questions

The vast majority of the questions in your assessment will be multiple choice questions. However, there may be a small number of objective test questions.

What is an objective test question?

An **OT** is made up of some form of **stimulus**, usually a question, and a **requirement** to do something.

(a)   Multiple choice questions

(b)   Filling in blanks or completing a sentence

(c)   Listing items, in any order or a specified order such as rank order

(d)   Stating a definition

(e)   Identifying a key issue, term, figure or item

(f)   Calculating a specific figure

(g)   Completing gaps in a set of data where the relevant numbers can be calculated from the information given

(h)   Identifying points/zones/ranges/areas on graphs or diagrams, labelling graphs or filling in lines on a graph

(i)   Matching items or statements

(j)   Stating whether statements are true or false

(k)   Writing brief (in a specified number of words) explanations

(l)   Deleting incorrect items

(m)   Choosing right words from a number of options

(n)   Complete an equation, or define what the symbols used in an equation mean

OT questions in CIMA assessment

CIMA has offered the following **guidance** about OT questions in the assessment.

*   Credit may be given for **workings** where you are asked to calculate a specific figure.

*   If you **exceed a specified limit on the number of words** you can use in an answer, you will **not be awarded any marks**.

Examples of OTs are included within each chapter, in the **quick quizzes** at the end of each chapter and in the **objective test question bank**.

BPP Learning Media's i-Pass for this paper provides you with plenty of opportunity for further practice of OTs.

BPP
LEARNING MEDIA

Part A

Comparison of English law with alternative legal systems

BPP
LEARNING MEDIA

Introduction to English Law

1

Introduction

The **English legal system** consists of practical and down-to-earth sets of procedures and rules designed to provide resolutions to ordinary problems. Publicity tends to focus on the higher courts, such as the Court of Appeal and the Supreme Court. However the vast majority of cases are heard in the Magistrates' Courts or the County Courts.

Many people, when they think of the law, have an image in their minds of judge and jury, or 'cops and robbers'. These are manifestations of **criminal** law. Business conduct is generally regulated by **civil** law, for example contract law and employment law. The distinction between criminal and civil law is fundamental to the English legal system.

There are **three principal sources of law** – the means by which law is brought into existence.

The historical interaction of **equity** and the **common law** led to the development of the first source of law, **case law**, which is based upon the system of **judicial precedent**. The second source is **legislation** – which is law created by Parliament.

Finally in this chapter we introduce the third source of law – **European Union Law**, whose influence on English Law is steadily increasing.

Topic list	Learning outcomes
1 Criminal and civil liability	D1(a)
2 Features and sources of English law	D1 (b)
3 Case law and judicial precedent	D1(b), D1(c)
4 Legislation	D1(b)
5 European Union law	D1(b)

1 Criminal and civil liability

FAST FORWARD

The distinction between **criminal liability** and **civil liability** is central to the English legal system and the way that the court system is structured.

1.1 Two types of liability

The distinction between **criminal** and **civil liability** is central to the legal system and to the way the court system is structured. It is often the **criminal law** that the general public has a clearer perception and a keener interest in. Some of the high profile criminal cases of London's Old Bailey are deemed extremely newsworthy. **Civil law**, on the other hand, receives less overt media coverage (with the exception of some high profile actions in tort, such as negligence or defamation). However, every time you buy or sell goods, or start or finish a contract of employment, your actions – and those of the other party – are governed by civil law. Therefore we can see that the **law manages the relationships** between members of society.

1.2 Criminal law

Key term

> A **crime** is conduct prohibited by the law. Criminal law exists to regulate behaviour in society.

In a **criminal case**, the **State prosecutes** the **accused** because it is the community as a whole which suffers as a result of the law being broken. The object is to **punish** the **offender** to help deter future crime and to offer the victim some retribution. Those **guilty** of crime may receive punishment in the form of **fines** payable to the State or **imprisonment**. However these punishments do not compensate the victim. For that they must seek a civil remedy and to that effect many criminal offences have a corresponding civil offence. As it is the State which initiates the proceedings, criminal law comes under the general heading of **public law**.

The initial decision to prosecute is usually taken by public bodies such as the **Police** or, **Crown Prosecution Service (CPS)**. No victim is needed for a criminal case to proceed – for example, unsuccessful car thefts or motoring offences such as dangerous driving where no one is hurt, may be victimless, but the fact that an offence was committed is enough to proceed with a prosecution.

Serious criminal trials are heard in front of a Judge (who decides on the law) and a **Jury** of twelve ordinary people (who decide on the evidence whether the accused is **guilty** or **not guilty** of the offence). The burden of proof to convict the **accused** rests with the **prosecution**, which must prove its case **beyond reasonable doubt**.

A criminal case might be referred to as *R v Smith*. The prosecution is brought in the name of the Crown (R signifying *Regina,* the Queen).

1.3 Civil law

Key term

> **Civil law** exists to regulate disputes over the rights and obligations of persons dealing with each other. It also acts as a control on behaviour in society as wrongdoers must pay compensation to the victim.

Civil proceedings are heard before a **Judge** who decides whether the defendant is **liable** or not **liable** for the wrong allegedly committed. The proceedings see a **claimant suing** a **defendant** for a **civil remedy**, such as the payment of **damages**. Cases must be proven on the **balance of probability**, the claimant must convince the court that their case is more probable than the defendant's. Terminology is different from that found in criminal cases. A civil case would be referred to as, for example, *Smith v Megacorp plc.* As it is the **claimant** who takes up the case privately, civil law comes under the general heading of **private law**.

One of the most important areas of civil liability for business, and accountants in particular, is the law of **contract**, which we shall study later.

1.4 Distinction between criminal and civil cases

It is **not an act** or **event** which **creates the distinction** between civil and criminal cases, but the **legal consequences**. A single event might give rise to criminal and civil proceedings. The two sorts of proceedings are distinguished by the fact the **courts**, **procedures** and the **terminology differ**.

1.4.1 Example

A broken leg caused to a pedestrian by a drunken driver is a single event which may give rise to:

- A criminal case (prosecution by the State for the offence of driving with excess alcohol), and
- A civil case (the pedestrian sues for compensation for pain and suffering).

Question	Criminal law

The criminal law aims

A   To compensate injured parties
B   To recover property which has been taken from the true owner
C   To enforce obligations
D   To penalise wrongdoers

Answer	

D   The criminal law aims to penalise wrongdoers.

Assessment focus point

Do not overlook any of the detail in this and the other chapters. Questions may focus on seemingly insignificant facts so beware, you have been warned!

2 Features and sources of English law

FAST FORWARD

There are a number of sources of English law. Two, **common law** and **equity**, may be classified as historical. Currently there are three main sources of law: **case law**, **legislation** and **EU law**.

2.1 Sources of law

There are three main current **sources of law**. These are the means by which law is brought into existence.

- **Case law**, which developed from historical common law and equity sources and based on the principle judicial precedent
- **Legislation**, made by or with the authority of Parliament
- **EU law**, as a result of Britain's membership of the European Union

2.2 Historical development of common law and equity

Common law (legal rights) is applied automatically and comprises a complete system of law.

Equity (equitable rights) is applied at the court's discretion and does not comprise a complete system of law.

2.2.1 Custom

The English legal system is often said to have its history in **local customs**. Some customs are still technically a source of law today, although almost all have been **superseded by common law** and **equity**. Customs are claims to rights, such as to use the land of another or to remove things from it, that may be established subject to certain conditions. It is possible for **local customs to override the common law** where they are legitimate, but a number of tests must be satisfied before this will be granted. In order to be **recognised**, a local custom must:

- Have existed from **'time immemorial'** – or 1189
- Have been **exercised continuously** since that date
- **Not have been opposed** – its exercise must have been **peaceably**
- Be **obligatory**
- Capable of **precise definition**
- **Be consistent** with other customs
- **Be reasonable**

2.2.2 Common law and equity

The '**common law**' which developed from customs still exists today and is constantly evolving as cases are brought before the courts. The effect of common law is to **add certainty** to the operation of law and we shall look at the concept of **judicial precedent** later.

Common law developed after the Norman invasion of 1066 where the Normans found no consistent set of laws which applied to the entire country. However, they did find local customs for dealing with legal problems, and where they could be **applied generally** throughout the kingdom they were made **common to all**. It is largely accepted that in this way, custom evolved into common law.

Equity was developed by the Court of Chancery, several hundred years later, as a system of law applied by the Chancellor in situations where justice did not appear to be done under the common law. It is based on the **principle of fairness**, and **remedies** are **discretionary**. The development of the **Law of Trusts** is attributable to equity.

Until the Judicature Acts (1873-75) equity and common law were practised in separate courts, today they are practised in the same courts. Where common law and equity conflict **equity will prevail** – equity is often referred to as the **gloss to the common law**.

Key terms

> **Common law** is the body of legal rules common to the whole country which is embodied in judicial decisions.
>
> **Equity** is a term which applies to a specific set of legal principles which were developed by the Court of Chancery to supplement (but not replace) the common law. It is based on fair dealings between the parties. It added to and improved on the common law by introducing the concept of fairness.

The **interaction** of **equity** and **common law** produced three major developments in the application of law in England.

(a) **New rights**. Equity recognised and protected rights for which the common law gave no safeguards.

(b) **Better procedure**. Equity may be more effective than common law in concluding disputed matters.

(c) **Better remedies**. The standard common law remedy for the successful claimant was the award of damages for his loss. The Chancellor developed remedies not available in other courts.

  (i) That the defendant must do what he had agreed to do (**specific performance**)
  (ii) That the defendant must abstain from wrongdoing (**injunction**)
  (iii) Alteration of a document to reflect the parties' true intentions (**rectification**)
  (iv) Restoration of the pre-contract status quo (**rescission**)

Question
Sources of law

Which of the following is an historical source of law?

A Equity
B Judicial precedent
C Legislation
D EU law

Answer

A Equity is an historical source of law, the others are current sources of law.

3 Case law and judicial precedent

FAST FORWARD

Decisions made in the courts are **case law**, which is judge-made law based on the underlying principle of consistency. Once a legal or equitable principle is decided by an appropriate court it is a **judicial precedent**.

3.1 Judicial decisions

When a judge hears a case before them, the following **three-stage procedure** is used to come to a decision.

(a) **Examine** all the facts to determine which are 'material' or most relevant to the decision
(b) **Consider the law** relating to the facts
(c) **Apply the law** to the facts and come to a decision

The application of the law will lead the judge to a decision which may or may not create a **judicial precedent**.

3.2 Judicial precedent

Key term

> A **precedent** is a previous court decision which another court is bound to follow by deciding a subsequent case in the same way.

A court's decision is expected to be **consistent with previous decisions** and to provide an opinion which can be used to direct future relationships. This is the basis of the system of **judicial precedent**.

Key term

> In any later case to which a principle is relevant, the same principle should (subject to certain exceptions) be applied. This doctrine of consistency, following precedent, is expressed in the maxim **stare decisis** which means 'to stand by a decision'.

3.2.1 Elements of judicial precedent

Judicial precedent is based on three elements.

Reports	There must be adequate and reliable reports of earlier decisions.
Rules	There must be rules for extracting a legal principle from a previous set of facts and applying it to current facts.
Classification	Precedents must be classified into those that are binding and those which are merely persuasive.

Key term

> The **doctrine of judicial precedent** is based on the view that the function of a judge is to decide cases in accordance with existing rules.

The doctrine of judicial precedent is designed to provide **consistency** in the law. Four things must be considered when examining a precedent before it can be applied to a case.

A decision must be based on a **proposition of law** before it can be considered as a precedent. It may **not** be a decision on a **question of fact**.
It must form part of the *ratio decidendi* of the case.
The **material facts** of each case must be the same.
The preceding court must have had a **superior (or in some cases, equal) status** to the later court, such that its decisions are binding on the later court.

3.3 *Ratio decidendi* and *obiter dicta*

FAST FORWARD

> In order that judicial precedent provides consistency in law, the **ratio decidendi** must be identified. The material facts must be the same. The status of the court which set the precedent must be such as to bind the present court. **Rationes decidendi** are the reasons for the decision being made – they alone are binding. **Obiter dicta** are comments made by the deciding judge in passing and are persuasive only.

A judgement will start with a **description of the facts** of the case and probably a **review of earlier precedents**. The judge will then make statements of law applicable to the legal problems raised by the material facts. It is these statements which form the basis for the decision (the *ratio decidendi*) and are the vital elements which bind future judges.

BPP
LEARNING MEDIA

'The **ratio decidendi** of a case is any rule of law expressly or impliedly treated by the judge as a necessary step in reaching his conclusion, having regard to the line of reasoning adopted by him, or a necessary part of his direction to the jury.'

(Cross: *Precedent in English Law*.)

Statements made by a judge are *ratio decidendi* or *obiter dicta*. There are two types of *obiter dicta*.

- A judge's statements of legal principle that do not form the basis of the decision.
- A judge's statements that are not based on material facts but on hypothetical facts.

Obiter dicta are words in a judgement which are said 'by the way'. They do not form part of the **ratio decidendi** and are not binding on future cases but are merely persuasive.

It is not always easy to identify the *ratio decidendi*. In decisions of appeal courts, where there are three or even five **separate judgements**, the members of the court may reach the same conclusion but give different reasons. Many judges indicate in their speeches which comments are *ratio* and which are *obiter*.

Not every decision made in every court is binding as a judicial precedent. The court's **status** has a significant effect on whether its decisions are binding, persuasive or disregarded.

3.4 The House of Lords and the Supreme Court

Until October 2009 the **House of Lords** had two roles – firstly as part of the process of **creating legislation**, and secondly as the **final appeal court** in the English court structure. However, the **Constitutional Reform Act 2005** severed the link between the **legislative** and **judicial** functions of the House of Lords.

A **Supreme Court** for the United Kingdom was established and opened for business in October 2009. It consists of **12 judges** known as *'Justices of the Supreme Court'* and its members include a **President** and a **Deputy President**

The **Supreme Court's role** is the same as the previous House of Lords' appellate function and the House of Lords continues with its existing **legislative role.**

As it is a new institution of the English legal system, you should expect the Supreme Court to be highly examinable.

3.5 The civil court structure

The **civil court structure** in England and Wales comprises the following.

- **Magistrates' Courts** mostly deal with small domestic matters.
- **County Courts** hear claims in contract and tort, equitable matters and land and probate disputes among others.
- The **Crown Court** hears appeals from Magistrates' Courts.
- The **High Court** is divided into three specialist divisions; **Queen's Bench**, **Family** and **Chancery**
- The **Court of Appeal** hears appeals from the County Court, the High Court, the Restrictive Practices Court, and the Employment Appeal Tribunal.
- The **Supreme Court** hears appeals from the Court of Appeal and the High Court.

3.5.1 The civil court structure

The diagram below sets out the English civil court structure.

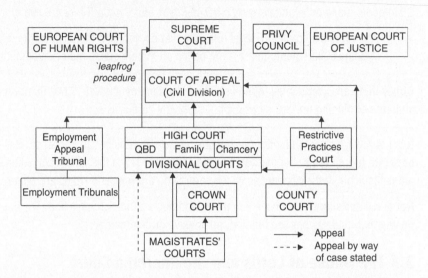

Appeals can be made from the County Court and High Court to the Court of Appeal (Civil Division) and to the Supreme Court if the point of law is in the **public interest**. If disputes involve **European law**, then any court may refer the case to the **European Court of Justice** for a 'preliminary ruling' on how the law should be applied or interpreted.

Note that the **Magistrates' Court** and the **Crown Court** are of **very limited importance** in the civil court system; it is the County Court and the High Court where most cases are heard. Cases generally start in the **County Court** unless the amount of money being claimed is substantial, such cases start in the High Court.

The High Court is split into the following **three divisions**, each dealing with a different area of law:

(a)   The **Queen's Bench Division** (QBD), which mainly deals with contract and tort cases.
(b)   The **Chancery Division**, which hears cases involving land, trusts, bankruptcy and company law.
(c)   The **Family Division**, which deals with matrimonial matters.

3.6 The criminal courts

The **criminal court structure** in England and Wales comprises the following.

- **Magistrates' Courts** hear summary offences and committal proceedings for indictable offences.

- The **Crown Court** tries serious criminal (indictable) offences and hears appeals from Magistrates' Courts.

- The **Divisional Court of QBD** hears appeals by way of case stated from Magistrates' Courts and the Crown Court.

- The **Court of Appeal** hears appeals from the Crown Court.

- The **Supreme Court** hears appeals from the Court of Appeal or a Divisional Court of QBD

Criminal cases begin at a **Magistrates' Court** and unless they are serious offences the Magistrate will hear them. If the case is serious, the Magistrate will decide if there is a case to answer and if so, refer it to the **Crown Court** where it will be heard by a judge and jury.

Appeals from the Magistrates' and Crown Courts are made by way of **'case stated'** to the **Divisional Court** of the Queen's Bench Division in the High Court. This appeal is in **writing** and sets out the **facts** of the case and the **law** applied to them - the object being to determine whether or not the law has been **correctly applied**. If it has not, the Magistrates' or Crown Court must apply the law correctly using an interpretation passed to them from the Divisional Court. Where the law has been correctly applied, an appeal can then be made to the **Court of Appeal** (Criminal Division) and then on to the **Supreme Court** if the point of law is of **public interest**.

3.6.1 The criminal court structure

The diagram below sets out the English criminal court structure. The two key courts in the criminal system are the **Crown Court** and the **Magistrates' Court**. A **court of first instance** is the court where a case is originally heard in full. The **appeal court** is the court to which an appeal is made against the ruling or the sentence.

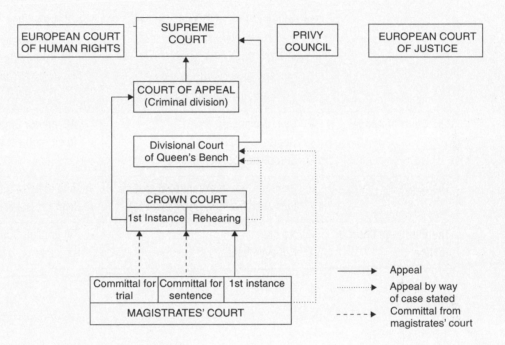

3.7 The hierarchy of the courts

The table below sets out the **status of each court** in determining how far they are bound by earlier decisions. For example, the County Court is bound by decisions of all courts above it in the civil court hierarchy, namely the High Court, the Court of Appeal, the Supreme Court and the European Court of Justice.

Court	Bound by	Decisions binding on
Magistrates' Court	<ul><li>High Court</li><li>The Court of Appeal</li><li>Supreme Court</li><li>European Court of Justice</li></ul>	<ul><li>No one</li><li>Not even itself</li></ul>
County Court	<ul><li>High Court</li><li>The Court of Appeal</li><li>Supreme Court</li><li>European Court of Justice</li></ul>	<ul><li>No one</li><li>Not even itself</li></ul>

BPP LEARNING MEDIA

Court	Bound by	Decisions binding on
Crown Court	• High Court (QBD) • The Court of Appeal • Supreme Court • European Court of Justice	• No one • However, its decisions are reported more widely and are more authoritative

The High Court consists of divisions:
• **Queen's Bench**
• **Chancery**
• **Family**
	• Judge sitting alone
	  – The Divisional Court
	  – The Court of Appeal
	  – Supreme Court
	  – European Court of Justice
		• Judge sitting alone
		  – Magistrates' Court
		  – County Court
		  – Crown Court

	• Judges sitting together
	  – Any Divisional Court
	  – The Court of Appeal
	  – Supreme Court
	  – European Court of Justice
		• Judges sitting together
		  – Magistrates' Court
		  – County Court
		  – Crown Court
		  – Divisional Courts

The Court of Appeal	• Own decisions • Supreme Court • European Court of Justice	• All inferior English courts • Itself (subject to the exception)
The Supreme Court	• Itself (except in exceptional cases) • European Court of Justice	• All English Courts • Itself (except in exceptional cases)
The European Court of Justice	• No one • Not even itself	• All English Courts

 Question

Binding precedents

Fill in the following table, then check your answer to the table above.

Name of court	Bound by	Decisions binding on
Magistrates' Court		
County Court		
Crown Court		
High Court		
Court of Appeal		
Supreme Court		
European Court of Justice		

BPP LEARNING MEDIA

3.8 Court of Appeal exception

In *Young v Bristol Aeroplane Co 1944*, it was decided that the **civil division** of the **Court of Appeal** is **usually bound** by its **own decisions** and those of the Supreme Court unless:

- Two of its previous decisions conflict, when it must decide which to follow

- The previous decision conflicts with a subsequent Supreme Court decision

- The previous decision was made with a lack of care (*per incuriam*)

Assessment focus point It is particularly important that you know the position of the Court of Appeal and the Supreme Court.

 Question

Previous decisions

Before a High Court judge is required to apply a previous decision to the case actually before him, he must

(i)   Decide whether the decision is binding or merely persuasive
(ii)   Distinguish the *obiter dicta* from the *ratio decidendi* and apply the former in his reasoning
(iii)   Determine that the material facts of the two cases are the same
(iv)   Be convinced that the decision was made by the County Court or Magistrates' court

A   (i) and (iii) only
B   (ii) and (iv) only
C   (i), (ii) and (iii) only
D   (i), (iii) and (iv) only

Answer

A   A High Court judge is only compelled to follow a previous decision if it is binding on him and if the material facts are the same. It is the *ratio decidendi* not the *obiter dicta* that must be applied in the Judge's reasoning.

3.9 Persuasive precedents

FAST FORWARD

The **Supreme Court binds itself** (but may exceptionally depart from its own decisions) and all lower courts. The Court of Appeal binds itself and all lower courts. The High Court binds all lower courts. Crown Court decisions may be of persuasive authority. The County Court and Magistrates' Courts do not make binding precedent.

Apart from binding precedents, reported decisions of any court may be treated as **persuasive precedents**. Persuasive precedents may be, but need not be, followed in a later case.

Point to note

Where an earlier decision was made by a lower court, the judges can **overrule** that earlier decision if they disagree with the lower court's statement of the law. **The outcome of the earlier decision remains the same, but will not be followed in future cases.**

If the decision of a lower court is appealed to a higher one, the higher court may **reverse** the decision if they feel the lower court has wrongly interpreted the law. **When a decision is reversed, the higher court is also overruling the lower court's statement of the law.**

3.10 Avoidance of a binding precedent

Even if a precedent appears to be binding, there are a number of grounds on which a court may decline to follow it.

(a) The precedent may be **overruled** by a superior court or subsequent legislation

(b) On appeal, a superior court may **reverse** the decision of a lower court which set the precedent

(c) The court may be able to **distinguish the facts**. Where significant differences appear between the material facts of the current case and the one which set the precedent, the court may **distinguish** the earlier case on the facts and thereby avoid following it as a precedent.

(d) It may declare the *ratio decidendi* **obscure**, particularly when a Court of Appeal decision by three or five judges gives as many *rationes*.

(e) It may declare the previous decision made *per incuriam*: without taking account of some essential point of law, such as an important precedent.

3.11 The advantages and disadvantages of precedent

Many of the strengths of judicial precedent as the cornerstone of English law also indicate some of its weaknesses.

Factor	Advantage	Disadvantage
Certainty	The law is decided fairly and predictably Like for like cases should have the same outcomes	Judges may sometimes be forced to make illogical distinctions to avoid an unfair result
Clarity	Following the reasoning of *ratio decidendi* should lead to statements of general legal principles	Sometimes, judgements may appear to be inconsistent with each other or legal principles followed
Flexibility	The system is able to develop with changing circumstances	The system can limit judges' discretion
Detail	Precedent states how the law applies to facts and should be flexible enough to allow for details to be different	The detail produces a vast body of reports to take into account Judges often distinguish on the facts to avoid a precedent
Practicality	Case law is based on experience of actual cases brought before the courts. This is an advantage over legislation which can be found impractical when tested	The law becomes reactive rather than proactive

What do you think are the advantages of case law as a source of law?

Answer

The law is decided **fairly** and **predictably**, so that individuals and businesses can regulate their conduct by reference to it. The **risk** of mistakes in individual cases is reduced by the use of precedents. Case law can **adapt** to changing circumstances in society, since it arises directly out of the actions of society. Case law, having been developed in **practical** situations, is suitable for use in other practical situations.

3.12 Other sources of case law and precedent

Case law from other **common law countries** such as Australia, Singapore and Canada, as well as other Commonwealth countries may be followed by English courts **if no English precedent exists**. Whilst foreign case law does not bind English judges, it may **persuade** them that the precedent is an accurate reflection of English law and so lead them to follow it.

In extremely rare circumstances, courts may even follow the hypothesis of **a textbook writer** who sets out how a certain law should be applied.

4 Legislation

FAST FORWARD

One of the major sources of law is **legislation**. UK statute law may take the form of Acts of Parliament or delegated legislation under the Acts, for example statutory instruments or bye-laws.

4.1 Statute law

Statute law is made by Parliament (or in exercise of law-making powers delegated by Parliament) and can be described as a **formal enactment of rules**. Statutes differ from case law as they are **purposively written** rather than developed over time in response to actual cases. Most legislation takes a long time to complete as it follows a set procedure through both the **House of Commons** and the **House of Lords** (see below).

In recent years however, **UK** membership of the **European Union** has restricted the previously unfettered power of Parliament. There is an obligation, imposed by the **Treaty of Rome**, to bring UK law into line with the Treaty itself and with directives.

Parliament enjoys **legislative sovereignty** which gives rise to a number of consequences. It may **repeal** earlier statutes, **overrule** case law developed in the courts, or **make new law** on subjects which have not been regulated by law before.

No Parliament can legislate so as to **prevent** a future Parliament changing the law.

4.1.1 Types of Statute law

Statute law can be categorised as follows.

Type of Act	Description
Public Acts	Legislation introduced by Government or MPs that affects the general public
Private Acts	Concern powers granted to individuals or institutions such as the power to acquire property through compulsory purchase orders
Enabling Acts	Confer power to delegated bodies, often known as delegated legislation
Consolidating legislation	Incorporates original statutes and their successive amendments into a single statute
Codifying legislation	Places case law onto a statutory basis

4.2 Parliamentary procedure

A proposal for legislation is originally aired in public in a **Government Green Paper**. After comments are received a **White Paper** is produced, which sets out the intended aim of the legislation. It is then put forward in draft form as a **Bill**, and may be introduced into either the House of Commons or the House of Lords. When the Bill has passed through one House it must then go through the same stages in the other House.

In each House the successive stages of dealing with the Bill are as follows.

Stage 1   **First reading**. Publication and introduction into the agenda. No debate.

Stage 2   **Second reading**. Debate and vote on the general merits of the Bill. No amendments at this stage.

Stage 3   **Committee stage**. The Bill is examined by a Standing Committee of about 20 members, representing the main parties and including some members at least who specialise in the relevant subject. If the Bill is very important, all or part of the Committee Stage may be taken by the House as a whole sitting as a committee.

Stage 4   **Report stage.** The Bill as amended in committee is reported to the full House for approval.

Stage 5   **Third reading.** This is the final approval stage and vote.

When it has passed through both Houses it is submitted for the **Royal Assent** which is given on the Queen's behalf by a committee of the Lord Chancellor and two other peers. It then becomes an Act of Parliament (or statute) but it does not come into operation until a commencement date is notified by statutory instrument.

There are some **exceptions** to this process, for example, each year's **Finance Act** is introduced following the Chancellor's speech.

Legislation remains in force until it is either **amended** or repealed by a **later Act**.

4.3 Statutory interpretation

Judges must follow the letter of the law when applying statutes in cases before them and (with one exception, below) **cannot question** whether or not Acts of Parliament are valid. They have to **interpret** statute law and they may find a meaning in a statutory rule which Parliament did not intend.

BPP
LEARNING MEDIA

Therefore a series of rules has developed concerning how judges should interpret statute. In general, they are required to consider the **purpose** of the statute and interpret the statute so that it achieves its purpose. Since the incorporation of the European Convention on Human Rights and Fundamental Freedoms into UK law in 1998, judges have also been required to interpret statute in a way that is **compatible** with the Convention, as far as is possible.

One **exception** to the rule that courts cannot question the validity of an Act does exist. As the UK is bound by EU law, any UK Act or provision which is found to be in **violation of EU law** can be suspended by the courts.

Question   Statutory interpretation

A key rule of statutory interpretation is that a court can never question the validity of an Act of Parliament.

True or False?

Answer

False. Where a UK Act contravenes EU law a court may suspend it.

4.4 Rules of language

The following **four rules** are available to judges to help them understand the words in a statute.

4.4.1 The eiusdem generis rule

Statutes often list a number of **specific things** and end the list with more **general words**. In that case the general words are to be limited in their meaning to other things of the same kind as the specific items which precede them.

> *Evans v Cross 1938*
>
> *The facts:* E was charged with driving his car in such a way as to 'ignore a traffic sign', having crossed to the wrong side of a white line. 'Traffic sign' was defined in the Act as 'all signals, warning signposts, direction posts, signs or other devices'.
>
> *Decision:* 'Other device' must be limited in its meaning to a category of such signs. A painted line was quite different from that category.

4.4.2 The in pari materia rule

The court may consider **other legislation** dealing with the **same matter** in order to interpret the statute in question.

4.4.3 The noscitur a sociis rule

This rule allows the **meaning** of a word to be discovered by the court considering **other words**.

4.4.4 The expressio unuis exclusio alterius rule

If the legislation **specifically states** what it affects, then anything else is not affected by it.

4.5 Other rules

There are also a number of important historical rules, summarised below. These contain principles which the courts apply in interpreting the words used in a piece of legislation. Those described below are the most important ones.

4.5.1 The literal rule

The **literal rule** means that words should be given their plain, ordinary or literal meaning. Normally a word should be construed in the same literal sense wherever it appears throughout the statute.

Whiteley v Chapell 1868

A statute aimed at preventing electoral malpractice made it an offence to impersonate 'any person entitled to vote' at an election. The accused was acquitted because he impersonated a dead person, who was clearly not entitled to vote.

4.5.2 The golden rule

The **golden rule** means that a statute should be construed to avoid a manifest absurdity or contradiction within itself. There is a principle, for instance, that a murderer cannot benefit under his victim's will.

Re Sigsworth 1935

The golden rule was applied to prevent a murderer from inheriting on the intestacy of his mother (his victim) although he was her only heir on a literal interpretation of the Administration of Estates Act 1925.

4.5.3 The mischief rule

The **mischief rule** allows a judge to interpret a statute in such a way to give it the legal effect for which it was intended. This is possible if the purpose of the statute was given in its preamble. This is called a **'purposive approach'** and takes into account of the mischief or weakness which the statute is explicitly intended to remedy.

Gardiner v Sevenoaks RDC 1950

The facts: The purpose of an Act was to provide for the safe storage of film wherever it might be stored on 'premises'. The claimant argued that 'premises' did not include a cave and so the Act had no application to his case.

Decision: The purpose of the Act was to protect the safety of persons working in all places where film was stored. If film was stored in a cave, the word 'premises' included the cave.

The **mischief rule** is sometimes referred to as 'the rule in *Heydon's Case*' 1584 which provides that judges should consider three factors.

- What the law was before the statute was passed
- What 'mischief' the statute was trying to remedy
- What remedy Parliament was trying to provide

BPP
LEARNING MEDIA

4.5.4 The contextual rule

The **contextual rule** means that a word should be construed in its context. It is permissible to look at the statute as a whole to discover the meaning of a word in it. This may seem to conflict to some extent with the rules described above, but the courts have been paying more attention to what Parliament intended in recent times. This is in order that the courts apply the law for the purpose for which it was enacted. A more purposive approach is also being taken because so many international and EU regulations come to be interpreted by the courts.

4.6 Presumptions (cannons) of statutory interpretation

There are a number of **core presumptions** that must be made when Acts are read, however they can be ignored if the Act concerned expressly rebuts them.

- A statute does not alter the existing common law.
- A statute does not have retrospective effect to a date earlier than its becoming law.
- If a statute deprives a person of his property, say by nationalisation, he is to be compensated for its value.
- A statute is not intended to deprive a person of his liberty.
- A statute does not bind the Crown.
- A statute has effect only in the UK and applies to the whole of the UK.
- A statute cannot impose criminal liability without proof of guilty intention.
- A statute does repeal other statutes.

4.7 Other interpretation aids

Judges may also use a number of other **aids** to help them **interpret statutes**. These include:

(a) **Intrinsic aids**

These are found **in the Act** itself.

(i) The **Title** (for example the Dangerous Dogs Act 1991) and the **long title** if there is one
(ii) The **Preamble** – the Act's intentions and objectives
(iii) The **Interpretation** section (schedules)
(iv) **Headings**
(v) **Notes** in the margins

(b) **Extrinsic aids**

These are found in sources **outside the Act**.

(i) The **Interpretation Act 1978** – defines words commonly found in statutes

(ii) **Hansard** – the official recording of Parliamentary debates can be used to understand the meaning or purpose of the Act, *Pepper v Hart (1993)*

(iii) A **Dictionary**

(iv) **Commission reports** such as Law Commission Reports

4.8 Delegated legislation

To save time in Parliament, Acts usually contain a section by which power is given to a minister, or public body such as a local authority, to make **subordinate or delegated legislation**. The government passes an **'enabling' Act** which sets out the overall objectives that the legislation is intended to achieve, but the actual detail of the Act is left to the body which the Act has delegated the power to.

Key term

> **Delegated legislation** means rules of law, often of a detailed nature, made by subordinate bodies to whom the power to do so has been given by statute.

4.8.1 Advantages of delegated legislation

There are a number of **advantages** to delegated legislation.

(a) **Timesaving**

As Parliament only sets out the overall policy and objectives of the legislation, valuable Parliamentary **time is saved**.

(b) **Speed**

Legislation can be passed **more quickly** than if all the detail was debated. This allows the law to respond quickly to a sudden crisis.

(c) **Expertise**

Delegation allows **technical specialists** or those with **local knowledge** (who may be better qualified than Parliament) to take on the task of writing the details of the Act.

(d) **Flexibility**

Delegated legislation is especially useful where the law is **complex** or **changes frequently**, such as the rules on motor vehicle construction.

4.8.2 Disadvantages of delegated legislation

However, there are some inherent **disadvantages** with delegated legislation.

(a) **Accountability**

The effect of delegated legislation is to allow unelected individuals or bodies to create law.

(b) **Scrutiny**

The overall volume of detail created by delegated legislation means that Parliament cannot scrutinise all the detail of the Act. However there are some parliamentary controls in place (see below).

(c) **Bulk**

Over 3,000 statutory instruments are passed each year which increases bureaucracy and compliance costs for businesses in the UK.

BPP
LEARNING MEDIA

Delegated legislation appears in various forms.

- Ministerial powers are exercised by **statutory instruments.** Statutory instruments are the most common form of delegated legislation.

- **Local authorities** are given statutory powers to make **bye-laws.**

- Parliament gives power to certain **professional bodies** to regulate their members' conduct.

- **Rules of Court** may be made by the judiciary to control court procedure.

- Emergency powers to make law are given to the Crown and Privy Council and are contained in **Orders in Council.** They allow laws to be passed quickly, bypassing the full Parliamentary process.

- The **Parliaments of Scotland** and **Wales** can legislate on certain matters which affect their own regions. This power has been delegated from the UK Parliament.

4.9 Control over delegated legislation

Parliament and the courts exercise **control** over delegated legislation as follows.

(a) **Parliament**

    (i) Most new legislation must be **laid before Parliament** for 40 days before automatically becoming law.

    (ii) Government **Scrutiny Committees** review statutory instruments.

    (iii) Parliament may **revoke** an enabling act.

(b) **Courts**

    (i) Courts may declare any piece of delegated legislation *ultra vires* (the delegated body abused the power given to it or acted beyond their capacity) and therefore **void.**

    (ii) The **Human Rights Act** allows courts to strike out any piece of delegated legislation which conflicts with the **European Convention on Human Rights**.

5 European Union law

FAST FORWARD

The sources of EU law may be described as **primary** or **secondary**. The primary sources of law are the **Foundation Treaties** themselves. The secondary sources of law are legislation, which takes three forms. **Regulations** are self-executing. **Directives** require national legislation to be effective, usually within two years. **Decisions** are immediately binding on the person to whom they are addressed.

The **European Union** (EU) consists of twenty-seven **independent states** which recognise the collective sovereignty of the EU. The UK joined the EC (now the EU) in 1972. It is not just a forum for the co-operation of governments (such as the United Nations), but nor is it a close federation of states (such as the USA).

Each independent state **surrendered the sovereignty** of its **parliament** and allows the EU to create laws which are binding on them.

5.1 Sources of European Union Law

The sources of EU Law may be described as primary or secondary. The **primary sources of law** are the **Foundation Treaties** themselves. These automatically become law in member states without the need for the further legislation to be passed by them.

- The **Treaty of Paris 1951**, which established the **ECSC**.
- The **First Treaty of Rome 1957**, which established the **EEC**
- The **Second Treaty of Rome 1957**, which established **EURATOM**.
- The **Merger Treaty of Brussels 1965**, which established a single **Commission** and single **Council**.
- The **Treaty of European Union 1992**, which introduced new forms of **co-operation** between **member states**.
- The **Treaty of Amsterdam 1997**, which **consolidated previous treaties**.
- The **Treaty of Nice 2001** which **reformed** some of the **EU's institutions**.
- The **Treaty of Lisbon 2007**, which attempted to make the EU more democratic. This Treaty attempted to establish a **constitution for Europe**, but this was never ratified.

Secondary legislation takes three forms, with the Council and Commission being empowered to do the following:

- Make **regulations**
- Issue **directives**
- Take **decisions**

They may also **make recommendations** and **deliver opinions** although these are only persuasive in authority.

5.2 Direct applicability and direct effect

To understand the importance of regulations, directives and decisions, it is necessary to appreciate the distinction between **direct applicability** and **direct effect**.

EU law which is directly applicable in member states comes into force without any act of implementation by member states. Law has direct effect if it confers rights and imposes obligations directly on individuals.

5.3 Regulations

Regulations may be issued by the Council and Commission. They have the force of law in every EU state without the need for national legislation to be passed. In this sense regulations are described as **directly applicable**. Their objective is to obtain uniformity of law throughout the EU.

Key term

> **Regulations** apply throughout the EU and they become part of the law of each member nation as soon as they come into force without the need for each country to make its own legislation.

Direct law-making of this type is generally restricted to matters within the **basic aims** of Treaty of Rome, such as the establishment of a single unrestricted market in the EU territory in manufactured goods.

Acts of implementation are actually prohibited, in case a member state alters the scope of the regulation in question.

5.4 Directives

Key term

Directives are issued to the governments of the EU member states by the Council and Commission requiring them within a specified period (usually two years) to alter the national laws of the state so that they conform to the directive.

Until a directive is given effect by a UK statute it does not usually affect legal rights and obligations of individuals. The wording of a directive may be cited in legal proceedings, but generally **statutory interpretation has been a matter for the UK courts**. However, as noted earlier, the courts are required to interpret UK legislation in a way which is compatible with the European Convention on Human Rights.

Important

Directives are the most significant and important means of importing EU law into the UK legal system.

5.5 Decisions

Decisions of an **administrative nature** are made by the European Commission in Brussels.

Key term

A **decision** may be addressed to a state, person or a company and is immediately binding, but only on the recipient.

5.6 Recommendations

Recommendations made by EU institutions are **not legally binding** but are **persuasive**.

5.7 Legislative procedure

The following bodies are responsible for European law development and application. Their power and responsibility is conferred by the **Foundation Treaties**. Treaties must be **ratified** by each nation before they become effective, this can be done either by a **referendum** of the people or by **national parliaments** passing laws.

Assessment focus point

The main law-making procedures used by these institutions are – **consultation**, **assent** and **co-decision**, the later being the most common. Ensure that you commit to memory all of the different types of EU law.

5.7.1 The European Parliament

The members of the European Parliament are **directly elected** by the public from their constituencies and serve five year terms. The number of members each member state is allocated depends on the size of the state.

The organisation supervises other EU institutions (such as approving budgets) and is also involved in **making legislation**. Its role in this case is to agree proposals with the Council of Ministers (under the '**co-decision**' procedure), but where there is disagreement the Parliament has the right of veto.

It may also pass a '**motion of censure**' that forces the European Commission to resign.

5.7.2 The European Council

The European Council is formed **twice-yearly** by Heads of State from all EU members and the President of the Commission. It has no legislative function itself but it does **set strategy** and **EU policy**. Its decisions are expressed as **Conclusions**, **Resolutions** and **Declarations**.

5.7.3 The European Commission

The European Commission is an **independent** body formed of commissioners from Member States (who do not however represent the interests of their state) and it fills the European Union's **executive function**. The organisation consists of several **Directorates-General** (DGs) each of which makes policy for a specific area.

5.7.4 The Council of Ministers ('The Council')

Member States are each represented by **ministers** at the Council of Ministers which performs the **legislative** and **decision-making functions** of the European Union by acting on proposals from the European Commission. Ministerial positions are not **'fixed'** placements, they are selected by the Member State depending upon the matter in hand (for example, Finance Ministers would be selected to represent the state in Finance matters). However, for **consistency** and to aid **co-ordination** of work where different areas (and therefore Ministers) are involved, there is a **General Affairs Council** that oversees matters. A **permanent body** of national representatives known as **Comitedes Représants Pérmanents** (COREPER) also provides support for the Council of Ministers.

5.7.5 The European Court of Justice (ECJ)

The ECJ **applies** EU law and provides **decisions** and **rulings** which are binding only on the parties concerned in the case. Judges are appointed from member states. As with English case law, precedents are formed which are binding in the future. Its role is to ensure European law is applied consistently across all member states (EU law is supreme over member state law) and gives rulings on matters brought before it in the following ways:

(a)   **Preliminary rulings**, where countries ask for advice on interpretation.

(b)   **Commission actions**, against states for failure to meet the terms of a treaty, or other obligation.

(c)   **Annulment actions**, to cancel an EU law if it is found illegal.

(d)   **Failure to act actions**, where a complaint is received that the other three institutions (above) have failed to meet a treaty obligation.

Question   Secondary legislation

Describe the three types of secondary legislation in EU law.

Answer

A **regulation** is a rule of law designed to obtain uniformity throughout the member states. It is directly applicable without the need for national legislation. A **directive** is issued to member states requiring them to make such changes to their own law as prescribed by the directive. A **decision** is binding in its entirety upon those to whom it is addressed, whether they be member states or corporate bodies. In the case of member states, a decision has direct effect.

5.8 The Human Rights Act 1998

The Human Rights Act 1998 incorporated into English law the **European Convention on Human Rights**. This affects 'public authorities' including the courts and Parliament. The **courts** are required to interpret UK legislation in a way that is compatible with the Convention. New laws drafted by **Parliament** must also be compatible.

Individuals and **companie**s may bring a case to court if they consider that their rights have been infringed. The **European Court of Human Rights**, which before the Act had no authority in the UK, is the final court of appeal for human rights cases after they have passed through the domestic courts.

BPP
LEARNING MEDIA

Chapter Roundup

- The distinction between **criminal liability** and **civil liability** is central to the English legal system and the way that the court system is structured.

- There are a number of sources of English law. Two, **common law** and **equity**, may be classified as historical. Currently, there are three main sources of law: **case law**, **legislation** and **EU law**.

- **Common law** (legal rights) is applied **automatically** and comprises a **complete system** of law.

- **Equity** (equitable rights) is applied **at the court's discretion** and does **not** comprise a **complete system** of law.

- Decisions made in the courts are **case law**, which is judge-made law based on the underlying principle of consistency. Once a legal or equitable principle is decided by an appropriate court it is a **judicial precedent**.

- In order that judicial precedent provides consistency in law, the **ratio decidendi** must be identified. The material facts must be the same. The status of the court which set the precedent must be such as to bind the present court. **Rationes decidendi** are the reasons for the decision being made – they alone are binding. **Obiter dicta** are comments made by the deciding judge in passing and are persuasive only.

- The **Supreme Court binds itself** (but may exceptionally depart from its own decisions) and all lower courts. The Court of Appeal binds itself and all lower courts. The High Court binds all lower courts. Crown Court decisions may be of persuasive authority. The County Court and Magistrates' Courts do not make binding precedent.

- One of the major sources of law is **legislation**. UK statute law may take the form of Acts of Parliament or delegated legislation under the Acts, for example statutory instruments or bye-laws.

- The sources of EU law may be described as **primary** or **secondary**. The primary sources of law are the **Foundation treaties** themselves. The secondary sources of law are legislation, which takes three forms. **Regulations** are self-executing. **Directives** require national legislation to be effective, usually within two years. **Decisions** are immediately binding on the person to whom they are addressed.

BPP
LEARNING MEDIA

Quick Quiz

1   **Fill in the blanks** in the statements below, using the words in the box.

- The distinction between (1) ~~Civil~~ and (2) ~~Criminal~~ liability is central to the English legal system.

- The sources of English law can be divided into two categories.

    - The historical sources are (3) ~~Common~~ and (4) ~~Equity~~

    - Currently, the three main sources are (5) ~~legislation~~ (6) ~~Case~~ and (7) ~~EU~~

• case law	• common law	• criminal
• equity	• civil	• legislation
• EU law		

2   Equity was developed by Parliament.

True ☐

False ☒

3   Which of the following statements is true of a criminal case?

A   A convicted person must pay compensation to his victim
B   The case must be proven beyond reasonable doubt
C   The Crown Prosecution Service is the claimant
D   Law reports of criminal cases are confidential

4   **Fill in the blanks** in the statements below, using the words in the box.

- In order that (1) ~~J.P~~ provides (2) ~~Consistency~~ in the law, a precedent must be carefully examined before it can be applied to a particular (3) ~~Case~~ It must be a proposition of (4) ~~Law~~ The (5) ~~ratio Decendi~~ must be identified. The (6) ~~material facts~~ must be the same.

- The (7) ~~Status~~ of the court which set the precedent must be such as to (8) ~~Bind~~ the present court.

• bind	• judicial precedent	• consistency
• case	• status	• material facts
• ratio decidendi	• law	

5   The primary sources of EU law are

A   Regulations
B   Foundation treaties
C   Directives
D   Decisions

6   Which of the following is attributed with the development of the Law of Trusts?

    A   The common law
    B   Equity
    C   European Union Treaties
    D   Delegated legislation

7   In 2010, Mr Justice Jeffries, a High Court judge is deciding a case which has similar material facts to one decided by the Court of Appeal in 1910. He can decline to be bound by this decision by showing that

    A   The status of the previous court is not such as can bind him
    B   The decision was taken too long ago to be of any relevance
    C   The decision does not accord with the rules of a statute passed in 1913
    D   The obiter dicta are obscure

8   The rule that a statute should be construed to avoid a manifest absurdity or contradiction within itself is known as the

literal rule	mischief rule
golden rule	contextual rule

9   Judicial precedent is based on the three elements. Which three?

- Reports of previous decisions
- The same judge being involved in the decision
- Facts of cases being classified
- Rules for extracting the legal principle from one set of facts to apply to a different set of facts
- Precedents being classified into those which are binding and those which are not.

10   Name the five stages of parliamentary procedure with regard to statutes.

Stage 1   .... Publication and introduction into the agenda. No debate.

Stage 2   .... Debate and vote on the general merits of the Bill. No amendments at this stage.

Stage 3   .... The Bill is examined by a Standing Committee of about 20 members, representing the main parties and including some members at least who specialise in the relevant subject. If the Bill is very important, all or part of the Committee Stage may be taken by the House as a whole sitting as a committee.

Stage 4   .... The Bill as amended in Committee is reported to the full House for approval.

Stage 5   .... This is the final approval stage and vote.

BPP
LEARNING MEDIA

Answers to Quick Quiz

1   (1) criminal (2) civil (3) common law (4) equity (5) case law (6) legislation (7) EU law

2   False. Equity was developed by the Court of Chancery.

3   B. Criminal cases must be proven beyond reasonable doubt. Fines are payable to the Government. The CPS is the prosecutor. Law reports are not confidential.

4   (1) judicial precedent (2) consistency (3) case (4) law (5) ratio decidendi (6) material facts (7) status (8) bind

5   B. Foundation Treaties are the primary sources of EU law.

6   B. Equity is attributed with the development of the Law of Trusts.

7   C. Subsequent statutes may override case law. The Court of Appeal decision will bind him. D is irrelevant as obiter dicta won't bind him.

8   Golden rule

9   • Reports **of previous decisions**
    • **Rules** for extracting the legal principle from one set of facts to apply to a different set of facts.
    • Precedents being **classified** into those which are binding and those which are not.

10 **Stage 1** **First reading**. Publication and introduction into the agenda. No debate.

    Stage 2 **Second reading**. Debate and vote on the general merits of the Bill. No amendments at this stage.

    Stage 3 **Committee stage**. The Bill is examined by a Standing Committee of about 20 members, representing the main parties and including some members at least who specialise in the relevant subject. If the Bill is very important, all or part of the Committee Stage may be taken by the House as a whole sitting as a committee.

    Stage 4 **Report stage**. The Bill as amended in committee is reported to the full House for approval.

    Stage 5 **Third reading**. This is the final approval stage and vote.

Now try the questions below from the Question Bank

Number
Q1
Q2
Q3
Q4
Q5

BPP
LEARNING MEDIA

The Tort of Negligence

Introduction

This chapter describes the tort of **negligence**, the most significant **tort** of modern times. Tort is an important branch of the law regulating business conduct, so this chapter begins with an introduction to the concept of tort, distinguishing it from criminal liability and liability in contract.

The **three essential elements** of a negligence claim are analysed by reference to the most important cases in each area, and a consideration of **negligent professional advice** appears at the end of the chapter. This is linked to the material in the previous chapter on judicial precedent to underline how the **doctrine of precedent** operates.

Topic list	Learning outcomes
1 Tort and other wrongs	D1(c)
2 The tort of negligence	D1(c)
3 Duty of care	D1(c)
4 Breach of duty of care	D1(c)
5 Causation	D1(c)
6 Professional advice	D1(c)

1 Tort and other wrongs

FAST FORWARD

> The law gives various rights to persons. When such a right is infringed the wrongdoer is liable in **tort**.

1.1 Tort

Tort is distinguished from other legal wrongs.

(a) It is **not a breach of contract**, where the obligation which is alleged to have been breached arose under an agreement between two parties.

(b) It is **not a crime**, where the object of proceedings is to punish the offender rather than compensate the victim.

Key term

> A **tort** is a civil wrong and the person wronged sues in a civil court for compensation. The claimant's claim generally is that he has suffered a loss, such as personal injury, at the hands of the defendant and the defendant should pay damages.
>
> **In tort no previous transaction or contractual relationship need exist** – the parties may be complete strangers as when a motorist knocks down a pedestrian in the street. The claim in tort is based on the general law of duties and rights.

Notwithstanding the distinction made above, note that the same event can easily give rise to more than one legal liability.

1.2 Examples

A road accident may lead to proceedings for both **crime** and **tort** and even in **contract** if, say, the driver is a hired chauffeur.

Bad professional advice may give rise to liability both in **tort** and in **contract**. We discuss the law of tort in relation to professional advisers later on.

1.3 Wrong and damage

The basis of a damages claim is that the claimant has **suffered a wrong**. In some torts, such as negligence, it is necessary to establish both the wrong and the loss resulting from the **damage**.

1.4 Cause and effect

When the claimant claims damages for the loss caused by the defendant's wrongful act two main issues of cause and effect may have to be considered.

(a) Was the loss **caused by a wrongful act** of the defendant himself? It may be a case of **inevitable accident** or there may be **contributory negligence** on the part of the claimant.

(b) How far down the **chain of consequences** should the court go in identifying the loss for which the claimant is entitled to recover damages? Therefore, it is necessary to have rules on **remoteness of damage**.

To be liable in tort, the claimant must prove which of the following?

A   They suffered loss as a consequence of a criminal act by the defendant
B   They suffered loss as a consequence of breach of contract by the defendant
C   They suffered a wrong as a consequence of the defendant's actions however caused
D   They suffered a wrong as a consequence of a criminal act or breach of contract by the defendant

Answer

C   In tort, no criminal act need be committed, nor does there need to be a breach of contract.

2 The tort of negligence

FAST FORWARD

Negligence is the most important modern tort. To succeed in an action for negligence the claimant must prove that:

- The defendant had a **duty of care** to avoid causing injury, damage or loss
- There was a **breach of that duty** by the defendant
- *In consequence* the claimant suffered **injury, damage or loss**

2.1 Definition

The **tort of negligence** can be defined as causing loss by a failure to take reasonable care when there is a duty to do so.

Assessment focus point

You must be aware of the academic requirements for negligence to be proved. The criteria for a successful negligence action are fundamental and should be learnt by all students.

3 Duty of care

FAST FORWARD

In the case of *Donoghue v Stevenson 1932* the House of Lords ruled that a person might **owe a duty of care to another with whom he had no contractual relationship** at all. The doctrine has been refined in subsequent rulings, but the principle is unchanged.

In the landmark case described below, the House of Lords established that a **general duty of care** could be applied to all subsequent cases and situations even where there is **no contract** between the parties – this duty states that everyone has a duty not to cause foreseeable harm to foreseeable victims. This duty is known as the **neighbour principle** and was given by Lord Atkin as guidance for the future cases.

> *Donoghue v Stevenson 1932*
>
> *The facts*: A purchased a bottle of ginger beer for consumption by B. B drank part of the contents, which contained the remains of a decomposed snail, and became ill. The manufacturer argued that as there was no contract between himself and B he owed her no duty of care and so was not liable.
>
> *Decision*: The House of Lords laid down the general principle that every person owes a duty of care to his 'neighbour', to 'persons so closely and directly affected by my act that I ought reasonably to have them in contemplation as being so affected'. The manufacturer was found liable to B for their illness.

It should be noted that the case was only decided by a 3 to 2 majority (House of Lords cases were heard by five Lords, each whom made an independent decision). As **Lord Atkin's** neighbour principle was wider than was required for the particular case, it can only be regarded as *obiter dictum*. In the same decision, **Lord Macmillan** set out the three features of the tort of negligence, a **duty of care**, **failure** to meet that duty and the fact that failure caused **damage**.

The consequence of this case is that the **scope of duty of care is very wide**. Whether or not a duty exists in any situation is generally decided by the courts on a case by case basis, with each new case setting a precedent based on its own particular facts. For example in *Home Office v Dorset Yacht Co Ltd 1970* it was held that the Home Office was liable for criminal damage caused by a group of young offenders under its supervision.

Assessment focus point

> Where cases were heard by the House of Lords in the past we shall continue to refer to the House of Lords. Cases decided by the Supreme Court will be described as such.

3.1 Development of the doctrine

This doctrine has been much refined in the years since the snail made its celebrated appearance. For any duty of care to exist, it was stated in *Anns v Merton London Borough Council 1977* that two stages must be tested:

- Is there sufficient **proximity** between the parties, such that the harm suffered was **reasonably foreseeable**?

- Should the duty be **restricted** or **limited** for reasons of economic, social or public policy?

The latest stage in the doctrine's development came in *Caparo Industries plc v Dickman and Others 1990*. We shall come back to this case when we study the duty of care of accountants and auditors, however it established a **three stage test** for establishing a duty of care that still stands:

- Was the harm **reasonably foreseeable**?
- Was there a **relationship of proximity** between the parties?
- Considering the circumstances, is it **fair, just and reasonable** to impose a duty of care?

3.1.1 Sufficient proximity

Individuals are **not automatically liable** for torts they may have committed. It must first be proved that a sufficiently close relationship existed between the parties – in other words there is **'sufficient proximity'**

Whether or not sufficient proximity exists depends on the facts of each case. A **reasonable boundary** must be drawn around the event to ensure only those people whose harm was **reasonably foreseeable** can take action

BPP
LEARNING MEDIA

against the defendant – otherwise the defendant could be liable for numerous torts which they could not possibly have contemplated.

When considering the boundary, lawyers for the defence will attempt to prove that it should be **restricted** so that the claimant falls outside the boundary and therefore the defendant does not owe a duty of care to them.

An example of the duty of care being restricted is *Alcock v Chief Constable of South Yorkshire Police 1991*. This was a case brought after the Hillsborough football disaster. It was ruled that the police did not owe a duty of care to people who witnessed their relatives dying on live television and suffered nervous shock as a result.

In *Bourhill v Young 1942* a lady heard a road accident but did not see it as her view was obstructed by another vehicle. She suffered shock and lost an unborn baby as a result. However, she lost her case as the fact that she did not see the accident firsthand excluded her from the foreseeable range of harm.

Other recent cases on this area include *Sutradhar v Natural Environment Research Council 2004* where a claimant attempted to sue the writer of a water survey report after drinking contaminated water and *London Borough of Islington v University College London NHS Trust 2004* where a local authority attempted to recover the costs of treating a stroke victim after receiving negligent medical advice. Both cases failed due to **insufficient proximity.**

3.1.2 Public policy

In certain circumstances an otherwise legitimate duty of care can be **ignored** on the grounds that it is **absurd** or otherwise **undesirable** on **public policy grounds**. In *Mulcahy v Ministry of Defence 1996*, a commanding officer was held not to owe an enforceable duty of care to a soldier when in action.

Assessment focus point

Reading cases and practising exam questions will help you judge whether or not a duty of care exists. Keeping in mind what you think is reasonable in the circumstances will also help.

Question   Duty of care

According to the judgement in the *Caparo* case, which of the following elements must be present for a duty of care to exist?

(i)   There must be a relationship of proximity between defendant and claimant
(ii)   It must be reasonable that the defendant should foresee that damage might arise from his carelessness
(iii)   The claimant must have acted in good faith and without carelessness
(iv)   It must be fair, just and reasonable for the law to impose liability

A   (i) and (ii) only
B   (iii) and (iv) only
C   (i), (ii) and (iii) only
D   (i), (ii) and (iv) only

Answer

D   The elements in options (i), (ii) and (iv) are the formulation of the tort of negligence in the *Caparo* case. If these are present then there is a right of action under the tort of negligence.

4 Breach of duty of care

FAST FORWARD

The second element that must be proven by a claimant in an action for negligence is that there was a **breach of the duty of care** by the defendant.

4.1 The basic rule

Breach of duty of care is the second issue to be considered in a negligence claim. An objective test to prove whether or not the **defendant acted reasonably** is carried out. The **standard of reasonable care** requires that the person concerned should do what a **reasonable person** would do. This will also mean the reasonable **employer**, or the reasonable **adviser**.

Those in **responsible positions** or who are **professionally qualified** will owe a **higher duty of care** than the ordinary person. Where the **consequences** of a person's actions are **serious** or the **likelihood of injury** is high, **more care** must be taken. However, a person is **not always expected to act** where the act is **impractical**, or where the **risk** of danger is **outweighed by the cost** of preventing it.

Generally **children** owe a **lower** standard of care than adults.

The rule has been developed as follows.

(a)   The test is one of **knowledge and general practice existing at the time**, not hindsight or subsequent change of practice.

(b)   In broad terms, a claim against a professional person will fail if he or she can point to a **body of opinion that supports the approach taken**.

(c)   In deciding what is reasonable care the **balance must be struck** between advantage and risk. The driver of a fire engine may exceed the normal speed on his way to the fire but not on the way back.

(d)   If A owes a duty of care to B and A knows that B is **unusually vulnerable** (for example, a child), a higher standard of care is expected. This is known as the '**thin skull principle**', 'you take your victim as you find them'.

Paris v Stepney Borough Council 1951

The facts: P was employed by K on vehicle maintenance. P was already blind in one eye. It was not the normal practice to issue protective goggles since the risk of eye injury was small. A chip of metal flew into P's good eye and blinded him.

Decision: There was a higher standard of care owed to P because an injury to his remaining good eye would blind him.

In *Glasgow Corporation v Taylor 1992* the local authority was held to be negligent when children ate poisonous berries in a park. A warning notice was not considered to be sufficient to protect children.

BPP
LEARNING MEDIA

Which of the following would owe a higher standard of care than an ordinary reasonable person?

(i)   Those who are professionally qualified
(ii)   Those whose actions have serious consequences
(iii)   Those caring for a vulnerable person
(iv)   Children

A   (i) and (ii) only
B   (i) and (iii) only
C   (i), (ii) and (iii) only
D   All of the above

Answer

C   Those who are professionally qualified, whose actions have serious consequences or who are caring for a vulnerable person owe a higher standard of care than the ordinary reasonable person. Children generally owe a lower standard of care than a reasonable person (an adult).

4.2 Res ipsa loquitur

In some circumstances the claimant may argue that **the facts speak for themselves** (*res ipsa loquitur*) – want of care being the only possible explanation for their loss or damage. If this is accepted then **negligence** on the part of the defendant must be **presumed**. The burden of proof is reversed and the **defendant** must **prove** that they were **not negligent**.

Key term

> **Res ipsa loquitur** can be defined as follows: The thing speaks for itself. Where an accident happens of which the most likely cause is negligence, the court may apply this maxim and infer negligence from mere proof of the facts. The burden of proof is reversed and the defendant must prove that they were not negligent.

For a claimant rely on this principle they must show:

(a)   The cause of the injury was under the **management and control** of the defendant.

(b)   The accident would not have occurred if the **defendant** used **proper care**. In *Richley v Fould 1965* the fact that a car skidded to the wrong side of the road was enough to indicate careless driving.

4.3 Example

In *Mahon v Osborne 1939* a surgeon was required to prove that leaving a swab inside a patient after an operation was not negligent.

5 Causation

FAST FORWARD

Finally the claimant must demonstrate that he **suffered injury** or **loss** as a result of the breach.

5.1 Damage or loss

This is the third element of a negligence claim. A claim will not succeed if **damage** or **loss** is not proved.

A person will only be compensated if they suffered actual loss, injury, damage or harm **as a consequence** of the defendant's actions. Examples of such loss may include:

- **Personal injury** including nervous shock.

- **Damage** to **property**

- **Financial loss** which is directly **connected to personal injury**, for example, loss of earnings

- **Pure financial loss** is **rarely recoverable** and usually limited to instances where the defendant is an identifiable person who acted in a professional capacity for the claimant .

In *Murphy v Brentwood DC 1990* the court held that a local authority was not liable for subsidence caused to a house built on land which the local authority approved as suitable for house building. The loss was found to be financial (ie an economic loss).

In *Boardman v Sanderson 1964* a father heard his son's screams from close by as he was hit by a car. The court held that the negligent driver was liable for the father's nervous shock as he was related to the victim and was in the immediate vicinity of the accident when it happened. This case contrasts with the *Bourhill* case that we saw earlier.

5.1.1 The 'But for' test

The '**But for**' test is used to decide if the defendant's breach of duty caused the harm suffered by the claimant. The test is simple; the claimant must prove that 'but for' the defendant's actions the damage would not have occurred.

In *Barnett v Chelsea and Kensington Hospital Management Committee 1968* the widow of a man who died from arsenic poisoning sued the defendant's hospital as he was negligently sent home without being properly treated. Whilst the hospital failed to meet its duty of care it was proved that the victim's death could not have been prevented even if he was treated correctly. Therefore the defendant was not liable.

Finally the claimant must prove that the **damage** is **not too remote** and is **reasonably foreseeable**.

5.1.2 Remoteness of damage

When a person commits a tort with the **intention of causing loss** or **harm**, the loss or harm can never be too remote.

If the tort committed was **unintentional**, the defendant's liability will be restricted if other events break the '**chain of causality**' between the defendant's act and the claimant's loss *(novus actus interveniens)*. In such circumstances, the defendant will only be liable for losses suffered up to the intervening act. Where there are **multiple possible causes** of the loss or damage, the defendant will only be liable if their act is the most likely to be the cause.

Examples of acts which may break the chain of causality include:

- A **third party** intervention
- **Natural events** such as a storm at sea
- Acts by the **claimant** themselves

5.1.3 Reasonable foresight

When there is a sequence of **physical cause** and effect **without human intervention**, the ultimate loss is too remote unless it could have been foreseen by the defendant that some loss of that kind might occur.

BPP
LEARNING MEDIA

> *The Wagon Mound 1961*
>
> *The facts:* A ship was taking on oil in Sydney harbour. By negligence oil was spilled onto the water and it drifted to a wharf 200 yards away where welding equipment was in use. The owner of the wharf carried on working because he was advised that the sparks were unlikely to set fire to the oil. Safety precautions were taken. A spark fell onto a piece of cotton waste floating in the oil, thereby starting a fire which damaged the wharf. The owners of the wharf sued the charterers of the ship.
>
> *Decision:* The claim must fail. Pollution was the foreseeable risk: fire was not.

5.2 Defences

The following defences are available to defendants to **avoid**, **reduce** or **limit** their liability for negligence.

5.2.1 Avoid liability

A defendant can avoid liability if another can be held **vicariously liable**. For example, an employee may avoid liability by claiming that their **employer** is liable for their negligence which occurred during the course of employment.

5.2.2 Reduce liability

There are two possible defences that will reduce a defendant's liability.

(a) **Contributory negligence**

   The courts may **reduce the amount of damages** owed by the defendant if the claimant **contributed** to their loss. This was the case in *Sayers v Harlow UDC 1958*, where a lady was injured while trying to climb out of a public toilet cubicle which had a defective lock. The court held that she had contributed to her injuries by the method that she used to climb out.

(b) **Volenti non fit injuria**

   Claimants may **voluntarily accept the risk of injury** and therefore **absolve the defendant** from liability for harm caused to them. Acceptance can be **express**, for example the signing of a waiver form before taking part in a dangerous activity, or **implied**, such as when a boxer takes part in a fight (they knew what they were going to do was dangerous but did it anyway).

5.2.3 Limit liability

Under the **Limitation Act 1980**, claims under tort must be brought within six years of the date of negligence. This is reduced to three years for personal injury claims.

Question

Causation

State three acts which may break the chain of causality.

BPP
LEARNING MEDIA

Third party interventions, natural events and acts by the claimant.

6 Professional advice

FAST FORWARD

The law on **negligent professional advice** is influenced strongly by the *Caparo* case. In this case, it was held that the auditors of a public limited company did not owe a duty of care to the public at large who relied upon the audit report when making an investment decision.

6.1 Development

We now consider how the law relating to negligent professional advice, and in particular **auditors**, has been developed through the operation of precedent, being refined and explained with each successive case that comes to court. It illustrates the often step-by-step development of English law, which has gradually refined the principles laid down in *Donoghue v Stevenson* to cover **negligent misstatements** which cause financial loss.

6.2 The special relationship

Before 1963, it was held that any liability for careless statements was limited in scope and depended upon the existence of a **contractual** or **fiduciary relationship** between the parties. Lord Denning's tests for a further (later termed 'special') relationship were laid down in his dissenting judgement on *Candler v Crane, Christmas & Co 1951*.

FAST FORWARD

According to Lord Denning, to establish a **special relationship** the person who made the statement must have done so in some professional or expert capacity which made it likely that others would rely on what he said. This is the position of an adviser such as an accountant, banker, solicitor or surveyor.

It follows that a duty could not be owed to complete strangers, but Lord Denning also stated at the time: 'Accountants owe a duty of care not only to their own clients, but also to **all those whom they know will rely on their accounts** in the transactions for which those accounts are prepared.' This was to prove a significant consideration in later cases.

However, Lord Denning's view was a dissenting voice in the 1951 *Candler* case, where the Court of Appeal held that the defendants were **not liable** (for a bad investment based upon a set of negligently prepared accounts) because there was **no direct contractual or fiduciary relationship** with the claimant investor.

It was twelve years later that the **special relationship** was accepted as a valid test. Our starting point is the **leading case** on negligent misstatement, outlined below, which was the start of a **new judicial approach** to cases involving negligent misstatement. You must make sure that you are familiar with it.

BPP
LEARNING MEDIA

Hedley Byrne & Co Ltd v Heller and Partners Ltd 1963

The facts: HB were advertising agents acting for a new client, Easipower Ltd. HB requested information from Easipower's bank (HP) on its financial position. HP returned non-committal replies, which expressly disclaimed legal responsibility, and which were held to be negligent misstatement of Easipower's financial resources.

Decision: While HP were able to avoid liability by virtue of their disclaimer, the House of Lords went on to consider whether there ever could be a duty of care to avoid causing financial loss by negligent misstatement where there was no contractual or fiduciary relationship. It decided that HP were guilty of negligence having breached the duty of care, because a special relationship did exist. Had it not been for the disclaimer, a claim for negligence would have succeeded.

The *Hedley* case is important as it saw liability for negligence **extended** from the *Donoghue* case. Up until this time, liability was **limited** to **acts or omissions** and **excluded financial losses**. After the *Hedley* case, liability now **included negligent statements** and **pure financial losses**. The key distinction is that in *Hedley*, advice was given to a specific person with the knowledge of how the advice would be used.

Another case which illustrates the point is *Smith v Eric S Bush 1989*. A house surveyor negligently produced a survey report for a potential buyer who relied upon it. The buyer did purchase the house and lost money as a result. The House of Lords found the surveyor liable for the financial loss caused by the negligent misstatement.

6.3 The Caparo decision

Point to note

The Caparo case is fundamental to an understanding of the current legal position of auditors.

This important and controversial case made considerable changes to the tort of negligence as a whole, and the negligence of professionals in particular. It set a precedent which now forms the foundation for courts to consider when deciding the **liability** of **professional advisers**.

Caparo Industries plc v Dickman and Others 1990

The facts: Caparo, which already held shares in Fidelity plc, bought more shares and later made a takeover bid, after seeing accounts prepared by the defendants that showed a profit of £1.3m. Caparo claimed against the directors (the brothers Dickman) and the auditors for the fact that the accounts should have shown a loss of £400,000. The claimants argued that the auditors owed a duty of care to investors and potential investors in respect of the audit. They should have been aware that a press release stating that profits would fall significantly had made Fidelity vulnerable to a takeover bid and that bidders might well rely upon the accounts.

Decision: The auditor's duty did not extend to potential investors nor to existing shareholders increasing their stakes. It was a duty owed to the body of shareholders as whole.

In the *Caparo* case it was decided that there were two very different situations facing a person giving professional advice.

(a)   Preparing information in the knowledge that a **particular person** was contemplating a transaction and would rely on the information in deciding whether or not to proceed with the transaction (the 'special relationship').

(b)   Preparing a statement for **general circulation**, which could forseeably be relied upon by persons unknown to the professional for a variety of different purposes.

It was held therefore that a public company's auditors owed **no duty of care to the public at large** who relied on the audit report when deciding to invest – and, in purchasing additional shares, an existing shareholder was in no different position to the public at large.

In *MacNaughton (James) Papers Group Ltd v Hicks Anderson & Co 1991*, it was stated that it was necessary to examine each case in the light of the following.

- Foreseeability
- Proximity
- Fairness

This is because there could be **no single overriding principle** that could be applied to the individual complexities of every case. Lord Justice Neill set out the matters to be taken into account in considering this.

- The purpose for which the statement was **made**
- The purpose for which the statement was **communicated**
- The **relationship** between the maker of the statement, the recipient and any relevant third party
- The **size** of any class to which the recipient belonged
- The **state of knowledge** of the maker
- Any **reliance** by the recipient

6.4 Non-audit role

The **duty of care** of **accountants** is **held** to be **higher** when **advising on takeovers than when auditing**. The directors and financial advisors of the target company in a contested takeover bid were held to owe a duty of care to a **known take-over bidder** in respect of express representations made about financial statements prepared for the purpose of contesting the bid in which they knew the bidder would rely: *Morgan Crucible Co plc v Hill Samuel Bank Ltd and Others 1991*.

In *Goldstein v Levy Gee (a firm) 2003*, the court held that liability for negligently valuing shares would exist if the defendant's valuation did not fall into the range that a reasonably **competent valuer** (without negligence) would produce. In this case, the auditors did negligently value shares, but escaped liability as the valuation they produced fell into the range expected of a reasonably competent valuer.

6.5 The law since *Caparo*

A more recent case highlighted the need for a cautious approach and careful evaluation of the circumstances when giving financial advice, possibly with the need to issue a disclaimer.

BPP
LEARNING MEDIA

ADT Ltd v BDO Binder Hamlyn 1995

The facts: Binder Hamlyn was the joint auditor of BSG. In October 1989, BSG's audited accounts for the year to 30 June 1989 were published. Binder Hamlyn signed off the audit as showing a true and fair view of BSG's position. ADT was thinking of buying BSG and, as a potential buyer, sought Binder Hamlyn's confirmation of the audited results. In January 1990, the Binder Hamlyn audit partner attended a meeting with a director of ADT. This meeting was described by the judge as the 'final hurdle' before ADT finalised its bid for BSG. At the meeting, the audit partner specifically confirmed that he 'stood by' the audit of October 1989. ADT proceeded to purchase BSG for £105m. It was subsequently alleged that BSG's true value was only £40m. ADT therefore sued Binder Hamlyn for the difference, £65m plus interest.

Decision: Binder Hamlyn assumed a responsibility for the statement that the audited accounts showed a true and fair view of BSG which ADT relied on to its detriment. Since the underlying audit work had been carried out negligently, Binder Hamlyn was held liable for £65m. The courts expect a higher standard of care from accountants when giving advice on company acquisitions since the losses can be so much greater.

This situation was different from *Caparo* since the court was specifically concerned with the **purpose of the statement made at the meeting**. Did Binder Hamlyn **assume any responsibility** as a result of the partner's comments? The court decided that it did. The court did not need to consider the question of duty to individual shareholders, because *Caparo* had already decided that there was none. Following the *ADT* case, another case indicated that a **higher standard of care** is expected when giving advice on **company takeovers** than when advising on an audit.

NRG v Bacon and Woodrow and Ernst & Young 1996

The facts: NRG alleged that the defendants had failed to suggest the possibility that certain companies it was targeting might suffer huge reinsurance losses. They had also failed to assess properly whether these losses could be protected against, because defective actuarial methods had been used. As a result, it overpaid for these companies by £255m.

Decision: The judge observed that accountants owe a higher standard of care when advising on company purchases, because the potential losses are so much greater, following *ADT*. However, applying this higher standard of care to the facts, it was decided that NRG had received the advice that any competent professional would have given, because the complex nature of the losses that the companies were exposed to were not fully understood at the time. In addition, the errors in assessment had not led directly to the losses, because NRG would have bought the companies anyway.

Assessment focus point

Liability in tort for negligent professional advice is a very topical subject, specifically highlighted in the syllabus, and is still developing through case law. It is of particular relevance for accountants and likely to be assessed regularly.

6.6 Limitation of liability

The **Companies Act 2006 s534** permits auditors to agree a **maximum liability** with the company in respect of negligent audit work and for default, or breach of duty or trust. s537 permits the liability to be limited to what is **'fair and reasonable in the circumstances'**. Therefore the Act has gone some way to protect auditors from liabilities which may put them out of business.

Question	Negligent misstatement

To show that the defendant owes them a duty of care not to cause financial loss by negligent misstatement, the claimant must prove:

(i)   The person making the statement did so in an expert capacity of which the claimant was aware
(ii)   The context in which the statement was given made it likely that the claimant would rely on it
(iii) In making the statement the defendant foresaw that it would be relied upon by the claimant
(iv)   The claimant had actually relied on the statement

A   (i) and (ii) only
B   (i), (ii) and (iii) only
C   (ii), (iii) and (iv) only
D   All of the above

Answer

D   In order to show a duty of care exists, a claimant must prove:

–   The person making the statement did so in an expert capacity of which the claimant was aware
–   The context in which the statement was given made it likely that the claimant would rely on it
–   In making the statement the defendant foresaw that it would be relied upon by the claimant
–   The claimant had actually relied on the statement

BPP
LEARNING MEDIA

Chapter Roundup

- The law gives various rights to persons. When such a right is infringed the wrongdoer is liable in **tort**.

- **Negligence** is the most important modern tort. To succeed in an action for negligence the claimant must prove that:
  - The defendant had a **duty of care** to avoid causing injury, damage or loss
  - There was a **breach of that duty** by the defendant
  - *In consequence* the claimant suffered **injury, damage or loss**

- In the case of *Donoghue v Stevenson 1932* the House of Lords ruled that a person might **owe a duty of care to another with whom he had no contractual relationship** at all. The doctrine has been refined in subsequent rulings, but the principle is unchanged.

- The second element that must be proven by a claimant in an action for negligence is that there was a **breach of the duty of care** by the defendant.

- Finally the claimant must demonstrate that he **suffered injury** or **loss** as a result of the breach.

- The law on **negligent professional advice** is influenced strongly by the *Caparo* case. In this case, it was held that the auditors of a public limited company did not owe a duty of care to the public at large who relied upon the audit report when making an investment decision.

- According to Lord Denning, to establish a **special relationship** the person who made the statement must have done so in some professional or expert capacity which made it likely that others would rely on what he said. This is the position of an adviser such as an accountant, banker, solicitor or surveyor

1   To be liable in tort no previous transaction or contractual relationship need exist.

        True   ☐

        False   ☐

2   The 'neighbour' principle was established by which case?

        A   Caparo v Dickman 1990
        B   Anns v Merton London Borough Council 1977
        C   Donoghue v Stevenson 1932
        D   The Wagon Mound 1961

3   **Fill in the blanks** in the statements below, using the words in the box.

        •   The law gives various rights to persons. When such a right is infringed the wrongdoer is liable in
                (1) ....

        •   (2) .... is the most important modern tort

        •   The law on negligent (3) .... advice is currently influenced strongly by the (4) ....
                case

        •   To succeed in a claim for negligent misstatement and resultant economic loss, it must be shown that there
                was a (5) .... of proximity and (6) .... on advice

• Caparo	• reliance	• relationship
• negligence	• tort	• professional

4   When the court applies the maxim *res ipsa loquitur*, it is held that the facts speak for themselves and the defendant
        does not have to prove anything, since the burden of proof is on the claimant.

        True   ☐

        False   ☐

5   According to the Limitation Act 1980, how long after negligence does a claimant have to bring a personal injury
        claim?

        A   1 year
        B   3 years
        C   5 years
        D   6 years

6   What three things must a claimant prove to succeed in an action for negligence?

        •   The defendant owed the claimant a ....

        •   There was a .... of the .... by the defendant

        •   In .... the claimant suffered ...., ... or ....

7   'A public company's auditors owe no duty of care to the public at large who rely on the audit report in deciding to invest.'

This is the decision from *Caparo*.

True ☐

False ☐

8   In certain circumstances, a court can rule that a legitimate duty of care can be ignored on the grounds that it is absurd or undesirable on public policy grounds.

True ☐

False ☐

9   Which of the following describes the 'thin skull' rule?

A   You take your victim as you find them

B   Defendants are not liable for injury where the claimant has a special vulnerability, if they did not know about that vulnerability when the damage was caused

C   Defendants are not liable for injury where the claimant has a special vulnerability, even if they did know about that vulnerability when the damage was caused

D   Those with special vulnerabilities have a duty to inform others about their vulnerability so steps can be taken to protect them

10 Sam agreed to take part in the extreme sport of crazyboarding whilst on holiday. Before taking part he signed a waiver form stating that he takes full responsibility for any injuries he may suffer. During the activity Sam was injured. No other party was involved in the incident. If Sam attempted to sue the organiser for his injuries as soon as he gets home, what defence would the organiser have that would absolve them from liability?

A   Contributory negligence
B   Volenti non fit injuria
C   Vicarious liability
D   Sam is time-barred under The Limitation Act 1980

Answers to Quick Quiz

1   True. A person can be liable in tort even if no previous transaction or contractual relationship exists.

2   C. In *Donoghue v Stevenson 1932*, Lord Atkin set out the 'neighbour principle'.

3   (1) tort (2) negligence (3) professional (4) Caparo (5) relationship (6) reliance

4   False. The burden of proof is reversed and it is up to the defendant to prove they were not negligent.

5   B. The period is 3 years for personal injury claims, 6 years for other claims.

6   Duty of care
    Breach, duty
    Consequence, injury, loss, damage

7   True. In the *Caparo* case it was held that auditors do not owe a duty of care to the public at large or those relying on audit reports for investment purposes.

8   True. For example the case of *Mulcahy v Ministry of Defence 1996*.

9   A. Defendants are liable to those with special vulnerabilities.

10 B. By signing the waiver form, Sam voluntarily accepted the risk of injury. Volenti is the only defence which can absolve a defendant from liability.

Now try the questions below from the Question Bank

Number
Q6
Q7
Q8
Q9
Q10

BPP
LEARNING MEDIA

3

Alternative legal systems and sources of law

Introduction

English common law became the basis of many legal systems around the world due to the expansion of the British Empire in the 18th and 19th centuries. However, common law is not the only basis for legal systems.

Many countries have a **Codified**, or **Civil law** system. Codified systems use statute law as a key source. Much of the law is stated as **general principles** rather than detailed rules. Judges simply **apply the law** rather than make it, and there is no concept of precedent.

Sharia law is explicitly based on the **religion of Islam** and is the source of law for many Muslim states. A key principle is that law is **God-given** and this has meant the law extends into areas of belief and religious practice.

We will also look other legal systems from around the world and other international regulations such as conventions and treaties.

Topic list	Learning outcomes
1 The purpose of legal systems	D2(a)
2 Types of legal system	D2(a)
3 Categories of law	D2(a)
4 Legal systems around the world	D2(a)
5 Sharia law	D2(b)
6 International law	D2(c)
7 Organisations that create international regulations for commerce and professional practice	D2(c)

1 The purpose of legal systems

FAST FORWARD

A **legal system** describes the **mechanism** for **administering** the **law** that has developed within a particular country.

The word law comes from an Old Norse word *lagu* and is used to describe the **rules** (or norms) that society has developed over time to **regulate** the **behaviour** of its citizens. It mandates, proscribes and permits **specified relationships** between individual people and organisations such as businesses. Its aim is to provide an **impartial** system that can be used to **settle disputes** and **punish** those who have not conducted themselves as the rules dictate.

All countries have some form of **legal system** which consists of **courts** where **judges** hear cases between parties that have a dispute. Judges apply **sets of rules** which developed within the country to achieve a **resolution** which is **just** and **fair**. It is the method of administering the law which is known as the legal system.

Legal systems vary between countries and we shall now look at some of the various types of legal system that can be found around the world.

2 Types of legal system

FAST FORWARD

The three main types of legal system that have developed are **common law**, **civil law**, and **Sharia law** legal systems.

Three main types of legal system have developed over time and can be found around the world today. These are:

- Common law
- Civil law
- Sharia law

2.1 Common law systems

FAST FORWARD

Common law systems are based on judge made law through the operation of **judicial precedent**.

Common law is **unwritten** and has developed over time (since the Anglo-Saxons) through the operation of **judicial precedent**. It is the basis of the **United Kingdom's** legal system and was spread through the British empire to countries such as **South Africa**, **Canada** and **Australia**. Its flexibility has led to it being adopted by mixed legal systems such as in **India** and **Nigeria** which also include religious and customary law.

2.2 Codified (civil) law systems

FAST FORWARD

Civil law systems seek to ensure **comprehensibility** and **certainty** by codifying laws via **statutes** and **administrative regulations**. Common law and custom no longer apply as all areas of law are covered by General Principles

Civil law is the **most widespread** legal system in the world with over 60% of all people living in a country which operates it. Civil tradition historically owes much to the **law of the Roman Empire**, and is sometimes given a date of origin as early as 450 BC.

In more recent times, a key period in the development of civil law was the era of **revolution** in Western Europe in the late 18th and early 19th Centuries. It was after these revolutions that **emerging nations** decided to **codify their law**, abolishing the mixture of common law and custom remaining from Roman times and establishing a **national law**.

BPP
LEARNING MEDIA

In France, the process of law-making can been seen in the period after the French Revolution in the years following 1789. The French Civil Code, the **Code Napoleon**, published in 1804, is the key example. Unlike most civil systems, this code only covers areas of **private law** (see later) – most other codes also cover **company law**, **tax**, **administrative** and **constitutional law**. Many Latin countries, and those once colonised by Spain or France, have codes which closely follow the Code Napoleon. Most Central and Eastern European, Scandinavian and East Asian states do not follow this code.

The **German Civil Code** was published in 1896 and shares its roots with Roman law, but was developed alongside established German legal traditions. Like many civil systems, the work of **legal scholars** has had significant influence over it.

2.2.1 Principles of civil law

Two key principles in civil law are **comprehensibility** and **certainty**. Law is **codified** in civil law systems which means it is written down and forms a civil code. The idea is to provide a comprehensive code of the enacted law in a certain area.

Therefore the key source of law is **statute**. Administrative regulations are also codified. Statute law is usually **drafted** as **general principles** and in **simple language** as far as possible, so as to ensure that the law is accessible. This is in stark contrast to English statutes, which are complex and drafted to cover many eventualities.

2.2.2 The role of judges in civil law

FAST FORWARD

In civil law systems, **judges simply apply the law** – they do not make law via judicial precedent, although they may perform **judicial review** to ensure that statutes are in line with the **constitution**.

The role of judges in a civil law system is significantly different from the role of a common law judge. There is a **distinct division** between those who **draft the law** and those who **apply the law**, judges being the latter.

There is no such thing as judge-made law. Whilst previous judicial decisions will be **persuasive** to other judges, they **do not create precedent** in the same way as in the common law system. However, in practice, judges do tend to follow their previous decisions.

2.3 Sharia law

Sharia law is founded in the religion of **Islam** and is adopted by a number of Muslim states. We shall look at Sharia law in more detail later on.

Question

Civil law

What are the features of a civil law system?

(i)   Codification under a civil law system is a comprehensive process where all law in a particular area is incorporated into a code.

(ii)   Civil law systems use the concept of precedent to allow judges to make law.

(iii)   Civil law distinguishes those who make the law and those who apply it.

(iv)   Civil law creates complex rules to cover many eventualities.

A   (i) and (iii) only
B   (ii) and (iii) only
C   (i), (iii) and (iv) only
D   All of the above

A   Codification under civil law systems is a comprehensive process where all law in a particular area is incorporated into a code. Civil law distinguishes those who make the law (the legislature) and those who apply it (the judges). Civil codes are usually drafted as general principles in simple language.

3 Categories of law

FAST FORWARD

Law can be **broken down** into four categories, **private**, **public**, **procedural** and **international**.

It is possible to break law down into four categories based on **who the disputing parties are**. These categories are:

- Private law
- Public law
- Procedural law
- International law

3.1 Private law

Most legal actions are between **private individuals** who are both within the same legal system. Such actions come under the term private law as the matter is private between the parties concerned. Common types of private actions include **contractual disputes** or those concerning **torts** or **company law**.

3.2 Public law

Some cases which are in the **public interest** are taken up by the **authorities** or **government** and are **against private individuals** (or vice versa) who are within the same legal system. These actions are **public law** actions. **Criminal** cases are the most common public law actions, but the state may take action against **breaches of regulations** as well. **Individuals** may take action against the state where their **rights** have been **violated** or where **legislation** has been **breached**. Such actions may be protected by the **constitution** of the country.

3.3 Procedural law

The **operation of law** such as **access to the legal system**, the **rights of disputing parties** and **complaints procedures** all come under **procedural law**. It is also known by the term **'adjective' law** as it deals with how other laws are applied. An example of procedural law are the **civil** and **criminal procedural rules** and the rules concerning the **submission of evidence**, **prison tariffs** for convicted criminals and **legal remedies** available to parties who have suffered harm.

3.4 International law

International law is quite different to the other types of law we have seen. This is because it deals with conduct **between nation states**, or **between individuals and organisations of different nation states**. All the other systems that have been discussed previously only affect individuals and organisations within a nation, as that is where their jurisdiction lies. It is important to remember that international law only works when it is recognised and accepted by states. **Treaties** and **international customs** are key sources of international law.

We shall study international law in greater detail later on.

Question

Which of the following types of law would deal with a dispute between an individual and the government of their nation?

A   Private law
B   Public law
C   Procedural law
D   International law

Answer

B   Public law deals with disputes between the state and an individual.

4 Legal systems around the world

FAST FORWARD

> **Legal systems** from around the world **vary greatly** and it is important to understand how and why they differ.

We shall now look in detail at a selection of **legal systems from around the world** split between those inside and outside the European Union.

Assessment focus point

Assessments will test your understanding of the sources, classifications and structure of the courts within each system.

4.1 Legal systems within the European Union

We have already looked at the English legal system, but we briefly summarise the main points below together with those of a number of other European countries.

4.1.1 England

In England the main sources of law are **case law**, created by the **judiciary,** and **legislation** created by **Parliament**.

The English legal system can be classified into, **civil law** (contract, tort and company law) and **criminal law**, or it can be split into **private** (effectively civil law) and **public** (including criminal law).

There is a **civil** and **criminal structure** to the court system. The courts to be found in each are:

(a)   **Civil law** – County Court, High Court (Queen's Bench division, Chancery division and Family division), Court of Appeal (civil division) and Supreme Court.

(b)   **Criminal law** – Magistrates' Court, Crown Court, Court of Appeal (criminal division) and Supreme Court.

4.1.2 Germany

The German constitution permits Parliament to create **codified law**. It is a democratic and social federal state in which **all are equal** before the law. A form of **delegated legislation** called **ordinances** or **statutory instruments** is also possible. These are created in the same way as in England (the right to create law is given by a Parent Act or Enabling Act). Where the constitution allows, legislation can be written by **public corporations** to allow the regulation of their own affairs.

Customary law plays some part in the German system as the judiciary must also follow established practices.

Courts interpret the law and issue **binding judgements** on the parties who are bound to follow the stated action. Judicial precedent is not created but lower courts will respect the earlier decisions of higher courts to prevent repeated consequences if similar cases are appealed.

4.1.3 Denmark

Denmark's legal system has strong **German** and **Nordic influences** and can trace its history back to the Middle Ages. In 1683 existing provincial laws were integrated into one system.

There are **four sources** of Danish law .

(a) **Constitutional Acts**. These determine the requirements for creating statutes and also regulate the relationships between the various state bodies. It is similar to the English system involving gaining approval from Parliament and Royal Assent.

(b) **Acts of Parliament**. Comparable to the English system.

(c) **Case law**. This is created by the courts, but unlike other common law systems, Danish case law exists to fill in the gaps where legislation has not been made and is therefore limited in effect.

(d) **Custom law**. The Danish system does reflect customs, however legislation can be created that overrides it and the courts may overrule customs which are deemed unreasonable.

International law such as treaties will be incorporated into Danish law. Denmark may hold a referendum before significant agreements are made.

Danish law can be classified into **Public law**, which deals with constitutional, administrative, international and criminal law, and **Civil law** that is concerned with individuals and legal persons such as companies.

The Danish court system is based on a **hierarchy**. The lowest courts are city courts, above them is the High Court and the Supreme Court. Unlike some other European countries, it does not have a constitutional or administrative court.

4.1.4 Poland

Like many European countries, Poland is a democratic republic which operates a **codified** legal system. Law is created by Parliament which like England is made up of two houses, a lower house, the *Sejm* and an upper house, the *Senate*. Other sources of law include **regulations**, which under the constitution require authorisation from permitted bodies as well as **international** and **local** laws.

The Polish system consists of **provincial** and **district courts** which hear civil and criminal cases with a **supreme court** of appeal. There is also a **high administrative court** which is held in ten districts and deals with public sector administration.

4.1.5 France

Most law in France is **codified**. The *Code Civile* was created by the people in 1904 and designed to be easily accessible by them. **Tort** is the exception, it is not codified but is created by the **judiciary**.

The French system is based on **Private** and **Public law**. Private law is the law of the people and includes criminal law (the judicial order). Public law is the law applicable to government and individuals (the administrative order).

French courts follow a similar structure to England. There is an **initial hearing level** and **two appeal levels**.

(a) **Trial level** – cases are heard at this level initially. It is split into six divisions which deal with specific areas such as ordinary and criminal jurisdiction, employment and commerce.

(b) **Appeal level** – cases are heard again and consider matters of fact and law. This level is also split into specialist divisions.

(c) **Supreme level** – similar to the appeal level, it forms a decision and sends it back down for the lower court to review. Its decision is final.

All individuals are entitled to legal representation. Cases follow **adversarial principles** (as in England) as well as **inquisitional principles**, where the judge will conduct the questioning within the court. Individuals are appointed judges when they commence their legal career, whereas in England they are appointed at the end of a successful legal career.

4.1.6 Italy

Another democratic republic. Italian law consists of **state law** (created by the state) and laws developed by its **autonomous** regions, municipalities and metropolitan cities. Any legislation passed in these locations must be consistent with the constitution, European law and Italy's international commitments.

Law is **codified** at state level and legislation must pass through two chambers. The **House of Representatives** (630 Representatives elected nationally) and **the Senate** (315 Senators elected regionally). The process of creating law is similar to England and legislation is subject to committee scrutiny and debate by both chambers.

The Italian system permits **delegated legislation** but it is strictly controlled through criteria being set on the area of law being developed and a strict time limit for its creation.

Courts handle distinct legal areas such as **criminal** and **civil law** (for which a hierarchy of courts exist), and **military**, **taxation**, **accounting** and **administrative**.

4.1.7 Cyprus

The history of Cyprus has resulted in a legal system which is influenced by a number of countries. From 1925 to 1959 it was a British colony and operated the English **common law system**. It then became an independent republic with a **constitution** which is the supreme source of law. Its system became complicated following the Turkish invasion - the northern part of the Island is recognised by Turkey as the Republic of Northern Cyprus. The Republic of Cyprus is a member of the **European Union** and is subject to its laws as well.

Therefore sources of Cypriot law are varied, the most important are, the **constitution**, **legislation**, **common law**, **Sharia law**, **Greek Orthodox law**, **EU law** and **international law**.

4.1.8 Greece

In 1975, the Greek presidential republic was formed. Its **codified** laws come from a number of sources including **French** and **Roman** traditions and customs as well as 19th century **continental codifications**. It has a **constitution** which is the supreme law.

Sources of Greek law include:

(a) **Legislation** (similar to the English system), but it is published and is enforceable within ten days of publication.

(b) **Codes**, including a civil code (and civil procedures), criminal procedures and statute law contained in the law of tribune

(c) **Case law**, similar to most European countries

In which year did Denmark integrate its laws into the one system which exists today?

A   1683
B   1783
C   1893
D   1993

Answer

A   Denmark integrated its system in 1683.

4.2 Legal systems outside the European Union

As we have already seen, many (mainly **commonwealth**) countries have adopted **English common law**, but many others have theirs based on **codified systems** developed by countries such as France and Spain. Indeed **Chile's** legal system is influenced by France and Spain as well as Austria! **Egypt's** system is a mixture of common and Sharia law and is also influenced by Napoleonic codes. We shall now look at other systems from around the world.

Assessment focus point

It is important to note any similarities you see between systems, as well as differences as this will help you in questions that require you to spot the 'odd one out'.

4.2.1 Russia

The Russian legal system is split into three branches: the **arbitration court system** headed by the **High Court of Arbitration**, a **regular court system** with the **Supreme Court** at the top of the hierarchy and the **Constitutional Court** as a single body with no courts under it.

Legal disputes between **business entities** are heard by the **Courts of Arbitration** (the business or economic courts). The system of these courts is on two levels topped by the **High Court of Arbitration**. There are **eighty-two courts of arbitration** with about two thousand judges handling about three hundred thousand disputes every year. Where a party to a civil case is a private individual, not involved in business activities, the dispute is heard by a court of general jurisdiction.

There are about fourteen thousand judges in some two thousand five hundred courts of general jurisdiction on various levels. Most cases in Russia are heard by these regular courts

The **regular court system** is the people's court, and each city district or rural district is represented. Apart from the arbitration court system, no courts of special jurisdiction in Russia exist (for example those handling domestic relations or probate disputes). These **district courts handle over ninety percent** of all civil and criminal cases.

Only a limited number of cases (such as those involving the most serious crimes) are heard by the next level of courts - the **Oblast** (provincial) courts. Cases are tried by one of several methods

- By a presiding, professional judge and two lay judges called 'people's assessors'
- By a panel of three professional judges
- By a single judge.

56   **3: Alternative legal systems and sources of law** | Part A Comparison of English law with alternative legal systems

BPP
LEARNING MEDIA

Relatively recently, Russia started to experiment with **jury trials** (panels of twelve jurors). A jury trial is only available in serious crimes where jurisdiction originates in the Oblast courts.

Decisions of the lower trial courts can be **appealed** through intermediate courts up to the Supreme Court.

Direct appeal to a higher court (through an appeals procedure called **'cassational review'**) is the main way for a party to complain against a court's decision. However, Russian law also allows citizens to appeal to higher courts even when the time limits prescribed for cassational review have expired.

Acting upon this appeal, the higher court (the **procurat**) exercise their supervisory powers and bring their own complaint (known as '**protest**') against the lower court's decision.

The **Constitutional Court** handles administrative cases and other matters related to the constitution of the state.

4.2.2 United States of America

The USA operates a **federal system** of law. It has a **national constitution** which is recognised as the supreme law and guarantees its citizens certain rights and freedoms. The interpretation of Federal law is undertaken by the Federal Courts.

The national government through the **United States Congress** introduces federal statutes and enactment follows broadly the same (two chamber and committee) procedure as the United Kingdom except for the need for Royal Assent.

International treaties and **federal statutes** have supreme status.

A form of **delegated legislation** (Executive Orders and Agency Rules) can be created by **administrative bodies** if Congress has authorised them.

In addition to Federal law, **individual states** can also create their own law through **statutes** and the operation of **common law** through the courts. Operation of common law is the same as in England with each case setting a precedent except in Louisiana. The **United States Supreme Court** is the ultimate appeal court. If state law ever **conflicts** with Federal law then Federal law will prevail.

4.2.3 China

The **traditional** Chinese legal system can be traced back to at least 500 BC and the time of the Chinese philosopher, **Confucius**. His philosophy was based upon **social relationships**, control, order, justice and sincerity. During this time, laws evolved to regulate the behaviour of individuals, but it was perceived as less important than **self-discipline**. Despite being viewed as poorly developed by the Europeans during the 18th Century, it is now recognised by historians as being at least as well developed as European legal systems of the same period.

Recent times have seen the Chinese push for **modernisation** and this has been reflected in changes to the legal system. Since 1979 the system of administering justice has been replaced and over three hundred new laws have been created.

There is little overall strategy for developing new laws. Very often specific areas of **activity** or **dealing** will identify the need for regulation and therefore law tends to develop on a **piecemeal** basis. China has resisted the option of importing laws from other legal systems and continues to develop in its own way. One feature of the Chinese style of development is the use of **trial periods** where new legislation is introduced and then redrafted after a period of time. This allows the impact and effect of the law to be reviewed and amendments made, but it has caused contradictions and gaps in the law.

The court system is made up of over 800,000 **mediation committees** which are found across the country in rural and urban areas. These committees hear both civil and criminal cases and are provided **free of charge**. Partly due to the large number of committees, most judges do not receive any legal training. These committees are hugely successful, hearing over **90%** of all cases in the country.

Since the 1990s, China has introduced further law reforms in areas such as **criminal law** and **human rights**, but it is considered to be at least half a century behind most countries. Interestingly, the previous Portuguese and British colonies of Macau and Hong Kong did not adopt Chinese law once they returned to Chinese sovereignty and still operate Portuguese and English legal systems.

4.2.4 Malaysia

Malaysian law is based upon **English common law** (developed by the courts) and, legislation (created by the legislature). Additionally, other laws such as **Sharia** will apply to Muslims and, **traditional laws** will also apply to other Malaysian people. The Federal government is responsible for the administration of justice.

There is a hierarchy of courts which is comparable to that of England. The lower level '**Subordinate**' courts include **Magistrates'** and **Sessions** courts. There are two mid level '**Superior**' courts: one is for the Malaysian states, *Sabah* and *Sarawak* and the other is for Peninsular Malaysia; both are of equal status. The **Federal Court** acts as a final appeal court.

A **Special Court** which hears alleged offences committed by the Monarchical heads of the various island states was formed in 1993. The constitutional Monarch (a '**paramount ruler**') would also appear in this court.

4.2.5 Sri Lanka

Sri Lanka operates a **Penal Code** based on **Indian law**. This system replaced the English legal system when the country gained independence from Britain in 1948 and became a republic. Sri Lanka's parliament consists of 168 elected members of whom 49 are ministers, forming the Prime Minister's Cabinet.

The courts' system is a typical **hierarchy** based on the English system. For example, in the criminal system cases begin in a Magistrates' Court and may be appealed to the High Court, Court of Appeal and finally the Supreme Court.

5 Sharia law

FAST FORWARD

> Sharia law is based on the religion of Islam. This means that the law extends into **areas of belief and religious practice** and that the **law is God-given** and so has **wider significance than social order**.

The major difference between Sharia law and other legal systems is that **Sharia law is explicitly based on**, and connected with, **the religion of Islam**. **Sharia** is 'a way to a watering place', in other words, a path to be followed. **Sharia law** is ordained by Allah as guidance for mankind.

Assessment focus point

> You may see Sharia law referred to as Shari'ah law in your assessment.

5.1 Development of Sharia law

Unlike other legal systems which are contained within one nation, **Sharia law** is the law of Muslims **regardless** of where they live. Over time many states have **incorporated** Sharia law into their legal systems to differing degrees. Similar to the spread to common law, **colonisation** has had an effect, resulting in some societies being highly Sharia and others less so. These states often replace elements of Sharia with **secular constitutions** and **laws** (Pakistan, Bangladesh and Indonesia are examples of such states). Some North African and Middle Eastern states have also developed systems of secular and religious courts.

BPP
LEARNING MEDIA

The **level of adoption** of Sharia law is related to the society and people of the nation. As with Fundamentalist Christians or Jews, individuals and societies with **Fundamentalist beliefs** would expect the law to apply to all those who share the faith. Where the society is **moderate**, law can be separated from religion allowing it to develop separately.

Differences in application of Sharia law include, rules on **evidence** and **burdens of proof** as well as the **strictness** and **nature of punishments** given to law-breakers. Many punishments such as amputation and stoning are seen as harsh by westerners, but is viewed as necessary to deter future criminals.

5.2 Areas of Sharia law

Sharia law is essentially in two parts. The first deals with **religion** and sets out rules on praying, fasting and the pilgrimage to Mecca. The second covers the **judicial process and administration of the law** such as the rules on the use of witnesses and evidence. As we have already seen, **Sharia law impacts on many areas of a Muslim's life**. The following are some of the most important:

- Family law (including rules of marriage, divorce, children, inheritance and endowments)
- Financial and business operations
- Peace and war
- Penal punishments
- Rules on food and drink

5.3 Principles of Sharia law

As can be seen above, the main princi0070le of Sharia law is that it is **the divine way** ordained for man to follow by Allah. The law, therefore, is **sourced directly from Allah** and this has a significant impact on how it is interpreted by judges. The **law is divine**, but it must be remembered that the opinions and decisions of the judges are not. By applying Sharia law people can live in **harmony** and a **just society** is sought.

5.3.1 Categories of behaviour

Muslims believe that Sharia law will provide them with **physical** and **spiritual wellbeing** and that it must therefore cover their lives **comprehensively**. There are five broad categories which govern a Muslim's actions. By knowing how a particular act is classified, a Muslim will know whether or not they **must** perform it (obligatory) or **must never** perform it (forbidden), or whether the act falls somewhere in between.

The **five categories** are:

- Obligatory
- Meritorious
- Permissible
- Reprehensible
- Forbidden

5.3.2 The Five Pillars of Islam

The **Five Pillars of Islam** are the duties that every Muslim is expected to perform during their life, and are:

- **Shahadah** – the profession of faith
- **Salat** – to pray five times a day
- **Zakat** – to give to charity
- **Sawm** – to fast during Ramadan
- **Hajj** – to take part in a pilgrimage to Mecca

BPP
LEARNING MEDIA

Part A Comparison of English law with alternative legal systems | **3: Alternative legal systems and sources of law** **59**

5.3.3 Examples of forbidden actions

The following are examples of some actions which are forbidden. It should be noted that whether an act is forbidden or not depends upon the **interpretation** of Sharia law which is taken.

(a) **Blasphemy**

Criticisms of the Prophet Muhammad are not acceptable and punishments are strict. In some countries this is seen as limiting an individual's freedom of speech.

(b) **Apostasy**

This is the conversion from Islam to another religion and is comparable to the crime of treason.

(c) **Diet**

There are strict rules on the consumption of meat – pork is prohibited.

Punishment for breaching these rules will vary on the country where the person lives. Those in western countries may face little or no punishment compared to those in Muslim states.

5.3.4 Women

Women are somewhat restricted regarding what **roles** they can perform, particularly in the areas of **work** and **religious practice**. As with other areas of Sharia law, these restrictions depend on the interpretation of the law and the society in which the woman lives. Indeed in Pakistan, women have held the positions of Head of State and Army General.

5.4 Sources of Sharia law

FAST FORWARD

The main sources of Sharia law are the **Quran** and the **Sunnah**. The secondary sources of law are the **Madhab**.

The **key source of law** in Sharia is the **Quran**, which contains various injunctions of a legal nature.

Key term

The **Quran** is Allah's divine revelation to his Prophet, Muhammad.

The Quran was revealed to the **Prophet Muhammad** during the last years of his life, around 619 – 632 CE. It was written down piecemeal during his lifetime but not fully collated until after his death.

The **Muslim calendar** is different from the Western systems of years BCE and CE. However, for the purposes of comparability with common and civil law systems, the CE dates are being used here.

The Quran includes various injunctions of a legal nature, but it does not cover every detail, so **another primary source of law** in Sharia is the **Sunnah**.

Key term

The **Sunnah** is 'the beaten track', in other words, what has come to be the acceptable course of conduct. It is derived from the sayings of the Prophet, known as **Ahadith** (known in singular as Hadith).

Some Muslims also consider the **unanimity of Muhammad's disciples** on certain issues to also be a primary source of Sharia law.

There are also five **major secondary sources** of law in the Muslim world, known as **Madhab**. These are schools of thought based on **writings and thoughts of major jurists** formed in the years immediately following the death of the Prophet and are named after those jurists:

- The **Shia** school
- The **Hanafi** school (Imam Abu Hanifa)
- The **Maliki** school (Imam Malik)
- The **Hanbali** school (Imam Ahmad Ibn Hanbal)
- The **Shafii** school (Imam As-Shafii)

Where the primary sources of Sharia law are silent, a process of **reasoning**, often using **analogies**, and what law exists is applied to the new situation. It is also possible for law to be found through consensus of the people or community.

There is also an element of **codification** of some Sharia practices which developed through customs.

5.5 The role of judges in Sharia law

FAST FORWARD

In **Sharia law**, **judges** may need to **interpret the law** (it cannot be changed). They do this in line with the Sunnah Ahadith (sayings of the Prophet) that are varyingly reliable. Fiqh is the process of further legal interpretation, using ijtihad. Judges may also perform a form of judicial review.

Due to the **religious nature** of Sharia law, **judges are often clerics**, known as Imam. This is the situation in **Iran**, for example. However, in other Muslim states, there are a **mixture of clerical judges and secular judges**.

Judges are required to apply the law to cases brought before them. However, given the **nature and source** of the law, there are **particular considerations** with regard to its **interpretation**.

5.5.1 Interpretation of Sharia law

The **Quran cannot be altered**, being the Word of Allah. It may only be **interpreted**. This leads to the problem in Islamic circles of who is **qualified to interpret** the Quran. Muhammad, as Allah's prophet, was qualified to do so.

When clear guidance cannot be obtained from the Quran, the judge may turn to the **Sunnah** to see **how the Quran was interpreted by the Prophet**. The Sunnah is used by Muslim jurists to:

- **Confirm** the law in the Quran
- **Explain** matters mentioned in the Quran in general terms
- **Clarify** verses in the Quran that may seem ambiguous
- **Introduce a rule where the Quran is silent**

The **Ahadith** that comprise the Sunnah were recorded some time after the death of the Prophet and are **classified according to reliability**. The authenticity of some is virtually certain: these are known as **muwatir**. Others are **less certain** and known as **mashtur**. Lastly, where there is **little certainty** as to their authenticity, Ahadith are called **ahad**.

Question

The unanimity of Muhammad's disciples is considered by many Muslims to be a secondary source of Sharia law.
True or False?

Answer

The correct answer is False.

The unanimity of the disciples is considered by many to be a primary source of Sharia law.

6 International law

FAST FORWARD

The main **sources** of **international law** are:

- Conventions and treaties
- International customary law
- General principles of law recognised by civilised nations

International law is quite different to the other legal systems we have seen. This is because it deals with conduct **between nation states**, or **between individuals and organisations of different nation states**. The other systems discussed previously only affect individuals and organisations within a state, as that is where their jurisdiction lies.

6.1 Types of international law

There are two types of international law:

- Public
- Private

6.2 Public international law

Public international law consists of **agreements between nations**. For example agreements regarding territory, human rights and decommissioning of nuclear weapons.

Sources of public international law include:

- **Conventions** and **treaties**
- **International customary law**
- **General principles of law recognised by civilised nations**

62   **3: Alternative legal systems and sources of law** | Part A Comparison of English law with alternative legal systems

BPP
LEARNING MEDIA

6.2.1 Conventions and treaties

FAST FORWARD

International conventions and treaties are **voluntary agreements** between nations that **create obligations** between them.

You can view treaties as contracts between nations, as they are binding under international law. Therefore parties are **legally liable** if they fail to meet their obligations. A central principle to treaty law is *maxim pacta sunt servanda* – 'pacts must be respected.'

6.2.2 International customary law

FAST FORWARD

Customary international law is founded on the basis that **consistent practice of certain principles** can **create an obligation** to continue to do so in the future.

Many legal systems around the world are based upon the same or similar general principles. These principles have been accepted as **binding norms** between countries during their relations over time. The consistant application of these principles has resulted in them becoming international customary law. The **Vienna Convention on the Law of Treaties** is an example of where customary law has been codified.

6.2.3 General principles of law recognised by civilised nations

Key principles of law from the major legal systems around the world can be used to **supplement international law** when necessary. For example, when a particular point of international law is unclear or disputed, seeing how it would have been dealt with by another civilised nation can help clarify the issue.

6.3 Private international law

Private international law describes a **nation's own national laws** that regulate the **international dealings** of its individuals and organisations where **another state** is involved.

6.3.1 Conflict of laws

FAST FORWARD

Conflict of laws occurs when people and organisations from different legal jurisdictions trade, or develop other relationships with each other. Conflicts arise when aspects of the different legal systems are fundamentally different.

As **domestic laws** within individual states **vary**, conflicts can occur when people and businesses from **different nations** trade, this is because each expects that their national laws will apply. But through international co-operation and agreement, regulations can be **harmonised**, differences eliminated and **fairness** to all can be achieved.

6.3.2 Example: conflict of laws

An individual in country A buys products from country B. Under the laws of their own state, the purchaser is entitled to a refund if the goods are faulty, but under country B's laws, they are only entitled to a replacement. If the goods turn out to be faulty, whose law will apply? Each country may insist their law applies and this may create a legal disagreement.

6.4 Who creates public international law?

Throughout history countries have developed **agreements**, **pacts** and **treaties** between each other as part of normal diplomatic relations. However this sometimes led to military or economic conflicts when countries broke agreements they made.

After the second world war, the **United Nations** was set up to provide the world with a body that nations can go to when disputes arise. Initially 51 countries joined, but now almost every nation on earth is represented.

There are other international bodies that exist to develop agreements between areas of the world, not just individual states. For example, the **United Nations Economic Commission for Europe** (UNECE) pursues harmonisation of policies and certain technical details within the EU.

Question   International law

Public international law deals with disputes between:

A   A nation and an individual in another nation
B   Two different nations
C   Individuals in different nations
D   Individuals in the same nation

Answer

B   Public international law deals with disputes between nations. Private international law deals with disputes between individuals in different nations.

7 Organisations that create international regulations for commerce and professional practice

FAST FORWARD There are **other bodies** which **create regulations** for **business** or **professions** that **operate internationally**.

These regulations are required because it is sometimes necessary for **common rules** to be in place in order for the business or profession to **operate properly**. Examples of bodies that create such international regulations include:

- International Federation of Accountants (IFAC)
- International Standardisation Organisation (ISO)
- Federation de Experts Comptable Europeen (FEE)

7.1 International Federation of Accountants (IFAC)

The **International Federation of Accountants** (IFAC) is an international body representing all the major accountancy bodies across the world. Its mission is to develop the high standards of professional accountants and enhance the quality of services they provide. We shall look at IFAC in more detail later in your studies.

BPP LEARNING MEDIA

7.2 International Standardisation Organisation (ISO)

The **International Standardisation Organisation** (ISO) is the world's largest issuer of International Standards It is a non-governmental organisation with members from 162 countries. Each country has one member/representative and there is a Central Secretariat in Geneva, Switzerland, that coordinates the system.

Standards are created by **technical committees** and **sub-committees** in a six-stage process:

- **Stage 1: Proposal stage** – confirmation that a new standard is actually needed.

- **Stage 2: Preparatory stage** – a working group of experts prepare a working draft.

- **Stage 3: Committee stage** – the draft is distributed, voted on and amendments made until the committee is happy with the new standard.

- **Stage 4: Enquiry stage** – the new draft is circulated among ISO's members and a five month consultation period begins. After five months the draft is voted on. If approved, the draft moves to the next stage, if not it returns to the technical committee for further work.

- **Stage 5: Approval stage** – final draft is put to an approval vote by ISO members.

- **Stage 6: Publication stage** – once approved, the standard is published. Very minor editorial changes may be made.

ISO's standards are applicable to **many types of business organisation** and they are updated periodically. The ISO 9000 2000 series of standards consists of four primary standards: ISO 9000, ISO 9001, ISO 9004, and ISO 19011.

(a) **ISO 9001:2000** contains ISO's current quality management system requirements. This is the standard you need to use if you wish to become certified (registered).

(b) **ISO 9000:2000 and ISO 9004:2000** contain ISO's quality management system guidelines. These standards explain ISO's approach to quality management presenting definitions and a set of guidelines for improving performance, but they are not intended to be used for certification purposes.

(c) **ISO 19011** covers quality auditing standards.

(d) **ISO 14001** relates to environmental management systems. It specifies a process for controlling and improving an organisation's environmental performance. Issues covered include:

   (i) Use and source of raw materials
   (ii) Waste
   (iii) Noise
   (iv) Energy use
   (v) Emissions

When a company claims that they are **ISO 9000 certified** or **registered**, they mean that an independent registrar has audited their processes and certified that they meet the ISO requirements.

When an organisation says that it is **ISO 9000 compliant**, they mean that they have met ISO's quality system requirements, but have not been formally certified by an independent registrar. In effect, they are self-certified. Of course, official certification carries more weight in the market place.

The ISO 9000 standards are **process standards**, not product standards. Organisations are granted certified or compliant status on the basis that their processes rather than their products and services meet ISO 9000 requirements. The logic is that high quality processes ensure high quality output.

7.3 Federation de Experts Comptable Europeen (FEE)

The **Federation de Experts Comptable Europeen** (FEE) is also known as The **Federation of European Accountants** and is the representative organisation for the **Europe's accountancy profession**. Its members are from 45 professional institutes of accountants from 33 countries, and representatives from each of the 27 Member States of the European Union are included. In total, over 500,000 European accountants are represented by FEE. Approximately 45% work in public practice and 55% work in industry, commerce, government and education.

The **organization commenced work on 1 January 1987** when it took over the activities previously carried out separately by the Union Européenne des Experts Comptables, Economiques et Financiers (UEC) and the Groupe d'Etudes des Experts Comptables de la CEE (Group d'Etudes). Both organisations had served the European accountancy profession since 1951 and 1961 respectively.

7.3.1 Objectives of FEE

FEE is a **non-profit association** with the **objectives** of:

(i)   **Promoting** and **advancing** the **interests** of the European accountancy profession in the broadest sense recognising the public interest in the work of the profession.

(ii)   Working towards the **enhancement**, **harmonisation** and **liberalisation** of the practice and regulation of accountancy, statutory audit and financial reporting in Europe in both the public and private sector, taking account of developments at a worldwide level and, where necessary, promoting and defending specific European interests.

(iii)   **Promoting co-operation** among the professional accountancy bodies in Europe in relation to issues of common interest in both the public and private sector;

(iv)   **Identifying developments** that may have an impact on the practice of accountancy, statutory audit and financial reporting at an early stage, to advise member bodies of such developments and, in conjunction with member bodies, to seek to influence the outcome;

(v)   Being the **sole representative** and consultative organisation of the **European accountancy** profession in relation to the EU institutions;

(vi)   **Representing** the **European accountancy profession** at the international level.

The **organisation** is **involved** in the following matters (amongst others):

- Accounting
- Anti-Money Laundering
- Auditing
- Banking and Insurance
- Capital Markets
- Company Law, Corporate Governance, Ethics and Sustainability
- Direct and Indirect Taxation
- Financial and Integrated Reporting

BPP
LEARNING MEDIA

7.3.2 Structure of FEE

FEE has **three main bodies**:

(a) The **General Assembly**

The General Assembly is made up of all the Member Bodies of the Federation. Its role is to make decisions on constitutional or membership issues, or other matters referred to it by Council. It also elects the President and Deputy President and approves expenditure and the annual accounts.

(b) The **Council**

The Council consists of representatives appointed by each country and is responsible for the management of the organisation. It meets four times a year during which strategic decisions are made,

(c) The **Executive**

FEE's Executive includes the President, the Deputy President, Vice-Presidents and the Chief Executive Officer. Its role is the implementation of Council decisions and the day-to-day management of the organisation.

Part A Comparison of English law with alternative legal systems | **3: Alternative legal systems and sources of law**   67

Chapter Roundup

- A **legal system** describes the **mechanism** for **administering** the **law** that has developed within a particular country.

- **The three main** types of legal system that have developed are **common law**, **civil law**, and **Sharia law** legal systems

- **Common law** systems are based on judge made law through the operation of **judicial precedent**.

- Civil law systems seek to ensure **comprehensibility** and **certainty** by codifying laws via **statutes** and **administrative regulations**. Common law and custom no longer apply as all areas of law are covered by General Principles

- In civil law systems, **judges simply apply the law** – they do not make law via judicial precedent, although they may perform **judicial review** to ensure that statutes are in line with the **constitution**

- **Law** can be **broken down** into four categories, **private**, **public**, **procedural** and **international**.

- **Legal systems** from around the world **vary greatly** and it is important to understand how and why they differ.

- Sharia law is based on the religion of Islam. This means that the law extends into **areas of belief and religious practice** and that the **law is God-given** and so has **wider significance than social order**.

- The main sources of Sharia law are the **Quran** and the **Sunnah**. The secondary sources of law are the **Madhab**

- In **Sharia law**, **judges** may need to **interpret the law** (it cannot be changed). They do this in line with the Sunnah Ahadith (sayings of the Prophet) that are varyingly reliable. Fiqh is the process of further legal interpretation, using ijtihad. Judges may also perform a form of judicial review.

- The main **sources** of **international law** are:
    - Conventions and treaties
    - International customary law
    - General principles of law recognised by civilised nations

- International conventions and treaties are **voluntary agreements** between nations that **create obligations** between them.

- Customary international law is founded on the basis that **consistent practice of certain principles** can **create an obligation** to continue to do so in the future.

- **Conflict of laws** occurs when people and organisations from different legal jurisdictions trade, or develop other relationships with each other. Conflicts arise when aspects of the different legal systems are fundamentally different.

- There are **other bodies** which **create regulations** for **business** or **professions** that **operate internationally**.

BPP LEARNING MEDIA

1   Fill in the blanks.

    In the civil law tradition, ... is the process of putting .... the law on a specific area together in a ....

2   French courts follow adversarial and inquisitional principles.

    True   ☐
    False   ☐

3   Under which type of law would a contractual dispute between a company in one country and a supplier in another country be heard?

    A   International public law
    B   International private law
    C   International procedural law
    D   International criminal law

4   Apostasy is a term which is related to which of the following under Sharia law?

    A   The restrictions on the role of women in religious practice
    B   The rules concerning the interpretation of the Quran
    C   The prohibition of criticising the Prophet Muhammad
    D   The conversion of Muslims to another religion

5   List three sources of international law.

6   Procedural law is also known as 'adjective' law.

    True   ☐
    False   ☐

7   FEE represents all the major accountancy bodies across the world?

    True   ☐
    False   ☐

8   ISO is the largest issuer of international standards regarding business processes?

    True   ☐
    False   ☐

9   IFAC represents the major European accountancy bodies?

    True   ☐
    False   ☐

10 ISO's General Secretariat is based in Geneva, Switzerland.

    True   ☐
    False   ☐

BPP
LEARNING MEDIA

Part A Comparison of English law with alternative legal systems | **3: Alternative legal systems and sources of law**   69

Answers to Quick Quiz

1   In the civil law tradition, **codification** is the process of putting **all** the law on a specific area together in a **code**

2   True. French courts follow adversarial principles where the lawyers question the parties, but judges are also permitted to conduct questioning under inquisitional principles.

3   B. Contractual disputes between individuals and organisations in different countries come under international private law.

4   D. Apostasy is the conversion from Islam to another religion and is comparable to treason.

5   Three sources of international law are:
   –   Conventions and treaties
   –   International customary law
   –   General principles of law recognised by civilised nations

6   True. Procedural law is also known as 'adjective' law as it deals with how other laws are applied.

7   False. IFAC represents all the major accounting bodies across the world.

8   True. ISO is the largest issuer of international standards regarding business processes.

9   False. FEE represents the major European accountancy bodies.

10 True. ISO's General Secretariat is based in Geneva, Switzerland.

Now try the questions below from the Question Bank

Number
Q11
Q12
Q13
Q14
Q15

BPP LEARNING MEDIA

Part B
Law of
Contract

BPP
LEARNING MEDIA

Establishing contractual obligations

4

Introduction

There are **three essential elements** to look for in the formation of a valid contract

The first essential element is **agreement**. To determine whether or not an agreement has been reached, the courts will consider whether one party has made a firm **offer** which the other party has **accepted**.

In most contracts, offer and acceptance may be made orally or in writing, or they may be implied by the conduct of the parties. The person making an offer is the offeror and the person to whom an offer is made is the offeree.

The second of the three essential elements of a contract is **consideration**. The promise which a claimant seeks to enforce must be part of a bargain to which the claimant has himself contributed. Related to consideration are the doctrines of **promissory estoppel** and **privity of contract**.

Finally, an agreement is not a binding contract unless the third element, **intention to create legal relations** is present. What matters is not what the parties have in their minds, but the inferences that reasonable people would draw from their words or conduct.

In this chapter we also look at the **form** of a contract. Only a small percentage of contracts must by law be in writing, and these are described. Good commercial practice dictates that many contracts that do not need to be in writing are in fact committed to paper.

The chapter concludes with a discussion of **misrepresentation** and its effect upon a contract.

Topic list	Learning outcomes
1 Contract basics	E1(a)
2 The form of a contract	E1(a)
3 Agreement	E1(b)
4 Consideration	E1(b)
5 Intention	E1(c)
6 Misrepresentation	E1(c)

1 Contract basics

FAST FORWARD

A **valid contract is a legally binding agreement**, formed by the mutual consent of two parties.

1.1 Definition

Key term

A **contract** may be defined as an **agreement which legally binds the parties.** The underlying theory is that a contract is the outcome of 'consenting minds'. Parties are judged by what they have said, written or done.

1.2 The essentials of a contract

There are **three essential elements** in any contract.

- **Agreement**. This is made by offer and acceptance.

- **Consideration**. There must be a bargain where the obligations of one party are supported by something of value given by the other.

- **Intention**. The parties must have intended to create legal relations between themselves.

These are the vital elements of a contract and are looked at in more detail later in the chapter.

Assessment focus point

The fact that a contract cannot exist unless the three essential elements are present is the most important thing for you to learn in relation to contract law.

1.3 Vitiating factors

Even if the essential elements can be shown, a contract may not necessarily be valid. The validity of a contract may also be affected by the following factors. These are sometimes referred to as vitiating factors.

Form. Some contracts must be made in a particular form.

Terms. In general the parties may enter into a contract on whatever terms they choose. However, terms must be incorporated properly into the contract. Some terms are also implied by statute.

Consent. A misrepresentation made by one party may affect the validity of a contract.

Legality. The courts will not enforce a contract which is deemed to be illegal or contrary to public policy.

Capacity. Certain artificial bodies such as local authorities can only make contracts in areas they are authorised to do so. Contracts outside of the authorised areas are deemed *ultra vires* and are void.

Individuals under 18 years of age lack capacity to enter into certain contracts such as credit agreements.

A contract which is not valid may be either **void**, **voidable** or **unenforceable**.

A **void contract** is not a contract at all. The parties are not bound by it and if they transfer property under it they can recover their goods sometimes even from a third party.

A **voidable contract** is a contract which one party may avoid. Property transferred before avoidance is usually irrecoverable from a third party.

An **unenforceable contract** is a valid contract and property transferred under it cannot be recovered even from the other party to the contract. But if either party refuses to perform or fulfil his side of the contract, the other party cannot compel him to do so. A contract is usually unenforceable when the required evidence of its terms, for example, written evidence of a contract relating to land, is not available.

Once a valid contract has been formed, it remains in existence until discharged. For your studies, the most important means of discharge is **breach of contract**.

Question   Essential elements

What are the essential elements of a binding contract?

Answer

There must be an agreement made by offer and acceptance. There must be consideration. There must be an intention to create legal relations.

1.4 Factors affecting the modern contract

FAST FORWARD

The law seeks to protect the idea of 'freedom of contract', although **contractual terms** may be regulated by **statute**, particularly where the parties are of unequal bargaining strength.

It is almost invariably the case that the two parties to a contract bring with them differing levels of **bargaining power**. Many contracts are made between experts and ordinary consumers. The law will intervene only where the former takes unfair advantage of his position. **Freedom of contract** is a term sometimes used and can be defined as follows.

> 'The principle that parties are completely unrestricted in deciding whether or not to enter into an agreement and, if they do so, upon the terms governing that relationship. In practice, this is not always the case because one may be in a much stronger economic position, and legislation has been introduced in order to redress the balance.'

> (CIMA, *Terminology of Business and Company Law*)

Mass production and nationalisation have led to the **standard form contract**.

Key term

The **standard form contract** is a document prepared by many large organisations setting out the terms on which they contract with their customers. The individual must usually take it or leave it.

1.5 Example

A customer has to accept his supply of electricity on the electricity supplier's terms – he is not likely to succeed in negotiating special terms, unless he represents a large consumer such as a factory.

1.6 Consumer protection

In the second half of the twentieth century, there was a surge of interest in **consumer matters**. The development of a mass market for often complex goods has meant that the consumer can no longer rely on his own judgement when buying sophisticated goods or services. Consumer interests are now served by two main areas.

- **Consumer protection agencies**, which include government departments (the Office of Fair Trading) and independent bodies (the Consumers' Association or Which?).

- **Legislation**, for example, the Consumer Credit Act 1974 and Unfair Contracts Terms Act 1977.

Question

Enforceable agreement

An agreement between Nigel and Rupert was brought before a court. The court found that neither Rupert nor Nigel should feel himself bound by the agreement and that property transferred from one party to the other, but subsequently transferred to Charles, should be recovered. The agreement was

A   Void
B   Voidable
C   Unenforceable
D   Illegal

Answer

A   Void. Property can only be recovered from void contracts.

2 The form of a contract

FAST FORWARD Although most contracts may be **made in any form**, some must be made in a particular form. A number of commercial contracts must be made in writing, for example.

2.1 Form of a contract

As a general rule, **a contract may be made in any form**. It may be written, or oral, or inferred from the conduct of the parties.

2.2 Example

A customer in a self-service shop may take his selected goods to the cash desk, pay for them and walk out without saying a word.

2.3 When is form important?

There are **circumstances in which a contract is not valid** unless the **correct form** is followed. **Writing is not usually necessary except** in the following circumstances.

- Some contracts must be by **deed.**
- Some contracts must be in **writing.**
- Some contracts must be **evidenced in writing.**

2.4 Contracts by deed

A contract by deed must be in **writing** and it must be **witnessed** and **signed**. **Delivery** must take place. Delivery is conduct indicating that the person executing the deed intends to be bound by it.

These **contracts** must be by **deed**.

- **Leases** for three years or more
- A **conveyance** or transfer of a legal estate in land (including a mortgage)
- A promise not supported by consideration (such as a **covenant**)

2.5 Contracts in writing

Some types of contract must be in the form of a **written document**, usually signed by at least one of the parties.

- A **transfer of shares** in a limited company
- The sale or disposition of an **interest in land** under the Law of Property (Miscellaneous Provisions) Act 1989.
- The **assignment of debts**
- **Bills of exchange, promissory notes** and **cheques**
- **Marine insurance** and **consumer credit** contracts

A contract for the sale or disposition of land promises to **transfer title** at a future date and must be in writing. The conveyance or transfer must be by deed and will therefore also be in writing.

In the case of **consumer credit** or **hire purchase transactions**, failure to make the agreement in the prescribed form (including providing information required by the Consumer Credit Act 1974) results in the agreement being unenforceable against the debtor.

2.6 Contracts evidenced in writing

Certain contracts may be made orally, but are not enforceable in a court of law unless there is written evidence of their terms. The most important contract of this type is the contract of **guarantee**.

2.7 Simple contracts and specialty contracts

A useful classification of contracts is to identify them as **simple** or **specialty contracts**.

(a) A **simple contract** is an agreement made orally or in writing with no special formalities. The vast majority of contractual agreements fall into this category.

(b) A **specialty contract** is a contract made by deed. As we saw above, a contract by deed serves to make a purely gratuitous promise enforceable.

Question

Which of the following contracts must be in the form of a deed?

A   Sale of shares

B   Consumer credit agreements

C   Sale of an interest in land

D   A covenant

Answer

D   Covenants must be in deed form. They should be in writing, signed by both parties and delivered.

3 Agreement

FAST FORWARD

The first essential element of a binding contract is **agreement**. This is usually evidenced by **offer and acceptance**. An offer is a definite promise to be bound on specific terms, and must be distinguished from the mere **supply of information** and from an **invitation to treat**. Acceptance must be unqualified agreement to all the terms of the offer. A **counter-offer** is a rejection of the original offer.

3.1 Offer

Key term

An **offer** is a **definite promise to be bound on specific terms**.

An offer does not have to be made to a **particular person**. It may be made to a **class of persons** or to the **world at large**, for example, as the offer of a reward for a lost item such as a cheque guarantee card, *First Sport Ltd v Barclays Bank plc 1993*.

Carlill v Carbolic Smoke Ball Co 1893

The facts: The manufacturers of a patent medicine published an advertisement by which they undertook to pay '£100 reward .... to any person who contracts .... influenza .... after having used the smoke ball three times daily for two weeks'. The advertisement added that £1,000 had been deposited at a bank 'showing our sincerity in this matter'. The claimant read the advertisement, purchased the smoke ball and used it as directed. She contracted influenza and claimed her £100 reward. In their defence the manufacturers argued against this.

    (a)   The offer was so vague that it could not form the basis of a contract, as no time limit was specified.

    (b)   It was not an offer which could be accepted since it was offered to the whole world.

Decision: The court disagreed.

    (a)   The smoke ball must protect the user during the period of use – the offer was not vague.

    (b)   Such an offer was possible, as it could be compared to reward cases.

	The case above, referred to as Carlill's case, is very important in the law of contract. Learn the legal point here before you learn any others.

An offer must be **distinguished** from other similar statements or actions. Only an offer in the proper sense may be accepted so as to form a binding contract.

Item	Distinguishing features
Supply of information	*Harvey v Facey 1893* *The facts:* The claimant telegraphed to the defendant 'Will you sell us Bumper Hall Pen? Telegraph lowest cash price'. The defendant telegraphed in reply 'Lowest price for Bumper Hall Pen, £900'. The claimant telegraphed to accept what he regarded as an offer; the defendant made no further reply. *Decision:* The defendant's telegram was merely a statement of his minimum price if a sale were to be agreed. It was not an offer which the claimant could accept. However, if in the course of negotiations for a sale, the vendor states the price at which he will sell, that statement may be an offer which can be accepted.
Statement of intention	Advertising that an event such as an auction will take place is not an offer to sell. Potential buyers may not sue the auctioneer if the auction does not take place: *(Harrison v Nickerson 1873)*
Invitation to treat *(see below)*	Where a party is initiating negotiations he is said to have made an invitation to treat. An **invitation to treat** cannot be accepted to form a binding contract. There are four types of invitation to treat. • **Auction** sales • **Advertisements** (eg, price lists or newspaper advertisements) • **Exhibition** of goods for sale • An **invitation** for tenders

3.1.1 Communication of offer

Offerees cannot accept offers that they were not aware of and therefore offers must communicated to them. For example, where a person returns a lost item to its owner, they cannot claim a reward if they were not aware at the time that one was being offered.

3.2 An invitation to treat

An **invitation to treat** can be defined as follows. 'An indication that a person is prepared to receive offers with a view to entering into a binding contract, for example, an advertisement of goods for sale or a company prospectus inviting offers for shares. It must be distinguished from an offer which requires only acceptance to conclude the contract.'

An **invitation to treat cannot be accepted** so as to form a binding contract. Four different categories of invitation to treat can be identified.

3.2.1 Auction sales

A **potential buyer's bid is the offer** which the auctioneer is free to accept or reject: *Payne v Cave 1789*. **Acceptance** is indicated by the **fall of the auctioneer's hammer**.

3.2.2 Advertisements

An advertisement of goods for sale is an attempt to **induce offers**.

> *Partridge v Crittenden 1968*
>
> *The facts:* Mr Partridge placed an advertisement for 'Bramblefinch cocks, bramblefinch hens, 25s each'. The RSPCA brought a prosecution against him for offering birds for sale in contravention of the Protection of Birds Act 1954. The justices convicted Partridge and he appealed.
>
> *Decision:* The conviction was quashed. Although there had been a sale in contravention of the Act, the prosecution could not rely on the offence of 'offering for sale', as the advertisement only constituted an invitation to treat.

Similarly, the circulation of a price list is an invitation to treat: *Grainger v Gough 1896* where it was noted:

> *'The transmission of such a price-list does not amount to an offer.... If it were so, the merchant might find himself involved in any number of contractual obligations to supply wine of a particular description which he would be quite unable to carry out, his stock of wine of that description being necessarily limited'.*

Care must be taken when **preparing adverts** which make outlandish claims regarding the **properties** of the goods or services provided. There is a fine line between **advertising puff** and a **contractual promise**.

3.2.3 Exhibition of goods for sale

Displaying goods in a **shop window**, on the **open shelves** of a self service shop, or **advertising goods for sale**, are **invitations to treat**.

> *Fisher v Bell 1961*
>
> *The facts:* A shopkeeper was prosecuted for offering for sale an offensive weapon by exhibiting a flick knife in his shop window.
>
> *Decision:* The display of an article with a price on it in a shop window is merely an invitation to treat.

> *Pharmaceutical Society of Great Britain v Boots Cash Chemists (Southern) 1952*
>
> *The facts:* Certain drugs could only be sold under the supervision of a registered pharmacist. The claimant claimed this rule had been broken by Boots who displayed these drugs in a self-service shop. Boots contended that there was no sale until a customer brought the goods to the cash desk and offered to buy them. A registered pharmacist was stationed at this point.
>
> *Decision:* The court found for Boots and commented that if it were true that a customer accepted an offer to sell by removing goods from the shelf, he could not then change his mind and put them back as this would constitute breach of contract.

BPP LEARNING MEDIA

3.2.4 Invitation for tenders

A **tender** is an estimate submitted in response to a prior request.

Question	Offer

Maud goes into a shop and sees a price label for £20 on an ironing board. She takes the board to the checkout but the till operator tells her that the label is misprinted and should read £30. Maud maintains that she only has to pay £20. How would you describe the price on the price label in terms of contract law?

A   An offer
B   A tender
C   An invitation to treat
D   An acceptance

Answer

C   The price shown on a label is an invitation to treat.

3.3 Termination of offer

An offer may only be accepted while it is still open. In the absence of an acceptance, an offer may be **terminated** in any of the following ways.

- Rejection
- Lapse of time
- Revocation by the offeror
- Failure of a condition to which the offer was subject
- Death of one of the parties

3.3.1 Rejection

Rejection terminates an offer. A counter-offer amounts to rejection.

A **counter-offer** is a final rejection of the original offer. If a counter-offer is made, the original offeror may accept it, but if he rejects it his original offer is no longer available for acceptance.

> *Hyde v Wrench 1840*
>
> *The facts:* The defendant offered to sell property to the claimant for £1,000 on 6 June. Two days later, the claimant made a counter-offer of £950 which the defendant rejected on 27 June. The claimant then informed the defendant on 29 June that he accepted the original offer of £1,000.
>
> *Decision:* The original offer of £1,000 had been terminated by the counter-offer of £950.

In *Neale v Merrett 1930* the attempted inclusion of credit terms into a sale of land by the offeree was deemed a counter-offer.

The following case demonstrates how complex counter-offers can be.

> *Pickfords Ltd v Celestica Ltd 2003*
>
> *The facts:* An original offer was made on 13 September. This was amended by a second offer on 27 September. On 15 October, the offeree accepted the original offer.
>
> *Decision:* The acceptance on the 15 October was not valid as the offer of the 27 September was a counter-offer which replaced the original offer of 13 September. A binding contract was created, but only due to the conduct of the parties and was held to be on the terms contained in the offer of 27 September.

3.3.2 Lapse of time

An offer may be expressed to last for a **specified time**. If, however, there is no express time limit set, it expires after a **reasonable time**.

> *Ramsgate Victoria Hotel Co v Montefiore 1866*
>
> *The facts:* The defendant applied to the company in June for shares and paid a deposit. At the end of November the company sent him an acceptance by issue of a letter of allotment and requested payment of the balance due. The defendant contended that his offer had expired and could no longer be accepted.
>
> *Decision:* The offer was for a reasonable time only and five months was much more than that. The offer had lapsed.

3.3.3 Revocation of an offer

The offeror may **revoke** his offer at any time before acceptance: *Payne v Cave 1789.* However, if he undertakes that the offer will remain open for a specified time, he may nonetheless revoke it within that time, unless he has bound himself to keep it open in another contract. In this case he will have broken the terms of this subsidiary contract only.

> *Routledge v Grant 1828*
>
> *The facts:* The defendant offered to buy the claimant's house for a fixed sum, requiring acceptance within six weeks. Within the six weeks specified, he withdrew his offer.
>
> *Decision:* The defendant could revoke his offer at any time before acceptance, even though the time limit had not expired.

Revocation may be an **express statement** or an **act of the offeror**. It does not take effect until it is communicated to the offeree. This raises two important points.

(a)   Firstly, **posting a letter is not a sufficient act of revocation**.

> *Byrne v Van Tienhoven 1880*
>
> *The facts:* The defendants were in Cardiff, the claimants in New York. The sequence of events was as follows.
>
> | | |
> |---|---|
> | 1 October | Letter posted in Cardiff, offering to sell 1,000 boxes of tinplates. |
> | 8 October | Letter of revocation of offer posted in Cardiff. |
> | 11 October | Letter of offer received in New York and telegram of acceptance sent. |
> | 15 October | Letter confirming acceptance posted in New York. |
> | 20 October | Letter of revocation received in New York. The offeree had meanwhile resold the goods. |
>
> *Decision:* The letter of revocation could not take effect until received (20 October). Therefore, it could not revoke the contract made by the telegram acceptance of the offer on 11 October.

BPP
LEARNING MEDIA

Ensure you learn how offers can be terminated. Mini scenarios may require you to decide whether or not an offer exists or has been ended.

(b) Secondly, **revocation of offer may be communicated by any third party who is a sufficiently reliable informant**.

Dickinson v Dodds 1876

The facts: The defendant, on 10 June, wrote to the claimant offering property for sale at £800, adding 'this offer is to be left open until Friday 12 June, 9.00 am.' On 11 June the defendant sold the property to another buyer, A. B, who had been an intermediary between Dickinson and Dodds, informed Dickinson that the defendant had sold the property to someone else. On Friday 12 June, before 9.00 am, the claimant handed to the defendant a formal letter of acceptance.

Decision: The defendant was free to revoke his offer and had done so by sale to a third party. The claimant could not accept the offer after he had learnt from a reliable informant of the revocation of the offer to him.

3.3.4 Failure of a condition

An offer may be **conditional**. If the condition is not satisfied, the offer is not capable of acceptance.

Financings Ltd v Stimson 1962

The facts: The defendant wished to purchase a car, and on 16 March signed a hire-purchase form. The form, issued by the claimants, stated that the agreement would be binding only upon signature by them. On 20 March the defendant, not satisfied with the car, returned it. On 24 March the car was stolen from the premises of the dealer, and was recovered badly damaged. On 25 March the claimants signed the form. They sued the defendant for breach of contract.

Decision: The defendant was not bound to take the car. His signing of the agreement was actually an offer to contract with the claimant. There was an implied condition in this offer that the car would be in a reasonable condition.

3.3.5 Termination by death

The **death of the offeree terminates the offer**. The offeror's death terminates the offer, unless the offeree accepts the offer in ignorance of the death, and the offer is not of a personal nature.

3.4 Acceptance

FAST FORWARD

Acceptance is generally not effective until **communicated** to the offeror. The principal exception to this is where the **'postal rule'** applies. In this case, acceptance is complete and effective as soon as notice of it is posted.

Key term

Acceptance may be defined as.

'An unconditional positive act by a person to whom an offer has been made which brings a binding contract into effect.'

Acceptance **'subject to contract'** means that the offeree is agreeable to the terms of the offer but proposes that the parties should negotiate a formal contract. Where a contract must be in writing, it is deemed that the parties did not intend to be bound until the written agreement is made: *Pitt v PHH Asset Management Ltd 1993*. Neither party is bound until the formal contract is signed. Agreements for the sale of land in England are usually made 'subject to contract'. **Letters of intent** are not usually legally binding.

In **commercial negotiations**, both parties often try to have their own standard terms and conditions included as the contract's terms by including them on all documents – this is known as **'battle of the forms'**. Since the terms of each party are unlikely to agree, no contract is formed until one party acts positively in performing under the 'agreement'. The first party to act in this way will be deemed to have accepted the terms of the other party.

The **place** of acceptance is important when parties are in different countries as it determines whose laws apply and which courts have jurisdiction.

Acceptance of an offer may only be made by a person **authorised** to do so. This will usually be the offeree or his authorised agents.

Powell v Lee 1908

The facts: The claimant was appointed to a post of headmaster but was informed of the appointment by an unauthorised manager. Later, it was decided to give the post to someone else. The claimant sued for breach of contract.

Decision: Since communication of acceptance was unauthorised, there was no valid agreement and hence no contract.

Acceptance may be by **express words**, by **action** or **inferred from conduct** but there must be some **act** on the part of the offeree to indicate his acceptance.

Bryen & Langley Ltd v Boston 2005

The facts: A tender for building work was not signed, but on the basis of an agreement made, the building work was started.

Decision: A binding contract existed as the commencement of the building work was a positive act, enough to imply acceptance.

Contrast this with the case below where **silence** did not imply a contract.

Felthouse v Bindley 1862

The facts: The claimant wrote to his nephew offering to buy the nephew's horse, adding 'If I hear no more about him, I consider the horse mine'. The nephew intended to accept his uncle's offer but did not reply. He instructed the defendant, an auctioneer, not to sell the horse. Owing to a misunderstanding the horse was sold to someone else. The uncle sued the auctioneer.

Decision: The action failed. The claimant had no title to the horse.

Goods which are sent or services which are rendered to a person who did not request them are not 'accepted' merely because he does not return them to the sender: **Unsolicited Goods and Services Act 1971**. The recipient may treat them as an **unsolicited gift** after **30 days**. A seller will be guilty of a criminal offence if they demand payment in these circumstances.

BPP
LEARNING MEDIA

Genuine acceptance must also be **distinguished** from other statements or actions.

    (a)   Acceptance must be **unqualified agreement to the terms of the offer**. A purported acceptance which introduces any **new terms** is a **counter-offer**.

    (b)   It is possible to respond to an offer by making a **request for information**. Such a request may be a request as to whether or not other terms would be acceptable. This does not constitute rejection of the offer.

Question
Contract?

Nicholas offers to sell his car to Derek for £700 on 1 June, but in reply Derek merely asks how old the car is, what its mileage is and how many owners it has had. Nicholas provides this information on 3 June and on that date states that the offer will be kept open only until 10 June. On 7 June Derek says he will take the car for £600. On 8 June Hughie buys the car from Nicholas for £700. On 10 June Derek agrees to buy the car for £700, and is told it has been sold. On 10 June, what is the state of the relations between Nicholas and Derek?

A   There is a contract to sell at £600 so Derek may recover the car from Hughie as his property

B   There is a contract to sell at £700 which has been terminated by Nicholas's breach when he sold the car to Hughie

C   There is an offer from Nicholas to sell for £700 which is still open for Derek to accept

D   There is an offer from Derek to buy at £700 which Nicholas cannot accept

Answer

D   Derek had made a counter offer on 7 June, which Nicholas rejected.

3.5 Communication of acceptance

The general rule is that acceptance **must be communicated** to the offeror and is not effective until this has been done. There are two exceptions.

    (a)   The offeror may **dispense** with the need for communication of acceptance. Such a waiver of communication may be express or may be inferred from the circumstances.

    (b)   The offeror may expressly or by implication indicate that he expects acceptance by means of a letter sent through the post. This is the important **postal rule**.

3.6 The postal rule

FAST FORWARD

The **postal rule** states that, where the use of the post is within the contemplation of both the parties, acceptance is complete and effective as soon as a letter of acceptance is posted. This is even though it may be delayed or even lost altogether in the post.

> *Adams v Lindsell 1818*
>
> *The facts:* The defendants made an offer by letter to the claimant on 2 September 1817 requiring an answer 'in course of post'. It reached the claimants on 5 September, who immediately posted a letter of acceptance that reached the defendants on 9 September. The defendants could have expected a reply by 7 September and assumed that the lack of one within the expected period indicated non-acceptance and sold the goods to another buyer on 8 September.
>
> *Decision:* The acceptance was made 'in course of post' (no time limit was imposed) and was effective when posted on 5 September.

The **intention to use the post** for communicating acceptance may be **deduced from the circumstances**, for example, if the negotiations have all been undertaken by letter. If the offeror expressly requires 'notice in writing', the postal rule does not apply.

Question

Postal rule

Under the postal rule, acceptance made by letter is complete and effective as soon as the letter is posted. Can the offeree subsequently withdraw his acceptance before the letter reaches the offeror?

Answer

No. Any such attempt should fail, as a binding contract is formed when the letter is posted.

If no mode of communication is prescribed during negotiations, the offeree must ensure that his acceptance is understood. This applies to any **instantaneous method of communication**.

> *Entores v Miles Far Eastern Corporation 1955*
>
> *The facts:* The claimants sent an offer by telex to the defendants' agent in Amsterdam and the latter sent an acceptance by telex. The claimants alleged breach of contract and wished to serve a writ.
>
> *Decision:* The acceptance took effect (and the contract was made) when the telex message was printed out on the claimants' terminal in London. A writ could therefore be issued.

3.6.1 Email communication

The use of **email** in business transactions has led to a number of cases involving this form of communication, however the overall position is yet to be decided.

In *NBTY Europe Ltd v Nutricia International BV 2005* the court held that an acceptance email did create a binding contract. The **EU directive on Electronic Commerce 2002** states that an offer is delivered when the email containing it is accessed by the intended recipient.

BPP
LEARNING MEDIA

4 Consideration

4.1 Definition

FAST FORWARD

Consideration is what each party brings to a contract. It is usually a **promise** in return for an **act** or **another promise**.

Key term

Consideration has been defined as:

'A valuable consideration in the sense of the law may consist either in some right, interest, profit or benefit accruing to one party, or some forbearance, detriment, loss or responsibility given, suffered or undertaken by the other.'

Currie v Misa 1875

4.2 Valid consideration

There are two broad types of valid consideration – **executed** and **executory**. If consideration is **past** then it is not enforceable. Each party does not need to provide the same type of consideration to each other as long as the consideration given is valid.

4.2.1 Executed consideration

Executed consideration is an act in return for a promise. The consideration for the promise is a performed, or executed, act. If A offers a reward for the return of lost property, his promise becomes binding when B performs the act of returning A's property to him. A is not bound to pay anything to anyone until the prescribed act is done. The claimant's act in Carlill's case, in response to the smoke ball company's promise of reward, was therefore executed consideration.

4.2.2 Executory consideration

Executory consideration is a promise given for a promise. The consideration in support of each promise is the other promise, not a performed act. If a customer orders goods which a shopkeeper undertakes to obtain from the manufacturer, the shopkeeper promises to supply the goods and the customer promises to accept and pay for them. Neither has yet done anything but each has given a promise to obtain the promise of the other. It would be breach of contract if either withdrew without the consent of the other.

4.2.3 Past consideration

Anything that has been done before a promise in return is given is past consideration. This, as a general rule, is not sufficient to make the promise binding.

Key term

Past consideration can be defined as follows.

'… something which has already been done at the time the promise is made. An example would be a promise to pay for work already carried out, unless there was an implied promise to pay a reasonable sum before the work began.'

> **Re McArdle 1951**
>
> *The facts:* Under a will the testator's children were entitled to a house after their mother's death. In the mother's lifetime one of the children and his wife lived in the house with the mother. The wife made improvements to the house. The children later agreed in writing to repay the wife 'in consideration of your carrying out certain alterations and improvements'. But at the mother's death they refused to do so.
>
> *Decision:* The work on the house had all been completed before the documents were signed. At the time of the promise the improvements were past consideration and so the promise was not binding.

However where **consideration can be implied at the outset** it will not be deemed as past.

> **Stewart v Casey 1892**
>
> *The facts:* The claimant was asked by the defendant to promote their patent. Once the work was finished the defendant promised to pay the claimant.
>
> *Decision:* Promotion work is normally paid for and this was implied at the outset. A valid contract therefore existed.

If there is an **existing contract** and one party makes a **further promise**, **no contract** will arise. Even if such a promise is directly related to the previous bargain, it will be held to have been made upon past consideration.

> **Roscorla v Thomas 1842**
>
> *The facts:* The claimant agreed to buy a horse from the defendant at a given price. When negotiations were over and the contract was formed, the defendant told the claimant that the horse was 'sound and free from vice'. The horse turned out to be vicious and the claimant brought an action on the warranty.
>
> *Decision:* The express promise was made after the sale was over and was unsupported by fresh consideration.

4.3 Adequacy and sufficiency

FAST FORWARD

Consideration need not be **adequate**, but it must be **sufficient**. This means that what is tendered as consideration must be capable in law of being regarded as consideration, but need not necessarily be equal in value to the consideration received in return.

Courts will seek to ensure that a particular act or promise can actually be deemed to be consideration. Learn these rules:

Consideration need not be adequate (that is, equal in value to the consideration received in return). There is no remedy at law for someone who simply makes a poor bargain.

Consideration must be sufficient. It must be capable in law of being regarded as consideration.

4.3.1 Adequacy

It is presumed that each party is capable of serving his own interests, and courts will not seek to **weigh up** the **comparative value** of the promises or acts exchanged.

BPP
LEARNING MEDIA

> **Thomas v Thomas 1842**
>
> *The facts:* By his will the claimant's husband expressed the wish that his widow should have the use of his house during her life. The defendants, his executors, allowed the widow to occupy the house (a) in accordance with her husband's wishes and (b) in return for her undertaking to pay a rent of £1 per annum. They later said that their promise to let her occupy the house was not supported by consideration.
>
> *Decision:* Compliance with the husband's wishes was not valuable consideration (no economic value attached to it), but the nominal rent was sufficient consideration.

4.3.2 Sufficiency

Consideration is sufficient if it has some **identifiable value**. The law only requires an element of bargain, not necessarily that it should be a good bargain.

> **Chappell & Co v Nestle Co 1960**
>
> *The facts:* As a sales promotion scheme, the defendant offered to supply a record to anyone who sent them a small sum of money and three wrappers from their chocolate bars. The claimants owned the copyright of the music. They sued for infringement of copyright. In the ensuing dispute over royalties the issue was whether the wrappers, which were thrown away when received, were part of the consideration for the promise to supply the record. The defendants offered to pay a royalty based on the small sum of money received for each record, but the claimants rejected this, claiming that the wrappers also represented part of the consideration.
>
> *Decision:* The wrappers were part of the consideration as they had commercial value to the defendants.

4.4 Performance of existing contractual duties

Performance of an **existing contractual obligation, or one imposed by statute** is no consideration.

> **Collins v Godefroy 1831**
>
> *The facts:* The claimant had been subpoenaed to give evidence on behalf of the defendant in another case. He alleged that the defendant promised to pay him for appearing.
>
> *Decision:* There was no consideration for this promise.

But if some **extra service** is given this may be sufficient consideration.

> **Glasbrook Bros v Glamorgan CC 1925**
>
> *The facts:* At a time of industrial unrest, colliery owners, rejecting the view of the police that a mobile force was enough, agreed to pay for a special guard on the mine. Later they repudiated liability saying that the police had done no more than perform their public duty of maintaining order, and that no consideration was given.
>
> *Decision:* The police had done more than perform their general duties. The extra services given, beyond what the police in their discretion deemed necessary, were consideration for the promise to pay.

In the *Glasbrook* case the threat to law and order was not caused by either of the parties. Where one party's actions lead to the need for a heightened police presence, and the police deem this presence necessary, they may also be entitled to payment.

> **Harris v Sheffield United F.C. Ltd 1988**
>
> *The facts:* The defendants (a football team) argued that they did not have to pay for a large police presence at their home matches.
>
> *Decision:* They had voluntarily decided to hold matches on Saturday afternoons when large attendances were likely, increasing the risk of disorder. They would therefore have to pay.

4.5 Promise of additional reward

If there is already a contract between A and B, and B promises **additional reward** to A if he (A) will perform his existing duties, there is no consideration from A to make that promise binding.

> **Stilk v Myrick 1809**
>
> *The facts:* Two members of the crew of a ship deserted in a foreign port. The master was unable to recruit substitutes and promised the rest of the crew that they would share the wages of the deserters if they would complete the voyage home short-handed. The ship-owners, however, repudiated the promise.
>
> *Decision:* In performing their existing contractual duties the crew gave no consideration for the promise of extra pay and the promise was not binding.

If a claimant does **more than perform an existing contractual duty**, this may amount to consideration.

> **Hartley v Ponsonby 1857**
>
> *The facts:* 17 men out of a crew of 36 deserted. The remainder were promised an extra £40 each to work the ship to Bombay. The claimant, one of the remaining crew-members, sued to recover this amount.
>
> *Decision:* The large number of desertions made the voyage exceptionally hazardous, and this had the effect of discharging the original contract. The claimant's promise to complete the voyage formed consideration for the promise to pay an additional £40.

The courts now appear to be taking a slightly different line on the payment of additional consideration. The principles of consideration may not be applied if the dispute can be dealt with on an alternative basis.

> **Williams v Roffey Bros & Nicholls (Contractors) Ltd 1990**
>
> *The facts:* The claimants agreed to do carpentry work for the defendants, who were engaged as contractors to refurbish a block of flats, at a fixed price of £20,000. The work ran late and so the defendants, concerned that the job might not be finished on time and that they would have to pay money under a penalty clause, agreed to pay the claimants an extra £10,300 to ensure the work was completed on time. They later refused to pay the extra amount.
>
> *Decision:* The fact that there was no apparent consideration for the promise to pay the extra was not held to be important, as in the court's view both parties derived benefit from the promise. The telling point was that the defendants' promise had not been extracted by duress or fraud: it was therefore binding.

BPP
LEARNING MEDIA

Re Selectmove 1994

The facts: A company which was the subject of a winding up order offered to settle its outstanding debts by instalment. An Inland Revenue inspector agreed to the proposal. The company tried to enforce it.

Decision: The court held that an agreement to pay in instalments is unenforceable. Even though the creditor may obtain some practical benefit, this is not adequate consideration to render the agreement legally binding.

4.6 Performance of existing contractual duty to a third party

If A promises B a reward if B will perform his **existing contract** with C, there is consideration for A's promise since he obtains a benefit to which he previously had no right, and B assumes new obligations. *Pao on v Lau Yiu Long 1979.*

4.7 Waiver of existing rights

If X owes Y £100 but Y agrees to accept a lesser sum, say £80, in full settlement of Y's claim, that is a promise by Y to waive his entitlement to the balance of £20. The promise, like any other, should be supported by consideration.

Foakes v Beer 1884

The facts: The defendant had obtained judgement against the claimant. Judgement debts bear interest from the date of the judgement. By a written agreement the defendant agreed to accept payment by instalments, no mention being made of the interest. Once the claimant had paid the amount of the debt in full, the defendant claimed interest, stating that the agreement was not supported by consideration.

Decision: She was entitled to the debt with interest. No consideration had been given by the claimant for waiver of any part of her rights against him.

There are, however, exceptions to the rule that the debtor (denoted by 'X' in the following paragraphs) must give consideration if the waiver is to be binding.

EXCEPTIONS	
Alternative consideration	If X offers and Y accepts anything to which Y is not already entitled, the extra thing is sufficient consideration for the waiver.
Anon 1495 *Pinnel's Case 1602*	• Goods instead of cash • Early payment
Bargain between the creditors *Woods v Robarts 1818*	If X arranges with creditors that they will each accept part payment in full entitlement, that is bargain between the creditors. X has given no consideration but can hold creditors individually to the agreed terms.
Third party part payment *Welby v Drake 1825*	If a third party (Z) offers part payment and Y agrees to release X from Y's claim to the balance, Y has received consideration from Z against whom he had no previous claim.
Promissory estoppel	Promissory estoppel may prevent Y from retracting a promise (see below).

Valid consideration

(i)   Must be of adequate and sufficient value
(ii)   Must move from the promisee
(iii) Must be given in every binding agreement
(iv) May be given before a promise in return

A   (ii) and (iii) only
B   (iii) and (iv) only
C   (i), (ii) and (iii) only
D   (ii), (iii) and (iv) only

Answer

A   Consideration need not be adequate. If it is given before a promise in return then it is invalid past
      consideration.

4.8 Promissory estoppel

FAST FORWARD

The principle of **promissory estoppel** was developed in *Central London Property Trust v High Trees House 1947*. It means that in some cases, where someone has made a promise they can be prevented from denying it.

Key term

The doctrine of **promissory estoppel** works as follows.

If a person makes a promise (unsupported by consideration) to another that is intended to be binding and acted upon, the other party acts on, or relies on it, the promisor is **estopped** from retracting his promise, unless the promisee can be restored to his original position.

Central London Property Trust v High Trees House 1947

The facts: In September 1939, the claimants let a block of flats to the defendants at an annual rent of £2,500 p.a. It was difficult to let the individual flats in wartime, so in January 1940 the claimants agreed in writing to accept a reduced rent of £1,250 p.a. No time limit was set on the arrangement but it was clearly related to wartime conditions. The reduced rent was paid from 1940 to 1945 and the defendants sublet flats during the period on the basis of their expected liability to pay £1,250 p.a. only. In 1945 the flats were fully let. The claimants demanded full rent of £2,500 p.a., both retrospectively and for the future. They tested this claim by suing for rent at the full rate for the last two quarters of 1945.

Decision: The agreement of January 1940 ceased to operate early in 1945. The claim was upheld. However, had the claimants sued for arrears for the period 1940-1945, the 1940 agreement would have served to defeat the claim.

If the defendants in the *High Trees* case had sued on the promise, they would have failed for want of consideration. The principle is **'a shield not a sword'**. Promissory estoppel only applies to a promise of waiver which is **entirely voluntary**.

D and C Builders v Rees 1966

The facts: The defendants owed £482 to the claimants who were in acute financial difficulties. The claimants reluctantly agreed to accept £300 in full settlement. They later claimed the balance.

Decision: The debt must be paid in full. Promissory estoppel only applies to a promise voluntarily given. The defendants had been aware of and had exploited the claimants' difficulties.

4.9 Privity of contract

FAST FORWARD

As a general rule, only a person who is a party to a contract has enforceable rights or obligations under it. This is the doctrine of **privity of contract**, as demonstrated in *Dunlop v Selfridge 1915*.

There is a maxim in contract law which states that **consideration must move from the promisee**. As consideration is the price of a promise, the price must be paid by the person who seeks to enforce the promise. If A promises B that A will confer a benefit on C, then C cannot as a general rule enforce A's promise since C has given no consideration for it.

Tweddle v Atkinson 1861

The facts: The claimant married the daughter of G. On the occasion of the marriage, the claimant's father and G exchanged promises that they would each pay a sum of money to the claimant. G died without making the promised payment and the claimant sued G's executor for the specified amount.

Decision: The claimant had provided no consideration for G's promise.

In *Tweddle's* case, each father could have sued the other but the claimant could not sue. The rule that consideration must move from the promisee overlaps with the rule that **only a party to a contract can enforce it**. No one may be entitled to or be bound by the terms of a contract to which he is not an original party: *Price v Easton 1833*.

Key term

Privity of contract can be defined as follows.

As a general rule, only a person who is a party to a contract has enforceable rights or obligations under it. Third parties have no right of action save in certain exceptional instances.

There are also **statutory exceptions**, particularly under the **Contract (Rights of Third Parties) Act 1999**. This provides a two-limbed test whereby a third party can have enforceable rights under a contract.

- If the contract so provides
- Where a term confers a benefit on a third party (unless the parties did not intend that he should enforce it)

This Act has a fundamental effect on the doctrine of **privity of contract** by setting out the circumstances in which a third party has a right to enforce a contract term or have it varied or rescinded, and introducing a right to the remedies available for breach of contract.

In *Nissin Shipping Co Ltd v Cleaves & Co Ltd and others 2003* a broker was held to have a valid claim for a commission payment against a ship's owners despite the fact they were a third party to the charter party. This was only possible due to the rights provided by the Act.

Other **statutory exceptions** include the principle under the **Road Traffic Act 1972** that a person injured in a road accident may claim against the other motorist's insurers.

BPP
LEARNING MEDIA

The **rules of consideration do not apply to contracts in deed form**. Therefore, deeds should be used where a **gratuitous promise** is to be binding – for example, donations to charity.

5 Intention

FAST FORWARD

Both parties to a contract must **intend** the agreement to give rise to legal obligations. Their intentions may be express – 'this agreement is not subject to legal jurisdiction' – or may be inferred from the circumstances. **Social, domestic and family** arrangements are not assumed to be legally binding unless the contrary is clearly shown. **Commercial** agreements are assumed to be legally binding unless the contrary is clearly demonstrated.

5.1 The basic presumptions

Where there is no express statement as to whether or not legal relations are intended, the courts apply one of two **rebuttable presumptions** to a case.

- **Social, domestic and family arrangements** are not usually intended to be binding.
- **Commercial agreements** are usually intended by the parties involved to be legally binding.

Key term

> **Intention to create legal relations** can be defined as follows.
>
> 'An agreement will only become a legally binding contract if the parties intend this to be so. This will be strongly presumed in the case of business agreements but presumed otherwise if the agreement is of a friendly, social or domestic nature.'

5.2 Domestic arrangements

5.2.1 Husband and wife

The fact that the parties are **husband** and **wife** does not mean that they cannot enter into a binding contract with one another. However, the court will assume that they have not, and this presumption must be disproved if an enforceable contract is to exist. The courts are more inclined to agree that legal relations exist if **property** is involved.

> *Balfour v Balfour 1919*
>
> *The facts:* The defendant was employed in Ceylon. He and his wife returned to the UK on leave but it was agreed that for health reasons she would not return to Ceylon with him. He promised to pay her £30 a month as maintenance. Later the marriage ended in divorce and the wife sued for the monthly allowance which the husband no longer paid.
>
> *Decision:* An informal agreement of indefinite duration made between husband and wife whose marriage had not at the time broken up was not intended to be legally binding.

BPP
LEARNING MEDIA

Merritt v Merritt 1970

The facts: The husband had left the matrimonial home, which was owned in the joint names of husband and wife, to live with another woman. The spouses met and held a discussion, in the course of which he agreed to pay her £40 a month out of which she agreed to keep up the mortgage payments. The wife made the husband sign a note of these terms and an undertaking to transfer the house into her name when the mortgage had been paid off. The wife paid off the mortgage but the husband refused to transfer the house to her.

Decision: In the circumstances, an intention to create legal relations was to be inferred and the wife could sue for breach of contract.

5.2.2 Relatives

Agreements between **other family members** may also be examined by the courts.

Jones v Padavatton 1969

The facts: The claimant wanted her daughter to move to England to train as a barrister, and offered to pay her a monthly allowance. The daughter did so in 1962. In 1964 the claimant bought a house in London. Part of the house was occupied by the daughter and the other part let to tenants whose rent was collected by the daughter for herself. In 1967 the claimant and her daughter quarrelled and the claimant issued a summons claiming possession of the house. The daughter sued for her allowance.

Decision: There were two agreements to consider. The daughter's agreement to read for the bar in exchange for a monthly allowance, and the agreement by which the daughter lived in her mother's house and collected the rent from tenants. It was held that neither agreement was intended to create legal relations.

5.2.3 Other domestic arrangements

Domestic arrangements extend to those between people who are not related but who have a **close relationship** of some form. The nature of the agreement itself may lead to the conclusion that legal relations were intended.

Simpkins v Pays 1955

The facts: The defendant, her granddaughter and the claimant, a paying boarder, took part together each week in a competition organised by a Sunday newspaper. The arrangements over postage and other expenses were informal and the entries were made in the grandmother's name. One week they won £750. The paying boarder claimed a third share, but the defendant refused to pay on the grounds that there was no intention to create legal relations.

Decision: There was a 'mutuality in the arrangements between the parties', amounting to a contract.

5.3 Commercial agreements

When business people enter into **commercial agreements** it is presumed that there **is an intention to enter into legal relations** unless this is expressly disclaimed or the circumstances indicate otherwise.

> **Rose and Frank v Crompton 1923**
>
> *The facts:* A commercial agreement by which the defendants appointed the claimant to be its distributor in the USA contained a clause described as 'the Honourable Pledge Clause' which expressly stated that the arrangement was 'not subject to legal jurisdiction' in either country. The defendants terminated the agreement without giving the required notice, and refused to deliver goods ordered by the claimants although they had accepted these orders when placed.
>
> *Decision:* The general agreement was not legally binding as there was no obligation to stand by any clause in it. However the orders for goods were separate and binding contracts. The claim for damages for breach of the agreement failed, but the claim for damages for non-delivery of goods ordered succeeded.

The words relied on by a party to a **commercial agreement** to show that legal relations are not intended are not always clear. In such cases, the burden of proof is on the party seeking to escape liability.

5.4 Transactions binding in honour only

If the parties state that an agreement is **'binding in honour only'**, this amounts to an express denial of intention to create legal relations.

> **Jones v Vernons Pools 1938**
>
> *The facts:* The claimant argued that he had sent to the defendant a football pools coupon on which his predictions entitled him to a dividend. The defendants denied having received the coupon. A clause on the coupon stated that the transaction should not 'give rise to any legal relationship … but … be binding in honour only'.
>
> *Decision:* This clause was a bar to an action in court.

Question

In which of the following circumstances would legal intention be inferred?

A   A husband promising to pay his wife a regular maintenance allowance.

B   A signed agreement between a separated husband and wife that the wife would pay the mortgage and the husband would transfer ownership of the house to the wife.

C   A mother agreeing to pay her daughter an allowance in return for the daughter taking legal exams.

D   An agreement between a father and son that the father would buy the son a car providing the son worked in the father's garden for a year.

Answer

B   The facts are the same as *Merritt v Merritt 1970*. Option A contains the same facts as in *Balfour v Balfour 1919* and option C has the same facts as *Jones v Padavatton 1969*. In both cases intention was not inferred.

   Option D would not be classed as commercial as it is an informal arrangement between father and son.

6 Misrepresentation

FAST FORWARD

A contract entered into following a **misrepresentation** is **voidable** by the person to whom the misrepresentation was made. A misrepresentation is a statement of fact, given **before the contract is made**, which is **untrue** and made by one party to the other in order to **induce** the latter to enter into the agreement.

6.1 Consent

A contract will not be valid if either of the two parties did not genuinely consent to the contract. This may occur, for example, where one party makes a **misrepresentation** to the other in the course of negotiations.

Key term

A **misrepresentation** is:

- A representation of **fact** which is **untrue**
- Made by one party to the other **before the contract is made**
- Which is an **inducement** to the party misled actually to enter into the contract

6.1.1 Representation of fact

In order to analyse whether a statement may be a **misrepresentation**, it is first of all necessary to decide whether it could have been a representation at all.

- A **statement of fact** is a representation.
- A **statement of law**, intention, opinion or mere 'sales talk' is not a representation.
- **Silence** does not usually constitute a representation.

Bisset v Wilkinson 1927

The facts: A vendor of land which both parties knew had not previously been grazed by sheep stated that it would support about 2,000 sheep. This proved to be untrue.

Decision: In the circumstances this was an honest statement of opinion as to the capacity of the farm, not a statement of fact.

Smith v Land and House Property Corporation 1884

The facts: A vendor of property described it as 'let to Mr Frederick Fleck (a most desirable tenant) at a rental of £400 per annum for 27½ years, thus offering a first-class investment'. In fact F had only paid part of the rent due in the previous six months by instalments after the due date and he had failed altogether to pay the most recent quarter's rent.

Decision: The description of F as a 'desirable tenant' was not a mere opinion but an implied assertion that nothing had occurred which could make F an undesirable tenant. As a statement of fact this was untrue.

A **statement of intention**, or a statement as to **future conduct**, is not actionable. If a person enters into a contract or takes steps relying on a representation, the fact that the representation is false entitles him to remedies at law. If he sues on a statement of intention he must show that the promise forms part of a valid contract if he is to gain any remedy.

6.1.2 Silence

As a **general rule** neither party is under any duty to disclose what he knows, however:

(a)   What is said must be **complete enough** to **avoid** giving a **misleading impression**.

(b)   There is a **duty to correct an earlier statement** which was true when made but **which becomes untrue** before the contract is completed.

> *With v O'Flanagan 1936*
>
> *The facts:* At the start of negotiations in January a doctor, who wished to sell his practice, stated that it was worth £2,000 per year. Shortly afterwards he fell ill and as a result the practice was almost worthless by the time the sale was completed in May.
>
> *Decision:* The defendant's illness and inability to sustain the practice's value falsified the January representation. His silence when he should have corrected the earlier impression constituted misrepresentation. The sale was set aside.

(c)   In contracts of **extreme good faith** (*uberrimae fidei*) there is a duty to disclose the material facts which one knows. Non-disclosure can lead to the contract being voidable for misrepresentation. For example:

(i)   Contracts of **insurance**
(ii)   Contracts preliminary to **family arrangements**
(iii)   Contracts in relation to **sale of land** (in regard to defects in title)
(iv)   Contracts where there is a **fiduciary relationship**, such as between solicitor and client
(v)   **Prospectuses inviting a subscription for shares** (in regard to statutory matters)

The person to whom a representation is made is entitled to rely on it without investigation.

6.1.3 Statement made by one party to another

Although, in general, a **misrepresentation** must have been made by the misrepresentor to the misrepresentee there are two exceptions to the rule.

- A misrepresentation can be made to the **public in general**, as where an advertisement contains a misleading representation.

- It is sufficient that the misrepresentor knows that the misrepresentation would be **passed on** to the relevant person.

6.1.4 Inducement to enter into the contract

A representation must have **induced** the person to enter into the contract.

- He knew of its existence.
- He allowed it to affect his judgement.
- He was unaware of its untruth.

In *Peekay Intermark Ltd v Australia and New Zealand Banking Group Ltd 2005* the court held that a regular customer could rely on information given to them during a telephone call as being contractual terms, even though he signed a contract with different terms, which he did not read.

BPP
LEARNING MEDIA

6.2 Types of misrepresentation

FAST FORWARD

Fraudulent misrepresentation is a statement made knowing it to be untrue, not believing it to be true or careless whether it be true or false. **Negligent misrepresentation** is a statement made in the belief that it is true but without reasonable grounds for that belief. **Innocent misrepresentation**, the residual category, is any statement made in the belief that it is true and with reasonable grounds for that belief.

Misrepresentation is classified for the purpose of determining what remedies are available as follows.

- **Fraudulent** – a statement made with knowledge that it is untrue, or without believing it to be true or careless whether it is true or false.

- **Negligent** – a statement made in the belief that it is true but without reasonable grounds for that belief.

- **Innocent** – a statement made in the belief that it is true and with reasonable grounds for that belief. It is a misrepresentation made without fault.

The **Misrepresentation Act 1967** provides the same remedy (damages) for a victim of non-fraudulent (ie negligent or innocent) representation as for a victim of fraudulent misrepresentation. The representor will escape liability if he can prove that he has reasonable grounds to believe that the facts represented were true.

Howard Marine and Dredging Co Ltd v A Ogden & Sons (Excavations) Ltd 1978

The facts: The defendants required two barges for use in an excavation contract. During negotiations with the claimants, the claimant's marine manager stated that the payload of two suitable barges was 1,600 tonnes. This was based on figures given by Lloyds Register, which turned out to be in error. The payload was only 1,055 tonnes. The defendants stopped paying the hire charges and were sued. They counterclaimed for damages at common law and under the Misrepresentation Act 1967.

Decision: The court was unable to decide on whether there was a duty of care (in the common law action), but the claimants had not discharged the burden of proof under the Act, as shipping documents in their possession disclosed the real capacity.

Misrepresentation can give rise to **criminal liability** if it comes under the scope of the Trades Description Act 1968.

6.3 Remedies for misrepresentation

There is a fundamental principle that the effect of a misrepresentation is to make a contract **voidable** and not void. The contract remains valid unless set aside by the representee. This means that the representee may choose either to **affirm** the contract (incorporating the misrepresented terms into the contract) or to **rescind** it.

Key term

Rescission can be defined as the act of repudiating or avoiding a contract which, for example, has been induced by misrepresentation or undue influence. It is not available if there has been undue delay, if the innocent party has affirmed the contract, or if the parties cannot be restored to their original positions.

Rescission entails setting the contract aside as if it had never been made. It is an equitable remedy that courts may not apply it if would be unfair.

6.3.1 Rescission

A contract is rescinded if the misrepresentee makes it clear that he refuses to be bound by its provisions - it is then terminated from the beginning ('*ab initio*'). The misrepresentee must rescind the contract **reasonably promptly** after they discovered (or should have discovered) the misrepresentation.

The misrepresenteee must **communicate his decision** to the misrepresentor, but there are two exceptions to this.

- If property has been delivered to the misrepresentor as a result of the misrepresentation, it is enough simply to take the property back again.

- If the misrepresentor disappears, the representee may announce his intention to rescind by some act that is reasonable in the circumstances.

The misrepresentee may alternatively **affirm** the contract.

- Declare his intention to proceed with it
- Perform some act from which such an intention may reasonably be inferred

---

Car & Universal Finance Co Ltd v Caldwell 1965

The facts: A car was purchased from the defendant by a rogue with a fraudulent cheque. The seller was unable to communicate with the rogue, but informed the police and the AA of the fraud. The rogue had resold the car. (The rogue had fraudulently misrepresented that the cheque would be honoured.)

Decision: The seller had rescinded the contract by taking all reasonable steps and the rogue did not transfer good title to the claimants in a subsequent sale.

Question

Rescission

In many cases, rescission is simply effected when the misrepresentee makes it clear that he refuses to be bound by the contract. When may it be advantageous to bring legal proceedings for an order of rescission?

Answer

Legal action may be desirable if the fraudulent party ignores the cancellation of the contract and fails to return what he has obtained under it. It may be necessary for a formal document, such as a lease, to be set aside by court order. There might also be a possibility that innocent third parties may act on the assumption that the contract still exists.

6.3.2 Damages

In some instances, there may be a right to **damages**, either instead of, or in addition to, the remedy of **rescission**. The available remedies vary depending on the type of misrepresentation.

The right to damages depends on showing that the statement made by the representor is either **fraudulent** or **negligent**.

In a case of **fraudulent misrepresentation** the party misled may in addition to, or instead of, rescinding the contract, recover damages for any loss by a common law action for the **tort of deceit**.

BPP
LEARNING MEDIA

Under the **Misrepresentation Act 1967** the court may, in the case of negligent or innocent misrepresentation, award damages instead of rescission as follows.

(a)   **Negligent misrepresentation**

An injured party may claim damages for **loss** caused by negligent misrepresentation. It is then up to the party who made the statement to prove that he had **reasonable grounds** for making it and that it was not negligent.

(b)   **Innocent misrepresentation**

In the case of **innocent misrepresentation** the remedy of damages is discretionary and awarded if the Court decides it is just and equitable to do so. An indemnity may be awarded, indemnifying the misrepresentee against any obligations created by the contract. The misrepresentee may of course choose instead to rescind the contract and refuse to perform his or her obligations.

Chapter Roundup

- A **valid contract is a legally binding agreement**, formed by the mutual consent of two parties.

- The law seeks to protect the idea of 'freedom of contract', although **contractual terms** may be regulated by **statute**, particularly where the parties are of unequal bargaining strength.

- Although most contracts may be **made in any form**, some must be made in a particular form. A number of commercial contracts must be made in writing, for example.

- The first essential element of a binding contract is **agreement**. This is usually evidenced by **offer and acceptance**. An offer is a definite promise to be bound on specific terms, and must be distinguished from the mere **supply of information** and from an **invitation to treat**. Acceptance must be unqualified agreement to all the terms of the offer. A **counter-offer** is a rejection of the original offer.

- **Acceptance** is generally not effective until **communicated** to the offeror, the principal exception being where the '**postal rule**' applies. In which case, acceptance is complete and effective as soon as notice of it is posted.

- The **postal rule** states that, where the use of the post is within the contemplation of both the parties, acceptance is complete and effective as soon as a letter is posted. This is even though it may be delayed or even lost altogether in the post.

- **Consideration** is what each party brings to a contract. It is usually a **promise** in return for an **act** or **another promise**.

- Consideration need not be **adequate**, but it must be **sufficient**. This means that what is tendered as consideration must be capable in law of being regarded as consideration, but need not necessarily be equal in value to the consideration received in return.

- The principle of **promissory estoppel** was developed in *Central London Property Trust v High Trees House 1947*. It means that in some cases, where someone has made a promise they can be prevented from denying it..

- As a general rule, only a person who is a party to a contract has enforceable rights or obligations under it. This is the doctrine of **privity of contract**, as demonstrated in *Dunlop v Selfridge 1915*.

- Both parties to a contract must **intend** the agreement to give rise to legal obligations. Their intentions may be express – 'this agreement is not subject to legal jurisdiction' – or may be inferred from the circumstances. **Social, domestic and family** arrangements are not assumed to be legally binding unless the contrary is clearly shown. **Commercial** agreements are assumed to be legally binding unless the contrary is clearly demonstrated.

- A contract entered into following a **misrepresentation** is **voidable** by the person to whom the misrepresentation was made. A misrepresentation is a statement of fact, given before the contract is made, which is **untrue** and made by one party to the other in order to **induce** the latter to enter into the agreement.

- **Fraudulent misrepresentation** is a statement made knowing it to be untrue, not believing it to be true or careless whether it be true or false. **Negligent misrepresentation** is a statement made in the belief that it is true but without reasonable grounds for that belief. **Innocent misrepresentation**, the residual category, is any statement made in the belief that it is true and with reasonable grounds for that belief.

BPP
LEARNING MEDIA

1   A valid contract is a legally binding agreement. The three essential elements of a contract are (1) ....,
     (2) .... and (3) ....

2   A conveyance must be evidenced by deed.

     True   ☐

     False   ☐

3   Which one of the following is **not** a means by which an offer is terminated?

     A   The period over which the offer is expressed to be kept open expires without acceptance by the offeree
     B   The offeror tells the offeree before the latter's acceptance that the offer is withdrawn
     C   The offer is accepted by the offeree
     D   The offeree responds to the offer by requesting further information

4   **Fill in the blanks** in the statements below, using the words in the box.

     •   As a general rule, acceptance must be (1) .... to the (2) .... and is not effective
          until this has been done.

     •   An (3) .... is a definite promise to be bound on specific terms, and must be distinguished from
          a supply of (4) .... and from an (5) ....

     •   A counter-offer counts as (6) .... of the original offer

• information	• offer	• invitation to treat
• rejection	• communicated	• offeror

5   As a general rule, silence cannot constitute acceptance.

     True   ☐

     False   ☐

6   If two offers, identical in terms, cross in the post

     A   Either party may accept, to form a contract
     B   The postal rule applies
     C   The first offer to arrive is the basis for the contract
     D   There is no contract as there is no acceptance

7   A misrepresentation is

     (i)   A statement of fact which proves to be untrue
     (ii)   A statement of law which proves to be untrue
     (iii) Made by one party to the other before the contract is formed in order to induce the latter to enter into the
            contract
     (iv)   A statement which affects the claimant's judgement

     A   (ii) and (iv) only
     B   (i), (iii) and (iv) only
     C   (i), (ii), and (iv) only
     D   All of the above

8   Past consideration, as a general rule, is not sufficient to make a promise binding.

True   ☐

False   ☐

9   Consideration need not be (1) ……………….. but it must be (2) ……………….. .

10   The rebuttable presumptions the courts will make with regard to parties' intention to create legal relations are: Social, domestic and family arrangements are generally intended to be binding. Commercial agreements are not generally intended to be binding.

True   ☐

False   ☐

Answers to Quick Quiz

1   Offer and acceptance, consideration, intention to create legal relations.

2   True. A conveyance must be evidenced by deed.

3   D. Requesting information does not terminate an offer. A is termination by lapse of time, B is revocation by the offeror and in C an offer is terminated when it is accepted.

4   (1) communicated (2) offeror (3) offer (4) information (5) invitation to treat (6) rejection

5   True. This is the position under the Unsolicited Goods and Services Act 1971.

6   D. An offer cannot also be acceptance.

7   B. A misrepresentation is

   • A statement of fact which proves to be untrue
   • Made by one party to the other before the contract is formed in order to induce the latter to enter into the contract
   • A statement which affects the claimant's judgement

8   True. Past consideration is not sufficient consideration.

9   (1) adequate, (2) sufficient

10   False. Social, domestic and family arrangements are **not generally intended** to be binding. Commercial agreements are **generally intended** to be binding.

Now try the questions below from the Question Bank

Number
Q16
Q17
Q18
Q19
Q20

BPP
LEARNING MEDIA

5

Performing
the contract

Introduction

In this chapter we consider how **terms** may be **incorporated** into a contract other than by offer and acceptance. We will also consider how one party to a contract may seek to exclude his liability under a contract by the use of a specific type of contract term: the **exclusion** clause.

(a) Statements made in pre-contract negotiations may become **terms** of the contract or remain as **representations**.

(b) In addition to the express terms of the agreement, additional terms may be implied by law. We consider **implied terms** too.

(c) The terms of the contract are usually classified as **conditions** or as **warranties** according to their importance.

(d) Sale of goods and supply of services **legislation** is a source of implied terms in many contracts.

(e) To be enforceable, terms must be **validly incorporated** into the contract.

(f) Terms which **exclude** or **restrict liability** for breach of contract may be restricted in their effect or be overridden by common law or statute.

Topic list	Learning outcomes
1 Contract terms	E1(d)
2 Express terms and implied terms	E1(d)
3 Conditions and warranties	E1(d)
4 Sale of goods and supply of services legislation	E1(e)
5 Exclusion clauses	E1(f)
6 Unfair contract terms regulations	E1(f)
7 Performance of the contract	E2(a)

1 Contract terms

FAST FORWARD

Statements made by the parties may be classified as **terms or representations**. Different **remedies** attach to breach of a term and to misrepresentation respectively.

1.1 Terms and representations

Many statements are made during the process of negotiation that leads to the formation of a contract. Statements may be classified as **terms** or as **representations**. It is important to be able to establish whether what has been said or written amounts to a contract **term**, or whether it is simply a **representation**.

If something said in negotiations proves to be untrue, the party misled can claim for breach of contract if the statement became a term of the contract. Otherwise his remedy is for **misrepresentation**.

The court will consider when the representation was made to assess whether it was designed as a contract term or merely as an incidental statement. If a statement is made with **special knowledge** it is more likely to be treated as a contract term.

A term which is **reasonable** may exclude liability for misrepresentation.

2 Express terms and implied terms

FAST FORWARD

As a general rule, the parties to a contract may include in the agreement whatever **terms** they choose. This is the principle of **freedom of contract**. Terms included in the contract are **express** terms. The law may complement or replace terms by **implying** terms into a contract. Terms may be implied by the **courts**, by **statute** or by **custom**.

2.1 Express terms

An **express term** is a term expressly stated by the parties to a contract to be a term of that contract. In examining a contract, the courts will look firstly at the terms expressly included by the parties.

A legally binding agreement must be **complete in its terms**. However, it is always possible for the parties to leave an essential term to be **settled by other means**.

2.2 Example

It may be agreed to sell at the **open market price** on the day of delivery, or to invite an arbitrator to determine a fair price. The price may be determined by the course of dealing between the parties.

> *Hillas & Co Ltd v Arcos Ltd 1932*
>
> *The facts:* The claimants agreed to purchase from the defendants '22,000 standards of softwood goods of fair specification over the season 1930'. The agreement contained an option to buy a further 100,000 standards in 1931, without terms as to the kind or size of timber being specified. The 1930 transaction took place but the sellers refused to supply any wood in 1931, saying that the agreement was too vague to bind the parties.
>
> *Decision:* The language used, when interpreted by reference to the previous course of dealings between the parties, showed an intention to be bound.

The courts will seek to uphold agreements by looking at the **intention of the parties**. In business, to save later confusion, contracts are often written in great detail.

2.3 Implied terms

There are occasions where certain terms are not **expressly adopted** by the parties, but may be implied from the context of the contract. Additional terms of a contract may be **implied** by **law**: by **custom**, **statute** or the **courts**.

Key term

> An **implied term** can be defined as follows.
>
> 'A term deemed to form part of a contract even though not expressly mentioned. Such terms may be implied by the courts as necessary to give effect to the presumed intentions of the parties. Other terms may be implied by statute, for example, the Sale of Goods Act.'

2.3.1 Terms implied by custom

The parties may enter into a contract subject to **customs of their trade**. Any express term overrides a term which might be implied by custom.

2.3.2 Terms implied by statute

Terms may be implied by statute. In some cases the statute may permit the parties to contract out of the **statutory terms**. In other cases the statutory terms are obligatory. The protection given by the **Sale of Goods Act 1979** to a consumer who buys goods from a trader cannot be taken away from him.

2.3.3 Terms implied by the courts

Terms may be implied if the court concludes that **the parties intended those terms to apply**.

> *The Moorcock 1889*
>
> *The facts:* The owners of a wharf agreed that a ship should be moored alongside to unload its cargo. It was well known that at low tide the ship would ground on the mud at the bottom. At low tide the ship settled on a ridge concealed beneath the mud and suffered damage.
>
> *Decision:* It was an implied term, though not expressed, that the ground alongside the wharf was safe at low tide since both parties knew that the ship must rest on it.

A **term of a contract** which is left to be **implied** and is not expressed is often **something that goes without saying**. Therefore if while the parties were making their contract an officious bystander were to suggest they make some express provision for the term, they would say 'why should we put that in? That's obvious'. This concept was put forward in *Shirlaw v Southern Foundries 1940* and is also described as terms being implied on the grounds of **business efficacy**.

The court may also imply terms to **maintain a standard of behaviour**.

> *Liverpool City Council v Irwin 1977*
>
> *The facts:* The defendants were tenants in a tower block owned by the claimants. There was no formal tenancy agreement. The defendants withheld rent, alleging that the claimants had breached implied terms because the lifts did not work and the stairs were unlit.
>
> *Decision:* Tenants can only occupy a building with access to stairs and/or lifts, so these terms needed to be implied.

Question

Name a statute which implies terms into contracts.

Answer

Sale of Goods Act 1979.

3 Conditions and warranties

FAST FORWARD

Statements which are classified as contract terms may be further categorised as **conditions** or **warranties**. A condition is a vital term going to the root of the contract, while a warranty is a term subsidiary to the main purpose of the contract. The remedies available for breach are different in each case.

3.1 The distinction

The **terms of the contract** are usually classified by their relative importance as **conditions** or **warranties**.

(a) **A condition is a vital term**, **going to the root of the contract**, breach of which deprives the injured party of what they substantially were entitled to under the contract. The injured party may treat the contract as **discharged** and claim damages.

Key term

A **condition** can be defined as follows.

'An important term which is vital to a contract so that its breach will destroy the basis of the agreement. It may arise from an express agreement between the parties or may be implied by law. For example, the condition that goods shall be of satisfactory quality in the Sale of Goods Act.'

(b) **A warranty is a term subsidiary to the main purpose of the contract**, breach of which only entitles the injured party to claim damages.

Key term

A **warranty** can be defined as follows.

'A minor term in a contract. If broken, the injured party must continue performance but may claim damages for the loss suffered.'

Poussard v Spiers *1876*

The facts: Mme Poussard agreed to sing in an opera throughout a series of performances. Owing to illness she was unable to appear on the opening night and the next few days. The producer engaged a substitute who insisted that she should be engaged for the whole run. When Mme Poussard recovered, the producer declined to accept her services for the remaining performances.

Decision: Failure to sing on the opening night was a breach of condition which entitled the producer to treat the contract for the remaining performances as discharged.

Bettini v Gye 1876

The facts: An opera singer was engaged for a series of performances under a contract by which he had to be in London for rehearsals six days before the opening performance. Owing to illness he did not arrive until the third day before the opening. The defendant refused to accept his services, treating the contract as discharged.

Decision: The rehearsal clause was subsidiary to the main purpose of the contract.

Classification may depend on the following issues.

(a) **Statute** often identifies implied terms specifically as conditions or warranties. An example is the Sale of Goods Act 1979.

(b) **Case law** may also define particular types of clauses as conditions.

(c) The **court** may construe the **intentions** of the parties at the time the contract was made as to whether a broken term was to be a condition or a warranty.

 Question

Contractual terms

Which of the following statements concerning contractual terms are true?

(i) Terms may be implied into contracts on the grounds of business efficacy

(ii) If a condition in a contract is not fulfilled, the whole contract is said to be discharged by breach

(iii) If a warranty in a contract is not fulfilled, the whole contract is said to be discharged by breach, but either party may elect to continue with his performance

(iv) Terms implied by custom override express terms on the same matter in the contract

A   (i) and (ii) only
B   (iii) and (iv) only
C   (i), (ii) and (iv) only
D   All of the above

Answer

A   Breach of a warranty does not discharge a contract. Terms implied by custom do not override express terms on the same matter.

3.2 Innominate terms

FAST FORWARD

It may not be possible to determine whether a term is a condition or a warranty. Such terms are classified by the courts as **innominate terms**. The court will only **construe** a broken term as a condition or warranty if the parties' intentions when the contract was formed are very clear.

Where it is not clear what the effect of breach of the term was intended to be, it will be classified by the court as **innominate**, **intermediate** or **indeterminate** (the three are synonymous).

The consequence of a term being classified as **innominate** is that the court must decide what is the actual effect of its breach. If the nature and effect of the breach is such as to deprive the injured party of most of his benefit from the contract then it will be treated as a breached condition.

The **injured party** may **terminate the contract** and **claim damages**.

Hong Kong Fir Shipping Co Ltd v Kawasaki Kisa Kaisha Ltd 1962

The facts: The defendants chartered a ship from the claimants for a period of 24 months. A term in the contract stated that the claimants would provide a ship which was 'in every way fitted for ordinary cargo service'. Because of the engine's age and the crew's lack of competence the ship's first voyage, from Liverpool to Osaka, was delayed for 5 weeks and further repairs were required at the end of it. The defendants purported to terminate the contract, so the claimants sued for breach. The defendants claimed that the claimants were in breach of a contractual condition.

Decision: The term was innominate and could not automatically be construed as either a condition or a warranty. The obligation of 'seaworthiness' embodied in many charterparty agreements was too complex to be fitted into one of the two categories. The ship was still available for 17 out of 24 months. The consequences of the breach were not so serious that the defendants could be justified in terminating the contract as a result.

Important

Do not over-emphasise innominate terms. Conditions and warranties are the key items to understand.

Question

To what is the injured party to a contract entitled in the event of breach of:

(a)   A condition by the other party?
(b)   A warranty by the other party?

Answer

(a)   He may treat the contract as discharged and rescind or terminate the contract, or alternatively he may go on with it and sue for damages.

(b)   He may claim damages only.

4 Sale of goods and supply of services legislation

FAST FORWARD

A particularly important source of implied terms is the **Sale of Goods Act 1979**. The Supply of Goods and Services Act 1982 extends these implied terms to cover goods bought by hire purchase, barter or exchange, and contracts for services.

4.1 Sale of Goods Act 1979

The terms implied by the **Sale of Goods Act 1979** have largely evolved from case law. Much depends on whether an implied term is a **condition** or a **warranty** and whether one party to the contract is dealing as a **consumer**.

4.2 Consumer

A definition of a consumer sale is contained in s 12 Unfair Contract Terms Act 1977.

Key term

'A party to a contract deals as **consumer** in relation to another party if:

(a)   He neither makes the contract in the course of a business nor holds himself out as doing so and

(b)   The other party does make the contract in the course of a business, and

(c)   In the case of a contract governed by the law of sale of goods ..... the goods are of a type ordinarily supplied for private use or consumption.'

4.3 Terms implied by the Sale of Goods Act

A sale of goods may be subject to **statutory rules** on the following.

- **Title**, or the seller's right to sell the goods: s 12
- **Description** of the goods: s 13
- **Quality** of the goods: s 14(2)
- **Fitness of the goods** for the purpose for which they are supplied: s 14(3)
- **Sale by sample**: s 15

Important

Of all the terms implied by the Sale of Goods Act the terms as to quality and fitness for purpose are the most important. Concentrate your reading on s 14 SGA 1979.

4.3.1 Title

Section 12(1) implies into contracts for the sale of goods an undertaking as to **title**, confirming that the seller has a right to sell. s 12(2) implies undertakings as to freedom from other claims, and quiet possession. The condition as to title is broken if the **seller can be stopped by a third party** from selling the goods. If the seller delivers goods to the buyer without having the right to sell, there is a total failure of consideration. If the buyer has to give up the goods to the real owner he may recover the entire price from the seller.

Rowland v Divall 1923

The facts: The claimant purchased a car from the defendant and both parties acted in good faith. Four months later the car was discovered to have been stolen and the claimant had to return it to the true owner. Upon being sued for the price, the defendant argued that damages should be reduced to reflect an allowance for use of the vehicle over the four month period.

Decision: There was no title to accept and therefore no acceptance. The claimant had paid for the property in the vehicle, not merely the right to use it. There had been a total failure of consideration, and as a result the claimant was entitled to recover the full purchase price.

This case has been criticised by some commentators who argue that it is unrealistic to refer to **a total failure of consideration** when the claimant in fact had four months' use of the vehicle.

4.3.2 Description

Section 13 applies to all sales. Sections 13(1) and (2) provide that where there is a contract for the **sale of goods by description**, there is an implied condition that the goods correspond with the description.

> *Beale v Taylor 1967*
>
> *The facts:* The defendant advertised a Triumph as a 'Herald convertible, white, 1961'. The claimant came to inspect the car and subsequently bought it. After buying the car he found that the back half had been welded to a front half which was part of an earlier model. The defendant relied on the buyer's inspection and argued that it was not a sale by description.
>
> *Decision:* The advertisement described the car as a 1961 Herald, and this formed part of the contract description.

It is not the case that all **descriptive words** used form the contract terms. However, Description is interpreted to include ingredients, age, date of shipment, packing, quantity, etc.

4.3.3 Satisfactory quality (s 14 (2))

There is an implied condition that goods supplied under a contract are of **satisfactory quality**. This condition applies only to goods sold in the course of a business, therefore private sales are excluded.

The condition applies to **all goods supplied under the contract**. Therefore it applies not only to the goods themselves but also to any packaging and instructions.

The Act (s 14(2B)) identifies **factors** which may in appropriate cases be aspects of the **quality of goods**.

- **Fitness for all the purposes** for which goods of the kind in question are commonly supplied
- **Appearance and finish**
- **Freedom from minor defects**
- **Safety**
- **Durability**, suggesting that goods will have to remain of **satisfactory quality** for a reasonable period.

The condition of satisfactory quality is excluded if the **buyer's attention** is drawn to defects before the contract is made, or the **buyer examines** the goods before the contract is made, and that examination ought to reveal the defects.

Similarly, if goods are bought **second-hand**, or very **cheaply**, it is not reasonable to expect the highest standards of quality: *Bartlett v Sidney Marcus Ltd 1965*. Conversely, if the product is of a **high price**, minor defects may make the quality unsatisfactory: *Rogers v Parish Ltd 1987*.

In *Clegg v Olle Andersson 2003* it was held that the buyer had a reasonable time to reject a yacht with an overweight keel since it affected its safety. The court also looked at other factors related to the time factor.

In addition to the usual remedies for breach of contract, a buyer who is a consumer has the added benefit of the **Sale and Supply of Goods to Consumers Regulations 2002**. These provide that a buyer may take into account **specific claims** made by a seller about the product when judging its quality. A buyer can also require the seller to **repair or replace faulty goods**, or goods that are not otherwise in conformity with the contract. They may also require the seller to reduce the purchase price or to rescind the contract.

4.3.4 Fitness for purpose

Section 14(3) implies a condition that the goods be **fit for any particular purpose** which the buyer expressly or by implication makes known to the seller. In *Grant v Australian Knitting Mills 1936*, a pair of pants were found not to be satisfactory quality for the purpose of wearing when the buyer contracted dermatitis from a chemical contained in them.

BPP
LEARNING MEDIA

Usually, a buyer must make known the **particular purpose** for which he wants the goods. If the goods have only one obvious purpose, the buyer by implication makes known his purpose merely by asking for the goods.

Where goods are required for a **particular purpose which is not obvious** to the seller or where there is some peculiarity about that purpose, the buyer must make these clear to the seller. However, a buyer may specify the 'particular purpose' quite broadly. Therefore, where a substance is commonly used as animal feedstuff it is sufficient to specify the latter without naming each kind of animal to which it might be fed: *Ashington Piggeries v Christopher Hill Ltd 1972*.

4.3.5 Sale by sample

Under s 15 of the Act there are requirements in a **sale by sample**. In the case of a contract for sale by sample there is an implied condition.

(a)   That the bulk will correspond with the sample in **quality**.

(b)   That the buyer will have a reasonable **opportunity of comparing** the bulk with the sample.

(c)   That the goods shall be free from any **defect** rendering their quality unsatisfactory which would not be apparent on reasonable examination of the sample.

4.3.6 Goods and services case law

The following cases provide an indication of how the legislation concerning the **supply of goods and services** is applied.

(a)   A pre-1961 car had its front replaced by a 1961 version and the whole car was described as a 1961 model. It was held that the description was incorrect: *Beale v Taylor 1967*.

(b)   Underpants which caused a skin condition were held not fit for purpose or of satisfactory quality: *Grant v Australian Knitting Mills 1936*.

(c)   Expensive repairs to a cheap secondhand car were held to mean the car was unsatisfactory for the price: *Bartlett v Sidney Marcus Ltd 1965*. This contrasts with *Rogers v Parish Ltd 1987* where even minor defects were held to be unsatisfactory for an expensive new car and *Feldaroll Foundry plc v Herries Leasing (London) Ltd 2004* where defects which cost very little to rectify meant the car was unsatisfactory as it was unfit to drive.

(d)   In *Frost v Aylesbury Dairy Co Ltd 1905* milk infected with typhoid was not fit for purpose. Even though the dairy had taken every possible precaution, it was liable as liability in this circumstance is strict.

4.4 Acceptance of goods by the buyer

Acceptance of goods deprives the buyer of his right to treat the contract as discharged by breach of condition on the part of the seller. But he may claim damages.

The **buyer is not deemed to have accepted** the goods until he has had a **reasonable opportunity** of examining them. The buyer is deemed to have accepted the goods in the following circumstances.

(a)   When he intimates to the seller that he has accepted them.

(b)   When the goods have been delivered to the buyer and he does any act in relation to them which is consistent with ownership, such as using or reselling them.

(c)   When after the lapse of a reasonable time he retains the goods without intimating to the seller that he has rejected them.

4.5 The Supply of Goods and Services Act 1982

The **Sale of Goods Act 1979**, including its provisions relating to implied terms under ss 12-15, applies only to contracts where goods are sold for money consideration. Other methods of obtaining goods (eg by hire purchase or barter), and the provision of services, are not protected. These areas are covered by the Supply of Goods and Services Act 1982. Part I of the Act affords the protection of statutory implied terms to all contracts for the supply of goods. Part II of the Act covers implied terms in contracts for services.

Hence the **Supply of Goods and Services Act 1982** covers the provision of **accountancy services** by accountants to their clients, which are covered by the wide statutory term that 'the supplier will carry out the service with **reasonable care and skill**'.

4.5.1 An accountant's duties under the Supply of Goods and Services Act

Under the Act, an accountant owes the following **implied duties**.

- **Demonstrate** the **level of skill** that has been **professed**
- **Honesty**
- **Good faith**
- **Obedience** to **client's instructions** (unless illegal)
- To **keep proper records**
- **Confidentiality**
- To take **reasonable care** - the standard of care is high.

Assessment focus point

> These duties could easily be examined in an assessment – learn them.

Question

Statement

During negotiations before entering into a contract for the sale of a car Howard says to Robbie 'the car will be ready for collection on the day you require it'. This statement is described as

A   A representation
B   A term
C   A warranty
D   An advertiser's puff

Answer

A   The statement is a representation as it was made during initial negotiations.

5 Exclusion clauses

FAST FORWARD

An **exclusion clause** may attempt to restrict one party's liability for breach of contract or for negligence. Because of inequality of bargaining power, the **Unfair Contract Terms Act 1977** renders **void** certain exclusion clauses in sale of goods or supply of services contracts and any clause which purports to exclude liability for death or personal injury resulting from negligence.

BPP
LEARNING MEDIA

5.1 The use of exclusion clauses

Key term

An **exclusion clause** can be defined as follows.

'A clause in a contract which purports to exclude liability altogether or to restrict it by limiting damages or by imposing other onerous conditions.' They are sometimes referred to as **exemption clauses**.

There has been strong criticism of the use of **exclusion clauses** in contracts made between manufacturers or sellers of goods or services and private citizens as consumers. The seller puts forward standard conditions of sale which the buyer may not understand, but which he must accept if he wishes to buy. With these so-called **standard form contracts**, the presence of exclusion clauses becomes an important consideration.

For many years the courts demonstrated the hostility of the common law to exclusion clauses by developing various rules of case law designed to restrain their effect. To these must now be added the considerable statutory safeguards provided by the **Unfair Contract Terms Act 1977** (UCTA) and the **Unfair Terms in Consumer Contracts Regulations** (UTCCR). However, the statutory rules do permit exclusion clauses to continue in some circumstances. Hence it is necessary to consider both the **older case law** and the **newer statutory rules**.

The **courts** have generally sought to protect consumers from the harsher effects of exclusion clauses in two ways.

- An exclusion clause must be properly **incorporated** into a contract before it has any legal effect.
- Exclusion clauses are **interpreted** strictly. This may prevent the application of the clause.

If an exclusion clause is made **void by statute (UCTA)** it is unnecessary to consider how other legal rules might affect it. Despite issues with exclusion clauses in contracts between businesses and individuals, they do have a legitimate use in **allocating risk** between businesses.

5.2 Incorporation of exclusion clauses

FAST FORWARD

The courts protect customers from the harsher effects of exclusion clauses by ensuring that they are properly **incorporated** into a contract and then by **interpreting** them strictly.

The general rules

- A clause may not usually be disputed if it is included in a document which has been signed.
- The clause must be put forward before the contract is made.
- Both parties must be aware of it.

Uncertainty often arises over which terms have actually been **incorporated** into a contract.

- The document containing notice of the clause must be an **integral part** of the contract.
- If the document is an integral part of the contract, a term may not usually be disputed if it is included in a document which a party has **signed**.
- The term must be put forward **before** the contract is made.
- It is not a binding term unless the person whose rights it restricts was made **sufficiently aware** of it at the time of agreeing to it.
- **Onerous terms** must be sufficiently highlighted.

5.2.1 Contractual documents

The term must be put forward in a document which gives **reasonable notice** that **conditions** are proposed by it. It must be shown that this document is an **integral part** of the contract and is one **which could be expected to contain terms**.

Chapelton v Barry UDC 1940

The facts: There was a pile of deck chairs and a notice stating 'Hire of chairs 2d per session of three hours'. The claimant took two chairs, paid for them and received two tickets which he put in his pocket. One of the chairs collapsed and he was injured. The defendant council relied on a notice on the back of the tickets by which it disclaimed liability for injury.

Decision: The notice advertising chairs for hire gave no warning of limiting conditions and it was not reasonable to communicate them on a receipt. The disclaimer of liability was not binding on the claimant.

Thompson v LMS Railway 1930

The facts: An elderly lady who could not read asked her niece to buy her a railway excursion ticket on which was printed 'Excursion: for conditions see back'. On the back it was stated that the ticket was issued subject to conditions contained in the company's timetables. These conditions excluded liability for injury.

Decision: The conditions had been adequately communicated and therefore had been accepted.

5.2.2 Signed contracts

If a person signs a document containing a term he is held to have agreed to the term even if he had not read the document. But this is not so if the party who puts forward the document for signature gives a misleading explanation of the term's legal effect.

L'Estrange v Graucob 1934

The facts: The defendant sold to the claimant, a shopkeeper, a slot machine under conditions which excluded the claimant's normal rights under the Sale of Goods Act 1893. The claimant signed the document described as a 'Sales Agreement' which included clauses in 'legible, but regrettably small print'.

Decision: The conditions were binding on the claimant since she had signed them. It was not material that the defendant had given her no information of their terms nor called her attention to them.

Curtis v Chemical Cleaning Co 1951

The facts: The claimant took her wedding dress to be cleaned. She was asked to sign a receipt on which there were conditions which she was told restricted the cleaner's liability and in particular placed on the claimant the risk of damage to beads and sequins on the dress. The document in fact contained a clause 'that the company is not liable for any damage however caused'. The dress was badly stained in the course of cleaning.

Decision: The cleaners could not rely on their disclaimer since they had misled the claimant. She was entitled to assume that she was running the risk of damage to beads and sequins only.

5.2.3 Prior information on terms

Each party must **be aware of the contract's terms at the time of entering into the agreement** if they are to be binding.

BPP
LEARNING MEDIA

Olley v Marlborough Court 1949

The facts: A husband and wife arrived at a hotel and paid for a room in advance. On reaching their bedroom they saw a notice on the wall by which the hotel disclaimed liability for loss of valuables unless handed to the management for safe keeping. The wife locked the room and handed the key in at the reception desk. A thief obtained the key and stole the wife's furs from the bedroom.

Decision: The hotel could not rely on the notice disclaiming liability since the contract had been made previously and the disclaimer was too late.

Complications can arise when it is difficult to determine at exactly what **point in time** the **contract is formed** so as to determine whether or not a term is validly included.

Thornton v Shoe Lane Parking Ltd 1971

The facts: The claimant wished to park his car in the defendant's automatic car park. He had seen a sign saying 'All cars parked at owner's risk' outside the car park and when he received his ticket he saw that it contained words which he did not read. In fact these made the contract subject to conditions displayed obscurely on the premises. These not only disclaimed liability for damage but also excluded liability for injury. When he returned to collect his car there was an accident in which he was badly injured.

Decision: The reference on the ticket to conditions was received too late for the conditions to be included as contractual terms. At any rate, it was unreasonable for a term disclaiming liability for personal injury to be presented so obscurely. Note that since the Unfair Contracts Terms Act 1977 the personal injury clause would be unenforceable anyway.

An exception to the rule that there should be prior notice of the terms is where the parties have had **consistent dealings** with each other in the past, and the documents used then contained similar terms.

J Spurling Ltd v Bradshaw 1956

The facts: Having dealt with a company of warehousemen for many years, the defendant gave it eight barrels of orange juice for storage. A document he received a few days later acknowledged receipt and contained a clause excluding liability for damage caused by negligence. When he collected the barrels they were empty and he refused to pay.

Decision: It was a valid clause as it had also been present in the course of previous dealings, even though he had never read it.

If the parties have had previous dealings, but **not on a consistent basis**, then the person to be bound by the term must be **sufficiently aware** of it at the time of making the latest contract.

Hollier v Rambler Motors 1972

The facts: On three or four occasions over a period of five years the claimant had repairs done at a garage. On each occasion he signed a form by which the garage disclaimed liability for damage caused by fire to customers' cars. The car was damaged by fire caused by negligence of garage employees. The garage contended that the disclaimer had, by course of dealing, become an established term of any contract made between them and the claimant.

Decision: The garage was liable. There was no evidence to show that the claimant knew of and agreed to the condition as a continuing term of his contracts with the garage.

Where a **term** is particularly **unusual** and **onerous it should be highlighted**. Failure to do so may mean that it does not become incorporated into the contract.

5.3 Interpretation of exclusion clauses

In deciding what an exclusion clause means, the courts interpret any ambiguity against the person at fault who relies on the exclusion. This is known as the **contra proferentem rule**. Liability can only be excluded or restricted by clear words.

In the *Hollier* case above, the court decided that as a matter of interpretation the disclaimer of liability could be interpreted to apply (a) only to accidental fire damage or (b) to fire damage caused in any way including negligence. It should therefore be interpreted against the garage in the narrower sense of (a) so that it did not give exemption from fire damage due to negligence. If a person wishes successfully to exclude or limit liability for loss caused by negligence the courts require that the word 'negligence', or an accepted synonym for it, should be included in the clause.

Alderslade v Hendon Laundry 1945

The facts: The conditions of contracts made by a laundry with its customers excluded liability for loss of or damage to customers' clothing in the possession of the laundry. By its negligence the laundry lost the claimant's handkerchief.

Decision: The exclusion clause would have no meaning unless it covered loss or damage due to negligence. It did therefore cover loss by negligence.

5.4 The 'main purpose' rule

When construing an exclusion clause the court will also consider the **main purpose rule**. By this, the court presumes that the clause was not intended to defeat the main purpose of the contract.

5.5 Fundamental breach

For more than twenty years there were conflicting judicial *dicta* on how far an exclusion clause can exclude liability in a case where the breach of contract was a failure to perform the contract altogether – that is, a **fundamental breach.**

Photo Productions v Securicor Transport 1980

The facts: The defendants agreed to guard the claimants' factory under a contract by which the defendants were excluded from liability for damage caused by any of their employees. One of the guards deliberately started a small fire which destroyed the factory and contents. It was contended that Securicor had entirely failed to perform their contract and so they could not rely on any exclusion clause in the contract.

Decision: There is no principle that total failure to perform a contract deprives the party at fault of any exclusion from liability provided by the contract. In this case the exclusion clause was drawn widely enough to cover the damage which had happened. As the fire occurred before the UCTA was in force, the Act could not apply here. But if it had done it would have been necessary to consider whether the exclusion clause was reasonable.

BPP
LEARNING MEDIA

Which of the following exclusion clauses would be binding?

(i)   A list of exclusion clauses provided in a hotel room

(ii)   Exclusion clauses listed on a car park ticket issued on entry through an automatic barrier

(iii)   Exclusion clauses that a customer was well aware of through previous dealings, although they did not sign a contract in this instance

(iv)   Exclusion clauses in a written document that was signed even though it was not read

A   (i) and (iv) only
B   (i) and (ii) only
C   (ii), (iii) and (iv) only
D   (iii) and (iv) only

Answer

D   Option (iii) refers to previous dealings and the customer was well aware of the terms. Option (iv) refers to the case of *L'Estrange v Graucob 1934*. Option (i) refers to *Olley v Marlborough Court 1949* and option (ii) relates to *Thornton v Shoe Lane Parking 1971*.

Assessment focus point

Reliance on exclusion clauses is an everyday occurrence in business dealings and is therefore important.

6 Unfair contract terms regulations

6.1 The Unfair Contract Terms Act 1977

FAST FORWARD

The application of UCTA 1977 depends to a great extent upon whether there is a **consumer sale**. A contract between business operations is considerably less affected by the Act. Both types often have to satisfy a statutory test of **reasonableness**.

When considering the **validity** of exclusion clauses the courts have had to strike a balance between:

- The principle that parties should have complete **freedom to contract** on whatever terms they wish, and
- The need to **protect the public** from unfair exclusion clauses

6.1.1 What is a consumer under UCTA 1977?

To be classed as a **consumer**, a person must be dealing as a **private buyer** with a **person in business**.

> **R&B Customs Brokers Co Ltd v United Dominions Trust Ltd 1988**
>
> *The facts*: R&B Customs purchased a car for the use of a director. The sales contract excluded an implied term from the Sale of Goods Act 1979. Such an exclusion would have been permitted if the contract was a commercial business contract. R&B Customs sought redress from the seller for faulty goods on the basis that it was a consumer.
>
> *Decision:* The purchase was made as a consumer as it was of an infrequent nature, and therefore could not be classed as trading. Had R&B been in the motor trade it would have been deemed a business contract.

Similar facts occurred in *Feldaroll Foundry plc v Herries Leasing (London) Ltd 2004*. In this case, exclusion clauses in a contract for a car were held to be invalid as the claimant purchased the car as a consumer.

However, it is important to note that **exclusion clauses** do have a proper place in business. They can be used to **allocate contractual risk**, and therefore to determine in advance who is to insure against that risk. Between businessmen with similar bargaining power exclusion clauses are a legitimate device.

Before we consider the specific terms of **UCTA**, it is necessary to describe how its **scope is restricted**.

(a)   In general the Act only applies to clauses inserted into agreements by **commercial concerns or businesses**. In principle, private persons may restrict liability as much as they wish.

(b)   The Act does **not apply** to some contracts.

    (i)   Contracts relating to the creation or transfer of **patents**
    (ii)   Contracts of **insurance** and **mortgages**
    (iii)   Contracts relating to the creation or transfer of an **interest in land**
    (iv)   Contracts relating to **company formation** or **dissolution**

The Act uses two techniques for controlling exclusion clauses - some types of clauses are **void**, whereas others are subject to a **test of reasonableness**. The main provisions of the Act are described below.

6.1.2 Exclusion of liability for negligence (s 2)

A person acting in the course of a business cannot, by reference to any contract term, restrict his liability for **death or personal injury** resulting from negligence. In the case of other loss or damage, a person cannot restrict his liability for negligence unless the term is **reasonable**.

6.1.3 Standard term contracts and consumer contracts (s 3)

The person who imposes the term, or who deals with the consumer, **cannot** (unless the term is reasonable) **restrict liability for his own breach or fundamental breach**. Also, they may not claim to be entitled to render substantially different performance or no performance at all.

6.1.4 Sale and supply of goods (ss 6-7)

No contract (consumer or non-consumer) for the sale or hire purchase of goods can exclude the implied condition that the seller has a **right to sell** the goods.

A **consumer contract** for the sale of goods, hire purchase, supply of work or materials or exchange of goods **cannot exclude** or **restrict liability** for breach of the conditions relating to description, quality, fitness and sample implied by the Sale of Goods Act 1979 and the Supply of Goods and Services Act 1982.

For a **non-consumer contract**, such **exclusions** are **subject to a reasonableness test**. The rules are set out in the table below.

		Exemption clauses in contracts for the supply of goods			
		Sale, HP, exchange and work + materials		Hire	
		Consumer transaction	Non-consumer transaction	Consumer transaction	Non-consumer transaction
Implied terms	Title	Void	Void	Subject to reasonableness test	Subject to reasonableness test
	Description	Void	Subject to reasonableness test	Void	Subject to reasonableness test
	Quality and suitability	Void	Subject to reasonableness test	Void	Subject to reasonableness test
	Sample	Void	Subject to reasonableness test	Void	Subject to reasonableness test

6.1.5 The statutory test of reasonableness (s 11)

The **term** must be **fair and reasonable having regard to all the circumstances** which were, or which ought to have been, known to the parties when the contract was made. The burden of proving reasonableness lies on the person seeking to rely on the clause. Statutory guidelines have been included in the Act to assist the determination of reasonableness. For instance, the court will consider the following.

(a)   The relative **strength** of the parties' bargaining positions.

(b)   Whether any **inducement** (eg a reduced price) was offered to the customer to persuade him to accept limitation of his rights.

(c)   Whether the customer **knew or ought to have known** of the existence and extent of the exclusion clause.

(d)   If **failure to comply** with a condition (eg failure to give notice of a defect within a short period) excludes or restricts the customer's rights, whether it was reasonable to expect when the contract was made that compliance with the condition would be practicable.

   In *R W Green Ltd v Cade Bros 1978* it was held that a three day limit to raise problems concerning seed potatoes was unreasonable as problems would not become apparent until after the seeds have started to grow.

(e)   Whether the goods were made, processed or adapted to the **special order** of the customer (UCTA Sch 2).

St Albans City and District Council v International Computers Ltd 1994

The facts: The defendants had been hired to assess population figures on which to base community charges (local government taxation). Their standard contract contained a clause restricting liability to £100,000. The database which they supplied to the claimants was seriously inaccurate and the latter sustained a loss of £1.3 million.

Decision: The clause was unreasonable. The defendants could not justify this limitation, which was very low in relation to the potential loss. In addition, they had aggregate insurance of £50 million. The defendants had to pay full damages.

The Unfair Contract Terms Act 1977 limits the extent to which it is possible to exclude or restrict *business liability*. What do you understand by the phrase business liability?

Answer

Business liability is liability, in tort or contract, which arises from things done or to be done in the course of a business or from the occupation of premises used for business purposes of the occupier. Business includes a profession and the activities of any government department or public or local authority.

Assessment focus point

A good way to look at UCTA is to write down which terms are void under UCTA and which are subject to a reasonableness test. It is vital you understand which contracts UCTA applies to.

6.2 The Unfair Terms in Consumer Contracts Regulations 1999

FAST FORWARD

The **Unfair Terms in Consumer Contracts Regulations 1999** define what is meant by an **unfair term**.

These regulations (UTCCR) implemented an **EU directive on unfair contract terms**. UCTA 1977 continues to apply as well as the common law. Therefore, there are three layers of law relevant to unfair contract terms.

(a)   The **common law**, which applies to all contracts, regardless of whether or not one party is a consumer

(b)   **UCTA 1977**, which applies to all contracts with specific provisions for consumer contracts

(c)   **The Regulations (UTCCR 1999)**, which apply to all types of unfair contract terms but only in relation to consumer contracts and to terms which have not been individually negotiated

The **regulations apply to contracts** for the **supply** of **goods** or **services**.

(a)   They apply to **terms** in **consumer contracts**.

Key term

A **consumer** is defined as 'a natural person who, in making a contract to which these regulations apply, is acting for purposes which are outside his trade, business or profession.'

(b)   They apply to **contractual terms** which have **not been individually negotiated**.

A key aspect of the regulations is the definition of an unfair term.

Key term

An **unfair term** is any term which contrary to the requirement of good faith, causes a significant imbalance in the parties' rights and obligations under the contract to the detriment of the consumer. Terms must be in plain, intelligible language.

In making an **assessment of good faith**, the courts will have regard to the following.

(a)   The **strength** of the **bargaining positions** of the parties
(b)   Whether the **consumer had an inducement** to agree to the term
(c)   Whether the **goods** or **services** were **sold** or **supplied** to the **special order of the consumer**
(d)   The extent to which the **seller** or **supplier** has **dealt fairly** and **equitably** with the **consumer**

BPP
LEARNING MEDIA

UCTCCR will apply when there is:

- A **consumer** – someone acting outside their trade or profession
- A lack of **good faith**
- An **imbalance** between the parties
- **Detriment** to the consumer

Unlike UCTA, **the 1999 regulations apply to insurance and mortgages**.

The effect of the regulations is to render certain terms in **consumer contracts unfair**.

(a)   Excluding or limiting liability of the seller when the consumer **dies** or **is injured**, where this results from an act or omission of the seller

(b)   Excluding or limiting liability where there is **partial** or **incomplete performance** of a contract by the seller

(c)   Making a contract binding on the consumer where the **seller can still avoid performing** the contract

Two forms of redress are available.

(a)   A consumer who has concluded a contract containing an unfair term can ask the court to find that the **unfair term should not be binding**.

(b)   A **complaint**, for example by an individual, a consumer group or a trading standards department can be made to the **Director General of Fair Trading**.

6.3 Other statutory protection

Some other statutes give **specific protection** against **unfair terms** in contracts:

(a)   Under the **Misrepresentation Act 1967** any term excluding liability for misrepresentation is void unless it is proved the exemption was fair and reasonable in the circumstances.

(b)   The **Consumer Credit Act 1974** protects the debtor during the payment period, for example, the debtor cannot be prevented from paying off what he owes at any time and a specific procedure should be followed if the debtor defaults. Under the **Consumer Credit Act 2006** consumers can challenge credit agreements on the grounds that the relationship between the parties is unfair.

7 Performance of the contract

FAST FORWARD

The normal method of discharge is **performance**. Obligations of the parties in the vast majority of commercial contracts are discharged by performance. Performance must be **complete and exact**. There is no right to receive payment proportionate to partially completed work unless one of the recognised exceptions applies.

7.1 Discharge by performance

This chapter has been concerned with the way in which the obligations of each party to a contract may be determined. Most business contracts are duly discharged in the way that the parties intended when establishing their respective contractual obligations. The obligations of each party are usually **discharged** by **performance**.

Performance is the normal method of discharge. Each party fulfils or performs his obligations and the agreement is then ended. As a general rule contractual obligations are discharged only by **complete and exact performance**.

Payment is the usual method of performance and the following rules apply.

- **Cash**. The debtor should seek the creditor at a reasonable time of day to offer payment.

- **Cheques** are conditional payments, not valid until honoured.

- **Credit cards** discharge a debt immediately the supplier receives the funds from the card company.

- **Post**. Where funds are posted, the risk of loss lies with the sender.

- **Multiple debts/part payments**. The debtor has the right to specify which debts each part payment relates to. If this right is not taken up then it passes to the creditor. The default position where neither takes up the right is that earlier debts are paid first.

Cutter v Powell 1795

The facts: The defendant employed C as second mate of a ship sailing from Jamaica to Liverpool at a wage for the complete voyage of 30 guineas. The voyage began on 2 August, and C died at sea on 20 September, when the ship was still 19 days from Liverpool. C's widow sued for a proportionate part of the agreed sum.

Decision: C was entitled to nothing unless he completed the voyage.

Bolton v Mahadeva 1972

The facts: The claimant agreed to install a central heating system in the defendant's home for £800. The work was defective as the system did not heat adequately and it gave off fumes. The defendant refused to pay for it.

Decision: The claimant could recover nothing.

In each of these cases the defendant might appear to have profited since he obtained part of what the claimant contracted to deliver without himself having to pay anything. The **courts** have **developed a number of exceptions** to the rule to ensure that the interests of both parties are protected.

The **exceptions** are as follows.

- The doctrine of **substantial performance**
- Where the promisee accepts **partial performance**
- Where the promisee **prevents performance**
- Where **time is not of the essence**
- **Severable contracts**

7.2 Substantial performance

The doctrine of **substantial performance** may be applied, especially in contracts for building work. If the building **contractor** has completed a very large part of the essential work, he **may claim** the **contract price less a deduction for the minor work outstanding**.

> **Sumpter v Hedges 1898**
>
> *The facts:* The claimant undertook to erect buildings on the land of the defendant for a price of £565. He partially erected the buildings, then abandoned the work when it was only completed to the value of £333. The defendant completed the work using materials left on his land. The claimant sued for the value of his materials used by the defendant and for the value of his work.
>
> *Decision:* The defendant must pay for the materials since he had elected to use them but he had no obligation to pay the unpaid balance of the charges for work done by the claimant before abandoning it. It was not a case of substantial performance of the contract.

However this case is in contrast to *Bolton v Mahadeva 1972* where a contract to install central heating for £560 was done so badly that it would cost £179 to remedy. This was not deemed substantial performance and the claimants were entitled to nothing when the defendants refused to pay.

> **Hoenig v Isaacs 1952**
>
> *The facts*: The defendant employed the claimant to decorate and furnish his flat at a total price of £750. There were defects in the furniture which could be put right at a cost of £56. The defendant argued that the claimant was only entitled to reasonable remuneration.
>
> *Decision*: The defendant must pay the balance owing of the total price of £750 less an allowance of £56, as the claimant had substantially completed the contract.

7.3 Partial performance

A **party may voluntarily accept partial performance and must then pay for it**. The principle here is that although the other party only partially fulfilled his contractual obligations, it may sometimes be possible to infer the existence of a fresh agreement by which it is agreed that payment will be made for work already done or goods already supplied. Mere performance by the promisor is not enough, it must be open to the promisee either to accept or reject the benefit of the contract.

Question   Performance

Why could the doctrine of partial performance not be applied in *Cutter v Powell*?

Answer

Partial performance can only be accepted by the promisee when he has a choice of acceptance or rejection. In *Cutter v Powell,* performance consisted of Cutter's services as second mate. Once he had provided those services, they could not be returned by the shipowners after his death.

7.4 Prevention of performance

The promisee may **prevent performance**. In that case the offer of performance is sufficient discharge. If one party is prevented by the other from performing the contract completely he may sue for damages for breach of contract, or alternatively bring a *quantum meruit* action to claim for the amount of work done.

> *Planché v Colburn 1831*
>
> *The facts*: The claimant had agreed to write a book on costumes and armour for the defendant. He was to receive £100 on completion. He did some research and wrote part of the book. The defendants then abandoned the series.
>
> *Decision*: The claimant was entitled to 50 guineas as reasonable remuneration on a quantum meruit basis.

7.5 Time of performance

If one party fails to perform at the agreed time he may perform the contract later unless **time is of the essence**. In that case the injured party may refuse late performance and treat the contract as discharged by breach. If the parties **expressly agree that time is of the essence** and so prompt performance is to be a condition, conclusive and late performance does not discharge obligations. If they make no such express stipulation the following rules apply.

(a) In a **commercial contract,** time of performance is usually treated as an essential condition.

(b) In a **contract for the sale of land**, equity may permit the claimant to have an order for specific performance even if he is late.

(c) If **time was not originally of the essence**, either party may make it so by serving on the other a notice to complete within a reasonable time.

7.6 Severable contracts

The contract may provide for performance by **instalments** with separate payment for each of them.

> *Taylor v Laird 1856*
>
> *The facts*: The claimant agreed to captain a ship up the River Niger at a rate of £50 per month. He abandoned the job before it was completed. He claimed his pay for the months completed.
>
> *Decision*: He was entitled to £50 for each complete month. Effectively this was a contract that provided for performance and payment in monthly instalments.

Note that not all contracts with **stage payments** are severable in this manner. Many **building contracts** require payment at various stages of completion (once the foundations are laid and when the roof is finished etc). In this case there is only **one contract** and a builder that fails to complete the contract would be liable for damages.

7.7 Sale of Goods Act 1979

As indicated above, acceptance of goods, or part of them (unless the contract is severable), deprives the buyer of his right to treat the contract as discharged by breach of condition on the part of the seller. But he may claim damages. Other **situations where the buyer loses his right to reject goods** include:

- He waives the breached condition.
- He elects to treat the breach of condition as a breach of warranty.
- He is unable to return the goods.

BPP
LEARNING MEDIA

Chapter Roundup

- Statements made by the parties may be classified as **terms or representations**. Different **remedies** attach to breach of a term and to misrepresentation respectively.

- As a general rule, the parties to a contract may include in the agreement whatever **terms** they choose. This is the principle of **freedom of contract**. Terms included in the contract are **express** terms. The law may complement or replace terms by **implying** terms into a contract. Terms may be implied by the **courts**, by **statute** or by **custom**.

- Statements which are classified as contract terms may be further categorised as **conditions** or **warranties**. A condition is a vital term going to the root of the contract, while a warranty is a term subsidiary to the main purpose of the contract. The remedies available for breach are different in each case.

- It may not be possible to determine whether a term is a condition or a warranty. Such terms are classified by the courts as **innominate terms**. The court will only **construe** a broken term as a condition or warranty if the parties' intentions when the contract was formed are very clear.

- A particularly important source of implied terms is the **Sale of Goods Act 1979**. The Supply of Goods and Services Act 1982 extends these implied terms to cover goods bought by hire purchase, barter or exchange, and contracts for services.

- An **exclusion clause** may attempt to restrict one party's liability for breach of contract or for negligence. Because of inequality of bargaining power, the **Unfair Contract Terms Act 1977** renders **void** certain exclusion clauses in sale of goods or supply of services contracts and any clause which purports to exclude liability for death or personal injury resulting from negligence.

- The courts protect customers from the harsher effects of exclusion clauses by ensuring that they are properly **incorporated** into a contract and then by **interpreting** them strictly.

- The general rules
    - A clause may not usually be disputed if it is included in a document which has been signed.
    - The clause must be put forward before the contract is made.
    - Both parties must be aware of it.

- The application of UCTA 1977 depends to a great extent upon whether there is a **consumer sale**. A contract between business operations is considerably less affected by the Act. Both types often have to satisfy a statutory test of **reasonableness**.

- The **Unfair Terms in Consumer Contracts Regulations 1999** define what is meant by an **unfair term**.

- The normal method of discharge is **performance**. Obligations of the parties in the vast majority of commercial contracts are discharged by performance. Performance must be **complete and exact**. There is no right to receive payment proportionate to partially completed work unless one of the recognised exceptions applies.

1   A term may be implied into a contract by

(i)   Statute
(ii)   Trade practice unless an express term overrides it
(iii)   The court to provide for events not contemplated by the parties
(iv)   The court to give effect to a term which the parties had agreed upon but failed to express because it was obvious

A   (ii) and (iii) only
B   (i), (ii) and (iv) only
C   (i), (ii) and (iii) only
D   (i), (iii) and (iv) only

2   **Fill in the blanks** in the statements below, using the words in the box.

•   A (1) ……………….. is a vital term, going to the root of the contract, breach of which entitles the injured party to treat the contract as (2) ……………….. and claim (3) ……………….. .

•   A (4) ……………….. is a term (5) ……………….. to the main purpose of the contract.

•   The consequence of a term being classified as innominate is that the court must decide what is the actual effect of its (6) ………………..

• breach	• condition	• subsidiary
• warranty	• damages	• discharged

3   Where cash is posted to settle a debt, the risk of loss is with the receiver.

True   ☐

False   ☐

4   Which of the following describes the proper use of exclusion clauses?

A   To limit an organisation's risk of being sued for causing personal injury
B   To limit an organisation's risk of being sued for causing death
C   To allocate risk between business organisations
D   To hide onerous obligations on consumers in the 'small print'

5   Exclusion clauses can be incorporated into a contact if the person whose rights are restricted is sufficiently aware of them.

True   ☐

False   ☐

6   Match the layers of law to their jurisdictions in the law of contract.

(a)   Common law   (1)   All contracts with specific provisions for consumer contracts

(b)   UCTA 1977   (2)   Applies only to consumer contracts and to non-negotiated terms

(c)   UTCCR 1999   (3)   All contracts

7   A sale of goods may be subject to statutory rules on which of the following?

- Title
- Description
- Price
- Quality
- Quantity
- Fitness for purpose
- Sale by sample

8   A term which is reasonable may exclude liability for misrepresentation.

True   ☐

False   ☐

9   What is the 'main purpose' rule in relation to exclusion clauses?

A   Exclusion clauses are intended to defeat the main purpose of a contact
B   Exclusion clauses are not intended to defeat the main purpose of a contact
C   The main purpose of an exclusion clause is to prevent one party from being liable for breach of contract
D   The main purpose of an exclusion clause is to allocate risk between contracting parties

10   What is the legal position where it is agreed between the parties that time is of the essence to their contract and one party fails to perform when the time for performance arrives?

A   The injured party must seek an order for specific performance to force the other party to perform
B   The party who failed to perform must do so as soon as possible
C   The injured party can refuse late performance by the other party and treat the contract as discharged by breach
D   The only remedy to the injured party is to sue the other party for damages due to late performance

1   B. A term may be implied into a contract by

    - Statute
    - Trade practice unless an express term overrides it
    - The court giving effect to a term which the parties had agreed upon but failed to express because it was obvious

2   (1) condition (2) discharged (3) damages (4) warranty (5) subsidiary (6) breach

3   False. The risk is with the sender.

4   C. Exclusion clauses cannot limit liability for personal injury or death. Onerous obligations must be sufficiently highlighted or they will be treated as not incorporated in the contract. However, they do have a legitimate use in business by allocating risk between organisations.

5   True. Such clauses are incorporated if the person who is restricted is sufficiently aware.

6   (a)   (3)
    (b)   (1)
    (c)   (2)

7   - Title
    - Description
    - Quality
    - Fitness for purpose
    - Sale by sample

8   True. A term which is reasonable may exclude liability for misrepresentation.

9   B. The 'main purpose' rule states that a court should assume that an exclusion clause is not intended to defeat the main purpose of the contact

10 C. By agreeing that time is of the essence, the time of performance becomes a condition of the contract. Breach of a condition allows the injured party to treat the contract as discharged.

Now try the questions below from the Question Bank

Number
Q21
Q22
Q23
Q24
Q25

Discharge of contract

Introduction

In Chapter 4 we saw how a contract comes into existence and in Chapter 5 we considered some of the factors which can affect a contract. We also looked at **performance** of a contract involving the discharge by each party of his contractual obligations. In this chapter we examine the other ways in which a contract may be **discharged** and the remedies when it is discharged incorrectly.

A party who is subject to the obligations of a contract may be discharged from those obligations in one of four ways. The four ways are **performance**, **agreement**, **frustration** and **breach**. Agreement, frustration and breach are discussed in the first half of this chapter.

You should remember from Chapter 5 that most business contracts are discharged by performance as the parties intended. However, if it is discharged by breach, the injured party will be able to seek remedies. There are a number of available remedies.

Damages and action for the price are **common law remedies** and are most frequently sought when a remedy is needed for breach of contract, since they arise as of right. The other types of remedy are **equitable remedies** which are only appropriate in specialised circumstances.

Topic list	Learning outcomes
1 Agreement	E2(a)
2 Frustration	E2(a), E2(b)
3 Breach of contract	E2(a)
4 Damages	E2(c)
5 Other common law remedies	E2(c)
6 Equitable remedies	E2(c)
7 Limitation to actions for breach	E2(c)

1 Agreement

FAST FORWARD The obligations of the parties may also be discharged by **agreement**.

Instead of performing the contract, **the parties may agree to cancel the contract before it has been completely performed** on both sides.

If there are unperformed obligations of the original contract on both sides, each party provides consideration for his own release by agreeing to release the other (**bilateral discharge**). Each party surrenders something of value.

But if one party has completely performed his obligations, his agreement to release the other from his obligations (**unilateral discharge**) requires consideration, such as payment of a cancellation fee (this is called **accord and satisfaction**).

If the parties enter into a **new contract** to replace the unperformed contract, the new contract provides any necessary consideration. This is called **novation** of the old contract - it is replaced by a new one.

A contract may include provision for its own discharge by imposing a **condition precedent**, which prevents the contract from coming into operation unless the condition is satisfied.

Alternatively, it may impose a **condition subsequent** by which the contract is discharged on the later happening of an event. A simple example of this is provision for termination by notice given by one party to the other. Effectively these are contracts whereby discharge may arise through agreement.

2 Frustration

FAST FORWARD If the parties to the contract assumed, at the time of the agreement, that certain underlying conditions would continue, the contract is discharged by **frustration** if these assumptions prove to be false. This is because the contract is fundamentally different in nature from the original agreement.

2.1 Definitions

If it is **impossible** to perform the contract when it is made, there is usually no contract at all. In addition, the parties are free to negotiate escape clauses or *force majeure* clauses covering impossibility which arises after the contract has been made. If they fail to do so, they are, as a general rule, in **breach** of contract if they find themselves unable to do what they have agreed to do.

The rigour of this principle is modified by the doctrine that in certain circumstances a contract may be discharged by **frustration**. If it appears that the parties assumed that certain underlying conditions would continue, the contract may be frustrated if their assumption proves to be false.

Key term

'The term **frustration** refers to the discharge of a contract by some outside event for which neither party is responsible which makes further performance impossible. It must be some fundamental change in circumstances such as the accidental destruction of the subject-matter upon which the contract depends. The contract is thereby brought to an end and the rights and obligations of the parties will, in many cases, be adjusted by the application of the Law Reform (Frustrated Contracts) Act 1943.'

BPP
LEARNING MEDIA

2.2 Destruction of the subject matter

In the case which gave rise to the doctrine of frustration, the **subject matter** of the contract was destroyed before performance fell due.

Taylor v Caldwell 1863

The facts: A hall was let to the claimant for a series of concerts on specified dates. Before the date of the first concert the hall was accidentally destroyed by fire. The claimant sued the owner of the hall for damages for failure to let him have the use of the hall as agreed.

Decision: Destruction of the subject matter rendered the contract impossible to perform and discharged the defendant from his obligations under the contract.

2.3 Personal incapacity to perform a contract of personal service

The principle that a physical thing must be available applies equally to a person, if that person's presence is a **fundamental requirement**. Not every illness will discharge a contract of personal service - personal incapacity must be established.

Condor v Barron Knights 1966

The facts: The claimant, aged 16, contracted to perform as drummer in a pop group. His duties, when the group had work, were to play on every night of the week. He fell ill and his doctor advised that he should restrict his performances to four nights per week. The group terminated his contract.

Decision: A contract of personal service is based on the assumption that the employee's health will permit him to perform his duties. If that is not so the contract is discharged by frustration.

2.4 Government intervention

Government intervention is a common cause of frustration, particularly in time of **war**. If maintenance of the contract would impose upon the parties a contract fundamentally different from that which they made, the contract is discharged.

Metropolitan Water Board v Dick, Kerr & Co 1918

The facts: The defendants contracted in July 1914 to build a reservoir for the claimants within six years, subject to a proviso that the time should be extended if delays were caused by difficulties, impediments or obstructions. In February 1916 the Minister of Munitions ordered the defendants to cease work and sell all their plant.

Decision: The proviso in the contract did not cover such a substantial interference with the contract. The interruption was likely to cause the contract, if resumed, to be radically different from that contemplated by the parties. The contract was discharged.

2.5 Supervening illegality

In many cases of government intervention, further performance of the contract becomes **illegal** - for example the outbreak of war.

Avery v Bowden 1855

The facts: The defendant entered into a contract to charter a ship from the claimant to load grain at Odessa within a period of 45 days. The ship arrived at Odessa and the charterer told the claimant that he did not propose to load a cargo. The master remained at Odessa hoping the charterer would change his mind. Before the 45 days (for loading cargo) had expired, the outbreak of the Crimean war discharged the contract by frustration.

Decision: The contract was discharged by frustration (the outbreak of war) without liability for either party.

2.6 Non-occurrence of an event if it is the sole purpose of the contract

Two contrasting examples of application of this doctrine are given by the so-called **coronation cases**.

Krell v Henry 1903

The facts: A room belonging to the claimant and overlooking the route of the coronation procession of Edward VII was let for the day of the coronation for the purpose of viewing the procession. The coronation was postponed owing to the illness of the King. The owner of the rooms sued for the agreed fee, which was payable on the day of the coronation.

Decision: The contract was made for the sole purpose of viewing the procession. As that event did not occur the contract was frustrated.

Herne Bay Steamboat Co v Hutton 1903

The facts: A steamboat was hired for two days to carry passengers, for the purpose of viewing a naval review and for a day's cruise round the fleet. The review had been arranged as part of the coronation celebrations. The naval review was cancelled owing to the King's illness but the steamboat could have taken passengers for a trip round the assembled fleet.

Decision: The royal review of the fleet was not the sole occasion of the contract, and the contract was not discharged. The owner of the steamboat was entitled to the agreed hire charge less what he had earned from the normal use of the vessel over the two day period.

2.7 Exceptions

A contract is not discharged by frustration in the following circumstances.

(a)   If an **alternative mode of performance** is possible.

> *Tsakiroglou & Co v Noblee and Thorl GmbH 1962*
>
> The facts: In October 1956 the sellers contracted to sell 300 tons of Sudanese groundnuts and transport them to Hamburg. The normal and intended method of shipment from Port Sudan (on the Red Sea coast) was by a ship routed through the Suez Canal to Hamburg. Before departure, the Suez Canal was closed. The sellers refused to ship the cargo arguing that it was an implied term that shipment should be via Suez or alternatively that shipment via the Cape of Good Hope would make the contract 'commercially and fundamentally' different, so that it was discharged by frustration.
>
> *Decision*: Both arguments failed. There was no evidence to support the implied term argument nor was the use of a different (although more expensive) route an alteration of the fundamental nature of the contract sufficient to discharge it by frustration.

(b)   If performance becomes suddenly more **expensive**.

(c)   If one party **has accepted the risk** that he will be unable to perform.

(d)   If one party **has induced frustration** by his own choice between alternatives.

2.8 The Law Reform (Frustrated Contracts) Act 1943

FAST FORWARD

> The common law consequences of frustration are modified by the **Law Reform (Frustrated Contracts) Act 1943**, which regulates the rights and obligations of the parties to a contract discharged by frustration.

Where a contract is frustrated, the **common law** provides that the occurrence of the frustrating event brings the contract automatically to an end. The consequences of this can be harsh.

> *Chandler v Webster 1904*
>
> *The facts:* The defendant agreed to let the claimant have a room for £141.15s for the purpose of viewing the coronation procession of Edward VII. The contract provided that the money was payable immediately. The coronation was postponed owing to the illness of the King. The claimant sued for the return of his £100 and the defendant counterclaimed for the unpaid amount of £41.15s.
>
> *Decision:* The obligation to pay rent had fallen due before the frustrating event. The claimant's action failed.

This case contrasts with *Krell v Henry 1903*, where the payment was due on the day of the procession.

> *Fibrosa v Fairbairn 1942*
>
> *The facts:* The claimant placed an order for machinery to be delivered in Poland. He paid £1,000 of the contract price of £4,800 with his order. Shortly afterwards the outbreak of the Second World War frustrated the contract since the German army occupied Poland. The claimant sued to recover the £1,000 which had been paid.
>
> *Decision:* The deposit was repayable since the claimant had received absolutely nothing for it - there had been a total failure of consideration.

Do not overlook the importance of statute law in the area of frustration.

In most cases now the **rights and liabilities of parties to a contract discharged by frustration** are regulated by the Law Reform (Frustrated Contracts) Act 1943 as follows.

(a)   Any money paid under the contract by one party to the other is to be repaid.

(b)   Any sums due for payment under the contract then or later cease to be payable.

(c)   If a person has to repay money under (a), or if he must forego payment earned, he may be able (at the court's discretion) to recover or set off expenses incurred up to the time the contract was frustrated.

(d)   If either party has obtained a valuable benefit (other than payment of money) under the contract before it is discharged, the court may in its discretion order him to pay to the other party all or part of that value.

Question   Frustration of contract

Which of the following is *not* a definition of the doctrine of frustration of contract?

A   Parties should be discharged from their contract if altered circumstances render the contract fundamentally different in nature from what was originally agreed

B   Parties should be discharged if an event, for which neither party is responsible, occurs which was not contemplated, which renders the contract fundamentally different and which results in a situation to which the parties did not originally wish to be bound

C   Parties who contract that something should be done are discharged if performance becomes more expensive

D   Parties who contract that something should be done are discharged if their assumption that certain conditions would continue proves to be false

Answer

C   Greater expense does not make the contract fundamentally different.

3 Breach of contract

FAST FORWARD

Breach of a condition in a contract may lead to the entire agreement being discharged by **fundamental breach**, unless the injured party elects to treat the contract as continuing and merely claim damages for his loss.

3.1 What is breach?

A party is said to be in breach of contract where, without lawful excuse, he does not perform his contractual obligations precisely.

A person sometimes has a **lawful excuse** not to perform contractual obligations.

- Performance is **impossible**, perhaps because of some unforeseeable event.
- He has tendered performance but this has been **rejected.**
- The **other party** has made it **impossible** for him to perform.
- The contract has been discharged through **frustration**.
- The parties have by **agreement** permitted **non-performance.**

Breach of contract gives rise to a secondary obligation to pay **damages** to the other party, but the **primary obligation to perform the contract's terms remains** unless breach falls into one of two categories.

(a) Where the party in default has **repudiated** the contract, either before performance is due or before the contract has been fully performed.

(b) Where the party in default has committed a **fundamental breach**.

Key term

> **Repudiation** can be defined as 'a rejection to avoid a contract or to bring a contract to an end for breach of condition. The term may also be applied to a situation where a party renounces his/her contractual obligations in advance of the date for performance.'

3.1.1 Repudiatory breach

Key term

> A **repudiatory breach** occurs where a party indicates, either by words or by conduct, that he does not intend to honour his contractual obligations. A repudiatory breach is a serious actual breach of contract.

It does not automatically discharge the contract - indeed the injured party has a choice.

(a) He can **elect to treat the contract as repudiated** by the other, recover damages and treat himself as being discharged from his primary obligations under the contract.

(b) He can **elect to affirm** the contract.

Courts may give the injured party time to consider their position. In *Marriot v Oxford and District Co-op 1970*, an employment case, an employee went back to work under protest for three weeks following a demotion while they considered what to do. The employee was still entitled to treat the contract as ended and themselves dismissed.

Repudiatory breach giving rise to a right either to terminate or to affirm arises in the following circumstances.

(a) **Refusal to perform (renunciation).** One party renounces his contractual obligations by showing that he has no intention to perform them: *Hochster v De la Tour 1853*

(b) **Failure to perform an entire obligation**. An entire obligation is said to be one where complete and precise performance of it is a precondition of the other party's performance.

(c) **Incapacitation.** Where a party prevents himself from performing his contractual obligations he is treated as if he refused to perform them. For instance, where A sells a thing to C even though he promised to sell it to B he is in repudiatory breach of his contract with B.

Genuine mistakes, even to one party's detriment, will not necessarily repudiate a contract. This was the decision in *Vaswani Motors (Sales and Services) Ltd 1996*. A seller of a motor vehicle, acting in good faith, mistakenly demanded a higher price than that specified in the contract. However, the buyer could not evade his responsibilities under the contract, since he could have offered to pay the original price.

3.2 Anticipatory breach

FAST FORWARD

If there is **anticipatory breach** (one party declares in advance that they will not perform their side of the bargain when the time for performance arrives) the other party may treat the contract as discharged forthwith, or continue with their obligations until actual breach occurs. Their claim for damages will then depend upon what they have actually lost.

Repudiation may be **explicit** or **implicit**. A party may break a condition of the contract merely by declaring in advance that he will not perform it, or by some other action which makes future performance impossible. The other party may treat this as **anticipatory breach** and treat the contract as discharged forthwith, or allow the contract to continue until there is an actual breach

> *Hochster v De La Tour 1853*
>
> *The facts:* The defendant engaged the claimant as a courier to accompany him on a European tour commencing on 1 June. On 11 May he wrote to the claimant to say that he no longer required his services. On 22 May the claimant commenced legal proceedings for anticipatory breach of contract. The defendant objected that there was no actionable breach until 1 June.
>
> *Decision:* The claimant was entitled to sue as soon as the anticipatory breach occurred on 11 May.

Where the injured party allows the contract to continue, it may happen that the parties are discharged from their obligations without liability if the contract is later frustrated: *Avery v Bowden 1855*. If the innocent party elects to treat the contract as still in force they may continue with their preparations for performance and **recover the agreed price** for their services. Any claim for damages will be assessed on the basis of what the claimant has really lost.

> *White & Carter (Councils) v McGregor 1961*
>
> *The facts:* The claimants supplied litter bins to local councils, and were paid not by the councils but by traders who hired advertising space on the bins. The defendant contracted with them for advertising of his business. He then wrote to cancel the contract but the claimants elected to advertise as agreed, even though they had at the time of cancellation taken no steps to perform the contract. They performed the contract and claimed the agreed payment.
>
> *Decision:* The contract continued in force and they were entitled to recover the agreed price for their services. Repudiation does not, of itself, bring the contract to an end. It gives the innocent party the choice of affirmation or rejection.

Question
Repudiation

Breach of a warranty will repudiate a contract.

True or false?

Answer

False. Only a breach of a condition counts as a repudiation.

Assessment focus point

Assessment questions may require you to distinguish between repudiatory and anticipatory breach.

3.3 Termination for repudiatory breach

To **terminate for repudiatory breach** the innocent party must **notify** the other of his decision. This may be by way of refusal to accept defects in performance, refusal to accept further performance or refusal to perform his own obligations.

(a) He is not bound by his future or continuing contractual obligations, and cannot be sued on them.

(b) He need not accept nor pay for further performance.

(c) He can refuse to pay for partial or defective performance already received.

(d) He can reclaim money paid to a defaulter if he can and does reject defective performance.

(e) He is not discharged from the contractual obligations which were due at the time of termination.

The innocent party can also **claim damages** from the defaulter. An innocent party who began to perform his contractual obligations but who was prevented from completing them by the defaulter can claim reasonable remuneration on a *quantum meruit* basis.

3.4 Affirmation after repudiatory breach

If a person is aware of the other party's repudiatory breach and of his own right to terminate the contract as a result but still decides to treat the contract as being in existence he is said to have **affirmed the contract**. The contract remains fully in force.

4 Damages

FAST FORWARD

Damages are a common law remedy intended to restore the party who has suffered loss to the position they would have been in had the contract been performed. The two tests applied to a claim for damages relate to **remoteness of damage** and **measure of damages**.

Key term

Damages are a common law remedy and are primarily intended to **restore the party who has suffered loss to the same position he would have been in if the contract had been performed**.

In a claim for damages the first issue is **remoteness of damage**. Here the courts consider how far down the sequence of cause and effect the consequences of breach should be traced before they should be ignored. Secondly, the court must decide how much money to award in respect of the breach and its relevant consequences. This is the **measure of damages**.

4.1 Remoteness of damage

FAST FORWARD

Remoteness of damage is tested by the **two limbs** of the rule in **Hadley v Baxendale 1854**.

- The first part of the rule states that the **loss must arise either naturally from the breach** (according to the usual course of things), **or in a manner which the parties may reasonably have contemplated** as a probable result of a breach.

- The second part of the rule provides that a **loss outside the usual course of events** will only be compensated if the exceptional circumstances which caused it were within the defendant's **actual or constructive knowledge** when they made the contract.

Under the rule in *Hadley v Baxendale 1854* damages may only be awarded in respect of loss as follows.

(a) (i)   The loss must **arise naturally** from the breach.

(ii) The loss must arise **in a manner which the parties may reasonably be supposed to have contemplated**, in making the contract, as the probable result of the breach of it.

(b) A loss **outside the natural course of events** will only be compensated if the **exceptional circumstances are within the defendant's knowledge** when he made the contract.

Hadley v Baxendale 1854

The facts: The claimants owned a mill at Gloucester whose main crank shaft had broken. They made a contract with the defendant for the transport of the broken shaft to Greenwich to serve as a pattern for making a new shaft. Owing to neglect by the defendant, delivery was delayed and the mill was out of action for a longer period. The defendant did not know that the mill would be idle during this interval. He was merely aware that he had to transport a broken millshaft. The claimants claimed for loss of profits of the mill during the period of delay.

Decision: Although the failure of the carrier to perform the contract promptly was the direct cause of the stoppage of the mill for an unnecessarily long time, the claim must fail since the defendant did not know that the mill would be idle until the new shaft was delivered. Moreover, it was not a natural consequence of delay in transport of a broken shaft that the mill would be out of action. The miller might have a spare.

The defendant is liable only if he knew of the **special circumstances** from which the abnormal consequence of breach could arise.

Victoria Laundry (Windsor) v Newman Industries 1949

The facts: The defendants contracted to sell a large boiler to the claimants 'for immediate use' in their business of launderers and dyers. Owing to an accident in dismantling the boiler at its previous site, delivery was delayed. The defendants were aware of the nature of the claimants' business and had been informed that the claimants were most anxious to put the boiler into use in the shortest possible space of time. The claimants claimed damages for normal loss of profits for the period of delay and for loss of abnormal profits from losing 'highly lucrative' dyeing contracts to be undertaken if the boiler had been delivered on time.

Decision: Damages for loss of normal profits were recoverable since in the circumstances failure to deliver major industrial equipment ordered for immediate use would be expected to prevent operation of the plant. The claim for loss of special profits failed because the defendants had no knowledge of the dyeing contracts.

Contrast this ruling with the case below.

The Heron II 1969

The facts: K entered into a contract with C for the shipment of a cargo of sugar belonging to C to Basra. He was aware that C were sugar merchants but he did not know that C intended to sell the cargo as soon as it reached Basra. The ship arrived nine days late and in that time the price of sugar on the market in Basra had fallen. C claimed damages for the loss due to the fall in market value.

Decision: The claim succeeded. It is common knowledge that market values of commodities fluctuate so that delay might cause loss.

BPP
LEARNING MEDIA

If the type of **loss** caused is **not too remote** the **defendant may be liable** for serious consequences.

H Parsons (Livestock) v Uttley Ingham 1978

The facts: There was a contract for the supply and installation of a large storage hopper to hold pig foods. Owing to negligence of the defendant supplier the ventilation cowl was left closed. The pig food went mouldy. Young pigs contracted a rare intestinal disease, from which 254 died. The pig farmer claimed damages for the value of the dead pigs and loss of profits from selling the pigs when mature.

Decision: Some degree of illness of the pigs was to be expected as a natural consequence. Since illness was to be expected, death from illness was not too remote.

4.1.1 Consequential loss

Parties may seek to **limit liability** by excluding consequential loss, in other words, loss or damage that occurs indirectly from breach of contract. **Such exclusion clauses can be allowed under UCTA 1977 if the contract is a commercial one**. The case below indicates how the courts have been interpreted what consequential losses can include.

Hotel Services v Hilton International 2000

The facts: Hotel Services supplied Hilton International with minibars for its guest rooms. The minibars were faulty and leaked ammonia. Hilton sought damages for repudiatory breach. Its claim included:

- Loss of profit from minibars
- Rental costs paid
- Removal and storing the units

Decision: Despite Hotel Services excluding liability for indirect or consequential loss, they were held liable. The Court decided the damage was direct rather than indirect.

4.2 Measure of damages

FAST FORWARD

The **measure of damages** is that which will **compensate for the loss incurred**. It is not intended that the injured party should profit from a claim.

As a **general rule** the amount awarded as **damages** is what is needed to **put the claimant in the position he would have achieved if the contract had been performed**. This is also referred to as protecting the claimant's **expectation interest**.

A claimant may alternatively seek to have his **reliance interest** protected. This refers to the position he would have been in had he not relied on the contract. This compensates for wasted expenditure. The onus is on the defendant to show that the **expenditure would not have been recovered** if the contract had been performed. However, if a contract is speculative, it may be unclear what profit might result.

Anglia Television Ltd v Reed 1972

The facts: The claimants engaged an actor to appear in a film they were making for television. He pulled out at the last moment and the project was abandoned. The claimants claimed the preparatory expenditure, such as hiring other actors and researching suitable locations.

Decision: Damages were awarded as claimed. It is impossible to tell whether an unmade film will be a success or a failure and, had the claimants claimed for loss of profits, they would not have succeeded.

The general principle is to compensate for **actual financial loss**.

Thompson Ltd v Robinson (Gunmakers) Ltd 1955

The facts: The defendants contracted to buy a Vanguard car from the claimants. They refused to take delivery and the claimants sued for loss of profit on the transaction. There was at the time a considerable excess of supply of such cars over demand for them and the claimants were unable to sell the car.

Decision: The market price rule, which the defendants argued should be applied, was inappropriate in the current market. The seller had lost a sale and was entitled to the profit.

Charter v Sullivan 1957

The facts: The facts were the same as in the previous case, except that the sellers were able to sell every car obtained from the manufacturers.

Decision: Only nominal damages were payable.

In some recent cases damages have been recovered for **mental distress** where that is the main result of the breach. It is uncertain how far the courts will develop this concept.

Jarvis v Swan Tours 1973

The facts: The claimant entered into a contract for holiday accommodation. What was provided was much inferior to the description given in the defendant's brochure. Damages on the basis of financial loss only were assessed at £32.

Decision: The damages should be increased to £125 to compensate for disappointment and distress.

4.3 Mitigation of loss

In **assessing the amount of damages** it is assumed that the claimant will take any reasonable steps to reduce or **mitigate** his loss. The burden of proof is on the defendant to show that the claimant failed to take a reasonable opportunity of mitigation.

Payzu Ltd v Saunders 1919

The facts: The parties had entered into a contract for the supply of goods to be delivered and paid for by instalments. The claimants failed to pay the first instalment when due, one month after delivery. The defendants declined to make further deliveries unless the claimants paid cash in advance with their orders. The claimants refused to accept delivery on those terms. The price of the goods rose, and they sued for breach of contract.

Decision: The seller had no right to repudiate the original contract. But the claimants should have mitigated their loss by accepting the seller's offer of delivery against cash payment. Damages were limited to the amount of their assumed loss if they had paid in advance, which was interest over the period of pre-payment.

An injured party does not need to take **discreditable** or **risky measures** to reduce his loss since these are not 'reasonable'.

BPP
LEARNING MEDIA

4.4 Contributory negligence

Where a duty of care exists, in addition to a contractual obligation, a **claimant's damages may be reduced** where they demonstrated **some contributory negligence**. In *Platform Home Loans Ltd v Oystonshipways Ltd 1999*, a surveyor was sued for an over-valuation of a property. However the claim was reduced as some of the claimant's losses were caused by them taking the property as security for a particularly risky loan. The losses were not all down to the over-valuation.

4.5 Liquidated damages and penalty clauses

To avoid future complicated calculations of loss, or disputes over damages payable, the parties may include up-front in their contract a formula (**liquidated damages**) for determining the damages payable for breach.

Key term

> **Liquidated damages** can be defined as 'a fixed or ascertainable sum agreed by the parties at the time of contracting, payable in the event of a breach, for example, an amount payable per day for failure to complete a building. If they are a genuine attempt to pre-estimate the likely loss, the court will enforce payment.'

A contractual term designed as a **penalty clause** to discourage breach is void and not enforceable. Such terms are not a genuine pre-estimate of losses and are inserted *in terrorem* of the party in breach and to pressurise them to perform or be liable for substantial losses that they would otherwise not be liable for. Relief from penalty clauses is an example of the influence of equity in the law of contract, and has most frequently been seen in consumer credit cases.

However, in *Alfred McAlpine Capital Projects Ltd v Tilebox Ltd 2005*, Judge Jackson J stated that in **commercial contracts** where a pre-estimate of losses is incorrect it might still be found as reasonable and therefore binding.

Key term

> A **penalty clause** can be defined as 'a clause in a contract providing for a specified sum of money to be payable in the event of a subsequent breach. If its purpose is merely to deter a potential difficulty, it will be held void and the court will proceed to assess unliquidated damages.'

 Question
Liquidated damages

What is a liquidated damages clause?

A   A penalty clause in a contract with a company
B   A penalty clause in a contract payable by instalments
C   A formula for pre-determining damages payable for breach
D   An onerous clause which will never be enforced by the courts

Answer

C   A liquidated damages clause is a formula for pre-determining damages payable for breach.

4.6 Sales of goods

Certain remedies are available to **buyers** and **sellers** in respect of the sale of goods.

4.6.1 Remedies for buyers

Where the **seller is in breach of contract**, the buyer has the following remedies.

- **Reject** the goods
- Claim **damages** for the **price of the goods**
- Claim **damages** for **non-acceptance** (where appropriate)

4.6.2 Remedies for sellers

The Sale of Goods Act 1979 gives the **seller rights over the goods sold**.

(a) **Lien**

If the goods are in the seller's possession, they may hold on to them until payment is received.

(b) **Stoppage in transit**

Where the buyer is insolvent, the seller has the right to stop delivery whilst the goods are being transported so they can be recovered.

(c) **Rescind and resell**

If the contract allows, or if the buyer is notified, the seller may rescind the contract and resell the goods if payment is not received in a reasonable time.

4.6.3 Romalpa clauses

These are not remedies but an attempt to protect the seller by using contract terms. They are **'reservation of title'** clauses which state that ownership of the goods will not pass to the buyer until they are paid for. Such clauses mean that in the event of the buyer's insolvency, the goods can be recovered rather than the seller becoming an unsecured creditor. Matters become complicated where the goods have been sold on to a third party or are mixed with other goods.

5 Other common law remedies

5.1 Action for the price

FAST FORWARD

A simple **action for the price** to recover the agreed sum should be brought if breach of contract is failure to pay the price. But property must have passed from seller to buyer, and complications arise where there is anticipatory breach.

If the breach of contract arises out of one party's **failure to pay the contractually agreed price** due under the contract, the creditor should bring a personal action against the debtor to recover that sum. This is a fairly straightforward procedure but is subject to two specific limitations.

The first is that an **action for the price** under a contract for the sale of goods may only be brought if property has passed to the buyer, unless the price has been agreed to be payable on a specific date: s 49 Sale of Goods Act 1979.

Secondly, whilst the injured party may recover an agreed sum due at the time of an anticipatory breach, **sums which become due after the anticipatory breach may not be recovered** unless he affirms the contract.

BPP
LEARNING MEDIA

5.2 Quantum meruit

FAST FORWARD

A **quantum meruit** is a claim which is available as an alternative to damages. The injured party in a breach of a contract may claim the value of his work. The aim of such an award is to restore the claimant to the position they would have been in had the contract never been made. It is a **restitutory award**.

In particular situations, a claim may be made on a *quantum meruit* basis as an alternative to an action for damages for breach of contract.

Key term

The phrase **quantum meruit** literally means **'how much it is worth'**. It is a measure of the value of contractual work which has been performed. The aim of such an award is to restore the claimant to the position he would have been in if the contract had never been made, and is therefore known as a **restitutory** award.

Quantum meruit is likely to be sought where one party has already performed part of his obligations and the other party then repudiates the contract.

De Barnardy v Harding 1853

The facts: The claimant agreed to advertise and sell tickets for the defendant, who was erecting stands for spectators to view the funeral of the Duke of Wellington. The defendant cancelled the arrangement without justification.

Decision: The claimant might recover the value of services rendered.

In most cases, a *quantum meruit* claim is needed because the other party has **unjustifiably prevented performance**: *Planché v Colburn 1831*.

Because it is **restitutory**, a *quantum meruit* award is usually for a smaller amount than an award of damages. However where only nominal damages would be awarded (say because the claimant would not have been able to perform the contract anyway) a *quantum meruit* claim would still be available and would yield a higher amount.

Question

Action for the price

Under an action for the price, what is the claimant claiming for?

A   The value of their work completed
B   The market value of the goods
C   The agreed sum in the contract
D   The recommended retail price of the goods

Answer

C   An action for the price is a claim for the agreed sum in the contract.

6 Equitable remedies

6.1 Specific performance

FAST FORWARD

An order for **specific performance** is an equitable remedy. The party in breach is ordered to perform their side of the contract. Such an order is only made where damages are inadequate compensation, such as in a sale of land, and where actual consideration has passed.

The court may at its discretion give an **equitable remedy** by ordering the defendant to perform his part of the contract instead of letting him 'buy himself out of it' by paying damages for breach.

Key term

Specific performance can be defined as 'an order of the court directing a person to perform an obligation. It is an equitable remedy awarded at the discretion of the court when damages would not be an adequate remedy. Its principal use is in contracts for the sale of land but may also be used to compel a sale of shares or debentures. It will never be used in the case of employment or other contracts involving personal services.'

An order will be made for specific performance of a contract for the sale of land since the claimant may need the land for a particular purpose and would **not be adequately compensated by damages** for the loss of his bargain. However, for items with no special features, specific performance will not be given, as damages would be a sufficient remedy.

The **order will not be made if it would require performance over a period of time** and the court could not ensure that the defendant did comply fully with the order. Therefore specific performance is not ordered for contracts of employment or personal service nor usually for building contracts.

6.2 Injunction

FAST FORWARD

An **injunction** is an equitable remedy which requires that a negative condition in the agreement be fulfilled.

Key term

An **injunction** is a discretionary court order and an equitable remedy, requiring the defendant to observe a negative restriction of a contract.

An **injunction** may be made to **enforce a contract of personal service**. This would be achieved by preventing a person from taking a course of action which would breach the contract.

Warner Bros Pictures Inc v Nelson 1937

The facts: The defendant (the film star Bette Davis) agreed to work for a year for the claimants and not during the year to work for any other producer nor 'to engage in any other occupation' without the consent of the claimants. She came to England during the year to work for a British film producer. The claimants sued for an injunction to restrain her from this work and she resisted arguing that if the restriction were enforced she must either work for them or abandon her livelihood.

Decision: The court would not make an injunction if it would have the result suggested by the defendant. But the claimants merely asked for an injunction to restrain her from working for a British film producer. This was one part of the restriction accepted by her under her contract and it was fair to hold her to it to that extent.

BPP LEARNING MEDIA

An injunction is limited to **enforcement of contract terms** which are in substance **negative restraints**. In other words, if a contract specifies acts which a party should not perform, an injunction can be granted to prevent them performing those acts.

However, an injunction will not be granted to prevent a person performing acts which seem **inconsistent** with the terms of a contract, if the contract does not specifically restrain them from doing so.

Question

Injunction

The purpose of an injunction is to

A   Enforce a negative restraint in a contract
B   Compel compliance with the contract's terms
C   Ensure timely and complete performance
D   Restrain acts inconsistent with the contract's obligations

Answer

A   Negative restraint means to stop someone from doing something.

6.3 Rescission

Strictly speaking the equitable right to **rescind** an agreement is not a remedy for breach of contract - it is a right which exists in certain circumstances, such as where a contract is **voidable** for misrepresentation.

Rescinding a contract means that it is **cancelled** or **rejected** and the parties are restored to their pre-contract condition. Four conditions must be met.

- It must be possible for each party to be returned to their pre-contract condition *(restitutio in integrum)*.

- An innocent third party who has acquired rights in the subject matter of the contract will prevent the original transaction being rescinded.

- The right to rescission must be exercised within a reasonable time of it arising.

- Where a person affirms a contract expressly or by conduct it may not then be rescinded.

7 Limitation to actions for breach

FAST FORWARD

The **right to sue** for breach of contract becomes statute-barred after six years from the date on which the cause of action accrued: s 5 Limitation Act 1980. The period is **twelve years** if the contract is by **deed**.

7.1 The Limitation Act 1980

The **right to sue** for breach of contract becomes statute-barred after **six years** from the date on which the cause of action accrued: s 5 Limitation Act 1980. The period is **twelve years** if the contract is **by deed**.

In three situations the six year period begins not at the date of the breach but later.

(a) If the **claimant is a minor** or under some other contractual disability (eg of unsound mind) at the time of the breach of contract, the six year period begins to run only when his disability ceases or he dies.

(b) If the **defendant or his agent conceals the right of action by fraud** or if the action is for relief from the results of a mistake, the six year period begins to run only when the claimant discovered or could by reasonable diligence have discovered the fraud, concealment or mistake: s 32 Limitation Act 1980. An innocent third party who acquired property which is affected by these rules is protected against any action in respect of them: s 32(4).

(c) The normal period of six years can be **extended** where **information** relevant to the possible claims is **deliberately concealed** after the period of six years has started to run.

Where the claim can only be for specific performance or injunction, the Limitation Act 1980 does not apply. Instead, the claim may be limited by the **equitable doctrine of delay or 'laches'**. This doctrine means that the party seeking an equitable remedy has a **very limited time** to do so. There is no rule on how much time a claimant has to claim, the amount will largely be governed by what is reasonable in the circumstances.

Allcard v Skinner 1887

The facts: The claimant entered a Protestant convent in 1868 and, in compliance with a vow of poverty, transferred property worth about £7,000 to the Order by 1878. In 1879 she left the order and became a Roman Catholic. Six years later she demanded the return of the balance of her gift, claiming undue influence by the defendant, the Lady Superior of the Protestant sisterhood.

Decision: This was a case of undue influence for which a right of rescission may be available, since the rule of the Order forbade its members from seeking the advice of outsiders. But the claimant's delay in making her claim debarred her from recovering her property.

7.2 Extension of the limitation period

The **limitation period may be extended** if the debt, or any other certain monetary amount, is either acknowledged or paid in part before the original six (or twelve) years has expired: s 29. Hence if a debt accrues on 1.1.2010, the original limitation period expires on 31.12.2015. But if part-payment is received on 1.1.2011, the debt is reinstated and does not then become 'statute-barred' until 31.12.2016.

(a) The **claim must be acknowledged as existing**, not just as possible, but it need not be quantified. It must be in writing, signed by the debtor and addressed to the creditor: s 30.

(b) To be effective, the **part payment must be identifiable with the particular debt**, not just a payment on a running account.

 Question

How long does a claimant have to bring an action for breach of a contract by deed?

A 3 years
B 6 years
C 9 years
D 12 years

Answer

D A claimant has twelve years to bring an action for breach of contact by deed.

 BPP
LEARNING MEDIA

Chapter Roundup

- The obligations of the parties may also be discharged by **agreement**.

- If the parties to the contract assumed, at the time of the agreement, that certain underlying conditions would continue, the contract is discharged by **frustration** if these assumptions prove to be false. This is because the contract is fundamentally different in nature from the original agreement.

- The common law consequences of frustration are modified by the **Law Reform (Frustrated Contracts) Act 1943**, which regulates the rights and obligations of the parties to a contract discharged by frustration.

- Breach of a condition in a contract may lead to the entire agreement being discharged by **fundamental breach**, unless the injured party elects to treat the contract as continuing and merely claim damages for his loss.

- If there is **anticipatory breach** (one party declares in advance that they will not perform their side of the bargain when the time for performance arrives) the other party may treat the contract as discharged forthwith, or continue with their obligations until actual breach occurs. Their claim for damages will then depend upon what they have actually lost.

- **Damages** are a common law remedy intended to restore the party who has suffered loss to the position they would have been in had the contract been performed. The two tests applied to a claim for damages relate to **remoteness of damage** and **measure of damages**.

- **Remoteness of damage** is tested by the **two limbs** of the rule in **Hadley v Baxendale 1854**.

  - The first part of the rule states that the **loss must arise either naturally from the breach** (according to the usual course of things), or **in a manner which the parties may reasonably have contemplated** as a probable result of a breach.

  - The second part of the rule provides that a **loss outside the usual course of events** will only be compensated if the exceptional circumstances which caused it were within the defendant's **actual or constructive knowledge** when they made the contract.

- The **measure of damages** is that which will **compensate for the loss incurred**. It is not intended that the injured party should profit from a claim.

- A simple **action for the price** to recover the agreed sum should be brought if breach of contract is failure to pay the price. But property must have passed from seller to buyer, and complications arise where there is anticipatory breach.

- A **quantum meruit** is a claim which is available as an alternative to damages. The injured party in a breach of a contract may claim the value of his work. The aim of such an award is to restore the claimant to the position they would have been in had the contract never been made. It is a **restitutory award**.

- An order for **specific performance** is an equitable remedy. The party in breach is ordered to perform their side of the contract. Such an order is only made where damages are inadequate compensation, such as in a sale of land, and where actual consideration has passed.

- An **injunction** is an equitable remedy which requires that a negative condition in the agreement be fulfilled.

- The **right to sue** for breach of contract becomes statute-barred after **six years** from the date on which the cause of action accrued: s 5 Limitation Act 1980. The period is **twelve years** if the contract is by **deed**.

1   Which of the following is **not** a lawful excuse to avoid performing contractual obligations?

    A   The contract has been discharged through frustration

    B   The parties have by agreement permitted non-performance

    C   One party has made it impossible for the other to perform

    D   One party will suffer financial loss.

2   Following an anticipatory breach of contract by the other party, the innocent party may elect to treat the contract as still in force and continue with their preparations for performance and recover the agreed price for their services.

    True   ☐

    False ☐

3   **Fill in the blanks** in the statements below, using the words in the box.

    (1) .... are a (2) .... remedy designed to restore the injured party to the position they would have been in had the contract been (3) ....

    A loss outside the natural course of events will only be compensated if the (4) .... circumstances are within the (5) ....'s knowledge at the time of making the contract.

    In assessing the amount of damage it is assumed that the (6) .... will (7) .... their loss.

    A contractual term designed as a (8) .... is (9) ....

• mitigate	• performed	• claimant
• penalty clause	• exceptional	• damages
• common law	• void	• defendant

4   The amount awarded as damages is what is needed to put the claimant in the position they would have achieved if the contract had been performed. What interest is being protected here?

expectation
reliance

5   Are each of the following remedies based on (i) equity or (ii) common law?

    (a)   Quantum meruit

    (b)   Injunction

    (c)   Action for the price

    (d)   Rescission

    (e)   Specific performance

6   State the statutory time limits for suing for breach of contract under the Limitation Act 1980.

7   Which one of the following is **not** a condition of rescinding a contract?

    A   The possibility of rescission must have been included in the original contract.

    B   It must be possible for each party to be returned to their pre-contract condition.

    C   No innocent third party has acquired rights in the subject matter of the contract.

    D   Rescission must take place within a reasonable time.

8   Once a contract is in force, the parties may not agree to cancel it before performance is complete.

      True   ☐

      False   ☐

9   In a sale of goods contract, at which point can a seller take an action for the price case against the buyer?

      A   At any time if the buyer refuses to pay
      B   At any time if the seller reasonably believes the buyer cannot pay
      C   At any time after the buyer has received the goods and any specific payment date has passed
      D   At any time after the contract payment date

10   Under the Sale of Goods Act 1979, sellers have the right of lien. Lien is:

      A   The right to halt delivery of the goods whilst a third party is transporting them to the buyer if payment has
            not been received

      B   The right to hold onto goods the buyer has ordered until their payment is received

      C   The right to rescind the contract and resell the goods if payment has not been received within a reasonable
            time

      D   The right to retain ownership of the goods until they are paid for

1   D. Financial loss does not remove an obligation to perform.

2   True. The innocent party may allow the contract to continue until actual breach occurs.

3   (1)   damages   (2)   common law   (3)   performed
        (4)   exceptional   (5)   defendant   (6)   claimant
        (7)   mitigate   (8)   penalty clause   (9)   void

4   Expectation

5   (a)   Common law
        (b)   Equity
        (c)   Common law
        (d)   Equity
        (e)   Equity

6   Six years unless the contract is by deed, in which case the period is twelve years.

7   A. It is not necessary for rescission to have been provided for in a contract for it to take place.

8   False. The parties can agree to discharge their obligations at any time.

9   C. To bring an action for the price case in a sale of goods contract, the buyer must be in possession of the goods and any specifically agreed payment date must have passed.

10   B. Lien is the seller's right to hold onto goods whilst they are still in their possession until the buyer's payment has been received.

Now try the questions below from the Question Bank

Number
Q26
Q27
Q28
Q29
Q30

Part C
Law of
Employment

BPP
LEARNING MEDIA

7

Employment contract

Introduction

The law of employment was developed under common law principles as an application of the law of contract. In recent years **statutory rules** have been enacted to give the **employee protection** both against dismissal and against unsafe or unhealthy working conditions. But the basic issues in employment law remain.

(a)   Is there an arrangement of a contract of service (**employment**) or only a contract for services (with an **independent contractor**)?

(b)   What are the **terms** of a contract of employment?

Topic list	Learning outcomes
1 What is an employee?	F1(a)
2 Why does it matter?	F1(a)
3 Employment contract: basic issues	F1(b)
4 Common law duties	F1(b)
5 Statutory duties	F1(b)
6 Varying the terms of an employment contract	F1(b)
7 Vicarious liability	F1(b)

1 What is an employee?

FAST FORWARD

It is important to distinguish between a **contract of service** (employment) and a **contract for services** (independent contractor). Each type of contract has different rules for taxation, health and safety provisions, protection of contract and vicarious liability in tort and contract.

A contract of service is **distinguished** from a contract for services usually because the parties **express** the agreement to be one of service. This does not always mean that an employee will not be treated as an independent contractor by the court, however; much depends on the three tests.

- Control test
- Integration test
- Economic reality test

A general rule is that an employee is someone who is employed under a **contract of service**, as distinguished from an independent contractor, who is someone who works under a **contract for services**.

However, it is important to note that some statutory provisions apply to '**workers**' and this term is wider than '**employees**' and includes those personally performing work or services unless they are truly self-employed.

Key terms

An **employee** is 'an individual who has entered into, or works under a contract of employment'. Employment Rights Act 1996 (ERA).

A **contract of employment** is 'a contract of service or apprenticeship, whether express or implied, and (if it is express) whether it is oral or in writing.'

In practice this distinction depends on many factors and it is important to know whether an individual is an employee or an independent contractor for a number of reasons. The courts will apply a series of **tests**.

Primarily, the court will look at the **reality of the situation**. This may be in spite of the form of the arrangement.

Ferguson v John Dawson & Partners 1976

The facts: A builder's labourer was paid his wages without deduction of income tax or National Insurance contributions and worked as a self-employed contractor providing services. His 'employer' could dismiss him, decide on which site he would work and direct him as to the work he should do. It also provided the tools which he used. He was injured in an accident and sued his employers on the basis that they owed him legal duties as his employer.

Decision: On the facts taken as a whole, he was an employee working under a contract of employment.

Where there is some **doubt** as to the nature of the relationship the courts will then look at any **agreement between the parties**.

Massey v Crown Life Assurance 1978

The facts: The claimant was originally employed by an insurance company as a departmental manager; he also earned commission on business which he introduced. At his own request he changed to a self-employed basis. Tax and other payments were no longer deducted by the employers but he continued to perform the same duties. The employers terminated these arrangements and the claimant claimed compensation for unfair dismissal.

Decision: As he had opted to become self-employed and his status in the organisation was consistent with that situation, his claim to be a dismissed employee failed.

BPP
LEARNING MEDIA

It can still be unclear whether a person is an employee or an independent contractor. Historically, the tests of **control, integration** into the employer's organisation, and **economic reality** (or the multiple test) have been applied in such cases.

The fundamental prerequisite of a contract of employment is that there must be **mutual obligations** on the employer to provide, and the employee to perform, work.

1.1 The control test

The court will consider whether the employer has **control** over the way in which the employee performs his duties.

Mersey Docks & Harbour Board v Coggins & Griffiths (Liverpool) 1947

The facts: Stevedores hired a crane with its driver from the harbour board under a contract which provided that the driver (appointed and paid by the harbour board) should be the employee of the stevedores. Owing to the driver's negligence a checker was injured. The case was concerned with whether the stevedores or the harbour board were vicariously liable as employers.

Decision: It was decided that the issue must be settled on the facts and not on the terms of the contract. The stevedores could only be treated as employers of the driver if they could control in detail how he did his work. But although they could instruct him what to do, they could not control him in how he operated the crane. The harbour board (as 'general employer') was therefore still the driver's employer.

1.2 The integration test

The courts consider whether the employee is so skilled that he cannot be controlled in the performance of his duties. Lack of control indicates that an employee is **not integrated** into the employer's organisation, and therefore not employed.

Cassidy v Ministry of Health 1951

The facts: The full-time assistant medical officer at a hospital carried out a surgical operation in a negligent fashion. The patient sued the Ministry of Health as the employer. The Ministry resisted the claim arguing that it had no control over the doctor in his medical work.

Decision: In such circumstances the proper test was whether the employer appointed the employee, selected him for his task and so integrated him into the organisation. If the patient had chosen the doctor, the Ministry would not have been liable as employer. But here the Ministry (the hospital management) made the choice and so it was liable.

The control and integration tests are important, but **no longer decisive** in determining whether a person is an employee.

1.3 The multiple (economic reality) test

Courts also consider whether the employee was **working on his own account** and this requires numerous factors to be taken into account.

Ready Mixed Concrete (South East) v Ministry of Pensions & National Insurance 1968

The facts: The driver of a special vehicle worked for one company only in the delivery of liquid concrete to building sites. He provided his own vehicle (obtained on hire purchase from the company) and was responsible for its maintenance and repair. He was free to provide a substitute driver. The vehicle was painted in the company's colours and the driver wore its uniform. He was paid gross amounts (no tax etc deducted) on the basis of mileage and quantity delivered as a self-employed contractor. The Ministry of Pensions claimed that he was in fact an employee for whom the company should make the employer's insurance contributions.

Decision: In such cases the most important test is whether the worker is working on his own account. On these facts the driver was a self-employed transport contractor and not an employee.

In the above case, Mackenna J held that a contract of service existed where:

- There is **agreement** from the worker that they will provide work for their master in exchange for remuneration.

- The worker agrees either expressly or impliedly that their master can exercise **control** over their performance.

- There are other **factors** included in the contract that make it **consistent** with a contract of service.

The fact that the drivers could appoint a **replacement** for themselves was a major factor in the decision that found them as contractors rather than employees.

1.4 Agency workers

The status of agency workers has been the subject of numerous cases in recent years as the numbers employed under such contracts have increased. Two key cases have considered **length of service** of agency workers and **control** that the client of the agency has over the worker.

(a) **Length of service**

In *Franks v Reuters Ltd 2003*, the agency worker had been providing services to the client for some **six years** engaged in a variety of jobs, and was effectively so thoroughly integrated with the employer's organisation as to be **indistinguishable** from the employer's staff.

Mummery LJ, said that an *'implied contract of employment did not arise simply by virtue of the length of the employment, but it could well be a factor in applying the overall tests appropriate to establish (or otherwise) an employment status'*.

The case was remitted to the tribunal for further consideration, but the length of an assignment of an agency worker clearly has implications for the development of other indications of an employment relationship, with those utilising the services of the worker forgetting the true nature of the relationship and behaving towards the work as if he or she was an employee. It may be that at this point the relevant approach also starts to involve the 'integration' test'.

BPP
LEARNING MEDIA

(b)   **Control over the worker**

Where the client of the agency has **sufficient control** over the employee provided by the agency, it could be held that they are in fact the true employer.

Motorola v Davidson and Melville Craig 2001

The facts: Davidson was contracted with the Melville Craig agency and was assigned to work for Motorola. Both the agency and Motorola had agreed that Davidson could be sent back to the agency if his work was unacceptable. Following a disciplinary hearing Davidson was found unacceptable and returned to the agency. Davidson took Motorola to an employment tribunal for unfair dismissal.

Decision: Motorola had sufficient control over Davidson to make them the employer. It was held that the court should look beyond the pure legal situation and look at the practical control aspects in such cases as well.

1.5 Relevant factors

Significant factors that you should consider when deciding whether or not a person is employed or self-employed are as follows.

- Does the employee use his **own tools and equipment** or does the employer provide them?

- Does the alleged employer have the power to **select or appoint** its employees, and may it dismiss them?

- **Payment of salary** is a fair indication of there being a contract of employment.

- **Working for a number of different people** is not necessarily a sign of self-employment. A number of assignments may be construed as 'a series of employments'.

- Can the 'employee' **delegate** their work to others? If so the courts are likely to conclude that a contract for employment does not exist.

In difficult cases, courts will consider whether there is restriction as to place of work, whether there is a **mutual obligation** and whether holidays and hours of work are agreed.

O'Kelly v Trusthouse Forte Plc 1983

The facts: The employee was a 'regular casual' working when required as a waiter. There was an understanding that he would accept work when offered and that the employer would give him preference over other casual employees. The employment tribunal held that there was no contract of employment because the employer had no obligation to provide work and the employee had no obligation to accept work when offered.

Decision: The Court of Appeal agreed with this finding. Whether there is a contract of employment is a question of law but it depends entirely on the facts of each case; here there was no 'mutuality of obligations' and hence no contract.

The decision whether to classify an individual as an employee or not is also influenced by **policy considerations**. For example, an employment tribunal might regard a person as an employee for the purpose of unfair dismissal despite the fact that the tax authorities treated him or her as self-employed.

> *Airfix Footwear Ltd v Cope 1978*
>
> *The facts:* The case concerned a classic outworking arrangement under which the applicant (having been given training and thereafter supplied with the necessary tools and materials) generally worked five days a week making heels for shoes manufactured by the respondent company. She was paid on a piece work basis without deduction of income tax or NIC.
>
> *Decision:* Working for some seven years, generally for five days a week, resulted in the arrangement being properly classified as employment under a contract of employment.

Question
'Of service' or 'for services'?

Which of the following factors indicate that an individual is likely to be independent contractor rather than an employee?

A   There is payment of a salary.

B   The 'employee' is not permitted to delegate his work.

C   The 'employee' provides the necessary tools and equipment to perform the work.

D   There are 'mutual obligations' on the employer to provide, and the employee to perform, work.

Answer

C   Where the 'employee' provides their own tools and equipment then it can indicate that they are an independent contractor. However, other factors would be taken into account too. The other options are clear indications of a contract of service.

2 Why does it matter?

FAST FORWARD

The distinction between **employed** and **self-employed** is important as to whether certain **rights** are available to an individual and how they are treated for **tax purposes**.

The first thing that it is important to note is that much of the legislation which gives protection to employees **extends further than employees**. Much of it is drafted to cover 'workers' a term which has a wide definition to cover most people providing services to others outside of the course of (their own) business. This has somewhat **reduced the importance** of the distinction between employees and independent contractors. However, there are several other **practical reasons** why the distinction between a contract of service and a contract for services is important.

BPP
LEARNING MEDIA

SIGNIFICANCE OF THE DISTINCTION		
	Employed	**Self-employed**
Social security	Employers must pay secondary Class 1 national insurance contributions on behalf of employees Employees make primary Class 1 national insurance contributions There are also differences in statutory sick pay and levies for industrial training purposes	Independent contractors pay Class 2 and 4 national insurance contributions
Taxation	Deductions for income tax must be made by an employer for income tax under PAYE from salary paid to employee	The self-employed are taxed under self-assessment for income tax and are directly responsible to the HM Revenue and Customs for tax due
Employment protection	There is legislation which confers protection and benefits upon employees under a contract of service, including • Minimum periods of notice • Remedies for unfair dismissal	Employment protection is not available for contractors
Tortious acts	Employers are generally vicariously liable for tortious acts of employees, committed in the course of employment even where an employee breaches their own statutory duty	Liability of the person hiring an independent contractor for the contractor's acts is severely limited unless they are negligent in selecting them
Implied terms	There are rights and duties implied by statute for employers and employees This will affect things such as copyrights and patents	These implied rights and duties do not apply to such an extent to a contract for services.
VAT	Employees do not have to register for or charge VAT	An independent contractor may have to register for, and charge VAT
Bankruptcy	In an employer's liquidation, an employee has preferential rights as a creditor for payment of outstanding salary and redundancy payments, up to certain limits	Contractors are treated as non-preferential creditors if their employer is liquidated
Health and safety	There is significant common law and legislation governing employers' duties to employees with regard to health and safety	The common law provisions and much of the legislation relating to employees also relates to independent contractors

BPP
LEARNING MEDIA

Assessment focus point

Ensure you understand the implications of an individual being classified as self-employed or an employee.

Question   Self-employed v employee

Self-employed contactors have their tax and national insurance contributions deducted by the employer from the money paid to them.

True or false?

Answer

False. The self-employed are responsible for paying their own tax and national insurance.

3 Employment contract: basic issues

FAST FORWARD

There are no particular legal rules relating to the commencement of employment – it is really **just like any other contract** in requiring offer and acceptance, consideration and intention to create legal relations.

A contract of service may be **express** or **implied**. If express, it can be either **oral** or **written**. In essence, then, an employment contract can be a simple, straightforward agreement. However, as we shall see later, some **rights** for employees are **provided by statute**. Employees and employers cannot 'opt-out' of these rights, even if they expressly agree to do so.

The contact must, of course, comply with the usual rules relating to the formation of a valid contract. **Illegal contracts** of employment (which are designed with tax avoidance in mind for example) are not enforceable and the employee may lose any statutory rights they would otherwise be entitled to.

Question   Essential elements of a contract of employment

As with any other contract, agreements for employment require offer and acceptance, consideration and the intention to create legal relations. How are these three essential elements manifested in a contract of employment?

Answer

Generally the offer comes from the employer and acceptance from the employee, who may write a letter or simply turn up for work at an agreed time. Consideration comprises the promises each party gives to the other – a promise to work for a promise to pay. If there is no consideration, a deed must be executed for there to be a contract of employment. The intention to create legal relations is imputed from the fact that essentially employment is a commercial transaction.

At the one extreme, an employment contract may be a **document** drawn up by solicitors and signed by both parties; at the other extreme it may consist of a **handshake** and a 'See you on Monday'. In such cases the court has to clarify the agreement by determining what the parties must be taken to have agreed.

Senior personnel may sign a contract specially drafted to include terms on **confidentiality** and **restraint of trade**. Other employees may sign a standard form contract, exchange letters with the new employer or simply agree terms orally at interview.

Each of these situations will form a valid contract of employment, subject to the requirements outlined below as to written particulars, as long as there is **agreement** on **essential terms** such as hours and wages. Nor should it be forgotten that even prior to employment commencing the potential employer has legal obligations, for example not to discriminate in recruitment.

3.1 Implied terms

Implied terms usually arise out of **custom** and **practice** within a profession or industry. In *Henry v London General Transport Services Ltd 2001* it was held that four requirements should be met before such terms can be read into a contract.

- The **terms** must be **reasonable**, **certain** and **notorious**

- They must **represent the wishes** of **both parties**

- **Proof of the custom or practice** must be provided by the party seeking to rely on the term

- A **distinction** must be made between implying terms that make **minor** and terms that make **fundamental changes** to the terms of the contract

Collective agreements between employers and unions can expressly be referred to in an employment contract, or be implied through their operation over time, *Grey, Dunn & Co Ltd v Edwards 1980*.

3.2 Requirement for written particulars

Within two months of the beginning of the employment the employer must give to an employee a written **statement of prescribed particulars** of his employment. Any **subsequent changes** should be notified within one month.

The statement should identify the following.

- The names of **employer** and **employee**

- The **date** on which employment began

- Whether any service with a previous employer forms part of the employee's **continuous period** of employment

- **Pay** – scale or rate and intervals at which paid

- **Hours** and **place** of work (including any specified 'normal working hours')

- Any **holiday** and **holiday pay** entitlement (the statutory minimum is 28 days which may include public holidays)

- **Sick leave** and **sick pay** entitlement

- **Pensions** and pension **schemes**

- Length of **notice** of termination to be given on either side

- The **title** of the job which the employee is employed to do (or a brief job description)

A **'principal statement'**, which must include the **first six items** above and the **title** of the job, must be provided, but other particulars may be given by way of separate documents.

If the employee has a **written contract of employment** covering these points and has been given a copy it is not necessary to provide him with separate written particulars.

The written particulars must also contain details of **disciplinary procedures** and **grievance procedures** or reference to where they can be found: s35 Employment Act 2002.

If the employer fails to comply with these requirements the employee may apply to an **employment tribunal** for a declaration of what the terms should be: s11 ERA. S38 Employment Act 2002 allows a tribunal to award compensation to an employee claiming unfair dismissal if the particulars are incomplete.

Question
Employee or independent contractor?

Charles saw a sign advertising vacancies at a local building site. He contacted the foreman and was told that he would be required but that, because work depended on the weather conditions, he would not be given an employment contract – he would be accountable for his own income tax and National Insurance. The foreman added that he would be provided with tools and that at the beginning of each day he would be told which site he would work on that day. Lateness or theft of materials would lead to his dismissal. Is Charles an employee?

Answer

Charles is an employee. Even though he does not receive an employment contract the facts indicate a contract of service since he is controlled by the employer in that the latter provides tools, tells him where to work and reserves the right to dismiss him.

4 Common law duties

FAST FORWARD

The **employer** has an implied **duty at common law** to take **reasonable care** of his employees; he must select proper staff, materials and provide a safe system of working.

The **employee** has a duty of **faithful service** and to exercise **care and skill** in performance of his duties.

4.1 Employee's duties

The employee has a **fundamental duty of faithful service** to his employer. All other duties are features of this general duty and **serious breaches** may justify the employer dismissing them. The **implied** duties include:

(a) **Reasonable competence** to do their job.

(b) **Obedience** to the **employer's instructions** unless they require him to do unlawful, dangerous or unreasonable acts: *Morrish v Henlys (Folkstone) Ltd 1973*.

(c) **Duty of good faith**. An employee has a duty of good faith to their employer. This includes

(i) Accounting for all money and property received during employment, except what it is **customary** to be received or if it is trivial: *Reading v Attorney General 1951*.

BPP
LEARNING MEDIA

> *Boston Deep Sea Fishing and Ice Co v Ansell 1888*
>
> *The facts*: The defendant, who was managing director of the claimant company, accepted personal commissions from suppliers on orders which he placed with them for goods supplied to the company. He was dismissed and the company sued to recover from him the commissions.
>
> *Decision*: The company was justified in dismissing the claimant and he must account to it for the commissions.

(ii)   Protecting confidential information

In *Fowler v Faccenda Chicken Ltd 1986,* the Court of Appeal considered what information should be considered confidential. It decided there are three categories.

(i)   **Not confidential** due to its trivial nature or easy accessibility.

(ii)   Information which is confidential, but becomes part of the employee's **skill and knowledge**.

(iii)   **Specific trade secrets**.

Once an employee leaves employment, they only have a duty to protect the last category.

(d)   **Reasonable care and skill** in the performance of his work: *Lister v Romford Ice and Cold Storage Co 1957*. What is reasonable depends on the degree of skill and experience which the employee professes to have.

(e)   **Personal service** – the contract of employment is a personal one and so the employee may not delegate his duties without the employer's express or implied consent.

(f)   The same duty of **fidelity** to an employer to whom he is seconded as to a **contractual employer**.

> *Hivac Ltd v Park Royal Scientific Instruments Ltd 1946*
>
> The facts: In their spare time certain of the claimant's employees worked for the defendant company, which directly competed with the claimant.
>
> *Decision*: Even though the employees had not passed on any confidential information, they were still in breach of their duty of fidelity to the claimants.

The importance of these common law implied duties on both parties is that:

(a)   **Breach of a legal duty**, if it is important enough, may entitle the injured party to treat the contract as **discharged** and to claim damages for breach of contract at common law, and

(b)   In an employee's claim for compensation for unfair dismissal, the employee may argue that it was a case of **constructive dismissal** by the employer, or the employer may seek to justify his express dismissal of the employee by reference to his conduct.

4.2 Restraint of trade

Some employment contracts seek to **restrict** the **activities** of employees after they leave service through the use of **restrictive covenants**.

In *Countryside Assured Financial Services v Pollard 2004*, such covenants were held to be **void**. They will be enforced only to the extent that they do the **minimum** to protect the interests of the employer.

Formation of a valid contract of employment requires

(i)   Offer and acceptance
(ii)   Intention to create legal relations
(iii) Consideration
(iv)   A written document

A   (i) and (ii) only
B   (i), (ii) and (iii) only
C   (ii) and (iii) only
D   All of the above

Answer

B   A valid employment contract does not have to be a written document.

4.3 Employer's duties

Employees have a right to expect their employers to **behave reasonably** and **responsibly** towards them within an overriding **duty of mutual trust and confidence.** Examples of where this duty have been breached include:

- A director calling his secretary 'an intolerable bitch on a Monday morning' – *Isle of Wight Tourist Board v Coombes 1976*

- Failure to investigate a sexual harassment claim – *Bracebridge Engineering v Darby 1990*

The **employer** usually also has the following duties at **common law**:

(a)   To **pay remuneration** to employees. If there is no rate fixed by the parties, this duty is to pay **reasonable** remuneration.

(b)   To **indemnify the employee** against expenses and losses incurred in the course of employment.

(c)   To take care of the employees' **health and safety** at work.

(d)   To **provide work**, where

- The employee is an apprentice

- The employee is paid with reference to work done

- The opportunity to work is the essence of the contract (for example, for actors)

- There is work available to be done (subject to contractual terms to the contrary) **and** the relevant employee is a skilled worker who needs work to preserve his or her skills – *William Hill Organisation v Tucker 1998*

- There is no breach of duty if there is **no work** available and the employer continues to pay its employees. However, if an employee was appointed to a **particular role** and no work was provided there may be a breach of duty to provide work if it denies the employee the opportunity to maintain his skills – *Collier v Sunday Referee Publishing Co Ltd 1940*

There is no duty to provide a **reference** when employees leave service. Employers may be liable under negligence for not taking reasonable care over accuracy and fairness if they do provide one: *Cox v Sun Alliance Life 2001*. There is no implied contractual term allowing an employee to smoke at work *Dryden v Greater Glasgow Health Board 1992*.

The importance of these common law implied duties on both parties is that:

- **Breach of a legal duty**, if it is important enough, may entitle the injured party to treat the contract as **discharged** and to claim damages for breach of contract at common law; and

- In an employee's claim for compensation for unfair dismissal, the employee may argue that it was a case of **constructive dismissal** by the employer, or the employer may seek to justify his express dismissal of the employee by reference to his conduct.

5 Statutory duties

FAST FORWARD

Statute implies terms into employment contracts, which may not usually be overridden, regarding pay, maternity leave and work-life balance generally, time off, health and safety and working time.

Various matters are implied into contracts of employment by statute. Some of them build upon the **basic matters** covered by the common law. Most of the employment statutes in this area implement European Directives on employment law issues. The employer has **statutory duties** in the following areas:

- Pay
- Time off work
- Maternity rights and the 'work-life balance'
- Health and safety
- Working time

5.1 Pay

There are two key pieces of legislation in relation to pay. These are the **Equal Pay Act 1970** and the **National Minimum Wage Act 1998**.

5.1.1 Equal Pay Act 1970

Under this Act, contractual **employment terms should be at least as favourable as those given to an employee of the opposite sex**. The Act covers terms such as sick pay, holiday pay and working hours, and it applies to all forms of full-time and part-time work.

5.1.2 National Minimum Wage Act 1998

A **national minimum wage** was introduced in the UK in 1999. The current **hourly rate** for those aged 21 and over (at October 2010) is £5.93. For persons between the ages of 18 and 20, the rate is £4.92 and for 16 and 17 year olds it is £3.64.

Under the **Employment Act 2008**, employers must reimburse employees for any underpayments and pay a penalty of up to 50% of the underpayments if found guilty of paying employees less than the minimum wage.

Assessment focus point

The national minimum wage rates from October 2011 are £6.08, £4.98 and £3.68 and from October 2012 are £6.19, £4.98 and £3.68 respectively.

5.1.3 Deductions and pay slips

The **Employment Rights Act 1996** contains provisions concerning deductions from pay.

Tax and **national insurance** must be deducted from pay. Other permissible deductions include:

- **Uniform** and **clothing**
- **Pension** contributions
- **Penalties** for **poor timekeeping** (if contractually agreed)
- **Stock losses** and **cash shortages** (retail only, limited to 10% of gross pay per payment period)

Any **unauthorised deductions** can be challenged at an employment tribunal.

Where an employer employs more than **20 staff**, they are obliged to provide an itemised **pay statement** for employees who work more than **8 hours** per week.

5.1.4 Sick pay

Employers must pay employees **statutory sick pay** for the first 28 weeks of illness payable at two levels depending on average salary. Employees also have a right to be paid for time off whilst recovering from an **occupational disease** or whilst **pregnant**.

5.2 Time off work

In addition to the rights relating to maternity and parental leave discussed below, statute lists **several occasions** when an **employee has a right to time off work**.

(a)   **Trade union officials** are entitled to time off on full pay at the employer's expense to enable them to carry out **trade union duties**: ss 168-169 Trade Union and Labour Relations (Consolidation) Act 1992.

(b)   An employee who has been given notice of dismissal for **redundancy** may have time off to look for work or to arrange training for other work.

(c)   A member of a recognised independent **trade union** may have time off work (without statutory right to pay) for **trade union activities**, for example, attending a branch meeting: s 170 TULRCA 1992.

(d)   Employees also have a duty to allow an employee to have reasonable time off to carry out certain **public duties**, for example performing his duties as a magistrate. There is **no statutory provision** entitling an employee to time off for jury service, but prevention of a person from attending as a juror is contempt of court.

(e)   Employees who are **suspended on medical grounds** after working with hazardous materials are entitled to full pay for 26 weeks if no suitable alternative employment can be found.

5.3 Maternity rights and the 'work-life balance'

A woman who is pregnant is given substantial rights under statute, including:

- The right to **time off work** for ante-natal care
- The right to **maternity leave**
- The right to **maternity pay**
- The right to **return to work** after maternity leave
- If dismissed, a claim for **unfair dismissal**

BPP LEARNING MEDIA

Much recent employment legislation, including provisions introduced by the Employment Act 2002, has been concerned with the introduction of **family-friendly** employment policies. There has been a specific focus on the so-called **'work-life balance'**. The law has developed as a result in the areas of maternity leave and pay, paternity leave, rights of adoptive parents and a right to request flexible working

5.3.1 Ante-natal care

An employee has a right not to be unreasonably refused time off for **ante-natal care** during working hours.

5.3.2 Maternity leave and pay

Every woman is given the right to **statutory maternity leave** which is **52 weeks** long, subject to her satisfying the requirement as to whether she qualifies as an 'employee'. She must also give her employer proper notice of her intentions.

If the woman has been employed for at least 26 weeks up to the 15th week before the baby is due and earns at least an average of £97 per week (£102 per week from April 2011) she is entitled to **statutory maternity pay**. This is paid for **39 weeks** during her statutory maternity leave.

(a)   The first six weeks are paid at 90% of weekly earnings

(b)   The remaining 33 weeks are paid at the lower of £124.88 per week (£128.73 from April 2011) or 90% of average weekly earnings.

(c)   Statutory maternity leave between 40 and 52 weeks is unpaid.

5.3.3 Paternity leave and pay

Eligible employees are entitled to take either **one week** or **two consecutive** weeks paid paternity leave. The leave must be completed within 56 days of the actual birth of the child.

Statutory paternity pay is paid during paternity leave. This will be paid at the same rate as statutory maternity pay.

5.3.4 Adoptive parents

The family-friendly employment policies introduced by the Employment Act 2002 extend to adoptive parents, who have similar rights to those provided under the maternity provisions. There is a right to **statutory adoption leave** (SAL) and **statutory adoption pay** (SAP). Statutory adoption leave may consist of 26 weeks of ordinary adoption leave and 26 weeks of additional adoption leave.

5.3.5 Flexible working

Employees have the **right** to apply for a change in terms and conditions of employment in respect of hours, time and place of work and not to be unreasonably refused.

The employer may **reasonably refuse** a request on the grounds of:

- The burden of additional cost
- A detrimental effect on ability to meet customer demand
- An inability to re-organise the work amongst existing staff or to recruit additional staff
- A detrimental impact on quality or performance
- Insufficiency of work during the periods the employee proposes to work or
- Planned structural changes

5.3.6 Parental leave

Any employee with a year's continuous service who has responsibility for a child is entitled to **unpaid parental leave** of 13 weeks to care for that child, for each child up until their 5th birthday: s 7 Employment Relations Act 1999. Parents of a disabled child may take up to 18 weeks up to that child's 18th birthday.

5.4 Health and safety

The key legislation under which an employer has a duty to his employees with regard to **health and safety** is the Health and Safety at Work Act 1974, which has been augmented by subsequent regulations, notably the Health and Safety at Work Regulations 1999.

5.5 Working time

The **Working Time Regulations 1998** provide broadly that a worker's **average working time in a 17 week period,** (including overtime) shall **not exceed 48 hours for each 7 days period**, unless the worker has agreed in writing that this limit shall not apply.

5.6 Immigration duty

Under the **Immigration, Asylum, and Nationality Act 2006** an employer may face a civil penalty of up to £2,000 or a criminal penalty of up to two years in prison and an unlimited fine for employing people who are not permitted to work in the United Kingdom.

Question

Paternity leave

What is the maximum period of absence that an employee is entitled to in respect of statutory paternity leave?

A   2 weeks
B   13 weeks
C   26 weeks
D   52 weeks

Answer

A   Statutory paternity leave is a maximum of 2 weeks.

6 Varying the terms of an employment contract

FAST FORWARD

A contract of employment can only be **varied** if the contract **expressly** gives that right, or if all parties consent to the variation.

It should be clear, from your earlier studies of general contract law, that a change in contract terms **can only be made with the consent of both parties** to the contract.

BPP
LEARNING MEDIA

6.1 Varying terms without changing the contract

There may be circumstances in which an employer can vary the terms of an employment contract without actually needing to vary the contract itself. For example, there may be an **express term** in the contract which itself gives rights of variation, for example to allow a change in area of work.

Alternatively, an **implied term** may act to vary the contract.

(a)   A sales representative may be required to take responsibility for such area as his employer considers necessary in order to meet changing market conditions

(b)   Terms may also be implied by custom, for example, where a steel erector is required at the request of his employer to change sites: *Stevenson v Teeside Bridge & Engineering Co Ltd 1971*

6.2 Changing the existing contract

The existing contract can be changed by **consent**. Consent might be demonstrated by **oral agreement** to new terms, by the **signing** of a new statement of terms and conditions or by the employee showing acceptance by **working** under the new terms. If an employee's contract is varied without consent, the employee may have a claim for **constructive dismissal**.

6.3 Signing a new contract

The third option open to the employer is to give contractual notice to the employee and then offer a new contract on the new terms. This opens the employer to a **potential claim** for unfair dismissal. It is generally best for the employer to obtain consent to vary the terms of an existing contract.

Question   Varying an employment contract

If an employee's employment contract is varied without their permission, they may have a claim for:

A   Wrongful dismissal
B   Unfair dismissal
C   Constructive dismissal
D   None of the above

Answer

C   If an employee's contract is varied without their permission, they may have a claim for constructive dismissal.

7 Vicarious liability

FAST FORWARD   >>   **Vicarious liability** means liability for the torts of others and arises because of a relationship between the parties.

7.1 Introduction

Circumstances when vicarious liability arises

- There is the **relationship** of employer and employee
- The employee's tort is committed in the **course of his employment**

Assessment focus point

You can see that negligence and employment law could overlap in a question in the form of vicarious liability.

7.2 Relationship of employer and employee

The existence of an employer/employee relationship is characterised by the features of a contract of service that we saw earlier.

7.3 Torts committed in the course of employment

The employer is only liable for the employee's torts **committed in the course of employment**. Liability arises even in the following circumstances:

(a)   If the employee **disobeys orders** as to how he shall do his work.

> *Limpus v London General Omnibus Co 1862*
>
> *The facts:* The driver of an omnibus intentionally drove across in front of another omnibus and caused it to overturn. The bus company resisted liability on the ground that it had forbidden its drivers to obstruct other buses.
>
> *Decision:* The driver was nonetheless acting in the course of his employment, so the employers were liable.

> *Beard v London General Omnibus Co 1900*
>
> *The facts:* The same employer forbade bus conductors to drive buses. A bus conductor caused an accident while reversing a bus.
>
> *Decision:* He was not doing the job for which he was employed and so the employers were not liable.

(b)   If, while engaged on his duties, the **employee does something for his own convenience**.

> *Century Insurance v Northern Ireland Road Transport Board 1942*
>
> *The facts:* A driver of a petrol tanker lorry was discharging petrol at a garage. While waiting he lit a cigarette and threw away the lighted match. There was an explosion.
>
> *Decision:* The employer was liable since the driver was, at the time of his negligent act, in the course of his employment.

If the employer allows the employee private use of the employer's vehicle, the employer is not liable for any accident which may occur. There is the same result when a driver disobeys orders by giving a lift to a passenger who is then injured.

> **Twine v Bean's Express 1946**
>
> The facts: In this case there was a notice in the driver's part of the van that the firm's drivers were forbidden to give lifts. The passenger was killed in an accident.
>
> Decision: The passenger was a trespasser and in offering a lift the driver was not acting in the course of his employment.

> **Rose v Plenty 1976**
>
> *The facts:* The driver of a milk float disobeyed orders by taking a 13 year old boy round with him to help with his deliveries. The boy was injured by the driver's negligence.
>
> *Decision:* The driver was acting in the course of his employment (presumably because the boy was not a mere passenger but was assisting in delivering milk).

If the employee, acting in the course of his employment, **defrauds a third party** for his own advantage, the employer is still vicariously liable.

> **Lloyd v Grace Smith & Co 1912**
>
> *The facts:* L was interviewed by a managing clerk employed by a firm of solicitors and agreed on his advice to sell property with a view to reinvesting the money. She signed two documents by which the property was transferred to the clerk who misappropriated the proceeds.
>
> *Decision:* The employers were liable. It was no defence that acting in the course of his employment the employee benefited himself and not them.

(c)   The employee commits a **criminal act** that is sufficiently **connected to their work**.

> **Lister v Hesley Hall Ltd 2001**
>
> *The facts:* Three former pupils claimed they were sexually abused by the warden at their school. The claim was based on the school's actual or constructive knowledge that abuse was taking place or that they were negligent in preventing it.
>
> *Decision:* The House of Lords held there was sufficient connection between the work the warden was employed to do and the abuse he committed. Accordingly, the school was liable.

This contrasts with *ST v North Yorkshire County Council 1999* where a school was not held liable for abuse committed by a deputy head teacher whilst on a school holiday. The court said it was an **independent act.**

> **Fennelley v Connex South Eastern 2001**
>
> *The facts:* A ticket inspector assaulted a train passenger following an argument.
>
> *Decision:* The employer was held liable since the company should have suitable training in place to help its employees to deal with difficult situations.

Contrast this with the following case.

Warren v Henleys 1948

The facts: A petrol pump attendant became involved in a quarrel with a customer and hit him.

Decision: The employer was not liable since the assault was not within the scope of the employment. It is not easy to distinguish this from the Century Insurance case above, but perhaps the main difference in the Warren case is that it was a violent personal act entirely unconnected with the employee's duty to sell petrol.

Where the employer is held to be vicariously liable, he may seek indemnity for the costs from his employee: *Lister v Romford Ice and Cold Storage Co 1957*.

7.4 Independent contractors

A person who has work done not by his employee but by an independent contractor, such as a freelance plumber used by a builder, is vicariously liable for torts of the contractor in the following **special circumstances**.

(a) If the operation creates a **hazard** for users of the highway.

(b) If the operation is exceptionally **risky**.

Honeywill & Stein v Larkin Bros 1934

The facts: Decorators who had redecorated the interior of a cinema brought in a photographer to take pictures of their work. The photographer's magnesium flare set fire to the cinema.

Decision: In commissioning an inherently risky operation through a contractor the decorators were liable for his negligence in causing the fire.

(c) If the duty is **personal**. For example, an employer has a common law duty to take reasonable care in providing safe plant and a safe working system. If they employ a contractor they remain liable for any negligence of the latter in their work.

(d) If there is **negligence in selecting** a contractor who is not competent to do the work entrusted to them. *Majrowski v Guy's and St Thomas's NHS Trust 2005*.

(e) If the operation is one for which there is **strict liability**.

Question   Vicarious liability

Employers are never liable for the actions of independent contractors.

True or false?

Answer

False. The circumstances where an employer may be liable are listed above.

Chapter Roundup

- It is important to distinguish between a **contract of service** (employment) and a **contract for services** (independent contractor). Each type of contract has different rules for taxation, health and safety provisions, protection of contract and vicarious liability in tort and contract.

- A contract of service is **distinguished** from a contract for services usually because the parties **express** the agreement to be one of service. This does not always mean that an employee will not be treated as an independent contractor by the court, however; much depends on the three tests.

  - Control test
  - Integration test
  - Economic reality test

- The distinction between **employed** and **self-employed** is important as to whether certain **rights** are available to an individual and how they are treated for **tax purposes**.

- There are no particular legal rules relating to the commencement of employment – it is really **just like any other contract** in requiring offer and acceptance, consideration and intention to create legal relations.

- The **employer** has an implied **duty at common law** to take **reasonable care** of his employees; he must select proper staff, materials and provide a safe system of working.

- The **employee** has a duty of **faithful service** and to exercise **care and skill** in performance of his duties.

- **Statute** implies terms into employment contracts, which may not usually be overridden, regarding pay, maternity leave and work-life balance generally, time off, health and safety and working time.

- A contract of employment can only be **varied** if the contract **expressly** gives that right, or if all parties consent to the variation.

- **Vicarious liability** means liability for the torts of others and arises because of a relationship between the parties.

1   What tests are applied by the courts to answer these questions?

- Has the employer control over the way in which the employee performs his duties?   (1) ....
- Is the skilled employee part of the employer's organisation? (2) ....
- Is the employee working on his own account? (3)....................

2   Give five reasons why the distinction between employed and self employed workers is important.

3   An employee who works seven hours per week in an organisation of 30 people is not entitled to receive an itemised pay slip.

True   ☐

False   ☐

4   In no more than 10 words, explain an employee's fundamental duty.

5   Which of these options are open to an employer who wishes to vary the terms of an employment contract?

(i)   Produce a wholly new contract
(ii)   Vary the terms without changing the contract
(iii)   Change the existing contract

A   (i) and (ii) only
B   (ii) and (iii) only
C   (iii) only
D   All of the above

6   Which of the following is **not** an implied duty of an employer?

A   To pay a reasonable wage
B   To provide a reasonable reference
C   To ensure a safe working environment
D   To reimburse expenses incurred in the course of employment

7   Delete where applicable

- The employer is vicariously liable for the employee's torts **in the course of his employment/at any time**.

- Employers are **liable/not liable** if an employee commits a tort whilst disobeying instructions during the course of their work.

- Employers are **liable/not liable** for torts committed in a company vehicle when the employee is undertaking private business.

- Employers are **liable/not liable** when an employee defrauds a client to his own advantage in the course of his employment.

8   The statutory minimum holiday entitlement for employees is:

A   20 days including public holidays
B   28 days including public holidays
C   20 days not including public holidays
D   28 days not including public holidays

9   The maximum statutory maternity leave period for employees is:

A   6 weeks
B   13 weeks
C   26 weeks
D   52 weeks

10 All employees with children have the right to flexible working which must be granted to them if they request it.

True   ☐

False ☐

1 (1) Control test
   (2) Integration test
   (3) Multiple (economic reality) test

2 Social security
   Taxation
   Employment protection
   Tortious acts
   Health and safety
   (also implied terms, VAT, rights in bankruptcy)

3 True. Employees working under 8 hours a week are not entitled to an itemised payslip, irrespective of the size of the employer.

4 Faithful service to his employer

5 D. All the options are available although care must be taken to avoid constructive or unfair dismissal cases.

6 B. Employers do not have a duty to provide a reference.

7 • The employer is vicariously liable for the employee's torts **in the course of his employment**

   • Employers are **liable** if an employee commits a tort whilst disobeying instructions during the course of their work.

   • Employers are **not liable** for torts committed in a company vehicle when the employee is undertaking private business.

   • Employers are **liable** when an employee defrauds a client to his own advantage in the course of his employment.

8 B. An employee is entitled to 28 days holiday per year, but this figure may include public holidays.

9 D. An employee is entitled to a maximum of 52 weeks of statutory maternity leave.

10 False. Employees have the right to request flexible working, but their employer is entitled to reasonably refuse it.

Now try the questions below from the Question Bank

Number
Q31
Q32
Q33
Q34
Q35

8

Employment protection

Introduction

The law of employment was developed under common law principles as an application of the law of contract. In recent years **statutory rules** have been enacted to give the **employee protection** both against dismissal, discrimination and against unsafe or unhealthy working conditions.

Topic list	Learning outcomes
1 Continuity of service	F1(b)
2 Discrimination at work	F1(b)
3 Health and safety	F2(a), F2(b)
4 Dismissal	F1(c)
5 Wrongful dismissal	F1(c)
6 Unfair dismissal	F1(c)

1 Continuity of service

FAST FORWARD

Certain employment rights are only available if an employee has a specified period of **continuous employment**.

1.1 The importance of continuity of service

Many of the rights given to employees under the Employment Rights Act 1996 in areas such as redundancy and unfair dismissal are only available if an employee has a specified period of **continuous employment**.

Employment is presumed to be continuous unless the contrary is proved. Continuity is preserved even where an employee's duties change within the period of service.

In **calculating length of service** (for all purposes including notice, redundancy pay and compensation for unfair dismissal) the following rules apply.

(a) A week is a week during which he is employed for at least **eight hours** or in which his employment is subject to a contract which involves employment for eight hours or more.

(b) Some **periods of absence are included** in reckoning continuity and length of service for example, when the employee is away from work sick or injured and they are then taken back on as an employee within 26 weeks of the contract being terminated

(c) If the employee has worked in the same business before its **transfer** to his present employer his previous service may be counted.

1.2 Transfer of undertaking

When an 'undertaking' – a business in the UK or a part of it – is transferred, the **employees of the business are automatically transferred (on the same terms and with unbroken service) to the employment of the new owner**.

(a) **There must be a real change in the ownership of the business**. If the business is carried on by a company and ownership is changed just by selling the share capital, rather than the business assets as a whole, the regulations do not apply.

(b) **There must be continuity in the business before and after the transfer**.

A transfer of business also includes '**service provision**' changes. For example where part of the business is outsourced/insourced to/from a contractor, or where provision of a service is transferred between contractors.

An employee cannot be compelled to accept continued employment in the service of a new employer. But his **refusal would be a resignation** which disentitles him from recovering redundancy pay or compensation for unfair dismissal.

If he does go over to the service of the transferee of the business, the employee has continuity of service.

A dismissal in connection with a transfer is **automatically unfair.**

The **only exception** to dismissal being unfair is if the dismissal is for an **economic**, **technical** or **organisational reason** (an ETO reason). The meaning of 'economic, technical or organisational reason' which renders a dismissal a fair dismissal for which no compensation must be given is not clear-cut.

BPP
LEARNING MEDIA

How many hours must be worked per week for them to be included in a calculation of continuous employment?

A   6
B   8
C   10
D   12

Answer

B   8 hours must be worked per week for them to be included in a calculation of continuous employment.

2 Discrimination at work

FAST FORWARD

Statute implies terms into employment contracts to prohibit discrimination in various categories. In addition to the longstanding legislation preventing discrimination on grounds of sex or race, there is new legislation which expands the framework considerably.

2.1 Introduction

In recent years, extensive new legislation has been passed to broaden the areas in which the law functions to prevent discrimination in the workplace. The **Equality Act 2010** (see below) identifies the following **protected characteristics; sex, race, disability, religion, sexual orientation, age, gender, marriage or civil partnership** and **pregnancy or maternity.**

Key term

Discrimination is the act of treating someone less favourably than another because of a protected characteristic.

Actions for discrimination are **not restricted** to the **period of employment**. For example, an individual may have been discriminated against at the recruitment stage. The burden of proof in discrimination cases is on the employer to prove they did not discriminate.

2.1.1 The Equality Act 2010

The **Equality Act 2010** brought previous **discrimination laws** (which we shall look at next) together into a **single Act**. From now on, discrimination judgements shall be viewed in light of a single '**justification' test.** This means employers need to prove their actions were a '**proportionate means of meeting a legitimate aim'**. What this means will be decided by the courts and employment tribunals, but it is expected that where previous legislation allowed or prevented certain types of discrimination, this will continue under the new Act.

Discrimination can be direct or indirect.

- **Direct discrimination**: treating people less favourably than others because of a protected characteristic.

- **Indirect discrimination**: applying a provision or practice which disadvantages people with a certain protected characteristic and which is not objectively justifiable.

The 'justification' test is based on **ACAS guidelines** which identifies what is meant by **proportionate** and **legitimate**.

Proportionate means:

- The discriminatory effect should be significantly outweighed by the benefits of achieving the aim.

- There is no reasonable alternative. If the aim can be achieved with less discrimination, that option should be followed.

Legitimate aims include:

- Business needs and efficiency.
- Health and safety reasons.
- Particular training requirements of the job.

Other behaviour which is prohibited includes harassment and victimisation.

- **Victimisation**: treating people less favourably because of some action they have taken in connection with the legislation.

- **Harassment**: indulging in unwanted conduct that violates an individual's dignity or creates an intimidating or degrading environment.

Assessment focus point | Previous anti-discrimination laws which have been amalgamated into the Equality Act 2010 are detailed below to help your understanding of how the law in this area has developed.

2.2 Sex discrimination

The law implies a number of terms into an employee's contract.

The Sex Discrimination Act 1975 **prohibits discrimination on the grounds of gender** against any employee, male or female, in recruitment, promotion, training, benefits or dismissal. A Code of Practice was drawn up in April 1985 under the Act. Discrimination may be direct, indirect or victimisation.

Direct discrimination occurs where an employer or prospective employer treats an employee or job applicant less favourably than another on grounds of sex. For example in *Shields v Coomes Ltd 1979* higher pay for a male clerk in a betting shop, on the basis of the potential need for him to deal with trouble, compared to a female clerk's pay was not justified.

Note that unfavourable treatment of a woman because she is pregnant will usually constitute discrimination.

The 1975 Act also prohibits **indirect** forms of discrimination such as **imposing a qualification** for promotion with which **fewer women** than men could comply unless the job demands it.

Price v Civil Service Commission 1978

The facts: The Civil Service Commission imposed a maximum age limit of 28 for appointment to the civil service grade of Executive Officer. A woman argued that this was indirectly discriminating against women since women in their twenties are often prevented by care of children from taking up employment.

Decision: The imposition of an age limit was indirect discrimination.

BPP LEARNING MEDIA

Section 7 of the Act gives permission to discriminate if there is **sufficient reason**. In some jobs, it is accepted that male sex is a 'genuine occupational qualification' (GOQ).

- An advertisement for a job abroad in a country whose laws and customs might make it difficult for a woman to perform her duties would be acceptable.

- Decency may require a male attendant in a male lavatory or sports facilities.

- Some occupations such as ministers of religion and police and prison officers are exempt from the statutory rules.

Minor differences, such as allowing women employees to leave work 5 minutes early to avoid a rush, may be ignored: *Peake v Automotive Products Ltd 1977*.

Victimisation arises when a person is discriminated against not because of his or her gender but because he or she has either brought proceedings under the Sex Discrimination Act or alleged a breach of the Act.

2.3 Developments in sex discrimination legislation

The Sex Discrimination Act 1975 is based on the EU's 1976 Equal Treatment Directive and it was recently amended by a directive in 2002 and regulations in 2008. **Gender equality** is at the heart of the EU's social policy agenda.

A new definition of sexual **harassment** is introduced:

'Sexual harassment shall be deemed to be discrimination on the grounds of sex at the workplace when an unwanted conduct related to sex takes place with the purpose or effect of affecting the dignity of a person and/or creating an intimidating, hostile, offensive or disturbing environment, in particular if a person's rejection of, or submission to, such conduct is used as a basis for a decision which affects that person.'

Note that it is conduct relating to the sex of the victim that is relevant, including **bullying**, **intimidation** and **threats**. (The treatment complained of does not have to be sexual in nature.)

The **Sex Discrimination (Amendment of Legislation) Regulations 2008** provides for employer liability for sexual harassment and benefits for women on maternity leave (such as pension and insurance rights, maternity leave and holiday entitlement).

2.4 Race discrimination

Discrimination on the grounds of race is prohibited by the Race Relations Act 1976. **Section 5** of the Act contains provisions similar to the Sex Discrimination Act 1975, although there are fewer grounds to justify discrimination.

- Authenticity in **entertainment, art or photography** is allowed – a black man to play Othello for instance.
- **Personal welfare services** – recruiting a Bangladeshi housing officer in a Bangladeshi area for example.
- Maintaining **ethnic authenticity** in a **bar or restaurant**.

Positive discrimination, the giving of preferential treatment to a particular racial group, counts as discrimination under the Act. However, some forms of **positive action** are permitted, for example encouraging a particular racial group to apply for particular work.

Which legislation includes provisions that provide valid reasons for discrimination?

(i)   Section 7 Sex Discrimination Act
(ii)   Section 5 Sex Discrimination Act
(iii)   Section 7 Race Relations Act
(iv)   Section 5 Race Relations Act

A   (i) and (iii)
B   (i) and (iv)
C   (ii) and (iii)
D   (ii) and (iv)

Answer

B   Section 7 of the Sex Discrimination Act and Section 5 of the Race Relations Act contain the provisions.

2.5 Disability discrimination

The **Disability Discrimination Act 1995** gives disabled people similar rights to those in relation to sex and race.

Key term

> **Disability** is defined by the Disability Discrimination Act as 'a physical or mental impairment which has a substantial and long-term adverse effect on the ability to carry out normal day-to-day activities'.

2.5.1 Determining disability

For the purposes of disability discrimination, disability is a legal term, and a **tribunal** must determine whether a person has a disability. However, the tribunal must not reject medical advice: *Kapadia v London Borough of Lambeth 2000.*

2.5.2 Disability Discrimination Act 1995

Disability discrimination arises when an individual is treated less favourably for a reason related to disability. The employer does not have to know of the disability.

If the employer is aware of the disability, he has a statutory duty to make **reasonable adjustments.** Failure by the employer to make **'reasonable adjustments'** without justification is classed as discrimination.

2.6 Discrimination on grounds of religion or belief

The **Employment Equality (Religion or Belief) Regulations 2003** cover all aspects of the employment relationship, including recruitment, pay, working conditions, training, promotion and dismissal.

The legislation follows the **framework** set out in earlier discrimination legislation. It outlaws the following:

- **Direct discrimination**: treating people less favourably than others because of their religion or belief.

- **Indirect discrimination**: applying a provision or practice which disadvantages people of a certain religion or belief and which is not objectively justifiable.

- **Victimisation**: treating people less favourably because of some action they have taken in connection with the legislation.

- **Harassment**: indulging in unwanted conduct that violates an individual's dignity or creates an intimidating or degrading environment.

2.7 Discrimination on grounds of sexual orientation

The **Employment Equality (Sexual Orientation) Regulations 2003 outlaw** discrimination on grounds of sexual orientation. This means it is unlawful to deny lesbian, gay or bisexual people jobs because of prejudice.

The legislation follows the framework set out above, and outlaws direct and indirect **discrimination**, **harassment** and **victimisation**.

2.8 Age discrimination

Legislation came into force in 2006 which targets ageism. The law now:

(a) **Prevents unjustified age discrimination in employment and training.**

Redundancy policies should not directly discriminate against older workers. Indirect discrimination, such as selecting part-time workers for redundancy when they are mostly older workers, is also prevented.

(b) **Prevents employers requiring employees to retire at 65.**

This means employers can no longer use fixed retirement dates as a fair reason for dismissal. However, in line with the justification rule of the Equality Act 2010, employers will be justified in applying a fixed retirement age if it is a proportionate means of achieving a legitimate aim. This may mean certain industries (such as in construction, the police or armed forces), fixed retirement dates may still be justified.

(c) **Removes upper limits for unfair dismissal and redundancy rights.**

Previously there was no entitlement to an employment tribunal for dismissal once a worker reached 65 or normal retirement age. Also workers under 18 or over 65 were not entitled to statutory redundancy payments unless included in their employment contract.

(d) **Removes lower age limits for workers.**

This is to prevent discrimination against younger people.

2.9 Trade unions

Employers may not discriminate against employees for **joining** an independent trade union or **refusing to join** a **workplace trade union**. It also applies to taking part or refusing to take part in trade union activities.

2.10 Remedies for discrimination

A person who believes that they have been discriminated against should make an application to an employment tribunal within **three months** of the discrimination taking place.

If the **employment tribunal** decides that discrimination has taken place, they can make the following orders.

(a)   Compensation.

(b)   Recommendation that the employer take action to correct the situation or limit the damage done to the applicant.

(c)   Appointment of an official from the Advisory, Conciliation and Arbitration Service (ACAS) to try to work out a settlement between the two parties.

The tribunal **cannot:**

- Force the employer to promote someone
- Insist the employer takes on a job applicant

2.11 The Equality and Human Rights Commission

This body oversees the law concerning **discrimination** on the grounds of sex, religion, belief, age and human rights. Complaints are heard by an **employment tribunal** which may obtain an injunction against employers who act illegally.

3 Health and safety

FAST FORWARD

Under s 2 of the **Health and Safety at Work Act 1974**, it is the duty of every employer, **as far as is practicable**, to ensure the health, safety and welfare of all employees.

In particular, they should:

- Provide and maintain plant and **systems of work** which are safe and without risk

- Make arrangements to ensure health and safety in relation to the use, handling, storage and transport of **articles and substances**

- Provide **adequate information**, instruction, training and supervision

- Maintain **safe places** of work

- Ensure there is **adequate access** in and out

- Provide a **safe and healthy working environment.**

3.1 The Health and Safety at Work Act 1974

The aims of the 1974 Act are:

(a)   To **integrate** and **extend the law** on health and safety at all places of work, that is, not only in factories

(b)   To reformulate the previously confused, incomplete or overlapping rules of common law and statute on safety at work. This is done by making **detailed regulations** to be enforced by sanctions of **criminal law**. A person who infringes the rules, more particularly safety rules, may also have a **civil liability** to the injured party for breach of statutory duty

(c)   To provide **effective means** of **shaping the policy** and regulations on health and safety at work and also effective machinery of enforcement

Under s 2 of the Act it is the **duty of every employer, as far as is practicable, to ensure the health, safety and well being of all his employees**.

- Provide and maintain plant and **systems of work** which are **safe** and without risk
- Make arrangements to ensure **safe use**, **handling**, **storage** and **transport** of articles and substances
- Provide **adequate information**, **instruction**, **training** and **supervision**
- Maintain **safe places of work** and ensure there is **adequate access** in and out
- Provide a **safe and healthy working environment**

Although the 1974 Act is intended mainly to safeguard employees it also **imposes duties**, for instance on occupiers of premises, to avoid creating risks to persons who may be near their premises but outside them or who may visit them. There are also rules to control or prohibit pollution of the environment by industrial processes.

A manufacturer, designer, importer or supplier of any article or substance for use at work must take **reasonable steps**, say by testing, to ensure that it is safe and that adequate information for safety purposes is provided for its use.

Every **employee** is required to take reasonable care at work for the health and safety of himself and others and to co-operate with his employer in the latter's compliance with his statutory obligations.

3.2 Recent regulations

There is a range of Regulations and Codes of Practice in the UK, most of them fairly recent. They have been issued under the Health and Safety Act 1974 to implement a number of **EU Directives** on health and safety, and have gradually replaced existing statutes.

3.3 Enforcement of health and safety conditions

FAST FORWARD

> The responsibility for making health and safety regulations rests on the government. A **Health and Safety Commission** oversees the working of the system. Its members include representatives of employers' organisations and of trade unions.

The responsibility for making regulations rests with the government. A **Health and Safety Commission**, acting through the **Health and Safety Executive**, oversees the working of the system. It advises on measures to be taken, promotes research and publishes information. Its members include representatives of employers' organisations and trade unions.

The **Health and Safety Executive (HSE)** is the headquarters of the inspectorate. Inspectors may, as part of routine enforcement of the safety code, issue formal notices or bring a criminal prosecution. These may be improvement notices or prohibition notices. Where remedial action is not taken, activities, or even premises, can be closed down and the employer may face criminal proceedings.

Employers must keep **records** concerning equipment testing and set up a **safety commission** if requested to do so by safety representatives nominated by a trade union. **Serious accidents** must be reported to the inspectorate.

Stark v Post Office 2002

The facts: A postman was injured when the brakes on his bike partially failed. The fault would not have been detected by routine inspection.

Decision: Despite the almost undetectable nature of the fault, the employer was held liable for faulty equipment.

Breach of the Health and Safety Act 1974 is a criminal act.

True or false?

Answer

True. Breach of the Act is a criminal offence.

3.4 Employment protection

Where there is a **breach of health and safety rules**, whether by employer or employee, this is usually regarded as serious by tribunals. In certain instances, employees have successfully claimed **constructive dismissal.**

(a) Where an employee needed safety goggles which could be worn over normal spectacles and the employer ignored repeated requests for such goggles: *British Aircraft Corporation v Austin 1978*

(b) Where an employee was obliged to work in very cold conditions: *Graham Oxley Tool Steels Ltd v Firth 1980.*

The **Public Interest Disclosure Act 1998** protects workers from being dismissed or penalised for bringing health and safety dangers to light. The right not to suffer a **detriment** means that the employee has a right not to be put under any disadvantage at work. The right not to be dismissed applies regardless of continuous employment.

Assessment focus point

> You should have an outline knowledge of the law in relation to health and safety at work and employers' responsibilities.

3.5 Employers' liability

Employees may bring claims under the **tort of negligence** against employers for:

- The employer's own acts
- Acts of employees which the employer is vicariously liable for

In such cases, the **standard rules of negligence apply**. The employee might be able to bring a case against an employer for breach of statutory duty, where the statute allows for such civil liability. For example, The Health and Safety at Work Regulations expressly exclude such civil liability.

In regard to negligence, employers have the three established **duties of care**.

(a) They **must take care** in **selecting**, **training** and **advising other employees** and to **dismiss those whose behaviour presents a risk** to others: *Hudson v Ridge Manufacturing Co Ltd 1957.*

(b) They **must take care** in **providing equipment** and **working materials** and **maintaining working equipment**: *Bradford v Robinson Rentals Ltd 1967.*

(c) **Provide a safe system** of work for staff.

The test for breach is what a **reasonable** and **prudent employer would have done** in the same situation. Where the risk of an accident or the potential for serious harm is great, extra care should be taken. It must be proved that the employee's harm was caused as a direct consequence of the employer's actions.

All employers are required under the **Employer's Liability (Compulsory Insurance) Act 1969** to insure themselves for any potential compensation claims. Alternatively, the employee may sue the employer for **breach of a statutory duty**, providing the legislation permits them to claim a civil remedy. The standard of care is similar to the common law standard.

Under the **Corporate Manslaughter and Homicide Act 2006**, a company's senior management can be liable for causing the death of those they owe a duty of care to. This includes employees as well as the company's customers. Failure to satisfy a relevant standard of care in respect of an employee or non-employee to whom the organisation owes a duty of care can lead to that organisation's senior management being prosecuted for the crime of **manslaughter**.

3.6 Social security

Other financial protection is available for employees injured at work or unable to work.

- **Statutory sick pay** and **incapacity benefit** whilst **away from work**
- **Disablement allowance** if 'loss of faculty' is over 14%
- **Other supplements** are available to dependants.

Where compensation is paid to the employee, the government can recoup **social security payments** paid in the last five years from the compensation payment.

4 Dismissal

4.1 Termination by notice

FAST FORWARD

Where employment is **terminated by notice** the period given must **not be less** than the **statutory minimum**.

As regards termination by **notice**, the following rules apply.

(a) The period of notice given must **not be less than the statutory minimum,** whatever the contract may specify.

(b) It **may be given without specific reason** for so doing, unless the contract requires otherwise.

(c) Where notice periods are not specified in the contract, **reasonable notice** should be given. This is usually regulated by reference to **trade practice**, **length of service** and **importance of the position** the employee was employed to perform.

Termination of a contract by notice is modified by the statutory code, which imposes a **minimum period of notice** of termination to be given on either side.

4.1.1 Notice due from employers

If an employer terminates the contract of employment by giving notice, the **minimum period of notice** to be given is determined by the employee's length of continuous service in the employer's service as follows: s 86.

- An employee who has been continuously employed for **one month or more** but less than two years is entitled to not less than **one week's** notice.

- An employee who has been continuously employed for **two years or more** but less than twelve years is entitled to **one week's notice for each year of continuous employment.**

- Any employee who has been employed for **twelve years** or more is entitled to **twelve weeks'** notice.

Garden leave may be offered to the employee. This is where the employer pays the employee, who is no longer required at the workplace, in lieu of notice.

4.1.2 Notice due from employees

Employers are entitled to **one week's notice** after one month of employment otherwise notice is the period specified in the employment contract.

4.2 Termination by dismissal

Summary dismissal and **constructive** dismissal are both examples of dismissal without proper notice.

Key terms

> In a case of **summary dismissal**, the employer dismisses the employee without notice. He may do this if the employee has committed a serious breach of contract.
>
> In a case of **constructive dismissal**, the employer commits a breach of contract, thereby causing the employee to resign.

4.2.1 Summary dismissal

Summary dismissal occurs where the employer dismisses the employee without notice. He may do this if the employee has committed a serious breach of contract and, if so, the employer incurs no liability. Misconduct by the employee in their own time may justify summary dismissal if it is relevant to their position.

However, if he has **no sufficient justification** the employer is liable for **breach of contract** and the employee may claim a remedy for wrongful dismissal. Whether the employee's conduct justifies summary dismissal will vary according to the circumstances of the case.

> *Pepper v Webb 1969*
>
> *The facts:* A gardener was asked to put in some plants, but refused to do so, using vulgar language.
>
> *Decision:* His summary dismissal was justified; he was in breach of contract for refusing to obey a lawful and reasonable order. He had a history of complaints against him for insolence.

> *Wilson v Racher 1974*
>
> *The facts:* A gardener swore at his employer using even choicer obscenities.
>
> *Decision:* His action for wrongful dismissal succeeded, as the employer's own conduct had provoked the outburst. This was a solitary outburst following a history of diligence and competence.

4.2.2 Constructive dismissal

Constructive dismissal occurs where the employer, although willing to continue the employment, repudiates some essential term of the contract and the employee resigns. The employer is liable for breach of contract. For example, the employer might seek unilaterally to impose a complete change in the employee's duties.

To **establish constructive dismissal**, an employee must show that:

- His employer has committed a serious breach of contract (a repudiatory breach).
- He left because of the breach.
- He has not 'waived' the breach, thereby affirming the contract.

BPP
LEARNING MEDIA

Examples of breaches of contract which have led to claims of constructive dismissal include the following.

- A reduction in pay
- A complete change in the nature of the job
- A failure to follow the prescribed disciplinary procedure
- A failure to provide a suitable working environment

The breach must be a **serious** one.

Question

Unless otherwise indicated in their employment contract, how much notice is an employee required to give their employer when they wish to terminate their employment?

A   1 day
B   1 week
C   1 month
D   1 year

Answer

B   Unless agreed otherwise in their employment contract, employees are required to give their employer one week's notice that they wish to terminate their employment.

5 Wrongful dismissal

FAST FORWARD

If an employee is dismissed with **shorter notice** than the statutory or contractual requirements, or without notice when summary dismissal is unjustified, the employer can be sued for **wrongful dismissal**.

5.1 Introduction

Key term

Wrongful dismissal is a common law concept arising in specific circumstances and which gives the employee an action for breach of contract, for example where insufficient notice has been given.

Where the employer has **summarily dismissed** an employee without notice (as where the employer becomes insolvent), there may be a claim for **damages** at common law for **wrongful dismissal**.

All employees, regardless of the length of employment, are entitled to claim wrongful dismissal but claimants have a maximum of **six years** to bring a claim.

5.2 Justification of dismissal

The following have been taken as justifiable circumstances.

(a)   **Wilful disobedience of a lawful order**. However it **must amount to wilful and serious defiance of authority**. A single act of disobedience may not justify immediate dismissal.

> **Laws v London Chronicle 1957**
>
> *The facts:* The claimant was called to a meeting by the managing director together with her immediate superior D. The managing director criticised D sharply and D walked out calling on the claimant to leave with him. She did so although the managing director ordered her to stay. She was dismissed.
>
> *Decision:* The dismissal was wrongful.

(b) **Misconduct**, in connection with the business or outside it if it is sufficiently grave. For example, acceptance of a secret commission, disclosure of confidential information, assault on a fellow employee or even financial embarrassment of an employee in a position of trust.

(c) **Dishonesty**, where the employee is in a position of particular trust.

(d) **Incompetence or neglect**, insofar as the employee lacks or fails to use skill which he professes to have.

(e) **Gross negligence**, depending on the nature of the job, for example, negligently landing an aeroplane.

(f) **Immorality**, only if it is likely to affect performance of duties or the reputation of the business.

(g) **Drunkenness**, only if it occurs in aggravated circumstances such as when driving a vehicle or is repeated.

5.3 Remedies for wrongful dismissal

Generally, the **only effective remedy available to a wrongfully dismissed employee is a claim for damages based on the loss of earnings**. The measure of damages is usually the **sum that would have been earned if proper notice had been given**. There is no limit to the amount of compensation available so this remedy is often used by those in senior positions who have large salaries.

As with any other case of compensation, the wronged party is expected to **mitigate** his loss by, say, seeking other employment.

Where breach of contract leaves the **employer** as the **injured party**, he may **dismiss the employee** and **withhold wages**. The employer may recover confidential papers, or apply for an injunction to enforce a valid restrictive covenant: *Thomas Marshall (Exporters) v Guinle 1978*.

Employment tribunals have jurisdiction to deal with wrongful dismissal cases, which formerly had to be heard in the civil courts.

Question
Wrongful dismissal

Damages are the only remedy available to an employee who takes their employer to court for wrongful dismissal. True or false?

Answer

True. Wrongful dismissal is a common law action for damages for breach of the employment contract.

6 Unfair dismissal

FAST FORWARD

Certain employees have a right not to be **unfairly dismissed**. Breach of that right allows an employee to claim compensation from a tribunal. To claim for unfair dismissal, the employee must satisfy certain criteria.

6.1 Introduction

Unfair dismissal is an extremely important element of employment protection legislation. The remedies available following a successful action for **wrongful dismissal** are **limited to damages** compensating for the sum which would have been earned **if proper notice had been given.** Unfair dismissal allows for a number of other remedies as well.

Key term

> **Unfair dismissal** is a statutory concept introduced by employment protection legislation. As a rule, every employee has the right not to be unfairly dismissed. Note that the distinction between wrongful and unfair dismissal depends not so much upon the nature of the dismissal, as on the **remedies available**.

6.2 Scope

Certain categories of employee are **excluded** from the statutory unfair dismissal code.

- Persons ordinarily employed **outside Great Britain**
- Employees dismissed while taking **unofficial strike** or other industrial action
- **Other categories**, including members of the police and armed forces

Subject to these exclusions, every employee who qualifies under (a) and (b) below has a statutory right not to be unfairly dismissed:

In order to obtain compensation or other remedies for unfair dismissal the employee must satisfy several criteria.

(a) Have been **continuously employed for one year** whether full-time or part-time.

(b) Have been **dismissed.** In the case of constructive dismissal, the tribunal may have to determine this.

(c) Have been **unfairly** dismissed. Dismissal may be unfair even if it is not a breach of contract by the employer. This is up to the tribunal to determine.

In some cases, a person need not have been employed for the year to claim unfair dismissal. These exceptions are:

- Where a **safety representative** is being penalised for carrying out legitimate health and safety activities
- Where an employee is being **denied a statutory right** (for example an unlawful deduction from wages)
- Where the employee is **pregnant**

The **effective date** of dismissal is reckoned as follows:

- Where there is termination by notice, the date on which the notice expires
- Where there is termination without notice, the date on which the termination takes effect
- Where an employee's fixed term contract is not renewed, the date on which that term expires

Assessment focus point

> The qualifying period that an employee must have worked before they can claim unfair dismissal has increased from one year to two years for those employed after 6 April 2012.

6.3 Making a claim

To claim **compensation** for unfair dismissal, there are three steps.

Step 1   The employee must apply to a tribunal **within three months** of being dismissed.

Step 2   The **employee** must show that

- He is a **qualifying employee,** and
- He has been **dismissed**

Step 3   Then the **employer** must demonstrate:

- What was the only or **principal reason for dismissal**
- That it was a **fair reason under the legislation (see below)**

6.4 What is dismissal?

Dismissal may be identified in three separate circumstances.

- **Actual dismissal** is usually fairly clear-cut and can be recognised from the words used by an employer.

- **Constructive dismissal**, involves a fundamental breach of the employment contract by the employer.

- **Expiry of a fixed-term contract** without renewal amounts to a dismissal.

The **employee must show that he has in fact been dismissed**. The courts often have to debate whether or not the use of four-letter words by employers constitutes mere abuse or indicates dismissal.

6.5 The reason for dismissal

FAST FORWARD

Dismissal must be **justified** if it related to the employee's capability or qualifications, the employee's conduct, redundancy, legal prohibition or restriction on the employee's continued employment or some other substantial reason. Some reasons for dismissal are **automatically** fair or unfair.

Employees with over one year's service are entitled to a **written reason** why they were dismissed. Employers must respond to such a request within **14 days**. If they fail to do this, the employee is entitled to **two weeks' pay** in **compensation.**

Under statute, there are **five potentially fair reasons** (justifications) for dismissal. There are also reasons for dismissal which are held to be **automatically fair**. The employer must state the principal reason for dismissal to the tribunal. If the reason is not one of the potentially fair or automatically fair reasons, the dismissal is unfair.

6.6 Potentially fair reasons for dismissal

To be able to justify dismissal as fair dismissal the employer must show that his reason related to one of the following.

(a)   The **capability or qualifications** of the employee for performing the work they were employed to do

(b)   The **conduct** of the employee

(c)   **Redundancy**

(d)   **Legal prohibition** or restriction by which the employee could not lawfully continue to work in the position which he held (for example, if a doctor employed as such is struck off the professional register)

(e)   **Some other substantial reason** which justifies dismissal

BPP
LEARNING MEDIA

6.6.1 Capability/qualifications

The Employment Rights Act 1996 (s 98(3)) states that

> '*Capability* is to be assessed by reference to skills, aptitude, health or any other physical or mental quality. '*Qualification*' means any academic or technical qualifications relevant to the position that the employee holds.'

6.6.2 Misconduct

It is usual to apply the common law distinction between **gross misconduct** which justifies summary dismissal on the first occasion, for example, theft, and **ordinary misconduct** which is not usually sufficient grounds for dismissal unless it is persistent.

For example, **assault on a fellow employee**, **conduct exposing others to danger** (for example, smoking in an area prohibited for safety reasons), **unpleasant behaviour towards customers** and **persistent absences** from work have all been treated as sufficient misconduct to justify dismissal.

6.6.3 Redundancy

If an employee is dismissed mainly or only on the ground of **redundancy**, he may claim remedies for unfair dismissal if he can show one of the following.

(a) There were one or more other employees in similar positions who might have been made redundant and that he was **selected for redundancy in breach of a customary arrangement or agreed procedure**.

(b) He was selected for a reason connected with **trade union membership**.

6.6.4 Other substantial reason

The category of **other substantial reason** permits the employer to rely on some factor which is unusual and likely to affect him adversely.

An employer has **justified dismissal** on specific grounds.

- The employee was married to one of his competitors.
- The employee refused to accept a reorganisation, for example, a change of shift working, made in the interests of the business and with the agreement of a large majority of other employees.

6.7 Automatically fair reasons for dismissal

Some reasons for dismissal are **automatically fair**.

- Taking part in **unofficial industrial action**
- Being a **threat to national security** (to be certified by the government)

An employee who strikes or refuses to work normally may be fairly dismissed unless the industrial action has been **lawfully organised** under the protection conferred by the Employment Relations Act 1999. Where dismissal results from a lock-out or a strike, the tribunal cannot deal with it unless victimisation is established.

6.8 Automatically unfair reasons for dismissal

Some reasons are **automatically unfair** (also known as **'inadmissible reasons'**.) The main ones are set out below:

- **Pregnancy** or other maternity-related grounds
- **Trade union membership** or **activities**
- **Transfer of an undertaking** (unless justified by economic, technical or organisational reasons)
- Taking steps to **avert danger** to **health** and **safety** at work
- Seeking to **enforce rights** relating to the **national minimum wage**
- **Exercising rights under** the **Working Time Regulations 1998**
- **Refusing** or **opting out of Sunday working** (in the retail sector)
- **Making a protected disclosure** under the **Public Interest Disclosure Act 1998**

6.8.1 Pregnancy

Dismissal on grounds of pregnancy or pregnancy-related illness is automatically unfair, regardless of length of service. It amounts to **gender discrimination** contrary to EC Directive 76/207: *Webb v Emo Air Cargo (UK) Ltd 1994*. If a pregnant woman cannot do her job adequately the employer may suspend the employee while the 'hazard' continues. The employee may complain to a tribunal if not offered suitable alternative work.

6.8.2 Trade union membership

Automatically unfair dismissal.

- **Membership** of an independent trade union
- **Taking part** at an appropriate time in the activities of such a trade union
- **Refusal** to be a member of a trade union: s 152 TULRCA 1992

6.9 Disciplinary process

The **Employment Act 2008** provides for the Advisory, Conciliation and Arbitration Service (ACAS) code of practice on disciplinary and grievance procedures dealing with workplace disputes. This recommends that employers and employees should try to resolve all **workplace disputes** by following a process:

- Employees with a grievance against their employer, or employers initiating disciplinary action against an employee, must set out the basis of their complaint in **writing**.

- The written statement must be followed by a **meeting** between the two parties. Employees have the right to be accompanied by a colleague or a trade union representative. After the meeting the employer must tell the employee how the employee's grievance is to be dealt with or what disciplinary action is to be taken

- The employee has the right to take the matter to an **appeal**

If the grievance goes to an **employment tribunal** and this procedure has not been followed, penalties may be imposed. There are a small number of **exceptions** where the process set out in the code does not have to be followed, for example when fear of violence, harassment or vandalism on the part of one of the parties makes it unreasonable for the two parties to deal together in this way.

Additionally, employees are not able to raise a grievance at an **employment tribunal** without first raising a formal grievance at work. This is so that the employee and the employer can try to fix the dispute internally first, before incurring the time and expenses of a tribunal. The 2008 Act also places a duty on ACAS to conciliate between parties.

BPP
LEARNING MEDIA

6.10 Reasonableness of employer

FAST FORWARD

Even where the reason for dismissal is justified or automatically fair, the tribunal must also decide whether the employer acted **reasonably** in the circumstances.

During an employment tribunal, employers must demonstrate **'reasonableness'** in their dealings with the employee.

- **Consultation** with employee to determine areas of difficulty
- Following the **ACAS Code of Practice** (failure to follow the ACAS code will make employers liable for an additional 25% compensation or may reduce employees' compensation by 25%)
- Allowing a **reasonable time** for improvement
- Providing **training** if necessary
- Considering **all alternatives** to dismissal

If the principal reason for dismissal is one of the potentially fair reasons, the tribunal will still investigate. This is because the dismissal may still be unfair **if the employer acted unreasonably** in dismissing the employee.

The **employment tribunal** is required to review the circumstances and to decide whether it was reasonable to dismiss the employee for the reasons given. Determining whether the employer has acted reasonably requires the tribunal to ask the following questions.

- Has the correct **procedure** been applied?
- Did the employer take all **circumstances** into consideration?
- What would any **reasonable employer** have done?

Not all disputes have to be heard formally. The **Employment Act 2008** allows parties to agree for proceedings to take place without a hearing, or where one party fails to respond to preliminary communications.

6.11 Remedies for unfair dismissal

FAST FORWARD

Remedies for **unfair dismissal** include:

- **Reinstatement**
- **Re-engagement**
- **Compensation**

An employee who alleges unfair dismissal must present his complaint to an **employment tribunal** within three months of the effective date of termination. The dispute is referred to a Conciliation Officer and only comes before the tribunal if his efforts to promote a settlement fail.

6.11.1 Reinstatement

If unfair dismissal is established, the tribunal first considers the possibility of making an order for reinstatement.

Key term

> **Reinstatement** is return to the same job without any break of continuity: s 114.

6.11.2 Re-engagement

The tribunal may alternatively order **re-engagement**. The new employment must be comparable with the old or otherwise suitable.

Re-engagement means that the employee is given new employment with the employer (or his successor or associate) on terms specified in the order.

In deciding whether to exercise these powers, the tribunal must take into account whether the complainant wishes to be reinstated and, whether it is practicable and just for the employer to comply. **Such orders are in fact very infrequent**.

6.11.3 Compensation

If the tribunal does not order reinstatement or re-engagement the tribunal may award **compensation**, which may be made in three stages as follows.

(a) A **basic award** calculated as follows. Those aged 41 and over receive one and a half weeks' pay up to a statutory weekly maximum for each year of service up to a maximum of 20 years. In other age groups the same provisions apply, except that the 22-40 age group receive one week's pay per year and the 21 and under age group receive half a week's pay.

(b) A **compensatory award** (taking account of the basic award) for any additional loss of earnings, expenses and benefits on common law principles of damages for breach of contract: s 124. This is limited to a statutory maximum by the Employment Rights Act 1996.

(c) If the employer does not comply with an order for reinstatement or re-engagement and does not show that it was impracticable to do so a **punitive additional award** is made of between 26 and 52 weeks' pay (again subject to a statutory weekly maximum).

The tribunal may **reduce the amount of the award** in any of the following circumstances.

- If the employee **contributed** in some way to his own dismissal: s 123(6)
- If he has **unreasonably refused** an offer of reinstatement
- If it is **just and equitable** by reason of some matter which occurred before dismissal: s 123(1)

Question   Dismissal

Which of the following are examples of dismissal?

(i)   An employee resigns following their employer's serious repudiatory breach of the employment contract
(ii)   An employer terminates an employee's contract with notice
(iii)   An employer fails to renew an employee's fixed term contract
(iv)   An employee is offered garden leave

A   (i), (iii) and (iv) only
B   (i) and (ii) only
C   (iii) only
D   All of the above

Answer

D   All the options are examples of dismissal.

- Certain employment rights are only available if an employee has a specified period of **continuous employment**.

- **Statute** implies terms into employment contracts to prohibit discrimination in various categories. In addition to the longstanding legislation preventing discrimination on grounds of sex or race, there is new legislation which expands the framework considerably.

- Under s 2 of the **Health and Safety at Work Act 1974**, it is the duty of every employer, **as far as is practicable**, to ensure the health, safety and welfare of all employees.

  In particular, they should

  - Provide and maintain plant and **systems of work** which are safe and without risk

  - Make arrangements to ensure health and safety in relation to the use, handling, storage and transport of **articles and substances**

  - Provide **adequate information**, instruction, training and supervision

  - Maintain **safe places** of work

  - Ensure there is **adequate access** in and out

  - Provide a **safe and healthy working environment**.

- The responsibility for making health and safety regulations rests on the government. A **Health and Safety Commission** oversees the working of the system. Its members include representatives of employers' organisations and of trade unions.

- Where employment is **terminated by notice** the period given must **not be less** than the **statutory minimum**.

- If an employee is dismissed with **shorter notice** than the statutory or contractual requirements, or without notice when summary dismissal is unjustified, the employer can be sued for **wrongful dismissal**.

- Certain employees have a right not to be **unfairly dismissed**. Breach of that right allows an employee to claim compensation from a tribunal. To claim for unfair dismissal, the employee must satisfy certain criteria.

- Dismissal must be **justified** if it related to the employee's capability or qualifications, the employee's conduct, redundancy, legal prohibition or restriction on the employee's continued employment or some other substantial reason. Some reasons for dismissal are **automatically** fair or unfair.

- Even where the reason for dismissal is justified or automatically fair, the tribunal must also decide whether the employer acted **reasonably** in the circumstances.

- Remedies for **unfair dismissal** include:

  - **Reinstatement**
  - **Re-engagement**
  - **Compensation**

1   Rick was employed by Chingtow Ltd, earning a salary of £24,000 pa and entitled to three month's notice from his employer. However, he was wrongfully dismissed with one month's notice. How much will the court award him as compensation?

    A   £2,000
    B   £4,000
    C   £6,000
    D   £8,000

2   How much notice is an employee with 5 years' continuous service entitled to?

3   The usual remedy for wrongful dismissal is

    A   Reinstatement
    B   Damages
    C   Redundancy pay
    D   Re-engagement

4   **Fill in the blanks** below, using the words in the box.

To claim (1) ………………….. for unfair dismissal, three issues have to be considered.

- The employee must show that he is a (2) ………………… employee and that he has been (3) …………………..

- The (4) ………………… must explain the (5) ………………… for dismissal

- Application has to be made to the (6) ………………… within (7) ………………… months of the dismissal

• qualifying	• dismissed	• employer
• reason	• three	• compensation
• employment tribunal		

5   Unfavourable treatment of a woman purely due to her pregnancy is classed as sex discrimination.

True ☐

False ☐

6   State an automatically unfair reason for dismissal.

7   John works for Netco's information technology (IT) department. To save costs, Netco has outsourced John's department to Intco, an unrelated business which provides IT services to a number of businesses. John's continuity of service is protected by the Transfer of Undertaking rules.

True ☐

False ☐

8   The Health and Safety Commission, working though the Health and Safety Executive, oversees the working of the Health and Safety system in the UK.

True ☐

False ☐

9   Employees who are summarily dismissed received how much notice?

   A   No notice
   B   1 day's notice
   C   1 week's notice
   D   1 month's notice

10   Except where agreed otherwise by an employment contract, what is the maximum notice period that an employee is entitled to?

   A   1 week's notice
   B   10 weeks' notice
   C   12 weeks' notice
   D   13 weeks' notice

Answers to Quick Quiz

1   B. 2/12 × £24,000. He was already given 1/12 (one month's notice) by Chingtow.

2   5 weeks (1 week for each year's continuous service).

3   B. Wrongful dismissal is a common law action and damages are the only remedy.

4   (1) compensation (2) qualifying (3) dismissed (4) employer (5) reason (6) employment tribunal (7) three

5   True. Unfair treatment of a woman by reason of her pregnancy is sex discrimination.

6   Any one from the following.

    • Pregnancy or other maternity-related grounds

    • Trade union membership or activities

    • Dismissal on transfer of an undertaking (unless there are 'economic, technical or organisational reasons'
      justifying the dismissal)

    • Taking steps to avert danger to health and safety at work

    • Seeking to enforce rights relating to the national minimum wage

    • Exercising rights under the Working Time Regulations 1998

    • Refusing or opting out of Sunday working (in the retail sector)

    • Making a protected disclosure under the Public Interest Disclosure Act 1998

7   True. Employees whose roles have been outsourced are protected by the Transfer of Undertaking rules.

8   True. This is the framework for health and safety in the UK.

9   A. Summary dismissal occurs when an employee is dismissed without notice. It would only be used where the
    employee has committed a serious disciplinary offence.

10 C. The maximum statutory notice period is 12 weeks and is given to employees with 12 years or longer service.

Now try the questions below from the Question Bank

Number
Q36
Q37
Q38
Q39
Q40

BPP
LEARNING MEDIA

Part D

Company formation

BPP
LEARNING MEDIA

BPP
LEARNING MEDIA

Organisations and corporate personality

9

Introduction

The concept of **legal personality** and in particular the legal status of a company as a separate legal personality is fundamental to an understanding of company law.

Questions about the legal personalities of different types of organisation are particularly popular in law assessments. You may be asked about the differences between **public** and **private** companies, **companies limited** by **shares** and **guarantee**, and **sole traders** and **partnerships**. Questions may also be asked about the **advantages** and **disadvantages** of **incorporation**.

The other main area this chapter covers is the concept and consequences of a company's **separate legal personality**. It also explains the main situations in which the **'veil of incorporation'** will be lifted and a company identified with its members or directors.

Topic list	Learning outcomes
1 Sole traders	G1(a), G1(e)
2 Partnerships	G1(a), G1(e)
3 Limited liability partnerships	G1(a), G1(e)
4 A company's legal identity	G1(a), G1(e)
5 Limited liability of members	G1(a), G1(e)
6 Types of company	G1(a), G1(b), G1(e)
7 Additional classifications	G1(a), G1(e)
8 Effect of legal personality	G1(a), G1(e)
9 Ignoring separate personality	G1(a), G1(e)
10 Comparison of companies and partnerships	G1(a), G1(e)

1 Sole traders

FAST FORWARD

In a **sole tradership**, there is no legal distinction between the individual and the business.

1.1 Introduction

A **sole trader owns** and **runs a business**. They contribute capital to start the enterprise, run it with or without employees, and earn the profits or stand the losses of the venture. Sole traders are found mainly in the retail trades (local newsagents), small scale service industries (plumbers), and small manufacturing and craft industries.

Assessment focus point

You may see the term 'sole practitionership' mentioned in your assessment. A sole practitionership is no different to a sole tradership, but the term can be used to describe sole trader businesses in which the owner practices a profession. For example an accountant may be a sole practitionership.

1.2 Legal status of the sole trader

Whilst the business is a separate accounting entity the business is **not legally distinct** from the person who owns it. In law, the person and the business are viewed as the same entity.

The **advantages** of being a sole trader are as follows.

- **No formal procedures** are required to set up in business. However, for certain classes of business a licence may be required (eg retailing wines and spirits), and VAT registration is often necessary.

- **Independence** and **self-accountability**. A sole trader need consult nobody about business decisions and is not required to reveal the state of the business to anyone (other than the tax authorities each year).

- **Personal supervision** of the business by the sole trader should ensure its effective operation. Personal contact with customers may enhance commercial flexibility.

- **All** the **profits** of the business **accrue** to the sole trader. This can be a powerful motivator, and satisfying to the individual whose ability/energy results in reward.

The **disadvantages** of being a sole trader include the following.

- If the business gets into debt, a sole trader's **personal wealth** (for example, private house) might be lost if the debts are called in, as they are the same legal entity.

- Expansion of the business is usually only possible by **ploughing back** the **profits** of the business as further capital, although loans or overdraft finance may be available.

- The business has a **high dependence** on the **individual** which can mean long working hours and difficulties during sickness or holidays.

- The **death** of the proprietor may make it **necessary** to **sell** the **business** in order to pay the resulting tax liabilities, or family members may not wish to continue the business anyway.

- The **individual** may **only have one skill**. A sole trader may be, say, a good technical engineer or craftsman but may lack the skills to market effectively or to maintain accounting records to control the business effectively.

- Other **disadvantages** associated with small size, lack of diversification, absence of economies of scale and problems of raising finance.

Question

All the profits of a sole tradership accrue to the owner.

True of false?

Answer

True. This is the main benefit of operating a business as a sole tradership.

2 Partnerships

FAST FORWARD

Partnership is defined as 'the relation which subsists between persons carrying on a business in common with a view of profit'. A partnership is *not* a separate legal person distinct from its members, it is merely a 'relation' between persons. Each partner (there must be at least two) is usually **personally liable** for all the debts of the firm.

Partnership is a common form of business association. It is **flexible**, because it can either be a **formal** or **informal** arrangement, so can be used for large organisations or a small husband and wife operation.

Partnership is normal practice in the **professions** as most professions prohibit their members from carrying on practice through limited companies, though some professions permit their members to trade as limited liability partnerships which have many of the characteristics of companies. Business people are not so restricted and generally prefer to trade through a limited company for the advantages this can bring.

Assessment focus point

You may be required to demonstrate knowledge of the legislation governing both limited and unlimited liability partnerships. You should therefore make careful note of the rules regarding the Partnership Act 1890, the Limited Partnership Act 1907 and the Limited Liability Partnership Act 2000.

2.1 Definition of partnership

Key term

'**Partnership** is the relation which subsists between persons carrying on a business in common with a view of profit.' S1 Partnership Act 1890.

We shall look at some points raised by this definition now.

2.1.1 The relation which subsists between persons

'**Person**' includes a corporation such as a **registered company** as well as an **individual** living person.

There must be at least **two** partners. If, therefore, two people are in partnership, one dies and the survivor carries on the business, that person is a sole trader. There is no longer a partnership.

2.1.2 Carrying on a business

Business can include every trade, occupation or profession. But three points should be noted.

(a)   A business is a **form of activity**. If two or more persons are merely the passive joint owners of revenue-producing property, such as rented houses, that fact does not make them partners.

(b)   A business can consist of a **single transaction**. These situations are often described as 'joint ventures'.

(c)   Carrying on a business must have a **beginning and an end**. A partnership begins when the partners agree to conduct their **business activity** together. This can be before the business actually begins to trade, such as when premises are leased and a bank account opened: *Khan v Miah 2001*.

2.1.3 In common

Broadly this phrase means that the partners must be associated in the business as **joint proprietors**. The evidence that this is so is found in their taking a share of the profits, especially **net profit**.

2.1.4 A view of profit

If persons enter into a partnership with a **view of making profits** but they actually suffer losses, it is still a partnership. The test to be applied is one of **intention**. If the intention of trading together is just to gain experience, for example, there is no partnership: *Davies v Newman 2000*.

2.2 Consequences of the definition

In most cases there is no doubt about the existence of a partnership. The partners declare their intention by such steps as signing a **written partnership agreement** and adopting a **firm name**. These outward and visible signs of the existence of a partnership are not essential however – a partnership can exist without them.

2.2.1 Terminology

The word 'firm' is correctly used to denote a partnership. It is **not** correct to apply it to a registered company (though the newspapers often do so).

The word 'company' may form part of the name of a partnership, for example, 'Smith and Company'. But 'limited company' or 'registered company' is **only** applied to a properly registered company.

2.3 Liability of the partners

Every partner is liable **without limit** for the debts of the partnership. It is possible to register a limited partnership in which one or more individual partners have limited liability, but the limited partners may not take part in the management of the business: **Limited Partnerships Act 1907**.

The **limited partnership** is useful where one partner wishes to invest in the activities of the partnership without being involved in its day-to-day operation. Such partners are entitled to inspect the accounts of the partnership.

Under the **Limited Liability Partnership Act 2000** it is possible to register a partnership with limited liability (an LLP).

2.4 Forming a partnership

FAST FORWARD   Partnerships can be **formed** very informally, but there may be complex formalities to ensure clarity.

A partnership can be a very **informal arrangement**. This is reflected in the procedure to form a partnership.

A partnership is **formed when two or more people agree to run a business together**. Partnerships can be formed in any trade or occupation or profession. In order to be a partnership, the business must be **'carried on in common'**, meaning that all parties must have **responsibility** for the business. In other words, there is **more than one proprietor**. A husband and wife who run a shop together are partners, but a shop owner and their employee are not.

In law then, the formation of a partnership is essentially straightforward. People **make an agreement** together to run a business, and **carry that agreement out**.

Imagine that two large firms of accountants wanted to merge. The partners agreed on 1 June 20X7 that they would merge and become a new partnership, known as the Biggest Accountancy Partnership. In law, this is straightforward. What problems do you think they might encounter?

Answer

In law, when the partners of the two firms agree to merge, then they have a new partnership. In practice, however, if two massive businesses such as two large firms decided to merge, the details of the formation of the new partnership would be far more complex than that. Here is a list of just some of the things that they would have to consider.

- Profit share
- Employees
- Partnership property
- Partner hierarchy

- Recruitment policy
- Future partners' policy
- Standard partners' authority to act in the new firm's name
- Fair trading and monopoly issues

In practice, the formation of such a new partnership would be an enormous operation.

2.4.1 Common formation formalities

In practice, the formalities of setting up a partnership may be more **complex** than simple agreement. Many professional people use partnerships. These business associations can be vast organisations with substantial revenue and expenditure, such as the larger accountancy firms and many law firms. Such organisations have so many partners that the relationships between them has to be **regulated**. Thus forming some partnerships can involve creating **detailed partnership agreements** which lay out terms and conditions of partnership.

2.4.2 The partnership agreement

A written partnership agreement is *not* legally required. In practice there are advantages in setting down in writing the terms of their association.

(a) It **fills** in the **details** which the law would not imply – the nature of the firm's business, its name, and the bank at which the firm will maintain its account for instance.

(b) A written agreement serves to **override terms** otherwise implied by the Partnership Act 1890 which are inappropriate to the partnership. The Act for example implies that partners share profits equally.

(c) Additional clauses can be developed. **Expulsion clauses** are an example and they provide a mechanism to expel a partner where there would be no ability to do so otherwise.

2.5 Termination of partnership

Partnerships may be **terminated** by passing of time, termination of the underlying venture, death or bankruptcy of a partner, illegality, notice, agreement or by order of the court.

Termination is when the partnership comes to an end. In this context, 'partnership' means the existing partners.

Illustration

Alison, Ben, Caroline and David are in partnership as accountants. Caroline decides to change career and become an interior designer. In her place, Alison, Ben and David invite Emily to join the partnership.

As far as third parties are concerned, a partnership offering accountancy services still exists. In fact, however, the old partnership (ABCD) has been dissolved, and a new partnership (ABDE) has replaced it.

2.5.1 Events causing termination

The Partnership Act 1890 states that partnership is terminated in the following instances.

- **Passing of time**, if the partnership was entered into for a fixed term
- **Termination of the venture**, if entered into for a single venture
- The **death or bankruptcy** of a partner (partnership agreement may vary this)
- **Subsequent illegality**
- **Notice** given by a partner if it is a partnership of indefinite duration
- **Order of the court** granted to a partner
- **Agreement** between the partners

In the event of the **termination** of a partnership, the partnership's **assets are realised** and the proceeds applied in this order.

- Paying off external debts
- Repaying to the partners any loans or advances
- Repaying the partners' capital contribution
- Anything left over is then repaid to the partners in the profit sharing ratio.

The partnership agreement can exclude some of these provisions and can **avoid dissolution** in the following circumstances.

- Death of a partner
- Bankruptcy of a partner

It is wise to make such provisions to give **stability** to the partnership.

2.6 Authority of partners

FAST FORWARD

The **authority** of partners to bind each other in contract is based on the principles of agency.

In simple terms, a partner is the **agent of the partnership and their co-partners**. This means that some of their acts bind the other partners, either because they have, or because they appear to have, authority. The **Partnership Act 1890 defines** the **authority** of a partner to make contracts as follows.

> **Authority of a partner**
>
> Every partner is an **agent** of the firm and his other partners for the purpose of the business of the partnership, and the acts of every partner who does any act for carrying on the **usual way** of business if the kind carried on by the firm of which he is a member **bind the firm** and his partners, **unless** the partner so acting has **in fact no authority** to act for the firm in the particular matter, **and the person with whom he is dealing** either **knows that he has no authority**, or **does not know or believe him to be a partner.**
>
> Where a partner pledges the credit of the firm for a **purpose apparently not connected** with the firm's ordinary course of business, the **firm is not bound, unless** he is in fact **specially authorised** by the other partners: but this section does not affect any personal liability incurred by an individual.
>
> If it has been **agreed between the partners** that any **restriction** shall be placed on the power of any one or more of them to bind the firm, **no act** done in contravention of the agreement is **binding** on the firm with respect to **persons having notice of the agreement.**

The key point to note about authority of partners is that, other than when the partner has actual authority, the authority often **depends on the perception of the third party**. If the third party genuinely believes that the partner has authority, the partner is likely to bind the firm.

Partners are also **jointly liable** for **crimes** and **torts** committed by one of their number in the course of business.

2.7 Liability of partners in an unlimited liability partnership

FAST FORWARD

Partners are **jointly liable** for all partnership debts that result from contracts that the partners have made which bind the firm.

Partners are **jointly liable** for all partnership debts that result from contracts made by other partners which bind the firm. The **Civil Liability Act 1978** provides that judgement against one partner does not prevent subsequent actions against other partners. The link between authority and liability can be seen in the following diagram.

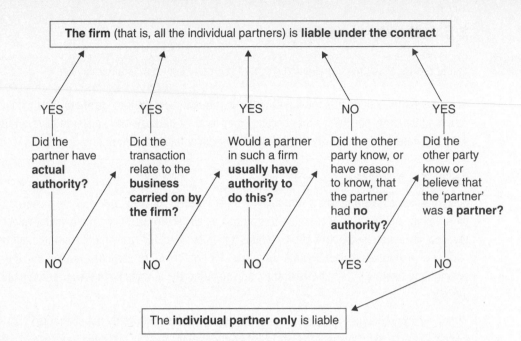

The firm (that is, all the individual partners) is **liable under the contract**

YES	YES	YES	NO	YES
Did the partner have **actual authority?**	Did the transaction relate to the **business carried on by the firm?**	Would a partner in such a firm **usually have authority to do this?**	Did the other party know, or have reason to know, that the partner had **no authority?**	Did the other party know or believe that the 'partner' was **a partner?**
NO	NO	NO	YES	NO

The **individual partner only** is liable

There are particular rules on liability for new and retiring partners.

Partner	Partner liability
New partners	A new partner admitted to an existing firm is liable for **debts incurred** only **after** they become a partner. They are not liable for debts incurred before they were a partner unless they agree to become liable.
Retiring partners	A partner who retires is still **liable** for any **outstanding debts** incurred while they were a partner, unless the creditor has agreed to release them from liability. They are also **liable** for debts of the firm **incurred after their retirement** if the creditor knew them to be a partner (before retirement) and has not had **notice** of their retirement.

Therefore, it is **vital** on retirement that a partner **gives notice** to all the creditors of the firm. The retiring partner may have an indemnity from the remaining partners with respect to this issue. |

2.8 Supervision and regulation

There is no formal **statutory supervision** or regulation of partnerships. Their accounts need not be in prescribed form nor is an audit necessary. The public has no means or legal right of inspection of the firm's accounts or other information such as companies must provide.

If, however, the partners carry on business under a firm name which is not the surnames of them all, say, 'Smith, Jones & Co', they are required to disclose the **names** of the **partners** on their letterheads and at their places of business. They are required to make a **return** of their **profits** for income tax and **usually** to **register** for VAT.

2.9 Property

Partnerships **can** grant a **mortgage** or **fixed charge** over property, but **cannot** grant **floating changes**.

BPP LEARNING MEDIA

Question

Partners in a traditional partnership have an agency relationship with each other. What is the effect of this arrangement?

Answer

Each partner acts as an agent of the partnership and all partners are jointly liable for a partner's actions.

3 Limited liability partnerships

FAST FORWARD

> **A limited liability partnership** formed under the 2000 Act combines the features of a traditional partnership with the limited liability and creation of legal personality more usually associated with limited companies.

3.1 Definition of limited liability partnership

The other form of partnership commonly used in England, particularly for professional partnerships, is the **limited liability partnership (LLP)**. This type of business association was created by the Limited Liability Partnership Act 2000.

LLPs are similar to limited companies in that they have separate legal identity and unlimited liability for debts, but the liability of the individual partners is **limited to the amount of their capital contribution**.

LLPs have similar requirements for governance and accountability as limited companies. They are generally set up by firms of professionals such as accountants and lawyers, who are required by the rules of their professions to operate as partnerships but who seek to have the protection of limited liability.

Key term

> A **limited liability partnership (LLP)** is a corporate body which has separate legal personality from its members and therefore some of the advantages and disadvantages of a company.

The main **advantage of an LLP** over a traditional partnership is that the LLP will be liable for its own debts rather than the partners. All contracts with third parties will be with the LLP.

3.2 Formation

A limited liability partnership may be formed by persons associating to carry on lawful business with a view to profit, but it **must be incorporated** to be recognised. LLPs can have an unlimited number of partners. To be incorporated, the subscribers must send an **incorporation document** and a **statement of compliance** to the Registrar of Companies.

The **document** must be **signed** and **state** the following:

- The **name** of the LLP
- The **location** of its **registered office** (England and Wales/Wales/Scotland)
- The **address** of the registered office
- The name and address of all the **members** of the LLP
- Which of the members are to be **designated members** (see below)

A **registration fee** is also payable.

3.3 Internal regulation

LLPs are more flexible than companies as they provide similar protection for the owners, but with less statutory rules on areas such as meetings and management. No board of directors is needed. As can be seen in the incorporation procedures, LLPs come under the supervision of the **Registrar of Companies** (the Registrar).

The members of the LLP are those who subscribe to the original incorporation document, and those admitted afterwards in accordance with the terms of the partnership agreement.

The rights and duties of the partners will usually be set out in a **partnership agreement**. In the absence of a partnership agreement, the rights and duties are set out in regulations under the Act.

LLPs must have **two designated members**, who take responsibility for the publicity requirements of the LLP.

With regard to publicity, the LLP's designated members must:

- **File** certain notices with the Registrar, such as when a member leaves and an annual return
- Sign and file **accounts**
- Appoint **auditors** if appropriate

The Registrar will maintain a file containing the **publicised documents** of the LLP at Companies House.

3.4 External relationships

Every member is an **agent** of the LLP. As such, where the member has authority, the LLP will be bound by the acts of the member.

The **LLP will not be bound by the acts of the member where:**

- They have no authority and the third party is aware of that fact
- They have ceased to be a member, and the third party is aware of that fact

3.5 Dissolution

An LLP **does not dissolve on a member leaving** it, in the same way that a traditional partnership does. Where a member has died or (for a corporate member) been wound up, that member ceases to be a member, but the LLP continues in existence.

3.6 Limited partnership

The other form of partnership that is seen, rarely, in the UK is the **limited partnership**. Under the Limited Partnership Act 1907, a partnership may be formed in which at least one partner (the general partner) must have **full, unlimited liability**. The other partners, which may include limited companies, have **limited liability** for the debts of the partnership beyond the extent of the capital they have contributed. The rules are as follows:

- Limited partners may not withdraw their capital

- Limited partners may not take part in the management of the partnership

- Limited partners cannot bind the partnership in a contract with a third party without losing the benefit of limited liability

- The partnership must be registered with Companies House

Question

Explain the publicity requirements that LLPs must meet.

Answer

The designated members must:

- File certain notices with the Registrar
- Sign and file accounts and an annual return
- Appoint auditors if appropriate

Assessment focus point

Partnership questions often revolve around a partner's authority to enter contracts and the liability of all the partners when debts are incurred.

4 A company's legal identity

FAST FORWARD

A company has a **legal personality** separate from its owners (known as members). It is a formal arrangement, surrounded by formality and publicity, but its chief advantage is that members' **liability** for the company's debts is typically **limited**.

A company is the most popular form of **business association**.

By its nature, a company is more **formal** than a partnership or a sole trader. There is often substantially **more legislation** on the formation and procedures of companies than any other business association, hence the weighting towards company law of most of the rest of this Study Text.

The key reason why the company is a popular form of business association is that the **liability of its members to contribute to the debts of the entity is significantly limited**. For many people, this benefit outweighs the disadvantage of the formality surrounding companies, and encourages them not to trade as sole traders or (unlimited) partnerships.

4.1 Definition of a company

Key terms

For the purposes of this Study Text, a **company** is an entity registered as such under the Companies Act 2006.

The key feature of a company is that it has a **legal personality** (existence) distinct from its members and directors.

4.2 Legal personality

A person possesses legal rights and is subject to legal obligations. In law, the term 'person' is used to denote two categories of legal person.

- An individual human being is a **natural person**. A sole trader is a natural person, and there is legally no distinction between the individual and the business entity in sole tradership

- The law also recognises **artificial persons** in the form of companies and limited partnerships. Unlimited partnerships are not artificial persons.

Corporate personality is a common law principle that grants a company a legal identity, separate from the members who comprise it. It follows that the property of a company belongs to that company, debts of the company must be satisfied from the assets of that company, and the company has perpetual succession until wound up.

A corporation is a **legal entity** separate from the natural persons connected with it, for example as members or directors. We shall come back to this later.

5 Limited liability of members

The fact that a company's members – not the company itself – have **limited liability** for its debts **protects** the **members** from the company's creditors and ultimately from the full risk of business failure.

A key consequence of the fact that the company is distinct from its members is that its members have **limited liability.**

Limited liability is a protection offered to members of certain types of company. In the event of business failure, the members will only be asked to contribute identifiable amounts to the assets of the business.

5.1 Protection for members against creditors

The **company** itself is **liable without limit for its own debts.** If the company buys plastic from another company, for example, it owes the other company money.

Limited liability is a benefit to members. They own the business, so might be the people whom the creditors logically ask to pay the debts of the company if the company is unable to pay them itself.

Limited liability prevents this by stipulating the **creditors** of a limited company **cannot demand payment of the company's debts** from members of the company.

It should be noted that in reality banks often request **personal guarantees** from the owners of small businesses which it can call upon if the business fails. In these cases, the owners' liability is not fully protected, but as the company grows and becomes profitable, requests for payment under such guarantees become less likely.

5.2 Protection from business failure

As the company is liable for all its own debts, limited liability only becomes an issue in the event of a business failure when the **company is unable to pay its own debts**.

This will result in the **winding up** of the company which will enable the creditors to be paid from the proceeds of any assets remaining in the company. It is at winding up that limited liability becomes most relevant.

5.3 Members asked to contribute identifiable amounts

Although the creditors of the company cannot ask the members of the company to pay the debts of the company, there are some amounts that **members are required to pay, in the event of a winding up**.

Type of company	Amount owed by member at winding up
Company limited by shares	Any **outstanding amount** from when they originally purchased their shares from the company. If the member's shares are fully paid, they **do not have to contribute anything in the event of a winding up**.
Company limited by guarantee	The **amount they guaranteed** to pay in the event of a winding up

Question

Limitations of liability

Hattie and two friends wish to set up a small business. Hattie is concerned that, following her initial investment, she will have no access to additional funds, and is worried what might happen if anything goes wrong. Advise her on the relative merits of a company and an unlimited partnership.

Answer

The question of liability appears to be important to Hattie. As a member of a limited company, her liability would be limited – as a member at least – to any outstanding amount payable for her shares. If the three friends decide to form an unlimited partnership, they should be advised that they will have **unlimited** liability for the debts of the partnership. (An unlimited partnership does **not** have a legal personality distinct from the partners.)

5.4 Liability of the company for tort and crime

As a company has a separate legal identity, it may also have liabilities in **tort** and **crime**. Criminal liability of companies in particular is a topical area but, is outside the scope of your syllabus.

6 Types of company

FAST FORWARD

Most companies are those **incorporated** under the **Companies Act**. However there are other types of company such as **corporations sole**, **chartered corporations**, **statutory corporations** and **community interest companies**.

Corporations are **classified** in one of the following categories.

Categories	Description
Corporations sole	A corporation sole is an **official position** which is filled by one person who is replaced from time to time. The Public Trustee and the Treasury Solicitor are corporations sole.
Chartered corporations	These are usually **charities** or bodies such as the Chartered Institute of Management Accounts, formed by Royal Charter.
Statutory corporations	Statutory corporations are formed by special Acts of Parliament. This method is little used now, as it is slow and expensive. It was used in the nineteenth century to form railway and canal companies.

Categories	Description
Registered companies	Registration under the Companies Act is the normal method of incorporating a commercial concern. Any body of this type is properly called a company.
Community Interest Companies (CICs)	A special form of company for use by 'social' enterprises pursuing purposes that are beneficial to the community, rather than the maximisation of profit for the benefit of owners, created by the Companies (Audit, Investigation and Community Enterprise) Act 2004. To become a CIC, the organisation must first register as a company, and then apply for CIC status.

6.1 Limited companies

The meaning of limited liability has already been explained. It is the **member**, not the company, whose liability for the company's debts may be limited.

6.1.1 Liability limited by shares

Liability is usually **limited by shares.** This is the position when a company which has share capital states in its constitution that 'the liability of members is limited'.

6.1.2 Liability limited by guarantee

A company may be **limited by guarantee.** Its constitution states the amount which each member **undertakes** to **contribute** in a winding up (also known as a liquidation). A creditor has no direct claim against a member under his guarantee, nor can the company require a member to pay up under his guarantee until it goes into liquidation.

In some cases, **ex-members** who left the organisation within the last 12 months may be required to contribute towards debts incurred whilst they were a member.

Companies limited by guarantee are appropriate to **non-commercial activities**, such as a charity or a trade association which is non-profit making but which wishes to have a form of reserve capital if it becomes insolvent. They do not have **share capital** but are required to submit an annual return and may be subject to an audit.

6.2 Unlimited liability companies

Key term

An **unlimited liability company** is a company in which members do not have limited liability. In the event of business failure, the liquidator can require members to contribute as much as may be required to pay the company's debts in full.

An unlimited company **can only be a private company**, as a **public company is always limited**, but it may or may not have share capital. An unlimited company need not **file** a copy of its **annual accounts** and reports with the Registrar, unless during the relevant accounting reference period:

    (a)   It is (to its knowledge) a **subsidiary** of a limited company.

    (b)   **Two** or more **limited companies** have **exercised rights** over the **company**, which (had they been exercised by only one of them) would have **made** the **company** a **subsidiary** of that one company.

    (c)   It is the **parent company** of a limited liability company.

BPP LEARNING MEDIA

The unlimited company certainly has its uses. It provides a **corporate body** (a separate legal entity) which can conveniently hold assets to which liabilities do not attach.

Question
Limited liability

Explain the liability of members of companies limited by guarantee.

Answer

Members of companies limited by guarantee are required to pay the amount they guaranteed if required when the company is wound up.

6.3 Public and private companies

FAST FORWARD

A company may be **private** or **public**. Only the latter may offer its share to the public.

Key terms

A **public company** is a company whose constitution states that it is public and that it has complied with the registration procedures for such a company.

A **private company** is a company which has not been registered as a public company under the Companies Act. The major distinction between a private and public company is that the former may not offer its securities to the public.

A **public** company is a company registered as such under the Companies Act with the Registrar. **Any company not registered as public is a private company**. A public company may be one which was **originally incorporated** as a public company or one which re-registered as a public company having been previously a private company. A company limited by guarantee and an unlimited company, **cannot** be public companies.

6.4 Conditions for being a public company

FAST FORWARD

To trade, a public company must hold a **Registrar's trading certificate** having met the requirements, including **minimum capital of £50,000**.

6.4.1 Registrar's trading certificate

Before it can trade a company originally incorporated as a public company must have a trading certificate issued by the Registrar. The conditions for this are:

- The **name** of the company identifies it as a public company by ending with the words 'public limited company' or 'plc' or their Welsh equivalents, 'ccc', for a Welsh company.

- The **constitution** of the company states that 'the company is a public company' or words to that effect.

- The **allotted share capital** of the company is not less than the authorised minimum which is currently £50,000.

- It is a **company** limited by shares.

With regard to the **minimum share capital** of £50,000.

- A company originally incorporated as a public company will not be permitted to trade until its **allotted** share capital is at least £50,000.

- A private company which re-registers as a public company will not be permitted to trade until it has **allotted** share capital of at least £50,000; this needs only be paid up to one quarter of its nominal value (plus the whole of any premium).

- A private company which has share capital of £50,000 or more may of course continue as a private company; it is always **optional** to become a public company.

6.4.2 Minimum membership and directors

A public company must have a minimum of **one member**. This is the same as a private company. However, unlike a private company it must have at least **two directors**. A private company must have just one. Directors do not usually have liability for the company's debts.

6.5 Private companies

A **private company** is the **residual category** and so does not need to satisfy any special conditions.

Private companies are generally small enterprises in which some if not all shareholders are also directors and **vice versa**. Ownership and management are combined in the same individuals. Therefore, it is unnecessary to impose on the directors complicated restrictions to safeguard the interests of members and so the number of rules that apply to public companies are reduced for private companies.

6.6 Differences between private and public companies

FAST FORWARD

The main differences between public and private companies relate to: **capital**, **dealings** in **shares**, **accounts**, **commencement of business**, **general meetings**, **names**, **identification**, and **disclosure requirements**.

The more important differences between public and private companies imposed by law relate to the following factors.

6.6.1 Capital

Although both types of company are only required to have one shareholder, there are a number of differences between them.

(a) There is a minimum amount of **£50,000** for a **public** company, but **no minimum** for a **private** company.

(b) A public company may **raise capital** by **offering** its **shares** or debentures to the public; a **private** company is **prohibited** from doing so.

(c) Both **public** and **private companies** must generally **offer** to **existing members first** any ordinary shares to be allotted for cash. However a **private** company **may permanently disapply** this rule.

6.6.2 Dealings in shares

Only a **public company** can obtain a listing for its shares on the **Stock Exchange** or other investment exchange. To obtain the advantages of listing the company must agree to elaborate conditions contained in particulars in a **listing agreement** with The Stock Exchange. However, not all public companies are listed.

6.6.3 Accounts

(a)   A **public** company has **six** months from the end of its accounting reference period in which to produce its statutory audited accounts. The period for a **private** company is **nine** months.

(b)   A **private** company, if qualified by its size, may have **partial exemption** from various **accounting provisions** (discussed later in this text). These exemptions are not available to a public company or to its subsidiaries (even if they are private companies).

(c)   A **listed public company** must publish its full accounts and reports on its **website**.

(d)   Public companies must lay their **accounts** and reports before a general meeting annually. Private companies have no such requirement.

6.6.4 Commencement of business

A **private** company can commence business **as soon** as it is **incorporated**. A **public** company if incorporated as such must first **obtain a trading certificate from the Registrar**.

6.6.5 General meetings

Private companies are not required to hold annual general meetings, (AGMs). **Public companies** must hold one within six months of their financial year end.

6.6.6 Names and Identification

The rules on identification as public or private are as follows.

- The word **'limited'** or **'Ltd'** in the name denotes a private company; **'public limited company'** or **'plc'** must appear at the end of the name of a public company.

- The **constitution** of a **public** company must state that it is a public company. A **private company** should be identified as private.

6.6.7 Disclosure requirements

There are **special disclosure and publicity requirements** for public companies. The main advantage of carrying on business through a public rather than a private company is that a public company, by the issue of listing particulars, may obtain a **listing** on The Stock Exchange and so mobilise capital from the investing public generally.

Attention!

> There is an important distinction between public companies and **listed public companies**. Listed (or quoted) companies are those which trade their shares (and other securities) on stock exchanges. Not all public companies sell their shares on stock exchanges (although, in law, they are entitled to sell their shares to the public). **Private** companies are not entitled to sell shares to the public in this way.
>
> In practice, only public companies meeting certain criteria would be allowed to obtain such a listing by the Stock Exchange.

Private companies may be broadly classified into two groups: independent (also called **free-standing**) private companies and **subsidiaries** of other companies.

7 Additional classifications

FAST FORWARD

There are a number of other ways in which companies can be **classified**.

7.1 Parent (holding) and subsidiary companies

The Companies Act draws a distinction between an 'accounting' definition, and a 'legal' definition in, s 1162. A company will be the **parent** (or **holding**) **company** of another company, its **subsidiary company**, according to the following rules.

Key term

> **Parent company**
>
> (a)   It holds a **majority of the voting rights** in the subsidiary.
>
> (b)   It **is a member of the subsidiary and has the right to appoint or remove a majority of its board of directors.**
>
> (c)   **It has the right to exercise a dominant influence over the subsidiary**:
>
>   (i)   By virtue of provisions contained in the subsidiary's articles.
>   (ii)   By virtue of a control contract.
>
> (d)   **It is a member of the subsidiary and controls alone**, under an agreement with other members, **a majority of the voting rights in the company.**
>
> (e)   **A company is also a parent if:**
>
>   (i)   It has the power to exercise, or actually exercises, a dominant influence or control over the subsidiary
>   (ii)   It and the subsidiary are managed on a unified basis
>
> (f)   **A company is also treated as the parent of the subsidiaries of its subsidiaries.**

A company (A Ltd) is a **wholly owned subsidiary** of another company (B Ltd) if it has no other members except B Ltd and its wholly owned subsidiaries, or persons acting on B Ltd's or its subsidiaries' behalf.

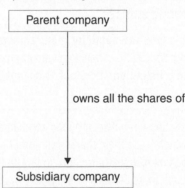

The diagram illustrates a **simple group**. In practice, such groups might be much larger and much more complex. The importance of the parent and subsidiary company relationship is recognised in company law in a number of rules.

(a)   A parent company must generally prepare **group accounts** in which the financial situation of parent and subsidiary companies is consolidated as if they were one person.

(b)   A subsidiary may **not ordinarily be a member** of its parent company.

(c)   Since directors of a parent company can **control** its **subsidiary**, some rules designed to regulate the dealings of companies with directors also apply to its subsidiaries, particularly loans to directors.

 BPP LEARNING MEDIA

7.2 Quoted companies

As we have seen public companies may seek a listing on a public exchange. This option is not open to private companies, who are not allowed to offer their shares for sale to the public. Listed companies are sometimes referred to as **quoted companies** (because their shares are quoted publicly).

7.3 Small companies regime

Small companies benefit from the **small companies regime's reduced legal requirements** in terms of filing accounts with the Registrar and obtaining an audit. The definitions of a small company for the purposes of accounting and auditing are almost identical.

In **accounting terms**, a company is small if it meets two of the following applicable criteria:

(a) Balance sheet total of not more than £3.26 million
(b) Turnover of not more than £6.5 million
(c) 50 employees or fewer on average

For **audit purposes**, a company is classed as small if it qualifies on the above criteria, but must **meet both** of conditions (a) and (b).

Assessment focus point

> Make sure you can identify the differences between private/public and quoted/unquoted companies.

7.4 Multinational companies

The vast majority of companies will simply operate in one country. However, some of the larger companies in the world will operate in more than one country. Such companies are **multinational**.

Key term

> A **multinational company** is a company that produces and markets its products in more than one country.

7.4.1 Examples: multinational companies

Three examples of large multinational companies include:

- Wal-mart Stores
- Royal Dutch Shell
- Exxon Mobil

Such companies sell their shares on stock exchanges around the world.

7.5 European companies

A European company is a **public company** which since **8 October 2004** can be **formed** under **European law**. The main requirement is that the **business must operate** in **two member states** and may be formed as a result of a merger of two companies in separate states.

Such companies are not likely to be a common form of business until rules on areas such as tax, insolvency and employment are harmonised across the European Union.

State the criteria that a company must meet to be classified as small.

Answer

A small company must meet two of the following criteria:

- Its balance sheet total must not exceed £3.26 million.
- Turnover must be no more than £6.5 million.
- It must employ fewer than 50 employees.

8 Effect of legal personality

FAST FORWARD

The case of *Salomon v Salomon & Co Ltd 1897* clearly demonstrates the **separate legal personality** of companies and is of great significance to any study of company law.

Salomon v Salomon & Co Ltd 1897

The facts: The claimant, S, had carried on business for 30 years. He decided to form a limited company to purchase the business so he and six members of his family each subscribed for one share.

The company then purchased the business from S for £38,782, the purchase price being payable to the claimant by way of the issue of 20,000 £1 shares, the issue of debentures, £10,000 of debentures and £8,782 in cash.

The company did not prosper and was wound up a year later, at which point its liabilities exceeded its assets. The liquidator, representing unsecured trade creditors of the company, claimed that the company's business was in effect still the claimant's (he owned 20,001 of 20,007 shares). Therefore he should bear liability for its debts and that payment of the debenture debt to him should be postponed until the company's trade creditors were paid.

Decision: The House of Lords held that the business was owned by, and its debts were liabilities of, the company. The claimant was under no liability to the company or its creditors, his debentures were validly issued and the security created by them over the company's assets was effective. This was because the company was a legal entity separate and distinct from S.

The principle of **separate legal personality** was confirmed in the following case.

Lee v Lee's Air Farming Ltd 1960

The facts: Mr Lee, who owned the majority of the shares of an aerial crop-spraying business, and was the sole working director of the company, was killed while piloting the aircraft.

Decision: Although he was the majority shareholder and sole working director of the company, he and the company were separate legal persons. Therefore he could also be an employee with rights against it when killed in an accident in the course of his employment.

8.1 Veil of incorporation

FAST FORWARD

Incorporation 'veils' members from outsiders' view but this veil may be lifted in **some circumstances**, so creditors and others can seek redress directly from members. The veil may be lifted: by statute to enforce the law; to prevent the evasion of obligations; and in certain situations where companies trade as a group.

Because a company has **separate legal personality** from the people who own or run it (the members/ shareholders/directors), people can look at a company and not know who or what owns or runs it.

The fact that members are 'hidden' in this way is sometimes referred to as the '**veil of incorporation'.** Literally, the members are 'veiled' from view.

9 Ignoring separate personality

FAST FORWARD

It is sometimes necessary by law to look at who the owners of a company are. This is referred to as **'lifting the veil'.**

Separate personality can be ignored to:

- **Identify** the **company** with its **members** and/or directors.
- Treat a **group of companies** as a **single commercial entity** (if a company is owned by another company).

The more important of these two reasons is the first one, although the second reason can sometimes be more complex. The main instances for lifting the veil are given below.

9.1 Lifting the veil by statute to enforce the law

Lifting of the veil is permitted under a number of statutes to enforce the law.

9.1.1 Liability for trading without trading certificate

A public company must obtain a trading certificate from the Registrar before it may commence to trade. Failure to do so leads to **personal liability** of the directors for any loss or damage suffered by a third party resulting from a transaction made in contravention of the trading certificate requirement. They are also liable for a fine.

9.1.2 Fraudulent and wrongful trading

When a company is wound up, it may appear that its business has been carried on with **intent** to **defraud creditors** or others. In this case the court may decide that the persons (usually the directors) who were knowingly parties to the **fraudulent trading** shall be **personally responsible** under civil law for debts and other liabilities of the company: s 213 Insolvency Act 1986.

Fraudulent trading is also a **criminal offence**; under s 993 of the Companies Act 2006 any person guilty of the offence, even if the company has not been or is not being wound up, is liable for a fine or imprisonment for up to 10 years.

If a company in insolvency proceedings is found to have traded when there is no reasonable prospect of avoiding insolvent liquidation, its directors may be liable under civil law for **wrongful trading**. Again a court may order such directors to make a contribution to the company's assets: s 214 Insolvency Act 1986.

9.1.3 Disqualified directors

Directors who participate in the management of a company in contravention of an order under the Company Directors Disqualification Act 1986 will be **jointly** or **severally liable** along with the company for the company's debts.

9.1.4 Abuse of company names

In the past there were a number of instances where directors of companies which went into **insolvent liquidation** formed another company with an identical or similar name. This new company bought the original company's business and assets from its liquidator.

The Insolvency Act 1986 (s 217) makes it a criminal offence and the directors personally liable where; they are a director of a company that goes into insolvent liquidation and; they become involved with the directing, managing or promoting of a business which has an **identical name** to the original company, or a **name similar** enough to suggest a connection.

9.2 Lifting the veil to prevent evasion of obligations

A company may be identified with those who control it, for instance to determine its residence for tax purposes. The courts may also ignore the distinction between a company and its members and managers if the latter use that distinction to **evade** their **existing legal obligations**. These are often known as **fraud or sham cases**.

> *Gilford Motor Co Ltd v Home 1933*
>
> *The facts:* The defendant had been employed by the claimant company under a contract which forbade him to solicit its customers after leaving its service. After the termination of his employment he formed a company of which his wife and an employee were the sole directors and shareholders. However he managed the company and through it evaded the covenant that prevented him from soliciting customers of his former employer.
>
> *Decision:* An injunction requiring observance of the covenant would be made both against the defendant and the company which he had formed as a 'a mere cloak or sham'.

9.2.1 Public interest and national emergency

In time of war a company is not permitted to trade with '**enemy aliens**'. The courts may draw aside the veil if, despite a company being registered in the UK, it is suspected that it is controlled by aliens.

The question of nationality may also arise in peacetime, where it is convenient for a foreign entity to have a British **facade** on its operations.

> *Re F G Films Ltd 1953*
>
> *The facts:* An English company was formed by an American company to 'make' a film which would obtain certain marketing and other advantages from being called a British film. Staff and finance were American and there were neither premises nor employees in England. The film was produced in India.
>
> *Decision:* The British company was the American company's agent and so the film did not qualify as British. Effectively, the corporate entity of the British company was swept away and it was exposed as a 'sham' company.

BPP
LEARNING MEDIA

9.2.2 Evasion of liabilities

The veil of may also be lifted where directors **ignore** the separate legal personality of two companies and transfer assets from one to the other in disregard of their duties in order to avoid an existing liability.

> *Re H and Others 1996*
>
> *The facts:* The court was asked to rule that various companies within a group, together with the minority shareholders, should be treated as one entity in order to restrain assets prior to trial.
>
> *Decision:* The order was granted. The court thought there was evidence that the companies had been used for the fraudulent evasion of excise duty.

9.2.3 Evasion of taxation

The court may lift the veil of incorporation where it is being used to **conceal** the nationality of the company.

> *Unit Construction Co Ltd v Bullock 1960*
>
> *The facts:* Three companies, wholly owned by a UK company, were registered in Kenya. Although the companies' constitutions required board meetings to be held in Kenya, all three were in fact managed by the holding company.
>
> *Decision:* The companies were resident in the UK and liable to UK tax. The Kenyan connection was a sham, the question being not where they ought to have been managed, but where they were actually managed.

9.2.4 Quasi-partnership

An application to wind up a company on the 'just and equitable' ground under the Insolvency Act 1986 may involve the court lifting the veil to reveal the company as a **quasi-partnership.** This may happen where the company only has a few members, all of whom are actively involved in its affairs. Typically the individuals have operated contentedly as a company for years but then fall out, and one or more of them seeks to remove the others.

The courts are willing in such cases to treat the central relationship between the directors as being that of partners, and rule that it would be unfair therefore to allow the company to continue with only some of its original members. This is illustrated by the case of *Ebrahimi v Westbourne Galleries Ltd 1973.*

Question	Quasi-partnerships

Sandy and Pat have carried on business together for twenty years, most recently through a limited company in which each holds 500 shares. They share the profits equally in the form of directors' remuneration. Pat's son Craig joins the business, buying 100 shares from each of Sandy and Pat. Disputes arise and Pat and Craig use their voting majority to remove Sandy from the board. Advise Sandy.

Answer

Sandy cannot prevent her removal from her directorship. However, a court may find that, on the basis of the past relationship, it is unjust and inequitable to determine the case solely on legal rights. It could, on equitable principles, order liquidation of the company. The veil of the company may be lifted to reveal a quasi-partnership.

9.3 Lifting the veil in group situations

The principle of the veil of incorporation extends to the holding (parent) company/subsidiary relationship. Although holding companies and subsidiaries are part of a group under company law, they retain their **separate legal personalities**. However, under **EU law**, the ECJ may treat groups of companies as **single economic units**.

Under English law, in *Adams v Cape Industries plc 1990*, three reasons were put forward for identifying the companies as one, and lifting the veil of incorporation. They are:

- The subsidiary is acting as **agent** for the holding company.
- The group is to be treated as a **single economic entity** because of statutory provision.
- The **corporate structure** is being used as a **facade** (or sham) to conceal the truth.

Adams v Cape Industries plc 1990

The facts: Cape, an English company, headed a group which included many wholly-owned subsidiaries. Some of these mined asbestos in South Africa, and others marketed the asbestos in various countries including the USA.

Several hundred claimants had been awarded damages by a Texas court for personal injuries suffered as a result of exposure to asbestos dust. The defendants in Texas included one of Cape's subsidiaries, NAAC. The courts also considered the position of AMC, another subsidiary, and CPC, a company linked to Cape Industries.

Decision: The judgement would not be enforced against the English holding company, either on the basis that Cape had been 'present' in the US through its local subsidiaries or because it had carried on business in the US through the agency of NAAC. Slade LJ commented in giving the judgement that English law 'for better or worse recognises the creation of subsidiary companies ... which would fall to be treated as separate legal entities, with all the rights and liabilities which would normally be attached to separate legal entities'.

Whether desirable or not, English law allowed a group structure to be used so that legal liability fell on an individual member of a group rather than the group as a whole.

Assessment focus point | Ensure you know the *Cape Industries* case and the three reasons for lifting the veil in groups which it sets out.

9.4 Summary of situations in which the veil can be lifted

The instances in which the veil will be lifted are as follows.

Lifting the veil by statute to enforce the law	<ul><li>Liability for trading without a trading certificate</li><li>Fraudulent and wrongful trading</li><li>Disqualified directors</li><li>Abuse of company names</li></ul>
Evasion of obligations	<ul><li>Evasion of legal obligations</li><li>Public interest</li><li>Evasion of liabilities</li><li>Evasion of taxation</li><li>Quasi-partnership</li></ul>
Group situations	<ul><li>Subsidiary acting as agent for the holding company</li><li>The group is to be treated as a single economic entity</li><li>The corporate structure is being used as a sham</li></ul>

BPP LEARNING MEDIA

9.5 Lifting the veil and limited liability

The above examples of lifting the veil include examples of where, if they have broken the law, **directors** can be made **personally liable** for a company's debts. This is very rare. If those directors are also members, then limited liability **does not apply**. This is the only time that limited liability is overridden and that the **member** becomes **personally liable** for the company's debts **due to their actions as a director.**

10 Comparison of companies and partnerships

FAST FORWARD Because it is a **separate legal entity**, a company has a number of features which are different from a partnership.

10.1 The differences

The following table sets out the key differences between companies and traditional partnerships.

Factor	Company	Traditional partnership
Entity	Is a legal entity separate from its members.	Has no existence outside of its members.
Liability	Members' liability can be limited	Partners' liability is usually unlimited
Size	May have any number of members	Some partnerships are limited to 20 members (not professional partnerships)
Succession	Perpetual succession – change in ownership does not affect existence	Partnerships are dissolved when any of the partners leaves it
Owners' interests	Members own transferable shares	Partners cannot assign their interests in a partnership
Assets	Company owns the assets	Partners own assets jointly
Management	Company must have at least one director (two for a public company)	All partners can participate in management
Constitution	Company must have a written constitution	A partnership may have a written partnership agreement, but also may not
Accounts	A company must usually deliver accounts to the Registrar	Partners do not have to send their accounts to the Registrar
Security	A company may offer a floating charge over its assets	A partnership may not usually give a floating charge on assets
Withdrawal of capital	Strict rules concerning repayment of subscribed capital	More straightforward for a partner to withdraw capital
Taxation	Company pays tax on its profit Directors are taxed through PAYE Shareholders receive dividends which are taxed 10 months after the tax year	Partners extract 'drawings' weekly or monthly. No tax is deducted. Income tax is payable on their share of the final profit for the year.
Management	Members elect directors to manage the company	All partners have a right to be involved in management

Chapter Roundup

- In a **sole tradership**, there is no legal distinction between the individual and the business.

- **Partnership** is defined as 'the relation which subsists between persons carrying on a business in common with a view of profit'. A partnership is *not* a separate legal person distinct from its members, it is merely a 'relation' between persons. Each partner (there must be at least two) is **personally liable** for all the debts of the firm.

- Partnerships can be **formed** very informally, but there may be complex formalities to ensure clarity.

- Partnerships may be **terminated** by passing of time, termination of the underlying venture, death or bankruptcy of a partner, illegality, notice, agreement or by order of the court.

- The **authority** of partners to bind each other in contract is based on the principles of agency.

- Partners are **jointly liable** for all partnership debts that result from contracts that the partners have made which bind the firm.

- **A limited liability partnership** formed under the 2000 Act combines the features of a traditional partnership with the limited liability and creation of a legal personality more usually associated with limited companies.

- A company has a **legal personality** separate from its owners (known as members). It is a formal arrangement, surrounded by formality and publicity, but its chief advantage is that members' **liability** for the company's debts is typically **limited**.

- The fact that a company's members – not the company itself – have **limited liability** for its debts **protects** the **members** from the company's creditors and ultimately from the full risk of business failure.

- Most companies are those **incorporated** under the **Companies Act**. However there are other types of company such as **corporations sole**, **chartered corporations**, **statutory corporations** and **community interest companies**.

- A company may be **private** or **public**. Only the latter may offer its shares to the public.

- To trade a public company must hold a **Registrar's trading certificate** having met the requirements, including **minimum capital** of £50,000.

- The main differences between public and private companies relate to: **capital**; **dealings** in shares, **accounts**; **commencement of business**; **general meetings**; **names**; **identification**; and **disclosure requirements**.

- There are a number of other ways in which companies can be **classified**.

- The case of *Salomon v Salomon & Co Ltd 1897* clearly demonstrates the **separate legal personality** of companies and is of great significance to any study of company law.

- Incorporation 'veils' members from outsiders' view but this veil may be lifted in **some circumstances**, so creditors and others can seek redress directly from members. The veil may be lifted: by statute to enforce the law; to prevent the evasion of obligations; and in certain situations where companies trade as a group.

- It is sometimes necessary by law to look at who the owners of a company are. This is referred to as **'lifting the veil'**.

- Because it is a **separate legal entity**, a company has a number of features which are different from a partnership.

BPP
LEARNING MEDIA

1   Only public companies can be quoted companies.

        True   ☐

        False   ☐

2   Which one of the following statements about traditional (unlimited) partnerships is incorrect?

        A   In England a partnership has no existence distinct from the partners.
        B   A partnership must have a written partnership agreement.
        C   A partnership is subject to the Partnership Act.
        D   Each partner is an agent of the firm.

3   An LLP dissolves when a member leaves.

        True   ☐

        False   ☐

4   Which two of the following statements are true? A private company

        A   Is defined as any company that is not a public company

        B   Sells its shares on the junior stock market known as the Alternative Investment Market and on the Stock Exchange

        C   Must have at least one director with unlimited liability

        D   Is a significant form of business organisation in areas of the economy that do not require large amounts of capital

5   Under which circumstance would a member of a limited company have to contribute funds on winding up?

        A   Where there is not enough cash to pay the creditors
        B   Where they have an outstanding amount from when they originally purchased their shares
        C   To allow the company to repurchase debentures it issued
        D   Where the company is a community interest company and the funds are required to complete a community project

6   A consequence of the principle of corporate personality is that company debts must be paid out of company assets.

        True   ☐

        False   ☐

7   Which of the following describes how a traditional (unlimited) partnership is taxed?

        A   The partnership pays tax on its profits
        B   The partners are taxed through the PAYE system
        C   The partners receive dividends on which they pay income tax
        D   Partners extract drawings on which they are subject to income tax

8   What was the name of the case that originally demonstrated the principle of separate legal personality?

9   Businesses in the form of sole traders are legally distinct from their owners.

True   ☐

False   ☐

10   Put the examples given below in the correct category box.

WHEN THE VEIL OF INCORPORATION IS LIFTED		
To enforce law	To enforce obligations	To expose groups

- Wrong use of company name
- Legal obligations
- Quasi-partnership
- Disqualified directors
- Fraudulent and wrongful trading
- Single economic entity
- Corporate structure a sham
- Public interest
- Trading without a trading certificate

Answers to Quick Quiz

1   True. Quoted companies are those listed on a stock exchange and therefore must be public companies.

2   B. A written agreement is not needed.

3   False. LLPs are only dissolved when they cease to trade.

4   A and D are correct. A private company cannot sell its shares to the public on any stock market, so B is incorrect. Directors need not have unlimited liability, so C is incorrect.

5   B. Members only have a liability for any outstanding amounts of share capital partly paid for.

6   True. Corporate personality is the principle that companies are legally distinct from their owners (the members).

7   D. In a partnership, the partners extract drawings on which they pay income tax. Partnerships do not themselves pay tax, partners are not employees and are therefore not taxed through the PAYE system, nor do they receive dividends from the partnership.

8   Salomon v Salomon Ltd 1897.

9   False. Sole trader businesses are not legally distinct from their owners.

10

WHEN THE VEIL OF INCORPORATION IS LIFTED		
To enforce law	**To enforce obligations**	**To expose groups**
Wrong use of company name Disqualified directors Fraudulent and wrongful trading Trading without a trading certificate	Legal obligations Quasi-partnership Public interest	Single economic entity Corporate structure a sham

Now try the questions below from the Question Bank

Number
Q41
Q42
Q43
Q44
Q45

Company formation

Introduction

Sections 1 to 3 of this chapter concentrate on the **procedural aspects** of **company formation**. Important topics in these sections include the **formalities** that a company must observe in order to be formed, and the liability of **promoters for pre-incorporation contracts**.

Sections 4 and 5 of this chapter consider the concept of the **public accountability** of **limited companies**. Later on in your coverage of the syllabus you will meet references to a company's obligation to publicise certain decisions, so it is important to understand at this stage how and why this should be done.

Topic list	Learning outcomes
1 Promoters and pre-incorporation contracts	G1(b), G1(e)
2 Pre-incorporation expenses and contracts	G1(b), G1(e)
3 Registration procedures	G1(b), G1(e)
4 Statutory books and records	G1(b), G1(e)
5 Statutory returns	G1(b), G1(e)

1 Promoters and pre-incorporation contracts

FAST FORWARD

> A promoter **forms** a company. They must act with **reasonable skill** and **care**, and if shares are to be allotted they are the agent of the company, with an agent's fiduciary duties.

A company cannot form itself. The person who forms it is called a '**promoter**'. A promoter is an example of an **agent**.

Key term

> A **promoter** is one who undertakes to form a company with reference to a given project and to set it going and who takes the necessary steps to accomplish that purpose: *Twycross v Grant 1877*.

In addition to the person who takes the procedural steps to get a company incorporated, the term 'promoter' includes anyone who makes **business preparations** for the company. **However** a person who acts **merely** in a **professional capacity** in company formation, such as a solicitor or an accountant, **is not** on that account a **promoter**.

1.1 Duties of promoters

Promoters have a general duty of **good faith** and to exercise **reasonable skill and care.**

If the promoter is to be the owner of the company there is no conflict of interest and it does not matter if the promoter obtains some advantage from this position, for example, by selling their existing business to the company for 100% of its shares.

If, however, **some or all the shares** of the company when formed **are to be allotted to other people**, the promoter is as **agent** of the company. This means they have the customary **duties** of an agent and the following fiduciary duties.

(a) A promoter must account for any **benefits obtained** through acting as a promoter.

(b) Promoters must not put themselves in a position where their own **interests conflict** with those of the company.

(c) A promoter must provide **full information** on their transactions and account for all monies arising from them. The promoter must therefore make **proper disclosure** of any personal advantage to **existing** and **prospective** company **members** or to an **independent board of directors**.

A promoter may make a **profit** as a result of their position.

(a) A **legitimate** profit is made by a promoter who acquires interest in property **before promoting** a company and then makes a profit when they sell the property to the promoted company, provided they disclose it.

(b) A **wrongful** profit is made by a promoter who enters into and makes a profit personally in a contract as a promoter. They are in breach of fiduciary duty.

A promoter of a public company makes their disclosure of **legitimate profit** through listing particulars or a prospectus. If they make proper disclosure of a legitimate profit, they may retain it.

BPP
LEARNING MEDIA

Which of the following describes the legal position concerning promoters making profits from their position in setting up a new company?

A   Promoters are not permitted to profit from their position

B   Promoters are only permitted to profit from selling property they own to the company providing their interest in the property is disclosed

C   Promoters are permitted to retain profits they make when setting up the company however they are obtained

D   Promoters are permitted to retain profits they make when setting up the company however they are obtained providing the directors approve it

Answer

B   Promoters are only permitted to make legitimate profit from their position. This means they can make a profit from selling the company property that they own, providing they disclose their interest.

2 Pre-incorporation expenses and contracts

FAST FORWARD
> A promoter has **no automatic right** to be reimbursed **pre-incorporation expenses** by the company, though this can be expressly agreed.

2.1 Pre-incorporation expenses

A promoter usually incurs **expenses** in preparations, such as drafting legal documents, made before the company is formed. They have **no automatic right to recover these 'pre-incorporation expenses'** from the company. However they can generally arrange that the first directors, of whom they may be one, **agree** that the company shall pay the bills or refund to them their expenditure. They could also include a special article in the company's constitution containing an indemnity for the promoter.

2.2 Pre-incorporation contracts

FAST FORWARD
> Pre-incorporation contracts **cannot** be ratified by the company. A new contract on the same terms must be created.

Key term

> A **pre-incorporation contract** is a contract purported to be made by a company or its agent at a time before the company has been formed.

In agency law a principal may ratify a contract made by an agent retrospectively. However, a company can **never ratify** a contract made on its behalf **before it was incorporated**. This is because it did not exist when the pre-incorporation contract was made.

2.3 Liability of promoters for pre-incorporation contracts

The company's **agent** is **liable** on a contract to which they are deemed to be a party. The agent may also be entitled to enforce the contract against the other party and so they could transfer the right to **enforce** the contract to the company. Liability is determined by s 51(1) of the Companies Act 2006.

'A contract that purports to be made by or on behalf of a company at a time when the company has not been formed has effect, subject to any agreement to the contrary, as one made with the person purporting to act for the company or as agent for it, and he is personally liable on the contract accordingly.'

2.4 Avoiding liability as a promoter for pre-incorporation contracts

There are various other ways for promoters to **avoid liability** for a pre-incorporation contract.

(a)   The contract remains as a **draft** (so not binding) until the company is formed. The promoters are the directors, and the company has the power to enter the contract. Once the company is formed, the directors take office and the company enters into the contract.

(b)   If the contract has to be finalised before incorporation it should contain a clause that the liability of promoters is to cease if the company, when formed, enters a **new contract** on identical terms. This is known as **novation**. However there must be **sufficient evidence** that the company has made a new contract. Mere recognition of the contract by performing it or accepting benefits under it is not the same as making a new contract.

(c)   A common way to avoid the problem concerning pre-incorporation contracts is to buy a company **'off the shelf'**. Even if a person contracts on behalf of the new company before it is bought the company should be able to ratify the contract since it existed 'on the shelf' at the time the contract was made.

(d)   A final method a promoter can use to avoid liability on pre-incorporation contracts is to **form the company ahead of any business activities** taking place. However, this may not be possible where the decision to setup a company and start trading is a 'spur-of-the-moment' decision.

Assessment focus point

A favourite question in law assessments is the status of a pre-incorporation contract.

Question   Promoter

Fiona is the promoter of Enterprise Ltd. Before the company is incorporated, she enters into a contract purportedly on its behalf. After the certificate of incorporation is issued, the contract is breached. Who is liable?

Answer

Fiona is liable as promoters are liable for pre-incorporation contracts: s 51(1).

BPP
LEARNING MEDIA

3 Registration procedures

FAST FORWARD

A company is **formed** and registered under the Companies Act 2006 when it is issued with a **certificate of incorporation** by the Registrar, after submission to the Registrar of a number of documents and a fee.

Most companies are registered under the **Companies Act 2006**.

A company is formed under the Companies Act 2006 by one or more persons subscribing to a **memorandum of association** who comply with the requirements regarding registration. A company may not be formed for an unlawful purpose.

3.1 Documents to be delivered to the Registrar

To obtain registration of a company limited by shares, an **application** for registration, **various documents** and a **fee** must be sent to the Registrar (usually electronically). If a quick service is required then **Companies House** operates a **same day incorporation service**. To take advantage of this, the promoter must complete and send in the necessary documentation by 3pm. This service is entirely different from purchasing an 'off-the-shelf' company where all the formalities for incorporation have already been completed.

3.1.1 Application for registration

S 9 requires an **application for registration** must be made and submitted to the Registrar with the other documents described in the table below.

The **application** must contain:

- The company's proposed name
- The location of its registered office (England and Wales, Wales, Scotland or Northern Ireland)
- That the liability of members is to be limited by shares or guarantee
- Whether the company is to be private or public.
- A statement of the intended address of the registered office.

Documents to be delivered	Description
Memorandum of association	This is a **prescribed form** signed by the subscribers. The memorandum states that the subscribers wish to form a company and they agree to become members of it. If the company has share capital each subscriber agrees to subscribe for at least one share.
Articles of association (only required if the company does not adopt model articles)	Articles are signed by the same subscriber(s), dated and witnessed. **Model articles** are provided by statute and can be adopted by a new company if: • No other articles are registered, or • If the articles supplied do not exclude or modify the model articles.
Statement of proposed officers	The statement gives the particulars of the proposed **director(s)** and **company secretary** if applicable. The persons named as directors must consent to act in this capacity. When the company is incorporated they are deemed to be appointed.
Statement of compliance	The statement that the **requirements** of the **Companies Act** in respect of registration have been **complied** with.

Documents to be delivered	Description
Statement of capital and initial shareholdings (only required for companies limited by shares)	A statement of capital and initial shareholdings must be delivered by all companies with **share capital**. Alternatively, a statement of guarantee is required by companies limited by guarantee.
Registration fee	A registration fee is also payable on registration.

Assessment focus point

Questions on incorporation could require you to identify the documents which should be sent to the Registrar.

3.2 Certificate of incorporation

The Registrar considers whether the documents are formally in order. If satisfied, the company is given a '**registered number**'. A **certificate of incorporation is** issued and notice of it is publicised.

A company is registered by the inclusion of the company in the register, and the issue of a **certificate of incorporation** by the Registrar. The certificate:

- Identifies the company by its name and registered number
- States that it is limited (if appropriate) and whether it is a private or public company
- States whether the registered office is in England and Wales, Wales, Scotland or Northern Ireland
- States the date of incorporation
- Is signed by the Registrar, or authenticated by the Registrar's official seal.

Key term

A **certificate of incorporation** is a certificate issued by the Registrar which denotes the date of incorporation, 'the subscribers, together with any persons who from time to time become members, become a body corporate capable of exercising all the functions of an incorporated company'.

The **certificate of incorporation** is **conclusive evidence** that:

- All the **requirements** of the **Companies Act** have been **followed.**
- The company is a **company authorised** to be **registered** and has been **duly registered.**
- If the certificate states that the company is a **public company** it is conclusive.

If irregularities in formation procedure or an error in the certificate itself are later discovered, the certificate is nonetheless **valid** and **conclusive:** *Jubilee Cotton Mills Ltd v Lewes 1924.*

Upon incorporation persons named as **directors** and **secretary** in the statement of proposed officers automatically become such officers.

3.3 Companies 'off the shelf'

FAST FORWARD

Buying a company '**off the shelf**' avoids the administrative burden of registering a company.

Because the registration of a new company can be a lengthy business, it is often easiest for people wishing to operate as a company to purchase an '**off the shelf**' company. This is possible by contacting enterprises specialising in registering a stock of companies, ready for sale when a person comes along who needs the advantages of incorporation.

Normally the persons associated with the company formation enterprise are registered as the company's subscribers, and its first secretary and director. When the company is purchased, the **shares** are **transferred** to the **buyer**, and the Registrar is notified of the director's and the secretary's resignation.

The principal **advantages** for the purchaser of purchasing an off the shelf company are as follows.

(a) The **following documents** will **not need** to be **filed** with the Registrar by the purchaser:

    (i) Memorandum and articles (unless the articles are not model articles)
    (ii) Application for registration
    (iii) Statement of proposed officers
    (iv) Statement of compliance
    (v) Statement of capital and initial shareholdings
    (vi) Fee

    This is because the specialist has already registered the company. It will therefore be a **quicker**, and very possibly **cheaper**, way of incorporating a business.

(b) There will be **no risk** of **potential liability** arising from pre-incorporation contracts. The company can trade without needing to worry about waiting for the Registrar's certificate of incorporation.

(c) **Formation dealers** may offer **advice** or **services**, such as acting as company secretary, which may be of great benefit to new companies and inexperienced directors.

The **disadvantages** relate to the changes that will be required to the off-the-shelf company to make it compatible with the members' needs.

(a) The off-the-shelf company is likely to have **model articles**. The directors may wish to amend these.

(b) The directors may want to **change** the **name** of the company.

(c) The **subscriber shares** will need to be **transferred**, and the transfer recorded in the register of members. Stamp duty will be payable.

Question
Documents required on formation of a company

What are the documents which must be delivered to the Registrar for registration of a company?

Answer

The memorandum of association (and articles if not in model form), application for registration, a statement of proposed officers, a statement of compliance, a statement of capital and initial shareholdings, and a fee.

3.4 Commencement of business rules

FAST FORWARD

To **trade** or **borrow**, a public company needs a **trading certificate**. Private companies may commence business on **registration**.

3.4.1 Public companies

A **public company** incorporated as such may not do business or exercise any borrowing powers unless it has obtained a **trading certificate** from the Registrar: s 761. This is obtained by sending an application to the Registrar. A private company which is re-registered as a public company is not subject to this rule.

The **application**:

- States the nominal value of the allotted share capital is not less than £50,000, or prescribed Euro equivalent (s 763)

- States the particulars of preliminary expenses and payments or benefits to promoters

- Must be accompanied by a statement of compliance.

If a public company does business or borrows before obtaining a certificate the other party is protected since the **transaction is valid**. However the company and any officer in default have committed an offence **punishable** by a **fine**. They may also have to indemnify the third party.

Under s 122 of the Insolvency Act 1986 a court may **wind-up** a public company which does not obtain a trading certificate within **one year** of incorporation.

3.4.2 Private company

A **private company** may do business and exercise its borrowing powers from the date of its incorporation. After registration the following procedures are important.

(a)   A **first meeting** of the directors should be held at which the chairman, secretary and sometimes the auditors are appointed, shares are allotted to raise capital, authority is given to open a bank account and other commercial arrangements are made.

(b)   A **return of allotments** should be made to the Registrar.

(c)   The company may give notice to the Registrar of the **accounting reference date** on which its annual accounts will be made up. If no such notice is given within the prescribed period, companies are deemed to have an accounting reference date of the **last day of the month** in which the **anniversary of incorporation** falls.

4 Statutory books and records

4.1 The requirement for public accountability

FAST FORWARD

The price of limited liability is greater **public accountability** via the Companies Registry, registers, the *London Gazette* and company letterheads.

Under company law the privileges of trading through a separate corporate body are matched by the duty to provide information which is available to the public about the company.

BPP
LEARNING MEDIA

Basic sources of information on UK companies

The Registrar keeps a file at **Companies House** which holds all documents delivered by the company for filing. Any member of the public, for example someone who intends to do business with the company, may inspect the file (usually electronically).

The **registers and other documents** which the company is required to hold at its registered office (or in some cases at a different address).

The *London Gazette*, a specialist publication, in which the company itself or the Registrar is required to publish certain notices or publicise the receipt of certain documents.

The **company's letterheads** and other forms which must give particulars of the company's place of registration, its identifying number and the address of its office.

4.2 The Registrar of Companies

The **Registrar of Companies** (the Registrar) and the Registrar's department within the Government is usually called Companies House (in full it is 'the Companies Registration Office').

For **English** and **Welsh** companies the Registrar is located at the Companies House in **Cardiff**; for **Scottish** companies the Registrar is in **Edinburgh**.

The company is identified by its **name** and **serial number** which must be stated on every document sent to Companies House for filing.

On first incorporation the company's file includes a copy of its **certificate of incorporation** and the **original documents** presented to secure its incorporation.

Once a company has been in existence for some time the **file** is likely to include the following.

- Certificate of incorporation
- Public company trading certificate
- Each year's annual accounts and return
- Copies of special and some ordinary resolutions
- A copy of the altered articles of association if relevant
- Notices of various events such as a change of directors or secretary
- If a company issues a prospectus, a signed copy with all annexed documents

4.3 Statutory books

FAST FORWARD

A company must keep **registers** of certain aspects of its constitution, including the registers of members, charges and directors.

Various people are entitled to have access to **registers** and copies of records that the company must keep, so the company must keep them at its registered office or another location permitted by the secretary of state if the Registrar is notified.

Register/copies of records	Relevant CA2006 section
Register of **members**	s 113
Register of **charges**	s 876
Register of **directors (and secretaries)**	s 162 and s 275
Records of **directors' service contracts and indemnities**	s 228 and s 237
Records of **resolutions and meetings** of the company	s 355
Register of **debentureholders**	s 743
Register of disclosed **interests** in shares (public company ONLY)	s 808

4.4 Register of members

Every company must keep a **register of members**. It must contain:

(a)   The **name** and **address** of **each member**

(b)   **The shareholder class** (if more than one) to which they belong unless this is indicated in the particulars of their shareholding

(c)   If the company has a share capital, the **number of shares** held by each member. In addition:

    (i)   If the shares have **distinguishing numbers**, the member's shares must be identified in the register by those numbers

    (ii)   If the company has more than one class of share the member's shares must be **distinguished** by their **class**, such as preference, ordinary, or non-voting shares

(d)   The date on which each member **became** and eventually the date on which they **ceased** to be a member

The company may choose where it keeps the register of members available for **inspection** from:

- The registered office
- Another office of the company
- The office of a professional registrar

Any **member of the company** can **inspect the register of members** of a company **without charge**. A member of the public must pay but has the right of inspection.

A company with more than 50 members must keep a **separate index** of those members, unless the register itself functions as an index.

4.5 Register of charges

The register of charges must contain:

- **Details of fixed or floating charges** affecting the company property or undertaking
- **Brief descriptions** of property charged
- The **amount** of the charge
- The **name** of the person entitled to the charge

A company must also keep copies of every **instrument creating a charge** at its registered office or some other designated place notified to the Registrar. Any person may inspect the instruments and the charges register; members and creditors may inspect free of charge.

BPP
LEARNING MEDIA

4.6 Register of directors

The **register of directors** must be held at the **company's registered office** and contain the following details in respect of a director who is an individual (that is, not a company).

- **Present** and **former** forenames and surnames
- A **service address** (may be the company's registered address rather than the director's home address)
- **Residency** and **nationality**
- **Business occupation** (if any)
- **Date of birth**

The register does not include **shadow directors**. It must be open to inspection by a member (free of charge), or by any other person (for a fee).

Note the company must keep a separate **register** of **directors' residential addresses** but this is not available to members or the general public.

4.6.1 Corporate directors

Where a **legal person** (such as a company) is a director, the register of directors must contain:

- The corporate or firm name
- Its registered or principal office

4.6.2 Records of directors' interests

Copies of **directors' interests in the company's shares and debentures** must be kept. All interests must be shown (for example, company charges and share options) and this includes the interests of spouses and children.

4.7 Records of directors' service contracts

The company should keep **copies** or written memoranda of all **service contracts** for its directors, including contracts for services which are not performed in the capacity of director. Members are entitled to view these copies for free, or request a copy on payment of a set fee.

Key term

> Under s 227 a director's **service contract**, means a contract under which:
>
> (a)   A director of the company undertakes personally to perform services (as director or otherwise) for a company, or for a subsidiary of the company, or
>
> (b)   Services (as director or otherwise) that a director of the company undertakes personally to perform are made available by a third party to the company, or to a subsidiary of the company.

4.8 Register of debentureholders

Companies with debentures issued nearly always keep a **register of debentureholders**, but there is no statutory compulsion to do so. If a register of debentureholders is maintained, it should be held at the **registered office** or another location permitted by the Secretary of State and notified to the Registrar.

4.9 Accounting records

FAST FORWARD

Companies must keep **sufficient accounting records** to explain the company's transactions and its financial position, in other words so a profit and loss account and balance sheet can be prepared.

A company is required to keep accounting records sufficient to **show and explain** the company's transactions. At any time, it should be possible:

- To **disclose** with reasonable accuracy the **company's financial position** at intervals of not more than six months

- For the directors to ensure that any accounts required to be prepared **comply** with the **Act** and **International Accounting Standards**

Certain **specific records** are required by the Act.

(a)   Daily entries of **sums paid** and **received**, with details of the source and nature of the transactions

(b)   A **record** of **assets** and **liabilities**

(c)   **Statements of stock** held by the company at the end of each financial year

(d)   **Statements of stocktaking** to back up the records in (c)

(e)   **Statements of goods bought and sold** (except retail sales), together with details of buyers and sellers sufficient to identify them

The requirements (c) to (e) above apply only to businesses involved in **dealing in goods**.

Accounting records must be kept for **three** years (in the case of a **private** company), and **six** years in that of a **public** one.

Accounting records should be kept at the company's **registered office** or at some other place thought fit by the directors. Accounting records should be open to **inspection** by the **company's officers**. Shareholders have **no statutory rights** to inspect the records, although they may be granted the right by the articles.

Failure in respect of these duties is an **offence** by the officers in default.

4.10 Annual accounts

FAST FORWARD

A registered company must prepare **annual accounts** showing a true and fair view, lay them and various reports before members, and file them with the Registrar following directors' approval.

For each **accounting reference period** (usually 12 months) of the company the directors must prepare accounts. Where they are prepared in Companies Act format they must include a statement of financial position (**balance sheet**) and income statement (**profit and loss account**) which give a **true and fair view** of the individual company's and the group's

- Assets
- Liabilities
- Financial position
- Profit or loss

The accounts can either be in **Companies Act format** or prepared in accordance with **International Accounting Standards**. Where international accounting standards are followed a note to this effect must be included in the notes to the accounts.

Most private companies are permitted to file **abbreviated accounts**.

The company's board of directors must **approve** the **annual accounts** and they must be signed by a director on behalf of the board. When directors approve annual accounts that do not comply with the Act or IAS they are **guilty** of an **offence.**

A public company is required to **lay its accounts**, and the **directors' report**, before **members** in **general meeting**. A quoted company must also lay the directors' remuneration report before the general meeting.

A company must file its annual accounts and its report with the **Registrar** within a maximum period reckoned from the date to which the accounts are made up. The standard permitted interval between the end of the accounting period and the filing of accounts is **six months** for a **public** and **nine months** for a **private company.**

The accounts must be **audited**. The **auditors' report** must be attached to the copies issued to members, filed with the Registrar or published. Exemptions apply to **small and dormant companies,** though members may require an audit. The accounts must also be accompanied by a **directors' report** giving information on a number of prescribed matters. These include (where an audit was necessary) a statement that there is no relevant information of which the auditors are unaware, and another statement from the directors that they exercised due skill and care in the period. Quoted companies must submit the **directors' remuneration report**.

Each **member** and **debentureholder** is entitled to be sent a copy of the **annual accounts**, together with the directors' and auditor's reports. In the case of public companies, they should be sent at least 21 days before the meeting at which they shall be laid. In the case of private companies they should be sent at the same time as the documents are filed, if not earlier.

Anyone else entitled to **receive** notice of a general meeting, including the company's auditor, should **also be sent** a copy. At any other time any member or debentureholder is entitled to a copy free of charge within **seven days** of requesting it.

All companies may prepare a summary financial statements to be circulated to members instead of the full accounts, subject to various requirements as to form and content being met. However, members have the right to receive full accounts should they wish to.

Quoted companies must make their annual accounts and reports available on a website which is maintained on the company's behalf and which identifies it. The documents must be made available as soon as reasonably practicable and access should not be conditional on the payment of a fee or subject to other restrictions.

Where the company or its directors **fail to comply** with the Act, they may be subject to a **fine**.

Question	Accounting records

To meet the minimum requirements of the Companies Act, how long should a public company keep its accounting records for?

A   1 year
B   3 years
C   6 years
D   7 years

C   Public companies are required to keep their accounting records for 6 years. The figure is 3 years for private companies.

5 Statutory returns

FAST FORWARD

Every company must make an **annual return** to the Registrar.

Every company must make an annual return each year to the Registrar which is made up to a 'return date'. This date is either the **anniversary of incorporation** or the **anniversary of the date** of the previous return (if this differs). The return must be delivered to the Registrar within **28 days** of the return date and be **accompanied** by a fee.

The **form of the annual return** prescribed for a company which has share capital is:

- The address of the **registered office** of the company

- The address (if different) at which the **register of members** or **debentureholders** is kept

- The type of company and its principal **business activities**

- The total number of **issued shares,** their **aggregate nominal value** and the amounts paid and unpaid on each share

- For each **class of share**, the **rights** of those shares, the **total number** of shares in that class and their **total nominal value**

- Particulars of **members** of the company

- Particulars of those who have **ceased** to be members since the last return

- The number of shares of each **class** held by members at the return date, and transferred by members since incorporation or the last return date

- The particulars of **directors,** and **secretary (if applicable)**

Question

Records and returns

Which of the following must be filed with the Registrar each year?

A   Accounts
B   Register of members
C   Copies of directors' service contracts
D   The annual return

Answer

A and D. Only the accounts and annual return would be filed. The register of members and copies of directors' service contracts are held by the company and are not required by the Registrar.

Chapter Roundup

- A promoter **forms** a company. They must act with **reasonable skill** and **care**, and if shares are allotted they are the agent of the company, with an agent's fiduciary duties.

- A promoter has **no automatic right** to be reimbursed pre-incorporation expenses by the company, though this can be expressly agreed.

- Pre-incorporation contracts **cannot** be ratified by the company. A new contract on the same terms must be created.

- A company is **formed and registered** under the Companies Act 2006 when it is issued with a **certificate of incorporation** by the Registrar, after submission to the Registrar of a number of documents and a fee.

- Buying a company **'off the shelf'** avoids the administrative burden of registering a company.

- To **trade** or **borrow**, a public company needs a **trading certificate**. Private companies may commence business on **registration**.

- The price of limited liability is greater **public accountability** is via the Companies Registry, registers, the *London Gazette* and company letterheads.

- A company must keep **registers** of certain aspects of its constitution, including the registers of members, charges and directors.

- Companies must keep **sufficient accounting records** to explain the company's transactions and its financial position, in other words so a profit and loss account and balance sheet can be prepared.

- A registered company must prepare **annual accounts** showing a true and fair view, lay them and various reports before members, and file them with the Registrar following directors' approval.

- Every company must make an **annual return** to the Registrar.

1   A company can confirm a pre-incorporation contract by performing it or obtaining benefits from it.

   True   ☐

   False ☐

2   If a public company does business or borrows before obtaining a trading certificate from the Registrar, the transaction is:

   A   Invalid, and the third party cannot recover any loss
   B   Invalid, but the third party may recover any loss from the directors
   C   Valid, and the directors are punishable by a fine
   D   Valid, but the third party can sue the directors for further damages

3   A company must keep a register of directors. What details must be revealed?

   A   Full name
   B   Service address
   C   Nationality
   D   Date of birth
   E   Business occupation

4   An accountant or solicitor acting in their professional capacity during the registration of a company may be deemed a promoter.

   True   ☐

   False ☐

5   If a certificate of incorporation is dated 6 March, but is not signed and issued until 8 March, when is the company deemed to have come into existence?

6   Within how many days of its return date must a company's annual return be submitted to the Registrar?

   A   7 days
   B   14days
   C   21 days
   D   28 days

7   Wooddan Ltd was registered on 6th March 20X7 by a business which specialises in setting up and selling 'off-the-shelf' companies. On 7th June 20X8 Woodan Ltd is brought by a promoter, Niall, who is setting up a new business. As part of setting up the business, Niall entered into a contract to lease some office space. This contract was signed on 4th April 20X7. Niall would like Woodan Ltd to ratify the contract for the lease so he is no longer liable on it.

   Which of the following describes the legal position?

   A   Wooddan Ltd cannot ratify the contract as Niall did not own the company when the lease was entered into

   B   Wooddan Ltd can ratify the contract as it existed when the contract was entered into

   C   Wooddan Ltd cannot ratify the contract because it only existed as an off-the-shelf company when the contract was signed and as such could not be party to it

   D   Wooddan Ltd can ratify the contract providing the company which set it up agrees

8   As part of the registration procedure for all companies, a statement of capital and initial shareholdings must be submitted.

True ☐

False ☐

9   Where is the Registrar of Companies for English and Welsh companies based?

A   London
B   Birmingham
C   Cardiff
D   Edinburgh

10   All directors must be natural (living) persons.

True ☐

False ☐

BPP LEARNING MEDIA

1   False. The company must make a new contract on similar terms.

2   C. The directors are punished for allowing the company to trade before it is allowed to.

3   All of them.

4   False. A person acting in a professional capacity will not be deemed a promoter.

5   6 March. The date on the certificate is conclusive.

6   D. Annual returns must be submitted to the Registrar within 28 days of the return date.

7   B. As long as the company is registered before the date that the contract (which the promoter wants it to be a party to) is signed, then the company can ratify that contract.

8   False. A statement of guarantee is required instead for companies limited by guarantee.

9   C. The Registrar of Companies for English and Welsh companies is based in Cardiff. The Registrar of Scottish companies is based in Edinburgh.

10 False. Companies and other legal persons may be directors.

Now try the questions below from the Question Bank

Number
Q46
Q47
Q48
Q49
Q50

A company's constitution

11

Introduction

This chapter considers the constitution of a company, which is mainly the **articles of association**. However, the memorandum has some historical importance.

Section 3 considers the **objects** of a company – these determine its legal capacity. If a company acts outside its legal capacity, the rights of third parties are protected.

Section 4 of this chapter introduces the **constitution as a contract** between the company and its members. It is important to realise that this contract only applies to members in their capacity as members, not as third parties.

Lastly in this chapter, we look at the rules concerning the choice of **company name** and on the **registered office**.

Topic list	Learning outcomes
1 Memorandum of association	G1(c), G1(e)
2 A company's constitution	G1(c), G1(e)
3 Company objects	G1(d), G1(e)
4 The constitution as a contract	G1(d), G1(e)
5 Company name and registered office	G1(b), G1(e)

1 Memorandum of association

FAST FORWARD

> The memorandum is a **simple document** which states that the subscribers wish to form a company and become members of it.

Before the Companies Act 2006, the **memorandum of association** was an extremely important document containing information concerning the relationship between the company and the outside world – for example its aims and purpose (its objects).

The position changed with the 2006 Act and much of the information contained in the old memorandum is now to be found in the Articles of Association, which we will come to shortly. The **essence** of the memorandum has been retained, although it is now a very simple historical document which states that the **subscribers** (the initial shareholders):

(a) Wish to **form a company** under the Act, and

(b) Agree to **become members** of the company and, to take at least one share each if the company is to have share capital.

The memorandum must be in the **prescribed form** and must be **signed** by each subscriber.

It has been deemed by the Companies Act 2006 that companies which were incorporated under a **previous** Act and whose memorandum contains provisions now found in the articles, shall have these provisions interpreted as if they are part of the articles.

2 A company's constitution

FAST FORWARD

> A **company's constitution** comprises the **Articles of Association** and any **resolutions and agreements** it makes which affect the constitution.

According to s 17 of the Companies Act 2006, the constitution of a company consists of:

- The **Articles of Association**
- **Resolutions and agreements** that it makes that affects the constitution

We shall consider resolutions and agreements first as an understanding of what they are is required to understand how the Articles of Association are amended.

2.1 Resolutions and agreements

In addition to the main **constitutional document** (the Articles of Association), **resolutions** and **agreements** also form part of a company's constitution.

Resolutions directly affect the constitution of a company as they are used to **introduce** new provisions, or to **amend** or **remove** existing ones. **Agreements** made, for example between the company and members of specific classes of share are also deemed as amending the constitution.

Copies of resolutions or agreements that amend the constitution must be sent to the Registrar within **15 days** of being passed or agreed. If a company fails to do this then every officer who is in default commits an offence punishable by fine. Where a **resolution** or **agreement** which affects a company's constitution is **not in writing**, the company is required to send the registrar a **written memorandum** that sets out the terms of the resolution or agreement in question.

2.2 Articles of Association

Key term

> **Articles of Association** consist of the internal rules that relate to the management and administration of the company.

The articles contain detailed **rules** and **regulations** setting out how the company is to be **managed** and **administered**. The Act states that the registered articles should be contained in a **single document** which is divided into **consecutively numbered paragraphs**. Articles contain rules on a number of areas, the most important being summarised below.

CONTENTS OF ARTICLES	
Appointment and dismissal of directors	Communication with members
Powers, responsibilities and liabilities of directors	Class meetings
Directors' meetings	Issue of shares
General meetings; calling, conduct and voting	Transfer of shares
Members' rights	Documents and records
Dividends	Company secretary

2.2.1 Model articles

Rather than each company having to draft their own articles, and to allow companies to be set up **quickly** and **easily**, the Act allows the Secretary of State to provide **model** (or standard) **articles** that companies can adopt. Different models are available for different types of company; most companies would adopt model **private** or **public company** articles.

Companies are free to use **any** of the model articles that they wish to by registering them on incorporation. If **no articles** are registered then the company will be **automatically incorporated** with the **default model articles** which are relevant to the type of company being formed. Model articles can be **amended** by the members and therefore tailored to the specific needs of the company.

Model articles are effectively a **'safety net'** which allow directors and members to take decisions if the company has failed to include suitable provisions in its registered articles or registered no articles at all. The following summarises the **model articles for a private limited company**. Do not try to learn the contents but use it to understand the type of information contained in them.

Model articles for private companies limited by shares

Index to the articles

Part 1 Definitions and interpretation

1. Defined terms
2. Liability of members

Part 2 Directors

Directors' powers and responsibilities

3. Directors' general authority
4. Shareholders' reserve power
5. Directors may delegate
6. Committees

Decision-making by directors

7. Directors to take decisions collectively
8. Unanimous decisions
9. Calling a directors' meeting
10. Participation in directors' meetings
11. Quorum for directors' meetings
12. Chairing of directors' meetings
13. Casting vote
14. Conflicts of interest
15. Records of decisions to be kept
16. Directors' discretion to make further rules

Appointment of directors

17. Methods of appointing directors
18. Termination of director's appointment
19. Directors' remuneration
20. Directors' expenses

Part 3 Shares and distributions

Shares

21. All shares to be fully paid up
22. Powers to issue different classes of share
23. Company not bound by less than absolute interests
24. Share certificates
25. Replacement share certificates
26. Share transfers
27. Transmission of shares
28. Exercise of transmittees' rights
29. Transmittees bound by prior notices

Dividends and other distributions

30. Procedure for declaring dividends
31. Payment of dividends and other distributions
32. No interest on distributions
33. Unclaimed distributions
34. Non-cash distributions
35. Waiver of distributions

Capitalisation of profits

36. Authority to capitalise and appropriation of capitalised sums

Part 4 Decision-making by shareholders

Organisation of general meetings

37. Attendance and speaking at general meetings
38. Quorum for general meetings
39. Chairing of general meetings
40. Attendance and speaking by directors and non-shareholders
41. Adjournment

Voting at general meetings

42. Voting: general
43. Errors and disputes
44. Poll votes
45. Content of proxy notices
46. Delivery of proxy notices
47. Amendments to resolutions

Part 5 Administrative arrangements

48. Means of communication to be used
49. Company seals
50. No right to inspect accounts and other records
51. Provision for employees on cessation of business

Directors' indemnity and insurance

52. Indemnity
53. Insurance

2.2.2 Alteration of the articles

FAST FORWARD

> The articles may be altered by a **special resolution**. The basic test is whether the alteration is for the **benefit of the company as a whole.**

Any company has a statutory power to alter its articles by **special resolution:** s 21. A private company may pass a **written resolution** with a **75% majority.** The alteration will be valid and binding on **all** members of the company. **Copies** of the amended articles must be sent to the **Registrar**, within 15 days of the amendment, taking effect.

2.2.3 Making the company's constitution unalterable

There are devices by which some provisions of the company's constitution can be made **unalterable** unless the member who wishes to prevent any alteration consents.

(a) The articles may give to a member **additional votes** so that he can block a resolution to alter articles on particular points (including the removal of his weighted voting rights from the articles): *Bushell v Faith 1970*. However, to be effective, the articles must also limit the powers of members to alter the articles that give extra votes.

(b) The articles may provide that when a meeting is held to vote on a proposed alteration of the articles the **quorum present must include** the **member concerned**. They can then deny the meeting a quorum by absenting themselves.

(c) Section 22 of the Act permits companies to **'entrench' provisions** in its articles. This means specific provisions may only be **amended** or **removed** if certain **conditions** are met which are more restrictive than a special resolution such as agreement of all the members. However, such 'entrenched provisions' **cannot** be drafted so that the articles can never be amended or removed.

2.2.4 Restrictions on alteration

Even when it is possible to hold a meeting and pass a special resolution, alteration of the articles is **restricted** by the following principles.

(a) The alteration is **void** if it **conflicts with the Companies Act** or with general law.

(b) In various circumstances, such as to protect a minority (s 994), the **court may order** that an alteration be made or, alternatively, that an existing article shall not be altered.

(c) An existing **member may not be compelled** by alteration of the articles to **subscribe for additional shares** or to accept increased liability for the shares which they hold unless they have given their consent: s 25.

(d) An alteration of the articles which varies the rights attached to a class of shares may only be made if the **correct rights variation procedure** has been followed to obtain the consent of the class: s 630. A 15 per cent minority may apply to the court to cancel the variation under s 633.

(e) A person whose **contract** is contained in the articles cannot obtain an injunction to prevent the articles being altered, **but** they may be entitled to **damages** for breach of contract: *Southern Foundries 1926 Ltd v Shirlaw 1940*. Alteration cannot take away rights already acquired by performing the contract.

(f) An alteration may be **void** if the **majority** who approve it are **not acting *bona fide* in what they deem to be the interests of the company as a whole** (see below).

The case law on the **bona fide test** is an effort to hold the balance between two principles:

(a) The **majority** is **entitled** to **alter articles** even though a minority considers that the alteration is prejudicial to its interests.

(b) A minority is entitled to protection against an alteration which is intended to **benefit** the **majority** rather than the company and which is **unjustified discrimination** against the minority.

Principle (b) tends to be **restricted** to cases where the majority seeks to expel the minority from the company.

The most elaborate analysis of this subject was made by the Court of Appeal in the case of *Greenhalgh v Arderne Cinemas Ltd 1950*. Two main propositions were laid down by Evershed MR.

(a) **'Bona fide for the benefit of the company as a whole'** is a **single test** and also a **subjective test** (what did the majority believe?). The court will not substitute its own view.

(b) 'The company as a whole' means, in this context, **the general body of shareholders.** The test is whether every 'individual hypothetical member' would in the honest opinion of the majority benefit from the alteration.

If the purpose is to benefit the company as a whole the alteration is valid even though it can be shown that the minority does in fact suffer special detriment and that other members escape loss. In *Allen v Gold Reefs of West Africa Ltd 1900* the articles were altered to extend the company's lien from just partly paid shares to all shares. In fact only one member held fully paid shares.

The court **overruled his objections** on the grounds that the:

- Alteration was for the **benefit of the company as a whole** and applied to any member who held fully paid shares.

- Members held their shares **subject to the constitution**, and were subject to any changes to those documents.

2.2.5 Expulsion of minorities

Expulsion cases are concerned with:

- Alteration of the articles for the purpose of **removing** a **director from office**

- Alteration of the articles to permit a majority of members to **enforce** a **transfer** to themselves of the shareholding of a minority

The action of the majority in altering the articles to achieve 'expulsion' will generally be treated as **valid** even though it is discriminatory, if the majority were concerned to **benefit the company** or to remove some detriment to its interests.

If on the other hand the majority was **blatantly seeking** to secure an **advantage** to themselves by their discrimination, the alteration made to the articles by their voting control of the company will be invalid. The cases below illustrate how the distinctions are applied in practice.

Shuttleworth v Cox Bros & Co (Maidenhead) Ltd 1927

The facts: Expulsion of director appointed by the articles who had failed to account for funds was held to be valid.

Sidebottom v Kershaw, Leese & Co Ltd 1920

The facts: The articles were altered to enable the directors to purchase at a fair price the shareholding of any member who competed with the company in its business. The minority against whom the new article was aimed did carry on a competing business. They challenged the validity of the alteration on the ground that it was an abuse of majority power to 'expel' a member.

Decision: There was no objection to a power of 'expulsion' by this means. It was a justifiable alteration if made *bona fide* in the interests of the company as a whole. On the facts this was justifiable.

Brown v British Abrasive Wheel Co 1919

The facts: The company needed further capital. The majority who held 98 per cent of the existing shares were willing to provide more capital but only if they could buy up the 2 per cent minority. As the minority refused to sell, the majority proposed to alter the articles to provide for compulsory acquisition on a fair value basis. The minority objected to the alteration.

Decision: The alteration was invalid since it was merely for the benefit of the majority. It was not an alteration 'directly concerned with the provision of further capital' and therefore not for the benefit of the company.

Dafen Tinplate Co Ltd v Llanelly Steel Co (1907) Ltd 1920

The facts: The claimant was a minority shareholder which had transferred its custom from the defendant company to another supplier. The majority shareholders of the defendant company sought to protect their interests by altering the articles to provide for compulsory acquisition of the claimant's shares.

The new article was not restricted (as it was in *Sidebottom's* case above) to acquisition of shares on specific grounds where benefit to the company would result. It was simply expressed as a power to acquire the shares of a member. The claimant objected that the alteration was invalid since it was not for the benefit of the company.

Decision: The alteration was invalid because it 'enables the majority of the shareholders to compel any shareholder to transfer his shares'. This wide power could not 'properly be said to be for the benefit of the company'. The mere unexpressed intention to use the power in a particular way was not enough.

Therefore if the majority intend that the power to acquire the shares of a minority is to be restricted to **specific circumstances** for the benefit of the company, they should ensure that this restriction is included in the new article.

Question

Explain the nature of the model articles of association under the Companies Act 2006.

Answer

The model articles are a single document containing model rules and regulations concerning the management and administration of a company. They can be amended by the company but do not need to be to have effect.

2.2.6 Filing of alteration

Whenever any alteration is made to the articles a copy of the altered articles must be delivered to the Registrar within **15 days**, together with a signed copy of the special resolution making the alteration.

2.2.7 Interaction of statute and articles

There are two aspects to consider.

(a) The Companies Act may permit companies to do something **if** their **articles** authorise it. If, however, they do not, then the company must **alter** the articles to include the **necessary power** before it may exercise the statutory power.

(b) The Companies Act will **override** the articles:

   (i)   If the Companies Act prohibits something

   (ii) If something is permitted by the Companies Act only by a special procedure (such as passing a special resolution in general meeting)

3 Company objects

FAST FORWARD

A **company's objects** are its aims and purposes. If a company enters into a contract which is outside its objects, that contract is said to be **ultra vires.** However the rights of third parties to the contract are protected.

3.1 The objects

The objects are the **'aims'** and **'purposes'** of a company. Under previous companies legislation they were held in a specific clause within the memorandum of association. This clause set out everything the company could do, including being a 'general commercial company' which meant it could pretty much do anything.

The 2006 Act changed matters. The objects could now be found in the **articles** but most articles will **not** mention any. This is because under the Act a company's objects are **completely unrestricted** (ie it can carry out any lawful activity). Only if the company wishes to restrict its activities is there an inclusion of those **restrictions** in the articles: s 31.

BPP
LEARNING MEDIA

3.1.1 Alteration of the objects

As a company's objects are located in its articles it may, under s 21, alter its objects by **special resolution** for any reason. The procedure is the same as for any other type of alteration.

3.2 Contractual capacity and *ultra vires*

FAST FORWARD

Companies may only act in accordance with their **objects**. If the directors permit an act which is restricted by the company's objects then the act is *ultra vires*.

Key terms

Ultra vires is where a company exceeds its objects and acts outside its capacity.

Companies which have **unrestricted objects** are highly unlikely to act *ultra vires* since their constitution permits them to do anything. Where a company has restrictions placed on its objects and it breaches these restrictions then it would be acting *ultra vires*.

Ashbury Railway Carriage & Iron Co Ltd v Riche 1875

The facts: The company had an objects clause which stated that its objects were to make and sell, or lend on hire, railway carriages and wagons and all kinds of railway plant, fittings, machinery and rolling stock; and to carry on business as mechanical engineers. The company bought a concession to build a railway in Belgium, subcontracting the work to the defendant. Later the company repudiated the contract.

Decision: Constructing a railway was not within the company's objects so the company did not have capacity to enter into either the concession contract or the sub-contract. The contract was void for *ultra vires* and so the defendant had no right to damages for breach. The members could not ratify it and the company could neither enforce the contract nor be forced into performing its obligations.

The approach taken by the Companies Act 2006 is to give **security** to commercial transactions for **third parties**, whilst preserving the rights of shareholders to restrain directors from entering an *ultra vires* action.

S 39 provides as follows:

'the validity of an act done by a company shall not be called into question on the ground of lack of capacity by reason of anything in the company's constitution.'

S 40 provides as follows:

'in favour of a person dealing with a company in good faith, the power of the directors to bind the company, or authorise others to do so, shall be deemed to be free of any limitation under the company's constitution.'

There are a number of points to note about s 40.

(a) The section applies in favour of the **person dealing with the company**, it does not apply to the members.

(b) In contrast with s 39 **good faith** is required on the part of the third party. The company has, however, to prove lack of good faith in the third party and this may turn out to be quite difficult: s 40(2).

(c) The **third party** is not required to **enquire** whether or not there are any **restrictions** placed on the power of directors: s 40(2). They are free to assume the directors have any power they profess to have.

(d) The section covers not only acts beyond the capacity of the company, but acts beyond **'any limitation under the company's constitution'**.

Whilst sections 39 and 40 deal with the company's transactions with **third parties**, the **members** may take action against the directors for permitting *ultra vires* acts. Their action will be based on the fact that the **objects specifically restricted** the particular act and under section 171, the **directors** must **abide** by the **company's constitution**.

The main problem for **members** is that they are most likely to be **aware** of the *ultra vires* act only **after** it has occurred. Therefore they are not normally in a position to prevent it, although in theory they could seek an **injunction** if they found out about the potential *ultra vires* act before it took place.

Question   Capacity to contract

Describe how a company's capacity to contract can be regulated and what third parties may assume when entering into a contract with the company.

Answer

A company's capacity to contract is regulated by its members passing resolutions which restrict its objects. Under section 40(2) of the Act, third parties can assume the directors have the necessary power to authorise the act.

Assessment focus point

Make sure you understand how s 39 and s 40 protect third parties.

3.3 Transactions with directors

S 41 of the Companies Act 2006 applies when the company enters into a contract with one of its **directors**, or its holding company, or any **person connected** with such a director. Contracts made between the company and these parties are **voidable** by the company if the director acts outside their capacity.

Whether or not the contract is avoided, the party and any authorising director is liable to repay any profit they made or make good any losses that result from such a contract.

4 The constitution as a contract

FAST FORWARD

The articles **constitute a contract** between:

- Company and members
- Members and the company
- Members and members

The articles **do not constitute** a contract between the **company** and **third parties**, or members in a **capacity** other than as **members** (the *Eley* case).

4.1 Effect

A **company's constitution bind**, under s 33:

- Members to company
- Company to members (but see below)
- Members to members

The company's constitution does **not** bind the company to third parties. This principle applies only to rights and obligations which affect members **in their capacity as members**.

Hickman v Kent or Romney Marsh Sheepbreeders Association 1915

The facts: The claimant (H) was in dispute with the company which had threatened to expel him from membership. The articles provided that disputes between the company and its members should be submitted to arbitration. H, in breach of that article, began an action in court against the company.

Decision: The proceedings would be stayed since the dispute (which related to matters affecting H as a member) must, in conformity with the articles, be submitted to arbitration.

The principle that only rights and obligations of members are covered by s 33 applies when an outsider who is also a member seeks to rely on the articles in support of a claim made as an **outsider**.

Eley v Positive Government Security Life Assurance Co 1876

The facts: E, a solicitor, drafted the original articles and included a provision that the company must always employ him as its solicitor. E became a member of the company some months after its incorporation. He later sued the company for breach of contract in not employing him as its solicitor.

Decision: E could not rely on the article since it was a contract between the company and its members and he was not asserting any claim as a member.

4.2 Constitution as a contract between members

S 33 gives to the **constitution** the effect of a contract made between (a) the **company** and (b) its **members individually**. It can also impose a contract on the members in their dealings with each other.

Rayfield v Hands 1958

The facts: The articles required that (a) every director should be a shareholder and (b) the directors must purchase the shares of any member who gave them notice of his wish to dispose of them. The directors, however, denied that a member could enforce the obligation on them to acquire his shares.

Decision: There was 'a contract ... between a member and member-directors in relation to their holdings of the company's shares in its articles' and the directors were bound by it.

Articles and resolutions are usually **drafted** so that each stage is a dealing between the company and the members, to which s 33 clearly applies, so that:

(a)   A member who intends to transfer his shares must give notice of his intention to the company.
(b)   The company must then give notice to other members that they have an option to take up his shares.

4.3 Constitution as a supplement to contracts

FAST FORWARD

The constitution can be used to **establish the terms** of a contract existing elsewhere.

If an outsider makes a **separate contract** with the company and that contract contains no specific term on a particular point but the constitution does, then the contract is deemed to incorporate the constitution to that extent.

One example is when services, say as a director, are provided under contract without agreement as to remuneration: *Re New British Iron Co, ex parte Beckwith 1898*.

If a contract incorporates terms of the articles it is subject to the company's **right** to **alter** its articles: *Shuttleworth v Cox Bros & Co (Maidenhead) Ltd 1927*. However a company's articles cannot be altered to deprive another person of a right already earned, say for services rendered **prior** to the alteration.

Point to note

> Remember the articles only create contractual rights/obligations in relation to rights **as a member**.

4.4 Shareholder agreements

FAST FORWARD

> **Shareholders' agreements** sometimes supplement a company's constitution.

Shareholder agreements are concerned with the **running of the company**; in particular they often contain terms by which the shareholders agree how they will vote on various issues.

They offer more protection to the interests of shareholders than do the articles of association. Individuals have a **power of veto** over any proposal which is contrary to the terms of the agreement. This enables a minority shareholder to protect his interests against unfavourable decisions of the majority.

Question   Constitution

State the parties who are bound by a company's articles.

Answer

The company is bound to the members, the members to the company and the members to the other members in their capacity as members.

5 Company name and registered office

FAST FORWARD

> Except in **certain circumstances** a company's name must end with the words limited (Ltd), public limited company (plc) or the Welsh equivalents.

A company's name is its **identity.** There are a number of rules which restrict the choice of name that a company may adopt.

5.1 Statutory rules on the choice of company name

FAST FORWARD

> No company may use a name which is:
>
> * The **same** as an existing company on the Registrar's index of company names
> * A **criminal offence, offensive,** or '**sensitive**'
> * Suggest a **connection** with the **government or local authority** (unless approved)

BPP
LEARNING MEDIA

The **choice of name** of a limited company must conform to the following rules.

(a) The name must **end** with the word(s):

    (i) **Public limited company** (abbreviated **plc**) if it is a public company

    (ii) **Limited** (or Ltd) if it is a private limited company, unless permitted to omit 'limited' from its name

    (iii) The **Welsh equivalents** of either (i) or (ii) may be used by a Welsh company

(b) No company may have a name which is the **same** as any other company appearing in the statutory index at Companies House. For this purpose two names are treated as 'the same' in spite of minor or non-essential differences. For instance the word 'the' as the first word in the name is ignored. 'John Smith Limited' is treated the same as 'John Smith' (an unlimited company) or 'John Smith & Company Ltd'. Where a company has a name which is the same or too similar to another, the Secretary of State may direct the company to **change its name**.

(c) No company may have a name the use of which would be a **criminal** offence or which is considered **offensive** or **'sensitive'** (as defined by the Secretary of State).

(d) Official approval is required for a name which in the Registrar's opinion suggests a **connection** with the **government** or a **local authority** or which is subject to **control**.

A name which suggests some professional expertise such as 'optician' will only be permitted if the appropriate representative association has been consulted and raises no objection.

The general purpose of the rule is to **prevent** a company **misleading** the public as to its real circumstances or activities. Certain names may be approved by the Secretary of State on written application.

5.2 Omission of the word 'limited'

A private company which is a charity and a company limited by shares or guarantee and licensed to do so before 25 February 1982 may omit the word 'limited' from its name if the following conditions are satisfied.

(a) The objects of the company must be the **promotion** of either commerce, art, science, education, religion, charity or any profession (or anything incidental or conducive to such objects).

(b) The memorandum or articles must require that the **profits** or other income of the company are to be **applied to promoting** its objects and no dividends or return of capital may be paid to its members. Also on liquidation the **assets** (otherwise distributable to members) are to be **transferred** to another body with similar objects. The articles must not then be altered so that the company's status to omit 'Limited' is lost.

5.3 Change of name

A company may decide to **change its name** by:

(a) Passing a **special resolution**

(b) By **any other means** provided for in the **articles** (in other words the company can specify its own procedure for changing its name).

Where a **special resolution** has been passed, the **Registrar** should be notified and a copy of the resolution sent. If the change was made by **any other procedure** covered by (b), the Registrar should be notified and a statement provided which states that the change has been made in accordance with the articles.

The change is effective from when a new **incorporation certificate is issued**, although the company is still treated as the same legal entity as before. The same limitations as above apply to adoption of a name by change of name as by incorporation of a new company.

5.4 Passing-off action

A person who considers that their rights have been infringed can apply for an injunction to restrain a company from using a name (**even if** the name has been duly registered). It can do this if the name suggests that the latter company is carrying on the business of the complainant or is otherwise connected with it.

A company can be **prevented** by an **injunction** issued by the court in a **passing-off action** from **using** its **registered name**, if in doing so it causes its goods to be confused with those of the claimant.

Ewing v Buttercup Margarine Co Ltd 1917

The facts: The claimant had since 1904 run a chain of 150 shops in Scotland and the north of England through which he sold margarine and tea. He traded as 'The Buttercup Dairy Co'. The defendant was a registered company formed in 1916 with the name above. It sold margarine as a wholesaler in the London area. The defendant contended that there was unlikely to be confusion between the goods sold by the two concerns.

Decision: An injunction would be granted to restrain the defendants from the use of its name since the claimant had the established connection under the Buttercup name. He planned to open shops in the south of England and if the defendants sold margarine retail, there could be confusion between the two businesses.

If, however, the two companies' businesses are different, confusion is unlikely to occur, and hence the courts will refuse to grant an injunction: *Dunlop Pneumatic Tyre Co Ltd v Dunlop Motor Co Ltd 1907*

The complaint will not succeed if the claimant lays claim to the exclusive use of a word which has a general use: *Aerators Ltd v Tollit 1902.*

5.5 Appeal to the Company Names Adjudicator

A company which feels that another company's name which is **too similar** to its own may object to the Company Names Adjudicator under the Companies Act. The Adjudicator will review the case and, within **90 days**, make their decision and provide their reasons for it in public. In most cases the Adjudicator will require the offending company to **change its name** to one which does not breach the rules. In some cases the **Adjudicator may determine** the new name.

An appeal against the decision may be made in Court. The Court may **reverse** the Adjudicator's decision, **affirm** it and may even **determine** a new name.

 Question

Company name

Do It Yourself Ltd was incorporated on 1 September 20X7. On 1 October 20X7 the directors received a letter from DIY Ltd stating that it was incorporated in 19X4, that its business was being adversely affected by the use of the new company's name, and demanding that Do It Yourself Ltd change its name.

Advise Do It Yourself Ltd.

BPP
LEARNING MEDIA

DIY Ltd may seek to bring a 'passing-off action'. This is a common law action which applies when one company believes that another's conduct (which may be the use of a company name) is causing confusion in the minds of the public over the goods which each company sells. DIY Ltd would apply to the court for an injunction to prevent Do It Yourself Ltd from using its name.

However, in order to be successful, DIY Ltd will need to satisfy the court that confusion has arisen because of Do It Yourself Ltd's use of its registered name and that it lays claim to something exclusive and distinctive and not something in general use: *Aerators Ltd v Tollit 1902*.

Appeal to Company Names Adjudicator

Alternatively DIY Ltd might object to the Company Names Adjudicator that the name Do It Yourself Ltd is too like its own name and is causing confusion, thus appealing to compel a change of name. In these circumstances, the Adjudicator would hear the case and make a decision. If they compel a name change Do It Yourself Ltd may appeal to the court.

5.6 Publication of the company's name

The **company's name** must appear **legibly** and **conspicuously**:

- Outside the registered office and all places of business.

- On all business letters, order forms, notices and official publications.

- On all receipts and invoices issued on the company's behalf.

- On all bills of exchange, letters of credit, promissory notes, cheques and orders for money or goods purporting to be signed by, or on behalf, of the company

- On its **website**

5.7 Business names other than the corporate name

Key term

> A **business name** is a name used by a company which is different from the company's corporate name or by a firm which is different from the name(s) of the proprietor or the partners.

Most companies trade under their own **registered names**. However a company may prefer to use some other name.

The rules require any person or organisation who carries on business under a **different name** from his own:

(a) To **state** its **name**, registered **number** and registered **address** on all **business letters (including emails)**, invoices, receipts, written orders for goods or services and written demands for payment of debts.

(b) To **display** its **name** and **address** in a **prominent position** in any **business premises** to which its customers and suppliers have access.

(c) On **request** from any **person** with whom it does business to give **notice** of its name and address.

5.8 Registered office

Section 86 of the Companies Act 2006 provides that a company must at all times have a **registered office** to which all communications and notices can be sent. Its location – in England and Wales, just in Wales or in Scotland – determines the company's domicile. It may **change its registered office** (not its country of domicile) under section 87 by notifying the Registrar, but for a period of 14 days after notice is served any person may validly present documents to the previous address.

BPP
LEARNING MEDIA

- The memorandum is a **simple document** which states that the subscribers wish to form a company and become members of it.

- A **company's constitution** comprises the **Articles of Association** and any **resolutions and agreements** it makes which affect the constitution.

- The articles may be altered by a **special resolution**. The basic test is whether the alteration is for the **benefit of the company as a whole**.

- A **company's objects** are its aims and purposes. If a company enters into a contract which is outside its objects, that contract is said to be **ultra vires**. However the rights of third parties to the contract are protected.

- Companies may only act in accordance with their **objects**. If the directors permit an act which is restricted by the company's objects then the act is *ultra vires*.

- The articles **constitute** a **contract** between:

    – Company and members
    – Members and the company
    – Members and members

- The articles **do not constitute** a contract between the **company** and **third parties**, or members in a **capacity** other than as **members** (the *Eley* case).

- The constitution can be used to **establish the terms** of a contract existing elsewhere.

- **Shareholders' agreements** sometimes supplement a company's constitution.

- Except in **certain circumstances** the name must end with the words limited (Ltd), public limited company (plc) or the Welsh equivalents.

- No company may use a name which is:

    – The **same** as an existing company on the Registrar's index of company names
    – A **criminal offence, offensive** or **'sensitive'**
    – Suggest a **connection** with the **government** or **local authority** (unless approved)

Quick Quiz

1   Percy Limited has recently formed a contract with a third party which is restricted by the objects in the company's constitution.

Which of the following statements is incorrect?

A   The validity of the act cannot be questioned on the grounds of lack of capacity by reason of anything in the company's constitution.

B   The act may be restrained by the members of Percy Ltd.

C   The act may be enforced by the company and the third party.

D   The directors have a duty to observe any limitation on their powers flowing from the company's constitution.

2   If a company wishes to restrict its objects, what kind of resolution is required?

A   Special resolution
B   Special resolution with special notice
C   Ordinary resolution with special notice
D   Ordinary resolution

3   A company has been formed within the last six months. Another long-established company considers that because of similarity between names there may be confusion between it and the new company. The only action the long-established company can take is to bring a passing-off action if it is to prevent the new company using its name.

True ☐

False ☐

4   Which of the following persons are not bound to one another by the constitution?

A   Members to company
B   Company to members
C   Members to members
D   Company to third parties

5   How long does a company have to file amended articles with the Registrar if they have been altered?

A   14 days
B   15 days
C   21 days
D   28 days

6   The memorandum of association is a document signed by the subscribers which states that they wish to form a company and that they all agree to become members of the company and to take at least one share (if the company is to have share capital).

True ☐

False ☐

7   Which of the following would be a valid alteration of a company's articles of association?

A   An alteration which permits the directors to defraud customers
B   An alteration which compels members to subscribe for additional shares
C   An alteration which benefits a small minority of members rather than the company as a whole
D   An alteration which gives members additional votes if they face removal from the company

8   A company's articles of association will always override the Companies Act 2006.

    True ☐
    False ☐

9   A limited company's name must always end with:

    A   Public Limited Company or PLC
    B   Limited Company or Ltd
    C   Co or Inc
    D   LLP

10 Once registered, a company may:

    A   Change the location of its registered office and its domicile
    B   Change the location of its registered office but not its domicile
    C   Change the location of its domicile but not its registered office
    D   Change neither the location of its registered office, nor its domicile

Answers to Quick Quiz

1   A, C and D are true. Members can only act before the contract is signed, so B is incorrect.

2   A. A special resolution is required to restrict the objects as with any alteration to the articles in general.

3   False. The long-established company can also complain to the Company Names Adjudicator.

4   A, B and C are correct: s 33. D is incorrect, illustrated by *Eley v Positive Government Security Life Assurance Co Ltd 1876.*

5   B. A company has 15 days to file amended articles with the Registrar.

6   True. This is the memorandum of association.

7   D. Such an alteration would be valid. Alterations may not contravene general law (as in A), compel members to subscribe for additional shares (B) or not be bona fide in the interests of the company as a whole.

8   False. The Companies Act 2006 will override a company's articles where it prohibits a company doing something.

9   B. A limited company's name must always end with Limited Company or Ltd.

10   B. A company may change the location of its registered office, but not its domicile (the part of the UK it is registered – England and Wales, Wales or Scotland).

Now try the questions below from the Question Bank

Number
Q51
Q52
Q53
Q54
Q55

Part E

Corporate administration and management

BPP
LEARNING MEDIA

12

Meetings and resolutions

Introduction

In this chapter we consider the **procedures** by which companies are managed and controlled, namely board and general meetings. **Board meetings** are where directors meet to discuss management issues. **General meetings** afford members a measure of protection of their investment in the company. There are many transactions which, under the Act, cannot be entered into without a **resolution** of the company in general meeting.

Moreover, a general meeting at which the annual accounts and the auditors' and directors' reports will be laid must normally be held annually, thus affording the members an opportunity of questioning the directors on their **stewardship**.

For the assessment you must be quite clear about the **different types of resolution**, when each type is used, and the percentage vote needed for each type to be passed.

Topic list	Learning outcomes
1 The importance of meetings	G1(f)
2 Board meetings	G1(f), G1(g)
3 General meetings	G1(f)
4 Types of resolution	G1(f), G1(h)
5 Calling a meeting	G1(f)
6 Proceedings at meetings	G1(f), G1(g)
7 Class meetings	G1(f)
8 Single member private companies	G1(f)

1 The importance of meetings

FAST FORWARD

Although the management of a company, is in the hands of the directors, the **decisions which affect the existence of the company**, its structure and scope are **reserved to the members** in general meeting.

The decision of a general meeting is only valid and binding if the meeting is **properly convened** by notice and if the **business** of the meeting is **fairly** and **properly conducted**. Most of the rules on company meetings are concerned with the issue of notices and the casting of votes at meetings to carry resolutions of specified types.

1.1 Control over directors

The members in general meeting can exercise **control over the directors**, though only to a limited extent.

(a) Under normal procedure **one half** of the **directors retire** at each annual general meeting though they may offer themselves for re-election. The company may remove directors from office by **ordinary resolution**: s 168.

(b) **Member approval** in general meeting is required if the directors wish to:

 (i) **Exceed their delegated power** or to use it for other than its given purpose
 (ii) **Allot shares** (unless private company with one class of shares)
 (iii) **Make a substantial contract** of sale or purchase with a director
 (iv) Grant a director a **long-service agreement**

(c) The **appointment and removal of auditors** is normally done in general meeting.

1.2 Resolution of differences

In addition, general meetings are the means by which **members resolve differences** between themselves by voting on resolutions.

2 Board meetings

FAST FORWARD

The directors can exercise their powers by holding **board meetings**.

2.1 Introduction

One of the basic principles of company law is that the powers which are delegated to the directors under the articles are given to them as a **collective body.** The **board meeting** is the proper place for the exercise of those powers.

Key term

> The **board of directors** is the elected representative of the shareholders acting collectively in the management of a company's affairs.

The directors can **unanimously assent** on issues without meeting by a 'signed resolution procedure' . Any resolution signed by all the directors entitled to attend a board meeting will be valid, as if it had been decided at a board meeting.

BPP LEARNING MEDIA

2.2 Content of the notice

Notice of the business, in the form of an agenda, is usually given. Some items of business are discussion of lengthy papers, such as management reports or proposals for new projects. Directors cannot usually discuss such matters adequately without having read the papers before the meeting.

The period of notice given to convene a board meeting need be **no longer** than is **reasonable** to enable directors to attend. Even five minutes' notice has been held reasonable, where the director in question was free to attend and close at hand.

2.3 Quorum for a board meeting

In order to constitute a board meeting, as any other a **properly appointed chairman** must preside, and a quorum must be present.

Most companies have model articles which provide that:

> '*The quorum for directors meetings may be fixed from time to time by a decision of directors and unless otherwise fixed shall be two.*'

Note also that on each item of business, any director who is disqualified from voting by having a **personal interest** may have to be excluded in reckoning the quorum for that item.

2.4 The chairman

The directors of a company may appoint one of their number to be **chairman** of the board of directors, and may at any time remove the chairman of the board from his office.

The chairman presides at meetings of the board, and is responsible for:

- **Ensuring** that the **functions** of the **board** are **carried out**

- Ensuring that the **meeting proceeds** in an **efficient manner**, without unnecessary or irrelevant discussion, and with a reasonable cross-section of views being heard

- **Providing** an **agenda** for the board meetings (and any necessary documentation, although the secretary would handle the paperwork)

2.5 Agenda for a board meeting

The agenda will **vary** according to the **type** and **formality** of the **meeting** and the particular business to be discussed. A typical agenda might include the following.

- Membership
- Apologies for absence
- Minutes of the last meeting
- Matters arising from the minutes
- Business of the present meeting, presentation of reports, resolutions etc.
- Any other business
- Date of the next meeting

2.6 Conduct of board meetings

There are some aspects of **procedure** which should be strictly observed.

(a) The discussion should **follow** the **sequence** of the **agenda**, and be confined at each stage to the item currently under discussion.

(b) Although it is not usually necessary to take a vote, the chairman should sum up **'the sense of the meeting'**, so that a suitably worded decision or conclusion may be formulated for inclusion in the minutes.

(c) If a vote does appear to be necessary, it will be along the lines of a show of hands or voice vote. The usual procedure is to **'go round the table'** inviting each member of the board to declare his vote for or against. If any member abstains, perhaps because a personal interest does not allow him to vote, this should be noted and recorded.

(d) Each member of the board, including the chairman, has **one vote**. The **articles** may provide otherwise, say by weighted voting or a veto given to a particular director. The chairman **may** also be given a casting vote, with which to resolve a tied issue.

2.7 Sole director and board meetings

In *Re Neptune Vehicle Washing Equipment Ltd 1995* it was held that a **sole director** could hold a meeting with a company secretary or by himself. Even if holding a meeting alone a director had to make and minute a declaration of interests in contracts, pausing for thought over potential conflicts of interest.

Question

Board meetings

According to model articles, what is the quorum for a board meeting?

A   1 director
B   2 directors
C   3 directors
D   4 directors

Answer

B   Unless altered, model articles provide that the quorum for a board meeting is 2 directors.

3 General meetings

FAST FORWARD

There are two kinds of general meeting of members of a company:

* **Annual general meeting (AGM)**
* **General meetings at other times**

3.1 Annual general meeting (AGM)

The **AGM** plays a major role in the life of a public company although often the business carried out seems fairly routine. It is a statutorily protected way for members to have a regular assessment and discussion of their company and its management.

Private companies are **not required** to have an **AGM** each year and therefore their business is usually conducted through **written resolutions**. However, members holding sufficient shares or votes can request a general meeting or written resolution.

Rules for directors calling an AGM	
Timing s 336	• Public companies must hold an AGM within **six months** of their year end
Notice s 337	• Must be in **writing** and in **accordance** with the **articles**
	• May be in **hard** or **electronic form** and may also by means of a **website** (s 308)
	• At least **21 days notice** should be given; a longer period may be specified in the articles
	• Shorter notice is only **valid** if all members agree
	• The notice must specify the **time**, **date** and **place** of the meeting and that the meeting is an AGM
	• Where notice is given on a **website** it must be available from the **date of notification** until the **conclusion of the meeting** (s 309)

The **business** of an **annual general meeting** usually includes:

- Considering the accounts
- Receiving the directors' report, the directors' remuneration report and the auditors' report
- Dividends
- Electing directors
- Appointing auditors

3.2 General meetings

3.2.1 Directors

The **directors** may have power under the articles to convene a general meeting whenever they see fit.

3.2.2 Members

The directors of **public and private** companies may be required to convene a general meeting by **requisition of the members:** s 303.

Rules for members requisitioning a general meeting (s 303)	
Shareholding	• The requisitioning members of public companies must hold at least **10%** of the **paid up share capital** holding **voting rights**. In private companies they need either **5%** or **10%**, depending on when there was last a meeting at which the members had a right to vote. Over 12 months ago = 5%; under 12 months = 10%
Requisition	• They must deposit a **signed requisition** at the registered office or make the request in electronic form
	• This must state the 'objects of the meeting': the **resolutions proposed** (s 303(5))

Rules for members requisitioning a general meeting (s 303)	
Date	• A notice conveying the meeting must be set out within **21 days** of the requisition
	• It must be held within **28 days** of the notice calling to a meeting being sent out.
	• If the directors have not called the meeting within 21 days of the requisition, the **members may convene** the meeting for a date within 3 months of the deposit of the requisition at the **company's expense**.
Quorum	• If **no quorum** is present, the meeting is **adjourned**.

3.2.3 Court order

The **court**, on the application of a director or a member entitled to vote, **may order that a meeting shall be held** and may give instructions for that purpose including fixing a quorum of one: s 306.

This is a method of last resort to resolve a **deadlock** such as the refusal of one member out of two to attend (and provide a quorum) at a general meeting.

3.2.4 Auditor requisition

An auditor who gives a **statement of circumstances** for their resignation or other loss of office in their written notice may also requisition a meeting to receive and consider their explanation: s 518.

3.2.5 Loss of capital by public company

The directors of a **public company** must convene a general meeting if the **net assets fall to half or less of the amount of its called-up share capital**: s 656.

Question

Public company meetings

Public companies must convene a general meeting if:

A   Requested to by any director
B   Requested to by any member
C   Its net assets fall to less than half of the amount of its called-up share capital
D   If the market value of its shares falls to less than half of the value its called-up share capital

Answer

C   A public company must convene a general meeting if its net assets fall to less than half the amount of its called-up share capital.

4 Types of resolution

FAST FORWARD

A meeting can pass two types of resolution. **Ordinary resolutions** are carried by a simple majority (more than 50%) of votes cast and requiring 14 days notice. **Special resolutions** require a 75% majority of votes cast and also 14 days notice.

BPP
LEARNING MEDIA

A meeting reaches a decision by passing a resolution (either by a show of hands or a poll). There are **two major kinds** of resolution, and an additional one for **private** companies.

Types of resolution	
Ordinary (s 282)	For most business Requires simple (50%+) majority of the votes cast 14 days notice
Special (s 283)	For major changes Requires 75% majority of the votes cast 14 days notice
Written (for private companies)	Can be used for all general meeting resolutions except for removing a director or auditor before their term of office expires. Either a simple (50%+) or 75% majority is required depending on the business being passed.

4.1 Differences between ordinary and special resolutions

Apart from the required size of the majority and period of notice, the main differences between the types of resolution are as follows.

(a) The **text** of **special resolutions** must be **set out** in **full** in the notice convening the meeting, and it must be described as a special resolution. This is not necessary for an ordinary resolution if it is routine business.

(b) A **signed copy** of every **special resolution** must be **delivered** to the **Registrar** for filing within **15 days** of being passed. **Some ordinary resolutions**, particularly those relating to share capital, have to be **delivered** for filing but many do not.

4.2 Special resolutions

A special resolution is required for **major changes** in the company such as the following.

- A change of name
- Restriction of the objects or other alteration of the articles
- Reduction of share capital
- Winding up the company
- Presenting a petition by the company for an order for a compulsory winding up

Question

Notice period

The period of notice for a general meeting at which a special resolution is proposed is:

A   14 days
B   28 days
C   21 days
D   42 days

Answer

A   A general meeting at which a special resolution is proposed requires 14 days notice.

4.3 Written resolutions

A private company can pass any decision needed by a **written resolution**, except for removing a director or auditor before their term of office has expired.

As we saw earlier, a private company is **not** required to hold an **AGM**. Therefore the Act provides a mechanism for directors and members to conduct business solely by **written resolution**.

4.3.1 Written resolutions proposed by directors

Copies of the resolution proposed by directors must be sent to **each member** eligible to vote by hard copy, electronically or by a website. Alternatively, the same copy may be sent to each member in turn. The resolution should be accompanied by a statement informing the member:

- How to **signify their agreement** to the resolution
- The **date** the resolution must be passed by

4.3.2 Written resolutions proposed by members

Members holding 5% (or lower if authorised by the articles) of the **voting rights** may request a written resolution providing it:

- **Would be effective** (not prevented by the articles or law)
- Is **not defamatory, frivolous** or **vexatious**

A **statement** containing no more than **1,000 words** on the subject of the resolution may accompany it.

Copies of the resolution, and statements containing information on the subject matter, how to agree to it and the date of the resolution must be sent to each member within **21 days** of the request for resolution.

Expenses for circulating the resolution **should be met by the members** who requested it unless the company resolves otherwise. The company may **appeal to the court** not to circulate the 1,000 word statement by the members if the rights provided to the members are being abused by them.

4.3.3 Agreement

The members may indicate their agreement to the resolution in **hard copy** or **electronically**.

If no **period for agreement** is specified by the articles, then the default period is **28 days** from the date the resolution was circulated. Agreement after this period is ineffective. Once agreed, a member **may not revoke** their decision.

Either a **simple** (50% plus one) or **75% majority** is required to pass a written resolution depending on the nature of the business being decided.

Three further points should be noted concerning **written resolutions**.

(a) Written resolutions can be used **notwithstanding any provisions** in the company's **articles**.

(b) A written resolution **cannot** be **used to remove a director or auditor** from office, since such persons have a right to **speak** at a **meeting**.

(c) **Copies of written resolutions** should be **sent to auditors** at or before the time they are sent to shareholders. Auditors do not have the right to object to written resolutions. If the auditors are not sent a copy, the resolution remains valid; however the directors and secretary will be liable to a fine. The purpose of this provision is to ensure auditors are kept informed about what is happening in the company.

Briefly explain the main features of the following types of resolution which may be passed at a general meeting of a company:

(a)   An ordinary resolution

(b)   A special resolution

Answer

(a)   Ordinary resolutions require a simple majority of votes cast (ie over 50%). 14 days notice is sufficient. Ordinary resolutions of a routine nature need not be set out in full in the notice of an annual general meeting, and most ordinary resolutions need not be filed with the Registrar.

(b)   Special resolutions require a 75% majority of votes cast and also require 14 days notice of the intention to propose such a resolution. The full text of the resolution should be set out in the notice.

5 Calling a meeting

FAST FORWARD

A meeting cannot make valid and binding decisions until it has been properly convened. Notice of general meetings must be given **14 days** in advance of the meeting. The notice should contain **adequate information** about the meeting.

Meetings must be called by a **competent person** or authority.

A meeting cannot make valid and binding decisions until it has been properly convened according to the company's articles, though there are also statutory rules.

(a)   The meeting must generally be **called by** the **board of directors** or other competent person or authority.

(b)   The notice must be issued to members in advance of the meeting so as to give them **14 days** 'clear notice' of the meeting. The members may agree to waive this requirement (see below).

(c)   The **notice** must be sent to every member (or other person) entitled to receive the notice.

(d)   The notice must include any information **reasonably necessary** to enable shareholders to know in advance what is to be done.

(e)   As we saw earlier members may require the directors to call a meeting if:

        (i)   They hold at least **10% of the voting rights** (5% for a private company if 12 months have elapsed since the last meeting)

        (ii)   They provide a **statement of the general business** to be conducted and the text of any proposed resolution

        The directors must within **21 days call a meeting** to be held no later than **28 days from the date of the notice** they send calling the meeting.

In most cases the notice need **not** be sent to a member whose only shares do not give him a right to attend and vote (as is often the position of **preference shareholders**).

5.1 Electronic communication

We have already seen that **notice** may be given by means of a **website** and in **electronic form** (s 308). Section 333 extends this by deeming that where a company gives an **electronic address** in a notice calling a meeting, any information or document relating to the meeting may be sent to that address.

5.2 Timing of notices

Clear notice must be given to members. **Notice** must be **sent to all members** entitled to receive it.

Members may – and in small private companies often do – waive the required notice. For **short notice** to be effective:

    (a)   All **members** of a public company must consent in respect of an **AGM**.

    (b)   In **any other case** a **majority of members** who hold at least **90 per cent** of the **issued shares** or voting rights must consent. 95% is required by a public company.

The following specific rules by way of exception should be remembered.

- When **special notice** of a resolution is given to the company to remove a director or auditor it must be given **28 days** in advance as prescribed.

- In a **creditors' voluntary winding up** there must be at least **7 days notice** of the **creditors' meeting** (to protect the interests of creditors). The members may shorten the period of notice down to 7 days but that is all: s 98 IA.

The **clear days rule** in s 360 provides that the day of the meeting and the day the notice was given are **excluded** from the required notice period.

5.3 Special notice of a resolution

Special notice of 28 days of intention to propose certain resolutions (removal of directors/auditors) must be given.

Key term

Special notice is notice of 28 days which must be given to a company of the intention to put certain types of resolution at a company meeting.

Special notice must be given **to the company** of the intention to propose a resolution for any of the following purposes.

- To **remove** an **auditor** or to **appoint** an **auditor other** than the **auditor** who was **appointed** at the **previous year's meeting**

- To **remove a director from office** or to appoint a substitute in their place after removal

A member may request a resolution to be passed at a particular meeting. In this case, the **member must give special notice** of their intention **to the company** at **least 28 days** before the date of the meeting. If, however, the company calls the meeting for a date less than 28 days after receiving the special notice that notice is deemed to have been **properly given**.

On receiving special notice a **public company may be obliged** to **include the resolution** in the **AGM notice** which it issues.

If the company gives notice to members of the resolution it does so by a **21 day notice** to them that special notice has been received and what it contains. If it is not practicable to include the matter in the notice of meeting, the company may give notice to members by newspaper advertisement or any other means permitted by the articles.

Where special notice is received of intention to propose a resolution for the removal of a director or to change the auditor, the company must send a copy to the **director** or **auditor**. This is to allow them to exercise their statutory right to defend themselves by issuing a memorandum and/or addressing the meeting in person.

The essential point is that a **special notice is given to the company**; it is **not a notice from the company to members** although it will be followed (usually) by such notice.

5.4 Members requisitioning a resolution

FAST FORWARD

Members rather than directors may be able to requisition resolutions. This may be achieved by requesting the directors call a meeting, or proposing a resolution to be voted on at a meeting already arranged.

The directors normally have the **right to decide** what resolutions shall be included in the notice of a meeting. However, apart from the requisition to call a general meeting, members can also take the initiative to requisition certain resolutions be considered at the AGM.

Rules for members requisitioning a resolution at the AGM	
Qualifying holding (s 338)	• The members must represent 5% of the voting rights, or • Be at least 100 members holding shares with an average paid up of £100, per member
Request (s 338)	• Must be in hard copy or electronic form, identify the resolution and be delivered at least 6 weeks in advance of an AGM or other general meeting
Statement (s 314)	• Members may request a statement (<1,000 words) be circulated to all members by delivering a **requisition**. Members with a qualifying holding may request a statement regarding their own resolution or any resolution proposed at the meeting • The company must send the statement with the notice of the meeting or as soon as practicable after

In either instance, the **requisitionists** must bear the incidental costs unless the company resolves otherwise.

Assessment focus point

The right of members to have resolutions included on the agenda of AGM or other meetings is asked frequently in law assessments. It is an **important consideration if some of the members disagree with the directors**.

5.5 Content of notices

FAST FORWARD

The **notice** convening the meeting must give certain details. The **date**, **time** and **place** of the meeting, and identification of AGM and special resolutions. Sufficient information about the business to be discussed at the meeting should be provided to enable shareholders to know what is to be done.

The **notice of a general meeting** must contain adequate information on the following points.

(a) The **date**, **time** and **place** of the meeting must be given.

(b) An **AGM** or a **special resolution** must be described as such.

(c) Information must be given of the business of the meeting **sufficient** to enable members (in deciding whether to attend or to appoint proxies) to **understand what will be done** at the meeting.

5.5.1 Routine business

In issuing the notice of an AGM it is standard practice merely to list the **items of ordinary or routine business** to be transacted, such as the following.

- Declaration of dividends (if any)
- Election of directors
- Appointment of auditors and fixing of their remuneration

The articles usually include a requirement that members shall be informed of any intention to **propose** the **election** of a director, other than an existing director who retires by rotation and merely stands for re-election.

Question	Removal of a director

How can members remove a director from office? What is the significance of special notice in this context?

Answer

A company may by ordinary resolution remove any director from office, notwithstanding any provision to the contrary in the articles or in a contract such as a director's service agreement.

However, this procedure requires that special notice shall be given to the company at least 28 days before the meeting of the intention to propose such a resolution. Moreover, the directors are not required to include the resolution in the notice of the meeting unless the person who intends to propose it has a sufficient shareholding.

If a company receives special notice it must send a copy to the director concerned who has the right to have written representations of reasonable length circulated to members. They may also speak before the resolution is put to the vote at the meeting.

Question	General meeting

When is a public company compelled to call a general meeting?

Answer

Members of a company who hold not less than one tenth of the company's paid up share capital carrying voting rights, or members representing one tenth of the voting rights, may requisition the holding of a general meeting. The directors are then required within 21 days to issue a notice convening the meeting to transact the business specified in the requisition. This must be within 28 days.

An auditor who resigns giving reasons for his resignation may requisition a general meeting so that he may explain to members the circumstances of his resignation.

If the net assets of a public company are reduced to less than half in value of its called-up share capital, the directors must convene a general meeting to consider what, if any, steps should be taken.

The court has statutory power in certain circumstances to direct that a meeting shall be held.

BPP
LEARNING MEDIA

6 Proceedings at meetings

6.1 How a meeting proceeds

FAST FORWARD

Company meetings need to be properly run if they are to be **effective** and within the **law**.

A meeting can only reach **binding decisions** if:

- It has been properly **convened** by notice
- A **quorum is present.**
- A **chairman presides**.
- The **business** is **properly transacted** and **resolutions** are **put to the vote.**

There is no obligation to allow a member to be present if their shares do not carry the right to attend and vote. However **full general meetings** and **class meetings** can be held when shareholders not entitled to vote are present.

Each **item of business** comprised in the notice should be taken separately, discussed and **put to the vote**.

Members may propose **amendments** to any resolutions proposed. The chairman should reject any amendment which is outside the limits set by the notice convening the meeting.

If the relevant business is an **ordinary resolution** it may be possible to amend the resolution's wording so as to **reduce its effect** to something less (provided that the change does not entirely alter its character). For example an ordinary resolution authorising the directors to borrow £100,000 might be amended to substitute a limit of £50,000 (but not to increase it to £150,000 as £100,000 would have been stated in the notice).

6.2 The chairman

FAST FORWARD

The meeting should usually be chaired by the **chairman** of the board of directors. They do not necessarily have a casting vote.

The articles usually provide that the **chairman** of the board of directors **is to preside** at general meetings; in their absence another director chosen by the directors shall preside instead. As a last resort a member chosen by the members present can preside.

The chairman derives their authority from the articles and they have **no casting vote unless** the **articles give them one**. Their duties are to **maintain order** and to **deal** with the **agenda** in a methodical way so that the business of the meeting may be properly transacted.

The chairman:

- **May dissolve** or **adjourn** the **meeting** if it has become disorderly or if the members present agree.
- Must **adjourn** if the meeting **instructs** them to do so.

6.3 Quorum

FAST FORWARD

The **quorum** for meetings may be two or more (except for single member private companies). **Proxies** can attend, speak and vote on behalf of members.

Key term

A **quorum** is the minimum number of persons required to be present at a particular type of (company) meeting. In the case of shareholders' meetings, the figure is usually two, in person or by proxy, but the articles may make other provisions.

There is a legal principle that a 'meeting means a coming together of more than one person'. Hence it follows that as a matter of law **one person generally cannot be a meeting.** The rule that at least two persons must be present to constitute a 'meeting' does not require that both persons must be members. Every member has a **statutory right to appoint a proxy** to attend as their representative.

In theory, **ultimate control** over a company's business lies with the **members** in a **general meeting**. One would obviously conclude that a meeting involved more than one person, and indeed there is authority to that effect in *Sharp v Dawes 1876*. In this case a meeting between a lone member and the company secretary was held not to be validly constituted. It is possible, however, for a meeting of only one person to take place and we shall consider this shortly.

6.3.1 Proxies

Key term

A **proxy** is a person appointed by a shareholder to vote on behalf of that shareholder at company meetings.

Any member of a company which has a share capital, provided they are entitled to attend and vote at a general or class meeting of the company, has a statutory right (s 324) to appoint an **agent**, called a **'proxy'**, to attend and vote for them.

Rules for appointing proxies	
Basic rule	• Any **member** may appoint a proxy • The proxy **does not** have to be a member • Proxies **may speak** at the meeting • A member may **appoint more than one proxy** provided each proxy is appointed in respect of a different class of share held by the member.
Voting	• Proxies **may vote** on a **poll** and on a **show of hands** • Proxies may **demand a poll** at a meeting • Most companies provide **two-way proxy cards** that the member can use to instruct a proxy how to vote, either for or against a resolution.
Notice	• Every notice of a meeting must **state** the member's right to a proxy • **Notice** of a proxy appointment should be given to the company at least 48 hours before the meeting (excluding weekends and bank holidays)

Hence one member and another member's proxy may together provide the quorum (if it is fixed, as is usual, at 'two members present in person or by proxy'). However one member who is also the proxy appointed by another member cannot by themselves be a meeting, since a **minimum of two individuals** present is required.

There may, however, be a meeting attended by **one person** only, if:

(a)   It is a **class meeting** and all the **shares** of that class are **held** by **one member.**

(b)   The **court**, in exercising a power to order a general meeting to be held, **fixes** the **quorum** at one. This means that in a two-member company, a meeting can be held with one person if the other deliberately absents themselves to frustrate business.

(c)   The company is a **single member private company**.

The articles usually fix a **quorum** for general meetings which may be as low as two (the minimum for a meeting) but may be more – though this is unusual.

If the articles do fix a quorum of two or more persons present, the meeting lacks a quorum (it is said to be an 'inquorate' meeting) if either:

- The **required number** is **not present** within a **stipulated time** (usually half an hour) of the appointed time for commencing a meeting.

- The **meeting begins** with a **quorum** but the **number present dwindles** to less than the quorum – unless the articles provide for this possibility.

The articles usually provide for automatic and compulsory **adjournment of an inquorate meeting**. The articles can provide that a meeting which begins with a quorum may continue despite a reduction in numbers present to less than the quorum level. However, there must still be **two or more persons present**.

6.4 Voting and polls

FAST FORWARD

Voting at general meetings may be on a **show of hands** or a **poll**.

The **rights of members** to **vote** and the **number of votes** to which they are entitled in respect of their shares are fixed by the **articles**.

One vote per share is normal but some shares, for instance preference shares, may carry no voting rights in normal circumstances. To shorten the proceedings at meetings the procedure is as follows.

6.4.1 Voting on a show of hands

Key term

> A **show of hands** is a method of voting for or against a resolution by raising hands. Under this method each member has one vote irrespective of the number of shares held, in contrast to a poll vote.

On putting a resolution to the vote the chairman calls for a **show of hands**. One vote may be given by each member present in person, including proxies. Unless a poll is then demanded, the chairman's declaration of the result is **conclusive**. However it is still possible to challenge the chairman's declaration on the grounds that it was fraudulent or manifestly wrong.

6.4.2 Voting on a poll

Key term

> A **poll** is a method of voting at company meetings which allows a member to use as many votes as their shareholding grants them.

If a **real test of voting strength** is required a poll may be demanded. The result of the previous show of hands is then disregarded. On a poll every member and also proxies representing absent members may cast the full number of votes to which they are entitled. A poll need not be held at the time but may be postponed so that arrangements to hold it can be made.

A poll may be **demanded** by:

- Not **less than five members**
- Member(s) **representing** not less than **one tenth** of the **total voting rights**
- Member(s) **holding shares** which **represent** not less than **one tenth** of the **paid-up capital**

Any provision in the articles is **void** if it seeks to prevent such members demanding a poll or to exclude the right to demand a poll on any question other than the election of a chairman by the meeting or an adjournment.

When a poll is held it is usual to appoint **'scrutineers'** and to ask members and proxies to sign voting cards or lists. The votes cast are checked against the register of members and the chairman declares the result.

Members of a quoted company may require the directors to obtain an **independent report** in respect of a poll taken, or to be taken, at a general meeting if:

- They represent at least 5% of the voting rights, or
- Are at least 100 in number holding at least £100 of paid up capital.

6.4.3 Result of a vote

In voting, either by show of hands or on a poll, the **number of votes cast determines the result**. Votes which are not cast, whether the member who does not use them is present or absent, are simply disregarded. Hence the majority vote may be much less than half (or three quarters) of the total votes which could be cast. Results of **quoted company polls** of must be made available on a **website**. The following information should be made available as soon as **reasonably practicable**, and should remain on the website for at least **two years**.

- Meeting date
- Text of the resolution or description of the poll's subject matter
- Number of votes for and against the resolution

6.4.4 Directors' voting rights

Directors do not have a **right to vote** at company meetings by virtue of their position in the company. However, if they are also **shareholders** of the company, they will enjoy the voting rights which attach to the **particular class of share** that they own.

6.5 Minutes of company meetings

Minutes must be kept of all **general, directors'** and **management meetings**.

Key term

> **Minutes** are a record of the proceedings of meetings. Company law requires minutes to be kept of all company meetings including general, directors' and managers' meetings.

Every company is **required to keep minutes** which are a formal written record of the proceedings of its general meetings for ten years: s 355. These minutes are usually kept in **book form**. If a loose-leaf book is used to facilitate typing there should be safeguards against falsification, such as sequential pre-numbering.

The chairman **normally signs** the minutes. If he does so, the signed minutes are admissible evidence of the proceedings, though evidence may be given to contradict or supplement the minutes or to show that no meeting at all took place. **Members** of the company have the **right to inspect** minutes of general meetings. The minutes of general meetings must be held at the registered office (or other permitted location) available for inspection by members, who are also entitled to demand copies.

290   **12: Meetings and resolutions** │ Part E Corporate administration and management

BPP
LEARNING MEDIA

6.6 The assent principle

A unanimous decision of the members is often treated as a substitute for a formal decision in general meeting properly convened and held, and is equally binding.

Question

A company has five members, each of whom are entitled to one vote on resolutions at general meetings. At the latest general meeting only two members turn up, Ally and Ben, who both vote against a particular resolution. The other three members send proxies to vote on their behalf for the resolution.

Will the resolution be passed?

A   No, as only votes made by members attending the meeting count towards passing or rejecting a resolution
B   No, as proxy votes are only counted where the number of member votes for and against a resolution are equal
C   Yes, as proxy votes carry equal weight to member votes
D   No, as one vote by a member counts as two votes by a proxy

Answer

C   All votes, whether by members or their proxies, have equal value.

7 Class meetings

FAST FORWARD

Class meetings are held where the interests of different groups of shareholders may be affected in different ways.

7.1 Types of class meeting

Class meetings are of two kinds.

(a)   If the company has more than one class of share it may be necessary to call a meeting of the holders of one class, to approve a proposed **variation** of the **rights** attached to their shares.

(b)   Under a **compromise** or **arrangements with creditors** (s 895), the holders of shares of the same class may nonetheless be divided into **separate** classes if the scheme proposed will affect each group differently.

When **separate meetings** of a class of members are held, the same procedural rules as for general meetings apply (but there is a different rule on quorum).

7.2 Quorum for a class meeting

The standard general meeting rules, on issuing notices and on voting, apply to a class meeting. However the **quorum** for a class meeting is fixed at two persons who hold, or represent by proxy, at least **one third** in nominal value of the issued shares of the class (unless the class only consists of a single member). If no quorum is present, the meeting is **adjourned** (under the standard adjournment procedure for general meetings). When the meeting resumes, the quorum is **one** person (who must still hold at least one third of the shares).

8 Single member private companies

FAST FORWARD

> There are **special rules** for **private companies** with only **one shareholder.**

If the sole member takes any decision that could have been taken in general meeting, that member shall (unless it is a written resolution) provide the company with a **written record** of it. This allows the sole member to conduct members' business informally without notice or minutes.

Filing requirements still apply, for example, in the case of alteration of articles.

Written resolutions **cannot** be used to remove a director or auditor from office as these resolutions require special notice.

Assessment focus point

> There are not too many ways meetings and resolutions can be tested. You are most likely to be asked about the general rules such as required majority and notice periods.

Chapter Roundup

- Although the management of a company is in the hands of the directors, the **decisions which affect the existence of the company**, its structure and scope are **reserved to the members** in general meeting.

- The directors exercise their powers by holding **board meetings**.

- There are two kinds of general meeting of members of a company:

    - **Annual general meeting (AGM)**
    - **General meetings at other times**

- A meeting can pass two types of resolution. **Ordinary resolutions** are carried by a simple majority (more than 50%) of votes cast and requiring 14 days notice. **Special resolution**s require a 75% majority of votes cast and also 14 days notice.

- A private company can pass any decision needed by a **written resolution**, except for removing a director or auditor before their term of office has expired.

- A meeting cannot make valid and binding decisions until it has been properly convened. Notice of general meetings must be given **14 days** in advance of the meeting. The notice should contain adequate information about the meeting.

- Meetings must be called by a **competent person** or authority.

- **Clear notice** must be given to members. **Notice** must be **sent to all members** entitled to receive it.

- **Special notice of 28 days** of intention to propose certain resolutions (removal of directors/auditors) must be given.

- **Members** rather than directors may be able to requisition resolutions. This may be achieved by requesting the directors call a meeting, or proposing a resolution to be voted on at a meeting already arranged.

- The **notice** convening the meeting must give certain details. The **date**, **time** and **place** of the meeting, and identification of AGM and special resolutions. Sufficient information about the business to be discussed at the meeting should be provided to enable shareholders to know what is to be done.

- Company meetings need to be properly run if they are to be **effective** and within the **law**.

- The meeting should usually be chaired by the **chairman** of the board of directors. They do not necessarily have a casting vote.

- The **quorum** for meetings may be two or more (except for single member private companies). **Proxies** can attend, speak and vote on behalf of members.

- Voting at general meetings may be on a **show of hands** or a **poll**.

- **Minutes** must be kept of all **general, directors'** and **management meetings**.

- **Class meetings** are held where the interests of different groups of shareholders may be affected in different ways.

- There are **special rules** for **private companies** with only **one shareholder**.

1   Which of the following decisions can only be taken by the members in general meeting?
    Select all that apply.

    A   Alteration of articles
    B   Change of name
    C   Reduction of capital
    D   Appointment of a managing director

2   Before a private company can hold a general meeting on short notice, members holding a certain percentage of the company's shares must agree. Which one of the following percentages is correct?

51%	90%
75%	95%

3   A plc must hold its AGM within six months of its year end.

    True   ☐

    False ☐

4   Which of the following matters is a quoted company not legally required to make available on a website?

    A   Notice of all its general meetings
    B   Text of resolutions voted on in a poll
    C   The number of proxies voting for and against a resolution
    D   The number of votes cast for and against a resolution

5   A member of a public company may only appoint one proxy, but the proxy has a statutory right to speak at the meeting.

    True   ☐

    False ☐

6   Which of the following is correct concerning the retirement of directors?

    A   At each AGM at least half of the directors must retire, but they may offer themselves for re-election
    B   At each AGM at least half of the directors must retire and they may not offer themselves for re-election
    C   At each AGM at least a third of the directors must retire, but they may offer themselves for re-election
    D   At each AGM at least a third of the directors must retire and they may not offer themselves for re-election

7   The notice of a general meeting must set out in full, the text of any ordinary resolutions that will be put to the vote during the meeting.

    True   ☐

    False ☐

8   The quorum for a class meeting is:

    A   Two members controlling at least one-third of the nominal value of the shares in the class
    B   Two members controlling at least half of the nominal value of the shares in the class
    C   Four members controlling at least one-third of the nominal value of the shares in the class
    D   Four members controlling at least half of the nominal value of the shares in the class

9   The minimum notice period for a plc's AGM is:

A   7 days
B   14 days
C   21 days
D   28 days

10   There are two circumstances where special notice is required to be given to a company in respect of proposed resolutions. The first is where the resolution seeks to remove a director from office, the other is:

A   To change the company's name
B   To reduce the company's share capital
C   To change the company's registered office
D   To remove the company's auditor from office

Answers to Quick Quiz

1   A, B and C. The board can appoint someone to be managing director, so D is incorrect.

2   90%

3   True. A plc must hold its AGM within six months of its year end.

4   C. The number of proxies voting for and against a resolution is not legally required to be made available on a website. Notice of meetings, text of resolutions and the total number of votes cast for and against the resolution are required.

5   False. Public company members can appoint more than one proxy. They have a statutory right to speak.

6   A. At each AGM at least half of the directors must retire, but they may offer themselves for re-election.

7   False. It is only the text of special resolutions which must be set out in full.

8   A. The quorum for a class meeting is two members controlling at least one-third of the nominal value of the shares in the class.

9   C. The minimum notice period for a plc's AGM is 21 days.

10   D. Special notice is required to be given to a company where a resolution proposes to remove directors or auditors from office.

Now try the questions below from the Question Bank

Number
Q56
Q57
Q58
Q59
Q60

13

Directors and secretaries

Introduction

In this chapter we turn our attention to the **appointment** and **removal**, and the **powers and duties of the directors**.

The important principle to grasp is that the **extent of directors' powers is defined by the articles**.

If **shareholders** do not approve of the directors' acts they must either **remove them** under s 168 or **alter the articles** to regulate their future conduct. However, they **cannot** simply **take over** the functions of the directors.

In a similar way to partners in a partnership, the directors act as **agents of the company**. The different types of authority a director can have (implied and actual) are important in this area.

We also consider the **duties** of directors (**duties of care and skill** and **fiduciary duties** of loyalty and good faith) and the common law and statutory **remedies for the breach of such duties**.

Statute also imposes some duties on directors, specifically concerning openness when transacting with the company.

Finally we look at the duties and powers of the **company secretary** and **auditor**.

Topic list	Learning outcomes
1 The role of directors	G2(d)
2 Appointment of directors	G2(d)
3 Remuneration of directors	G2(d)
4 Vacation of office	G2(d)
5 Disqualification of directors	G2(d)
6 Powers of directors	G2(e)
7 Powers of the managing director	G2(e)
8 Powers of an individual director	G2(e)
9 Duties of directors	G2(e), G2(f)
10 The company secretary	G2(i)
11 The company auditor	G2(i)

1 The role of directors

FAST FORWARD Any person who occupies the position of director is treated as such, the test being one of **function**.

Key term

> A **director** is a person who is responsible for the overall direction of the company's affairs. In company law, director means any person occupying the position of director, by whatever name called.

Any person who occupies the position of director is treated as such. The test is one of **function**. The directors' function is to take part in **making decisions** by **attending meetings** of the board of directors. Anyone who does that is a director whatever they may be called.

A person who is given the title of director, such as 'sales director' or 'director of research', to give them status in the company structure is not a director in company law. This is unless by virtue of their appointment they are a **member** of the **board** of **directors**, or they carry out functions that would be properly discharged only by a director. Anyone who is held out by a company as a director, and who acts as a director although not validly appointed as one, is known as a **de facto** director.

1.1 Shadow directors

A person might seek to **avoid the legal responsibilities of being a director** by avoiding appointment as such but using his power, say as a major shareholder, to manipulate the acknowledged board of directors.

Company law seeks to prevent this abuse by extending several statutory rules to **shadow directors**. Shadow directors are directors for legal purposes if the board of directors are accustomed to act in **accordance with their directions** and **instructions**. This rule does not apply to professional advisers merely acting in that capacity.

1.2 Alternate directors

A director may, if the articles permit, appoint an **alternate director** to attend and vote for them at board meetings which they are unable to attend. Such an alternate may be another director, in which case they have the vote of the absentee as well as their own. More usually they are an outsider. Company articles could make specific provisions for this situation.

1.3 Executive directors

Key term

> An **executive director** is a director who performs a specific role in a company under a **service contract** which requires a regular, possibly daily, involvement in management.

A director may also be an **employee** of his company. Since the company is also his **employer** there is a potential conflict of interest which in principle a director is required to avoid.

To allow an individual to be **both a director and employee** the articles usually make express provision for it, but prohibit the director from voting at a board meeting on the terms of their own employment.

Directors who have additional management duties as employees may be distinguished by **special titles**, such as 'Finance Director'. However (except in the case of a managing director) **any such title does not affect their personal legal position**. They have two distinct positions as:

- A member of the board of directors; and
- A manager with management responsibilities as an **employee**

1.4 Non-executive directors

Key term

A **non-executive director** does not have a function to perform in a company's management but is involved in its governance.

In **listed companies**, corporate governance codes state that boards of directors are more likely to be fully effective if they comprise both **executive directors** and strong, independent **non-executive directors**.

The **main tasks** of the **NEDs** are as follows:

- **Contribute** an **independent view** to the board's deliberations
- **Help the board provide** the company with **effective leadership**
- **Ensure** the **continuing effectiveness** of the **executive directors** and management
- **Ensure high standards** of **financial probity** on the part of the company

Non-executive and shadow directors are subject to the **same duties** as executive directors.

1.5 The managing director

Key term

A **managing director** is one of the directors of the company appointed to carry out overall day-to-day management functions.

If the articles provide for it the board may appoint one or more directors to be **managing directors**. A managing director ('MD') does have a special position and has wider apparent powers than any director who is not appointed an MD.

Assessment focus point

Assessments may require the identification of differences between the different types of director.

1.6 Number of directors

Every company must have at least **one** director and for a **public** company the minimum is **two**. There is no statutory maximum in the UK but the articles usually impose a limit. At least one director must be a **natural person**, not a body corporate.

A **company** may be a director. In that case the director company sends an individual to attend board meetings as its representative.

1.7 The board of directors

Companies are run by the directors collectively, in a **board of directors**.

Key term

The **board of directors** is the elected representative of the shareholders acting collectively in the management of a company's affairs.

One of the basic principles of company law is that the **powers** which are delegated to the directors under the articles are given to them as a **collective body.**

The **board meeting** is the **proper place for the exercise of the powers,** unless they have been validly passed on, or 'sub-delegated', to committees or individual directors.

A person who is held out by a company to be a director although not validly appointed as such is:

A   An executive director
B   A non-executive director
C   A shadow director
D   A de facto director

Answer

D   Executive and non-executive directors are validly appointed. A shadow director is anyone who is not appointed as a director, but are able to use their power to manipulate the appointed board.

2 Appointment of directors

FAST FORWARD

The method of appointing directors, along with their rotation and co-option is **controlled** by the **articles.**

A director may be **appointed expressly**, in which case they are known as a *de jure* director.

Where a person acts as a director without actually being appointed as such (a *de facto* or **shadow director**) they incur the obligations and have some of the powers of a proper director. In addition, a shadow director is subject to many of the duties imposed on directors.

2.1 Appointment of first directors

The application for registration delivered to the Registrar to form a company includes **particulars of the first directors**, with their consents. On the formation of the company those persons become the first directors.

2.2 Appointment of subsequent directors

Once a company has been formed further directors can be appointed, either to **replace** existing directors or as **additional** directors.

Appointment of further directors is carried out **as the articles provide**. Most company articles allow for the appointment of directors:

- By **ordinary resolution** of the shareholders, and
- By a **decision** of the directors.

However the articles do not have to follow these provisions and may impose **different methods** on the company.

When the appointment of directors is proposed at a general meeting of a public company a **separate** resolution should be proposed for the election of **each director**. However the rule may be waived if a resolution to that effect is first carried without any vote being given against it.

2.3 Publicity

In addition to giving notice of the first directors, every company must within **14 days** give **notice** to the **Registrar** of any change among its directors. This includes any changes to the register of directors' residential addresses.

2.4 Age limit

The **minimum age** limit for a director is **16** and, unless the articles provide otherwise, there is no upper limit.

Question	Shadow directors

A shadow director, although not validly appointed, still owes the same duties as directors who have been validly appointed.

True/false?

Answer

True. All those who fulfil the role of director, whether validly appointed or not, owe the same duties.

3 Remuneration of directors

FAST FORWARD

> Directors are entitled to **fees** and **expenses** as directors as per the articles, and **emoluments** (and compensation for loss of office) as per their service contracts (which can be inspected by members). Some details are published in the directors' remuneration report along with accounts.

Details of directors' remuneration is usually contained within their **service contract**. This is a contract where the director agrees to personally perform services for the company.

3.1 Directors' expenses

Most articles state that directors are entitled to **reimbursement** of **reasonable expenses** incurred whilst carrying out their duties or functions as directors. In addition, most directors have **written service contracts** setting out their entitlement to emoluments and expenses. Where service contracts **guarantee employment** for longer than **two years** then an **ordinary resolution** must be passed by the members of the company that the contract is with.

3.2 Compensation for loss of office

Any director may receive **non-contractual** compensation for loss of office paid to him voluntarily. Any such compensation is lawful **only if** approved by members of the company in general meeting after proper disclosure has been made to all members, whether voting or not. However, approval is not required where the company is contractually bound to make the payment.

Compensation paid to directors for loss of office is distinguished from any payments made to directors **as employees**. For example to settle claims arising from the premature termination of the service agreements. These are contractual payments which do not require approval in general meeting.

3.3 Directors' remuneration report

Quoted companies are required to include a **directors' remuneration report** as part of their annual report, part of which is subject to audit. The report must cover:

- The details of each **individual directors' remuneration package**
- The company's **remuneration policy**
- The **role** of the **board** and **remuneration committee** in deciding the **remuneration** of **directors**

Under s 421(3), it is the duty of the directors (including those who were a director in the preceding five years) to provide any information about themselves that is necessary to produce this report. **Quoted companies** are required to allow a vote by members on the directors' remuneration report. The vote is purely advisory and does not mean the remuneration should change if the resolution is not passed. A negative vote would be a strong signal to the directors that the members are unhappy with remuneration levels.

Items not subject to audit

- Consideration by the directors (remuneration committee) of matters relating to directors' remuneration
- Statement of company's policy on directors' remuneration
- Performance graph (share performance)
- Directors' service contracts (dates, unexpired length, compensation payable for early termination)

Items subject to audit

- Salary/fees payable to each director
- Bonuses paid/to be paid
- Expenses
- Compensation for loss of office paid
- Any benefits received
- Pensions, share options and long term incentive schemes – performance criteria and conditions
- Excess retirement benefits
- Compensation to past directors
- Sums paid to third parties in respect of a director's services

3.4 Inspection of directors' service agreements

A company must make available for inspection by members a copy or particulars of **contracts of employment** between the company or a subsidiary with a director of the company. Such contracts must cover all services that a director may provide, including services outside the role of a director, and those made by a third party in respect of services that a director is contracted to perform.

Contracts must be **retained** for **one year** after expiry and must be available either at the **registered office**, or any other location permitted by the Secretary of State.

Prescribed particulars of **directors' emoluments** must be given in the accounts and also particulars of any **compensation for loss of office** and directors' **pensions**.

BPP
LEARNING MEDIA

4 Vacation of office

FAST FORWARD A director may vacate office as director due to: **resignation**; **not going** for **re-election**; **death**; **dissolution** of the company; **removal**; **disqualification**.

A **director may leave office** in the following ways.

- **Resignation**
- Not **offering themselves for re-election** when their term of office ends
- **Death**
- **Dissolution of the company**
- Being **removed** from office
- Being **disqualified**

A form should be filed with the **Registrar** whenever and however a director vacates office.

4.1 Retirement and re-election of directors

The model articles for **public companies** provide the following rules for the **retirement** and **re-election** of all **directors** except the managing director ('rotation').

(a) Every year **half** (or the number nearest to half) shall **retire**; at the first AGM of the company they all retire.

(b) **Retiring directors** are **eligible** for **re-election**.

(c) Those retiring shall be those **in office longest** since their last election.

(d) When calculating which directors are required to retire by rotation, directors who were **appointed to the board** during the year (and therefore are obliged to stand for re-election) and those **retiring** and **not seeking re-election** are **not included** in the calculation.

Question

Rotation of directors

The board of Teddy plc has the following directors at the start of its AGM on 31 December 20X7.

	Age	When last re-elected
Mrs Clare	42	31 December 20X4
Mr Paul	64	31 December 20X5
Mr Bob	27	31 December 20X5
Mr Nick	30	31 December 20X5
Miss Alison	60	31 December 20X6
Mr Maurice	38	31 December 20X6
Mrs Pippa	34	31 December 20X6
Mr Gordon	43	2 May 20X7
Mrs Helen	41	2 May 20X7

At a board meeting on 2 May 20X7 Mr Gordon and Mrs Helen were appointed to fill casual vacancies and Mrs Clare was appointed managing director.

Which directors would be due for re-election at the AGM on 31 December 20X7?

Mr Gordon and Mrs Helen must stand for re-election since they have been appointed during the year.

Calculation of who is to retire by rotation excludes Mr Gordon, Mrs Helen and Mrs Clare (as Managing Director), thus leaving six directors. Three of those must therefore retire, and as Mr Paul, Mr Bob and Mr Nick have been in office the longest, it must be them.

4.2 Removal of directors

In addition to provisions in the articles for removal of directors, a director may be removed from office by **ordinary** resolution at a meeting of which **special notice** to the company has been given by the person proposing it: s 168.

On receipt of the special notice the company must send a copy to the director who may require that a **memorandum of reasonable length** shall be issued to members. They also have the **right to address the meeting** at which the resolution is considered.

The articles and the service contract of the director **cannot override the statutory power**. However, the articles can **permit dismissal without the statutory formalities** being observed, for example dismissal by a resolution of the board of directors.

The power to remove a director is **limited** in its effect in four ways.

Restrictions on power to remove directors	
Shareholding qualification to call a meeting	In order to propose a resolution to remove a director, the shareholder(s) involved must call a general meeting. To do this they must hold: • Either, 10% of the paid up share capital • Or, 10% of the voting rights where the company does not have shares
Shareholding to request a resolution	Where a meeting is already convened, 100 members holding an average £100 of share capital each may request a resolution to remove a director: s 338.
Weighted voting rights	A director who is also a member may have weighted voting rights given to them under the constitution for such an eventuality, so that they can automatically defeat any motion to remove them as a director: *Bushell v Faith 1970*
Class right agreement	It is possible to draft a shareholder agreement stating that a member holding each class of share must be present at a general meeting to constitute quorum. If so, a member holding shares of a certain class could prevent a director being removed by not attending the meeting.

Assessment focus point

> The courts have stressed that the s 168 power of members to remove directors is an important right, but you should remember the ways in which members' intentions might be frustrated.

The dismissal of a director may also entail payment of a **substantial sum** to settle their claim for breach of contract if they have a service contract. Under s 168(5), no resolution may deprive a removed director of any compensation or damages related to their termination to which they are entitled to.

BPP
LEARNING MEDIA

> **Southern Foundries (1926) Ltd v Shirlaw 1940**
>
> *The facts:* In 1933 S entered into a written agreement to serve the company as managing director for ten years. In 1936 F Co gained control of the company and used their votes to alter its articles to confer on F Co power to remove any director from office. In 1937 F Co exercised the power by removing S from his directorship and thereby terminated his appointment as managing director (which he could only hold so long as he was a director).
>
> *Decision:* The alteration of the articles was not a breach of the service agreement but the exercise of the power was a breach of the service agreement for which the company was liable.

Question   Resolution for removal of director

A company has three members who are also directors. Each holds 100 shares. Normally the shares carry one vote each, but the articles state that on a resolution for a director's removal, the director to be removed should have 3 votes per share. On a resolution for the removal of Jeremy, a director, Jeremy casts 300 votes against the resolution and the other members cast 200 votes for the resolution. Has Jeremy validly defeated the resolution?

Answer

Yes. This was confirmed in a case called *Bushell v Faith 1970.*

5 Disqualification of directors

FAST FORWARD

> Directors may be required to vacate office because they have been disqualified on grounds dictated by the articles. Directors **may** be disqualified from a wider range of company involvements under the Company Directors Disqualification Act 1986 (CDDA).

A person cannot be appointed a director or continue in office if he is or becomes **disqualified** under the articles or statutory rules as explained below.

The articles often embody the statutory grounds of disqualification and add some optional extra grounds. Public company model articles provide that a director must vacate office if:

    (a)   They are **disqualified** by the **Act** or any rule of law.

    (b)   They become **bankrupt** or enter into an arrangement with creditors.

    (c)   They become of **unsound mind**.

    (d)   They **resign** by notice in writing.

    (e)   They are **absent** for a period of **three consecutive months** from board meetings held during that period, without obtaining leave of absence **and** the other directors resolve that they shall on that account vacate office.

Unless the court approves it, an **undischarged bankrupt** cannot act as a director nor be concerned directly or indirectly in the management of a company. If they do continue to act, they become personally liable for the company's relevant debts.

5.1 Disqualification under statute

The **Company Directors Disqualification Act 1986** (CDDA 1986) provides that a **court may** formally **disqualify a person from being a director** or in any way directly or indirectly being concerned or taking part in the promotion, formation or management of a company: s1.

Therefore the terms of the disqualification order are very wide, and include acting as a consultant to a company. The Act, despite its title, is not limited to the disqualification of people who have been directors. **Any person** may be disqualified if they fall within the appropriate grounds.

In addition to the grounds of disqualification described above, the articles may provide that **a director shall automatically vacate office** if they are **absent** from **board meetings** (without obtaining the leave of the board) for a **specified period** (three months is usual). The effect of this disqualification depends on the words used.

- If the articles refer merely to 'absence' this includes involuntary absence due to illness.
- The words 'if they shall absent himself' restrict the disqualification to periods of voluntary absence.

The period of **three months** is reckoned to begin from the **last meeting** which the absent director did attend. The normal procedure is that a director who foresees a period of absence, applies for leave of absence at the last board meeting which they attend; the leave granted is duly minuted. They are not then absent 'without leave' during the period.

If they fail to obtain leave but later offer a reasonable explanation the other directors may let the matter drop by simply not resolving that they shall vacate office. The general intention of the rule is to **impose a sanction against slackness**; a director has a duty to attend board meetings when they are able to do so.

Question

Disqualification of directors

Which of the following are grounds provided for a director being compelled to leave office?

A   Becoming bankrupt
B   Entering into an arrangement with personal creditors
C   Becoming of unsound mind
D   Resigning by notice in writing
E   Being absent from board meetings for six consecutive months without obtaining leave of absence

Answer

All of them.

5.2 Grounds for disqualification of directors

FAST FORWARD

Directors may be **disqualified** from acting as directors or being involved in the management of companies in a number of circumstances. They must be disqualified if the company is insolvent, and the director is found to be unfit to be concerned with management of a company.

BPP LEARNING MEDIA

Under the CDDA 1986 the court **may** make a disqualification order on any of the following grounds.

(a) **Where a person is convicted of an indictable offence in connection with the promotion, formation, management or liquidation of a company or with the receivership or management of a company's property** (s 2).

An indictable offence is an offence which may be tried at a Crown Court; it is therefore a serious offence. It need not actually have been tried on indictment but if it was the maximum period for which the court can disqualify is 15 years, compared with only 5 years if the offence was dealt with summarily (at the Magistrates' Court).

(b) **Where it appears that a person has been persistently in default in relation to provisions of company legislation.**

This legislation requires any return, account or other document to be filed with, delivered or sent or notice of any matter to be given to the Registrar (s 3). Three defaults in five years are conclusive evidence of persistent default.

The maximum period of disqualification under this section is five years.

(c) **Where it appears that a person has been guilty of fraudulent trading**. This means carrying on business with intent to defraud creditors or for any fraudulent purpose whether or not the company has been, or is in the course of being, wound-up.

The person does not actually have to have been convicted of fraudulent trading. The legislation also applies to anyone who has otherwise been guilty, of any fraud in relation to the company or of any breach of their duty as an officer (s 4).

The maximum period of disqualification under this section is 15 years.

(d) **Where the Secretary of State acting on a report made by the inspectors or from information or documents obtained under the Companies Act, applies to the court for an order believing it to be expedient in the public interest.**

If the court is satisfied that the person's conduct in relation to the company makes that person unfit to be concerned in the management of a company, then it may make a disqualification order (s 8). Again the maximum is 15 years.

(e) **Where a director was involved in certain competition violations**. Maximum – 15 years.

(f) **Where a director of an insolvent company has participated in wrongful trading (s 10)**. Maximum – 15 years.

The court **must** make an order where it is satisfied that the following apply:

(a) A person has been a director of a company which has at any time become **insolvent** (whether while they were a director or subsequently).

(b) Their conduct as a director of that company makes them **unfit** to be **concerned** in the **management** of a company. The courts may also take into account their conduct as a director of other companies, whether or not these other companies are insolvent. Directors can be disqualified under this section even if they take no active part in the running of the business.

In such cases the **minimum** period of disqualification is two years.

Offences for which directors have been disqualified include the following.

(a) **Insider dealing**: *R v Goodman 1993*

(b) **Failure** to **keep proper accounting records**: *Re Firedart Ltd, Official Receiver v Fairall 1994*

(c) **Failure to read the company's accounts**: *Re Continental Assurance Co of London plc 1996*

(d) **Loans** to another company for the purposes of purchasing its own shares with **no grounds for believing the money would be repaid**: *Re Continental Assurance Co of London plc 1996*

(e) **Loans** to associated companies on **uncommercial terms** to the detriment of creditors: *Re Greymoat Ltd 1997*

5.3 Disqualification periods

In *Re Sevenoaks Stationers (Retail) Ltd 1991* the Court of Appeal laid down certain 'disqualification brackets'. The appropriate period of disqualification which should be imposed was a **minimum of two to five years** if the conduct was not very serious, **six to ten years** if the conduct was serious but did not merit the maximum penalty, and **over ten years** only in particularly serious cases.

Disqualification as a director need not mean disqualification from all involvement in management: (*Re Griffiths 1997),* and it may mean that the director can continue to act as an **unpaid director** (*Re Barings plc 1998*), but only if the court gives leave to act.

5.3.1 Mitigation of disqualification

Examples of circumstances which have led the court to imposing a lower period of disqualification include the following.

- **Lack of dishonesty**: *Re Burnham Marketing Services Ltd 1993*
- **Loss of director's own money** in the company: *Re GSAR Realisations Ltd 1993*
- **Absence of personal gain**, for example excessive remuneration: *Re GSAR Realisations Ltd 1993*
- **Efforts to mitigate** the situation: *Re Burnham Marketing Services Ltd 1993*
- **Likelihood of re-offending**: *Re Grayan Building Services Ltd 1995*
- **Proceedings hanging over director** for a long time: *Re Aldermanbury Trust 1993*

5.4 Procedures for disqualification

Company administrators, **receivers** and **liquidators** all have a statutory duty to **report directors** to the Government where they believe the conditions for a disqualification order have been satisfied.

The Secretary of State then decides whether to apply to the **court** for an order, but if they do decide to apply they must do so within two years of the date on which the company became insolvent.

Question   **Disqualificatic**

In what circumstances may a court make a disqualification order against a director of a company?

BPP
LEARNING MEDIA

The provisions for disqualification of directors are contained in the Company Directors Disqualification Act 1986. A court may, by order, disqualify a person from being a director, liquidator, administrator, receiver or manager of a company, and from being concerned in the promotion or management of any company.

The order may be made in any one of the following circumstances.

(a)   The director concerned is convicted of an indictable offence in connection with a company.

(b)   The director concerned has been persistently in default in relation to company law requirements requiring the delivery to the Registrar of annual accounts, the annual return and other documents. A previous decision of a court on three previous occasions in five years that the person concerned has been in default in compliance with these requirements is conclusive evidence of 'persistent' default.

(c)   The director concerned has been guilty of fraudulent trading.

(d)   The Secretary of State applies for disqualification in the public interest. This would arise from an investigation by Government inspectors or documents obtained under the Companies Act.

(e)   The director has been found to be in breach of certain aspects of competition law.

(f)   The director has participated in wrongful trading in insolvency.

In general, disqualification may be ordered for up to 15 years. But the maximum is 5 years in case (b) above or when the order is made by a magistrates' court. A person subject to disqualification may apply to the court for remission of the order.

Bankruptcy

An undischarged bankrupt may not, without leave of the court, act as a director of a company or be concerned in the management or promotion of a company.

Here the disqualification is the automatic result of the bankruptcy order made against him by the court.

6 Powers of directors

FAST FORWARD
> The **powers** of the directors are **defined** by the **articles**.

The powers of the directors are **defined by the articles**. The directors are usually authorised 'to manage the company's business' and 'to exercise all the powers of the company for any purpose connected with the company's business'.

Therefore they may take **any decision which is within the capacity** of the company **unless** either **the Act** or **the articles** themselves **require** that the **decision shall be taken by the members in general meeting**.

6.1 Restrictions on directors' powers

FAST FORWARD
> Directors' powers may be restricted by statute or by the articles. The directors have a duty to exercise their powers in what they honestly believe to be the **best interests** of the company and for the **purposes** for which the powers are given.

6.1.1 Statutory restrictions

Many transactions, such as an alteration of the articles or a reduction of capital must by law be effected by passing a **special resolution**. If the directors propose such changes they must secure the passing of the appropriate resolution by shareholders in a general meeting.

6.1.2 Restrictions imposed by articles

As an example, the articles often set a maximum amount which the directors may borrow. If the directors wish to exceed that limit, they should **seek authority** from a **general meeting**.

When the directors clearly have the necessary power, their decision may be challenged if they exercise the power in the wrong way. They must exercise their powers:

- In what they **honestly believe to be the interests of the company:** *Re Smith v Fawcett Ltd 1942*
- For a **proper purpose**, being the purpose for which the power is given: *Bamford v Bamford 1969.*

We shall come back to these points when we consider **directors' duties**.

6.1.3 Members' control of directors

There is a **division of power** between the board of directors who manage the business and the members who as owners take the major policy decisions at general meetings. How, then, do the owners seek to 'control' the people in charge of their property?

- The members **appoint** the directors and may **remove** them from office under s 168, or by other means.

- The members can, by **altering the articles** (special resolution needed), re-allocate powers between the board and the general meeting.

- Articles may allow the members to pass a **special resolution ordering** the **directors to act** (or **refrain from acting**) in a **particular way**. Such special resolutions cannot invalidate anything the directors have already done.

Remember that **directors are not agents of the members.** They cannot be instructed by the members in general meeting as to how they should exercise their powers. **The directors' powers are derived from the company as a whole** and are to be exercised by the directors as they think best in the **interests of the company**.

6.1.4 Control by the law

Certain powers must be exercised **'for the proper purpose'** and all powers must be exercised ***bona fide* for the benefit of the company**. Failure by the directors to comply with these rules will result in the **court setting aside their powers** unless the shareholders **ratify** the directors' actions by **ordinary resolution** (50 % majority).

Question | Control of directors

Directors are the appointed agents of the members and as such the members are entitled to control how the directors exercise their powers.

True/false?

False. Directors are agents of the company as a whole. Members cannot control how they exercise their powers.

7 Powers of the managing director

FAST FORWARD

One or more directors may be appointed by the board as **managing director**. The managing director has **apparent** authority to make business contracts on behalf of the company. The managing director's **actual** authority is whatever the board gives them.

Assessment focus point

Assessments may refer to the Chief Executive Officer (CEO) instead of managing director (MD). Both terms can be used interchangibly.

If the articles provide for it the **board** may appoint one or more directors to be **managing directors**.

In their dealings with outsiders the managing director has **apparent authority** as agent of the company to **make business contracts**. No other director, even if they work full time, has that **apparent** authority as a director, though if they are employed as a manager they may have apparent authority at a slightly lower level.

The managing director's **actual authority** is whatever the board gives them.

Although a managing director (MD) has this special status, their appointment as MD may be **terminated** like that of any other director (or employee); they then revert to the position of an ordinary director. Alternatively the company in general meeting may **remove them from their office of director** and they immediately cease to be MD since being a director is a necessary qualification for holding the post of MD.

7.1 Agency and the managing director

The directors are **agents of the company, not the members**. Where they have **actual or usual** authority they can **bind the company**. In addition a director may have **apparent authority** by virtue of **holding out**.

Holding out is a basic rule of the law of agency. This means, if the principal (the company) holds out a person as its authorised agent they are estopped from denying that they are its **authorised agent**. They are bound by a contract entered into by them on the company's behalf.

Key term

Apparent authority is the authority which an agent appears to have to a third party. A contract made within the scope of such authority will bind the principal even though the agent was not following their instructions.

Therefore if the board of directors **permits a director** to behave as if he were a **managing director** duly appointed when in fact they are not, the company may be bound by their actions.

A managing director has, by virtue of their position, **apparent authority** to make commercial contracts for the company. Moreover if the board allows a director to enter into contracts, being aware of their dealings and taking no steps to disown them, the company will usually be bound.

> **Freeman & Lockyer v Buckhurst Park Properties (Mangal) Ltd 1964**
>
> *The facts:* A company carried on a business as property developers. The articles contained a power to appoint a managing director but this was never done. One of the directors of the company, to the knowledge but without the express authority of the remainder of the board, acted as if he were managing director. He found a purchaser for an estate and also engaged a firm of architects to make a planning application. The company later refused to pay the architect's fees on the grounds that the director had no actual or apparent authority.
>
> *Decision:* The company was liable since by its acquiescence it had represented that the director was a managing director with the authority to enter into contracts that were normal commercial arrangements, and which the board itself would have been able to enter.

Assessment focus point

> Situations with facts similar to the *Freeman & Lockyer* case may appear in assessments so be prepared to spot them.

In the *Freeman & Lockyer* case, Diplock L J laid down four conditions which must be satisfied in claiming under the principle of **holding out**.

The **claimant** must show that:

(a)   A **representation** was made to them that the **agent had** the **authority** to enter on behalf of the company into the contract of the kind sought to be enforced.

(b)   Such **representation** was **made by a person** who had **'actual' authority** to **manage** the **business** of the company.

The board of directors would certainly have actual authority to manage the company. Some commentators have also argued that the managing director has actual or apparent authority to make representations about the extent of the actual authority of other company agents. (However a third party cannot rely on the representations a managing director makes about their own actual authority).

(c)   They were **induced** by the **representation** to enter into the contract; they had in fact relied on it.

(d)   There must be **nothing** in the **articles** which would prevent the company from giving valid authority to its agent to enter into the contract.

Question

Directors' powers

Under the articles of association of Recycle Ltd the directors of the company need the consent of the general meeting by ordinary resolution to borrow sums of money in excess of £50,000. The other articles are all standard model articles.

Mary has been appointed managing director of the company and she holds 1% of the issued shares of the company. Early in May 20X5 Mary entered into two transactions for the benefit of Recycle Ltd. First, she arranged to borrow £100,000 from Conifer Bank Ltd, secured by a floating charge on the company's assets. She had not sought the approval of the members as required by the articles. Secondly, she placed a contract worth £10,000 with Saw Ltd to buy some agricultural machinery.

Advise the directors of Recycle Ltd whether they are bound by the agreements with Conifer Bank Ltd and Saw Ltd.

The enforceability of the loan agreement and floating charge by Conifer Bank Ltd against Recycle Ltd is determined by reference to s 40. The transaction is *intra vires* the company, but beyond the authority of the managing director. Mary failed to obtain an ordinary resolution of the company as required by its articles of association.

S 40 provides that, in favour of a person dealing in good faith with a company, the power of the board of directors to bind the company or (importantly in this case) to authorise others to do so, shall be deemed to be free of any limitation under the company's constitution.

There is no suggestion that Conifer Bank Ltd has not acted in good faith and it will be presumed that it has in fact acted in good faith unless the contrary is proved by the company.

The articles allow the board to appoint a managing director. In that position, Mary has apparent authority as agent of the company to make business contracts including the type of transaction entered into with Saw Ltd.

Under the Act, the restriction placed on her actual authority (by the article requiring an ordinary resolution) shall be deemed not to exist in favour of the third party, Conifer Bank Ltd. The power of the board to authorise Mary to bind the company is deemed to be free of any constitutional limitation.

In conclusion, Recycle Ltd will be bound to the contracts with both Conifer Bank Ltd and Saw Ltd.

8 Powers of an individual director

The position of any other individual director (not an MD) who is also an employee is that:

(a)   They **do not have the apparent authority to make general contracts** which attaches to the position of MD, but they have **whatever apparent authority attaches** to their **management position**.

(b)   **Removal** from the office of director may be a **breach** of their **service contract** if that agreement stipulates that they are to have the status of director as part of the conditions of employment.

9 Duties of directors

FAST FORWARD ▶▶ | The Company's Act 2006 sets out the **seven principal duties** of **directors**

The Company's Act 2006 sets out the **principal duties** that directors owe to their company. Many of these duties developed over time through the operation of **common law** and **equity,** or are **fiduciary duties** which have now been codified to make the law clearer and more accessible.

Point to note

When deciding whether a duty has been broken, the courts will consider the Companies Act primarily. All case law explained in this section applied before the 2006 Act and is included here to help you understand the types of situation that arise and how the law will be interpreted and applied by the courts in the future.

> **Fiduciary duty** is a duty imposed upon certain persons because of the position of trust and confidence in which they stand in relation to another. The duty is more onerous than generally arises under a contractual or tort relationship. It requires full disclosure of information held by the fiduciary, a strict duty to account for any profits received as a result of the relationship, and a duty to avoid conflict of interest.

Broadly speaking directors must be **honest** and **not allow their personal interests to conflict with their duties as directors**. The directors are said to hold a **fiduciary position** since they make contracts as **agents** of the company and have control of its property.

The duties included in the Companies Act 2006 form a **code of conduct** for directors. They do not tell them what to do but rather create a framework that sets out how they are expected to **behave** generally. This code is important as it addresses situations where:

- A director may put their **own interests** ahead of the company's, and
- A director may be **negligent** and liable to an action in tort.

9.1 Who are the duties owed to?

Section 170 makes it clear that directors owe their duties to the company, **not** the members. This means that the **only company itself can take action against a director** who breaches them. However, it is possible for a member to bring a derivative claim against the director on behalf of the company.

The effect of the **duties are cumulative**, in other words, a director owes **every duty** to the company that could apply in any given situation. The Act provides guidance for this. Where a director is offered a bribe for instance they will be breaking the duty not to accept a benefit from a third party and they will also not be promoting the company for the benefit of the members. When deciding whether or not a director has breached a duty, the court should consider their actions in the context of **each individual duty** in turn.

9.2 Who are the duties owed by?

Every person who is **classed as a director** under the Act owes the duties that are outlined below. Certain aspects of the duties regarding conflicts of interest and accepting benefits from third parties also apply to **past directors**. This is to prevent directors from exploiting a situation for their own benefit by simply resigning. The courts are directed to apply duties to **shadow directors** where they would have been applied to them previously under common law and equity. Directors must at all times continue to **act in accordance with all other laws**; no authorisation is given by the duties for a director to breach any other law or regulation.

9.3 The duties and the articles

The **articles** may provide more **onerous regulations** than the Act, but they may not reduce the level of duty expected unless it is in the following circumstances:

- If a director has **acted in accordance with the articles** they cannot be in breach of the duty to exercise independent judgement.

- Some **conflicts of interest by independent directors** are permissible by the articles.

- Directors will not be in breach of duty concerning **conflicts of interest** if they follow any **provisions in the articles for dealing with them** as long as the provisions are lawful.

- The company may **authorise anything** that would otherwise be a breach of duty.

9.4 The duties of directors

The **statutory duties** owed by directors are to:

- Act within their powers
- Promote the success of the company
- Exercise independent judgement
- Exercise reasonable skill, care and diligence
- Avoid conflicts of interest
- Not to accept benefits from third parties
- Declare an interest in a proposed transaction or arrangement

We shall now consider the duties placed on directors by the Act. Where cases are mentioned it is to **demonstrate** the previous common law or equitable principle that courts will follow when interpreting and applying the Act.

9.4.1 Duty to act within powers (s 171)

The directors owe a duty to act in accordance with the company's constitution, and only to exercise powers for the purposes for what they were conferred. They have a **fiduciary duty to the company to exercise their powers bona fide in what they honestly consider to be the interests of the company**: Re *Smith v Fawcett Ltd 1942*. This honest belief is effective even if, in fact, the interests of the company were not served.

This duty is owed **to the company** and **not generally to individual shareholders**. The directors will not generally be liable to the members if, for instance, they purchase shares without disclosing information affecting the share price: *Percival v Wright 1902*.

In exercising the powers given to them by the articles the directors have a fiduciary duty not only to act *bona fide* **but also only to use their powers for a proper purpose.** *Bamford v Bamford 1969*.

The powers are restricted to the **purposes** for **which they were given**. If the directors infringe this rule by exercising their powers for a collateral purpose the transaction will be invalid **unless** the **company** in **general meeting authorises it, or subsequently ratifies it**.

Most of the directors' powers are found in the **articles,** so this duty means that the directors must not act outside their power or the capacity of the company (in other words *ultra vires*).

If the irregular use of directors' powers is in the **allotment of shares** the votes attached to the new shares may not be used in reaching a decision in general meeting to sanction it.

Howard Smith Ltd v Ampol Petroleum Ltd 1974

The facts: Shareholders who held 55% of the issued shares intended to reject a takeover bid for the company. The directors honestly believed that it was in the company's interest that the bid should succeed. The directors therefore allotted new shares to a prospective bidder so that the shareholders opposed to the bid would then have less than 50% of the enlarged capital and the bid would succeed.

Decision: The allotment was invalid. 'It must be unconstitutional for directors to use their fiduciary powers over the shares in the company purely for the purpose of destroying an existing majority or creating a new majority which did not previously exist'.

Any **shareholder** may **apply to the court** to declare that a transaction in breach of s 171 should be set aside. However the practice of the courts is generally to **remit the issue** to the **members in general meeting** to see if the members wish to confirm the transaction. If the majority approve what has been done (or have authorised it in advance) that decision is treated as a proper case of **majority control** to which the minority must normally submit.

Hogg v Cramphorn 1966

The facts: The directors of a company issued shares to trustees of a pension fund for employees to prevent a takeover bid which they honestly thought would be bad for the company. The shares were paid for with money belonging to the company provided from an employees' benevolent and pension fund account. The shares carried 10 votes each and as a result the trustees and directors together had control of the company. The directors had power to issue shares but not to attach more than one vote to each. A minority shareholder brought the action on behalf of all the other shareholders.

Decision: If the directors act honestly in the best interests of the company, the company in general meeting can ratify the use of their powers for an improper purpose, so the allotment of the shares would be valid. But only one vote could be attached to each of the shares because that is what the articles provided.

Bamford v Bamford 1969

The facts: The directors of Bamford Ltd allotted 500,000 unissued shares to a third party to thwart a takeover bid. A month after the allotment a general meeting was called and an ordinary resolution was passed ratifying the allotment. The holders of the newly-issued shares did not vote. The claimants (minority shareholders) alleged that the allotment was not made for a proper purpose.

Decision: The ratification was valid and the allotment was good. There had been a breach of fiduciary duty but the act had been validated by an ordinary resolution passed in general meeting.

These cases can be distinguished from the *Howard Smith* case (where the allotment was invalid) in that in the *Howard Smith* case the original majority would not have sanctioned the use of directors' powers. In the *Bamford* case the decision could have been sanctioned by a vote which excluded the new shareholders.

Ratification is not effective when it attempts to validate a transaction when

- It constitutes **fraud on a minority**.
- It involves **misappropriation of assets**.
- The transaction **prejudices creditors' interests** at a time when the company is insolvent.

Under s 239, any resolution which proposes to **ratify the acts of a director** which are negligent, in default or in breach of duty or trust regarding the company must exclude the director or any members connected with them from the vote.

Most of the cases discussed above concern the **duty of directors** to exercise their power to allot shares. This is only one of the powers given to directors that are subject to this **fiduciary duty**. Others include:

- Power to borrow
- Power to give security
- Power to refuse to register a transfer of shares
- Power to call general meetings
- Power to circulate information to shareholders

9.4.2 Duty to promote the success of the company (s 172)

An overriding theme of the Companies Act 2006 is the principle that the **purpose of the legal framework** surrounding companies should be **to help companies do business**. Their main purpose is to create wealth for the shareholders.

This theme is evident in the **duty of directors to promote the success of a company**. During the development of the Act, the independent Company Law Review recommended that company law should consider the interests of those who companies are run for. It decided that the new Act should embrace the principle of **'enlightened shareholder value'**.

In essence, this principle means that the law should encourage **longtermism** and **regard for all stakeholders** by directors and that **stakeholder interests** should be **pursued** in an **enlightened** and **inclusive** way.

To achieve this, a duty of directors to act in a way, which, in **good faith**, promotes the success of the company for the benefit of the members as a whole, was created.

The requirements of this duty are difficult to define and possibly problematic to apply, so the Act provides directors with a **non-exhaustive list** of issues to keep in mind.

When exercising this duty **directors should consider**:

- The **consequences of decisions** in the long term.
- The **interests of** their **employees**.
- The need to **develop good relationships** with **customers** and **suppliers**.
- The **impact of the company** on the **local community** and the **environment**.
- The desirability of **maintaining high standards of business conduct** and a **good reputation**.
- The need to **act fairly as between all members** of the company.

The list identifies areas of **particular importance** and **modern day expectations** of **responsible business behaviour**. For example the interests of the company's employees and the impact of the company's operations on the community and the environment.

The **Act does not define** what should be regarded as the **success of a company**. This is down to a director's judgement in good faith. This is important as it ensures that business decisions are for the directors rather than the courts.

No guidance is given for what the **correct course of action** would be where the various s172 **duties conflict**. For example a decision to shut down an office may be in the long term best interests of the company but it is certainly not in the interests of the employees affected, nor the local community in which they live. Conflicts such as this are inevitable and could potentially leave directors open to breach of duty claims by a wide range of stakeholders if they do not deal with them carefully.

9.4.3 Duty to exercise independent judgement (s 173)

This is a simple duty that states directors must **exercise independent judgement.** They should **not delegate** their powers of decision-making or be **swayed by the influence of others**. Directors may delegate their functions to others, but they must continue to make independent decisions.

This duty is not infringed by acting in accordance with any agreement by the company that restricts the exercise of **discretion** by directors, or by acting in a way authorised by the company's constitution.

9.4.4 Duty to exercise reasonable skill, care and diligence (s 174)

Directors have a **duty of care** to show **reasonable skill, care and diligence**.

Section 174 provides that a director 'owes a duty to his company to exercise the same standard of 'care, skill and diligence that would be exercised by a reasonably diligent person with:

(a) *The general knowledge, skill and experience that may reasonably be expected of a person carrying out the functions carried out by the director in relation to the company; and*

(b) *The general knowledge, skill and experience that the director has.*

There is therefore a **reasonableness test** consisting of two parts:

(a) An **objective test**

Did the director act in a manner reasonably expected of a person performing the same role?

A director, when carrying out his functions, must show such **care** as could **reasonably** be expected from a **competent person** in that role. If a 'reasonable' director could be expected to act in a certain way, it is no defence for a director to claim, for example, lack of expertise.

(b) A **subjective test**

Did the director act in accordance with the skill, knowledge and experience that they actually have?

In the case of *Re City Equitable Fire and Insurance Co Ltd 1925* it was held that a director is expected to show the **degree of skill** which may **reasonably be expected** from a person of his knowledge and experience. The standard set is personal to the person in each case. An accountant who is a director of a mining company is not required to have the expertise of a mining engineer, but they should show the expertise of an accountant.

The duty to be competent extends to **non-executive directors**, who may be liable if they fail in their duty.

Dorchester Finance Co Ltd v Stebbing 1977

The facts: Of all the company's three directors S, P and H, only S worked full-time. P and H signed blank cheques at S's request who used them to make loans which became irrecoverable. The company sued all three; P and H, who were experienced accountants, claimed that as non-executive directors they had no liability.

Decision: All three were liable, P's and H's acts in signing blank cheques were negligent and not showing the necessary objective or subjective skill and care.

In other words, the **standard of care** is an objective 'competent' standard, plus a higher 'personal' standard of application. If the director actually had particular expertise that leads to a higher standard of competence being reasonably expected.

The company may recover damages from its directors for loss caused by their negligence. However something more than imprudence or want of care must be shown. It must be shown to be a case of **gross negligence**. This was defined in *Overend Gurney & Co v Gibb 1872* as conduct such that 'no men with any degree of prudence, acting on their own behalf, would have entered into such a transaction as they entered into'.

Therefore, in the absence of fraud it was difficult to control careless directors effectively. The **statutory provisions** on disqualification of directors of insolvent companies and on liability for wrongful trading therefore both set out how to judge a director's competence, and provide more effective enforcement (discussed below).

The company by decision of its **members in general meeting** decides whether to sue the directors for their negligence.

BPP
LEARNING MEDIA

Even if it is a case in which they could be liable **the court has discretion under s 1157 to relieve directors of liability** if it appears to the court that:

- The directors acted **honestly** and **reasonably**
- They **ought**, having regard to the circumstances of the case, **fairly to be excused**.

Re D' Jan of London Ltd 1993

The facts: D, a director of the company, signed an insurance proposal form without reading it. The form was filled in by D's broker. An answer given to one of the questions on the form was incorrect and the insurance company rightly repudiated liability for a fire at the company's premises in which stock worth some £174,000 was lost. The company became insolvent and the liquidator brought this action under s 212 of the Insolvency Act 1986 alleging D was negligent.

Decision: In failing to read the form D was negligent. However, he had acted honestly and reasonably and ought therefore to be partly relieved from liability by the Court under s 727 of the Companies Act 1985, (now s 1157 under the Companies Act 2006).

In the absence of **fraud**, **bad faith** or **ultra vires** the members may vote unanimously to forgive the director's negligence, even if it is those negligent directors who control the voting and exercise such forgiveness: *Multinational Gas & Petrochemical Co v Multinational Gas and Petrochemical Services Ltd 1983.* Where there is no fraud on the minority, a majority decision is sufficient: *Pavlides v Jensen 1956.*

9.4.5 Duty to avoid conflicts of interest (s 175)

Directors have a **duty to avoid circumstances** where their **personal interests conflict**, or may possibly conflict, **with the company's interests**. It may occur when a director makes personal use of information, property or opportunities belonging to the company, whether or not the company was able to take advantage of them at the time.

Therefore directors must be careful not to breach this duty when they **enter into a contract** with their company or if they **make a profit in the course of being a director**.

This duty does not apply to a conflict of interest in relation to a transaction or arrangement with the company, provided the director declared an interest.

As **agents,** directors have a **duty to avoid a conflict of interest**. In particular:

- The directors must **retain their freedom of action** and **not fetter their discretion** by agreeing to vote as some other person may direct.
- The directors owe a fiduciary duty to **avoid a conflict of duty and personal interest.**
- The directors **must not obtain any personal advantage** from their position as directors **without the consent of the company** for whatever gain or profit they have obtained.

The following cases are important in the area of **conflict of interest**.

> *Regal (Hastings) Ltd v Gulliver 1942*
>
> *The facts:* The company owned a cinema. It had the opportunity of acquiring two more cinemas through a subsidiary to be formed with an issued capital of £5,000. However the company could not proceed with this scheme since it only had £2,000 available for investment in the subsidiary.
>
> The directors and their friends therefore subscribed £3,000 for shares of the new company to make up the required £5,000. The chairman acquired his shares not for himself but as nominee of other persons. The company's solicitor also subscribed for shares. The share capital of the two companies (which then owned three cinemas) was sold at a price which yielded a profit of £2.80 per share of the new company in which the directors had invested. The new controlling shareholder of the company caused it to sue the directors to recover the profit which they had made.
>
> *Decision:*
>
> (a) The directors were **accountable** to the company for their profit since they had obtained it from an opportunity which came to them as directors.
>
> (b) It was **immaterial** that the **company** had **lost nothing** since it had been unable to make the investment itself.
>
> (c) The directors might have kept their profit if the company had **agreed** by resolution passed in general meeting that they should do so. The directors might have used their votes to approve their action since it was not fraudulent (there was no misappropriation of the company's property).
>
> (d) The chairman was not accountable for the profit on his shares since he did not obtain it for himself. The solicitor was not accountable for his profit since he was **not a director** and so was not subject to the rule of accountability as a director for personal profits obtained in that capacity.

> *Industrial Development Consultants Ltd v Cooley 1972*
>
> *The facts:* C was managing director of the company which provided consultancy services to gas companies. A gas company was unlikely to award a particular contract to the company but C realised that, acting personally, he might be able to obtain it. He told the board of his company that he was ill and persuaded them to release him from his service agreement. On ceasing to be a director of the company C obtained the contract on his own behalf. The company sued him to recover the profits of the contract.
>
> *Decision:* C was accountable to his old company for his profit.

Directors will not be liable for a breach of this duty if:

- The **members** of the company **authorised** their actions

- The **situation cannot reasonably be regarded** as likely to give rise to a conflict of interest

- The **actions have been authorised by the other directors**. This only applies if they are genuinely independent from the transaction and:

    - If the company is private - the articles do not restrict such authorisation, or
    - If it is public - the articles expressly permit it.

9.4.6 Duty not to accept benefits from third parties (s 176)

This duty **prohibits the acceptance of benefits** (including bribes) from third parties conferred by reason of them being director, or doing, (or omitting to do) something as a director. Where a director accepts a benefit that may also create or potentially create a conflict of interest, they will also be in breach of their s 175 duty (see above).

BPP
LEARNING MEDIA

Unlike s 175, an act which would potentially be in breach of this duty **cannot be authorised** by the **directors**, but **members do have the right to authorise it**. Directors will not be in breach of this duty if the acceptance of the benefit **cannot reasonably** be regarded as likely to give rise to a conflict of interest.

9.4.7 Duty to declare interest in proposed transaction or arrangement (s 177)

Directors are required to disclose to the other directors the nature and extent of any interest, direct or indirect, that they have in relation to a **proposed transaction** or **arrangement** with the **company**. Even if the director is not a party to the transaction, the duty may apply if they are aware, or ought reasonably to be aware, of the interest. For example, the interest of another person in a contract with the company may require disclosure under this duty if that other person's interest is a direct or indirect interest on the part of the director.

Directors are required to disclose their interest in any transaction **before** the company enters into the transaction. Disclosure can be made by:

- Written notice
- General notice
- Verbally at a board meeting

Disclosure to the **members** is **not** sufficient to discharge the duty. Directors must declare the **nature** and **extent** of their interest to the **other directors** as well.

If the declaration becomes **void** or **inaccurate**, a **further declaration** should be made.

No declaration of interest is required if the director's interest in the transaction **cannot reasonably** be regarded as likely to give rise to a conflict of interest.

9.5 Consequences of breach of duty

Breach of duty comes under the **civil law** rather than criminal law and, as mentioned earlier, the company itself must take up the action. This usually means the other directors starting proceedings.

Consequences for breach include:

- **Damages** payable to the company where it has suffered loss.
- **Restoration** of company property
- **Repayment of any profits** made by the director
- **Rescission of contract** (where the director did not disclose an interest)

9.6 Declaration of an interest in an existing transaction or arrangement (s 182)

Directors have a statutory obligation to declare any **direct** or **indirect interest** in an **existing transaction** entered into by the company. This obligation is almost identical to the duty to disclose an interest in a proposed transaction or arrangement under s 177 (see above). However, this section is relevant to transactions or arrangements that have already occurred.

A declaration under s 182 is **not** required if:

- It has **already been disclosed** as a proposed transaction under s 177

- The director is **not aware** of either

  - **The interest** they have in the transaction, or
  - In **the transaction** itself

- The director's interest in the transaction **cannot reasonably** be regarded as likely to give rise to a conflict of interest

- The **other directors are aware** (or reasonably should be aware) of the situation

- It concerns the **director's service contract** and it has been considered by a board meeting or committee

Where a declaration is required it should be made as soon as **reasonably practicable** either:

- By written notice
- By general notice
- Verbally at a board meeting

If the declaration becomes **void** or **inaccurate**, a **further declaration** should be made.

9.7 Other controls over directors

The table below summarises other statutory controls over directors included in the Companies Act 2006.

CA06 Ref	Control
188	Directors' service contracts lasting more than two years must be approved by the members.
190	Directors or any person connected to them may not acquire a non-cash asset from the company without approval of the members. This does not apply where the asset's value is less than £5,000, or less than 10% of the company's asset value. All sales of assets with a value exceeding £100,000 must be approved.
197	Any loans given to directors, or guarantees provided as security for loans provided to directors, must be approved by members, if over £10,000 in value.
198	Expands section 197 to prevent unapproved quasi-loans to directors (public companies only) of over £10,000 in value.
201	Expands section 197 to prevent unapproved credit transactions by the company for the benefit of a director (public companies only) of over £15,000 in value.
204	Directors must seek approval of members where the company loans them over £50,000 to meet expenditure required in the course of business.
217	Non-contractual payments to directors for loss of office must be approved by the members.

9.8 Examples of remedies against directors

Remedies against directors for breach of duties include accounting to the company for a **personal gain**, **indemnifying the company**, and **rescission of contracts** made with the company. The type of remedy varies with the breach of duty.

(a) The director may have to **account for a personal gain**: *Regal (Hastings) Ltd v Gulliver 1942*.

(b) They may have to **indemnify the company** against loss caused by their negligence such as an unlawful transaction which they approved.

(c) If they contract with the company in a conflict of interest the **contract may be rescinded by the company**. However under common law rules the company cannot both affirm the contract and recover the director's profit: *Burland v Earle 1902*.

(d) The court may declare that a transaction is *ultra vires* or unlawful: *Re Lee Behrens & Co 1932*.

BPP
LEARNING MEDIA

A company may, either by its **articles** or by **passing a resolution** in general meeting, **authorise or ratify** the conduct of directors in breach of duty. There are some limits on the power of members in general meeting to **sanction a breach of duty** by directors or to release them from their strict obligations.

(a) If the directors **defraud** the company and vote in general meeting to approve their own fraud, their votes are invalid (*Cook v Deeks 1916*).

(b) If the directors **allot shares** to alter the balance of votes in a general meeting the votes attached to those shares may not be cast to support a resolution approving the issue (see *Bamford's* case above).

9.9 Directors' liability for acts of other directors

A director is **not liable** for acts of fellow directors. However if they become aware of serious breaches of duty by other directors, they may have a duty to inform members of them or to take control of assets of the company without having proper delegated authority to do so.

In such cases the director is **liable for their own negligence** in what they allow to happen and not directly for the misconduct of the other directors.

9.10 Directors' personal liability

As a general rule a director has no personal liability for the debts of the company. But there are certain exceptions.

- Personal liability **may arise** by **lifting the veil** of incorporation.

- A **limited company** may by its articles or by **special resolution** provide that its directors shall have unlimited liability for its debts

- A director may be **liable** to the **company's creditors** in certain circumstances.

Can a director be held personally liable for **negligent advice** given by his company? The case below shows that they can, but only when they assume responsibility in a personal capacity for advice given, rather than simply giving advice in their capacity as a director.

Williams and Another v Natural Life Health Foods Ltd 1998

The facts: The director was sued personally by claimants who claimed they were misled by the company's brochure. The director helped prepare the brochure, and the brochure described him as the source of the company's expertise. The claimants did not however deal with the director but with other employees.

Decision: The House of Lords overruled the Court of Appeal, and ruled that the director was not personally liable. In order to have been liable, there would have had to have been evidence that the director had assumed personal responsibility. Merely acting as a director and advertising his earlier experience did not amount to assumption of personal liability.

 Question

Statutory duties of directors

Which of the following is a statutory duty of directors?

A   Promote the success of the company
B   Accept benefits from third parties
C   Maximise company profitability
D   Fulfil corporate social responsibility obligations

A   This is a statutory duty under s172 of the Companies Act 2006.

10 The company secretary

FAST FORWARD

Every public company must have a **company secretary**, who is one of the officers of a company and may be a director. Private companies are not required to have a secretary.

Every public company must have a **company secretary**, who is one of the officers of a company and may be a director. Private companies are not required to have a secretary. In this case the roles normally done by the company secretary may be done by one of the directors, or an approved person. The secretary of state may require a public company to appoint a secretary where it has failed to do so.

10.1 Appointment of a company secretary

To be appointed as a company secretary to a plc, the directors must ensure that the candidate should be qualified (s 273) by virtue of:

- **Employment** as a plc's secretary for **three out of the five years** preceding appointment
- **Membership** of one of a list of **qualifying bodies**: CIMA, ACCA, ICAEW, ICSA, ICAI or CIPFA
- **Qualification** as a **solicitor**, **barrister** or **advocate** within the UK
- **Employment** in a position or **membership** of a professional body that, in the opinion of the directors, **appears to qualify that person** to act as company secretary

They should also have the *'necessary knowledge and experience'* as deemed by the directors.

A **sole director** of a private company cannot also be the company secretary, but a company can have **two** or more joint secretaries. A **corporation** can fulfil the role of company secretary. A register of secretaries must be kept.

Under the **UK Corporate Governance Code**, the appointment of the company secretary is a matter for the board as a whole.

10.2 Duties of a company secretary

The specific **duties** of each company secretary are **determined by the directors** of the company. As a company officer, the company secretary is responsible for ensuring that the company complies with its statutory obligations. In particular, this means:

- **Establishing** and **maintaining** the company's **statutory registers**
- **Filing accurate returns** with the Registrar on time
- **Organising** and **minuting** company and **board meetings**
- **Ensuring** that **accounting records** meet **statutory requirements**
- **Ensuring** that **annual accounts** are **prepared** and **filed** in accordance with **statutory requirements**
- **Monitoring statutory requirements** of the company
- **Signing company documents** as may be required by law

BPP
LEARNING MEDIA

Under the **UK Corporate Governance Code**, the company secretary must:

- **Ensure good information flows** within the board and its committees
- **Facilitate induction of board members** and assist with professional development
- **Advise** the **chairman** and the **board** on all **governance issues**

10.3 Powers and authority of a company secretary

The **powers of the company secretary** have historically been very limited. However, the common law increasingly recognises that they may be able to act as agents to exercise apparent or **ostensible authority**, therefore, they may enter the company into contracts connected with the administrative side of the company.

Panorama Developments (Guildford) Ltd v Fidelis Furnishing Fabrics Ltd 1971

The facts: B, the secretary of a company, ordered cars from a car hire firm, representing that they were required to meet the company's customers at London Airport. Instead he used the cars for his own purposes. The bill was not paid, so the car hire firm claimed payment from B's company.

Decision: B's company was liable, for he had apparent authority to make contracts such as the present one, which were concerned with the administrative side of its business. The decision recognises the general nature of a company secretary's duties.

Question

Qualifications of company secretaries

Ownership of which of the following qualifications would entitle an individual to be appointed as a company secretary?

A   A degree in Accountancy
B   An NVQ in Business Studies
C   CIM
D   ICAEW

Answer

D   Qualified accountants, such as members of CIMA, ACCA and ICAEW are entitled to be appointed as company secretaries. Degrees, NVQs or non-specified professional qualifications such as CIM, do not entitle an individual to act as a company secretary. A qualified solicitor or barrister can act as a company secretary.

11 The company auditor

FAST FORWARD

Every company (apart from certain small companies) must appoint appropriately qualified **auditors**. An audit is a check on the stewardship of the directors.

Every company (except a dormant private company and certain small companies) must **appoint auditors** for each financial year: s 475.

11.1 Appointment

The **first auditors** may be appointed by the directors, to hold office until the **first general meeting** at which their appointment is considered.

Subsequent auditors may not take office until the previous auditor has ceased to hold office. They will hold office until the end of the next financial period (private companies) or the next accounts meeting (public companies) unless re-appointed.

Appointment of auditors	
Members	• Usually appoint an auditor in general meeting by ordinary resolution. • Auditors hold office from 28 days after the meeting in which the accounts are laid until the end of the corresponding period the next year. This is the case even if the auditors are appointed at the meeting where the accounts are laid. • May appoint in general meeting to fill a casual vacancy.
Directors	• Appoint the first ever auditors. They hold office until the end of the first meeting at which the accounts are considered. • May appoint to fill a casual vacancy.
Secretary of State	• May appoint auditors if members fail to. • Company must notify Secretary of State within 28 days of the general meeting where the accounts were laid.

11.1.1 Eligibility as auditor

Membership of a **Recognised Supervisory Body** is the main prerequisite for eligibility as an auditor. An audit firm may be either a body corporate, a partnership or a sole practitioner. The Act requires an auditor to hold an **'appropriate qualification'**. A person holds an 'appropriate qualification' if they:

- Have satisfied **existing criteria** for appointment as an auditor
- Hold a **recognised qualification** obtained in the UK
- Hold an **approved overseas qualification**

11.1.2 Ineligibility as auditor

Under the Companies Act 2006, a person may be ineligible on the grounds of **'lack of independence'**. A person is ineligible for appointment as a company auditor if they are:

- An **officer** or **employee** of the company being audited

- A **partner** or **employee** of such a person

- A **partnership** in which such a person is a partner

- **Ineligible** by virtue of the above for appointment as auditor of any parent or subsidiary undertaking where there exists a **connection** of any description as may be specified in regulations laid down by Secretary of State.

11.1.3 Effect of lack of independence or ineligibility

No person may act as auditor if they lack independence or become ineligible. If during their term of office an auditor loses their independence or eligibility they must **resign** with immediate effect, and **notify** their client of their resignation giving the reason. A person continuing to act as auditor despite losing their independence or becoming ineligible is **liable to a fine**. However it is a defence if they can prove they were not aware that they lost independence or became ineligible.

BPP LEARNING MEDIA

The **legislation does not disqualify** the following from being an auditor of a limited company:

- A shareholder of the company
- A debtor or creditor of the company
- A close relative of an officer or employee of the company

However, the **regulations** of the **accountancy bodies** applying to their members are **stricter than statute in this respect**.

11.1.4 Reappointing an auditor of a private company

The above rules on appointment make reference to a **meeting** where the accounts are laid. This is not always relevant for private companies as under the Act they are not required to hold an AGM or lay the accounts before the members. Therefore **auditors of private companies are deemed automatically reappointed** unless one of the following circumstances apply.

- The auditor was **appointed by the directors** (most likely when the first auditor was appointed).

- The **articles require formal reappointment**.

- **Members holding 5% of the voting rights** serve notice that the auditor should not be reappointed s 488.

- A **resolution** (written or otherwise) has been passed that prevents reappointment.

- The **directors have resolved that auditors should not be appointed** for the forthcoming year as the company is likely to be exempt from audit.

11.2 Auditor remuneration

Whoever appoints the auditors has power to **fix their remuneration** for the period of their appointment. It is usual when the auditors are appointed by the general meeting to leave it to the directors to fix their remuneration (by agreement at a later stage). The auditors' remuneration must be **disclosed** in a **note to the accounts**.

11.3 Exemption from audit

Certain **companies** are exempt from audit provided the following conditions are fulfilled.

(a) A company is totally exempt from the annual audit requirement in a financial year if its turnover for that year is **not more** than **£6.5m** and its **balance sheet total** is **not more than £3.26m**.

(b) The exemptions do not apply to **public companies**, **banking** or **insurance companies** or those subject to a **statute-based regulatory regime**.

(c) The company is a **non-commercial**, **non-profit making public sector body** which is subject to audit by a **public sector auditor**.

(d) **Members** holding **10%** or more of the capital of any company can veto the exemption.

(e) **Dormant companies** which qualify for exemption from an audit as a dormant company.

11.4 Duties of auditors

The **statutory duty** of auditors is to report to the members whether the accounts give a **true and fair view** and have been properly prepared in accordance with the Companies Act.

They **must also**:

- **State** whether or not the **directors' report** is **consistent** with the **accounts**.

- For **quoted companies**, **report** to the members on the **auditable** part of the **directors' remuneration report** including whether or not it has been properly prepared in accordance with the Act.

- Be **signed** by the **auditor**, stating their **name**, and **date**. Where the auditor is a firm, the **senior auditor** must sign in their **own name** for, and on behalf, of the auditor.

To fulfil their duties, the auditors **must carry out such investigations as are necessary** to form an opinion as to whether:

(a) **Proper accounting records** have been kept and proper returns adequate for the audit have been received from branches.

(b) The **accounts** are in **agreement** with the **accounting records**.

(c) The **information** in the **directors' remuneration report** is consistent with the **accounts**.

The auditors' report must be **read** before any general meeting at which the accounts are considered and must be open to inspection by members. Auditors have to make disclosure of other services rendered to the company and the remuneration received.

Where an auditor **knowingly** or **recklessly** causes their report to be **materially misleading**, **false** or **deceptive**, they commit a criminal offence and may be liable to a **fine**: s 507.

11.5 Rights of auditors

FAST FORWARD

The Companies Act provide **statutory rights** for auditors to enable them to carry out their duties.

The **principal rights** of auditors, excepting those dealing with resignation or removal, are set out in the table below, and the following are notes on more detailed points.

Access to records	A right of access at all times to the books, accounts and vouchers of the company: S 499 (1)
Information and explanations	A right to require from the company's officers, employees or any other relevant person, such information and explanations as they think necessary for the performance of their duties as auditors: S 499 (1)
Attendance at/notices of general meetings	A right to attend any general meetings of the company and to receive all notices of and communications relating to such meetings which any member of the company is entitled to receive: s 502 (2)
Right to speak at general meetings	A right to be heard at general meetings which they attend on any part of the business that concerns them as auditors: s 502 (2)
Rights in relation to written resolutions	A right to receive a copy of any written resolution proposed: s 502 (1)

If auditors have **not received** all the information and explanations they consider necessary, they should state this fact in their audit report.

The Act makes it an **offence** for a company's officer knowingly or recklessly to make a **statement** in any form to an auditor which **conveys** or **purports to convey** any **information or explanation** required by the auditor and **is materially misleading**, **false** or **deceptive**. The **penalty** is a maximum of two years' imprisonment, a fine or both.

11.6 Auditors' liability

Under s 532 any **agreement** between an auditor and a company that seeks to **indemnify the auditor** for their own negligence, default, or breach of duty or trust is **void**. However under s 534, an agreement can be made which **limits the auditor's liability** to the company. Such **liability limitation agreements** can only stand for **one financial year** and must therefore be replaced annually. Liability can only be **limited** to what is **fair and reasonable** having regard to the auditor's responsibilities, their contractual obligations and the professional standards expected of them. Such agreements must be approved by the members and **publicly disclosed** in the **accounts** or **directors' report**.

11.7 Termination of auditors' appointment

FAST FORWARD

> Auditors may leave office in the following ways: **resignation**; **removal from office** by an ordinary resolution with special notice passed before the end of their term; **failing** to **offer themselves** for **re-election**; and **not being re-elected** at the general meeting at which their term expires.

Departure of auditors from office can occur in the following ways.

(a) Auditors may **resign** their appointment by giving notice in writing to the company delivered to the registered office.

(b) Auditors may **decline reappointment**.

(c) Auditors may be **removed** from office before the expiry of their appointment by the passing of an ordinary resolution in general meeting. Special notice is required and members and auditors must be notified. **Private companies cannot remove an auditor by written resolution;** a meeting must be held.

(d) Auditors **do not have to be reappointed** when their term of office expires, although in most cases they are. Special notice must be given of any resolution to appoint auditors who were not appointed on the last occasion of the resolution, and the members and auditor must be notified.

Where a private company resolves to **appoint** a replacement auditor by **written resolution**, copies of the resolution must be sent to the proposed and outgoing auditor. The outgoing auditor may circulate a **statement of reasonable length** to the members if they notify the company within 14 days of receiving the copy of the written resolution.

11.7.1 Resignation of auditors

However auditors leave office they must either: **state** there are **no circumstances** which should be brought to members' and creditors' attention; **or list those circumstances**. Auditors who are resigning can also: circulate a statement about their resignation to members; requisition a general meeting'; or speak at a general meeting.

Procedures for resignation of auditors	
Statement of circumstances	Auditors must deposit a statement at the registered office with their resignation stating: • For quoted companies – the circumstances around their departure. • For non-quoted public companies and all private companies – there are no circumstances that the auditor believes should be brought to the attention of the members or creditors. • If there are such circumstances the statement should describe them. • Statements should also be submitted to the appropriate audit authority.

Procedures for resignation of auditors	
Company action	• The company must send notice of the resignation to the Registrar. • The company must **send** a copy of the statement of circumstances to **every person entitled to receive a copy of the accounts.**
Auditor rights	If the auditors have deposited a statement of circumstances, they may: • Circulate a statement of reasonable length to the members • Requisition a general meeting to explain their reasons: s 518 • Attend and speak at any meeting where appointment of successors is to be discussed.

If the auditors decline to seek reappointment at an AGM, they must nevertheless fulfil the requirements of a **statement of the circumstances** just as if they had resigned. The reason for this provision is to prevent auditors who are unhappy with the company's affairs keeping their suspicions secret. The statement must be deposited not less than **14 days** before the time allowed for next appointing auditors.

11.7.2 Removal of the auditor from office

Procedures for removal from office	
Auditor representations	If a resolution is proposed either to: • Remove the auditors before their term of office expires or • Change the auditors when their term of office is complete the auditors have the right to make representations of reasonable length to the company
Company action	The company must: • Notify members in the notice of the meeting of the representations • Send a copy of the representations in the notice • If it is not sent out, the auditors can require it is read at the meeting
Attendance at meeting	Auditors removed before expiry of their office may: • Attend the meeting at which their office would have expired • Attend any meeting at which the appointment of their successors is discussed
Statement of circumstances	If auditors are removed at a general meeting they must: • Make a statement of circumstances for members and creditors as above.

Question

Auditors

Who appoints a company's first auditors?

A   Directors
B   Subscribers
C   Members
D   Senior managers

Answer

A   Directors appoint a company's first auditors and they hold office until the first meeting where the accounts are considered. From then on, the members usually appoint the auditors each year by ordinary resolution.

- Any person who occupies the position of director is treated as such, the test being one of **function**.

- The method of appointing directors, along with their rotation and co-option is **controlled** by the **articles.**

- Directors are entitled to **fees** and **expenses** as directors as per the articles, and **emoluments** (and compensation for loss of office) as per their service contracts (which can be inspected by members). Some details are published in the directors' remuneration report along with the accounts.

- A director may vacate office as director due to: **resignation**; **not going** for **re-election**; **death**; **dissolution** of the company; **removal**; **disqualification**.

- Directors may be required to vacate office because they have been disqualified on grounds dictated by the articles. Directors **may** be disqualified from a wider range of company involvements under the Company Directors Disqualification Act 1986 (CDDA).

- Directors may be **disqualified** from acting as directors or being involved in the management of companies in a number of circumstances. They must be disqualified if the company is insolvent, and the director is found to be unfit to be concerned with management of a company.

- The **powers** of the directors are **defined** by the **articles**.

- Directors' powers may be restricted by statute or by the articles. The directors have a duty to exercise their powers in what they honestly believe to be the **best interests** of the company and for the **purposes** for which the powers are given.

- One or more directors may be appointed by the board as **managing director**. The managing director has **apparent** authority to make business contracts on behalf of the company. The managing director's **actual** authority is whatever the board gives them.

- The Company's Act 2006 sets out the **seven principal duties** of **directors**.

- The **statutory duties** owed by directors are to:

  - Act within their powers
  - Promote the success of the company
  - Exercise independent judgement
  - Exercise reasonable skill, care and diligence
  - Avoid conflicts of interest
  - Not accept benefits from third parties
  - Declare an interest in a proposed transaction or arrangement

- Every public company must have a **company secretary**, who is one of the officers of a company and may be a director. Private companies are not required to have a secretary.

- Every company (apart from certain small companies) must appoint appropriately qualified **auditors**. An audit is a check on the stewardship of the directors.

- The Companies Act provide **statutory rights** for auditors to enable them to carry out their duties.

- Auditors may leave office in the following ways: **resignation**; **removal from office** by an ordinary resolution with special notice passed before the end of their term; **failing** to **offer themselves** for **re-election**; and **not being re-elected** at the general meeting at which their term expires.

1 Which of the following are correct rules on retirement and re-election of directors?
Select all that apply.

   A   Every year one third of the directors (or the nearest number thereto) shall retire.

   B   The managing director and any other director holding executive office are not subject to retirement by rotation and are excluded from the reckoning of the one third figure.

   C   Those retiring will be those in service longest since their last election.

   D   Directors appointed to the board during the year are not included in the calculation.

2 **Fill in the blanks** in the statements below.

   Under model articles directors are authorised to m..................... the b..................... of the company, and e..................... the p.....................of the company.

3 Under which of the following grounds may a director be disqualified if he is guilty, and under which must a director be disqualified?

   A   Conviction of an indictable offence in connection with a company

   B   Persistent default with the provisions of company legislation

   C   Wrongful trading

   D   Director of an insolvent company whose conduct makes him unfit to be concerned in the management of the company

4 What is the extent of a managing director's actual authority?

5 What is the minimum age that a person must have to be a director of a company?.

   A   14
   B   16
   C   18
   D   21

6 A public company must have two directors, a private company only needs one.

   True ☐

   False ☐

7 Describe the subjective test that directors must pass in order to meet their duty of care.

8 A private company with a sole director is not legally required to have a company secretary, but if it does, the sole director cannot also be the company secretary.

   True ☐

   False ☐

9 State two reasons why a person would be ineligible to be an auditor under Companies Act 2006.

   (1)   ....

   (2)   ....

10   The directors remuneration report of which type of company must be put to a vote of the members?

    A   Private companies only

    B   All public companies

    C   Quoted companies only

    D   Companies limited by guarantee

11   Individual directors, who are not managing directors, have the authority to enter their company into any general commercial contract.

True   ☐

False   ☐

Answers to Quick Quiz

1   C and D are correct. One half of the directors shall retire each year. Executive directors excluding the MD are subject to retirement by rotation.

2   Under model articles directors are authorised to **manage** the **business** of the company, and **exercise all** the **powers** of the company.

3   A to C are grounds under which a director may be disqualified; D is grounds under which a director must be disqualified.

4   The actual authority is whatever the board gives them.

5   B. Directors must be a minimum of 16 years old.

6   True. Private companies only need one director.

7   A director is expected to show the degree of skill, knowledge and expertise that he or she actually has in order to meet the subjective test.

8   True. Sole directors cannot be company secretaries. Private companies are not required to have a company secretary.

9   Any of:

    (1) Is an officer/employee of the company being audited, (2) A partner or employee of a person in (1), (3) A partnership in which (1) is a partner, (4) Ineligible by (1), (2) and (3) to be auditor of any of the entity's subsidiaries

10   C. The directors remuneration report of quoted companies must be put to a vote of the members.

11   False. They only have the authority which attaches to their management position.

Now try the questions below from the Question Bank

Number
Q61
Q62
Q63
Q64
Q65

14

Majority control and minority protection

Introduction

Every member of a company is bound by the articles to the company and to his fellow members as we saw in an earlier chapter. By implication, a member agrees to be bound by the decisions of the **majority** as expressed at a general meeting. This principle of majority rule was established in *Foss v Harbottle*.

However, while *directors* must exercise their power *bona fide* for the benefit of the company, shareholders are under no such obligation. Clearly shareholders may exercise their votes in their own interests and not those of the company. There must, therefore, be some restraint on the power of those able to command a majority vote. Minorities are therefore protected by **common law** and **statute**, and the various rules are all covered in this chapter.

You should concentrate more on the **statutory rules for minority protection** under s 994 than on the common law rules.

This topic may be examined along with the **duties of directors** and other actions a shareholder may take, including a shareholder's right to remove directors under s 168.

Topic list	Learning outcomes
1 The rule of the majority	G2(g)
2 Statutory protection for the minority	G2(g)
3 Other protection for the minority	G2(g)

1 The rule of the majority

FAST FORWARD Ultimate **control** of a company rests with its members voting in general meeting.

1.1 Majority control

Directors owe their duties to company (the members as a body in general meeting), not to individual members. Therefore, if they breach their duties, it is the company which should bring proceedings.

> *Foss v Harbottle 1843*
>
> *The facts:* A shareholder (Foss) sued the directors of the company alleging that the directors had defrauded the company by selling land to it at an inflated price. The company was by this time in a state of disorganisation and efforts to call the directors to account at a general meeting had failed.
>
> *Decision:* The action must be dismissed.
>
> (a) The **company** as a person separate from its members is the **only proper claimant** in an action to protect its rights or property.
>
> (b) The **company** in **general meeting** must decide whether to bring such legal proceedings.

In laying down the general principles of procedure the court did nonetheless recognise that 'the claims of justice' must prevail over 'technical rules'. A shareholder majority may have an effective voice in general meeting, and if **directors or majority shareholders** make use of this fact to **take a course of action** which is **detrimental to the minority**, then the minority must have some **protection** against them.

The protection of a minority in various situations is provided by (most importantly) **statute**, and (rarely in modern times) in common law by making **exceptions** to the rule laid down in *Foss v Harbottle*.

2 Statutory protection for the minority

FAST FORWARD The principal **statutory** remedy for minorities is a s 994 action alleging the company's affairs have been conducted in an **unfairly prejudicial manner.** The court may make **whatever order** it sees fit to settle a s 994 action (generally purchase of the petitioner's shares).

Other statutory protection is available such as **derivative claims** and **proceedings** under **insolvency legislation**.

2.1 Unfairly prejudicial conduct: S 994

Any member may apply to the court for relief under s 994 on the grounds that the company's affairs are being or have been conducted in a manner which is **unfairly prejudicial** to the interests of the members **generally or of some part** of the members, including at least himself. Application may also be made in respect of an actual or proposed single prejudicial act or omission.

There is **no statutory definition** of what constitutes **unfairly prejudicial conduct**. Applications against unfairly prejudicial conduct often arise from:

(a) **Exclusion of a director** from participation in the management of a quasi-partnership company (A 'quasi-partnership' company is a small, generally private and often family-owned company where essentially the relationship between the directors and members is equivalent to partners in a partnership.)

(b) **Discrimination against a minority**

 BPP LEARNING MEDIA

2.2 Examples of conduct that has been held to be unfairly prejudicial

Examples of conduct that has been held to be **unfairly prejudicial** include the following.

- **Exclusion** and **removal from the board**
- **Improper allotment** of **shares**
- **Failure** to **call a meeting**
- **Making** an **inaccurate statement** to **shareholders**
- **A managing director using assets** for **his own personal benefit** and the personal benefit of his family and friends
- **Diversion** of the **company's business** to a director-controlled company
- **Making a rights issue** which **minority shareholders could not take up**
- Payment of **excessive directors' bonuses** and **pension contributions**

The courts will not generally intervene in cases of **management** (even bad management). However, on occasions the courts have intervened where continued mismanagement caused serious financial damage to the company and the minority's interests.

There are **other instances** where the courts have held that conduct was **not unfairly prejudicial**.

- Late presentation of accounts
- Failure by a parent company to pay the debts of a subsidiary
- Non-compliance with the Stock Exchange rules, the City Code and UK Corporate Governance rules

The **limits on the application** of s 994 are debatable. It has been argued for example that a s 994 action could be used as a check on excessive board remuneration packages.

2.3 Court orders

When a petition is successful the **court** may make whatever order it deems fit. Courts may make, under s 996:

(a) An order regulating the **future conduct** of the company's affairs, for example that a controlling shareholder shall conform to the decisions taken at board meetings: *Re H R Harmer Ltd 1958*

(b) An authorisation to any person to bring **civil proceedings** on behalf of the company; the company is then responsible for the legal costs

(c) An order requiring the company to **refrain** from doing or continuing an act complained of, or to do an act that it has omitted to do.

(d) Provision for the **purchase of shares** of the **minority**

(e) A requirement that the **company should not make any**, or any **specified**, **alterations** to its **articles** without the court's leave

Perhaps the **most common type of relief** is an order that either the controlling shareholder or the company shall purchase the petitioner's shares at a fair price; this ends a relationship which has probably broken down beyond repair.

- The shares should be valued on the basis of their **worth before** the controlling shareholders' conduct had diminished it
- The **court** may determine what is **fair**; in particular no allowance need be made because the shares to be bought are only a minority holding and do not give control

Question

James is the majority shareholder in Elan Ltd, holding 52% of the issued shares. The other shareholders are Chris, Martin, Jennifer and Henry, each of whom holds 12% of the shares. The minority shareholders feel that James has been abusing his position as majority shareholder and have lost confidence in him. They approach you for general advice.

Advise them on the nature of the action available under s 994 of the Companies Act 2006 on the basis of unfair prejudice to the minority.

Answer

Under s 994, any member may apply to the court for relief on the grounds that the company's affairs are being or have been conducted in a manner which is unfairly prejudicial to the interests of the members generally or some part of the members or in respect of a particular act or omission which has been or will be prejudicial. Applications are commonly made in cases of discrimination against a minority or exclusion of a partner in a quasi-partnership company.

The prejudice complained of must affect the claimant-member in his capacity as member and not as an employee or unpaid creditor. The member need not prove bad faith or even an intention to discriminate.

The court will take into account the surrounding circumstances including the parties' conduct and may make such orders as it deems fit. It might regulate the company's future affairs in some way, order the purchase of the minority's shares by the majority or by the company itself, authorise some person to bring civil proceedings on the company's behalf, order the company to refrain from doing the act complained of or to do an act omitted, or not to alter the articles without the court's leave.

The types of conduct that have been held to be unfairly prejudicial are as follows.

(a) Exclusion and removal from the board

(b) A managing director using assets for his own personal benefit and the personal benefit of his family and friends

(c) The improper allotment of shares

(d) The failure to call a meeting as requisitioned by the petitioner-minority

(e) Payment to directors of excessive remuneration

(f) The diversion of a company's business to a director-controlled company or the making of a rights issue which minority shareholders were not permitted to take up or the payment of excessive directors' bonuses and pension contributions.

Point to note

A shareholder who is unhappy about the conduct of the company's affairs will often try to obtain a remedy under s 994.

2.4 Derivative claims

As we saw earlier, under section 170 of the Act directors owe their **general duties** to the company as a whole rather than to an individual member and therefore the company is the only proper claimant which can enforce them.

Under English common law members may, under certain circumstances, bring an action on behalf of a company that they are a member of. This is known as a **derivative claim**. The purpose of such claims is to enforce liability for breach of duty by one of the directors. After all, if the company itself is the only proper claimant and the directors take the decisions on behalf of the company, it is unlikely that they would want to take action against one of their number!

Sections 260 to 269 of the 2006 Act provide a **statutory basis** for deciding whether or not a member has a right to bring a **derivative claim**. They do not replace the rule in *Foss v Harbottle*, but instead set out new rules that allow a derivative claim for negligence, default, breach of trust or breach of duty against a director or other person, even if the director has not benefited personally.

The sections introduce a **two-stage procedure** for derivative claims.

(a) The applicant presents a *prima facie* case for their claim and the court considers the issues on the basis of the evidence filed by the applicant only. At this stage courts can dismiss applications if the applicant cannot establish a *prima facie* case.

(b) If a *prima facie* case is established then the court shall consider a range of other matters before giving permission for a substantive claim.

Under a substantive claim, the claimant brings an action on behalf of the company to **enforce the company's rights** or to recover its property. Any **benefits** received from the claim will **accrue to the company** and not to the member.

The claimant would usually combine the derivative action with a **representative action** (on behalf of the other members who are not defendants) and a **personal claim** for damages.

2.5 S122 Insolvency Act 1986

A member who is dissatisfied with the directors or controlling shareholders over the management of the company may petition the court for a winding up on the **just and equitable ground**.

For such a petition to be successful, the member must show that no other remedy is available. It is not enough for a member to be dissatisfied to make it just and equitable that the company should be wound up, since winding up what may be an otherwise healthy company is a drastic step. This makes it very **rare**, given the protection for the minority under s 994 Companies Act 2006, discussed above.

Orders have been made for winding up in the following situations.

(a) The **substratum of the company has gone** – the only or main object(s) of the company (its underlying basis or substratum) cannot be or can no longer be achieved.

> *Re German Date Coffee Co 1882*
>
> *The facts:* The objects clause specified very pointedly that the sole object was to manufacture coffee from dates under a German patent. The German government refused to grant a patent. The company manufactured coffee under a Swedish patent for sale in Germany. A contributory petitioned for compulsory winding up.
>
> *Decision:* The company existed only to 'work a particular patent' and as it could not do so it should be wound up.

(b)   The **company was formed for an illegal or fraudulent purpose** or there is complete deadlock in the management of its affairs. *Re Yenidje Tobacco Co Ltd 1916*

(c)   The **understandings between members or directors** which were the basis of the association have been **unfairly breached by lawful action**.

Ebrahimi v Westbourne Galleries Ltd 1973

The facts: E and N carried on business together for 25 years, originally as partners and for the last 10 years through a company in which each originally had 500 shares. E and N were the first directors and shared the profits as directors' remuneration; no dividends were paid. When N's son joined the business he became a third director and E and N each transferred 100 shares to N's son. Eventually there were disputes; N and his son used their voting control in general meeting (600 votes against 400) to remove E from his directorship under the power of removal given by the Companies Act.

Decision: The company should be wound up. N and his son were within their legal rights in removing E from his directorship, but the past relationship made it 'unjust or inequitable' to insist on legal rights and the court could intervene on equitable principles to order liquidation.

Re A company 1983

The facts: The facts were similar to those in Ebrahimi's case but the majority offered and the petitioner agreed that they would settle the dispute by a sale of his shares to the majority. This settlement broke down however because they could not agree on the price. The petitioner then petitioned on the just and equitable ground.

Decision: An order for liquidation on this ground may only be made 'in the absence of any other remedy'. As the parties had agreed in principle that there was an alternative to liquidation the petition must be dismissed.

(d)   The **directors deliberately withheld information** so that the **shareholders have no confidence** in the **company's management**: *Loch v John Blackwood Ltd 1924*.

2.6 Government investigations

The **Government** has **statutory power to appoint an inspector** (or joint inspectors) to investigate:

- The **affairs** of a company

- The **ownership** of a company

- Suspected **infringement** by directors of **statutory** rules relating to their interests or dealings in options over shares or debentures of their company

- **Suspected insider dealing**

The Government **must** appoint inspectors to investigate the company if the **court** makes an **order** to that effect.

BPP
LEARNING MEDIA

The Government **may** in its discretion appoint inspectors to investigate the company in any of the following situations.

(a) If the **company** itself **applies**

(b) If application is made by members:

(i) Who are **not less than 200** in number

(ii) Who **hold at least one tenth** of the **issued shares**

(iii) If the company has no share capital, by at **least one fifth** of the **members**

(c) If the Government considers that the affairs of the company have been conducted in a **fraudulent or unlawful manner** (or that it was formed for a fraudulent or unlawful purpose) or in a manner **unfairly prejudicial** to some part of its members or that members have not been given all the information with respect to its affairs which they might reasonably expect.

Under the Companies Act 2006 the Secretary of State has powers to give directions to **inspectors** on to the subject matter of the investigation and actions to be taken. He may also order the investigation to be terminated.

The inspectors submit a **report** to the Government. Their report is usually published and may well contain severe criticism of the shortcomings of the persons involved.

The outcome of the investigation may be **civil** or **criminal proceedings** or a petition for compulsory winding up of the company or for a court order for the protection of a minority.

Assessment focus point

You should learn the circumstances when the Government may investigate a company.

3 Other protection for the minority

FAST FORWARD

A number of **common law** exceptions to the principle of majority rule for the protection of the minority have been accepted since *Foss v Harbottle*.

3.1 Non-statutory protection

Case law recognises a number of limitations to the principle of **majority control** (the rule in *Foss v Harbottle*). In those cases a minority can bring legal proceedings.

(a) No majority vote can be effective to sanction an act of the company which is **illegal**.

(b) If those who control the company use their control to **defraud** it (or possibly to **act oppressively** to a minority) the minority may bring legal proceedings against the fraudulent (or oppressive) majority.

(c) If the company under majority control deprives a member of his **individual rights of membership**, he may sue the company to enforce his rights.

3.2 Illegal decisions

Illegal decisions taken in general meeting are not binding because a majority of members cannot decide that the company shall break the law. If they attempt to do so any member may apply to the court for a declaration that the decision is void and (if necessary) for an **injunction** to restrain the company from acting on the decision.

3.3 Fraud on the company

The **exception to the rule** (in *Foss v Harbottle*) over fraud by a controlling majority is to protect the company (by a member's action) since the company cannot protect itself. It must be shown that:

- What was taken belonged to the company
- It passed to those against whom the claim is made
- Those who appropriated the company's property are in control of the company

3.3.1 Diversion of contracts

To divert away from the company **profitable contracts** which it was about to make, is to deprive it of its 'property.

> *Cook v Deeks 1916*
>
> *The facts:* The directors, who were also controlling shareholders, negotiated a contract in the name of the company. They took the contract for themselves and passed a resolution in general meeting declaring that the company had no interest in the contract. A minority shareholder sued them as trustees for the company of the benefit of the contract.
>
> *Decision:* The contract 'belonged in equity to the company' and the directors could not, by passing a resolution in general meeting, bind the company to approving this action of defrauding it.

3.3.2 Passing of property to controlling shareholders

Likewise passing property to controlling shareholders (though **not** to **other third parties**: *Pavlides v Jensen 1956*) may well be equivalent to fraud even though no dishonesty is shown.

> *Daniels v Daniels 1978*
>
> *The facts:* The company was controlled by its two directors, husband and wife. It bought land for £4,250 (probate value) from the estate of a deceased person and later resold it at the same price to the lady director. She re-sold it for £120,000. A minority shareholder sued the directors but did not allege fraud. Objection was raised that a member could not sue the directors on the company's behalf for negligence but only for fraud.
>
> *Decision:* The circumstances required investigation and a member might sue the directors and controlling shareholders for negligence if one of them secured benefit from the company by reason of it. This is now enshrined in statute: s 260.

3.3.3 Discrimination against minority

Courts take **fraud** to mean not just **misappropriation** of company property, but also **discrimination** against the minority.

> *Clemens v Clemens Bros Ltd 1976*
>
> *The facts:* A and B (who were aunt and niece) held 55% and 45% respectively of the shares with voting rights. A proposed to vote in favour of ordinary resolutions to increase the authorised share capital and to approve the allotment of new shares to or for the benefit of employees of the company. No more shares would be allotted to A or B but the effect of the scheme would be to reduce B's shareholding from 45% to 24.5% with the object of depriving B of her power to block a special resolution to alter the articles as A desired. B sought a declaration that A could not use her votes in this way.

BPP LEARNING MEDIA

Decision: A should be restrained from using her votes to deprive B of her 'negative control' (her ability to block an alteration of the articles to which B objected).

3.4 Enforcement of individual rights of membership

A member may sue the company to enforce his personal rights against it. This is a different kind of minority action. In the other cases the minority is usually seeking to protect **the company** (and their interests in it) against others. In protecting his personal rights the member is **protecting himself against** the company.

Pender v Lushington 1877

The facts: The articles gave members one vote for each 10 shares held by them but subject to a maximum of 100 votes for each member. A company which was a large shareholder transferred shares to the claimant to increase its voting power. At the meeting the chairman rejected the claimant's votes. The claimant sued and the company relied on the argument that only the company itself could object to an irregularity of voting procedure.

Decision: The claimant's votes were a 'right of property' which he was entitled to protect by proceedings against the company.

The principle of *Pender's* case is restricted to protection of **personal rights** of **membership** such as the right to vote or receive a due dividend.

Question

Derivative action

Austen Ltd has three directors: Darcy, Bingley and Benett. Together they own 85% of the shares in the company. They agree to sell a plot of land to Wickham for £50,000 which is what they honestly believe it to be worth. They do not, however, have the land professionally valued until later when it is shown to be worth nearer £100,000. Elizabeth and Jane are two minority shareholders who are considering bringing an action against the directors and the company.

Advise Elizabeth and Jane whether they are likely to be successful.

Answer

The type of action open to Elizabeth and Jane would be a derivative action, that is one brought by Elizabeth or Jane on behalf of the company, with the directors as defendants. However, they would be unlikely to succeed. The facts of this case resemble those of *Daniels v Daniels 1978*. In this case it was held that mere negligence did not justify a minority action to protect the company's rights. Thus, in the absence of fraud, the sale could legitimately be approved by a majority of the shareholders.

Assessment focus point

Unless members are aware of directors discriminating against them or acting against the best interests of the company, there is very little they can do to prevent such actions taking place.

Chapter Roundup

- **Ultimate control** of a company rests with its members voting in general meeting.

- The principal **statutory** remedy for minorities is a s 994 action alleging the company's affairs have been conducted in an **unfairly prejudicial manner.** The court may make **whatever order** it sees fit to settle a s 994 action (generally purchase of the petitioner's shares).

- Other statutory protection is available, such as **derivative claims** and proceedings under **insolvency legislation**.

- A number of **common law** exceptions to the principle of majority rule for the protection of the minority have been accepted since *Foss v Harbottle*.

BPP
LEARNING MEDIA

Quick Quiz

1   *Foss v Harbottle* established the rights of minority shareholders to obtain relief from oppressive acts by the majority.

    True ☐

    False ☐

2   **Fill in the blanks** in the statements below.

    S 994 gives relief to a minority on the grounds that the company's affairs are being or have been conducted in a manner that is ……………….. to the interests of ……………….. or ……………….. .

3   What is the position of a minority shareholder who wishes to bring an action in the company's name against the directors, who are the majority shareholders and have purchased company assets at a considerable under-valuation?

    A   No action may be brought by the minority.

    B   An action may only be brought if there is deliberate fraud on the part of the directors.

    C   An action will only be allowed if the articles of association permit.

    D   An action will be permitted since the directors have used their position to make personal gain at the expense of the company.

4   **Fill in the blanks** in the statements below.

    Petitions under s 994 often arise from exclusion of a director from participation in the management of a ……………….. company, or ……………….. against a minority.

5   What point of law was confirmed by the case of *Pender v Lushington 1877*?

6   Which of the following is an example of conduct which the courts have held to be unfairly prejudicial?

    A   Failure by a parent company to pay the debts of a subsidiary
    B   Non-compliance with Stock Exchange or Corporate Governance rules
    C   Failure to call a meeting
    D   Late presentation of accounts

7   A common remedy for a member who has been the subject of unfairly prejudicial conduct is for the controlling shareholder, or the company, to purchase their shares at a fair price.

    True ☐

    False ☐

8   A member who brings a petition to the court for the just and equitable winding up of their company does so under:

    A   s170 Companies Act 2006
    B   s994 Companies Act 2006
    C   s122 Insolvency Act 1986
    D   Common law principles of contract law

BPP
LEARNING MEDIA

Part E Corporate administration and management | **14: Majority control and minority protection**   **345**

9   What action can a member take where their company takes an illegal decision in a general meeting and they wish to prevent the company from acting on it?

    A   Sue the company for breach of the articles of association

    B   Apply to the court for relief under s994 Companies Act 2006

    C   Petition the court for a winding up order

    D   Request an injunction from the court

10   A court can order the Government to investigate the affairs of a company.

    True   ☐

    False   ☐

BPP
LEARNING MEDIA

Answers to Quick Quiz

1 False. *Foss v Harbottle* emphasised the principle of majority rule. (It was thus evident that the minority needed protection.)

2 S 994 gives relief to a minority on the grounds that the company's affairs are being or have been conducted in a manner that is **unfairly prejudicial** to the interests of **members generally** or **some part of the members**.

3 D. An action will be permitted since the directors have used their position to make personal gain at the expense of the company.

4 Petitions under s 994 often arise from exclusion of a director from participation in the management of a **quasi-partnership** company, or **discrimination** against a minority.

5 That a member's votes are a right of property which can be protected by proceedings against a company.

6 C. Failure to call a meeting has been held to be unfairly prejudicial conduct. The other examples have been held not to be unfairly prejudicial.

7 True. In most cases this is the preferred remedy as the relationship between the member and the company/majority shareholders would have broken down.

8 C. Winding up petitions would be taken under s122 of the Insolvency Act 1986.

9 D. Only an injunction can prevent a company from acting on a decision.

10 True. Courts can order Government investigations.

Now try the questions below from the Question Bank

Number
Q66
Q67
Q68
Q69
Q70

Part F

Corporate finance

BPP
LEARNING MEDIA

Share capital and capital maintenance

15

Introduction

In this chapter the nature of share capital is explained. You should note (and **not** confuse) the different types of capital that are important for company law purposes.

The rest of the chapter discusses procedural matters relating to the **issue** and **transfer** of shares. You will see that there are built-in safeguards to protect members' rights, **pre-emption rights** and the necessity for directors to be **authorised** to **allot** shares. There are also safeguards that ensure that a company receives **sufficient consideration** for its shares. This is an aspect of **capital maintenance**.

Capital maintenance is a fundamental principle of company law, the price that members of a limited company pay for limited liability. There are a number of rules governing how capital must be maintained, which we explore in the second half of this chapter.

Topic list	Learning outcomes
1 Members	G2(a)
2 The nature of shares and capital	G2(a)
3 Types of share	G2(a)
4 Allotment of shares	G2(a)
5 Capital maintenance	G2(b)
6 Reduction of share capital	G2(b)
7 Issuing shares at a premium or at a discount	G2(a), G2(b)
8 Redemption and purchase by a company of its own shares	G2(b)
9 Financial assistance for the purchase of shares	G2(a)

1 Members

FAST FORWARD

A member of a company is a person who has **agreed to become a member**, and whose name has been **entered** in the **register of members**. This may occur by: subscription to the memorandum; applying for shares; the presentation to the company of a transfer of shares to the prospective member applying as personal representative of a deceased member or a trustee of a bankrupt.

1.1 Becoming a member

Key term

> A **member** of a company is a person who has agreed to be a member and whose name has been entered in the register of members.

Entry in the register is **essential**. Mere delivery to the company of a transfer does not make the transferor a member – until the transfer is entered in the register.

1.2 Subscriber shares

Subscribers to the memorandum are deemed to have agreed to become members of the company. As soon as the company is formed their names should be entered in the register of members.

Other persons may acquire shares and become **members**:

- By **applying** and being allotted shares
- By presenting to the company for registration a **transfer** of shares to them
- By applying as **personal representative** or **trustee** of a:
    - Deceased member
    - Bankrupt member

1.3 Ceasing to be a member

A member **ceases to be a member** in any of the following circumstances.

- He **transfers** all his shares to another person and the transfer is registered.
- The member **dies**.
- The **shares** of a bankrupt member are **registered** in the name of his trustee.
- A **member who is a minor repudiates his shares**.
- The **trustee** of a **bankrupt member disclaims** his shares.
- The **company forfeits** or **accepts** the **surrender of shares**.
- The **company** sells them in exercise of a lien.
- The **company is dissolved** and **ceases to exist**.

1.4 The number of members

FAST FORWARD

Public and **private companies** must have a minimum of **one** member (s 7). There is **no maximum** number.

Public and private companies must have a minimum **of one member** (s 7). There is **no maximum** number.

Where a company has a **sole member**, the following rules will apply.

(a) The **register of members** must contain a statement that there is **only one member** and give his address.

(b) **Quorum**. The Act **automatically permits** a **quorum of one** for general meetings.

Question

Members

The first shareholders of a company are known as:

A Initial shareholders
B Subscriber shareholders
C Member shareholders
D Trustee shareholders

Answer

B The first shareholders are known as subscribers as they subscribe to the memorandum.

2 The nature of shares and capital

FAST FORWARD

A **share** is a transferable form of property, carrying rights and obligations, by which the interest of a member of a company limited by shares is measured.

2.1 Shares

Key term

A **share** is 'the interest of a shareholder in the company measured by a sum of money, for the purpose of a liability in the first place, and of interest in the second, but also consisting of a series of mutual covenants entered into by all the shareholders *inter se*': *Borland's Trustee v Steel Bros & Co Ltd 1901*.

The **key points** in this definition are:

- The share must be **paid for** ('liability'). The nominal value of the share fixes this liability, it is the base price of the share eg a £1 ordinary share.

- It gives a **proportionate entitlement** to dividends, votes and any return of capital ('interest').

- It is a form of **bargain** ('mutual covenants') between shareholders which underlies such principles as majority control and minority protection.

Key term

A share's **nominal value** is its face value. So a £1 ordinary share for instance, has a nominal value of £1. No share can be issued at a value below its nominal value.

A share is a form of personal property, carrying rights and obligations. It is by its nature **transferable**. A member who holds one or more shares is a **shareholder**. However some companies (such as most companies limited by guarantee) do not have a share capital. So they have members who are not also shareholders.

BPP
LEARNING MEDIA

Part F Corporate finance | **15: Share capital and capital maintenance** 353

Information about any **special rights** attached to shares is obtainable from one of the following documents which are on the file at Companies House:

- The **articles**, which are the normal context in which share rights are defined.

- A **resolution** or agreement incidental to the creation of a new class of shares (copies must be delivered to the Registrar).

- A **statement of capital** given to the Registrar within one month of **allotment**, together with the return of allotment.

2.2 Types of capital

FAST FORWARD

> The term **'capital'** is used in several senses in company legislation, to mean issued, allotted or called up share capital or loan capital.

2.2.1 Authorised share capital

Under previous company legislation, companies had to specify a **maximum authorised share capital** that it could issue. Under the 2006 Act, the concept of authorised share capital was removed.

2.2.2 Issued and allotted share capital

Key terms

> **Issued** and **allotted share capital** is the type, class, number and amount of the shares issued and allotted to specific shareholders, including shares taken on formation by the subscribers to the memorandum

A company need not issue all its share capital at once. If it retains a part, this is **unissued share capital**.

Issued share capital can be **increased** through the allotment of shares (s 617).

Rights issues and the issue of **bonus shares** (see later) will also increase the amount of a company's capital.

2.2.3 Called up and paid up share capital

Key terms

> **Called up share capital** is the amount which the company has required shareholders to pay now or in the future on the shares issued.
>
> **Paid up share capital** is the amount which shareholders have actually paid on the shares issued and called up.

For example, a company has issued and allotted 70 £1 (nominal value) shares, has received 25p per share on application and has called on members for a second 25p. Therefore its issued and allotted share capital is £70 and its **called up** share capital is £35 (50p per share). When the members pay the call, the **'paid up'** share capital is then £35 also. Capital not yet called is **'uncalled capital'**. Called capital which is not yet paid is termed **'partly paid'**; the company therefore has an outstanding claim against its shareholders and this debt is transferred to the new shareholder if the share is transferred.

As we saw earlier, on allotment **public companies** must receive at least **one quarter** of the **nominal value** of the shares paid up, plus the whole of any premium.

2.2.4 Loan capital

Key term

> **Loan capital** comprises debentures and other long-term loans to a business.

Loan capital, in contrast with the above, is the term used to describe **borrowed money** obtained usually by the issue of debentures. **It is nothing to do with shares**.

2.3 Market value

Shares of a **public company** are freely transferable (providing the appropriate procedures are followed) and therefore may be subsequently sold by some or all of the shareholders. The sale price will not necessarily be the nominal value, rather it will reflect the prospects of the company and therefore may be greater or less than the nominal value.

Question

Shares

Zing Ltd issued and allotted 100 shares on 1/6/20X8. For each share, 30p was received on application, 70p was called-up on 1/8/20X8, 50p was paid-up on 30/8/20X8 and as at 30/9/20X8 the company had uncalled capital per share of 50p. No premium was payable on the nominal value.

What is the nominal value of Zing Ltd's shares?

A 50p
B £1
C £1.50
D £2

Answer

C As no premium was paid, the nominal value of Zing Ltd's shares consists called-up capital and uncalled capital (30p + 70p + 50p). Paid-up capital is that part of the called-up capital which the company has received payment from the shareholders for.

3 Types of share

FAST FORWARD

If the constitution of a company states no differences between shares, it is assumed that they are all **ordinary** shares with parallel rights and obligations. There may, however, be other types, notably **preference shares** and **redeemable shares**.

3.1 Ordinary shares (equity)

If no differences between shares are expressed then all shares are equity shares with the **same rights**, known as ordinary shares.

Equity is the residual interest in the assets of the company after deducting all its liabilities. It comprises issued share capital excluding any part of that does not carry any right to participate beyond a specified amount in a distribution.

Equity share capital is a company's issued share capital less capital which carries preferential rights.

Ordinary shares are shares which entitle the holders to the remaining divisible profits (and, in a liquidation, the assets) after prior interests, eg creditors and prior charge capital, have been satisfied.

3.2 Class rights

Class rights are rights which are attached to particular types of shares by the company's constitution.

A company may at its option attach **special rights** to different shares regarding:

- Dividends
- Return of capital
- Voting
- The right to appoint or remove a director

Shares which have different rights from others are grouped together with others carrying identical rights to form a **class**.

The most **common types of share capital** with different rights are **preference shares** and **ordinary shares**. There may also be ordinary shares with voting rights and ordinary shares without voting rights.

Class rights may be attached to a class of shares by:

- The **articles**
- A **special resolution** of the company in **general meeting**
- A **shareholders' agreement**

Owning a share does not entitle the shareholder to participate in the management of the company, not does it impose any specific duties on the shareholder (shareholders who are not also directors do not owe the duties of directors).

3.3 Preference shares

The most common right of **preference shareholders** is a **prior right** to receive a fixed dividend. This right is not a right to **compel payment** of a dividend, but it is **cumulative** unless otherwise stated. Usually, preference shareholders **cannot participate** in a dividend over and above their fixed dividend and **cease to be entitled to arrears of undeclared dividends** when the company goes into liquidation.

Preference shares are shares carrying one or more rights such as a fixed rate of dividend or preferential claim to any company profits available for distribution.

A preference share may and generally will carry a **prior right** to receive an annual dividend of fixed amount, say a dividend of 6% of the share's nominal value.

Ordinary and preference shares are deemed to have **identical rights**. However, a company's articles or resolutions may create differences between them.

As regards the priority **dividend entitlement,** four points should be noted.

(a) **The right is merely to receive a dividend at the specified rate before any other dividend may be paid or declared**. It is **not** a right to compel the company to pay the dividend, *(Bond v Barrow Haematite Steel Co 1902)*. The company can decline to pay the dividend if it decides to transfer available profits to reserves instead of using the profits to pay the preference dividend.

(b) **The right to receive a preference dividend is deemed to be cumulative unless the contrary is stated.** If, therefore, a 6% dividend is not paid in Year 1, the priority entitlement is normally carried forward to Year 2, increasing the priority right for that year to 12% – and so on.

When arrears of cumulative dividend are paid, the holders of the shares at **the time when the dividend is declared** are entitled to the whole of it even though they did not hold the shares in the year to which the arrears relate.

An intention that preference shares should not carry forward an entitlement to arrears is usually expressed by the word **'non-cumulative'**.

(c) **If a company which has arrears of unpaid cumulative preference dividends goes into liquidation, the preference shareholders cease to be entitled to the arrears unless:**

    (i) A **dividend** has been **declared** though **not yet paid** when liquidation commences.

    (ii) The **articles** (or other terms of issue) **expressly provide** that in a liquidation arrears are to be paid in priority to return of capital to members.

(d) **Holders of preference shares have no entitlement to participate in any additional dividend over and above their specified rate.** If, for example, a 6% dividend is paid on 6% preference shares, the entire balance of available profit may then be distributed to the holders of ordinary shares.

This rule also may be expressly overridden by the terms of issue. For example, the articles may provide that the preference shares are to receive a priority 6% dividend and are also to participate equally in any dividends payable after the ordinary shares have received a 6% dividend. Preference shares with these rights are called **participating preference shares**.

In all other respects preference shares carry the **same** rights as ordinary shares **unless otherwise stated**. If they do rank equally they carry the same rights, no more and no less, to return of capital distribution of surplus assets and voting.

In practice, it is unusual to issue **preference shares** on this basis. More usually, it is expressly provided that:

(a) The preference shares are to carry a **priority right** to **return of capital**.

(b) They are **not to carry a right to vote, or voting is permitted in specified circumstances**. For example failure to pay the preference dividend, variation of their rights or a resolution to wind up.

When preference shares carry a **priority right** to **return** of **capital** the result is that:

(a) The amount paid up on the **preference shares**, say £1 on each £1 share, is to be **repaid** in liquidation **before anything is repaid to ordinary shareholders**.

(b) Unless otherwise stated, the holders of the **preference shares** are **not entitled to share in surplus assets** when the ordinary share capital has been repaid.

3.3.1 Advantages and disadvantages of preference shares

The advantages of preference shares are **greater security of income** and (if they carry priority in repayment of capital) **greater security of capital**. However in a period of persistent inflation, the benefit of entitlement to fixed income and to capital fixed in money terms is an illusion.

A number of other **drawbacks** and pitfalls, such as loss of arrears, winding up and enforced payment, have been indicated above. Preference shares may be said to fall between the two stools of risk and reward (as seen in ordinary shares) and security (debentures). If a company wishes to raise capital for a particular period and at a fixed cost, it could issue **redeemable preference shares**. These are issued and then bought back by the company after a certain period of time and offer an alternative to loan stock or debentures.

3.4 Variation of class rights

FAST FORWARD

> The holders of **issued shares** have **vested rights** which can only be varied by using a strict procedure. The standard procedure is by **special resolution** passed by at least **three quarters** of the votes cast at a **separate class meeting** or by written consent.

Key term

> A **variation of class rights** is an alteration in the position of shareholders with regard to those rights or duties which they have by virtue of their shares.

The holders of issued shares have **vested rights** which can only be varied by the company with the consent of all the holders or with such consent of a majority as is specified (usually) in the articles. The standard procedure for variation of class rights requires that a **special resolution** shall be passed by a **three quarters majority** cast either at a **separate meeting** of the class, or by **written consent**: s 630. If any other requirements are imposed by the company's articles then these must also be followed.

3.4.1 When variation rules apply

FAST FORWARD

> It is **not** a variation of class rights to issue shares to new members, to subdivide shares of another class, to return capital to preference shareholders, or to create a new class of preference shareholders.

It is only necessary to follow the variation of class rights procedure **if what is proposed amounts to a variation of class rights**. There are many types of transaction that do not actually constitute a variation of class rights.

3.4.2 Examples: Not a variation of class rights

(a)   **To issue shares of the same class to allottees who are not already members of the class** (unless the defined class rights prohibit this).

> *White v Bristol Aeroplane Co Ltd 1953*
>
> *The facts:* The company made a bonus issue of new ordinary and preference shares to the existing ordinary shareholders who alone were entitled under the articles to participate in bonus issues. The existing preference shareholders objected. They stated that reducing their proportion of the class of preference shares (by issuing the bonus of preference shares) was a variation of class rights to which they had not consented.
>
> *Decision:* This was not a variation of class rights since the existing preference shareholders had the same number of shares (and votes at a class meeting) as before.

(b)   **To subdivide shares of another class with the incidental effect of increasing the voting strength of that other class.**

> *Greenhalgh v Arderne Cinemas Ltd 1946*
>
> *The facts:* The company had two classes of ordinary shares, 50p shares and 10p shares. Every share carried one vote. A resolution was passed to subdivide each 50p share into five 10p shares, thus multiplying the votes of that class by five.
>
> *Decision:* The rights of the original 10p shares had not been varied since they still had one vote per share as before.

(c)   **To return capital to the holders of preference shares**: *House of Fraser plc v ACGE Investments Ltd 1987.*

(d)   **To create and issue a new class of preference shares with priority over an existing class of ordinary shares**: *Re John Smith's Tadcaster Brewery Co Ltd 1953.*

The cases cited in the preceding paragraph illustrate the principle that without a '**literal variation**' of class rights there is no alteration of rights to which the safeguards of proper procedure and appeal to the court apply. The fact that the **value** of existing rights may be affected will not concern the court if the rights are unchanged.

Assessment focus point

Knowledge of what does **not** constitute a variation of class rights is vital in this area.

3.4.3 Special situations

To deal with unusual special situations which in the past caused some difficulty, the following rules apply.

(a)   If the class rights are set **by the articles and** they **provide** a **variation procedure**, that procedure must be followed for any variation even if it is less onerous than the statutory procedure.

(b)   If class **rights** are **defined otherwise than by the articles** and there is **no variation procedure**, consent of a **three quarters majority** of the class is both necessary and sufficient.

The rules on notice, voting, polls, circulation of resolutions and quorum relating to general meetings relate also to class meetings when voting on alteration of class rights.

3.4.4 Minority appeals to the court for unfair prejudice

FAST FORWARD

A **dissenting minority** holding 15% or more of the issued shares may apply to the court within 21 days of class consent to have the variation cancelled as 'unfairly prejudicial'.

Whenever class rights are varied under a procedure contained in the constitution, a minority of holders of shares of the class may apply to the court to have the variation cancelled. The objectors together must:

- Hold **not less** than **15%** of the **issued shares** of the class in question
- **Not** themselves have **consented** to or voted in favour of the variation
- **Apply** to the court within **21 days** of the consent being given by the class s 633.

The court can either approve the variation as made or cancel it as '**unfairly prejudicial**'. It cannot, however, modify the terms of the variation.

To establish that a variation is 'unfairly prejudicial' to the class, the minority must show that the majority was seeking **some advantage** to themselves as **members** of a **different class** instead of considering the interests of the class in which they were then voting.

3.5 Redeemable shares

Redeemable shares are shares issued on terms that they may be bought back by a company either at a future specific date or at the shareholder's or company's option. They remain in existence until the company is wound up, but can be bought and sold between shareholders just like any other share.

3.6 Treasury shares

These are created when a **public limited company** whose shares are listed on the stock exchange or AIM, **legitimately purchases its own shares out of distributable profit** (see later). Up to **10%** of its shares can be held '**in treasury**' which means the company can **re-issue** them **without** the usual **formalities**. They can only be sold for cash and the company cannot exercise the voting rights which attach to them.

3.7 Deferred shares

This type of share is also known as **management** or **founder shares** and is rarely used. Holders of deferred shares are not entitled to a dividend until the fixed dividend on preference shares and a certain amount or percentage is paid on ordinary shares. As with other types of share, the rights are set out in the terms of issue or the company's constitution.

Question

Types of shares

Give brief definitions of the following types of share.

(a) Equity share
(b) Ordinary share
(c) Preference share

Answer

(a) An equity share is a share which gives the holder the right to participate in the company's surplus profit and capital. In a winding up the holder is entitled to a repayment of the nominal value plus a share of surplus assets. The term equity share embraces ordinary shares but also includes preference shares when the terms of issue include either the right to an additional dividend or the right to surplus assets in a winding up.

(b) An ordinary share is the more common type of equity share, as discussed in (a) above. The dividend is payable only when preference dividends, including arrears, have been paid.

(c) Preference shares carry a prior right to receive an annual dividend of a fixed amount, usually as a percentage of the share's nominal value. There are no other implied differences between preference and ordinary shares, although there may be express differences between them. For example, preference shares may carry a priority right to return of capital. Generally preference shares do not carry voting rights in the company other than those relating to their own class. Unless otherwise stated, dividends allocated to preference shares are assumed to be cumulative. This means that, if the company does not make sufficient profits to pay a dividend in one year, the arrears are carried forward to future years.

BPP
LEARNING MEDIA

3.8 Statement of capital

We have already seen that a return known as a **statement of capital** is required to be made to the **Registrar** in certain circumstances.

The statement of capital must give the following details in respect of the **share capital** of the company and be **up to date** as of the statement date.

(a) The **total number of shares** of the company

(b) The **aggregate nominal value** of the shares

(c) For each class of share:

    (i) The **prescribed particulars** of any rights attached

    (ii) The **total number of shares** in the class

    (iii) The **aggregate nominal value** of shares in the class

(d) The **amount paid up** and the **amount (if any) unpaid** on each share, either on account of the nominal value of the share or by way of premium.

(e) **Information that identifies the subscribers to the memorandum of association**.

(f) In respect of **each subscriber**, the **number**, **nominal value** and **class of shares** taken by them on formation and the **amount** to be **paid up**.

4 Allotment of shares

FAST FORWARD

Directors exercise the **delegated power** to allot shares, either by virtue of the articles or a resolution in general meeting.

4.1 Definition

Key term

> **Allotment of shares** is the issue and allocation to a person of a certain number of shares under a contract of allotment. Once the shares are allotted and the holder is entered in the register of members, the holder becomes a member of the company. The member is issued with a share certificate.

The allotment of shares is a **form of contract**. The intending shareholder applies to the company for shares, and the company accepts the offer.

The terms **'allotment'** and **'issue'** have slightly different meanings.

(a) A share is **allotted** when the person to whom it is allotted acquires an unconditional right to be entered in the register of members as the holder of that share. That stage is reached when the board of directors (to whom the power to allot shares is usually given) considers the application and formally resolves to allot the shares.

However if the directors imposed a condition, for instance that the shares should be allotted only on receipt of the subscription money, the allotment would only take effect when payment was made.

(b) The **issue** of shares is not a defined term but is usually taken to be a later stage at which the allottee **receives** a **letter of allotment** or share certificate issued by the company.

The allotment of shares of a private company is a simple and immediate matter. The name of the **allottee** is usually entered in the register of members soon after the allotment of shares to him. They then become a member.

4.2 Public company allotment of shares

There are various methods of selling shares to the public.

Key terms

Public offer: where members of the public subscribe for shares directly to the company.

Offer for sale: an offer to members of the public to apply for shares based on information contained in a prospectus

Placing: a method of raising share capital where shares are offered in a small number of large 'blocks', to persons or institutions who have previously agreed to purchase the shares at a predetermined price.

In order to encourage the public to buy shares in a public company, it may issue a **prospectus**, or in the case of a company listed on the Stock Exchange, listing particulars. Listing particulars are subject to rules set down by the UK Listing Authority (part of the Financial Services Authority).

4.3 Allotment procedure

Public companies listed on the **Stock Exchange** usually follow a two-stage procedure.

(a)   They first issue a **renounceable allotment letter** which the original allottee may for a limited period (up to six weeks) transfer to another person by signing a **form of renunciation** (included in the letter) and delivering it to the transferee. The original allottee, or the ultimate renouncee, sends in the allotment letter with a completed application for registration of the shares in his name.

(b)   On receipt of the **application for registration** the company enters the name of the applicant in the register of members and delivers a **return of allotment** to the Registrar made up to show who is then on the register. The applicant becomes a member **by entry on the register of members** and receives a share certificate from the company.

Public companies face the restriction that no allotment can be made unless either:

(a)   The shares offered are **subscribed** for in **full**, or

(b)   The offer states that even if the capital is not subscribed for in full, the **amount** of the **capital subscribed** for may be **allotted** in **any event**, or in the event of the conditions specified in the offer being satisfied.

If (a) applies, money must be returned to applicants at the expiry of **40 days** after the first issue of the prospectus.

4.3.1 Prospectus

The Companies Act definition of a prospectus covers all **public advertisements** for shares – under contract law these are invitations to treat. A prospectus has to comply with certain legal requirements under the Financial Services and Markets Act 2000.

4.3.2 Listing particulars

This document is similar to a prospectus, but, as mentioned above, it is governed by the rules of the UK Listing Authority. A public company can only obtain a listing if it has **existed** for over **five years**, has **filed audited accounts** for the last **three years**, can **carry on business at arms length** from any shareholder with a **controlling (30%) interest** and its **securities** have a **minimum market value of £700,000** of which **25% are distributed** to the **public**.

4.4 Private company allotment of shares

The allotment of shares in a private company is more straightforward. The rule to remember is that **private companies cannot sell shares to the public**. An application must be made to the directors directly. After that shares are allotted and issued, and a return of allotment made to the Registrar, as for a public company.

BPP
LEARNING MEDIA

4.5 Directors' powers to allot shares

Directors of **private companies** with **one class of share** have the **authority** to allot shares **unless restricted** by the articles.

Directors of **public companies** or **private companies with more than one class of share may not allot shares** (except to subscribers to the memorandum and to employees' share schemes) **without authority from the members.**

Authority may be given either by the **articles** or by **ordinary resolution** passed in general meeting in accordance with the conditions in the following table.

Directors who allot shares **without authority** commit an **offence** under s549 Companies Act 2006 and may be fined. However, the allotment remains **valid**.

Directors' power to allot shares	
Timescale	<ul><li>Authority to allot must be given until a **specified date**</li><li>Authority to allot must be given for a **specified period**</li><li>Authority can be given by **ordinary resolution** in general meeting even if it would require the articles being amended</li><li>Extension cannot be for more than **five years**</li></ul>
Maximum	Must specify a **maximum number of shares** which may be allotted.
Additional conditions	May give **additional** conditions.
Resolution	An **ordinary** resolution is required. A copy must be sent to the Registrar within 15 days.
General authority	Directors may have been given general authority to allot by the articles without further reference to general meeting. A **general meeting** must be called if <ul><li>**No authority** has been given in advance</li><li>Authority is subject to certain **conditions**</li><li>Authority has **lapsed** or been used up</li></ul>
Documents	Allotments of shares to be recorded in the **register of members** within two months. A return of allotment containing **prescribed particulars** and a **statement of capital** to be sent within one month to the Registrar.

Assessment focus point

Remember the basic distinction that (a) directors can only allot shares if they have the power to do so (given by the articles, generally as part of their power of management) *and* (b) if they have the authority to *exercise* the power (given by the articles or ordinary resolution).

4.5.1 Issuing shares: factors to consider

Before issuing shares, the directors should consider whether the company has **sufficient expertise** relating to share issues to handle the procedure itself, or whether **outside experts** should be brought in to help.

The **key factors** requiring attention are the **type of share** to issue and the **rights** and **conditions** attaching to them.

BPP LEARNING MEDIA

Other considerations then follow and include:

- **The issue price**. If the asking price is too high then the shares may not be purchased; if it is to low the company may be overwhelmed and be subject to costs of returning cheques for unsuccessful applications.

- **Issue costs**. The number of people to be offered shares will increase the cost of issue.

- **Other factors**. The amount of capital for investment circulating in the market is finite. Therefore share issues by other companies will be competing with that of the company concerned.

4.6 Pre-emption rights: s 561

FAST FORWARD

> If the directors propose to allot 'equity securities' wholly for cash, there is a general requirement to offer these shares to **holders** of **similar shares** in proportion to their holdings.

Key term

> **Pre-emption rights** are the rights of existing ordinary shareholders to be offered new shares issued by the company *pro rata* to their existing holding of that class of shares.

If a company proposes to allot ordinary shares wholly for cash, it has a **statutory obligation** to offer those shares first to holders of similar shares in **proportion to their holdings** and on the same or more favourable terms as the main allotment. This is known as a **rights issue**.

4.7 Rights issues

Key term

> A **rights issue** is a right given to a shareholder to subscribe for further shares in the company, usually *pro rata* to their existing holding in the company's shares.

A rights issue must be made **in writing** (hard copy or electronic) in the same manner as a notice of a general meeting is sent to members. It must specify a period of **not less than 21 days** during which the offer may be accepted but may not be withdrawn. If not accepted or renounced in favour of another person within that period the offer is deemed to be declined.

Equity securities which have been offered to members in this way but are **not accepted** may then be allotted on the same (or less favourable) terms to non-members.

If equity securities are allotted in breach of these rules the members to whom the offer should have been made may within the ensuing two years recover **compensation** for their loss from those in default. The allotment will generally be valid.

4.7.1 Exclusion of pre-emption rights: s567

A **private** company may by its articles permanently exclude these rules so that there is no statutory right of first refusal.

4.7.2 Disapplication of pre-emption rights: s 570

Any company may, by special resolution resolve that the statutory right of first refusal shall not apply: s 570. Such a resolution to 'disapply' the right may either:

(a) Be combined with the grant to directors of authority to allot shares, or

(b) Simply permit an offer of shares to be made for cash to a non-member (without first offering the shares to members) on a particular occasion

In case (b) the directors, in inviting members to 'disapply' the right of first refusal, must issue a circular. This sets out their reasons, the price at which the shares are to be offered direct to a non-member and their justification of that price.

4.8 Issues for an improper purpose

We have already seen that directors may issue shares for a proper purpose, and that issues to manipulate the company's shareholdings were void, unless approved by the members in general meeting. Remember that holders of shares that have been issued irregularly **cannot vote** in a general meeting to sanction the directors' actions.

4.9 Bonus issues

Key term

> A **bonus issue** is the capitalisation of the reserves of a company by the issue of additional shares to existing shareholders, in proportion to their holdings. Such shares are normally fully paid-up with no cash called for from the shareholders.

A **bonus issue** is more correctly but less often called a **'capitalisation issue'** (also called a **'scrip' issue**). The articles of a company usually give it power to apply its reserves to paying up unissued shares wholly or in part and then to allot these shares as a bonus issue to members.

Question	Sale of shares

Which of the following is not a method that a public company can use to sell shares to the public?

A   Public offer
B   Offer for sale
C   Placing
D   Subscription

Answer

D   Subscription is the acceptance of an offer for shares made by the purchaser.

5 Capital maintenance

The rules which dictate how a company is to manage and maintain its capital exist to maintain the delicate balance between the **members' enjoyment of limited liability** and the **creditors' requirements that the company shall remain able to pay its debts**.

Key term

Capital maintenance is a fundamental principle of company law, that limited companies should not be allowed to make payments out of capital to the detriment of company creditors. Therefore the Companies Act contains many examples of control upon capital payments. These include provisions restricting dividend payments, and capital reduction schemes.

Assessment focus point

The rules affecting the possible threats to capital are complicated in certain areas. However, provided you know the rules, questions on capital maintenance tend to be straightforward.

5.1 Controls

The Companies Act contains many examples of **control upon capital payments**. These include provisions restricting dividend payments, financial assistance to aid share purchases, the uses to which share premiums may be put, the freedom of a company to purchase its own shares, and capital reduction schemes.

The capital which a limited company obtains from its members as consideration for their shares is sometimes called **'the creditors' buffer'**.

No one can prevent an unsuccessful company from losing its capital by trading at a loss. However, what capital the company does have must be **held for the payment of the company's debts** and may not be returned to members (except under procedures which safeguard the interest of creditors). However, there are some other aspects of capital maintenance for you to be aware of before you consider these detailed rules. The first is **dividends** and the second is the issue of **loss of capital in a plc**.

5.2 Dividends

As discussed earlier, ownership of a share gives the member a right to receive any **dividends** declared by the directors. There are certain rules governing the payment of dividends.

Dividends may only be paid by a company out of profits available for the purpose. In other words, they may not be paid out of capital. In the event of liquidation, a **liquidator** may take action against directors who have paid dividends out of capital. A **company** may recover unlawful dividends from members if the member knew the distribution was unlawful.

Key terms

Profits available for distribution are accumulated realised profits (which have not been distributed or capitalised) less accumulated realised losses (which have not been previously written off in a reduction or reorganisation of capital).

A public company may only make a distribution if its **net assets** are equal to or greater than the aggregate of its called up share capital and undistributable reserves.

Undistributable reserves are:

- Share premium account
- Capital redemption reserve
- Revaluation reserve
- Any reserve restricted by the articles

5.3 Loss of capital in a plc

If the **net assets** of a **public limited company** are **half or less of the amount of its called up share capital** there must be a general meeting: s 656.

Where the directors' duty arises they must issue a notice to **convene a meeting** within **28 days** of becoming aware of the need to do so. The meeting must be convened for a date within 56 days of their coming to know the relevant facts.

The purpose of this procedure is to enable shareholders to consider 'whether any, and if so what, measures should be taken to deal with the situation'. If the capital falls below £50,000, the company must re-register as private.

Question	Capital maintenance

A public company must re-register as private if:

A   It trades at a loss
B   The market value of its shares falls below their nominal value
C   Its capital falls below £50,000
D   It is unable to pay a dividend to its shareholders

Answer

C   A public company must re-register as private if its capital falls below £50,000.

6 Reduction of share capital

FAST FORWARD

> Reduction of capital can be achieved by: **extinguishing/reducing liability on partly-paid shares; cancelling paid-up share capital**; or **paying off part of paid-up share capital**. Court confirmation is required for public companies. The court considers the interests of creditors and different classes of shareholder. There must be power in the articles and a special resolution.

A limited company is permitted without restriction to cancel **unissued shares** as that change does not alter its financial position.

If a limited company with a share capital wishes to **reduce** its **issued share capital** it may do if:

- It has **power** to do so in its articles. (If it does not have power in the articles, these may be amended by a **special resolution).**

- It passes a **special resolution**. (If the articles have been amended, this is another special resolution)

- It obtains **confirmation** of the reduction **from the court** (in the case of public companies).

6.1 Solvency statement

A private company need not apply to the court if it supports its special resolution with a solvency statement. A **solvency statement** is a **declaration** by the directors, provided **15 days** in advance of the meeting where the special resolution is to be voted on. It states there is **no ground** to suspect the company is currently **unable** or will be **unlikely to be able** to pay its debts for the next **twelve months**. All possible liabilities must be taken into account and the statement should be in the prescribed form, naming all the directors.

6.2 Why reduce share capital?

A company may wish to **reduce its capital** for one or more of the following reasons.

- The company has suffered a **loss** in the **value** of its **assets** and it reduces its capital to reflect that fact.

- The company wishes to **extinguish** the **interests** of some members entirely.

- The capital reduction is part of a **complicated arrangement** of capital which may involve, for instance, replacing share capital with loan capital.

There are **three basic methods** of reducing share capital specified in s 641 of the Act.

Method	What happens	Effects
Extinguish or reduce liability on partly paid shares	Eg Company has nominal value £1 shares 75p paid up. Either (a) reduce nominal value to 75p; or (b) reduce nominal value to a figure between 75p and £1.	Company gives up claim for amount not paid up (nothing is **returned** to shareholders).
Pay off part of paid-up share capital out of surplus assets	Eg Company reduces nominal value of fully paid shares from £1 to 70p and repays this amount to shareholders	Assets of company are reduced by 30p in £.
Cancel paid-up share capital which has been lost or which is no longer represented by available assets.	Eg Company has £1 nominal fully paid shares but net assets only worth 50p per share. Difference is a debit balance on reserves. Company reduces nominal value to 50p, and applies amount to write off debit balance	Company can resume dividend payments out of future profits without having to make good past losses.

6.3 Role of the court in reduction of share capital

When the court receives an application for reduction of capital by a public company its **first concern** is the effect of the reduction on the company's ability to pay its debts, that is, that the creditors are protected.

If the reduction is by extinguishing liability or paying off part of paid-up share capital, the court requires that **creditors** shall be **invited** by advertisement to state their objections (if any) to the reduction. Where paid-up share capital is cancelled, the court **may** require an invitation to creditors.

Normally the company persuades the court to dispense with advertising for creditors' objections (which can be commercially damaging to the company).

Two possible approaches are:

- To **pay off** all **creditors** before application is made to the court; or, if that is not practicable

- To produce to the court a **guarantee**, say from the company's bank, that its existing debts will be paid in full

The **second** concern of the court, where there is more than one class of share, is whether the reduction is fair in its effect on different classes of shareholder.

If the reduction is, **in the circumstances**, a **variation of class rights** the **consent** of the class must be obtained under the variation of class rights procedure.

BPP
LEARNING MEDIA

Within each class of share it is usual to make a **uniform reduction** of every share by the same amount per share, though this is **not** obligatory.

The court may also be concerned that the **reduction should not confuse or mislead people who may deal with the company in future**. It may insist that the company add 'and reduced' to its name or publish explanations of the reduction.

6.3.1 Confirmation by the court

If the court is satisfied that the reduction is in order, it confirms the reduction for the public company by making an order to that effect. A **copy of the court order** and a **statement of capital**, approved by the court, to show the altered share capital is delivered to the Registrar who issues a certificate of registration.

Question	Maintenance of capital

Which one of the following statements is incorrect in relation to the maintenance of capital rule?

A   Share capital must be put aside as a fund to pay creditors in the event of the company becoming insolvent.

B   A company cannot simply give share capital back to its members.

C   Share capital may be returned to members following an approved reduction of capital scheme.

D   Share capital should be used to further the company's lawful objects.

Answer

A   Money raised as share capital can always be used in the company's business, and thus the company may lose it through its trading activities.

7 Issuing shares at a premium or at a discount

FAST FORWARD

In issuing shares, a company must fix a **price** which is **equal** to or **more than** the **nominal value of the shares**. It may not allot shares at a discount to the nominal value.

Every share has a **nominal value** and **may not be allotted at a discount** to that: s 580.

In allotting shares every company is required to obtain in money or money's worth, consideration of a value at least equal to the nominal value of the shares plus the whole of any premium. To issue shares **'at par'** is to obtain equal value, say, £1 for a £1 share.

> *Ooregum Gold Mining Co of India v Roper 1892*
>
> *The facts:* Shares in the company, although nominally £1, were trading, at a market price 12.5p. In an honest attempt to refinance the company, new £1 preference shares were issued and credited with 75p already paid, so the purchasers of the shares were actually paying twice the market value of the ordinary shares. When, however, the company subsequently went into insolvent liquidation the holders of the new shares were required to pay a further 75p.

If shares are allotted at a discount on their nominal value the allottee (and subsequent owners of the shares) must nonetheless pay the **full nominal value** with **interest** at the appropriate rate. Any subsequent holder of such a share who knew of the underpayment must make good the shortfall: s 588.

Consideration for shares	
Partly-paid shares	The no-discount rule only requires that, in allotting its shares, a company shall not fix a price which is less than the nominal value of the shares. It may leave part of that price to be paid at some later time. Thus £1 shares may be issued partly-paid – 75p on allotment and 25p when called for or by instalment. The unpaid capital passes with the shares. If transferred, they are a debt payable by the holder at the time when payment is demanded.
Underwriting fees	A company may pay underwriting or other commission in respect of an issue of shares if so permitted by its Articles. This means that, if shares are issued at par the net amount received will be below par value. This is not a contravention of s 580 (prohibiting allotment of shares at a discount).
Bonus issue	The allotment of shares as a 'bonus issue' is for full consideration since reserves, which are shareholders' funds, are converted into fixed capital and are used to pay for the shares.
Money's worth	The price for the shares may be paid in **money** or **'money's worth'**, including goodwill and know-how: s 582. It need not be paid in cash and the company may agree to accept a **'non-cash' consideration** of sufficient value. For instance, a company may issue shares in payment of the price agreed in the purchase of a property.

7.1 Private companies

A private company may allot shares for **inadequate consideration** by acceptance of goods or services at an over-value. This loophole has been allowed to exist because in some cases it is very much a matter of opinion whether an asset is or is not of a stated value.

The **courts** therefore have **refused** to overrule directors in their valuation of an asset acquired for shares if it appears **reasonable** and **honest**: *Re Wragg 1897*. However a blatant and unjustified overvaluation will be declared **invalid**.

7.2 Public companies

More stringent rules apply to public companies.

(a) The company must, at the time of allotment, receive **at least one quarter of the nominal value** of the shares and the **whole** of any premium: s 586.

(b) Any **non-cash consideration** accepted must be **independently valued** (see below).

(c) **Non-cash consideration** may **not** be accepted as payment for shares if an undertaking contained in such consideration is to be, or may be, **performed more than five years after the allotment.** This relates to, say, a property or business in return for shares. To enforce the five year rule the law requires that:

    (i) At the time of the allotment the **allottee** must **undertake** to **perform** his side of the agreement within a specified period which must not exceed five years. If no such undertaking is given the **allottee** becomes **immediately liable** to pay cash for his shares as soon as they are allotted

    (ii) If the **allottee later fails** to **perform** his undertaking to transfer property at the due time he becomes liable to pay **cash** for his shares when he defaults

(d) An **undertaking to do work or perform services is not to be accepted as consideration**. A public company may, however, allot shares to discharge a debt in respect of services already rendered.

If a public company does accept future services as consideration the holder must pay the company their **nominal value** plus any **premium** treated as paid-up, and **interest** at 5% on any such amount.

BPP LEARNING MEDIA

(e)   Within **two years of receiving its trading certificate**, a public company **may not receive a transfer of non-cash assets from a subscriber** to the memorandum. This is unless its value is less than 10% of the issued nominal share capital and it has been independently valued and agreed by an ordinary resolution.

7.2.1 Valuation of non-cash assets

When a public company allots shares for a non-cash consideration the company must usually obtain a **report on its value** from an independent valuer.

The **valuation report** must be made to the company within the six months before the allotment. On receiving the report the company must send a copy to the proposed allottee and later to the Registrar.

The independent valuation rule does not apply to an allotment of shares made in the course of a **takeover bid**.

7.3 Allotment of shares at a premium

Key term

> **Share premium** is the excess received, either in cash or other consideration, over the nominal value of the shares issued.

An established company may be able to obtain consideration for new shares in excess of their nominal value. The excess, called 'share premium', must be credited to a **share premium account**.

If a company obtains non-cash consideration for its shares which exceeds the nominal value of the shares the excess should also be credited to the **share premium account.**

7.3.1 Example: Using a share premium account

If a company allots its £1 (nominal) shares for £1.50 in cash, £1 per share is credited to the share capital account, and 50p to the share premium account.

Illustration

We will use the above example to illustrate the effects of the transaction on the balance sheet. The company has issued 100 shares.

	Before share issue £	After share issue £
Cash	100	250
Share capital	100	200
Share premium	–	50
	100	250

The general rule is that reduction of the share premium account is subject to the **same** restrictions as reduction of share capital. You should learn the fact that **a company cannot distribute any part of its share premium account as dividend**.

7.4 Uses of the share premium account

The **permitted uses of share premium** are to pay:

- **Fully paid shares under a bonus issue** since this operation merely converts one form of fixed capital into another

- **Issue expenses** and **commission** in respect of a **new share issue**

> **Point to note**
>
> The prohibition on offer of shares at a discount on *nominal* value is often confused with a company issuing shares at a price below *market* value (which is not prohibited).

Question   Increasing a company's share capital

Explain the rule concerning issuing shares at a discount to their nominal value.

Answer

Shares may not be issued at a discount to their nominal value: s 580. However shares may be issued 'partly paid' with, for example, 75p of a £1 share paid up. The 25p balance remains a liability that the shareholder must pay when demanded.

Question   Share premium account

Which of the following are permissible uses of the share premium account under the Companies Act 2006?

(i)   Payment of issue costs in respect of a new share issue
(ii)   Payment of fully paid bonus shares allotted to existing members
(iii) Payment of dividends
(iv)   Payment of commission in respect of a new share issue

A   (i) and (ii) only
B   (i), (ii) and (iv) only
C   (ii) and (iii) only
D   (ii) and (iv) only

Answer

B   Dividends must be paid out of distributable profit.

BPP
LEARNING MEDIA

8 Redemption and purchase by a company of its own shares

FAST FORWARD Specific rules govern the ability of private and public companies to **redeem** or **purchase** their own shares.

8.1 The basic rule

S 658 states that **a company cannot acquire its own shares** by purchase, subscription or other method. To do so is an **offence**, and the purported acquisition is **void**.

The **prohibition** is subject to exceptions in s659. A company may:

- Purchase its own shares in compliance with a **court order**
- Issue and redeem **redeemable** shares
- **Purchase** its **own shares** under certain specified procedures
- Forfeit, or **accept** the **surrender** of, its shares

8.2 Redeemable shares

Both ordinary and preference shares may be issued on terms which allow the company to **redeem them**. The expression redeemable shares means only shares which are redeemable from the time of issue, so shares not issued as redeemable cannot later be made so.

Key term

> **Redeemable shares** are shares which are issued on terms which may require them to be bought back by the issuer at some future date, either at the discretion of the issuer or of the holder.　　(CIMA, *Official Terminology*)

The conditions for the issue and redemption of **redeemable shares** are set out in ss 684 and 687. The rules for private and public companies differ slightly so you should read them carefully.

The articles of a public company must give **authority** for the issue of redeemable shares. If the articles do not, they must be altered before the shares are issued. In private companies the directors have authority to allot redeemable shares unless restricted by the articles.

Redeemable shares may only be issued if, at the time of issue, the company also has **issued shares** which are **not redeemable**. A company's capital may not consist entirely of redeemable shares.

Redeemable shares may only be redeemed if they are **fully paid**.

The terms of redemption must provide for **payment on redemption** or on a later date.

The shares may be redeemed out of:

- **Distributable profits**
- The **proceeds of a new issue** of shares
- **Capital** (if it is a **private** company)

Any **premium payable on redemption** must generally be provided out of **distributable profits**.

The company may redeem shares on such **terms** and in such manner as may be provided by the company's **articles** or company **resolution** subject only to the specific provisions set out in the Act.

When shares are **redeemed** they are cancelled and may not be reissued.

(a)   The amount of the company's **issued** share capital is **reduced** by the **nominal amount** of the shares.

(b)   Any new shares issued to raise money to redeem shares are treated as a **replacement** for them to the extent that the nominal value of the new shares does not exceed the nominal value of the shares redeemed.

(c)   If shares are redeemed wholly out of profits an amount equal to the nominal value of shares redeemed must be transferred to a **capital redemption reserve** which is to be treated as if it were share capital, except that it may be applied in paying up unissued shares as a bonus issue: s 733.

8.3 Purchase of own shares

A company limited by shares may **purchase its own fully paid shares**:

- **Out of distributable profits or the proceeds of an issue of new shares** under the redemption of shares rules.
- If it is a **private company,** out of **capital**: s 692.

A **company cannot**, however, purchase ordinary shares if, as a result, **only redeemable shares are left**.

An **unlimited** company can reduce its share capital or purchase its own shares without statutory restriction.

There are **two methods** of carrying out the purchase; **off-market** or **market purchase**. Either can be used for any type of share, but only public companies can use the market method, as private companies will not have shares available on a public market.

- **Market purchase** is purchase under the normal market arrangements of a recognised investment exchange.

- **Off-market purchase** is any other purchase, usually by private treaty. This will apply to shares of private companies, but it can also apply to public companies.

Market purchase of own shares (s 701)	

Authority	The purchase must be authorised by ordinary resolution specifying
	
	• Maximum number of shares to be acquired
	
	• Maximum and minimum prices to be paid
	
	  – By global sum, or
	  – By price formula
	
	• Specify a date (< 18 months after resolution) on which authority expires

Filing	A return must be sent to the Registrar within 28 days
Changes	The authority may be varied, revoked or renewed by ordinary resolution

BPP
LEARNING MEDIA

Off market purchase of own shares (s 694)	
Authority	A contract for the purchase of shares must be approved in advance by special resolution
Inspection	A copy of the proposed contract must be available for inspection by members • At the registered office • For 15 days before the meeting for approval • At the meeting It must disclose the names of the sellers. If the resolution is a written one a copy of the contract must be sent to all eligible members.
Voting	The members who intend to sell the shares should not vote If they do vote and the resolution would not have been carried without their vote, it is invalid They may cast votes attached to other shares which they are not selling
Public company	A public company may only be given authority for a limited period (max 18 months)
Filing	The company must make a return to the Registrar giving prescribed particulars including a statement of capital within 28 days of making the purchase and cancelling the shares: s 708
Changes	The authority may be varied, revoked or renewed by special resolution

Question

Purchase of shares

A limited company may without restriction purchase its own shares providing the purchase is out of profits or an issue of new shares.

True or false?

Answer

False. Such an action is prevented if the purchase would only leave redeemable shares.

8.4 Payment for shares out of capital – private companies only

A private limited company which has a share capital may redeem or purchase its shares 'out of capital' by a **'permissible capital payment'** to which elaborate rules apply: s 709. These rules are designed to ensure that the company does not make itself insolvent.

The conditions are as follows.

(a)   There must be **no restrictions** in the **articles** for redemption or purchase of shares out of capital.

(b)   Capital may only be used to **'top up'** distributable profits and the proceeds of any issue of new shares in cases where those resources, fully used, do not suffice to make up the required amount,

(c) A **capital redemption reserve** must be created where the amount of the permissible capital payment is less than the nominal amount of the shares redeemed or purchased: s 734.

If the payment is greater than the nominal amount then the capital redemption reserve, share premium account, share capital or revaluation reserve of the company may be reduced by the excess.

(d) A **statutory declaration of the directors** must be made and supported by a **report of the auditors** to the effect that after the payment is made the company will be able to pay its debts and to carry on its business for at least a year to come: s 714.

(e) Shareholders must approve the payment by passing a **special resolution s 716**. In this decision any vendor of shares may **not** use the votes attached to the shares which he is to sell to the company: s 717.

(f) A member who did not vote for the resolution and a creditor (for any amount) may within five weeks **apply to the court to cancel the resolution**, which may not be implemented until the five weeks have elapsed: s 721.

(g) A **notice** must be placed in the *Gazette* and in an appropriate national newspaper, **or** every creditor must be informed: s 719.

If the company goes into insolvent liquidation within a year of making a payment out of capital the persons who received the payment and the directors who authorised it may have to make it good to the company.

8.5 Subsidiary not to be a member of its holding company

The restrictions on acquisition by a company of its own shares are extended by a general prohibition against a subsidiary being a member of its holding company: s 136.

9 Financial assistance for the purchase of shares

FAST FORWARD

A **public** company may not give **financial assistance** to a third party to purchase shares in the company. A private company can do so.

9.1 The rule against financial assistance

The general rules apply to all public companies only.

(a) A company is **prohibited** from **giving** any **financial assistance** for the **purpose** of the **acquisition** of **shares** either of the company or of its holding company or to **discharge liabilities** incurred in making the acquisition: s 678

(b) **'Financial assistance'** is elaborately defined to mean:

(i) A loan or gift

(ii) A guarantee indemnity or security

(iii) A release from debt or a wavier

(iv) 'Any other financial assistance given by a company which reduces to a material extent, its net assets': s 677

Key term

Financial assistance is the provision of benefit by a company to a person to put that person in funds so that s/he may purchase shares in the company.

A **public company** may give a person **financial assistance** if its principle purpose in doing so is not to reduce or discourage the person's liability, or if it is an incidental part of a larger purpose of the company, *and* if it is done in good faith: s 678(4). Two main tests have to be applied to any suspect transaction.

What was its **purpose**? It is not objectionable if its **principal purpose** was **not** to give financial assistance for the purchase of the shares nor if it was an incidental part of some **larger purpose** of the company.

What was the state of mind of the directors in approving the transaction? Did they act in **good faith** in what they deemed to be the interests of the company and not of a third party?

9.2 Group companies

Under the **Act**:

- A **private subsidiary** may give assistance to purchase its own shares and that of its parent (if it also is a private company)

- A **public subsidiary** may not give assistance to purchase its own shares or that of its parent (even if the parent is a private company)

9.3 Other exceptions from the financial assistance rules

Three other **specific exceptions** are also made. By s 682 a company is not prohibited from entering into any of the following transactions provided it is either a private company, or it is a public company and either its net assets are not reduced by giving the assistance, or it gives the assistance out of distributable profit.

(a) Making a loan if **lending is part of its ordinary business**, and the loan is made in the ordinary course of its business; this exception is restricted to money-lending companies

(b) Providing money in good faith and in the best interests of the company for the purpose of an **employees' share scheme** or for other share transactions by *bona fide* employees or connected persons

(c) **Making loans** or providing assistance to persons (other than directors) employed in good faith by the company with a view to those **persons acquiring fully paid shares** in the company or its holding company to be held by them as beneficial owners

Question   Financial assistance

Which of the following transactions for assistance to purchase a company's own shares are allowable under the Companies Act 2006? Select all that apply.

A   A private subsidiary can give assistance to a private parent.
B   A public subsidiary can give assistance to a private parent.
C   A private company may give assistance to a third party company.
D   A public company may give assistance to a third party company.

Answer

A and C. Public companies may never give assistance in these circumstances. Private companies can.

Chapter Roundup

- A member of a company is a person who has **agreed to become a member**, and whose name has been **entered** in the **register of members**. This may occur by: subscription to the memorandum; applying for shares; the presentation to the company of a transfer of shares to the prospective member; applying as personal representative of a deceased member or a trustee of a bankrupt.

- **Public** and **private companies** must have a minimum of **one member** (s 7). here is **no maximum** number.

- A **share** is a transferable form of property, carrying rights and obligations, by which the interest of a member of a company limited by shares is measured.

- The term **'capital'** is used in several senses in company legislation, to mean issued, allotted or called up share capital or loan capital.

- If the constitution of a company states no differences between shares, it is assumed that they are all **ordinary** shares with parallel rights and obligations. There may, however, be other types, notably **preference shares** and **redeemable shares**.

- The most common right of **preference shareholders** is a **prior right** to receive a fixed dividend. This right is not a right to **compel payment** of a dividend, but it is **cumulativ**e unless otherwise stated. Usually, preference shareholders cannot **participate** in a dividend over and above their fixed dividend and **cease to be entitled to arrears of undeclared dividends** when the company goes into liquidation.

- The holders of **issued shares** have **vested rights** which can only be varied by using a strict procedure. The standard procedure is by **special resolution** passed by at **least three quarters** of the votes cast at a **separate class meeting** or by written consent.

- It is **not** a variation of class rights to issue shares to new members, to subdivide shares of another class, to return capital to preference shareholders, or to create a new class of preference shareholders.

- A **dissenting minority** holding 15% or more of the issued shares may apply to the court within 21 days of class consent to have the variation cancelled as 'unfairly prejudicial'.

- Directors exercise the **delegated power** to allot shares, either by virtue of the articles or a resolution in general meeting.

- If the directors propose to allot 'equity securities' wholly for cash, there is a general requirement to offer these shares to **holders** of **similar shares** in proportion to their holdings.

- The rules which dictate how a company is to manage and maintain its capital exist to maintain the delicate balance between the **members' enjoyment of limited liability** and the **creditors' requirements that the company shall remain able to pay its debts**.

- Reduction of capital can be achieved by: **extinguishing/reducing liability on partly-paid shares**; **cancelling paid-up share capital;** or **paying off part of paid up share capital**. Court confirmation is required for public companies. The court considers the interests of creditors and different classes of shareholder. There must be power in the articles and a special resolution.

- In issuing shares, a company must fix a **price** which is **equal** to or **more than** the **nominal value of the shares**. It may not allot shares at a discount to the nominal value.

- Specific rules govern the ability of private and public companies to **redeem** or **purchase** their own shares..

- A **public** company may not give **financial assistance** to a third party to purchase shares in the company. A private company can do so.

1   If a company fails to pay preference shareholders their dividend, they can bring a court action to compel the company to pay it.

    True ☐

    False ☐

2   If a company issues new ordinary shares for cash, the general rule is that:

    A   The shares must first be offered to existing members in the case of a public but not a private company.
    B   The shares must first be offered to existing members whether the company is public or private.
    C   The shares must first be offered to existing members in the case of a private but not a public company.
    D   The shares need not be issued to existing members.

3   **Fill in the blanks** in the statements below.

    A .... issue is an allotment of additional shares to existing members in exchange for consideration payable by the members.

    A .... issue is an allotment of additional shares to existing members where the consideration is paid by using the company's reserves.

4   No company may give financial assistance for the purchase of its own shares unless that assistance is for certain specified purposes.

    True ☐

    False ☐

5   What is the minimum number of members that a plc must have?

    A   One
    B   Two
    C   Three
    D   Four

6   Match the definitions to the correct type of capital

    (a)   Issued share capital
    (b)   Called up share capital
    (c)   Paid up share capital

    (i)   The amount which the company has required shareholders to pay on shares issued.
    (ii)   The type, class, number and amount of the shares held by the shareholders.
    (iii)   The amount which shareholders have actually paid on the shares issued and called up

7   Where application is made to the court for confirmation of a reduction in capital, the court may require that creditors should be invited by advertisement to state their objections. In which of the following ways can the need to advertise be avoided?
    Select all that apply.

    A   Paying off all creditors before application to the court
    B   Producing a document signed by the directors stating the company's ability to pay its debts
    C   Producing a guarantee from the company's bank that its existing debts will be paid in full
    D   Renouncement by existing shareholders of their limited liability in relation to existing debts

8   A share premium account can be used for bonus issues of shares or issue costs for new share issues.

        True   ☐

        False   ☐

9   Which of the following is a distributable reserve?

        A   General profit reserve
        B   Capital redemption reserve
        C   Revaluation reserve
        D   Share premium account

10   An unlimited company can reduce its share capital and purchase its own shares without statutory restriction.

        True   ☐

        False   ☐

1   False. The company may decide not to pay any dividend, or may be unable to because it does not have any distributable profits. What the preference shareholders have is a right to receive their dividends before other dividends are paid or declared.

2   B. The shares must be first offered to existing members whether the company is public or private.

3   A **rights issue** is an allotment of additional shares to existing members in exchange for consideration payable by the members.

    A **bonus issue** is an allotment of additional shares to existing members where the consideration is effectively paid by using the company's reserves.

4   False. A private company may give financial assistance for any reason providing it follows the procedures in the Companies Act.

5   A. All companies must have a minimum of one member (s 7).

6   (a)   (ii)
       (b)   (i)
       (c)   (iii)

7   A and C. The only guarantee that the courts will accept is from the company's bank.

8   True. Both are acceptable uses for the share premium account.

9   A. The use of general profit reserves are not restricted and so a company can distribute them.

10   True. Unlimited companies are not subject to such statutory restrictions.

Now try the questions below from the Question Bank

Number
Q71
Q72
Q73
Q74
Q75

BPP
LEARNING MEDIA

16

Borrowing and loan capital

Introduction

The last chapter was concerned with share capital. In this chapter on **borrowing and loan capital**, you should note that the interests and position of a lender are very different from that of a shareholder.

This chapter covers how loan capital holders protect themselves, specifically through taking out **fixed or floating charges**.

You need to understand the differences between **fixed** and **floating charges**, and also how they can protect loan creditors, for example by giving chargeholders the ability to appoint a receiver.

Topic list	Learning outcomes
1 Borrowing	G2(c)
2 Debentures and loan capital	G2(c)
3 Charges	G2(c)
4 Registration of charges	G2(c)
5 Debentureholders' remedies	G2(c)
6 Transactions at an undervalue and preferences	G2(f)

1 Borrowing

FAST FORWARD Companies have an **implied power** to borrow for purposes incidental to their trade or business.

All companies registered under the Companies Act 2006 have an **implied power to borrow** for purposes **incidental to their trade or business**. A company formed under earlier Acts will have an implied power to borrow if its object is to carry on a trade or business.

In delegating the **company's power to borrow** to the directors it is usual, and essential in the case of a company whose shares are quoted on the Stock Exchange, to impose a **maximum limit** on the **borrowing** arranged by directors.

A **contract to repay borrowed money** may in principle be unenforceable if either:

- It is money borrowed for an **ultra vires** (or restricted) purpose, and this is known to the lender.
- The directors **exceed their borrowing powers** or have no powers to borrow.

However:

- In both cases the lender will probably be **able** to **enforce** the contract.
- If the contract is within the capacity of the company but beyond the delegated powers of the directors the company may **ratify** the **loan contract**.

Case law has determined that if a company has power to borrow, it also has power to **create charges** over the company's assets as **security** for the loan. *Re Patent File Co 1870.*

2 Debentures and loan capital

2.1 Loan capital

FAST FORWARD **Loan capital** comprises all the longer term borrowing of a company. It is distinguished from share capital by the fact that, at some point, borrowing must be repaid. Share capital on the other hand is only returned to shareholders when the company is wound up.

A company's **loan capital** comprises all amounts which it borrows for the long-term, such as:

(a) Permanent overdrafts at the bank
(b) Unsecured loans, from a bank or other party
(c) Loans secured on assets, from a bank or other party

Companies often issue long-term loans as capital in the form of **debentures**.

2.2 Debentures

FAST FORWARD A **debenture** is a document stating the terms on which a company has borrowed money. There are three main types.

- A **single debenture**

- **Debentures issued as a series** and usually registered

- **Debenture stock** subscribed to by a large number of lenders. Only this form requires a **debenture trust deed**, although the others may often incorporate one

BPP
LEARNING MEDIA

Key term

A **debenture** is the written acknowledgement of a debt by a company, normally containing provisions as to payment of interest and the terms of repayment of principal. A debenture may be secured on some or all of the assets of the company or its subsidiaries.

A debenture may create a **charge** over the company's assets as security for the loan. However a document relating to an unsecured loan is also a debenture in company law.

2.3 Types of debenture

A **debenture** is usually a **formal legal document**, often in printed form. Broadly, there are three main types.

(a) **A single debenture**

If, for example, a company obtains a secured loan or overdraft facility from its bank, the latter is likely to insist that the company seals the bank's standard form of debenture creating the charge and giving the bank various safeguards and powers.

(b) **Debentures issued as a series and usually registered**

Different lenders may provide different amounts on different dates. Although each transaction is a separate loan, the intention is that the lenders should rank equally *(pari passu)* in their right to repayment and in any security given to them. Each lender therefore receives a debenture in identical form in respect of his loan.

The debentures are **transferable securities**.

(c) **The issue of debenture stock subscribed to by a large number of lenders**

Only a public company may use this method to offer its debentures to the public and any such offer is a prospectus; if it seeks a listing on The Stock Exchange then the rules on listing particulars must be followed.

Each lender has a right to be **repaid** his **capital** at the **due time** (unless they are perpetual) and to receive **interest** on it until **repayment**. This form of borrowing is treated as a single loan 'stock' in which each debenture stockholder has a specified fraction (in money terms) which they or some previous holder contributed when the stock was issued. Debenture stock is transferable in multiples of, say, £1 or £10.

One advantage of debenture stock over debentures issued as single and **indivisible loan transactions** is that the holder of debenture stock can sell part of his holding, say £1,000 (nominal), out of a larger amount.

Debenture stock must be created using a **debenture trust deed** though single and series debenture's may also use a debenture trust deed.

2.4 Debenture trust deed

Major elements of a debenture trust deed for debenture stock
The appointment usually of a trustee for prospective debenture stockholders. The trustee is usually a bank, insurance company or other institution but may be an individual.
The nominal amount of the debenture stock is defined, which is the maximum amount which may be raised then or later. The date or period of repayment is specified, as is the rate of interest and half-yearly interest payment dates.
If the debenture stock is secured **the deed creates a charge or charges** over the assets of the company.

Major elements of a debenture trust deed for debenture stock
The trustee is authorised to **enforce the security** in case of default and, in particular, to appoint a receiver with suitable powers of management.
The company enters into **various covenants**, for instance to keep its assets fully insured or to limit its total borrowings; breach is a default by the company.
There may be elaborate provisions for **transfer of stock** and **meetings** of debenture stockholders.

Advantages of a debenture trust deed for debenture stock
The **trustee** with appropriate powers can **intervene promptly** in case of default.
Security for the debenture stock in the form of charges over property can be **given to a single trustee**.
The **company** can **contact a representative of the debentureholders** with whom it can negotiate.
By calling a **meeting of debentureholders**, the trustee can consult them and obtain a decision binding on them all.
The **debentureholders** will be able to **enjoy the benefit of a legal mortgage** over the company's land.

2.5 Register of debentureholders

Company law does not specifically require a **register of debentureholders** be maintained. However, a company is normally required to maintain a register by the debenture or debenture trust deed when debentures are issued as a series or when debenture stock is issued.

When there is a **register of debentureholders**, the following regulations apply.

(a) The company is required by law to keep the **register** at its registered office, or at an **address** notified to the registrar: s 743.

(b) The register must be open to **inspection** by **any person** unless the constitution or trust deed provide otherwise. Any person may obtain a copy of the register or part of it for a fee. A holder of debentures issued under a trust deed may require the company (on payment) to supply them with a copy of the deed: s 749.

Under s 745 a company has **five days** to respond to an inspection request or seek exemption to do so from the court.

(c) The register should be **properly kept** in accordance with the requirements of the Companies Act.

2.6 Rights of debentureholders

The position of **debentureholders** is best described by comparison with that of shareholders. At first sight the two appear to have a great deal in common.

- Both **own transferable company securities** which are usually long-term investments in the company.

- The **issue procedure** is much the same. An offer of either shares or debentures to the public is a prospectus as defined by the Act.

- The **procedure** for **transfer** of registered shares and debentures is the same.

But there are **significant differences**.

BPP
LEARNING MEDIA

Differences	Shareholder	Debentureholder
Role	Is a proprietor or owner of the company	Is a creditor of the company
Voting rights	May vote at general meetings	May not vote
Cost of investment	Shares may not be issued at a discount to nominal value	Debentures may be offered at a discount to nominal value
Return	Dividends are only paid • Out of distributable profits • When directors declare them	Interest must be paid when it is due
Redemption	Statutory restrictions on redeeming shares	No restriction on redeeming debentures
Liquidation	Shareholders are the last people to be paid in a winding up	Debentures must be paid back before shareholders are paid

From the investor's standpoint debenture stock is often **preferable to preference shares**. Although both yield a fixed income, debenture stock offers greater security.

2.6.1 Advantages and disadvantages of debentures (for the company)

Advantages	Disadvantages
Easily traded	May have to pay high interest rates to make them attractive
Terms clear and specific	Interest payments mandatory
Assets subject to a floating charge may be traded	Interest payments may upset shareholders if dividends fall
Popular due to guaranteed income	Debentureholder's remedies of liquidators or receivers may be disastrous for the company
Interest tax-deductible	Crystallisation of a floating charge can cause trading difficulties for a company
No restrictions on issue or purchase by a company	

 Question

Rights of shareholders and debentureholders

Unlike paying shareholders dividends, a company is obliged to pay debentureholders interest.

True/False?

Answer

True. Paying interest payments on debentures is mandatory.

3 Charges

FAST FORWARD

A charge over the assets of a company gives a creditor a **prior claim** over other creditors to payment of their debt out of these assets.

Charges may be either **fixed**, which attach to the relevant asset on creation, or **floating**, which attach on 'crystallisation'. For this reason it is not possible to identify the assets to which a **floating** charge relates (until **crystallisation**).

3.1 Definition

Key term

A **charge** is an encumbrance upon real or personal property granting the holder certain rights over that property. They are often used as security for a debt owed to the charge holder. The most common form of charge is by way of legal mortgage, used to secure the indebtedness of borrowers in house purchase transactions. In the case of companies, charges over assets are most frequently granted to persons who provide loan capital to the business.

A charge **secured** over a company's assets gives to the creditor (called the 'chargee') a prior claim (over other creditors) to payment of their debt out of those assets. Charges are of two kinds, fixed and floating.

3.2 Fixed charges

Key term

A **fixed charge** is protection given to secured creditors relating to specific assets of a company. The charge grants the holder the right of enforcement against the identified asset (in the event of default in repayment or some other matter) so that the creditor may realise the asset to meet the debt owed. Fixed charges rank first in order of priority in liquidation.

Fixed (or specific) charges attach to the relevant asset as soon as the charge is created. By its nature a fixed charge is best suited to assets which the company is likely to retain for a long period. A mortgage is an example of a fixed charge. If the company disposes of the charged asset it will either **repay the secured debt** out of the proceeds of sale so that the charge is discharged at the time of sale, or **pass the asset over to** the purchaser still subject to the charge.

3.3 Floating charges

Key term

A **floating charge** has been defined, in *Re Yorkshire Woolcombers Association Ltd 1903*, as:

(a)   A charge on a class of assets of a company, present and future …
(b)   Which class is, in the ordinary course of the company's business, changing from time to time and …
(c)   Until the holders enforce the charge the company may carry on business and deal with the assets charged.

Floating charges do not attach to the relevant assets until the charge crystallises. A floating charge is **not restricted** to assets such as **receivables** or **inventory**. A floating charge over 'the undertaking and assets' of a company (the most common type) applies to future as well as to current assets.

3.4 Identification of charges as fixed or floating

It is not always immediately apparent whether a charge is fixed or floating. Chargees often do not wish to identify a charge as being floating as it may get paid later than preferential debts in insolvency proceedings. A charge contract may declare the charge as fixed, or fixed and floating, whether it is or not. **The label attached** by parties in this way is **not a conclusive statement of the charge's legal nature**.

The general rule is that a **charge over assets will not be registered as fixed if it envisages that the company will still be able to deal with the charged assets without reference to the chargee**.

> *R in Right of British Columbia v Federal Business Development Bank 1988*
>
> *The facts:* In this Canadian case the Bank had a charge over the company's entire property expressed as 'a fixed and specific mortgage and charge'. Another term allowed the company to continue making sales from stock in the ordinary course of business until notified in writing by the bank to stop doing so.
>
> *Decision:* The charge was created as a floating, not a fixed, charge.

However, the courts have found **exceptions** to the general rule concerning permission to deal.

(a) In *Re GE Tunbridge Ltd 1995* it was held that as the three criteria stated in the *Yorkshire Woolcombers* case applied. The charge over certain fixed assets was a floating charge even though the company was required to obtain the chargee's permission before dealing with the assets.

(b) In *Re Cimex Ltd 1994* the court decided that the charge in dispute was a fixed charge. The assets did not in the ordinary course of business change from time to time. This was despite the company being able to deal with the assets without the chargee's permission.

3.4.1 Charges over receivables

Charges expressed to be fixed which cover **present and future receivables** (book debts) are particularly tricky.

Again the **general rule** applies. If the company is allowed to deal with money collected from customers without notifying the charge, the courts have decided that the charge is floating. If the money collected must be paid to the chargee, say in reduction of an overdraft, the courts have determined that the charge is fixed: *Siebe Gorman & Co Ltd v Barclays Bank Ltd 1979*. In 2005 the House of Lords held in *Re Spectrum Plus* that there can be no fixed charge over a company's book debts.

3.5 Creating a floating charge

A **floating charge** is **often created by express words**. However no special form of words is essential. If a **company** gives to a chargee rights over its assets while **retaining freedom to deal with them in the ordinary course of business** until the charge crystallises, that will be a charge which 'floats'. The particular assets subject to a floating charge cannot be identified until the charge attaches by crystallisation.

3.6 Crystallisation of a floating charge

FAST FORWARD

Floating charges **crystallise** or harden (convert into a fixed charge) on the happening of certain relevant events.

Key term

Crystallisation of a floating charge occurs when it is converted into a fixed charge: that is, a fixed charge on the assets owned by the company at the time of crystallisation.

Events causing crystallisation
The **liquidation** of the company
Cessation of the company's **business**
Active intervention by the chargee, generally by way of appointing a receiver
If the **charge contract so provides**, when notice is given by the chargee that the charge is converted into a fixed charge (on whatever assets of the relevant class are owned by the company at the time of the giving of notice)
The **crystallisation** of **another floating charge** if it causes the company to cease business.

Floating charge contracts sometimes make provision for 'automatic crystallisation'. This is where the charge is to crystallise when a **specified event** – such as a breach of some term by the company – occurs, regardless of whether:

- The chargee learns of the event.
- The chargee wants to enforce the charge as a result of the event.

Such clauses have been accepted by the courts if they state that, on the event happening, **the floating charge is converted to a fixed one**. Clauses which provide only that a company is to cease to deal with charged assets on the occurrence of a particular event have been rejected.

3.7 Comparison of fixed and floating charges

FAST FORWARD

Floating charges rank **behind** a number of other creditors on liquidation, in particular preferential creditors such as employees.

A **fixed charge** is normally the more satisfactory form of security since it **confers immediate rights** over identified assets. A **floating charge** has some advantage in being applicable to **current assets which may be easier to realise** than long term assets subject to a fixed charge. If for example a company becomes insolvent it may be easier to sell its inventory than its empty factory.

The principal disadvantages of floating charges
The **holder** of a floating charge **cannot be certain** until the charge crystallises which assets will form his security.
Even when a floating charge has crystallised over an identified pool of assets the **chargeholder** may find themselves **postponed** to the claim of **other creditors** as follows.
(a) A **judgement creditor or landlord** who has seized goods and sold them may retain the proceeds if received before the appointment of the debentureholder's receiver: s 183 IA.
(b) **Preferential debts** such as wages may be paid out of assets subject to a floating charge unless there are other uncharged assets available for this purpose: ss 40 and 175 IA.
(c) The **holder** of a **fixed charge** over the same assets will usually have priority over a floating charge on those assets even if that charge was created before the fixed charge (see below).
(d) A creditor may have sold goods and delivered them to the company on condition that he is to retain legal ownership until he has been paid (a **Romalpa** clause).
A **floating charge** may become **invalid automatically** if the company creates the charge to secure an existing debt and goes into liquidation within a year thereafter (s 245 IA). The period is only six months with a fixed charge.

3.8 Priority of charges

If more than one charge exists over the **same class of property** then legal rules must be applied to see which takes priority in the event the company goes into liquidation.

Different charges over the **same** property may be given to different creditors. It will be necessary in such cases to determine which party's claim has **priority**.

Illustration

If charges are created over the same property to secure a debt of £5,000 to X and £7,000 to Y and the property is sold yielding only £10,000, either X or Y is paid in full and the other receives only the balance remaining out of £10,000 realised from the security.

Priority of charges
Fixed charges rank according to the **order of their creation**. If two successive fixed charges over the same factory are created on 1 January and 1 February the earlier takes priority over the later one.
A floating charge created before a fixed charge will only take priority if, when the latter was created, the **fixed chargee** had **notice** of a clause in the floating charge that prevents a later prior charge.
A fixed charge created before a **floating one** has **priority**.
Two floating charges take priority according to the **time of creation**.

If a floating charge is existing and a fixed charge over the **same property** is created later the fixed charge has priority. This is unless the fixed chargeholder knew of the floating charge. The **fixed** charge ranks **first** since it attached to the property at the time of **creation** but the **floating** charge attaches at the time of **crystallisation**. Once a floating charge has crystallised it becomes a fixed charge and a fixed charge created subsequently ranks after it.

A floating chargeholder may seek to protect himself against losing his priority by including in the terms of his floating charge a prohibition against the company creating a fixed charge over the same property (sometimes called a **'negative pledge clause'**).

If the company **breaks that prohibition** the creditor to whom the fixed charge is given nonetheless obtains priority, unless at the time when his charge is created he has **actual** knowledge of the prohibition.

If a company sells a charged asset to a **third party** the following rules apply.

- A chargee with a fixed charge still has recourse to the property in the hands of the third party – the **charge** is **automatically** transferred with the property.
- Property only remains charged by a floating charge if the **third party** had **notice** of it when he acquired the property.

Assessment focus point

You should be aware of what fixed and floating charges are and what the implications are of the differences between them.

Question

A floating charge is created on 1 January 20X1. A fixed charge over the same property is created on 1 April 20X1. Assuming both are registered correctly, which ranks first?

Answer

The fixed charge attaches to the asset on creation; the floating charge only attaches on crystallisation, and the effect of crystallisation is not retrospective. Therefore the fixed charge ranks first.

4 Registration of charges

FAST FORWARD

To be valid and enforceable, charges must be **registered** within **21 days** of creation by the Registrar.

Certain types of **charge** created by a company **should be registered** within **21 days** with the Registrar by either the company or a person interested in it (eg the debenture trustee). Charges securing a **debenture issue** and **floating charges** are **specifically registrable**.

Other charges that are **registrable** include charges on:

- Uncalled share capital or calls made but not paid
- Land or any interest in land, other than a charge for rent
- Receivables (book debts)
- Goodwill or any intellectual property
- Ships or aircraft or any share in a ship

4.1 The registration process

The **company is responsible for registering the charge** but the charge **may** also **be registered** as a result of an application **by another person** interested in the charge.

The Registrar should be sent **the instrument** by which the charge is created or evidenced. The Registrar also has to be sent **prescribed particulars of the charge**.

- The date when the charge was created
- The amount of the debt which it secures
- Short particulars of the property to which the charge applies
- The person entitled to it

The Registrar files the particulars in the companies 'charges' register and notes the date of delivery. They also issue a **certificate** which is **conclusive evidence** that the **charge had been duly registered**.

The 21 day period for registration runs from the **creation** of the **charge**, or the acquisition of property charged, and not from the making of the loan for which the charge is security. Creation of a charge is usually effected by **execution of a document**.

4.2 Rectification of register of changes

A mistake or omission in **registered particulars** can only be rectified by the court ordering an extension of the period for registration, and with the subsequent rectification of the register. The court will only make the order if the error or omission was accidental or if it is just equitable to do so.

4.3 Failure to deliver particulars

The duty to deliver particulars falls upon the **company** creating the charge and if no one delivers particulars within 21 days, the **company and its officers are liable to a fine**: s 860. Non-delivery in the time period results in the **charge** being **void** against an administrator, liquidator or any creditor of a company: s 874. Non-delivery of a charge means that the sum secured by it is **payable forthwith on demand**: s 874.

4.3.1 Late delivery of particulars

The rules governing late delivery are the **same** as governing registration of **further particulars**, that is, a **court order** is required for registration. A charge can only be registered late if it does not prejudice the creditors or shareholders of the company. Therefore a correctly registered fixed charge has priority over a fixed charge created earlier but registered after it, if that charge is registered late. s 873.

4.4 Register of charges

As you already know, every company is under an obligation to keep a copy of **documents creating charges**, and a **register of charges**, at its registered office or any other location permitted by the Secretary of State.

Assessment focus point

Ensure that you are abolsutely clear on the rules relating to the registration of charges as they are a regular source of assessment questions.

Question
                                                                              Registering charges

A company creates a charge over a property in favour of Margaret on 1 May 20X7. It creates a further charge of the same type in favour of Chris over the same property on 13 May 20X7. The company has Chris's charge registered on 25 May 20X7, and Margaret's charge on 29 May 20X7.

Whose charge ranks first, and why?

Answer

Margaret's charge would have taken precedence because it was created first, had it been registered within the allowed period of 21 days, up to 22 May. However it was not registered until 29 May, and Chris's charge was legitimately registered in the period between 22 and 29 May when Margaret's charge was void. The court would probably have allowed late registration of Margaret's charge but not at the expense of Chris's rights per s 873.

---

5 Debentureholders' remedies

5.1 Rights of unsecured debentureholders

FAST FORWARD

A debentureholder **without security** has the same rights as any other creditor.

Any **debentureholder** is a creditor of the company with the normal remedies of an unsecured creditor. He could:

- **Sue** the company for debt and seize its property if his judgement for debt is unsatisfied
- Present a petition to the court for the **compulsory liquidation** of the company
- Apply to the court for an **administration order**, that is, a temporary reprieve to try and rescue a company

5.2 Rights of secured debentureholders

FAST FORWARD

A **secured** debentureholder may enforce the security if the company defaults on payment of interest or repayment of capital. They may take possession of the asset subject to the charge and sell it or apply to the court for its transfer to their ownership by a foreclosure order. They may also appoint a receiver or administrator of it. A floating charge holder may place the company into administration.

A **secured** debentureholder (or the trustee of a debenture trust deed) may enforce the security. They may:

- Take **possession of the asset** subject to the charge if they have a fixed charge (if they have a floating charge they may only take possession if the contract allows)

- **Sell it** (provided the debenture is executed as a deed)

- Apply to the court for its **transfer** to their ownership by foreclosure order (rarely used and only available to a legal chargee)

- Appoint a **receiver** of it, provided an administration order is not in effect or (in the case of floating charge holders), appoint an administrator without needing to apply to the court.

6 Transactions at an undervalue and preferences

FAST FORWARD

A **transaction at an undervalue** is a gift or a transaction in the two years before liquidation or administration, by which the company gives consideration of greater value than it received: s 238 IA. Such a transaction is **void** unless the company acted in good faith and for the purpose of carrying on its business, and believed on reasonable grounds that it would benefit the company.

A company gives **preference** to a creditor or to a guarantor of its debts if it acts so as to benefit that person's position should the company go into insolvent liquidation *and* does so with the intention of producing that result: s 239 IA. The transaction will be void if it was created within the 6 months before the commencement of liquidation.

6.1 Introduction

When a company goes into liquidation the court may avoid **transactions at an undervalue** and **preferences**. A transaction **'at an undervalue'** is a gift or a transaction in the two years previous to liquidation (or administration), by which the company gives consideration of greater value than it receives, for instance a sale at less than full market price: s 238 IA. Such a transaction is void if it was effected within a certain time period (see below). However, such a transaction does **not** become void if the company enters into it:

- In good faith
- For the purpose of carrying on its business
- Believing on reasonable grounds that it will benefit the company

A company **'gives preference'** to a creditor or guarantor of its debts if it does anything by which his position will be benefited should the company go into insolvent liquidation *and* the company does this with the intention of producing that result: s 239 IA. The transaction is **void** if it was effected within a certain time period (see below).

If, at the time of the undervalue or preference, the company was **unable to pay its debts**, or became so by reason of the transaction, and the company later goes into liquidation or administration, the liquidator or the administrator can apply to the court for an **order** to restore the position to what it would have been if no such transaction had taken place. The relevant **period** which brings the **avoidance** powers into operation in relation to a transaction are as follows.

(a) **Undervalues: two years** before the commencement of liquidation

(b) **Preferences**

(i) With a person **unconnected** with the company: **six months** before the commencement of liquidation

(ii) With a person **connected** with the company: **two years** prior to commencement

Unless the person in whose favour the undervalue or preference operates is connected with the company, the company must be **insolvent** at the time of entering into the disputed transaction, or must have become so in consequence of it, if it is to be disputed by the court. If the court is satisfied that a **preference** has been given it can (under s 241 IA):

- **Order return** of **property** or of the proceeds of its sale
- **Discharge any security** given
- **Order payment** in respect of benefit to the liquidator
- **Renew guarantee obligations** discharged by the preference
- **Charge property**

The term **'connected persons'** appears in the law both in the context of preferences and transactions at an undervalue and also in relation to floating charges. A person is **'connected'** with the company if he is:

- A **director** or **shadow director** of the company
- An **associate** of a director, shadow director or the company itself

These **provisions** are summarised below.:

Transaction with		Transactions at an undervalue	Preference
Unconnected person	Time period before commencement	2 years	6 months
	Company insolvent at that time?	Yes	Yes
Connected person	Time period before commencement	2 years	2 years
	Company insolvent at that time?	Yes	No

 Question

A transaction at an undervalue can be a gift made in the two years before a company is liquidated where it gave more consideration than it received.

True or false?

Answer

True. This is an example of a transaction at an undervalue.

Chapter Roundup

- Companies have an **implied power** to borrow for purposes incidental to their trade or business.

- **Loan capital** comprises all the longer term borrowing of a company. It is distinguished from share capital by the fact that, at some point, borrowing must be repaid. Share capital on the other hand is only returned to shareholders when the company is wound up.

- A **debenture** is a document stating the terms on which a company has borrowed money. There are three main types.

  - A **single debenture**
  - **Debentures issued as a series** and usually registered
  - **Debenture stock** subscribed to by a large number of lenders. Only this form requires a **debenture trust deed**, although the others may often incorporate one

- A charge over the assets of a company gives a creditor a **prior claim** over other creditors to payment of their debt out of these assets.

- Charges may be either **fixed**, which attach to the relevant asset on creation, or **floating**, which attach on 'crystallisation'. For this reason it is not possible to identify the assets to which a **floating** charge relates (until **crystallisation**).

- Floating charges **crystallise** or harden (convert into a fixed charge) on the happening of certain relevant events.

- Floating charges rank **behind** a number of other creditors on liquidation, in particular preferential creditors such as employees.

- If more than one charge exists over the **same class of property** then legal rules must be applied to see which takes priority in the event the company goes into liquidation.

- To be valid and enforceable, charges must be **registered** within **21 days** of creation by the Registrar.

- A debentureholder **without security** has the same rights as any other creditor.

- A **secured** debentureholder may enforce the security if the company defaults on payment of interest or repayment of capital. They may take possession of the asset subject to the charge and sell it or apply to the court for its transfer to their ownership by a foreclosure order. They may also appoint a receiver or administrator of it. A floating charge holder may place the company into administration.

- A **transaction at an undervalue** is a gift or a transaction in the two years before liquidation or administration, by which the company gives consideration of greater value than it received: s 238 IA. Such a transaction is void unless the company acted in good faith and for the purpose of carrying on its business, and believed on reasonable grounds that it would benefit the company.

- A company gives **preference** to a creditor or to a guarantor of its debts if it acts so as to benefit that person's position should the company go into insolvent liquidation *and* does so with the intention of producing that result: s 239 IA. The transaction will be void if it was created within the 6 months before the commencement of liquidation.

1   Which of the following are correct statements about the relationship between a company's ordinary shares and its debentures?
     Select all that apply.

     A   Debentures do not confer voting rights, whilst ordinary shares do.
     B   The company's duty is to pay interest on debentures, and to pay dividends on ordinary shares.
     C   Interest paid on debentures is deducted from pre-tax profits, dividends are paid from net profits.
     D   A debentureholder takes priority over a member in liquidation.

2   A fixed charge

     A   Does not attach to assets until they crystallise
     B   Can be a legal mortgage
     C   Can only attach to land, shares or book debts
     D   Cannot attach to land

3   What are the elements of the definition of a floating charge?

4   Company law requires a company to maintain a register of charges, but not a register of debentureholders.

     True   ☐

     False   ☐

5   In which of the following situations will crystallisation of a floating charge occur?
     Select all that apply.

     A   Liquidation of the company
     B   Disposal by the company of the charged asset
     C   Cessation of the company's business
     D   After the giving of notice by the chargee if the contract so provides

6   Certain types of charges need to be registered within 28 days of creation.

     True   ☐

     False   ☐

7   What steps can a fixed debentureholder take to enforce their security? (Max 30 words).

8   All companies have the implied power to borrow for any purpose.

     True   ☐

     False   ☐

9   How long does a company have to respond to a request by a shareholder to inspect the register of debentureholders?

     A   5 days
     B   7 days
     C   14 days
     D   21 days

10   Where an individual, who is connected to a company, is given a preference and the company subsequently becomes insolvent, the liquidator can apply for them to return the benefit they received so that the company is restored to the position it would have been in if the transaction had never taken place. This is the case where the transaction occurred within which time period before the insolvency?

A   6 months
B   12 months
C   18 months
D   24 months

Answers to Quick Quiz

1   A, C and D are correct. Whilst the company has a contractual duty to pay interest on debentures, there is no duty on it to pay dividends on shares. B is therefore incorrect.

2   B. A mortgage is an example of a fixed charge. It can extend to, for instance, plant and machinery as well as land. Floating charges do not attach to assets until they crystallise.

3   The charge is:

(a)   A charge on a class of assets, present and future
(b)   Which class is in the ordinary course of the company's business changing from time to time
(c)   Until the holders enforce the charge, the company may carry on business and deal with the assets charged

4   True. A register of charges must be kept, a register of debentureholders is not required to be kept by the Act.

5   A, C and D are true. As the charge does not attach to the asset until crystallisation, B is untrue.

6   False. Certain charges such as charges securing a debenture issue and floating charges need to be registered within 21 days.

7   Take possession of the asset subject to the charge
Sell it
Apply to the court for a transfer to his ownership
Appoint a receiver of it

8   False. All companies have an implied power to borrow for purposes incidental to their trade or business.

9   A. Companies have 5 days to respond to a request to inspect the register of debenureholders.

10   D. For persons connected to a company, the relevant period is 2 years (24 months).

Now try the questions below from the Question Bank

Number
Q76
Q77
Q78
Q79
Q80

Part G
Ethics and business

BPP
LEARNING MEDIA

17

The importance of ethics

Introduction

This chapter introduces the subject of **ethics**.

You have probably not come across ethics before in your studies, but you may have some idea of what the subject is about already from your personal life.

> **Important**
>
> It is vital that you do not 'pigeon hole' or categorise this subject as being self-contained. Although you will have your knowledge of ethics specifically tested in this exam, you should realise that ethical ideas and concepts flow through everything you do as an accountant. It is certain that they will be incorporated into other exams at Operational, Management and Strategic levels.

The chapter begins by considering why society developed a framework of rules. It goes on to discuss what ethics is, and why it is relevant to businesses and accountants. We then look into ethical codes including **CIMA's ethical guidelines** and the qualities accountants should demonstrate.

Finally we look at the importance of **personal development** and the concept **of lifelong learning**.

Topic list	Learning outcomes
1 A framework of rules	A1(a), A1(b)
2 What are ethics?	A1(a), A1(c)
3 Accountants and ethics	A1(a), A1(c), A1(d)
4 A code of ethics for accountants	A1(a), A2(e)
5 CIMA's ethical guidelines	A1(a), A2(c), A2(e)
6 Qualities of an accountant	A1(a), A2(b), A2(d)
7 Personal development and lifelong learning	A1(a), A2(a)

1 A framework of rules

Humans have developed a **framework of rules** to regulate behaviour.

The society we live in could not exist without **rules and standards**. Think about it, what would life be like if everyone went about doing exactly what they felt like?

People may decide not to turn up for work. This would mean shops not opening, and that you could not buy food. What we consider **crime would spiral out of control** as members of the public decide to take what they want and the police would only tackle criminals if they felt like it. **Businesses would not function** and the financial markets could not operate.

As society developed from prehistoric tribes to the complex interrelationships we have today, **rules regulating behaviour** had to evolve also. This is because humans recognised the need for everyone to work together for the good of the group.

1.1 Developments of society

Imagine our prehistoric tribe. They would have started as individuals, roaming for food and shelter to keep themselves alive. By working as a group, some could **find shelter**, while others **hunted** for things to eat. It would be no good if the hunters ate all the food they found, and those who found shelter refused to let the hunters into the shelter. The shelter finders would **starve** to death while the hunters would **freeze**.

Humans have evolved from these tribes and have built a strong society that has revolutionised our planet. This has only been possible because **individuals have worked together**, guided by rules.

1.2 A need for rules

Back in prehistoric times, there were no laws, no courts and no police. Rules would have **developed through need**. The tribe would have a collective idea of what was **right** and **wrong** for the good of the group and would have **punished** a group member who stepped out of line, for example by taking food from others.

Further rules developed as society grew and eventually the first **laws** were laid down to control the larger populations. **Religion** played a major role in developing the rules for the individual, and many of these rules are still in place today.

Business law is relatively new, and has only developed over the last couple of hundred years with **industrialisation** and the needs that grew from it.

1.3 How do the rules fit together?

Your syllabus focuses on **three main sources of rules** that regulate behaviour of individuals and businesses. These are:

- The law (criminal and civil)
- Regulations
- Codes of conduct

The table below identifies the differences of approach each source takes.

Source	Explanation	Creator and form				Enforcement and penalty		
		Parliament (Acts of Parliament)	Court (case law)	Regulatory bodies (statutory rules)	Professional bodies (guidance, rules and principles)	Police (fines and prison)	Lawyers (compensation and enforceable agreements)	Regulatory or professional body (disciplinary hearings fines, compensation)
Law (criminal)	Handles serious threats against the public or the public administration. Attempts to protect the public by deterring and stigmatising offenders.	✓	✓	☐	☐	✓	☐	☐
Law (civil)	Handles loss or damage to individuals caused by the actions, or failure to comply with legal obligations, of others. Attempts to compensate the victim.	✓	✓	☐	☐	☐	✓	☐
Regulations	Handles anything which requires procedures or practice to be followed. Attempts to provide detailed rules for specific activities.	✓	☐	✓	✓	☐	☐	✓
Codes of practice	Handles guidance for professionals. Attempts to provide practical rules on how to perform work or deal with certain situations.	☐	☐	✓	✓	☐	☐	✓

BPP LEARNING MEDIA

The diagram below shows how the sources of regulation fit together and the relationship ethics has with them.

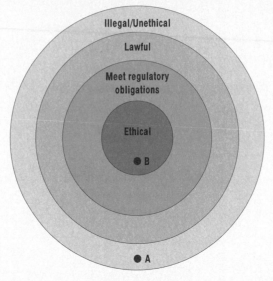

Point A shows a company's current behaviour. It indicates that it is currently breaking the law. It could be treating its employees in an illegal way such as breaking health and safety laws.

The company wants to move to **point B**. This means (in the case of health and safety) taking the **maximum care of employees** that is expected by society. To get to this point, the company needs to meet its legal and non-legal obligations first.

The **law is the minimum level of behaviour required by society**. Any standard of behaviour below it is considered illegal and warrants punishment by society.

By **meeting non-legal regulations** (such as the rules of your workplace), you meet a **higher level of behaviour** than just the legal requirements.

Ethical behaviour is seen as the **highest level of behaviour** that society expects. Your behaviour goes further than just meeting your legal and non-legal obligations.

Question

Rules

Which of the following sources of rules can be created by both Parliament and regulatory bodies?

A   Criminal law
B   Civil law
C   Regulations
D   Codes of practice

Answer

C   Regulations can either be created by Parliament or regulatory bodies. Criminal and civil law can be created by Parliament or the courts. Codes of practice can be created by regulatory or professional bodies.

BPP
LEARNING MEDIA

2 What are ethics?

FAST FORWARD

Ethics are a set of **moral principles** that **guide behaviour**.

Individuals have **moral values** and beliefs about what constitutes **'right'** and **'wrong'** behaviour. These values often reflect those of the individual's **family, culture** and **educational environment** they are brought up in.

Ethics are not the same thing as **law** or the rules of **religion**.

Ethics and morals are concerned with **right** and **wrong** and how conduct should be judged to be good or bad. It is about how we should live our lives and, in particular, how we should behave towards other people. It is therefore relevant to all forms of human activity.

Morals differ from ethics in the sense that they derive from a **person's individual beliefs** and are often linked to religious views. They are not derived from **professional ethics** which are the **views** and **rules** of the **professional organisation** that an individual is a member of.

Therefore it is perfectly possible for an individual to find an action to be **justified ethically** (in terms of professional ethics) **but be immoral** (to their personal views).

Where an individual's morals clash with their professional ethics they can **protest** or **resign** – but this will have **consequences** for them professionally and therefore is the hardest choice that a professional may face. The law will provide the individual some protection if they make an ethical protest. Where an individual follows their professional ethics, they may not be taking (to them) the correct course of action, but they will be afforded the protection of their profession.

The problem professions have regarding promoting ethical behaviour by their members is that **individuals must choose** to behave ethically. This was identified by the philosopher and modern ethical thinker **Emmanuel Kant** as **'the good will'**. Individuals must be motivated to behave ethically rather than taking the usually more easy, convenient or personally acceptable option.

The ancient philosopher **Aristotle** suggested that ethical behaviour can be developed by individuals who have a strong foundation of **fundamental virtues** such as honesty, integrity and openness. Such individuals not only practice these virtues in everyday life, but they also have an **ethical compass**.

CIMA's ethical code, which we shall study later, attempts to develop strong fundamental virtues in CIMA members. By doing this it is hoped that **CIMA members** will **practice the good virtues** and therefore have a strong sense of what is ethically right and wrong.

Question

Ethics

Consider the following situations. Do you think the person is behaving ethically?

(a)   Somebody who claims unemployment benefit from the state, but who also works part-time, as they cannot otherwise afford to feed their children.

(b)   An airline pilot who decides to risk an emergency landing in severe bad weather for a passenger who is gravely ill and will die if not treated very soon.

(c)   A lottery winner who decides to keep all the winnings for themselves and not to share it with their family.

There is never any single answer to ethical questions. Everyone will have his or her own ideas about 'right' and 'wrong'. All you can do is to look at the facts and come to your own conclusion.

(a) The person is clearly breaking the law and this in itself can be considered unethical behaviour. However, some may consider the reason is ethical and that 'the end justifies the means'. You might consider the reason to be unethical since it puts the parent at risk of prosecution, and this may harm the children in the long run.

(b) The pilot may be risking the lives of everyone onboard the aircraft to save the life of just one. You could consider this unethical, but the pilot may have many years of experience in dealing with bad weather, so they consider the risk to be low. Pilots will have their own guidelines for dealing with these situations. Ignoring them may constitute unethical behaviour.

(c) You may feel the size of the lottery win determines whether the action is ethical or not. Society may expect those with 'small' wins to keep it for themselves, but if they win millions, they should share it. If the winner comes from a wealthy family, the action may be considered perfectly ethical. For a less well-off family, the apparent selfishness may seem completely unethical.

2.1 Businesses and ethics

Key term

> **Ethics in business**: 'The application of ethical values to business behaviour'. CIMA

Businesses also have ethical values, based on the **norms** and **standards** of **behaviour** that their leaders believe will best help them express their identity and achieve their objectives. Some of these ethical values may be **explicit**, for example, expressed in a mission statement or in employee training programmes. Others may be **unwritten rules and customs** that form part of the organisations' culture: 'the way we do things around here'.

Business life is a fruitful source of **ethical dilemmas** because its whole purpose is material gain, the making of profit. Success in business requires a constant, avid search for potential advantage over others and business people are under pressure to do whatever yields such advantage.

The table below summarises **three elements** to ethics.

Element	Explanation
I	Ethics concern an individual's professional responsibility to act.
DO	Ethics concern the 'real world' practical actions an individual can take. It is important to consider how an individual acts and not always what they do.
BEST	Ethics concern choices between different courses of action. These may involve taking a course of action which is less unpalatable than another.

2.1.1 An issue of trust

Whatever the situation, there is a public expectation (especially regarding professionals) that organisations will act ethically. This is known as the **'trust me'** model and was the case for many years when most businesses were owned by families. Times have now changed and most companies are now run by directors and mangers rather than fathers and sons and the model changed to **'involve me'** as more evidence was needed of their ethical credentials.

In recent times, trust in business has fallen and increasingly more evidence is required to demonstrate it. The **'Show me'** stage required some demonstration of trust, **'Prove to me'** required independent verification and assurance and the final stage of **'Obey me'** would exist when the law creates legislation to cure instances of unethical behaviour. We are some way off this point currently.

What caused this trust to disintegrate? Since the 1980s, the UK has seen a procession of corporate disasters including the names of **Barings Bank**, **Polly Peck** and **Maxwell**. The US has seen scandals concerning **Worldcom**, **Enron** and **Tyco**. Europe did not escape and has seen its share of problems with **Parmalat** and in Asia, **Mitsubishi Motors** and **Daewoo** have had issues too. All these scandals have severely knocked public confidence and trust in major corporations.

In an attempt to counter this lack of trust, many corporations have developed **ethical strategies** and **policies** to provide **guidance** and **training** for their employees. The strategy is set by the leadership and this will feed into all areas of the business and become part of the cultural DNA of the organisation.

2.1.2 Corporate Responsibility Policies and Reports

An ethical strategy is not always visible to outsiders, and many companies now produce **Corporate Responsibility Policies (CRPs)** and **Corporate Responsibility Reports (CRRs)** for their stakeholders to demonstrate their commitment and to manage its relationships in the wider community. They reflect the view that an organisation has responsibilities beyond that of its shareholders.

(a)   **Corporate (Social) Responsibility policies**

Corporate Responsibility policies are also known as Corporate Social Responsibility policies. These are policies in which the organisation decides how to help the local community that it is part of and which charities to support. However, they also deal with the wider community, and policies often focus on reducing the environmental impact the organisation has and where to recruit new employs from. These policies must be consistent with the overall aims of the organisation to ensure support continues even when the organisation faces its own problems such as a downturn in profit.

(b)   **Corporate Responsibility Reports**

Many new technological advances allow for the reporting of statistics as carbon footprints and a company's impact on the environment. These can be added to more conventional assessments such as staff turnover to provide a quite detailed report on the organisation.

Such **corporate values** also guide staff as to the expectations that employers have regarding their behaviour. The aim is to end up with consistent behaviour across the workforce in terms of personal conduct and professionalism. These policies are enforced on a voluntary basis and results are monitored through audits, surveys and interviews.

The changing ethical environment

The surreal dilemmas sound like they could be drawn from a magazine advice column for paranoid lawyers: can I provide sacrificial goats for my customers in the Middle East? What if the client asks us to procure internal organs for his sick relative? Is it ok for me to donate cash at a Korean funeral?

These are real life scenarios under discussion by senior executives responsible for setting policies for corporate hospitality and gifts in an increasingly strict US regulatory environment.

The conclusion of the executives, who recently gathered in New York for a summit on the problem, was that the fine grey line that separates acceptable generosity from the darker world of bribery and corruption has narrowed substantially.

What lies behind their nervousness is the growing impact of Sarbanes-Oxley corporate governance legislation on the already strict rules of the US Foreign Corrupt Practices Act. Combine this with increasingly active enforcement agencies and the rapid globalisation of US business and there is a recipe for multinational angst on a grand scale.

Where minor local transgressions might once have been swept under the carpet, they are now likely to emerge as so-called 'material weaknesses' in internal control reports requiring sign-off from a chief executive and finance director worried about their own liability.

Some rules are clear-cut. Schering Plough makes a rule not to pay for spouses to attend medical conferences, for example. Other policies can be difficult. Rule one is no cash – yet there are countries in Asia where token payments in envelopes are still expected at certain social situations such as funerals or Chinese New Year.

In contrast, Northrop Grumman, the US defence manufacturer, takes a more rule-bound approach – perhaps in keeping with the military background of many of its employees.

Trace International, which advises its member companies on differing international standards, recently conducted a survey of corporate lawyers that found a wide range of in-house policies. 13 per cent of companies had no policy for gifts and hospitality, 17 per cent left it to the discretion of local managers and 34 percent simply required prior approval for any 'reasonable' expenditure. Only 3 per cent demanded approval if the monetary value was above a pre-determined threshold, while 3 per cent applied a blanket ban on anything above their threshold.

This is likely to change quickly as companies realise the impact of the changing regulatory climate. Provisions to protect whistleblowers and ensure full disclosure are also likely to increase the number of cases that come to the surface.

The trend in fines is also going up. Last July, two divisions of ABB's oil, gas and petrochemicals business pleaded guilty to charges of bribing Nigerian government officials – including with cash and pedicures – and agreed with the Department of Justice to pay fines of $10.5m (£5.4m). Separately, ABB, the Swiss-Swedish engineering group, resolved civil charges brought by the SEC and agreed to pay an additional $5.9m fine.

The Changing Ethical Environment. Dan Roberts. Financial Times, 20 April 2005

BPP
LEARNING MEDIA

3 Accountants and ethics

FAST FORWARD

As an accountant, your values and attitudes **flow through** everything you do professionally. They contribute to the **trust** the wider community puts in the profession and the **perception** it has of it.

We have seen in earlier chapters that the law provides a mechanism for **serious offences** to be punished and compensation sought by those who have suffered. This mechanism is **inappropriate** to handle the day-to-day decisions that accountants make, as the **level of unacceptable behaviour** is high and it is highly unlikely that the amount of proof required to establish guilt or liability would be found.

The problem of lack of proof stems from the fact that accountancy is about **making decisions** and **forming judgements**. These decisions and judgements are **personal** to the accountant concerned and (unless the error is substantial) the **time** and **cost** involved in bringing an accountant to account for their actions is likely to be **prohibitive**.

Therefore, as we shall see later, the accountancy profession has developed a **code of ethics** that all accountants are bound by. Should an individual's behaviour fall short of these rules they may be brought to account at a **disciplinary hearing** which is **cheaper** and **quicker** to organise than a court action.

Key reasons for accountants to behave ethically:

- Ethical issues may be a matter of law and regulation and accountants are expected to apply them.

- The profession requires members to conduct themselves and provide services to the public according to certain standards. By upholding these standards, the profession's reputation and standing is protected.

- An accountant's ethical behaviour serves to protect the public interest.

- Consequences of unethical behaviour include disciplinary action against the accountant by their employer or CIMA and adverse affects on jobs, financial viability and business efficacy of their organisation.

- Accountants employed in the public sector have a duty to protect tax-payers' money.

It is not enough just to behave ethically, the **values of society** will **change** over time. Working in the **public interest** means that accountants must keep **up to date** with the expectations of society in order to fulfil their role and build **confidence** in the profession.

3.1 Approaches to accountancy ethics

Professionals will have their own idea of what behaviour is ethical and what is not. Although there will be differences, collectively there are common views and values that shine through.

In the UK, the **Financial Reporting Council (FRC)** has taken a lead role in **ethical reporting** and building **confidence** in the accountancy profession. It also monitors the **accountability** of professional accountants. This work is undertaken by two sub-bodies.

   (a)   **The Professional Oversight Board for Accountancy (POB)**

       Its role is to **regulate specific activities** of the accountancy bodies regarding their members':

       (i)   **Registration** and **monitoring**
       (ii)   **Training** and **education**
       (iii)   **Continuous professional development (CPD)**
       (iv)   **Conduct** and **discipline**

(b)   **The Auditing Practices Board (APB)**

Its role is mainly in conjunction with **audit practices**. Examples of the role it plays includes:

(i)   Issuing **audit standards** containing principles and procedures that auditors in the UK and Republic of Ireland must comply with.

(ii)   Issuing **advice** on **the application** of **audit standards** and assistance with dealing with **emerging issues**.

(iii)   Developing **standards** for accountants who provide **assurance services.**

(iv)   Issuing **ethical standards** concerning the key principles of **independence, objectivity** and **integrity**.

(v)   Assisting the **development of legislation** and other **regulations** nationally and internationally when required.

(vi)   Developing the **public's understanding** of the role and responsibilities of auditors – including research and sponsorship.

The **International Federation of Accountants** (IFAC) oversees accountancy worldwide and has published a **code of ethics for professional accountants**. All members of professional bodies that are part of IFAC must apply this code and the bodies themselves ensure the efficacy of the rules by consulting with firms of accountants and other interested parties.

Finally, increasing numbers of **corporations** are developing codes of ethics for their employees which must be followed during the course of their employment.

3.2 The Seven Principles of Public Life

The UK government's **Committee of Standards in Public Life** set out seven principles that individuals employed in the public sector must follow.

(a)   **Selflessness**

Individuals should act solely in the public interest and not for personal gain or that of friends and family.

(b)   **Integrity**

Individuals should avoid actions which would place them under financial or other obligations whereby the person holding their obligation could influence their public duties.

(c)   **Objectivity**

All choices, especially those regarding awarding contracts, rewarding or providing benefits to others and making public appointments must be made purely on merit.

(d)   **Accountability**

Individuals are responsible for their own actions and are accountable to others. They must subject themselves to whatever scrutiny comes with their office.

(e)   **Openness**

Individuals must be open about their decisions and actions. Information regarding the reasons for their decisions must be freely available. Restrictions on information are only permitted when it is in the wider public interest.

BPP
LEARNING MEDIA

(f)   **Honesty**

Where individuals have private interests which relate to their public ones, they should declare them and seek to resolve any conflict to protect the public interest.

(g)   **Leadership**

Individuals must promote and respect the other six principles through leadership and example.

Accountants must also follow these principles. Where they appear to be in a situation which **conflicts** with their legal, regulatory or other ethical frameworks they must ensure their concerns are heard.

3.3 Codes of conduct

FAST FORWARD

Professional institutions (such as CIMA) have an overriding duty to **protect the public interest**. To ensure members act in a manner which achieves this, most have developed codes of conduct to guide behaviour.

To help professionals judge whether or not they are acting ethically in particular circumstances, guidance is often given (usually by a governing body) that clarifies the matter. Such guidance is usually known as a **'Code of ethics'** or **'Code of conduct'**.

If such codes **conflict** with **legislation** or other legally enforceable rules, the **legal position** will **prevail**.

Key term

Code of ethics. 'Set of standards governing the conduct of members of a certain profession, by specifying expected standards for competence, professional behaviour and integrity'. (*CIMA Official Terminology*)

There are two theoretical approaches that can be followed when developing a code of ethics.

- **Compliance-based** approach (also known as **rules-based**)
- **Ethics-based** approach (also known as **framework-based**)

Whatever approach is taken, members either comply '**formally**' or '**actually**'. Members who follow the code **formally** follow the **letter of the law**, doing the minimum necessary to meet their obligations. Those who follow the code **actually go beyond the minimum** and seek to **achieve** the **overall purpose** of the code – they embody it.

3.3.1 Compliance-based approach

Under this approach, the governing body will attempt to anticipate every possible ethical situation and lay down specific rules for members to follow. As with law, members are expected to follow the rules and will be accountable if they breach them – effectively members are **legally bound**.

It is often called a **'tick box'** approach to ethics and is well established in the US. The **Sentencing Guidelines for Judges** gives judges the power to mitigate fines against companies if they can prove that it had published ethical guidelines and attempted to guide employee behaviour.

Advantages	Disadvantages
Rules are specific to each circumstance	Long and lengthy rulebooks
Encourages consistent application of rules	Members cannot 'learn' every rule
Rule breaches are clearly identifiable	Can be seen to reduce members to robots, just following a set of rules

3.3.2 Ethics-based approach

Under this approach, principles are set out which describe the **fundamental values** and **qualities** that members should embody. There is no attempt to prescribe detailed rules, however, general guidelines are developed to give advice on how certain situations should be handled. This approach means members follow **voluntary guidelines** which are examples of **good** or **best-practice**.

Advantages	Disadvantages
Encourages proactive members, issues have to be addressed rather than passively following the law	Interpretation of rules can lead to lengthy, complex disciplinary hearings
Treats members as professionals and enables them to make their own decisions	Potential for inconsistent application of rules
Best-suited to deal with complex situations and evolving environments where it is difficult to think up rules for every possible case	Ambiguous rules may confuse members
Makes it harder for members to search for ways round the rules	'General guidelines' may become detailed rules over time

3.3.3 Differences in approach

Under the **compliance** approach, individuals have a **clear perception** of the expected behaviour and can consult a **rule book** if necessary, but there is a limit to the amount of rules which can be legislated for and in many cases individuals would be forced to make their own decisions. To cover these **'grey'** areas some indication of the expected behaviour should be provided to give individuals something to judge their actions against.

The **ethics** approach is more organic and allows the **individual to decide** what behaviour is appropriate in all circumstances. This approach is more wide ranging than the compliance-based approach as the principles can be applied in many circumstances, more than a compliance-based rule book could cover.

The following phrases may be used to describe the **characteristics** of each approach.

Characteristic	Compliance-based	Ethics-based
Enforceability	Mandatory	Discretionary
Choices	Obedience/disobedience	Judgement
Standards	Explicit	Implicit
Motivation	Fear-driven	Values-driven
Approach	Law-based	Principles-based
Objective	Detection	Prevention
Measure	Rules	Principles (values)

3.4 Codes of conduct for business organisations

The approaches to codes of conduct described above can also be applied by **businesses** wishing to develop an **ethical code** for their employees.

BPP
LEARNING MEDIA

There are **three elements** to creating an effective ethical programme.

(a)   **Active leadership**

The programme should be supported by the very top of the organisation. A senior board member should be appointed as 'Ethical Champion' whose initial role is to persuade all other senior executives to lead by example.

(b)   **Buy-in**

The Champion's next role is to organise a consultation process with members of staff to achieve their 'buy-in' of the new ethical culture. All staff should understand that the ethical code gives them principles and values that should be reflected in their everyday activities and will help them deal with any ethical issues they come across whilst at work.

(c)   **Training**

Once employees understand the need for ethical behaviour and embrace the change in culture, training should be provided to ensure all understand what is expected of them and to further instil the ethical message. Helplines may be set up to provide employees with advice for dealing with ethical problems.

3.5 Why develop an ethical code?

Organisations such as companies and accountancy firms have several **reasons for introducing ethical codes**, aside from the public interest issues.

(a)   **Communication**

Ethical codes communicate the standard of behaviour expected of employees.

(b)   **Consistency of conduct**

With the message effectively communicated, the behaviour of employees can be standardised or made consistent across all operations and locations. Customers, suppliers and other stakeholders will receive similar treatment wherever they are.

(c)   **Risk reduction**

Standardised behaviour reduces the risk of unethical actions as employees who are unethical will 'stand out' and can be dealt with. This reduces the risk of a few employees irrevocably damaging the reputation of the organisation and the trust people have in it.

(d)   **Compliance with UK Corporate Governance rules**

The Cadbury Report on corporate governance recommended that businesses draw up codes of conduct which are published internally and externally to the organisation. The purpose is to ensure employees know what is expected of them. Corporate governance is an important issue for businesses, particularly those which are listed on the London Stock Exchange so these recommendations are important to them.

Question

Which of the following are included in the seven principles of public life?

Selflessness
Boldness
Honesty
Obedience
Leadership

Answer

Selflessness – is included
Boldness – is not included
Honesty – is included
Obedience – is not included
Leadership – is included

4 A code of ethics for accountants

FAST FORWARD The **International Federation of Accountants** (IFAC) is an international body representing all the major accountancy bodies across the world. Its mission is to develop the **high standards** of professional accountants and enhance the quality of services they provide.

To enable the **development of high standards**, IFAC's ethics committee established a **code of ethics** which has aligned standards globally. The code (which CIMA has adopted) has the aim of **identifying the responsibilities** that a person employed as an accountant takes on, in return for a traditionally well paid career with high status. The code identifies potential situations where pitfalls may exist and offers advice on how to deal with them. By doing this the code indicates a minimum level of conduct that all accountants must adhere to and it is split into three parts:

(a)   **Part A – General Application of the Code**

       This introduces the fundamental principles which we shall study below.

(b)   **Part B – Professional Accountants in Public Practice**

       This section provides guidance on applying the principles that is relevant to those who work in public practice, for example issues of appointment, conflicts of interest, second opinions, fees and remuneration, marketing, hospitality, gifts, looking after client assets and objectivity and independence.

(c)   **Part C – Professional Accountants in Business**

       This section provides guidance that is particularly relevant to those who work in commerce. Such as the preparation of information, acting with sufficient experience, financial interests and inducements.

As a member of IFAC, **CIMA** released its own **code of ethics** that are almost the same as IFAC's but with some amendments that reflect local regulations. Additionally, CIMA has its own reasons for upholding high ethical standards.

- As a **Chartered Institute**, it has an overriding commitment to protect the public interest. This requires members to act ethically

- High ethical standards contribute to the integrity of the CIMA qualification which enhances the **employability** of CIMA members

5 CIMA's ethical guidelines

FAST FORWARD

CIMA's ethical guidelines give the **fundamental principles** that members should follow in their professional lives.

In June 2006, CIMA launched its code of ethics – or ethical guidelines. These ethical guidelines give the **fundamental principles** that members should follow in their professional lives. Fundamental means the principles form the **bedrock of professional judgements**, **decisions**, **reasoning** and **practice**. CIMA members must not only **know** them, but also **apply** them in their everyday work. In this respect we can see that **CIMA's ethical code** is **framework** or **ethics based**, This is typical of profession codes as it **helps** the professional rather than **directing** them. There are **serious consequences for failing to follow them**, quite apart from the unacceptability of failure. Whenever a complaint is made against a member, failure to follow the contents of the fundamental principles will be taken into account when a decision is made as to whether a *prima facie* case exists of professional misconduct. The code reflects the standards CIMA expects from its **members** and **students**.

As we saw earlier, professionals must meet the public's expectation for keeping themselves up to date with current developments, to this end it has also created a **Professional Development framework**. This reflects the inescapable truth that issues accountants face will change over time.

CIMA took a **framework approach** because compliance-based rules are not always particularly effective and the organisation preferred to operate by trust and **self-regulation** rather than strict enforcement of rules.

Important!

CIMA's ethical guidelines are available at www.cimaglobal.com. Ensure you study them.

5.1 Fundamental principles

The **fundamental principles**, which must be observed by all members, are as follows.

5.1.1 Integrity

Integrity is the important principle of honesty and requires accountants to be **straightforward** in all **professional** and **business relationships**. Particular care must be taken when reporting figures and statements. Omitting key information, obscuring the facts or making calculations and decisions without due care could result in false or misleading information being produced and integrity being breached.

Integrity goes further than the work an accountant produces. It also requires the **accountant to act** in a **professional**, **consistent manner**. The accountant must treat everyone the same rather than being friendly to some colleagues but cold to others. It also means that they should not back down over their personal or professional values just to avoid a difficult situation.

5.1.2 Objectivity

Objectivity is a combination of impartiality, intellectual honesty and a freedom from conflicts of interest. Accountants should act fairly and not allow prejudice or bias or the influence of others to affect their judgements. It contrasts with subjectivity (meaning an individual takes matters into consideration which are important to them, eg friendship and loyalty.)

Objectivity is the core value that an accountant brings to their organisation. It is often difficult to separate one's personal interest from a decision, but as accountants it is expected.

Circumstances which may leave accountants in particular risk of breaching this principle include accepting **excessive hospitality** or forming **illicit relationships** which could cause embarrassment and the risk of blackmail. Where a threat to objectivity exists, it can be reduced or eliminated by **withdrawal**, **terminating the relationship**, **involving others** in the process and **discussing** the problem with others in higher positions.

5.1.3 Professional competence and due care

Professional competence and due care means accountants should refrain from performing any services that they cannot perform with **reasonable care knowledge**, **competence**, **diligence** and a full **awareness** of the **important issues**. There is a duty to remain **technically up-to-date** and apply appropriate technical and professional standards when providing professional services.

Where others perform work on the accountant's behalf, the accountant must ensure that such staff also have adequate experience and qualifications, and that they are supervised. **Limitations** and problems found should be **disclosed** to those who the accountant is reporting to. **Fact** and **opinion** should be **clearly identified** to avoid misunderstandings.

5.1.4 Confidentiality

Accountants have a duty to safeguard the security of information in their possession unless there is a **legal or professional right or duty to disclose**. Also this means not using information obtained in the course of work for personal advantage or for the benefit of others.

Breaches of confidentiality often occur when information is **inadvertently disclosed** to friends and family and where the accountant has recently **changed employers**. Care must be taken to keep confidential all information found in the course of performing a professional duty and where a new job is commenced, prior experience may be used in the new role, but not prior information.

CIMA's code of conduct lists circumstances where **confidential information may be disclosed**, examples include:

- Disclosure is **permitted by law**
- Disclosure is **authorised by the client or employer**
- Disclosure is **required by law**, such as providing evidence in legal proceedings or assisting public authorities when legal infringements have occurred. This would, for example, occur when an accountant has a duty to report knowledge or suspicion of money laundering activities by their employer or client.
- Disclosure is **permitted by a professional duty or right**, such as complying with technical or ethical requirements, protecting the professional interests of an accountant in a legal action, when dealing with their professional body in an investigation or to comply with a professional body's quantity review

In some **special circumstances**, for example where an accountant is involved in the **provision of legal advice** or is acting in respect of litigation, then they may be covered by **legal professional privilege**. This means they will have a defence to a charge of failing to report an offence they become aware of whilst dealing with their client. However, there must be no intention on their part to further a criminal purpose.

BPP LEARNING MEDIA

5.1.5 Professional behaviour

Professional behaviour means, in essence, not doing anything that might discredit the profession and to comply with all relevant laws and regulations. This is defined by the profession as *'actions which a reasonable and informed third party, having knowledge of all relevant information, would conclude negatively affects the good reputation of the profession.'*

Remember a quote from **Benjamin Franklin**, 'Glass, china and reputations are easily cracked and never well mended'.

5.2 Threats and safeguards

As well as identifying fundamental principles, CIMA's ethical guidelines identify **five types of threat** to those principles. These threats are self-interest threats, self-review threats, advocacy threats, familiarity threats and intimidation threats.

Type of threat	Description of threat
Self-interest	The risk that a financial or other interest may influence the accountant's judgment or behaviour. Also known as 'conflict of interest' threats.
Self-review	The risk that an accountant may not appropriately re-evaluate their (or a colleague's) previous work (including judgments made or services performed) when relying on the work when performing a current service.
Advocacy	The risk that an accountant promotes a client's or employer's position to the point that their objectivity is compromised.
Familiarity	The risk that due to a long or close relationship with a client or employer, an accountant will be too sympathetic to their interests or too ready to accept their work.
Intimidation	The risk that an accountant will be deterred from acting objectively because of actual or perceived pressures, including attempts to exercise undue influence over them.

CIMA's ethical guidelines take a **'threats and safeguards'** approach to dealing with ethical issues. They state that where a threat is identified, the member should assess whether or not they are significant and then take action to remove or mitigate it. Further advice for dealing with ethical issues will be covered later on in your studies.

5.3 Rules

As a **CIMA member** you are expected to go beyond following the rules and to achieve this it is important for you to understand some theory.

(a) **Rules are a cut-off point**

Either an individual is inside a rule (ie complying) or is not (disobeying). This creates a strong divide between acceptable and unacceptable behaviour.

(b) **Rules have a meaning**

To maintain the boundary between acceptable and unacceptable behaviour it is important to agree on the exact meaning of a rule. However there is nearly always argument as naturally one person (who may have broken a rule) is interested in their self-preservation while another is seeking to find them guilty.

(c) **Rules need enforcement**

To administer rules, an objective third party must be available to interpret the rule and (where it deems a rule has been broken) ensure the guilty party finds their actions are met with appropriate consequences.

Consider each of the fundamental principles. Try to think of one example of a situation where someone would be acting unethically.

Answer

There is a huge range of possible answers. Here are some examples, you probably thought of others.

- Integrity – handing over work to a colleague that you know contains errors
- Objectivity – allowing personal feelings about something to cloud your judgement
- Professional competence and due care – taking on work you are not qualified to do
- Confidentiality – leaving sensitive or confidential information where anyone can look at it
- Professional behaviour – cheating in professional exams

Assessment focus point | These fundamental principles will be tested at length in the assessment. Learning definitions is not enough, you must be able to spot situations which breach the fundamental principles.

6 Qualities of an accountant

In meeting the **fundamental principles**, certain qualities are expected of accountants, these can be classed as:

- Personal qualities
- Professional qualities

6.1 Personal qualities expected of an accountant

FAST FORWARD

The **personal qualities** that an accountant should demonstrate are:

- Reliability
- Responsibility
- Timeliness
- Courtesy
- Respect

6.1.1 Reliability

An accountant's clients and colleagues **trust** them to be dependable. When taking on work, they must ensure it is consistently **delivered on time** and is what was **asked for**.

6.1.2 Responsibility

Accountants should take **'ownership'** of their work and be **accountable** for their actions and decisions. They should not expect others to do their work for them and must be willing to personally respond to queries regarding their decisions.

6.1.3 Timeliness

Clients and work colleagues rely on accountants to produce work within a **specified time frame** and therefore prioritisation and work management skills are important. They also rely on work **meeting their expectations**. Accountants should **be on time** for work and appointments - **failure** to do so wastes both their time and that of others.

6.1.4 Courtesy

Accountants should conduct themselves with **courtesy**, **consideration** and **general good manners** towards their clients, colleagues, and others that they come into contact with during the performance of their work. Poor behaviour reflects on both the **accountant** and the **accountancy profession**, so it is important to leave acquaintances with a good impression.

6.1.5 Respect

Accountants should respect others by developing **constructive relationships** and recognising their **values** and **rights**. This involves **listening** and understanding their **point of view**. It is perfectly reasonable to disagree with them, but the disagreement should not become personal. Virtues such as regard, admiration, esteem and deference should be developed.

6.2 Professional qualities expected of an accountant

FAST FORWARD

The **professional qualities** an accountant should demonstrate are:

- Independence
- Scepticism
- Accountability
- Social responsibility

6.2.1 Independence

The principle of objectivity requires an **'independent mind'**. This means putting all considerations not relevant to the task in hand to one side - enabling the completion of work free from bias or prejudice. It allows the professional to act with **integrity**, **objectivity** and **professional scepticism**.

Accountants must also be seen to be independent. This is known as **'independence in appearance'**, and means they should demonstrate their independence by avoiding situations that could cause a reasonable observer to question their integrity, objectivity or professional scepticism.

Examples of **situations** which may **reduce an accountant's independence** include:

- Accepting a valuable gift from an audit client that is about to be reported on
- Auditing a client which they were recently employed by
- Having a large amount of fee income reliant on one client
- Knowing an audit client for a long period of time socially
- Having a domineering manager who is a friend of an audit client

Assessment focus point

You may be required to identify qualities of an accountant from a description provided to you.

6.2.2 Professional Scepticism

The principle of integrity means that accountants should develop a healthy sense of scepticism. Therefore, **accountants should question information given to them**. They should ask questions such as, does the information make sense, is there other evidence that supports it, where did it come from, and why was it given to me?

By questioning, accountants form their own opinion about its quality and reliability, reducing the risk of misinformation.

6.2.3 Accountability

Accountants should recognise that they are **accountable** for their own **judgements** and **decisions**. Where these are called into question they should not pass undue responsibility onto others. Accountability is monitored in the UK by the FRC, POB and APB that we studied earlier. In most cases, accountability is exercised through the **disciplinary procedures** put in place by employers and the professional bodies.

6.2.4 Social responsibility

We saw earlier that corporate responsibility is an outward manifestation of an ethical policy. Accountants have a public (social) duty as well as a duty to their employer or clients. This public duty can also be referred to as social responsibility – the provision of specific benefits to society as a whole. **CIMA's ethical code** requires members to follow the **socially responsible principles** of integrity, respect, courtesy and due care.

Accountants should be aware that **their work may affect** their **company's stakeholders** or **the public** in some way. Examples include:

(a) **Audit work**. This may affect an entity's financial result which members of the public use when making investment decisions. The public rely on audits to ensure the accounts are correct and free from error.

(b) **Accountancy work**. For example the preparation of sole trader or limited company accounts will affect their profit and therefore the amount of tax collected.

(c) **Investment decisions**. Accountants may be asked to work on a major investment decision that their company will be making. The wrong decision could cost the company significant sums of money, and shareholders their dividends.

Remember – although the effect one accountant has on society may be small, collectively, accountants have a significant influence.

Question

Professional qualities

Which of the professional qualities has the accountant in the scenario below failed to display?

An accountant found substantial financial misstatements during the audit of a major client who provides their practice with 55% of its total audit fee income. The relationship between the practice and the client has been strained recently and because of this the accountant ignored the misstatements and ensured the client stayed with the firm.

Answer

Independence. The accountant is not independent due to the reliance on the client for a large amount of its income. This has caused them to ignore irregularities when they should have reported them.

7 Personal development and lifelong learning

FAST FORWARD

Personal development is the development of personal qualities such as communication skills, assertiveness, time management and relationship building. They are skills that have to be developed by an individual and must come from deep within them.

Lifelong learning is the concept that an individual never stops learning and should be open to new ideas, decisions, skills or behaviours.

7.1 Why is professional development necessary?

The fundamental ethical principles of **professional competence and due care** require accountants to develop and maintain their knowledge and technical skills.

This requirement is driven by **public expectations**. After all, medical professionals are expected to keep up to date with new diseases and treatments, so why should accountants not have a similar duty with accountancy rules and techniques?

7.2 CIMA's professional development cycle

One approach to personal development and lifelong learning is **CIMA's professional development cycle** that it introduced from January 2006.

Stages in **CIMA's professional development** cycle:

- **Define**, members should define their current and desired roles
- **Assess**, a member's current capabilities and competences should be assessed and any knowledge gaps should be identified. These will form the learning objectives the member needs to achieve
- **Design**, members should construct an activity programme that meets the learning objectives
- **Act**, members should undertake the learning activities.
- **Reflect**, members should reflect on the activities, consider what was learnt, how it should be applied and if further training is needed
- **Evaluate**, members should assess the actual development against the learning objectives. If any additional training is required, it should be carried over to the next cycle

7.2.1 What counts as development?

The cycle recognises that development is a **continuous process** and gives members a framework to follow. It also recognises that professional development comes from a wide range of sources.

The following activities count as **CPD** under the scheme:

- Reading professional publications and study for professional or academic qualifications
- Computer based training and training colleagues and students
- Research and project work
- Attending CIMA events

7.3 Other approaches to professional development

Other accountancy bodies such as the **ICAEW** and **ACCA** have their own development requirements. Rather than following a cycle, they require members to complete a certain number of hours of CPD each year that should be **relevant to their role**.

CPD is classified as **verified** or **unverified**. Verified CPD covers development that can be supported by evidence such as course notes or work produced. Unverified CPD covers development such as reading journals that cannot be supported with evidence.

Question

Professional development

Accountants should stay technically up-to-date because the public expects them to.

True or false?

Answer

True. Public expectation has driven the need for continuing professional development.

Chapter Roundup

- Humans have developed a **framework of rules** to regulate behaviour.

- **Ethics** are a set of **moral principles** that **guide behaviour**.

- Individuals have **ethical values** and beliefs about what constitutes **'right'** and **'wrong'** behaviour. These values often reflect those of the individual's **family**, **culture** and **educational environment** they are brought up in.

- Ethics are not the same thing as **law** or the rules of **religion**.

- As an accountant, your values and attitudes **flow through** everything you do professionally. They contribute to the **trust** the wider community puts in the profession and the **perception** it has of it.

- **Professional institutions** (such as CIMA) have an overriding duty to **protect the public interest**. To ensure members act in a manner which achieves this, most have developed codes of conduct to guide their behaviour.

- The **International Federation of Accountants** (IFAC) is an international body representing all the major accountancy bodies across the world. Its mission is to develop the **high standards** of professional accountants and enhance the quality of services they provide.

- CIMA's ethical guidelines give the **fundamental principles** that members should follow in their professional lives.

- The **personal qualities** that an accountant should demonstrate are:

  - Reliability
  - Responsibility
  - Timeliness
  - Courtesy
  - Respect

- The **professional qualities** an accountant should demonstrate are:

  - Independence
  - Scepticism
  - Accountability
  - Social responsibility

- **Personal development** is the development of personal qualities such as communication skills, assertiveness, time management and relationship building. They are skills that have to be developed by an individual and must come from deep within them.

- **Lifelong learning** is the concept that an individual never stops learning and should be open to new ideas, decisions, skills or behaviours.

1   Ethics are a set of ……… …………… that ……….. ………..

2   The table below indicates some of the characteristics of compliance and integrity-based approaches to business ethics. Complete the table using the phrases below.

Characteristic	Compliance	Ethics
Enforceability		
Choices		
Standards		
Motivation		
Approach		
Objective		
Measure		

Obedience / disobedience	Rules	Principles based	Mandatory
Implicit	Values driven	Explicit	Law based
Fear driven	Discretionary	Detection	
Prevention	Judgement	Principles (values)	

3   Which two of the following are methods that businesses may use to demonstrate to their stakeholders that they have an ethical strategy?

(i)   Corporate Responsibility Policy
(ii)   Corporate Responsibility Plan
(iii)   Corporate Responsibility Report
(iv)   Corporate Responsibility Recommendation

A   (i) and (iii)
B   (i) and (iv)
C   (ii) and (iii)
D   (ii) and (iv)

4   Which of the following are fundamental principles in CIMA's ethical guidelines?

(i)   Confidentiality
(ii)   Scepticism
(iii)   Integrity
(iv)   Independence

A   (i) and (ii) only
B   (i), (ii) and (iii) only
C   (i) and (iii) only
D   All of the above

5   List five personal qualities expected of an accountant.
(i)   R……….
(ii)   R……….
(iii)   T………..
(iv)   C………..
(v)   R………..

6   Behaving ethically is the minimum level of behaviour expected of an individual by society.

    True   ☐

    False ☐

7   Which part of IFAC's code of ethics is particularly relevant to professional accountants in business?

    A   Part A
    B   Part B
    C   Part C
    D   Part D

8   Which stage follows Design in CIMA's professional development cycle?

    A   Define
    B   Act
    C   Reflect
    D   Evaluate

9   Which of the following are both sub-bodies of the Financial Reporting Council (FRC)?

    A   POB and APB
    B   POB and IFAC
    C   APB and IFAC
    D   CIMA and POB

10   If an organisation's code of conduct is in conflict with the law, the legal position will prevail.

    True   ☐

    False ☐

1   Moral principles, guide behaviour

2

Characteristic	Compliance-based	Ethics-based
Enforceability	Mandatory	Discretionary
Choices	Obedience/disobedience	Judgement
Standards	Explicit	Implicit
Motivation	Fear-driven	Values-driven
Approach	Law-based	Principles-based
Objective	Detection	Prevention
Measure	Rules	Principles (values)

3   A. Corporate Responsibility Policies and Reports are the correct names for the two methods.

4   C. Scepticism and independence are professional qualities expected of an accountant not fundamental principles

5   (i)   Reliability
(ii)   Responsibility
(iii)   Timeliness
(iv)   Courtesy
(v)   Respect

6   False. The law is the minimum level of behaviour expected by society.

7   C   Part C is particularly relevant to professional accountants in business. There is no part D.

8   B   Act follows Design in CIMA's professional development cycle.

9   A   The Professional Oversight Board (POB) and Auditing Practices Board (APB) are sub-bodies of the FRC.

10   True. The law always takes priority over other rules.

Now try the questions below from the Question Bank

Number
Q81
Q82
Q83
Q84
Q85

18

Ethical conflict

Introduction

We begin this chapter by discussing what the consequences of behaving unethically are, not just to you, but also to the accountancy profession and society as a whole.

The chapter moves on to identify practical situations that can result in ethical dilemmas. It is vital that you are able to spot potential problems so you can avoid them.

Finally, we present you with a framework to help you resolve ethical issues.

Topic list	Learning outcomes
1 Consequences of unethical behaviour	A1(a), B1(b)
2 Ethical conflicts	A1(a), B2(a)
3 Resolution of ethical conflicts	A1(a), B2(b)

1 Consequences of unethical behaviour

FAST FORWARD

Unethical behaviour will have consequences for

- You as an accountant
- The accountancy profession
- Society as a whole

1.1 You as an accountant

Any unethical behaviour risks being discovered at some stage. If it is discovered, then you risk:

- Being subject to a professional disciplinary hearing
- Being fined or being struck off as an accountant
- Losing your job, either through an employer disciplinary hearing or being unable to practice
- Your actions becoming public knowledge and your personal reputation damaged
- Prosecution if the behaviour is criminal
- Being sued for damages by an affected party

Even if your behaviour is not discovered, you will have to live with your actions for the rest of your life, and the threat that one day they will be discovered.

1.2 The accountancy profession

Accountants have a high degree of trust placed in them by society. Therefore any breaches will have severe consequences on the profession. These may include:

- Loss of reputation, and therefore
- Reduced employability of accountants
- Pressure by outside bodies to tighten up regulations and penalties
- Government intervention if it is thought the profession is incapable of self-regulation
- Accountancy bodies losing their 'Chartered' status

1.3 Society as a whole

We discussed earlier how an accountant's work has consequences for the public. There are many wider implications of a profession of unethical accountants.

- The work of all accountants would be called into question

- Unethical companies would eventually fail as they will lose public confidence

- The financial markets would be affected if investors could not rely on audit reports and financial statements

- The tax authorities may question tax computations, affecting the amount of tax collected

- Criminals may gravitate towards the profession to make money from fraud or other financial crime

- Commercial organisations would not function if they are unable rely on their accountants' work

In short, society could not function as we know it without ethical accountants!

State three consequences to the accountancy profession of allowing unethical behaviour by accountants.

Answer

Any three of:

- Loss of the profession's reputation
- Reduced employability of accountants
- Pressure by outside bodies to tighten up regulations and penalties
- Increased regulation by the government
- Accountancy bodies losing their 'chartered' status

2 Ethical conflicts

 FAST FORWARD

Ethical conflicts are situations where two ethical values or requirements seem to be incompatible. They can also arise where two conflicting demands or obligations are placed on an individual.

A **conflict of interest** arises where an individual has a duty to two or more parties. Whilst working, information or other matters may arise that mean they cannot continue work for one party without harming another.

We have discussed the **need** for accountants to be ethical, and the **consequences** of being unethical. It is therefore important that they can spot an **ethical problem** and be able to deal with it effectively and appropriately. Many dilemmas challenge both **personal integrity** and **business skills** and therefore a strong ethical understanding is important. We now consider potential situations where accountants have to make ethical decisions, and how they should resolve them.

2.1 Ethical conflicts and conflicts of interest

Ethical conflicts are situations where two ethical values or requirements seem to be incompatible. They can also arise where two conflicting demands or obligations are placed on an individual.

A **conflict of interest** arises where an individual has a duty to two or more parties. Whilst working, information or other matters may arise that mean they cannot continue work for one party without harming another. Conflicts of interest are not wrong in themselves but they will become a problem if a professional continues with a course of action whilst being aware of, and not declaring them.

2.2 Situations where ethical conflicts and conflicts of interest occur

Ethical conflicts occur as a result of **tensions** between four sets of values.

- **Societal values** – the law.
- **Personal values** – values and principles held by the individual.
- **Corporate values** – the values and principles of the organisation where the individual works, often laid down in ethical codes.
- **Professional values** – the values and principles of the professional body that the individual is a member of, often laid down in ethical codes.

Where society believes that businesses are not conducting themselves correctly, **laws may be introduced** to ensure a **minimum level** of **behaviour** is followed. Examples of this include laws created to deal with environmental issues, cartels, unfair competition as well as fraud, insider dealing, bribery and corruption.

Ethical conflicts involve **unclear choices** of what is right and wrong. In fact the choice could be what is the **least wrong** course of action to take. In such circumstances there is little an individual can do but to **seek advice** and trust their own **instincts** to make the correct choice.

Remember that **laws** do not necessarily help an individual to resolve an ethical issue – indeed many members of society feel torn when their **personal ethics** lead them to feel following a particular **law** is **immoral**. This said, where a professional duty conflicts with statute, CIMA's advice is clear – the **law overrides** it every time.

2.2.1 Ethics and contractual obligations

Contractual obligations differ from statute in the sense that an individual enters into a contract **voluntarily**, there is no voluntary element to statutory obligations.

This means an individual may break contractual obligations without breaking the law. For this reason, professional **ethics should be followed even if this is at the expense of a contractual obligation**. Logically this means that given the choice of breaking professional ethics or a term in your contract of employment you must give the profession priority. The law and employment tribunals will support an employee whose employer required them to break their professional ethics – the problem is that many employees would not want to go to court over such matters.

2.2.2 Examples of ethical tensions

The following are examples of how tensions between sets of values can be created.

(a) **Societal values and corporate values**

An individual may be asked by their employer to act in an illegal way, for example to discriminate against a disabled or ethnic employee.

(b) **Personal values and corporate values**

An individual may not agree with certain activities of their organisation, such as the use of child labour in foreign factories. Whilst not necessarily illegal it goes against their own moral beliefs.

(c) **Professional values and corporate values**

An individual is put into a position by their employer where they are required to amend a set of accounts to improve the profit figure. Such amendments go against the code of conduct of their accountancy body.

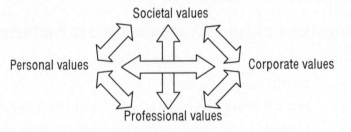

BPP
LEARNING MEDIA

2.3 Spotting an ethical dilemma

Accountants will encounter situations throughout their professional life that presents them with an **ethical dilemma** or **conflict of interest**. The following questions will help develop your ability to identify problems in the future. Use the information given to identify the ethical principles at stake.

Assessment focus point

The key to answering exam questions in this area is to apply CIMA's fundamental principles. Also, you will probably get a feeling of whether a situation is unethical or not. Use the principles and your instinct to come to your own conclusion.

Question
Time pressure

You are under time pressure to complete this month's management accounts. Important sales information is provided by the sales department, usually in good time for you to incorporate it into the final figures. The sales report is delayed this month due to staff sickness and you will not receive the information until a few hours before the accounts are due for presentation to the finance director.

Answer

There is an **integrity** issue here. Whilst you may have time to include the information in the management accounts, it is unlikely that you will be able to check its accuracy as well. Therefore you risk misinforming the finance director of the month's sales.

Question
Tax advice

During your lunch break, your company's human resources manager has asked you for some help. She has recently inherited a considerable sum of money and would like you to calculate her inheritance tax and capital gains tax liabilities. She has also asked you for advice on how she should invest the money.

Answer

The issues here are **professional competence and due care**. Unless you are a tax expert, it is unlikely that you would have sufficient competence to calculate the tax liabilities. Giving financial advice can be a minefield, and you may need to be qualified under the financial services regulations before you could do so.

Even if you did have the required competence, it is probable that you could not offer due care as any advice you give would be on-the-spot, and you would not have been able to look into the matter in enough detail.

Question
Holiday cover

You have been asked to cover the duties of one of your colleagues while he is on holiday. One of his duties is to distribute the management accounts to the department managers a few days before they hold the monthly accounts meeting. Before he left, your colleague told you, 'Just print off the accounts and put them on each manager's desk'.

Answer

Confidentiality is the issue here. Management accounts are usually only for the eyes of top management, so you should reduce the risk of them getting into the hands of anyone else. Leaving unprotected copies on a desk makes them vulnerable. Ideally they should be handed directly to the manager concerned, or sealed in a confidential envelope if they must be left on their desk.

Question

Cunning plan

Your finance director has asked you to join a team planning a takeover of one of your company's suppliers. An old school friend works as an accountant for the company concerned, the finance director knows this, and has asked you to try and find out 'anything that might help the takeover succeed, but it must remain secret'.

Answer

There are three issues here. Firstly you have a **conflict of interest** as the finance director wants you to keep the takeover a secret, but you probably feel that you should tell your friend what is happening as it may affect their job.

Second, the finance director is asking you to deceive your friend. Deception is unprofessional behaviour and will break your ethical guidelines. Therefore the situation is presenting you with **two conflicting demands**. It is worth remembering that no employer can ask you to break your ethical rules.

Finally, the request to break your own ethical guidelines constitutes **unprofessional behaviour** by the finance director. You should consider reporting him to their relevant body.

Question

Bonus time

Your company runs a cost-saving initiative whereby the department head that saves the most cost in the year receives a bonus. Your role is to collect the cost-saving data from each department and to present the results to the finance director.

After the initiative is over, the successful department head presents you with tickets to see your favourite music group in a sold-out concert.

Answer

The issue here is **objectivity**. The other department heads could see the gift as a reward for 'fixing' the result, or for 'special favours'. It may also bias your future work and therefore should be refused.

Assessment focus point

> Assessment questions in this area are likely to require you to fill in missing words of sentences which describe each principle, or to identify a principle from a scenario.

3 Resolution of ethical conflicts

Ethical conflicts may arise from:

- Pressure from an overbearing colleague or from family or friends
- Members asked to act contrary to technical and/or professional standards
- Divided loyalties between colleagues and professional standards
- Publication of misleading information
- Members having to do work beyond their degree of expertise or experience they possess
- Personal relationships with other employees or clients
- Gifts and hospitality being offered

We have seen there are many situations that could cause ethical conflicts, ranging from the trivial to the very serious (such as fraud or illegal acts). The method of resolving them that CIMA sets out for its members and students is laid down in its **ethical code**, however many organisations propose an alternative process to evaluate a decision.

Individuals should ask themselves:

(a) **Transparency**

Do I feel comfortable with others knowing about my decision, is my decision defensible?

(b) **Effect**

Have I considered all parties who may be affected by the decision and have all factors been taken into account such as mitigating circumstances?

(c) **Fairness**

Would a reasonable third party view the decision as fair?

Question

Dealing with ethical dilemmas

Which of the following would NOT be a suitable question to ask yourself when resolving an ethical dilemma?

A   Would my colleagues think my solution is reasonable?
B   Have I thought about all the possible consequences of my solution?
C   Could I defend my solution under public scrutiny?
D   Does my solution benefit my career?

Answer

D   The best solution to an ethical dilemma should be taken whether or not it improves your career.

3.1 Raising and dealing with ethical dilemmas

A number of options are available for accountants wishing to raise ethical issues, for example:

- **Direct** with their accountancy body
- Within their organisation via a **help or whistleblower line**
- To **external organisations** such as customers, suppliers or agents
- **Anonymously**

However they choose to proceed, CIMA members and students should ensure it is **consistent** with CIMA's Ethical Code.

The following steps suggests an approach for **conflict resolution** based in the **CIMA's Ethical Checklist**.

Step 1 Gather and record facts
- Identify all relevant facts
- Do not rely on assumptions, word of mouth or gossip

Step 2 Decide if the issue is ethical
- How does it feel?
- What would you think if it was reported in the media or those close to you find out about it?
- Refer to CIMA's Ethical Code
- Consult your organisation's rules and policies on the matter

Step 3 Decide if the issue is legal in nature
- Find out if the issue is covered by any laws
- Check to see if it is covered by government or professional regulations

Step 4 Identify any of CIMA's Fundamental Principles that may be affected
- Integrity, objectivity, professional behaviour, professional competence and due care, confidentiality

Step 5 Identify any affected parties
- Those affected may be individuals, organisations or other stakeholders
- How are they affected (and is their any conflict between them)
- What happens if you don't take any action?

Step 6 Consider possible courses of action
- Consider internal grievance procedures
- Potential escalation to legal or professional advisers, or company auditor
- Ensure all actions to resolve the issue are documented

Step 7 If necessary seek professional or legal advice
- CIMA's ethics helpline
- Personal legal advice
- Whistleblower hotlines

Step 8 Refuse to be associated with the conflict
- Move departments
- Set out in writing that you do not wish to be associated with the issue
- May affect your employment status
- Take advice if you are in any way implicated in the matter

If ultimately the CIMA member is **unable to resolve** the ethical conflict, or disassociate themselves from the issue by moving departments, then they may, as a last resort, have to consider **resigning** from their position.

Where a **resolution** to an ethical problem **breaches**, or risks breaching, the **principle of confidentiality**, the member should **seek legal advice** or consult **CIMA**.

Members should **document** all **meetings**, **conversations** and **actions** they have in relation to their ethical problem as they may be required at a later date to show how they dealt with the matter.

Chapter Roundup

- **Unethical behaviour** will have consequences for:

    - You as an accountant
    - The accountancy profession
    - Society as a whole

- **Ethical conflicts** are situations where two ethical values or requirements seem to be incompatible. They can also arise where two conflicting demands or obligations are placed on you.

- A **conflict of interest** arises where you have a duty to two or more parties. Whilst working, information or other matters may arise that mean you cannot continue work for one party without harming another.

- **Ethical conflicts** may rise from:

    - Pressure from an overbearing colleague or from family or friends
    - Members asked to act contrary to technical and/or professional standards
    - Divided loyalties between colleagues and professional standards
    - Publication of misleading information
    - Members having to do work beyond their degree of expertise or experience they possess
    - Personal relationships with other employees or clients
    - Gifts and hospitality being offered

BPP
LEARNING MEDIA

1   State four consequences for an accountant of behaving unethically

2   Ethical conflicts are situations where .... or requirements seem to be ....

3   A conflict of interest arises where you have a duty to .... or more parties. Matters arise which mean you cannot continue to work for one party without .... the other.

Using CIMA's ethical guidelines, identify the fundamental principles at stake in the following two situations.

4   You work for a manufacturing company producing various electronic components. Your role within the management accounts department is to produce various reports on costings and variances for the directors.

    Five management accountants submit their variance analysis to you so you can compile them into a larger report. You are the most senior, four others have yet to take any of their CIMA exams and have been with the company for about six months. Your other colleague has been with the company about the same time as you, and has recently passed their management accounts exam, scoring 85%.

    The deadline for your latest report has been brought forward, and you do not have time to check all five reports without having to work late.

5   You work for a large public company listed on the London Stock Exchange. While working on the management accounts, it is becoming clear that the company is making significant losses in the last quarter before the year-end.

    Your father owns shares in your company and you think it is only fair to warn him.

6   Corporate values are the values and principles of the organisation where an individual works. They may be set out in ethical codes.

    True ☐

    False ☐

7   Jack works for a large organisation as head of the accounts department. The company has recently introduced a policy which discriminates against disabled people during the recruitment process. Jack has no moral objections to the policy and applied it when he recently filled a vacancy in his department.

    This is an example of ethical tensions between which sets of values?

    A   Professional and corporate
    B   Personal and corporate
    C   Societal and corporate
    D   None – there are no ethical tensions in the scenario

8   Statutory obligations differ from contractual obligations as fulfilling them is voluntary.

    True ☐

    False ☐

9   Being objective as an accountant is an example of a:

    A   Societal value
    B   Professional value
    C   Corporate value
    D   Contractual obligation

10   CIMA has an ethical hotline which students and members can use to access help with any ethical issues they may face.

True ☐

False ☐

Answers to Quick Quiz

1   Any four from the following

- Professional disciplinary hearing
- Being fined or struck off
- Losing job
- Damage to personal reputation
- Prosecution
- Liable for damages
- Having to live with themselves afterwards

2   Two ethical values, incompatible

3   Two, harming

4   The issue is **integrity**. To avoid working late there is a temptation to rely on the work of the colleague who has passed their exam, and not check it. However, individuals can make mistakes and there is a risk of passing on misinformation to the directors. If you cannot work late then you should arrange for an extension to the deadline to ensure your work is accurate.

5   The issue is **confidentiality**. You have a duty to your employer not to disclose sensitive information to anyone, even your family. Passing on market-sensitive information regarding a public company is also known as **insider-dealing**, a criminal offence for which you could be prosecuted.

6   True. This is a description of corporate values.

7   C. Whilst Jack has no moral objections to the policy, he has been required to act in an illegal way by his employer. There is therefore tension between societal values (the law) and corporate values (the employment policy).

8   False. It is contractual obligations which are voluntary to fulfil.

9   B. Objectivity is a professional value.

10   True. CIMA has such an ethical helpline.

Now try the questions below from the Question Bank

Number
Q86
Q87
Q88
Q89
Q90

BPP
LEARNING MEDIA

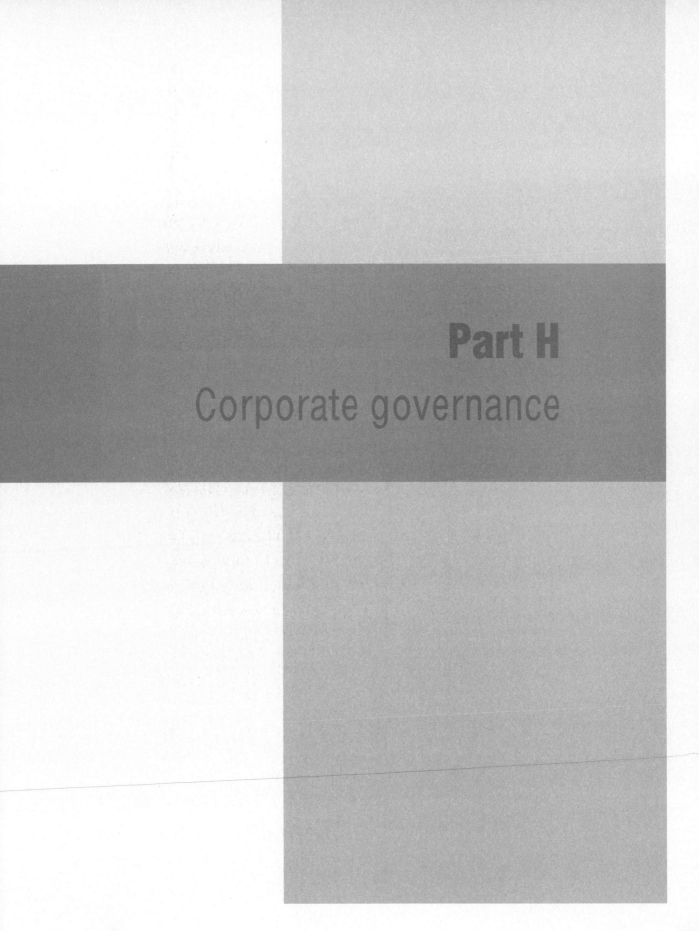

Part H

Corporate governance

BPP
LEARNING MEDIA

BPP
LEARNING MEDIA

19

Corporate governance

Introduction

This chapter introduces you to the concept of **corporate governance**, a major issue facing companies today.

Corporate governance is concerned with how **companies** are **directed** and **controlled**. We consider how the concept relates to ethics and company law, why in recent years there has been a need for corporate governance rules to develop, and what the current regulatory framework contains.

Remember, the **main issues** and **principles** are **most important**, so you need to make sure you understand them thoroughly.

Topic list	Learning outcomes
1 What is corporate governance?	C1(a)
2 Causes of poor corporate governance	C1(c)
3 The need for greater corporate governance	C1(c)
4 Corporate governance development in the USA, South Africa, UK and Europe	C1(c)
5 Symptoms of poor corporate governance	C2(c)
6 The UK regulatory framework	C2(c), C2(d)
7 Principles vs rules	C1(d)
8 Role of the board	C2(a), C2(b), G2(h)
9 Ethics, law and governance	B1(a), C1(b)

1 What is corporate governance?

FAST FORWARD **Corporate governance** is the system by which organisations are directed and controlled. *The Cadbury Committee.*

Corporate governance was defined by the UK **Cadbury Committee** as *'the system by which organisations are directed and controlled'*. In other words, how companies are run. Companies with good governance have **effective controls** over their **operations** and **business efficacy**, and **management** are **held accountable** to stakeholders.

Despite the strict controls over companies that you have already studied, a number of **high-profile corporate failures** have occurred in recent years and these have **damaged the confidence** that the public has in listed companies. As these companies are often financed by **pension funds** and other individual or corporate **investments** and because they **employ** thousands of people, it is important that these companies do not go out of business.

Causes of **corporate failure** are numerous, but are quite often due to **ineffective control** over **directors**, resulting in **mismanagement**, **fraudulent behaviour** and **excessive remuneration packages**. Many countries are now establishing legal and non-legal controls over directors and the way companies are run in an attempt to prevent future disasters.

Although mostly discussed in relation to large quoted companies, **governance** is an **issue for all corporate bodies** - private and public, commercial and not for profit.

2 Causes of poor corporate governance

FAST FORWARD Corporate governance problems can result from the **agency problem** and **lack of shareholder activism**.

Governance problems are often caused by **lack of control** over the **directors** and **senior management**. This lack of control may mean that negligent mismanagement of the company's affairs is not discovered and/or that the directors are able to get away with fraud.

The **agency problem** and **lack of shareholder activism** can lead to poor control of directors.

2.1 The agency problem

Governance problems are often considered to be caused by the **separation of power** between the **owners** of the company (the shareholders) and the **management** of the company (the board of directors). You should note that in most private companies the directors are also the shareholders so the agency problem is less prevalent.

Due to their **size** and the **expertise** required to run them, most public companies employ directors to run the company on the shareholders' behalf. Therefore **directors** become **agents** of the shareholders and they are entrusted to form contractual agreements with third parties. This allows the shareholders to step away from the management of the company and focus on their main interests - capital growth of their shares and dividend income from them.

BPP
LEARNING MEDIA

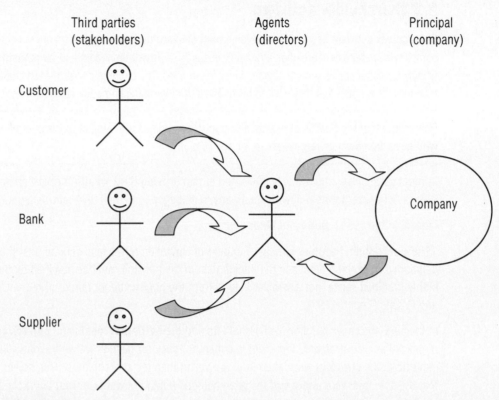

Third parties
(stakeholders)

Agents
(directors)

Principal
(company)

Customer

Bank

Supplier

Company

2.1.1 Stakeholders

The term stakeholder is used to describe any **person** or **organisation** with an **interest** in the company. There are two types of stakeholder which can be identified.

(a) **Financial stakeholders** are those with a **financial relationship** with the organisation, in other words, should financial problems occur to the organisation then these stakeholders will **suffer**.

(b) **Interest stakeholders** are **interested in how the organisation behaves** and are very often more powerful than the financial stakeholders due to the influence they have over it.

The following table lists the various types of financial and interest stakeholder.

Financial stakeholders	Interest stakeholders
Shareholders and other investors – investment	Media – publicity and reporting events
Employees – job and wages	Non-government organisations – impact on their activities
Customers – own or have ordered goods and services	Activist groups – environmental impact
Suppliers – owed money for goods and services supplied	Competitors – strategy and development
Government/community – taxation	Regulators – fair trading, stock exchange

Assessment focus point

The assessment could easily test your understanding of stakeholders by requiring you to identify which are financial and which are interest. Ensure you learn them.

2.2 Shareholder activism

Shareholder activism describes the **involvement of shareholders** in the affairs of the company and its management. A company's shareholders are often a mix of thousands of **private investors** and **large institutions**. They own shares, usually for either capital growth, dividend income or both. The circumstances of each shareholder will be different and therefore the amount that they wish to be involved in running the company will be different too.

Assessment focus point

Remember that the boards of private and public companies are subject to the overall control of the shareholders who have the power to remove them for any reason.

In most cases, investors are only interested in **maximising their wealth** through share price growth and dividends. It does not matter to them how the company is managed, only that they receive a good return on their investment.

Indeed, in the 1930s, **Berle** and **Means** wrote:

'(The stockholder) becomes simply a supplier of capital on terms less definite than those customarily given or demanded by bondholders; and the thinking about his position must be qualified by the realization that he is, in a highly modified sense, not dissimilar in kind from the bondholder or lender of money.' *The Modern Corporation and Private Property 1932*.

In the past, the sheer **number** of shareholders and their **different ideals** and **objectives** prevented them from being mobilised as a co-ordinated force with a coherent policy for taking on the directors. Therefore, even though small in number, the **directors** were often more **powerful** than the shareholders. This power was reinforced by the fact that the directors were aware that the shareholders would not want **internal conflicts** and the subsequent publication of information which would be detrimental to the share price. To this extent, directors have had (and possibly still do) an opportunity to get away with mismanaging the company or indeed, fraud.

In very recent years, the typical **shareholder has changed** from **individuals**, to **institutions** such as pension funds or insurance companies and now around 60% of shares in the UK and USA are held by such organisations. This has caused a change in the **balance of power** between shareholders and directors as fund managers are legally obliged to actively manage investments on their clients' behalf and this has helped swing the balance in favour of increased shareholder activism. However the **company law review** and the **2001 Myners report** in the UK still concluded that institutional investors are less involved in terms of taking actions in their clients' interests as they should be.

Question

Stakeholders

Which of the following is not a financial stakeholder?

A Competitor
B Supplier
C Customer
D The government

Answer

A Financial stakeholders are those who will suffer harm if the company experiences financial difficulties. If such difficulties occur, suppliers may not get paid, customers may not receive goods or services they paid for and the government may not receive taxation due to it. Competitors would benefit from the situation.

3 The need for greater corporate governance

Key drivers for the development of corporate governance.

- Increasing internationalisation and globalisation
- Issues concerning financial reporting
- An increasing number of high profile corporate scandals and collapses

Corporate governance issues came to prominence in the USA, UK and Europe from the late 1980s. In general the main, but not the only, drivers associated with the increasing demand for the development of governance were:

(a) **Increasing internationalisation and globalisation** which meant that investors, and institutional investors in particular, began to invest outside their home countries. For international share trading to be successful, investors needed to have confidence of management and reporting standards in all countries.

(b) Issues concerning **financial reporting** were raised by many investors and were the focus of much debate and legal action. In many cases, confidence in the management and reporting of companies was eroded. The introduction of codes of conduct was seen as necessary to rebuild it.

(c) An increasing number of **high profile corporate scandals** and collapses prompted the development of governance codes in the early 1990s.

It is important to realise that **corporate governance is dynamic** and will continue to develop over time to meet society's needs and to tackle new issues as they arise.

4 Corporate governance development in the USA, South Africa, UK and Europe

FAST FORWARD

The **USA, UK** and **Europe** have taken **different approaches** to corporate governance.

We shall now consider the **development of corporate governance rules** in the USA, South Africa, UK and Europe.

4.1 USA

Corporate governance rules in the USA have developed from relatively little to the complex **Sarbanes-Oxley Act** of 2002. Three main drivers for this were:

(a) **Active management**

Increasing shareholder activism from institutional investors and in particular fund managers brought the actions and behaviour of senior corporate managers to the public's attention. This was driven in part by the increasingly protective practices of directors in preventing takeovers which some investors thought went against their best interests.

(b) **Enron, Arthur Andersen and Worldcom**

The collapses of Enron (see case study below) and Worldcom encouraged the US government to take action to restore public confidence and trust in large corporations. The Sarbanes-Oxley Act of 2002 introduced measures to protect investors from further corporate disasters by implementing reporting procedures aimed at increasing the accuracy of disclosures and the openness of corporations.

While Enron no longer exists, Worldcom did survive and merged with MCI International following successfully emerging from bankruptcy.

(c)   **Close relationships between auditors and clients**

Enron also revealed that far from being independent, auditors often enjoyed very close relationships with their clients, In Enron's case, its auditor (Arthur Andersen) undertook lucrative consultancy work. The threat of losing this valuable income compromised the auditor's ability to give a truly independent report.

Andersen was found guilty of obstructing justice as a result of the investigation into the scandal (although the decision was subsequently quashed). Andersen still exists today but it is very small and mainly deals with lawsuits against it.

The Public Company Accounting Oversight Board was created by the Sarbanes-Oxley Act and was given the role of policing auditors. All auditors of public companies must be registered and comply with strict rules on ethics and audit procedures. Restrictions are in place to prevent auditors performing certain audit and non-audit work for clients and they must disclose audit and non-audit income separately.

Case Study

In a relatively short period of time Enron grew from nowhere to the seventh largest company in the USA, It was a major multinational corporation and employed 21,000 staff in over 40 countries.

However this growth was too good to be true. Its expansion was fuelled by massive debts which it hid from its own balance sheet by using subsidiary companies. This deception allowed it to appear creditworthy and generated confidence in the stock market where Enron's share price grew swiftly.

The bubble soon burst and in December 2001, Enron filed for bankruptcy under the USA's Chapter 11 rules with debts of approximately £3 Billion. The following investigation also uncovered criminal behaviour including fraud, money laundering and insider dealing by senior executives and its auditors.

4.2 South Africa

Like other nations, **South Africa** has seen its share of corporate governance failures. To help prevent repeats, and to provide confidence and some assurance for investors, it has been developing corporate governance rules since the mid-1990s and now has some of the most **sophisticated practices** and **rules** among the emerging **market economies**.

In common with the UK, South Africa has adopted a **self-regulation** of corporate governance approach, in a comply-or-explain format of compliance with the **King Report** (the South African equivalent of the UK Corporate Governance Code). The first edition of the King Report was released in 1994, a second version was produced in 2002 and a third in 2009.

The reports are the result of work done by the **King Committee**, led by a former High Court Judge (**Mervyn King**) and require all companies listed on South Africa's JSE Security Exchange to comply with the contents of the King Report or explain why they have not. The 2009 version of the report also requires such companies to produce an integrated report in place of a financial report and sustainability report.

In addition to the King Report, a new **Companies Act** was enacted in 2009 and came into effect on 1st July 2010. The Act enhances corporate governance and empowers shareholders. It also codifies the standard for directors' conduct and holds directors accountable where the standard is not met.

4.3 UK

Three significant government committees (**Cadbury**, **Greenbury** and **Hampel**), were commissioned during the 1990s in response to the increased need for good corporate governance in light of several corporate scandals including the collapse of Asil Nadir's **Polly Peck**, the pension scandal of Robert Maxwell's **Mirror Group** and **Guinness's** illegal share support scheme involving Ernest Saunders. Other UK corporate scandals involved Barings Bank and BA.

Corporate collapses such as those mentioned above not only affect the **stakeholders** involved – such scandals **reduce overall investor confidence** in the markets, as directors are not being seen to be effectively controlled. For a country such as the UK which has a tradition of investment and respected financial markets, resolving this issue was massively important economically.

The recommendations of the committees were incorporated into the **1998 Combined Code** which companies listing on the London Stock Exchange were required to comply. Since then, three further committees reported (**Turnbull**, **Higgs** and **Smith**) and their recommendations were incorporated into the **2003 Combined Code**. This Code was itself revised in **2008**.

In 2010, the Combined Code was renamed the **UK Corporate Governance Code** and some further amendments were made.

The development of UK corporate governance

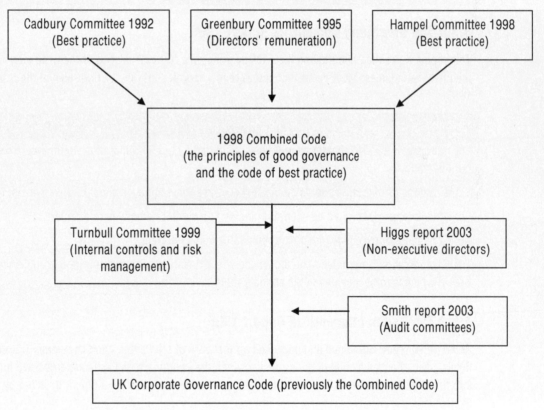

4.3.1 The Cadbury Committee Report 1992

A **joint initiative** between the Financial Reporting Council, the accountancy profession and the London Stock Exchange saw a code of practice created that all listed companies should follow as a **condition to being admitted to the stock exchange**. The committee developed the 'comply or explain' approach to corporate governance and the table below sets out its main recommendations.

Recommendations of the Cadbury Report
Boards of listed companies should include independent non-executive directors.
A nomination committee consisting of independent non-executive directors should vet new appointments to the board.
Service contracts of executive directors should be limited to three years unless approved by shareholders.
A remuneration committee consisting of mostly non-executive directors should approve executive director remuneration.
An audit committee consisting of mostly non-executive directors should monitor the finances of the company.
The role of Chairman and Chief Executive should not be performed by one person to ensure the board is separated from the day to day running of the company.

4.3.2 The Greenbury Committee Report 1995

This report was aimed at curtailing the publicly unpopular **'fat cat'** salaries of many directors, especially those in the privatised utilities. Most of the findings were incorporated into the Listing rules of the Stock Exchange in late 1995.

Recommendations of the Greenbury Report
The interests of the shareholders should be considered by the Remuneration Committee when setting directors' remuneration.
Share options for directors should be disallowed and annual bonuses should not be pensionable.
Shareholder approval should be sought if long-term incentives are given to directors.
Notice periods for executive directors should not exceed one year.
The Remuneration Committee should produce a report stating compliance or non-compliance to the Greenbury Report which is to be included in the annual report.

4.3.3 The Hampel Committee Report 1998

The Hampel report combined and improved on the work of the Cadbury and Greenbury Committees. In June 1998 it was given effect as a code of good practice when the London Stock Exchange embodied its recommendations into the **1998 Combined Code**. Failure to follow the code could result in a fine or delisting by the London Stock Exchange.

BPP
LEARNING MEDIA

Recommendations of the Hampel Report
All directors, both executive and non-executive, should owe the same duties and should receive suitable information and instruction as to their duties.
Executive directors must be suitably experienced to understand the nature and interests of their company.
The board should consist of at least one-third non-executive directors of which the majority are independent.
The roles of Chairman and Chief Executive should not be performed by one person.
Nomination committees should be involved in recommending new board appointments and directors should be re-elected at least every three years.
Directors' remuneration should be based upon the recommendations of a remuneration committee consisting entirely of non-executive directors. Remuneration should not be excessive.
Service contracts of directors should be no longer than twelve months.

4.3.4 The Turnbull Committee Report 1999

This report decided that the **board of directors** should be more **active** and involved in **internal control procedures** and risk management. In particular, the board should be responsible for:

(a) **Evaluating sources** and **types of risk** that the company is faced with.

(b) **Providing effective safeguards** and **internal controls** to manage, prevent or reduce the risks.

(c) **Ensuring the transparency** of **internal controls** and providing an annual risk assessment.

4.3.5 The Higgs Report 2003

The Higgs report identified the need for **non-executive directors** to play an increasingly **important role** in the running of a company, and that the board as a whole should accept **collective responsibility** for the results of the company and its actions. It recommended the use of the **unitary board structure** instead of other structures common in French and German corporations. This report was the UK's response to the Enron disaster in the USA.

4.3.6 The Smith Report 2003

The Smith Report produced guidelines to help **audit committees** perform their role effectively and also contained **essential requirements** that all committees should meet. The 'comply or explain' principle applies to these requirements, but the report also states that best practice involves going over and above these requirements.

 Case Study

In the UK the Cadbury committee was set up in May 1991 because of the lack of confidence which was perceived in financial reporting and in the ability of external auditors to provide the assurances required by the users of financial statements. The main difficulties were considered to be in the relationship between external auditors and boards of directors. In particular, the commercial pressures on both directors and auditors caused pressure to be brought to bear on auditors by the board and the auditors often capitulated. Problems were also perceived in the ability of the board of directors to control their organisations. The lack of board accountability in many of these company collapses demonstrated the need for action.

4.4 Europe

The **European Commission** has taken the view that corporate governance matters should be left as a matter for individual states to deal with and was the subject of an announcement in 2003. The Commission did recognise that a common approach was necessary for certain fundamental issues (such as directors' remuneration, disclosure and access to financial information and the management of independent non-executive directors) so it developed a series of Directives as a basis for all states to follow.

In October 2004 the **EU Corporate Governance Forum** was established with 15 members representing various stakeholders from across the EU with the objective of co-ordinating corporate governance between all member states.

By 2010 the organisation's structure had been amended to 14 members and part of its work is now in connection with the **evaluation** of the **effectiveness** of **monitoring** and **enforcement systems** that member states have in place in connection with their **national corporate governance codes**.

Question
UK corporate governance

Which of the following were recommendations of the Greenbury Committee?

(i)   Share options for directors should be disallowed and annual bonuses should not be pensionable.

(ii)   All directors, both executive and non-executive, should owe the same duties and should receive suitable information and instruction as to their duties.

(iii)   Shareholder approval should be sought if long-term incentives are given to directors.

(iv)   Notice periods for executive directors should not exceed one year.

A   (i) and (ii)
B   (i), (ii) and (iii)
C   (i), (iii) and (iv)
D   All of the above

Answer

C   Option 2 was a recommendation of the Hampel Committee.

5 Symptoms of poor corporate governance

FAST FORWARD

The following **symptoms** can indicate poor corporate governance.

- Domination by a single individual
- Lack of involvement of board
- Lack of adequate control function
- Lack of supervision
- Lack of independent scrutiny
- Lack of contact with shareholders
- Emphasis on short-term profitability
- Misleading accounts and information

There are a **number of elements** in **corporate governance**:

(a) The **management** and **reduction of risk**.

(b) The notion that **overall performance is enhanced** by **good supervision** and **management** within **set best practice guidelines**.

(c) Good governance provides a **framework** for an organisation to pursue its strategy in an **ethical and effective** way from the perspective of all stakeholder groups affected, and offers safeguards against misuse of resources, physical or intellectual.

(d) Good governance is not just about externally established codes, it also requires a willingness to **apply the spirit** as well as the letter of the law.

(e) **Accountability** is generally a major theme in all governance frameworks.

The scandals over the last 25 years have highlighted the need for guidance to tackle the various risks and problems that can arise in organisations' systems of governance.

5.1 Domination by a single individual

A feature of many corporate governance scandals has been boards **dominated by a single senior executive** with other board members merely acting as a rubber stamp. Sometimes the single individual may bypass the board to action his **own interests**. The report on the UK Guinness case suggested that the Chief Executive, Ernest Saunders paid himself a £3m reward without consulting the other directors.

Even if an organisation is not dominated by a single individual, there may be other weaknesses. The organisation may be **run by a small group** centred round the Chief Executive and Chief Financial Officer, and appointments may be made by personal recommendation rather than a formal, objective process.

5.2 Lack of involvement of board

Boards that meet irregularly or fail to consider systematically the organisation's activities and risks are clearly weak. Sometimes the failure to carry out proper oversight is due to a **lack of information** being provided.

5.3 Lack of adequate control function

An obvious weakness is a **lack of internal audit.**

Another potential weakness is a **lack of adequate technical knowledge** in key roles, for example in the audit committee or in senior compliance positions. A rapid turnover of staff involved in accounting or control may suggest inadequate resourcing, and will make control more difficult because of lack of continuity.

5.4 Lack of supervision

Employees who are not properly supervised can create large losses for the organisation through their own incompetence, negligence or fraudulent activity. The behaviour of Nick Leeson, the employee who caused the collapse of Barings bank was not challenged because he appeared to be successful, whereas he was using unauthorised accounts to cover up his large trading losses. Leeson was able to do this because he was in charge of dealing and settlement, a systems weakness of **lack of segregation of key roles** that featured in other financial frauds.

5.5 Lack of independent scrutiny

External auditors may not carry out the necessary questioning of senior management because of **fears of losing the audit**, and **internal audit** do not ask awkward questions because the Chief Financial Officer determines their **employment prospects**. Often corporate collapses are followed by criticisms of external auditors, such as the Barlow Clowes affair where poorly planned and focused audit work failed to identify illegal use of client monies.

5.6 Lack of contact with shareholders

Often, board members grow up with the company and **lose touch** with the interests and views of shareholders. One possible symptom of this is the payment of remuneration packages that do not appear to be warranted by results.

5.7 Emphasis on short-term profitability

Emphasis on success or getting results can lead to the **concealment of problems or errors,** or **manipulation of accounts** to **achieve desired results**.

5.8 Misleading accounts and information

Misleading figures are often symptomatic of other problems (or are designed to conceal other problems) but clearly poor quality **accounting information** is a major problem if markets are trying to make a fair assessment of the company's value. Giving out misleading information was a major issue in the UK's Equitable Life scandal where the company gave contradictory information to savers, independent advisers, media and regulators.

Question   Governance

Techpoint Plc is a medium sized public company that produces a range of components used in the manufacture of computers. The board of directors consists of Chairman Max Mallory, Chief Executive Richard Mallory, Finance Director Linda Mallory (all of whom are siblings) and five other unrelated executive directors. All directors receive bonuses based on sales. The company's sales are made by individual salesmen and women each of whom have authority to bind the company into contracts of unlimited value without the need to refer to a superior or consult with other departments. It is this flexibility that has enabled the company to be very profitable in past years. However, a number of bad contracts in the current year have meant that the Finance Director has re-classed them as 'costs' to maintain healthy sales and to protect the directors' bonuses.

What are the corporate governance issues at Techpoint Plc?

The main corporate governance issues are:

(a) **Domination by a small group**

All the key directors are related which gives them power over the other executives.

(b) **Short-term view**

Directors' bonuses are based on short-term sales which caused the manipulation of accounts to achieve them.

(c) **Lack of supervision**

The sales force can tie the company into large loss-making contracts without any checks. There is no authorisation or communication with other departments which means the company may take on contracts that it cannot fulfil. The company has been hit hard with bad contracts in the current year.

6 The UK regulatory framework

6.1 The UK Corporate Governance Code

FAST FORWARD

The **main source** of corporate governance in the **UK** at this time is the **UK Corporate Governance Code**.

It is important to recognise that following the **UK Corporate Governance Code** is **not a legal requirement**. However, the London Stock Exchange requires all **listed companies** to include in their annual reports a **statement of compliance** or **non-compliance** with the code. All other companies are encouraged to follow it as an example of 'best practice'. Companies may find pressure from their stakeholders if they do not adopt it.

6.2 Stakeholder benefits

When studying the detail which follows about the **UK Corporate Governance Code**, think about what the principles are trying to achieve, and in particular how they **benefit** an organisation's stakeholders.

Examples of benefits include:

- **Encouraging** all involved in a company to **accept their legal obligations**. This includes the board of directors (including non-executive directors), the auditors and the shareholders.

- **Encouraging** the **scrutiny** of **corporate stewardship** so that those involved in running the business know that if they act inappropriately they are likely to be caught.

- **Imposing** certain **checks and controls** on executive directors but without restricting the commercial enterprise aspect of governance.

- **Improving** the **transparency** surrounding how the organisation is run. This is to encourage scrutiny (as mentioned above), but it should also mean those running the company would not act inappropriately in the first place.

- **Reducing** the **risk** to all **stakeholders**. More transparency, scrutiny, checks and controls should help reduce the risk of poor decision making and corporate failure.

6.3 Detail of the UK Corporate Governance Code

The **UK Corporate Governance Code** is set out as a series of **main principles**, some of which have **supporting principles** and all of which have **provisions**. It contains five main sections:

A   Leadership
B   Effectiveness
C   Accountability
D   Remuneration
E   Relations with shareholders

6.4 Leadership: the role of the board (main principle A1)

Every company should be headed by an **effective board** which is **collectively responsible** for the long-term success of the company.

6.4.1 Supporting principles for the role of the board

The board's role is to provide **entrepreneurial leadership** of the company within a framework of prudent and effective controls which enables risk to be assessed and managed. The board should:

- Set the company's **strategic aims**.

- Ensure that the **necessary financial and human resources** are in place for the company to meet its objectives.

- **Review management performance.**

- Set the company's **values and standards** and ensure that its **obligations** to its shareholders and others are understood and met.

- **All directors** must act in what they consider to be the best interests of the company, consistent with their statutory duties.

6.4.2 Provisions supporting the role of the board

- The board should **meet sufficiently regularly** to discharge its duties effectively, with a formal schedule of matters specifically reserved for its decision.

- The **annual report** should include a statement of how the board operates, including a high level statement of which types of decision are taken by the board and which are delegated to management.

- The annual report should identify the board's **Chairman**, the **Deputy Chairman** (where there is one), the **Chief Executive**, the **senior independent (non-executive) director** and the **chairmen and members of the board committees**. It should also set out the number of meetings of the board and its committees and individual attendance by directors.

- The company should arrange appropriate **insurance cover** in respect of **legal action against its directors**.

6.5 Leadership: division of responsibilities (main principle A2)

There should be a clear **division of responsibilities** at the head of the company between the **running of the board** and the executive responsibility for the **running of the company's business**. No one individual should have **unfettered powers of decision**.

6.5.1 Provision supporting the division of responsibilities

The roles of the Chairman and Chief Executive should **not be exercised by the same individual**. The division of responsibilities between them should be clearly established, set out in writing and agreed by the board.

6.6 Leadership: the Chairman (main principle A3)

The **chairman** is responsible for **leadership of the board** and ensuring its effectiveness in all aspects of its role.

6.6.1 Supporting principle for the Chairman

The **Chairman**:

- Is responsible for setting the board's **agenda** and ensuring that adequate **time** is available for discussion of all agenda items, in particular strategic issues.

- Should promote a **culture of openness and debate** by facilitating the effective contribution of non-executive directors in particular and ensuring **constructive relations** between executive and non-executive directors.

- Is responsible for ensuring that the **directors receive accurate, timely and clear information**.

- Should ensure **effective communication with shareholders**.

6.6.2 Provision supporting the Chairman

The Chairman should, on appointment, **meet the independence criteria** set out in the provisions to main principle B1 below. **A Chief Executive should not go on to be Chairman of the same company**. If, exceptionally, a board decides that a Chief Executive should become Chairman, the board should consult major shareholders in advance and should set out its reasons to shareholders at the time of the appointment and in the next annual report.

6.7 Leadership: non-executive directors (main principle A4)

As part of their role as members of a unitary board, non-executive directors should **constructively challenge and help develop proposals on strategy**.

6.7.1 Supporting principle for non-executive directors

Non-executive directors should:

- **Scrutinise the performance of management** in meeting agreed goals and objectives

- **Monitor the reporting of performance**

- Satisfy themselves on the **integrity of financial information** and that **financial controls** and systems of **risk management** are robust and defensible

- Be responsible for determining appropriate levels of **remuneration of executive directors**

- Have prime roles in **appointing** and **removing executive directors**, and in **succession planning**

6.7.2 Provisions supporting the non-executive directors

The board should appoint one of the independent non-executive directors to be the **senior independent director**:

- To provide a **sounding board for the chairman** and

- To serve as an **intermediary for the other directors** when necessary.

The **senior independent director** should be available to shareholders if they have concerns which contact through the normal channels of Chairman, Chief Executive or other executive directors have failed to resolve, or for which such contact is inappropriate.

The **Chairman should hold meetings with the non-executive directors without the executives present**. Led by the senior independent director, the non-executive directors should meet without the Chairman present at least annually to **appraise the Chairman's performance** and on such other occasions as deemed appropriate.

Where directors have concerns which cannot be resolved about the running of the company or a proposed action, they should ensure that their concerns are recorded in the **board minutes**.

On resignation, a non-executive director should provide a **written statement** to the Chairman, for circulation to the board, if they have any such concerns.

6.8 Effectiveness: the composition of the board (main principle B1)

The board and its committees should have the **appropriate balance of skills**, **experience**, **independence** and **knowledge** of the company to enable them to discharge their respective duties and responsibilities effectively.

6.8.1 Principles supporting the composition of the board

The board should be **big enough** that the requirements of the business can be met, and that changes to the board's composition can be managed without undue disruption. The board should **not be so large** as to be unwieldy.

The board should include an appropriate combination of **executive and non-executive directors** (and in particular **independent non-executive directors**) such that no individual or small group of individuals can dominate the board's decision taking.

Committee membership must be refreshed and undue reliance should not be placed on particular individuals. This should be taken into account in deciding chairmanship and membership of committees.

Only the **committee chairman** and **members** are entitled to be present at meetings of the nomination, audit or remuneration committees, though others may attend at the invitation of the committee.

6.8.2 Provisions supporting the composition of the board

The board should identify in the annual report each **non-executive director** (including the Chairman of the board) it considers to be **independent**.

The board should determine whether the director is **independent in character and judgement** and whether there are relationships or circumstances which are likely to affect, or could appear to affect, the director's judgement. The board should state its reasons if it determines that a director is independent notwithstanding the existence of relationships or circumstances which may appear relevant.

BPP
LEARNING MEDIA

A director **may** be determined as being **not independent** if they:

- Have been an **employee** of the company within the last **five years**.

- Have, or have had within the last **three years**, a **material business relationship** with the company either directly, or as a partner, shareholder, director or senior employee of a body that has such a relationship with the company.

- Have received or receives additional **remuneration** from the company apart from the director's fee, participates in the company's **share option** or a **performance-related pay scheme**, or is a member of the company's **pension scheme**.

- Have close **family ties** with any of the company's advisors, directors or senior employees.

- Hold **cross directorships** or have significant links with other directors through involvement in other companies or bodies.

- **Represent a significant shareholder**.

- Have served on the board for more than **nine years** from the date of their first election.

At least **50% of the board**, excluding the Chairman, should comprise **independent non-executive directors**. A smaller company (below the FTSE 350 threshold throughout the year immediately prior to the reporting year) should have at least **two** independent non-executive directors.

6.9 Effectiveness: appointments to the board (main principle B2)

There should be a formal, rigorous and transparent procedure for the **appointment of new directors** to the board.

6.9.1 Principles supporting board appointments

The search for **board candidates** and their appointment to the board should be made:

- **On merit** and
- Against **objective criteria** and
- With due regards to the **benefits of diversity** on the board, including gender.

The board should satisfy itself that plans are in place for orderly **succession of appointments** to the board and to senior management, so as to **maintain an appropriate balance of skills and experience** within the company and on the board and to ensure progressive refreshing of the board.

6.9.2 Provisions supporting board appointments: the nomination committee

- There should be a **nomination committee** which should lead the process for board appointments and make recommendations to the board.

- **Over 50%** of members of the **nomination committee** should be **independent non-executive directors**.

- The board Chairman or an independent non-executive director should **chair the nomination committee**, but the board Chairman should not chair the nomination committee when it is dealing with the appointment of a successor to the Chairmanship.

- The nomination committee should make available its **terms of reference**, explaining its role and the authority delegated to it by the board. This can be done via an appropriate website.

- The nomination committee should evaluate the **balance of skills, knowledge, independence and experience on the board** and, in the light of this evaluation, prepare a description of the role and capabilities required for a particular appointment.

- Non-executive directors should be appointed for **specified terms** subject to re-election and to statutory provisions relating to the removal of a director. **Any term beyond six years for a non-executive director should be subject to particularly rigorous review**, and should take into account the need for progressive refreshing of the board.

- A separate section of the **annual report** should describe the work of the nomination committee, including the process it has used in relation to board appointments.

- An explanation should be given if neither an **external search consultancy** nor **open advertising** has been used in the appointment of a Chairman or a non-executive director.

6.10 Effectiveness: commitment (main principle B3)

All directors should be able to allocate **sufficient time** to the company to discharge their responsibilities effectively.

6.10.1 Provisions supporting commitment

- For the **appointment of the board Chairman**, the nomination committee should prepare a job specification, including an assessment of the time commitment expected, recognising the need for availability in the event of crises.

- A Chairman's other **significant commitments** should be disclosed to the board before appointment and included in the annual report. Changes to such commitments should be reported to the board as they arise, and included in the next annual report.

- The **terms and conditions of appointment of non-executive directors** should be made available for inspection at the registered office and at the annual general meeting (AGM).

- The letter of appointment for non-executive directors should set out the expected **time commitment**. Non-executive directors should undertake that they will have sufficient time to meet what is expected of them.

- Non-executive directors should disclose their **other significant commitments** to the board before appointment, with a broad indication of the time involved, and the board should be informed of subsequent changes.

- The board should not agree to a **full-time executive director** taking on more than one non-executive directorship in a FTSE 100 company nor the Chairmanship of such a company.

6.11 Effectiveness: development (main principle B4)

All directors should receive **induction** on joining the board and regularly **update and refresh** their skills and knowledge.

BPP
LEARNING MEDIA

6.11.1 Principles supporting development

The Chairman should ensure that the **directors continually update their skills** and the knowledge and familiarity with the company required to fulfil their role both on the board and the board committees. The company should provide the necessary resources for developing and updating its directors' knowledge and capabilities.

To function effectively, all directors need **appropriate knowledge** of the company and access to its operations and staff.

6.11.2 Provisions supporting development

- The Chairman should ensure that new directors receive a **full, formal and tailored induction on joining the board**. As part of this, directors should avail themselves of opportunities to meet **major shareholders**.

- The Chairman should regularly review and agree with each director their **training and development needs**.

6.12 Effectiveness: information and support (main principle B5)

The board should be supplied in a **timely** manner with **information in a form and of a quality** appropriate to enable it to discharge its duties.

6.12.1 Principles supporting information and support

The Chairman is responsible for ensuring that the directors receive **accurate, timely and clear information**. Management has an obligation to provide such information but **directors should seek clarification or amplification where necessary**.

Under the direction of the Chairman, the **company secretary's** responsibilities include ensuring good information flows within the board and its committees and between senior management and non-executive directors, as well as facilitating induction and assisting with professional development as required. The company secretary should also be responsible for advising the board through the Chairman on all **governance matters**.

6.12.2 Provisions supporting information and support

- The board should ensure that directors, especially non-executive directors, have access to **independent professional advice** at the company's expense where they judge it necessary to discharge their responsibilities as directors.

- **Committees** should be provided with **sufficient resources** to undertake their duties.

- All directors should have access to the advice and services of the **company secretary**, who is responsible to the board for ensuring that board procedures are complied with.

- Both the **appointment and removal of the company secretary** should be a matter for the board as a whole.

6.13 Effectiveness: evaluation (main principle B6)

The board should undertake a formal and rigorous annual **evaluation of its own performance** and that of its **committees** and individual **directors**.

6.13.1 Principles for evaluation

The Chairman should **act on the results of the performance evaluation** by recognising the strengths and addressing the weaknesses of the board. Where appropriate the Chairman should propose that **new members** be appointed to the board, or should seek the **resignation of directors**.

Individual evaluation should aim to show whether each director continues to contribute effectively and to demonstrate commitment to the role (including commitment of **time** for board and committee meetings and any other duties).

6.13.2 Provisions for evaluation

- The board should state in the **annual report** how performance evaluation of the board, its committees and its individual directors has been conducted

- Evaluation of the board of FTSE 350 companies should be **externally facilitated** at least every three years. A statement should be made available of whether an external facilitator has any other connection with the company

- The **non-executive** directors, led by the senior independent director, should be responsible for performance evaluation of the Chairman taking into account the views of executive directors

6.14 Effectiveness: re-election (main principle B7)

All directors should be submitted for **re-election** at **regular intervals**, subject to continued satisfactory performance.

6.14.1 Provisions for re-election

All **directors of FTSE 350 companies** should be subject to **annual election** by shareholders

With regards to the **directors of other companies**:

- Directors should be subject to election by shareholders at the **first AGM** after their appointment and re-election thereafter at intervals of **no more than three years**.

- Non-executive directors who have served longer than nine years should be subject to **annual re-election**

The names of directors submitted for election or re-election should be accompanied by sufficient **biographical details** and any other relevant information to enable shareholders to take an informed decision on their election.

Accompanying a resolution to **elect a non-executive director** should be papers from the board setting out why they believe an individual should be elected. The Chairman should confirm to shareholders when proposing re-election that, following formal performance evaluation, the individual's **performance** continues to be effective and to demonstrate commitment to the role.

6.15 Accountability: financial and business reporting (main principle C1)

The board should present a **balanced and understandable assessment of the company's position and prospects**.

BPP
LEARNING MEDIA

6.15.1 Principles supporting financial and business reporting

The board's responsibility to present a balanced and understandable assessment extends to:

- **Interim reports**
- **Other price-sensitive public reports**
- Reports to **regulators**
- The statutory **financial statements**

6.15.2 Provisions supporting financial and business reporting:

- The directors should explain in the annual report:

    - their responsibility for preparing the annual report and accounts

    - the basis on which the company generates or preserves value over the longer term (the business model) and the strategy for delivering the objectives of the company

- The **auditors** should explain their reporting responsibilities in the annual report

- The directors should report that the business is a **going concern**, with supporting assumptions or qualifications as necessary

6.16 Accountability: risk management and internal control (main principle C2)

The board is responsible for determining the nature and extent of the significant risks it is willing to take in achieving its strategic objectives. The board should maintain **sound risk management and internal control systems**.

6.16.1 Provision supporting risk management and internal control

The board should, at least annually, conduct a **review of the effectiveness of the company's risk management and internal control systems** and should report to shareholders that they have done so. The review should cover all material controls, including **financial, operational and compliance controls**.

6.17 Accountability: audit committee and auditors (main principle C3)

The board should establish formal and transparent arrangements for considering how they should **apply the corporate reporting and risk management and internal control principles** and for maintaining an appropriate relationship with the company's **auditors**.

6.17.1 Provisions supporting the audit committee and auditors

- The board should establish an **audit committee** of at least **three** or, in the case of smaller companies, **two independent non-executive directors**. In smaller companies the Chairman may be a member of, but not chair, the committee in addition to the independent non-executive directors, provided he or she was considered independent on appointment as Chairman.

- At least one member of the audit committee should have **recent and relevant financial experience**.

BPP
LEARNING MEDIA

- Roles and responsibilities of the audit committee should be set out in written terms of reference and should include:

    - monitoring the **integrity of the financial statements** of the company, and any formal announcements relating to the company's financial performance, reviewing significant financial reporting judgements contained in them

    - reviewing the company's **internal financial controls** and, unless expressly addressed by a separate board risk committee composed of independent directors, or by the board itself, to review the company's internal control and risk management systems

    - monitoring and reviewing the **effectiveness of the company's internal audit function**

    - making recommendations to the board and thereby to shareholders for their approval in general meeting regarding the **appointment, re-appointment and removal of the external auditor** and to approve the **remuneration and terms of engagement of the external auditor**

    - reviewing and monitoring the external auditor's **independence and objectivity** and the effectiveness of the audit process, taking into consideration relevant UK professional and regulatory requirements

    - developing and implementing policy on the engagement of the external auditor to supply **non-audit services**, taking into account relevant ethical guidance regarding the provision of non-audit services by the external audit firm, and to report this to the board, identifying any matters in respect of which it considers that action or improvement is needed and making recommendations as to the steps to be taken

- The audit committee's **terms of reference**, including its role and the authority delegated to it by the board, should be made available (via a website if desired).

- A separate section of the **annual report** should describe the work of the audit committee in discharging its responsibilities.

- The audit committee should review arrangements by which staff of the company may, in confidence, raise concerns about **possible improprieties** in matters of financial reporting or other matters. Arrangements should be in place for the proportionate and independent investigation of such matters and for appropriate follow-up action.

- The audit committee should monitor and review the effectiveness of the **internal audit** activities. Where there is no internal audit function, the audit committee should consider annually whether there is a need for an internal audit function and make a recommendation to the board, and the reasons for the absence of such a function should be explained in the relevant section of the annual report.

- The audit committee should have primary responsibility for making a recommendation on the appointment, re-appointment and removal of **external auditors**. If the board does not accept the audit committee's recommendation, it should include in the annual report, and in any papers recommending appointment or re-appointment, a statement from the audit committee explaining the recommendation and should set out reasons why the board has taken a different position.

- The annual report should explain to shareholders how, if the auditor provides **non-audit services**, auditor objectivity and independence are safeguarded.

BPP
LEARNING MEDIA

6.18 Remuneration: level and components of remuneration (main principle D1)

Levels of remuneration should be sufficient to **attract, retain and motivate directors** of the quality required to run the company successfully, but a company should avoid paying more than is necessary for this purpose. A significant proportion of executive directors' remuneration should be structured so as to **link rewards to corporate and individual performance**.

6.18.1 Principle supporting the level and components of remuneration

The **performance-related elements** of **executive directors'** remuneration should be **stretching** and designed to promote the **long-term success of the company**. The **remuneration committee** should judge where to position their company relative to other companies, but they should use such comparisons with caution. They must avoid **an upward ratchet of remuneration levels with no corresponding improvement in performance**. They should also be sensitive to pay and employment conditions elsewhere in the company, especially when determining annual salary increases.

6.18.2 Provisions supporting the level and components of remuneration

- In designing schemes of **performance-related remuneration** for executive directors, the remuneration committee should follow the guidance provided in Schedule A of the Code. This guidance states that:

    - Performance conditions for **annual bonuses** should be relevant, stretching and designed to promote the long-term success of the company

    - Shares granted under **share option schemes** etc should not vest in or be exercisable by the director in less than three years

    - Any new proposed **long-term incentive scheme** should be approved by shareholders, and the total potentially available rewards of all schemes should not be excessive

    - **Payouts** etc should be subject to challenging performance criteria linked to the company's objectives, and should be compatible with risk policies and systems

    - Consideration should be given to mechanisms for **clawing back** some **performance-related remuneration** in exceptional circumstances of mis-statement or misconduct

    - Only **basic salary** should generally be **pensionable**

- Levels of remuneration for **non-executive directors** should:

    - Reflect the **time commitment** and **responsibilities** of the role

    - **Not include share options or other performance-related elements** (as these can undermine independence) unless shareholder approval is sought in advance and any shares acquired by exercise of the options are held until at least one year after the non-executive director leaves the board. Holding of share options could be relevant to the determination of a non-executive director's (lack of) independence

- Where an executive director is released to serve as a non-executive director elsewhere, the **remuneration report** should include a statement as to whether or not the director will retain such earnings and, if so, what the remuneration is

- The remuneration committee should carefully consider what **compensation commitments** (including pension contributions and all other elements) their directors' terms of appointment would entail in the event of early termination. The aim should be to avoid rewarding poor performance. They should take a robust line on reducing compensation to reflect departing directors' obligations to mitigate loss

- Notice or contract periods should be set at **one year or less**. If it is necessary to offer longer notice or contract periods to new directors recruited from outside, such periods should reduce to one year or less after the initial period

6.19 Remuneration: procedure (main principle D2)

There should be a formal and transparent procedure for developing **policy on executive remuneration** and for fixing the remuneration packages of individual directors. **No director should be involved in deciding his or her own remuneration**.

6.19.1 Principles supporting procedure

The **remuneration committee** should:

- Consult the Chairman and/or Chief Executive about their proposals relating to the remuneration of other executive directors

- Be responsible for appointing any consultants in respect of executive director remuneration

Where executive directors or senior management are involved in advising or supporting the remuneration committee, care should be taken to recognise and avoid **conflicts of interest**. The board Chairman should ensure that the company maintains contact as required with its **principal shareholders** about remuneration in the same way as for other matters.

6.19.2 Provisions supporting procedure

- The board should **establish a remuneration committee** of **at least three, or in the case of smaller companies two, independent non-executive directors**.

- **The board Chairman may be a member of, but not chair**, the remuneration committee if they were considered independent on appointment as Chairman.

- The remuneration committee should make available its **terms of reference**, on a website if desired, explaining its role and the authority delegated to it by the board.

- Where **remuneration consultants** are appointed, a statement should be made available as to whether they have any other connection with the company.

- The remuneration committee should have delegated responsibility for **setting remuneration for all executive directors and the Chairman**, including pension rights and any compensation payments.

- The committee should also recommend and monitor the level and structure of remuneration for **senior management**. The definition of 'senior management' for this purpose should be determined by the board but should normally include the first layer of management below board level.

- The board itself or, where required by the company's Articles, the shareholders should **determine the remuneration of the non-executive directors** within the limits set in the Articles. Where permitted by the Articles, the board may however delegate this responsibility to a committee, which might include the Chief Executive.

- **Shareholders** should be invited specifically to approve all new **long-term incentive schemes** and significant changes to existing schemes.

BPP
LEARNING MEDIA

6.20 Relations with shareholders: dialogue with shareholders (main principle E1)

There should be a **dialogue with shareholders** based on the **mutual understanding of objectives**. The board as a whole has responsibility for ensuring that a satisfactory dialogue with shareholders takes place.

6.20.1 Principles supporting dialogue with shareholders

Most shareholder contact is with the Chief Executive and Finance Director, but the board Chairman should ensure that all directors are made aware of their major shareholders' **issues and concerns**. The board should keep in touch with shareholder opinion in whatever ways are most practical and efficient.

6.20.2 Provisions supporting dialogue with shareholders

- The board Chairman should ensure that the **views of shareholders** are communicated to the board as a whole.

- The Chairman should **discuss governance and strategy** with major shareholders.

- **Non-executive directors** should be offered the opportunity to attend scheduled meetings with major shareholders and should expect to attend meetings if requested by major shareholders.

- The **senior independent director** should attend sufficient meetings with a range of major shareholders to listen to their views in order to help develop a balanced understanding of the issues and concerns of major shareholders.

- The board should state in the **annual report** the steps they have taken to ensure that the members of the board and, in particular, the non-executive directors, develop an understanding of the views of major shareholders about the company, for example through direct face-to-face contact, analysts' or brokers' briefings and surveys of shareholder opinion.

6.21 Relations with shareholders: constructive use of the AGM (main principle E2)

The board should use the AGM to **communicate with investors** and to **encourage their participation**.

6.21.1 Provisions supporting the use of the AGM

- At any general meeting, the company should propose **a separate resolution on each substantially separate issue**, and should in particular propose a resolution at the AGM relating to the **report and accounts**.

- For each resolution, **proxy appointment forms** should provide shareholders with the option to direct their proxy to vote either for or against the resolution or to withhold their vote.

- The proxy form and any announcement of the results of a vote should make it clear that a **'vote withheld'** is not a vote in law and will not be counted in the calculation of the proportion of the votes for and against the resolution.

- The company should ensure that all **valid proxy appointments** received for general meetings are properly recorded and counted.

- For each resolution, after a vote has been taken, except where taken on a poll, the company should ensure that the following **information is given at the meeting and on the company's website**:
    - The number of shares in respect of which proxy appointments have been validly made
    - The number of votes for the resolution
    - The number of votes against the resolution
    - The number of shares in respect of which the vote was directed to be withheld.

- The chairman should arrange for the **chairmen of the audit, remuneration and nomination committees** to be available to answer questions at the AGM, and for **all directors to attend**.

- The company should arrange for the Notice of the AGM and related papers to be sent to shareholders at least **20 working days** before the meeting.

6.22 Compliance with the Code

The **London Stock Exchange** requires listed companies to include in their accounts:

(a) A narrative statement of how they **applied** the **principles** set out in the UK Corporate Governance Code. This should provide explanations which enable their shareholders to assess how the principles have been applied.

(b) A statement as to whether or not they **complied throughout** the **accounting period** with the provisions set out in the UK Corporate Governance Code. Listed companies that did not comply throughout the accounting period with all the provisions must specify the provisions with which they did not comply, and give **reasons** for **non-compliance**.

Question

The Code

State three recommendations that the UK Corporate Governance makes for each of the following.

(a) Balance and independence of the board
(b) Appointments to the board
(c) Re-electing directors

Answer

(a) See Section 6.8
(b) See Section 6.9
(c) See Section 6.14

The provisions of the code should be learnt as they can easily be tested in your assessment.

7 Principles vs rules

There is continuing debate over the form corporate governance guidance should take. Some believe in **fundamental principles**, others that **detailed rules** are required.

We have already seen that the **United Kingdom** has adopted a **principles-based** approach with its Corporate Governance Code. This was the preferred option recommended by the Hampel committee when it reported.

The **United States** has firmly come down on the side of a prescriptive **rules-based** approach. This is most evident from the Sarbanes-Oxley Act that requires a large amount of compliance work by companies to ensure they meet very detailed rules.

466   **19: Corporate governance** | Part H Corporate governance

BPP
LEARNING MEDIA

There are many **arguments** for and against both approaches.

Arguments in favour of a principles-based approach:

- Companies are **highly regulated** already - further regulation would stifle their development.
- There is a **high cost** involved when complying with detailed rules.
- It is not **practical** to apply an identical set of rules to individual companies.
- Companies may have **valid reasons** for non-compliance with rules.

Arguments in favour with a rules-based approach:

- **General guidance is of little use** to ensure companies have robust procedures in place.
- **Disasters are less likely** to strike companies who are 100% compliant as they are unlikely to be satisfied with mere token compliance.
- The **cost of compliance** may be high, but it is likely to be **less than** the cost of a **major fraud** occurring.
- The '**comply or explain**' requirement of a principles-based approach requires a high degree of **shareholder activism** to be a deterrent.

8 Role of the board

FAST FORWARD

> The board should be responsible for taking major **policy** and **strategic** decisions.
>
> Directors should have a **mix of skills** and their **performance** should be assessed regularly.
>
> Appointments should be conducted by formal procedures administered by a **nomination committee**.

8.1 Scope of role

In addition to running a company's business activities, a key role of the board of directors is to **establish** the organisation's **corporate governance standards**. The **UK Corporate Governance Code** provides the following description of the role of the board:

'The board's role is to provide **entrepreneurial leadership** of the company within a framework of prudent and effective controls which enables risk to be assessed and managed. The board should set the company's strategic aims, ensure that the necessary financial and human resources are in place for the company to meet its objectives and review management performance. The board should set the company's values and standards and ensure that its obligations to its shareholders and others are understood and met.'

If the board is to act effectively, its role must be defined carefully. The UK Corporate Governance Code states that the board should have a **formal schedule of matters** specifically reserved to it for decision. Some would be decisions such as **mergers and takeovers** that are **fundamental** to the business and hence should not be taken just by executive managers. Other decisions would include **acquisitions and disposals of assets of the company** or its subsidiaries that are material to the company and **investments, capital projects, bank borrowing** facilities, **loans** and their repayment, foreign currency transactions, all above a certain size (to be determined by the board). However the role of boards has grown and they are no longer there just to add value for the shareholders.

Other **tasks the board should perform** include:

- **Monitoring** and even **dismissing** the **Chief Executive Officer**
- **Overseeing strategy**
- **Monitoring risks** and **control systems**
- **Monitoring** the **human capital** aspects of the company in regard to succession, morale, training, remuneration etc.
- **Ensuring** that there is **effective communication** of its strategic plans, both internally and externally
- Develop **corporate social responsibility policies** and to ensure they are met.

8.1.1 Role of the shareholders

As we have seen above, the role **directors** is to **decide on how the business should be run**. This means they are involved in the **day-to-day running** of the business as well as setting out its **corporate governance policy** and overall **strategy**.

Shareholders only become involved in a company's affairs at a **high level**. They have no right to tell the directors how to run the company, but if they do not agree with how business is conducted then they can remove a particular director or the board at the appropriate time.

The role of the shareholders is to agree on changes to the **company's constitution** and take part in decisions if and when the directors deem it important that they do so. Certain decisions (such as winding up the company or changing its name) have to be put to the shareholder vote.

We have already seen that shareholders do have the **right to take action themselves** (by calling a meeting and a resolution), but this is not common as it would mean that relations between the directors and shareholders would have broken down.

8.2 Attributes of directors

In order to carry out effective scrutiny, directors need to have **relevant expertise** in industry, the company's functional areas and governance. The board as a whole needs to contain a **mix of expertise** and show a **balance** between **executive management** and **independent non-executive directors**. New and existing directors should also have **appropriate training** to develop the knowledge and skills required.

8.2.1 Nomination committee

In order to ensure that **balance of the board** is maintained, the board should set up a **nomination committee,** to oversee the process for board appointments and make recommendations to the board. The nomination committee needs to consider the balance between executives and independent non-executives, the skills possessed by the board, the need for continuity and the desirable **size** of the board. Recent corporate governance guidance has laid more stress on the need to attract board members from a **diversity** of backgrounds.

8.3 Possession of necessary information

In many corporate scandals, boards of directors were not given full information before making key decisions. The UK's Higgs report stressed that it is the responsibility both of the chairman, to decide what information should be made available, and directors, to satisfy themselves that they have **appropriate information** of **sufficient quality** to make sound judgements.

BPP LEARNING MEDIA

The South African **King report** highlights the importance of the board receiving **relevant non-financial information**, going beyond assessing the financial and qualitative performance of the company, looking at **qualitative measures** that involve **broader stakeholder interests**.

8.4 Performance of board

Appraisal of the board's performance is an important control over it. The Higgs report recommended that **performance of the board** should be **assessed** once a year. **Separate appraisal** of the chairman and chief executive should also be carried out, with links to the remuneration process.

8.5 UK board structures

FAST FORWARD

The choice of **board structure** in the UK can be split into three options according to *Tricker (1996)*.

- All executive directors
- Majority executive directors
- Majority non-executive directors

A fourth option of **all non-executive directors** is not practical as the board needs input from those running the day-to-day operations when making decisions.

Most companies in the UK operate a **unitary board system** where a singular board is in control of the organisation. Companies are free to have as many directors as they feel necessary. Executive directors must beware of **'two hat' syndrome** whereby their roles of **management** and **governance conflict**. A common example occurs during board meetings. These should be reserved for addressing governance issues, but the risk is that they become just another management meeting.

8.5.1 All executive directors

As the name suggests, the board comprises **solely** executive directors. It is common for **small private companies** or **subsidiaries** whose directors are also the shareholders to adopt this structure. A crucial drawback with this approach is that directors both **monitor** and **supervise** their **own performance**.

Without external shareholders to protect, there is little need for non-executive directors as the executives are only **responsible to themselves**. This is not to say that the directors could benefit from the knowledge and experience that non-executive directors would bring to the company.

8.5.2 Majority executive directors

This is the most common board structure in the UK for **publicly listed companies** and is often found in well established organisations. There is a mixture of executive directors (as employees under a contract of service) and non-executive directors (these are not employees and they work under a contract for services). As the name suggests, the executive directors are in the majority numerically.

The **public shareholders** benefit from the independent scrutiny that the non-executives bring, and the board benefits from their knowledge and experience.

Boards tend to be **weighted numerically in favour of executive directors** as executives may feel their security is threatened by being outnumbered. This should not pose a corporate governance problem providing the non-executives have suitably strong personalities.

8.5.3 Majority non-executive directors

Some organisations such as **mutual building societies** adopt this least common board structure. Unlike large, publicly listed organisations whose shareholders are mainly powerful, influential City institutions, mutuals are owned by their members who are normally just individuals.

These **members have little power** by themselves and the organisation may look after their life savings, so it is important for them to have a high proportion of non-executives to ensure decisions are made that **protect their interests**. This board structure is often found in **American** and **Australian** public companies.

8.5.4 Number of directors

Aside from the statutory minimum of one director for any company, there is no maximum number. This can give rise to the **'two-hat syndrome'**. Directors must be careful to act correctly depending on the role they are performing – ie to keep **board meetings** for their **governance functions** and to save **management functions** for the rest of their time.

 Case Study

The Yorkshire Building Society's financial statements to 31 December 2011 states that its board consists of four executive directors and eight non-executive directors.

8.6 German, French and American board structures

Some **jurisdictions** take the split between executive and other directors to its furthest extent.

8.6.1 German boards

Institutional arrangements in German companies are based on a two-tiered board.

(a) A Supervisory Board (Aufsichstrat) consists of 20 members elected by the shareholders. Its role is to monitor the management of the company and is responsible for safeguarding **stakeholders'** interests. A feature of German boards is that employees are elected and sit as members on them. It is not uncommon for shareholders to elect two-thirds of the board and employees one-third. Joint stock (AG) companies with over 2,000 employees divide the votes equally between shareholders and employees. The Chairman of this board is elected by the shareholders and has a deciding vote.

(b) A **Management Board** (Vorstand), is responsible for **independently running** the business and for adding value to it. The board reports to the Supervisory Board in areas such as strategy, profitability, material transactions (on profitability or liquidity) and general business policy.

The board also:

- **Ensures** the business **meets** all its **regulatory obligations**.
- **Prepares resolutions** for meetings.
- **Provides financial statements** for the general meeting.

Members are elected for **five year** terms by the Supervisory Board who advise them and are responsible for their supervision and dismissal. The number of directors depends on the size of the organisation. Small companies have three to five, large companies five to ten.

BPP
LEARNING MEDIA

8.6.2 French boards

Most **French companies** use one of the following three board structures.

(a) **Unitary board** (Conseil D'administration) with the roles of Chairman and Chief Executive Officer rolled into one (the President Director General or PDG). Alternatively, the roles may be separated.

(b) **Unitary board** with the roles of Chairman and Chief Executive Officer separated.

(c) A **two-tier structure** similar to the German model. The Supervisory Board (Conseil De Surveillance) is led by the Chairman and the Management Committee (Directoire) involves the Chief Executive Office (Directeur General).

Boards consist of between **3 and 18 members** and listed companies must comprise two-thirds non-executive officers.

8.6.3 American boards

Most boards in the USA are **unitary** with increasing numbers of non-executive directors as well as directors who are women or from ethnic minorities.

Proposals to introduce **two** (or more**) tier boards** have been particularly **criticised** in the UK and USA as leading to **confusion** and a **lack of accountability**. This has affected the debate on enhancing the role of non-executive directors, with critics claiming that moves to increase the involvement of non-executive directors are a step on the slippery slope towards two-tier boards.

8.7 Directors' duties under corporate governance rules

FAST FORWARD

Corporate governance rules have **not changed** directors' **fiduciary** and **statutory duties**, or their duties of skill and care under common law.

During our study of company law, we saw that **directors owe a number of duties** to the company and its shareholders. You may wish to revisit this area to refresh your memory. This chapter has demonstrated how corporate governance principles although not legally binding, seek to increase the duties of directors still further. These **corporate governance rules do not affect a director's duty under the Companies Act or common law,** but they are far wider reaching. It is possible that a director could breach their duty of care but still comply with corporate governance principles.

8.8 Directors' behaviour

FAST FORWARD

Corporate governance requirements **affect directors' behaviour** in two main areas:

- Increased accountability and responsibility
- Performance related pay

8.8.1 Increased accountability and responsibility

Corporate governance and Companies Act rules created standards of **'best practice'** and a legal code of conduct that all companies, not just listed ones, should follow.

These standards have raised **public expectations** of directors' conduct, and widened the range of stakeholders taking an interest in a company's governance.

Directors now **face increased risk** of:

- **Legal action**, as they are accountable for their actions and responsible to a wider range of stakeholders.

- **Dismissal**, as service contracts are shorter in length and directors must stand for re-election more often.

Directors have had to alter their **behaviour** to counter these increased risks. They are devoting more time to meeting the requirements of 'best practice', to stakeholder relations and their legal duties.

However, this may result in **directors' attention being diverted away** from making the company profitable, potentially damaging the long-term success of the business.

8.8.2 Performance related pay

The use of **performance related pay** has encouraged directors to take decisions that are aligned with the **goals of their shareholders**. For example, shareholders want their company's share price to increase over time. Linking directors' bonuses to an increase in share value can encourage directors to take decisions that will increase the share price.

However, this may mean directors taking **short-term decisions** to achieve bonuses, which in **the long-term may harm** the company. An example of this would be directors cutting prices to achieve higher short-term sales, without a view to future long-term profitability.

Question   Board of directors

Which of the following countries allow the election of employees to boards of directors?

(i)   Germany
(ii)   France
(iii)   USA
(iv)   UK

A   (i) only
B   (i) and (ii)
C   (ii) and (iii)
D   All of the above

Answer

A   Only Germany allows the election of employees to boards of directors.

9 Ethics, law and governance

FAST FORWARD

Ethics, law and corporate governance are all interrelated.

9.1 A brief recap

Following a study of law, we saw that ethics are a set of **moral principles** that guide the behaviour of individuals and businesses. We all have a free choice of how to act, and we look to the standards and norms of our society or profession for advice when we are unsure what is acceptable.

BPP
LEARNING MEDIA

This chapter has developed the concept of **corporate governance**. As management and owners of companies are not necessarily the same people, it is important for management to be encouraged to act in the best interests of the owners and other stakeholders.

9.2 Interaction of ethics, law and corporate governance

By pulling together all we have already studied, we find that ethics are values and principles that society **expects** companies and individuals to follow and laws are rules that the legislators have determined that companies and individuals **must** follow.

Corporate governance requirements may be viewed as **additional rules** and guidance for companies and individuals. They bridge the gap between what the law requires and what society expects.

9.2.1 The law and ethics

Ethical and moral behaviour is very often **codified** and therefore legally binding. This occurs where the ethical position is so important that the legislators decide that it must be protected by the force of law.

For example, society believes it is **ethically wrong** for those who commit crimes (such as drug smuggling) to profit from their illegal actions. Legislation was brought in and now it is now an offence in the UK to **launder the proceeds of crime**, in other words making illegal gains appear legitimate.

The rules on **insider dealing**, where those who possess 'inside information' about a company and who gain by the sale or purchase of its shares whilst using this information, is another example. Society believes it is **unfair** for those 'lucky' individuals with inside knowledge to take advantage of their position at the expense of others.

However we have also seen that legislators have been unwilling or unable to legislate in all areas of business. For reasons of **public policy** or **sheer complexity** areas such as auditors taking on lucrative consultancy work (and thereby potentially compromising their independence) are not regulated by law. In such cases, **regulators** (such as in this case, the APB) step in to provide guidance and professional standards that '**fill the gaps**' left by legislation. We have also seen how the UK Corporate Governance Code performs a similar role in corporate governance.

9.2.2 The law and corporate governance

The **law** provides the **structure** for the internal regulation of companies, such as the duty of directors to be open about their dealings and it also provides a **mechanism** of control, for example the ability of shareholders to dismiss the directors and to exercise control of the company through the articles and meetings.

The **main legal regulations** that affect companies are as follows.

Name	Contains rules on:
Companies Act 2006	Registering, administering and operating companies..
Model articles of association	Interaction between the shareholders and directors
Company Directors Disqualification Act 1986	Behaviour and conduct of directors. Breach of its rules may lead to the disqualification of directors.
The Criminal Justice Act 1993 and Money Laundering Regulations 2007	Criminal activities such as money laundering and insider dealing.
Insolvency Act 1986 (amended by the Enterprise Act 2002)	Individual and corporate insolvency and administration - the alternative to winding up.
UK Listing Authority Listing Rules	Listing rules such as admission and disclosure requirements

Name	Contains rules on:
(previously the Stock Exchange Listing Regulations 1984)	
EU Council Directives 2004/25 and 2004/109	Take-overs (2004/25) and transparency requirements for listed companies (2004/109)

However, these regulations are often **circumvented** and **loopholes** may be found that allow unscrupulous directors to bend the rules. To that extent, the law has been unsuccessful and must be supplemented by **corporate governance**.

We have already seen that in the UK, corporate governance is contained in the UK Corporate Governance Code. *Gower and Davies* describe such rules as '**soft law**' due to the fact that companies may avoid compliance with the code if they explain why. This leaves a problem. What can be done if a company avoids compliance with the code? Is there anyway of enforcing it? Without any legal teeth, **nothing legally** can be done. At present, the government or any of its bodies (such as the FSA) cannot interfere. Only the shareholders can take action against boards of directors. The Stock Exchange listing rules will enforce the '**comply or explain**' procedure, but this will not stop non-compliance providing it is disclosed. However, if enough companies continue with non-compliance, the government may step in and make the rules legally binding. As companies tend to prefer **voluntary codes**, this threat might be enough to ensure compliance in most organisations.

However, the law is moving to catch up with corporate governance rules and the **2006 Companies Act** introduced new rules that should:

(a)   Encourage **shareholder activism** and involvement and encourage a **long-term investment culture**
(b)   Encourage a **think small first** approach and **better regulation** of companies
(c)   Make companies **quicker to set up** and **easier to run**
(d)   Improve **flexibility** for the future

The only group with any real power currently are **shareholders**. In theory they could remove directors if they do not agree with their non-compliance. However, as we have seen, shareholder apathy might allow the directors to get away with things. In reality it is probably **market forces** which acts to maintain compliance. Non-compliant companies are more **risky** investments as controls over directors and operations are poor. This may reduce the number of willing investors, causing a **fall in share price** – something directors would not want as it may mean lower bonuses for them.

9.2.3 Business ethics – a grey area

The law has had even less effect on the area of **business ethics**. These are **contemporary principles** regarding **morality**, **ethics** and **standards of behaviour**, that are not enforceable by the law. For example, in theory auditors have no real reason to report financial or control problems that they find in a company. They are more interested in the company continuing to operate and employing them as auditors. Publicising problems may be disastrous for confidence in the company, possibly causing it to fail. The fact that the auditors published the problems would antagonise the directors and may lead them to taking their business elsewhere. It is the role of **professional codes of ethics** (such as CIMA's) to **regulate the behaviour** of members and ensure the ethical approach is taken.

9.2.4 Corporate social responsibility

Businesses, particularly large ones, are subject to increasing expectations that they will exercise **social responsibility**. This is an ill-defined concept, but appears to focus on the provision of **specific benefits** to society in general, such as charitable donations, the creation or preservation of employment, and spending on environmental improvement or maintenance. A great deal of the pressure is created by the activity of **minority action groups** and is aimed at businesses because they are perceived to possess extensive resources.

BPP
LEARNING MEDIA

The momentum of such arguments is now so great that the notion of social responsibility has become almost inextricably confused with the matter of ethics. It is important to remember the distinction. Social responsibility and ethical behaviour **are not** the same thing.

In this context, you should remember that a business managed with the sole objective of maximising shareholder wealth can be run in just as **ethical** a fashion as one in which far wider stakeholder responsibility is assumed. On the other hand, there is no doubt that many large businesses have behaved irresponsibly in the past and some continue to do so.

9.3 Levels of regulation

Another way of examining how the **subjects are related** is to look at how regulated they are.

The relationship between law, governance, social responsibility and ethics			
Law	Corporate governance	Social responsibility	Ethics
Mandatory rules that individuals and companies **must follow**. The **minimum level of behaviour** society allows.	**Publicly listed companies only** are regulated. Others are **encouraged** to follow 'best practice'.	**No regulation.** Individuals and companies have a free choice. **Some social pressure** to act in a socially responsible manner.	**Values and principles.** Individuals and companies are **expected to follow**. Adopting an ethical position is down to free choice.
More regulation, less freedom of choice.		Less regulation more freedom of choice.	

From the table above we can see that the law is highly regulated, corporate governance is less regulated and, social responsibility and ethics have no regulation as adoption is down to free choice. In practice, **corporate governance and social responsibility policies** are developed from **ethical codes of practice** and are related to the needs of financial and interest stakeholders, the environment, community and any philanthropic activities which the organisation supports.

9.3.1 Ethical codes and the law

There is an important **distinction** to be drawn between **behaviour** which is **regulated by ethics** (such as codes of conduct or ethical codes) and **behaviour** which is **regulated by the law** (such as contracts or criminal law). The distinction should be quite obvious – the state, or other individuals cannot enforce behaviour covered by ethical codes or codes of conduct because they have no right to do so in law. An ethical code or code of conduct is not legally binding.

In **contract law**, another organisation or individual can take action against another party that they have a contract with because the contract created a **legal obligation** to behave in a particular way. There is a similar obligation created in the **law of tort** and **criminal law**, although the medium which sets out the rules on behaviour is common law (in the case of tort) and common law and statute (in the case of criminal law) rather than a contract.

9.4 Effect on corporate behaviour

Perhaps more importantly, we should examine the effect each has on **corporate behaviour**. An important point to remember is that companies **do not** make decisions by themselves. Human individuals (usually the directors) make the significant policy choices.

The following diagram demonstrates the **interaction** of law, ethics and social responsibility on the company.

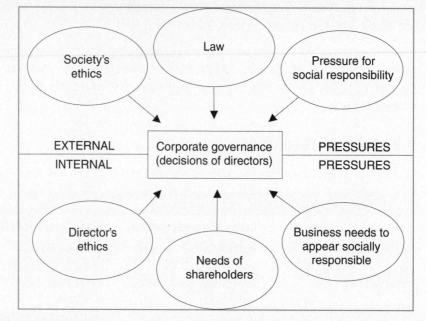

We can see that many factors influence the behaviour of a company. The main external influence is the **law** as it sets the minimum level of behaviour expected. Society's **ethical views** and needs for **social responsibility** will have an influence as companies will respect them as far as necessary to remain profitable.

Directors are greatly influenced by the need to deliver the results that shareholders require, for example increasing the company's share price or dividend. To achieve this may require breaking their own **personal ethical beliefs**.

Remember, **businesses do not necessarily have to act ethically**. In most cases they are run for the benefit of the owners (the shareholders) rather than for the benefit of society as a whole.

Question

UK regulations

Which of the following contains legislation concerning the registration, administration and operation of UK companies?

A   The Enterprise Act 2002
B   The Financial Services Act 1986
C   The Insolvency Act 1986
D   The Companies Act 2006

Answer

D   The Companies Act 2006 contains rules concerning the registration, administration and operation of companies in the UK.

9.5 Offences in relation to running a business

In response to the risk that those involved in running a business **act in their own interests** or **against the interests of others**, the law has introduced two number of offences – fraudulent and wrongful trading.

9.5.1 Fraudulent trading

This **criminal offence** occurs under the **Companies Act 2006** where a company has traded with **intent to defraud creditors** or for any fraudulent purpose. Offenders are liable to imprisonment or a fine (s 993).

There is also a **civil offence** of the same name under s 213 of the Insolvency Act 1986 but it only applies to companies which are in liquidation. Under this offence courts may declare that **any persons** who were knowingly parties to carrying on the business in this fashion shall be liable for the debts of the company.

Various rules have been established to determine **what is fraudulent trading**:

(a)   Only persons who **take the decision** to carry on the company's business in this way or play some active part are liable.

(b)   **'Carrying on business'** can include a single transaction and also the mere payment of debts as distinct from making trading contracts.

(c)   The offence relates not only to **defrauding creditors**, but also to carrying on a business for the purpose of any kind of fraud: *R v Kemp 1988.*

Under the civil offence, if the liquidator considers that there has been fraudulent trading they should apply to the court for an order that those responsible are liable to make good to the company all or some specified part of the **company's debts**.

9.5.2 Wrongful trading

The problem which faced the creditors of an insolvent company before the introduction of **'wrongful trading'** was that it was exceptionally difficult to prove fraud. Therefore a further civil liability for 'wrongful trading' was introduced, which means that the director will have to make such contribution to the company's assets as the court sees fit.

Directors will be liable if the **liquidator** proves the following.

(a)   The director(s) of the insolvent company **knew**, or **should have known**, that there was **no reasonable prospect** that the **company** could **have avoided going into insolvent liquidation**. This means that directors cannot claim they lacked knowledge if their lack of knowledge was a result of failing to comply with Companies Act requirements, for example preparation of accounts: *Re Produce Marketing Consortium 1989* (see below).

(b)   The director(s) did not take **sufficient steps** to minimise the potential loss to the creditors.

Directors will be deemed to know that the company could not avoid insolvent liquidation if that would have been the conclusion of a **reasonably diligent person** with the **general knowledge**, **skill and experience** that might reasonably be expected of a person carrying out that particular director's duties. If the director has greater than usual skill then he will be judged with reference to his own capacity.

Chapter Roundup

- **Corporate governance** is the system by which organisations are directed and controlled. *The Cadbury Committee.*

- Corporate governance problems can result from the **agency problem** and **lack of shareholder activism**.

- **Key drivers** for the development of corporate governance.

  - Increasing internationalisation and globalisation
  - Issues concerning financial reporting
  - An increasing number of high profile corporate scandals and collapses

- The **USA, UK** and **Europe** have taken **different approaches** to corporate governance.

- The following **symptoms** can indicate poor corporate governance.

  - Domination by a single individual
  - Lack of involvement of board
  - Lack of adequate control function
  - Lack of supervision
  - Lack of independent scrutiny
  - Lack of contact with shareholders
  - Emphasis on short-term profitability
  - Misleading accounts and information

- The **main source** of corporate governance in the **UK** at this time is the **UK Corporate Governance Code**.

- There is a continuing debate over the form corporate governance should take. Some believe in **fundamental principles**, others that **detailed rules** are required.

- The board should be responsible for taking major **policy** and **strategic** decisions.

- Directors should have a **mix of skills** and their **performance** should be assessed regularly.

- Appointments should be conducted by formal procedures administered by a **nomination committee**.

- The choice of **board structure** in the UK can be split into three options, according to *Tricker (1996).*
  - All executive directors
  - Majority executive directors
  - Majority non-executive directors

- **Corporate governance** rules have **not changed** directors' **fiduciary** and **statutory duties**, or their duties of skill and care under common law.

- Corporate governance requirements are **affecting directors' behaviour** in two main areas:

  - Increased accountability and responsibility
  - Performance related pay

- **Ethics**, **law** and **corporate governance** are all **interrelated**.

BPP
LEARNING MEDIA

1   Corporate governance is the system by which organisations are .... and ....

2   Which two of the following are symptoms of poor corporate governance?

    A   Lack of board involvement

    B   Bonuses for directors

    C   The finance director also performing the role of company secretary

    D   Inadequate supervision

3   The Turnbull Committee findings were incorporated into the 1998 Combined Code.

    True   ☐

    False   ☐

4   According to the UK's Corporate Governance Code: Independent .... should be appointed to balance the board.

5   Which of the following is often cited as the main cause of corporate governance problems?

    A   Increasing profitability of listed companies

    B   The separation of ownership and control in companies

    C   'Fat cat' salaries of executive directors

    D   Lack of enforcement of the UK Corporate Governance Code

6   Audit committees are generally staffed by a company's auditors.

    True   ☐

    False   ☐

7   Gower and Davies described the UK regulations on corporate governance as.

    A   Hard law

    B   Natural law

    C   Universal law

    D   Soft law

8   German companies operate a .... board consisting of a .... board and a...................... board.

9   The UK has taken a rules-based approach to corporate governance whereas the USA has taken a principles-based approach.

    True   ☐

    False   ☐

10   Corporate Governance issues came to prominence in the USA, UK and Europe after the Year 2000.

    True   ☐

    False   ☐

1   Directed, controlled

2   A. Lack of board involvement. D. Inadequate supervision.

3   False – they were incorporated in the 2003 Combined Code

4   Non-executive directors.

5   B. The main cause cited is the agency problem as a result of the separate of ownership and control of companies.

6   False. They are generally staffed by non-executive directors.

7   D. They describe the rules as 'soft law'.

8   Two-tiered, supervisory, management.

9   False. The UK has taken a principles-based approach as seen in its Corporate Governance Code whereas the American approach is to use rules, embodied in the Sarbanes-Oxley legislation.

10 False. Corporate governance issues came to prominence in the 1980s,

Now try the questions below from the Question Bank

Number
Q91
Q92
Q93
Q94
Q95

Question bank

BPP
LEARNING MEDIA

1   What is the burden of proof in civil proceedings?

A   The decision of the majority
B   Beyond all reasonable doubt
C   A unanimous decision
D   On the balance of probabilities

2   Which of the following statements about judicial precedent is incorrect?

A   A County Court cannot create binding precedents
B   A statement *obiter dicta* is of persuasive authority
C   Decisions of the European Court of Justice bind all English courts except the Supreme Court
D   The Supreme Court is entitled to depart from its own precedents in exceptional cases

3   What is the correct name of the approval given to all new Acts of Parliament?

A   Crown Assent
B   Prime Minister's Assent
C   Royal Assent
D   Judiciary Assent

4   Judges may use a number of aids to help them interpret statutes. Which of the following is an intrinsic aid?

A   The preamble
B   Hansard
C   A dictionary
D   The Interpretation Act 1978

5   Which of the following types of European Union law is directly applicable on a member state?

A   Regulations
B   Directives
C   Annulment actions
D   Failure to act actions

6   Which of the following must the claimant show, amongst other things, in order to succeed in an action for negligence?

(i)   The defendant owed him a duty of care
(ii)   There was no contractual relationship between the parties
(iii)   There was a breach of the duty of care
(iv)   There was no contributory negligence

A   (i), (ii) and (iii)
B   (i), (iii) and (iv)
C   (i) and (iii)
D   (ii) and (iii)

7   Since the decision in *The Wagon Mound 1961* the test for the recoverability of damages in general tort is that

A   The loss or damage was reasonably foreseeable by the defendant only

B   The loss or damage was reasonably foreseeable by both claimant and defendant

C   The loss or damage was the direct and natural consequence of the defendant's breach of duty

D   The loss or damage caused by something under the defendant's control was of a kind which would not have been suffered but for the defendant's negligence

8   Which of the following summarises the decision in *Caparo v Dickman 1990*?

A   The auditor's duty extends to potential investors and to existing shareholders increasing their stakes

B   The auditor's duty extends to potential investors but not to existing shareholders increasing their stakes

C   The auditor's duty does not extend to potential investors but only to existing shareholders increasing their stakes

D   The auditor's duty does not extend to potential investors nor to existing shareholders increasing their stakes

9   Which of the following are true circumstances that are enough for courts to ignore an otherwise legitimate duty of care?

Circumstance	True	False
Against public policy		
No case law to support duty		
Insufficient proximity		
Lack of judicial support for duty		

10   Solid Products (SP) Ltd makes a range of industrial machines. It sold its latest product 'CVY 18' to Perkplex (P) Ltd for use in its factory. Soon after installation it malfunctioned causing injury to the employee operating it, who was not wearing the specified safety helmet and clothing.

Which of the following statements is correct?

A   The employee cannot sue SP Ltd as the machine was sold to P Ltd.

B   SP Ltd will be found liable for damages to the employee if negligence can be proved. However, the amount of damages may be limited.

C   P Ltd will be found negligent but can recover any damages it is liable for by suing SP Ltd.

D   SP nor P Ltd will be liable for the injuries as the employee failed to use the safety equipment.

11   Which statement regarding codified legal systems is correct?

A   There is no distinction between those who draft the law and those who apply it
B   Judges decisions can never be influenced by previous cases
C   Codified law is detailed and complex
D   Judges are involved in judicial review

BPP
LEARNING MEDIA

12   Judges in which European country are appointed at the start of their legal career?

   A   Germany
   B   Greece
   C   Denmark
   D   France

13   The role of the United Nations Economic Commission for Europe (UNECE) is to:

   A   Standardise investment procedures between the UN and EU
   B   Harmonise policies and technical details within the EU
   C   Develop trade relations between the EU and nations outside the EU
   D   Integrate the EU within the wider global economy

14   Which country's legal system involves mediation committees?

   A   Sri Lanka
   B   China
   C   Malaysia
   D   Russia

15   Which of the following is not a category of behaviour recognised by Muslims under Sharia law?

   A   Tolerated
   B   Obligatory
   C   Meritorious
   D   Reprehensible

16   There are three essential elements to a valid contract. Which of the following is **not** an essential element?

   A   All parties must be in agreement.
   B   All parties must intend to create legal relations.
   C   All contracts must be written.
   D   All parties must provide consideration.

17   In which of the following circumstances has a valid contract been created?

   A   X places an advert in his local paper for a cabinet for sale priced at £50. Y Sees the advert, phones X and tells him she will pay £45 and will come round the next day to collect it.

   B   X places a sign on his boat that states it is for sale at a price of £10,000. Y says she will pay him £8,000 but X refuses. Y agrees to the original price of £10,000.

   C   X tells Y that she can buy his music collection for £500 and that the offer is open until Monday. On Monday Y accepts X's offer but finds that the music was sold on Sunday.

   D   X offers to sell Y his car and keeps the offer open until Friday. Y emails acceptance on Wednesday but X does not access the message until Saturday.

18 Fill in the missing words using the box below.

.... consideration is a promise given for a promise.

.... consideration is anything done before a promise in return.

.... consideration is an act in return for a promise.

Consideration must be ....

Executed	Past
Executory	Sufficient

19 Which of the following statements is/are correct?

(i)   The parties to a social or domestic arrangement are presumed not to have intended the arrangement to be legally enforceable

(ii)   The parties to a commercial transaction are presumed to have intended the arrangement to be legally enforceable

A   (i) only
B   (ii) only
C   Both (i) and (ii)
D   Neither (i) nor (ii)

20 Which of the following remedies is available for fraudulent misrepresentation but not negligent misrepresentation?

A   Rescission of the contract
B   Damages under the Misrepresentation Act 1967
C   Damages under an action for the tort of deceit
D   Damages under common law

21 Which of the following statements is inaccurate?

A   Conditions and warranties are the two basic types of express term

B   A contract must expressly contain all essential terms

C   A representation is something which induces the formation of a contract but which does not become a term of the contract

D   Terms can be implied into a contract from trade practice or custom

22 DTZ Ltd has broken a contractual term contained in its contract with EVT Ltd. The term which has been broken is a warranty. Which of the following remedies are true remedies in this situation?

Remedy	True	False
EVT Ltd can recover damages from DTZ Ltd and avoid the contract.		
EVT may only recover damages.		
EVT can consider the contract as repudiated.		
EVT may consider the contract as repudiated or recover damages.		

BPP
LEARNING MEDIA

23   Which of the following types of contract does the Unfair Contract Terms Act 1977 apply to?

    A   Business contracts
    B   Contracts for insurance
    C   Contracts for the transfer of patents
    D   Contracts for the transfer of an interest in land

24   Which of the following is **not** an implied condition in contracts for the sale of goods?

    A   The seller has a right to sell the goods
    B   The goods correspond with the description
    C   The goods are of merchantable quality
    D   (In the case of a sale by sample) The bulk corresponds with the sample provided

25   Complete and exact performance is the normal method of discharging a contract, but a number of exceptions have been developed by the courts to ensure that the interests of both parties are protected. Which of the following is not one of those exceptions?

    A   Where the promisor substantially performs the contract
    B   Where the promisee accepts partial performance
    C   Where the promisee prevents performance by the promisor
    D   Where one party performs later than agreed and time is of the essence

26   The Law Reform (Frustrated Contracts) Act 1943 sets out a number of rules as to the effect of a frustrated contract. Which of the following rules are contained in the Act?

    (i)   Any money paid by X to Y before frustration is to be repaid

    (ii)   Sums actually due under the contract at the time of frustration remain payable but the court may order them to be cancelled

    (iii)   A party liable to repay sums may, at his option, set off his expenses incurred in performance up to the time of frustration

    (iv)   A party whose right to sums due which is cancelled may recover expenses at the court's discretion

    A   (i), (ii) and (iv) only
    B   (i) and (iii) only
    C   (i) and (iv) only
    D   All of the above

27   In a case of anticipatory breach, which of the following is open to the injured party?

    (i)   To treat the contract as discharged
    (ii)   To allow the contract to continue until there is an actual breach

    A   (i) only
    B   (ii) only
    C   (i) or (ii)
    D   Neither (i) nor (ii)

28 Fill in the missing words using the box below.

.... is a simple action to recover the agreed sum if the breach of contract is failure to pay the price.

.... is an equitable remedy which requires that a negative condition in the agreement be fulfilled.

.... is a claim where the injured party claims the value of their work.

......................is a remedy which requires the party in breach to fulfil their side of the contract.

Injunction	Action for the price
Specific performance	Quantum meruit

29 If an injured party wishes to rescind the contract they must do so within

A   A reasonable time
B   Three months
C   Six months
D   One year

30 Bertram is in breach of his contractual obligation to repair Alexander's car. In respect of which of the following might Alexander recover damages?

(i)   Loss of enjoyment
(ii)   Inconvenience
(iii)   Distress
(iv)   Cost of repairing the car elsewhere

A   (i), (ii) and (iv) only
B   (ii) and (iv) only
C   (iv) only
D   All of the above

31 Which factors may a court look at when deciding if a person is employed or self employed? Select all that apply.

A   Is the person paid a salary?
B   Does the person have control over the way they perform their duties?
C   Does the person have a business bank account?
D   Does the employer provide the tools for the employee to work with?

32 Employees have implied duties to their employers, which one of the following is **not** an implied duty?

A   Reasonable competence
B   Personal service
C   Obedience to instructions
D   Indemnify the employer against loss or damage caused while working

33 Employers are often vicariously liable for the acts of their employees. In what circumstance would they **not** be held liable?

A   When the employee is a self-employed contractor and the work is exceptionally risky
B   When the employee disobeys orders as to how they shall perform the work
C   When the employee commits a crime outside the course of their employment
D   When the employee defrauds a third party whilst working

BPP
LEARNING MEDIA

34 Which of the following can be found on an employee's written statement of particulars of their employment?

Select all that apply.

A The employer and employee's name
B The date the employment commenced
C The employee's hours of work
D Health and safety rules

35 Which of the following is an employee permitted to do after leaving a particular employer?

A Use special skills that they acquired as a result of the employment
B Act against a restraint of trade clause which is reasonable
C Disclose specific trade secrets to obtain new employment
D Disclose specific trade secrets to third parties without restriction

36 Which of the following is an example of indirect sex discrimination?

A Advertising a job abroad where local laws or customs make it difficult for a woman to perform her duties
B Imposing qualification requirements for promotion that men are more likely to have than women
C Stating 'men only should apply' for a lavatory attendant's position in a male lavatory
D Not promoting a woman because she is pregnant

37 How many weeks statutory notice is an employee entitled to after one month's continuous employment?

A No notice
B One week
C Two weeks
D Four weeks

38 Unfair dismissal protection is usually only available to employees with a certain period of continuous service. Which of the following are exceptions to the rule? Select all that apply.

A Where the employee is a safety representative and has been penalised for carrying out legitimate health and safety activities

B When an employee is denied a statutory right

C When an employee is dismissed for taking part in an unofficial strike

D When the employee is pregnant

39 In the context of unfair dismissal, what is a punitive award?

A An award of compensation calculated on the same scale as redundancy pay

B An award given on common law principles of damages for breach of contract so that loss may be compensated

C An award compensating the employee for loss caused by the employer's refusal to reinstate the employee following an order from the tribunal

D An award compensating the employee for loss and for distress caused by dismissal on the grounds of race and/or sex

40   Which of the following are rights that are enjoyed by all females under employment law?

Select all that apply.

A   Pregnancy as an automatically unfair reason for dismissal regardless of length of employment.

B   Equal entitlement to training as male employees.

C   Equal chance of promotion as male employees.

D   Equal chance of being recruited as male employees.

41   Which of the following statements is an inaccurate description of a partnership?

A   A partnership is a relationship which subsists between parties carrying on a business in common with a view of profit

B   A partnership business may be any trade, occupation or profession but must be more than a single transaction

C   Every partner is liable without limit for the debts of the partnership (except in the case of a registered limited partnership)

D   A written partnership agreement is not a legal requirement

42   What important rule of law was established in the case of *Salomon v Salomon & Co Ltd 1897*?

A   A solicitor who is also a shareholder cannot rely on the articles of association in his capacity as solicitor

B   Acts beyond the capacity of the company are *ultra vires* and void

C   A company is a separate legal person distinct from its members

D   The company, acting in general meeting, is the only proper claimant in an action to protect its rights or property

43   Which of the following is **not** a difference between public and private companies?

A   A public company has six months after its accounting reference period to produce its statutory accounts; a private company has nine months.

B   A public company must hold an AGM within six months of their financial year-end, a private company must hold one every calendar year.

C   Public companies can offer their shares to the public, private companies cannot.

D   Public companies must have two directors, private companies just need one.

44   Indicate which of the following are circumstances where the court will ignore the concept of separate legal personality to enforce the law.

Circumstance	True	False
To find the directors of a public company personally liable for allowing the company to trade without a trading certificate.		
To reveal a quasi-partnership.		
Where the company has breached advertising standards rules.		
Where it is in the public interest.		

BPP
LEARNING MEDIA

45 Some business organisations do not have share capital but instead the members undertake to contribute to the liabilities of a company on winding-up. Such an organisation is known as

    A   A Community Interest Company
    B   A Company Limited by Guarantee
    C   An Unlimited Liability Company
    D   A Statutory Corporation

46 Which of the following statements concerning the formation of a company is correct?

    A   The company exists once the Articles of Association have been sent to the registrar.

    B   The company legally exists when the promoters send the Certificate of Incorporation to the registrar.

    C   All companies must submit a Memorandum of Association to the registrar as part of the formation process.

    D   A registration fee is payable to the registrar by the company on receipt of the Certificate of Incorporation.

47 Is a promoter of a company ever permitted to make a profit from their position?

    A   No. Promoters may not profit from their position.

    B   Yes, if they acquire property before becoming promoter and disclose the profit if they sell the property to the company they promoted.

    C   Yes, promoters are permitted to profit as a result of their position without the need to disclose it.

    D   Yes, providing it is in the normal course of business.

48 How long does a company have to deliver its Annual Return after the return date?

    A   7 days
    B   14 days
    C   21 days
    D   28 days

49 A public company should keep accounting records for

    A   Three years
    B   Six years
    C   Nine years
    D   Twelve years

50 Which of the following registers is a company required by law to keep?
Select all that apply.

    A   Register of Directors' home addresses.
    B   Register of Debentureholders.
    C   Register of Members
    D   Register of Charges

51 A business has been registered under the name 'The Mark Jones Partnership Co Ltd'. What type of business organisation must this be?

    A   A partnership
    B   A private limited company
    C   A public limited company
    D   Any of the above as this is a business name

52 Which bodies are bound by the articles of association?

(i)   The members are bound to the company
(ii)   The members are bound to other members
(iii)   The company is bound to third parties
(iv)   The members are bound to third parties

A   (i) and (ii)
B   (i) and (iii)
C   (i), (ii) and (iv)
D   All of the above

53 What are the consequences of a company failing to provide Articles of Association when it applies to the registrar for formation?

A   It does not legally exist until Articles are registered.

B   It will be incorporated with standard articles relevant to the type of company formed.

C   It will be incorporated with standard articles which must be amended by the members as soon as practicable after registration.

D   It exists legally but is not permitted to trade.

54 Which of the following describe the default objects of a company?

A   They are completely unrestricted, any lawful activity is permitted.
B   They permit general commercial activities.
C   They permit any activities set out in the constitution of the company.
D   They permit any activities that the directors have authority to contract the company to.

55 Which of the following statements are true or false?

Statement	True	False
A company may change its name by special resolution.		
A company may change its name by any procedure its constitution allows		

56 How much paid up share capital do the members of a public company need before they can requisition a general meeting?

A   5%
B   10%
C   15%
D   20%

57 Which of the following resolutions needs special notice?

A   An increase in share capital
B   To wind up the company
C   To remove an auditor
D   To elect a new director

BPP
LEARNING MEDIA

58   Which of the following do **not** need to be passed by special resolution?

A   To reduce a company's share capital
B   To add restrictions to a company's objects
C   To wind up a company
D   To agree the company's accounts

59   Who has the authority to call a company general meeting?

Select all that apply.

A   The company secretary
B   The members holding the required share capital or voting rights
C   A court
D   An auditor

60   What is the most common resolution passed by private companies formed under Companies Act 2006?

A   Ordinary
B   Special
C   Written
D   Ordinary with special notice

61   Which of the following is **not** automatically qualified under the Companies Act to be company secretary to a company?

A   A member of CIMA
B   A person who has been secretary of a public company for two of the five years previous to appointment
C   Any person who appears to the directors to be capable of being company secretary by virtue of having held any other position
D   A solicitor in the UK

62   A director may be removed from office under s 168 of the Companies Act 2006 by:

A   Ordinary resolution with the usual notice
B   Special resolution with the usual notice
C   Ordinary resolution with special notice
D   Special resolution with special notice

63   The directors of a company have used their powers for an improper purpose, although they have acted *bona fide*. A general meeting can:

A   Do nothing that will retrospectively authorise the action
B   Authorise the action by ordinary resolution
C   Authorise the action by special resolution only
D   Authorise the action by special resolution with special notice

64   Which of the following is **not** an example of conduct leading to disqualification of a director?

A   Insider dealing
B   Failure to keep proper accounting records
C   A breach of statutory provisions requiring accounts and other documents to be registered
D   Failure to read the company's accounts

65 Which of the following are statutory duties of directors under the Companies Act 2006?

Select all that apply.

A   Duty to promote the success of the company
B   Duty to promote the health and safety of employees
C   Duty to exercise independent judgement
D   Duty to avoid conflicts of interest

66 Which of the following is a correct summary of the rule in *Foss v Harbottle 1843*?

A   The company as a person separate from its members is the only proper claimant in an action to protect its rights or property and the company in general meeting must decide whether to bring such legal proceedings

B   Any member of a company may apply to the court for relief on the grounds that the company's affairs are being conducted in a manner which is unfairly prejudicial to the interests of the members

C   A member who is dissatisfied with the directors or controlling shareholders over the management of the company may petition the court for a winding up on the ground that it is just and equitable to do so

D   A member may sue the company to enforce his personal rights against it, for example the right to vote

67 In an action brought on the grounds of fraud on the minority, it must be shown that:

A   Those who appropriated the company's property are in control of the company

B   Those who appropriated the company's property held sufficient voting rights to exert a 'significant influence' over the company's affairs

C   Those who are bringing the action hold at least 5% of the voting rights

D   Those who are bringing the action hold at least 5% of the voting rights and have suffered a personal loss in their capacity as members

68 Benefits from a derivative action under s260 of the Companies Act 2006 accrue to

A   The company only
B   The members only
C   The company and the members only
D   The members and the directors only

69 A minority of members feel that their company has been managed in a way which unfairly prejudices them. Which of the following remedies are available to them?

Select all that apply.

A   Petition for a court order instructing the company to purchase their shares
B   Petition the court for the company to be wound up
C   Sue the wrongdoers. This option is always available to minorities
D   Take up a derivative action

70 Courts will intervene in cases where conduct has found to be to be unfairly prejudicial. Which one of the following is **not** unfairly prejudicial conduct?

A   Failure to call a meeting
B   Non-compliance with Stock Exchange listing rules
C   Making an inaccurate statement to shareholders
D   Payment of excessive directors bonuses

BPP
LEARNING MEDIA

71 Which of the following defines 'issued share capital'?

A   The type, class, number and amount of the shares which a company may issue as empowered by its constitution

B   The type, class, number and amount of the shares held by the shareholders

C   The amount which the company has required shareholders to pay on the issued shares of the company

D   The amount which shareholders are deemed to have paid on the shares issued and called up

72 Which of the following is prohibited by law in the case of private companies?

A   The issue of shares as fully paid up in consideration for less than their nominal value

B   The issue of shares in consideration of goodwill

C   The issue of shares for goods which are overvalued notwithstanding that the directors are acting honestly and reasonably

D   The issue of shares for more than their nominal value

73 When purchasing its own shares, a private company cannot use

A   Capital
B   Distributable profits
C   Directors' loans
D   Proceeds from a fresh issue

74 Which of the following statements regarding the provision of financial assistance by a company to purchase its own shares are true or false?

Statement	True	False
Private companies are generally permitted to give assistance to third parties.		
Public companies are generally not permitted to give assistance to third parties.		
A private company in a group may always give assistance to its holding company.		
A public subsidiary company may never give assistance to its parent company.		

75 Which of the following statements best describes a shareholder's pre-emption rights?

A   The right to request the company repurchases their shares.
B   The right to be offered new shares issued by the company pro rata to their existing shareholding.
C   The right of first refusal when another shareholder wishes to sell their shares.
D   The right to a dividend payment before other classes of share.

76 Shares and debentures have much in common. Which one of the following is **not** true of the two forms of capital?

A   Both are transferable company securities
B   An offer of either to the public is a prospectus under the Financial Services Act 1986
C   The procedure for the transfer of registered shares and debentures is the same
D   The holders of both are proprietors of the company

77 Which of the following are **not** classed as loan capital?

A   Permanent bank overdrafts
B   Preference shares
C   Unsecured loans
D   Secured loans

78 Which of the following statements regarding fixed charges are correct?

Select all that apply

A   To be valid, a fixed charge must be registered within 21 days of creation.
B   Fixed charges for land must be registered with HM Land Registry.
C   Fixed charges rank for priority on order of value, highest value takes priority over lowest value.
D   A holder of a fixed charge has priority over all other creditors.

79 How long has a company to respond to an inspection request to see the register of debentureholders?

A   Five days
B   Seven days
C   Nine days
D   Fourteen days

80 Which of the following is **not** an event which causes a floating charge to crystallise?

A   The liquidation of the company.
B   Cessation of business.
C   Appointment of a receiver by the chargee.
D   The crystallisation of another floating charge.

81 How does a framework-based approach to a code of ethics differ from a rules-based approach?

A   A rules-based approach is based around general principles

B   A framework-based approach prescribes general guidelines on how to handle certain situations

C   A rules-based approach is designed to cope with constantly evolving circumstances

D   A framework-based approach requires members to learn specific rules covering every conceivable situation

82 Which statement describes the ethical principle of integrity?

A   The principle of straightforwardness and honesty in all dealings
B   The principle of freedom from conflicts of interest
C   The principle of ensuring work is as accurate as possible
D   The principle of maintaining security of information

83 Which statement describes the ethical principle of objectivity?

A   The principle of avoiding situations that may discredit the profession
B   The principle of ensuring you are capable of performing the work
C   The principle of impartiality and avoiding the influence of others whilst working
D   The principle of avoiding the use of information obtained in the course of work for your own advantage

BPP
LEARNING MEDIA

84   Independence is an important quality for accountants to demonstrate when providing assurance services. The two key elements of independence are

    A   Mind and appearance
    B   Thought and appearance
    C   Mind and thought
    D   None of the above

85   The Committee of Standards in Public Life set out seven principles that individuals employed in the public sector should follow. Which of the following are included in these principles?

    Select all that apply.

    A   Selflessness
    B   Openness
    C   Professionalism
    D   Objectivity

86   Donald's company is moving offices. During the move he finds his computer (which contains the payroll budgets) has been moved and he will not have access to it for a couple of days. The human resources director has requested information from the budgets for an important meeting today. Donald thinks he can remember the information but is not 100% sure of it. What should Donald do?

    A   Refuse to provide the information
    B   Provide the information from memory
    C   Provide the information with a disclaimer on its accuracy
    D   Re-calculate the information quickly

87   What ethical principle should CIMA members take particular care of protecting when seeking professional help to resolve an ethical conflict?

    A   Objectivity
    B   Confidentially
    C   Professional behaviour
    D   Due care

88   What should a solution to an ethical conflict be?

    A   Acceptable to the employer
    B   Authorised by CIMA
    C   Expressly permitted in IFAC's ethical code
    D   Consistent with fundamental principles

89   When should a CIMA member consider resigning from their job due to an ethical conflict with their employer?

    A   If their employer suggests it is a good idea
    B   Before consulting with senior people in the organisation
    C   If changing roles or departments is not an option or will not end their association with the issue
    D   Resignation should never be considered

90 Many ethical dilemmas occur due to conflicting sets of values. Which of the following values may cause such dilemmas?

Select all that apply.

A   Personal values
B   Societal values
C   Professional values
D   Corporate values

91 According to the UK Corporate Governance Code, what two board committees should companies have?

A   Nomination and remuneration
B   Audit and election
C   Remuneration and compliance
D   Nomination and disclosure

92 What does the UK Corporate Governance Code recommend regarding the roles of chairman and chief executive?

A   The roles must be combined

B   The chief executive should not go on to be chairman at a later date

C   The chairman's role must be performed by a non-executive director and the chief executive's by an executive director

D   Individuals selected for either role must hold a professional qualification

93 What does the UK Corporate Governance Code recommend regarding the number of non-executive directors on the board?

A   They should be the majority
B   They should be the minority
C   They are not required on the main board
D   They should have enough of a presence so that power and information is not concentrated in one or two individuals

94 A two-tier board of directors comprises

A   An executive board and a management board
B   A supervisory board and a management board
C   A management board and a stakeholder board
D   An executive board and a stakeholder board

95 A company may have a diverse group of stakeholders, all with an interest in it. Indicate which of the following are interest stakeholders and which are financial stakeholders.

Stakeholder	Interest	Financial
Employees		
Competitors		
Customers		
Suppliers		

BPP
LEARNING MEDIA

Answer Bank

BPP
LEARNING MEDIA

1	D	B is the burden of proof in criminal cases. Even in jury cases, in civil proceedings, the judge will direct the jury to decide liability on the balance of probabilities.
2	C	Decisions of the European Court of Justice bind all English Courts including the Supreme Court.
3	C	Royal Assent is given by the King or Queen of England for all Acts of Parliament.
4	A	The Preamble to an Act is found within the Act and is therefore an intrinsic aid.
5	A	Regulations are directly applicable on member states.
6	C	As well as showing the duty of care and breach the claimant must also show that he suffered loss, damage or injury as a consequence of the breach. Where a contractual relationship exists, there may also be a cause of action for breach of contract. Contributory negligence may reduce the amount of damages recoverable but is not a bar to an action being brought.
7	A	In B, the claimant is not required to foresee the results of an act or omission by the defendant. 'Reasonable foresight' is the test, therefore C and D are wrong.
8	D	The duty is owed to the body of shareholders as a whole not individually.
9		

Circumstance	True	False
Against public policy	✓	
No case law to support duty		✓
Insufficient proximity	✓	
Lack of judicial support for duty		✓

The only true answers are: Against public policy and insufficient proximity. A lack of case law or judicial support are not valid reasons.

10	B	SP Ltd is still liable even though it sold the equipment to P Ltd due to the neighbour principle. Contributory negligence on behalf of the employee may reduce the damages it is liable for.
11	D	In civil law systems there is a distinction between those who draft the law (the legislature) and those who apply it (the Judges). Laws are usually general principles drafted in simple language. Previous decisions may be persuasive to judges in similar cases. Judges can review statute law to check it is in accordance with the constitution.
12	D	French legal professionals are appointed judges at the commencement of their legal career.
13	B	The role of the UNECE is to harmonise policies and technical details within the EU.
14	B	China uses mediation committees in rural and urban areas to hear the vast majority of cases.
15	A	'Tolerated' is not a category of behaviour recognised by Muslims under Sharia law.
16	C	Contracts do not always have to be in writing.
17	C	A contract was formed within the time allowed, Y can sue X for breach of contract. In A there is no agreement, in B, Y's counter-offer terminates X's original offer and in D the acceptance was communicated too late – emails are deemed communicated once the recipient accesses them.
18		Executory, Past, Executed, Sufficient.
19	C	These are the two rebuttable presumptions of intention to create legal relations.
20	C	Seeking damages under the tort of deceit is only available for claims of fraudulent misrepresentation.

21   B   The parties are entitled to leave an essential term to be settled by other means, for example setting the price by reference to open market value, arbitration or a previous course of dealing.

22

Remedy	True	False
EVT Ltd can recover damages from DTZ Ltd and avoid the contract.		✓
EVT may only recover damages.	✓	
EVT can consider the contract as repudiated.		✓
EVT may consider the contract as repudiated or recover damages.		✓

The only true remedy available for breach of warranty is to recover damages.

23   A   UCTA 1977 applies to all contracts, including business contracts. Whether it applies in a particular case depends on the circumstances. Options B, C and D are examples of contracts that the Act expressly states it does not apply to.

24   C   The test is one of 'satisfactory quality'.

25   D   Where time is not of the essence, the party may perform later than the agreed time. If time is of the essence and prompt performance is a condition of the contract, conclusive and late performance will not discharge obligations.

26   C   The rules in the 1943 Act state that:

- All money paid must automatically be repaid. All amounts owing automatically cease to be payable.

- A party liable to repay and a party whose right to be paid which has been cancelled may apply to the court to set off or recover the whole or part of expenses incurred up to the limit of the amount payable/amount due.

- Valuable benefit may be repayable at the court's discretion.

Hence option (ii) is incorrect because cancellation of the amounts due for payment is automatic; option (iii) is incorrect because permission is required from the court to set off expenses.

27   C   The injured party may treat the contract as discharged or may continue with it until actual breach occurs.

28   Action for the price, injunction, quantum meruit, specific performance.

29   A   Parties who have the right to rescind a contract must exercise their right within a reasonable time.

30   C   Damages should only compensate for the loss incurred.

31   A,B,D   Whether or not a person has a business bank account does not affect whether the contract is an employment contract or not.

32   D   There is no implied duty to indemnify the employer.

33   C   Employers are not liable for acts committed outside the course of employment.

34   A,B,C   Health and safety rules need not be given although in practice they often are.

35   A   Employees cannot be prevented from using special skills acquired in the course of employment.

36   B   Indirect sex discrimination involves setting conditions that favour one sex ahead of the other. Answers A and C are examples where discrimination is permitted Answer D is direct discrimination.

BPP
LEARNING MEDIA

37	B	Employees are entitled to one week's notice after one month of continuous employment.
38	A,B,D	Option C is an example of a category of employee excluded from unfair dismissal protection.
39	C	A punitive award compensates the employee for loss caused by the employer's refusal to reinstate or re-engage the employee following an order from the tribunal.
40	A,B,C,D	They are all rights enjoyed by females under employment law.
41	B	A partnership can consist of a single transaction (such businesses are often described as joint ventures).
42	C	A company is distinct from its members.
43	B	Private companies are not required by the Companies Act 2006 to hold an AGM.

44

Circumstance	True	False
To find the directors of a public company personally liable for allowing the company to trade without a trading certificate.	✓	
To reveal a quasi-partnership.	✓	
Where the company has breached advertising standards rules.		✓
Where it is in the public interest.	✓	

45	B	Members of companies limited by guarantee are obliged to contribute to the liabilities of the company on winding-up. The amount they are liable for is the amount that they guarantee.
46	C	The Memorandum is sent as part of the formation process along with the registration fee and Articles of Association. The legal existence of the company is confirmed when the registrar sends the Certificate of Incorporation.
47	B	Promoters can make legitimate profit if they acquired the property before becoming promoter and disclose the profit when they sell it to the property.
48	D	Companies have 28 days to file their annual return after the return date.
49	B	Public companies should keep accounting records for six years, private companies for three.
50	A,C,D	The company is not required by law to keep a register of debentureholders although in practice many do.
51	B	The 'Ltd' in the title indicates this. D is incorrect as the registered name indicates the type of business it is.
52	A	The articles do not bind the company or its members to a third parties.
53	B	Standard articles are provided by the Secretary of State and will be applied to any company which fails to submit Articles on registration. They do not have to be amended.
54	A	The default objects are completely unrestricted.

55

Statement	True	False
A company may change its name by special resolution.	✓	
A company may change its name by any procedure its constitution allows	✓	

A company may change its name by any procedure permitted by its articles. The default position is by special resolution.

56   B   Members of a public company must hold 10% of the paid up share capital before they can requisition a general meeting.

57   C   The removal of directors and auditors are the two occasions where special notice is required.

58   D   Ordinary business does not need to be passed by special resolution.

59   B,C,D   The company secretary does not have the authority to call a general meeting.

60   C   Private companies do not have to hold general meetings and therefore the most common resolution is written.

61   B   The requirement is for 3 of the previous 5 years.

62   C   This is the key ordinary resolution for which special notice must be given.

63   B   If the directors acted for improper purpose although *bona fide* the members can ratify the actions: *Hogg Cramphorn 1966.*

64   C   Breach of such provisions is not a valid reason for disqualification.

65   A,C,D   Promoting the health and safety of employees is not a director's statutory duty under the Companies Act 2006.

66   A   The company as a person separate from its members is the only proper claimant. You must make sure that you know this rule.

67   A   The test is control. The action can be brought by individual members, so C and D are incorrect.

68   A   The benefits of a derivative action accrue to the company only.

69   A,B,D   Minorities are not normally permitted to sue the wrongdoers as the company is the only proper claimant.

70   B   Non-compliance with Stock Exchange listing rules was not found to be unfairly prejudicial conduct.

71   B   A: made up. C: called up share capital. D: paid up share capital.

72   A   If shares are allotted at a discount on their nominal value, the allottee must nonetheless pay the full nominal value with interest at the appropriate rate.

73   C   The other three are permitted sources for purchasing own shares by a private limited company.

BPP
LEARNING MEDIA

74

Statement	True	False
Private companies are generally permitted to give assistance to third parties.	✓	
Public companies are generally not permitted to give assistance to third parties.	✓	
A private company in a group may always give assistance to its holding company.		✓
A public subsidiary company may never give assistance to its parent company.	✓	

Private companies can generally give assistance to any third party, unless it is its public holding company. Public companies cannot generally give assistance to third parties even if it is its private holding company.

75   B   Under s561 pre-emption rights, a shareholder has the right to be offered new shares issued by the company pro-rata to their existing holding so that their overall percentage holding of shares remains the same.

76   D   Debentureholders are not proprietors.

77   B   Preference shares are classed as share capital.

78   A,B,D   Fixed charges rank for priority on the order of creation not value.

79   A   A company has five days to respond to a request to inspect the register of debentureholders.

80   D   This option is only correct if the other crystallisation causes the company to cease business.

81   B   A framework-based approach sets out general principles of behaviour and general guidelines giving advice on how to handle certain circumstances.

82   A   Integrity describes the principle of straightforwardness and honesty and not being party to the supply of false information. Option B describes objectivity, C relates to professional competence and D relates to confidentiality.

83   C   Objectivity requires an accountant to avoid bias, conflicts of interest or the influence of others in their work.

84   A   Independence should be in mind and appearance.

85   A,B,D   Professionalism is not list among the seven principles of public life. The other options are.

86   A   Donald should not make himself party to inaccurate information. Options B and C potentially make him party to such misinformation. Option D could mean him breaking the principle of due care by rushing a calculation.

87   B   CIMA members must take particular care not to break their duty of confidentiality to their employers when consulting professional help when resolving an ethical conflict.

88   D   Any solution must be consistent with fundamental ethical principles. They do not have to be authorised by CIMA or expressly permitted in IFAC's code. An ethical solution may be unacceptable to an employer who is behaving unethically.

89   C   Resignation should only be considered as a last resort once all other attempts to resolve the situation have failed. It may be the only way for the member to disassociate themselves from the issue.

90   A,B,C,D They are all values which may cause ethical dilemmas if they conflict.

91   A   An organisation should set up a nomination committee to make recommendations on all new board appointments and a remuneration committee to review the pay of executive directors. It should also have an audit committee.

92   B   The UK Corporate Governance Code states that the chief executive should not go on to be chairman at a later date.

93   D   The UK Corporate Governance recommends the non-executives have enough of a presence to prevent domination of the board by small groups or individuals.

94   B   Two-tier boards consist of a management board responsible for the day-to-day operations and a supervisory board.

95

Stakeholder	Interest	Financial
Employees		✓
Competitors	✓	
Customers		✓
Suppliers		✓

Employees have a financial interest as their financial security depends on their job, customers own or have ordered goods from the company for which they have paid and suppliers are owed money for goods and services they have provided. Competitors are interested in the company's strategy and development.

BPP
LEARNING MEDIA

Index
and Cases

BPP
LEARNING MEDIA

BPP
LEARNING MEDIA

A

B

C

D

E

BPP
LEARNING MEDIA

F

G

H

BPP
LEARNING MEDIA

BPP
LEARNING MEDIA

Note. **Key terms** and their page references are given in **bold**.

BPP
LEARNING MEDIA

BPP
LEARNING MEDIA

BPP
LEARNING MEDIA

BPP
LEARNING MEDIA

BPP
LEARNING MEDIA

BPP
LEARNING MEDIA

BPP
LEARNING MEDIA

BPP
LEARNING MEDIA

BPP
LEARNING MEDIA

BPP
LEARNING MEDIA

BPP
LEARNING MEDIA

Review Form – Paper C05 Fundamentals of Ethics, Corporate Governance and Business Law

Please help us to ensure that the CIMA learning materials we produce remain as accurate and user-friendly as possible. We cannot promise to answer every submission we receive, but we do promise that it will be read and taken into account when we up-date this Study Text.

Name: _____   Address: _____

_____

_____

How have you used this Interactive Text?
(Tick one box only)

☐ Home study (book only)

☐ On a course: college _____

☐ With 'correspondence' package

☐ Other _____

Why did you decide to purchase this Interactive Text? *(Tick one box only)*

☐ Have used BPP Texts in the past

☐ Recommendation by friend/colleague

☐ Recommendation by a lecturer at college

☐ Saw information on BPP website

☐ Saw advertising

☐ Other _____

Which BPP products have you used?

Text	☑	Home Study Package	☐
Kit	☐	Interactive Passcard	☐
Passcard	☐	i-Pass	☐

During the past six months do you recall seeing/receiving any of the following?
(Tick as many boxes as are relevant)

☐ Our advertisement in *Financial Management*

☐ Our advertisement in *PQ*

☐ Our brochure with a letter through the post

☐ Our website www.bpp.com

Which (if any) aspects of our advertising do you find useful?
(Tick as many boxes as are relevant)

☐ Prices and publication dates of new editions

☐ Information on Text content

☐ Facility to order books off-the-page

☐ None of the above

Your ratings, comments and suggestions would be appreciated on the following areas.

	Very useful	Useful	Not useful
Introductory section (Key study steps, personal study)	☐	☐	☐
Chapter introductions	☐	☐	☐
Key terms	☐	☐	☐
Quality of explanations	☐	☐	☐
Case studies and other examples	☐	☐	☐
Assessment focus points	☐	☐	☐
Questions and answers in each chapter	☐	☐	☐
Fast forwards and chapter roundups	☐	☐	☐
Quick quizzes	☐	☐	☐
Question Bank	☐	☐	☐
Answer Bank	☐	☐	☐
Index	☐	☐	☐
Icons	☐	☐	☐

	Excellent	Good	Adequate	Poor
Overall opinion of this Study Text	☐	☐	☐	☐

Do you intend to continue using BPP products?   Yes ☐   No ☐

On the reverse of this page are noted particular areas of the text about which we would welcome your feedback.

The BPP author of this edition can be e-mailed at: lmfeedback@bpp.com

Please return this form to: BPP Publishing Services, Aldine Place, 142-144 Uxbridge Road, London, W12 8AA

Review Form (continued)

TELL US WHAT YOU THINK

Please note any further comments and suggestions/errors below